Exchanges

A Global History Reader
Volume I, to 1500

TREVOR R. GETZ
RICHARD J. HOFFMAN
JARBEL RODRIGUEZ
ALL OF SAN FRANCISCO STATE UNIVERSITY

PEARSON
Prentice Hall

Upper Saddle River, New Jersey 07458

Library of Congress Cataloging-in-Publication Data

Getz, Trevor R.
  Exchanges: a global history reader / Trevor R. Getz, Richard J. Hoffman, Jarbel Rodriguez.
      v. cm.
  Contents: v. 1. To 1500
  ISBN 978-0-321-35508-9 (alk. paper)
  1. World history—Textbooks. 2. World history—Sources. I. Hoffman, Richard
J. (Richard Joseph) II. Rodriguez, Jarbel III. Title.
  D21.G45 2008
  909—dc22   2008031900

Executive Editor: Charles Cavaliere
Editorial Director: Leah Jewell
Editorial Assistant: Lauren Aylward
Project Manager: Rob DeGeorge
Senior Marketing Manager: Laura Lee Manley
Marketing Assistant: Athena Moore
Senior Managing Editor: Ann Marie McCarthy
Production Liaison: Fran Russello
Permissions Supervisor: Sherry Hoesly/The Permissions Group
Senor Operations Supervisor: Mary Ann Gloriande
Cover Design: Margaret Kenselaar
Cover Illustration: Volume I: By Permission of the British Library.
AV Project Manager: Mirella Signoretto
Illustrator/Cartography: Maps.com
Manager, Rights and Permissions: Zina Arabia
Manager, Visual Research: Beth Brenzel
Manager, Cover Visual Research & Permissions: Karen Sanatar
Image Permission Coordinator: Jan Marc Quisumbing
Composition/Full-Service Project Management: Elm Street Publishing Services
Printer/Binder: RR Donnelley & Sons Company

Credits and acknowledgments borrowed from other sources and reproduced, with permission, in this textbook appear on p. 355, which constitutes an extension of the copyright page.

Pearson Education LTD., London
Pearson Education Singapore, Pte. Ltd
Pearson Education, Canada, Inc.
Pearson Education–Japan
Pearson Education Australia PTY, Limited

Pearson Education North Asia, Ltd., Hong Kong
Pearson Educación de Mexico, S.A. de C.V.
Pearson Education Malaysia, Pte. Ltd.
Pearson Education, Upper Saddle River, New Jersey

10 9 8 7 6 5 4 3 2 1

ISBN-(10):   0-321-35508-3
ISBN-(13): 978-0-321-35508-9

Contents

Preface

We originally wrote this textbook for our students. Although we were trained in different fields of history, we have shared many of the same experiences in teaching undergraduate courses in western civilizations, world history, classical history, and area studies courses. In so doing, we have found that many of our students, both history majors and nonmajors, understood history largely as a set of dates and facts, within which there were several subsets categorized by geography and chronology. Students generally agreed that history was largely known and its stories all told. Many of them further felt that history was mostly irrelevant to their day-to-day experiences.

Yet we gradually became aware that in most cases, our students' surface disenchantment with history as a discipline masked a hunger to understand the historical roots of the world around them and of their own individual and collective heritage. Moreover, it became clear that many students understood that these histories were interpreted differently not only by various historians but also by the people who lived them. In fact, we found that most students who enrolled in our survey courses were ready to be guided beyond the "history as fact" stage to an understanding of "history as debate." They were also increasingly ready to see the world around them not as the end of history but as part of an unguided, ongoing global human experience. The 9/11 terrorist attacks in the United States and subsequent events around the world especially emphasized the significance of global history. Students wanted to know *why* these events were happening—to understand the relationships between events and trends in different times and in different parts of the world. This textbook is the result of the challenge our students gave us to rethink our approaches to teaching history.

We also wrote this textbook for ourselves and for other instructors like us who have watched the discipline of world history evolve. In many cases, we were the first generation of history students to have taken classes that featured the relationships between societies as their main themes. Many of us have discovered world history on our own. We were usually trained as regional specialists, but in conducting research in small rural communities or great capitals we have ascertained that we cannot tell our stories without reference to the influence of factors originating *outside* of our research area. Or we stumbled upon world history through being required to teach world history surveys, especially if we were trained in "non-western" fields. Our shared discovery is that the history of the world is as much about the relationships *among* societies as it is about transformations and continuities *within* societies. It is about diffusion as much as invention. This is not to say that invention doesn't happen, just that replication, exchange, confrontation, and diffusion are more prevalent and probably more important in the history of the world. This has led us to reinterpret invention more as the result of long collaborative and competitive processes than the spark of a moment. It is an interpretation that seems obvious to some of us today, but if so it is a secret kept by professional historians and only rarely shared with undergraduate students. It is disappointing that, while monographs and texts aimed at graduate students have embraced a new sense of interaction in the past and present, most world history readers still cling to the notion of *civilizations* as rigidly defined, isolatable aggregations of tradition, a notion that we challenge in the introduction to this text.

Instead, this reader is underpinned by three axioms. They are axioms that every student should understand at the conclusion of a world history survey. They are concepts that we believe will help students achieve academic success, as well as comprehend the world around them. The first is that any event in history can be interpreted differently even by two people who witness it directly. Thus the sources in this text are not intended to impart truth to the students, but rather to be interrogated as flawed and biased accounts that reveal as much about the author as the subject. It is for this reason that we have written a great deal of guiding text in each chapter and have developed questions that link sources, chapters, and parts.

The second, related idea is that history is both created and debated by historians. It is for this reason that we hope instructors will direct students to read the sources together rather than separately. In each chapter, polemical works are matched with documentary evidence and with contrasting interpretations so that students will learn to disassemble and to question the work of scholars and nonscholars alike.

Finally, world history is much more than just comparative history or "big" history. It is not merely the sum of nation-state or civilizational histories. It is something all its own, a field made up of attempts to understand the relationships among regions, states, and societies. This text asks students to investigate the flow of people, things, and ideas between societies. In this perspective, borders become zones of interaction as well as exclusion. Distinctions between "tribes," "nations," and "races" become opaque instead of polarizing. Societies are connected, rather than merely compared.

This reader is designed as an introduction to world history as a discipline. Its scope is vast: the entirety of the human experience before about 1500 C.E. Geographically it covers the world, bounded only by the availability of sources and the limits of space. The structure is geared toward achieving coherence: Not all regions are covered evenly in every part, nor do all periods receive the same attention. The goal of the text is to help students look beyond strictly delineated regionalism and chronological structures to understand history as a product of ongoing debates. Thus the text is structured as a series of interconnected themes and debates. Each part revolves around a global inquiry investigated and debated by world historians, defined partly by chronology but also by topic. The parts are divided into chapters, each of which highlights an issue or approach within the part-level topics. Within each chapter are both secondary and primary sources, matched to each other in an opposing, supporting, and/or evidentiary relationship. Although the distinction between primary and secondary sources is useful, we found in writing the two volumes that make up this series that it is sometimes problematic to try to rigidly distinguish between them. This is true not only because it leads students to miss the role perspective plays in historians' accounts but also because some sources can easily be considered to fit into both categories. Thus we have not sought to identify between them. In combination, the sources provide students with the tools not only to question assumptions and arguments but also to understand historians' methods. Each chapter contains significant introductory material, and each source is accompanied by explanatory text. The chapters conclude with two types of questions: Mastering the Material questions, which help students to analyze, evaluate, and compare the sources, are suitable for assigning as homework or chapter exams. Making Connections questions ask students to connect sources both across chapters and across parts. These questions are designed to be used for midterms, unit exams, and final exams.

Scholars at the center of the study of interaction claim for their work the title "the new world history" because they feel their approach is truly a breakthrough. Perhaps instructors and students will question just how revolutionary the transformation from nation-state–based history to the new world history really is. Nevertheless, world historians convey a certain sense of excitement at these attempts to explain why the human experience has been shaped as it has. We hope that excitement will rub off on students.

This textbook would not have been possible if not for the input of friends, students, and peers. We would especially like to thank our colleagues at San Francisco State who helped us in both volumes of this series to identify sources in areas and periods of history about which we knew little. Chris Chekuri and Pi-Ching Hsu deserve to be especially thanked. Julyana Peard, Abdiel Oñate, Maziar Berhooz, Frank Kidner, and Sarah Curtis were also obliging in pointing us in the direction of obscure texts and major works. Anthony D'Agostino, Arturo Arrieta, and William Issel helped us shape our understanding of world history, but not always by agreeing with our approach. None of the errors or failings of this text are their fault, but many of the important features are to their credit. In addition, several former students made contributions to this text. We were further assisted by the contributions of historians and history instructors who read and commented on portions of the text: Kenneth Wilburn, East Carolina University; Valerie Emanoil, Ohio State University; William Bakken, Rochester Community College; Brian Catlos, University of California Santa Cruz; Jennifer Kolpacoff Deane, University of Minnesota—Morris; Gayle Brunelle, California State University—Fullerton; Anthony Cheeseboro, Southern Illinois University—Edwardsville; Aviel Roshwald, Georgetown University; Eric Hetherington, New Jersey Institute of Technology; David Perry, Macalester College; Arthur T. Coumbe, Troy University; Patricia Ali, Morris College; Carolyn R. Dupont, Eastern Kentucky University; and Polly Detels, Texas A&M University—Commerce. These scholars helped us to avoid egregious errors and identify pertinent points.

We also owe thanks to all of the historians, modern and ancient, whose work appears in this book. There are four especially to whom we owe a large intellectual debt. William H. McNeill's 1963 *The Rise of the West* introduced the thematic approach to world history. His 2003 *The Human Web,* cowritten with J. R. McNeill, reflects the advances made over the past forty years and places him once again at the front of the pack. Patrick Manning's *Navigating World History* is the field's concise and authoritative defining text. Ross E. Dunn's edited volume, *The New World History: A Teacher's Companion* is an instructor's delight. Finally, Andre Gunder Frank's insistence that world history can be useful for understanding periods long past was a pioneering contribution. Many other scholars have contributed to the creation of a truly global discourse on world history, but the input of these four scholars stand out. Although none of them saw this text in production, it could not have existed without them.

Finally, it is hardly possible to give sufficient credit to our editors at Pearson: Janet Lanphier, who shepherded this project for four years, and Charles Cavaliere, who saw it to fruition. Without their patience, perseverance, and belief in this project we could not have succeeded.

Trevor R. Getz
Richard J. Hoffman
Jarbel Rodriguez

A Note on Spelling

Because of the wide diversity of human languages and texts, the transliteration of terms and names into the English language and the Roman alphabet is not a simple matter. As authors, we recognize that these words can be transliterated in a variety of ways. Our two guiding principles in this book have been to respect schemes recognized by the major scholars of and from each region on the one hand, and to adopt transliterations that are most useful for students.

Sometimes these goals are in conflict with one another, and we have had to try to forge a compromise.

Several of these compromise solutions deserve somewhat more explanation. In the interests of students, in cases where terms are very recognizable we have stuck to familiar formulations like "Rome," rather than the more strictly correct "Roma." We have also decided strictly not to use diacritical symbols and accent marks that are unfamiliar to most of our readers. Thus, for example, we write "Timur" for the name of the great Turkic leader rather than the more Europeanized "Tamerlane" or the phonic "Tīmūr" or "Temür". Chinese terms present a unique problem, as the sources in this book variously adopt two different systems of transliteration. In our commentary and discussion of sources, we have chosen to adopt the Pinyin system, which was developed in China and which became the international standard in 1979. Where our sources use the older Wide-Giles system of transliteration developed in late nineteenth century Britain, we preserve the integrity of the texts by presenting the terms as spelled in the source followed by the Pinyin spelling in brackets.

Introduction

What Is World History?: An Introduction for Students of the Premodern World

The field of world history developed as a new way to seek answers to questions that were beyond the scope of regional specialists. As the globalization of the world became increasingly evident in the second half of the twentieth century, scholars came to recognize the importance of global trends and events in shaping the national histories on which they were working. They began to search for global answers to questions they had only previously contemplated on local levels. While some of these questions dealt with the relatively recent past, others reached back into ancient history. Historians of sub-Saharan Africa began to contemplate how technologies like metallurgy and cultivation spread from one region to another. Archaeologists in Mesopotamia, India, and Latin America asked why humans developed cities, and why these developed first in certain regions. Historians of Rome and Han China compared how these two empires emerged and how they interacted with each other and with other states. Researchers in Central Asia asked questions about how people learned to trade with each other across long distances. Investigations of these issues on an intercontinental level led historians to explore wider issues. Why are some societies wealthy and others impoverished? How did the great empires manage to conquer much of the world? Why do wars happen? How do complex societies arise, and why do some fall? What is the role of identity—ethnicity, gender, race, age, class status, and group affiliation—in influencing the decisions people make? What scholars found, quite quickly, was that by studying several human societies comparatively, they could add a new layer to their understanding of each of them. Some then even further, suggesting that there are untold stories in the way societies related to each other and that the telling of these stories is the task of world historians.

The underlying premise of world history is that the interaction among human societies resembles not the relationships among building blocks or billiard balls, but rather among bacteria. Building blocks can be stacked next to or on top of each other, but they rarely if ever affect their neighbors' shapes or composition. Similarly, billiard balls careening around the table may collide and affect each other's trajectories, but they do not actually change each other: The eight ball is an eight ball even after it is struck by the cue ball. Bacteria, however, fundamentally shape each other as they interact. Because the membranes covering bacteria are full of pores, bacteria can exchange genetic information and can even fundamentally alter each other's basic make-up when they touch. Similarly, human societies in contact affect each other's development. World historians, recognizing this, seek to understand human history through studying both developments within societies and the way in which societies relate to each other. They look not only at the process of invention but also at the key role played by the diffusion of people, things, and ideas around the world. Rather than invalidating the work of historians who take a more regional approach this work adds a new layer of complexity to the understanding of societies, states, and cultural groups around the world.

Questions and Connections: The World before c. 1500 C.E.

Most two-semester world history courses divide at about 1500 C.E. Thus in the first semester instructors often cover well over 5500 years of recorded human history, and merely 500 in the second. Several justifications are normally given for this division. The first is that humanity was divided into several isolated worlds prior to Columbus' voyages of 1492–1493 C.E. and unified afterward. The second is that the pace of change in the human experience has greatly accelerated in the last 500 years. Thus, it is implied, the "modern" era is more complex and demands greater attention than previous periods.

In fact, however, the premodern world was complex. Its societies were intricate, its social networks sophisticated, and the stories of its inhabitants are both fascinating and valuable to us today. If this has not always been widely understood, it is because we know less about the inhabitants of pre-Columbian Mesoamerica or Zhou Dynasty China than we do about nineteenth-century Britain, for example. For a long time, historians had little understanding of these periods because few written records survived. More recently, however, new sources of information have begun to emerge through the application of techniques borrowed from archaeology, linguistics, and other disciplines. Moreover, more and more documentary sources are being unearthed and interpreted from these periods. These new sources of information reveal not only the complexity of societies around the world but also the sophistication of their trading and exchange networks.

This is not to say that the world did not change dramatically from the reconnecting of its two largest landmasses in 1492 C.E. Indeed, the two volumes that make up this textbook are divided at that point exactly because there *are* a number of compelling arguments for this division. However, there are compelling arguments for other dividing points as well. The seemingly uneven division of most courses—and this text—at around 1500 C.E. is more a reflection of how little we know about earlier periods of human history than of their importance or complexity.

Geography and Periodization

The geography and ecology of the world before 1400 C.E. is of fundamental importance to human history. These factors played a pivotal role in determining human settlement patterns, shaping culture, and influencing trade and interaction. Evidence suggests that humans evolved on the earth only once—in eastern Africa—and then spread to populate the world. Their diffusion to other parts of Africa and to other continents was funneled by geographical opportunities and obstacles. The most significant obstacles were vast oceans, although at times ice sheets and deserts played a role as well. Even as humans populated the globe, however, they found some areas more amenable to settlement than others based both on weather and the availability of local resources. This differentiation was increased when human societies began to develop **cultivation** (the systematic planting and harvesting of plants) and **pastoralism** (the herding of domesticated animals). Only some regions provided the correct environmental conditions to raise the animals and plants that were domesticatable by humans. Thus, cultivators especially began to congregate in environmental zones where they could grow crops, like the Valley of Mexico, the highlands of Peru, Mesopotamia, and the Yellow (Huanghe), Nile, and Indus river valleys. In these areas and a few others, dense populations made possible by high-calorie diets slowly created a **sedentary** (settled, nonnomadic) lifestyle that led to the development of cities. In many other areas, human populations found it more advantageous to live as nomadic herders or as foraging societies. Although none of these lifestyles was intrinsically better than another, each led society to develop certain cultural attributes.

One of the effects of the shift in some areas to cultivation and pastoralism was the development of long-range commerce. As peoples in different regions developed their local resources, they began to take notice of resources available to populations elsewhere. This in turn led to resource exchanges, which over time led to long-distance trading. This trading in resources resulted not only in commercial ties but also in the exchange of ideas, species, technologies, and humans among societies. However, while evidence of commerce can be found across the globe, such ties were not evenly distributed. Geography especially played a role in shaping and limiting commercial interaction. Several great geographic divisions are evident in human history. Populations in the Americas, largely cut off from other landmasses by two great oceans, could trade with each other but not with societies outside of the Americas. Similarly, societies in western and central Africa were for a time cut off from their neighbors to the north by the drying of the Sahara Desert and by the Atlantic Ocean, at least until camels arrived from the eastern Mediterranean to aid passage across the desert. Finally, many Polynesian societies and Oceanian societies were relatively isolated. The largest concentrations of humans in sustained contact with each other for most of human history were the populations of Europe, Asia, and North and East Africa, populations inhabiting a vast connected landmass that was not interrupted by uncrossable geographic barriers.

Both by invention and by diffusion, human societies in all parts of the world underwent change over time, and understanding the role of time is as important to the historian's task as is comprehending the role of geography. The process by which historians divide history into ages and eras is called **periodization.** Periodization is a useful tool that tells us how scholars interpret the world of the past. For example, historians of Europe often divide the history of that continent according to the spreading and ebbing of large states, especially the Roman Empire. On other occasions they use terms and periods borrowed from art history, such as **archaic** to refer to early stages of a society's development. World historians have found it necessary to adopt a very flexible chronology, because great changes occur at different times in different regions even if they spread from one region to another. In this book, therefore, the periodization is merely a guideline that makes use of benchmarks commonly accepted by many researchers. Two such big transitions were the interrelated development of agricultural technology and cities. These innovations occurred separately only about a half-dozen times in human history and then subsequently spread around the world. An additional important transformation was the almost simultaneous series of intellectual, spiritual, and political developments that gave birth to what are often called "classical" states and empires. A fourth was the collapse of many of these large-scale societies and their replacement by successor states. In this text, we use these changes to give shape to each part. It is important to remember, however, that in some cases these transformations were very gradual and even incomplete. Also, similar events may have occurred at different dates in different regions, thus inviting comparison across periods.

Along with periodization, historians are also concerned with calendars and dates. Although dates may seem absolutely fixed, that is not the case. Every culture has a mechanism for reckoning time: some very precise, like the Maya calendar, and others more suggestive, like that of the Nuer in southern Sudan. Not all calendars are based on $365^1/_4$ days, meaning that dates in different years fall at different times, as with the Islamic calendar. Very commonly societies have no strict chronology at all, but measure time by either the number of years a monarch has ruled or by the names of chief office holders. Still others create systems that combine a key event, like the Founding of the City of Rome or the Flight of the Prophet Mohammed, with the holder of high office. To add to the confusion for today's students, the first day of any new year varies considerably among societies, resulting in hyphenated years for some events. For example, January 1 was not made the first day of the new year in Rome until 153 B.C.E. Until then, March 1 began the year—that is why the months from September, "the seventh month," to December, "the tenth month," are so called, even though they are actually months ten through twelve. Following the Roman practice, we designate January 1 as New Year's Day and continue to name the months as Rome did. But over the years the calendar got out of sequence with the seasons and had to be reformed. In North America, the British colonies did not accept the reformed calendar of Pope Gregory XIII until 1752; continental Europe and Britain had had two different calendrical systems since 1583 when England went over to the new system. As a result, George Washington has two birth dates, depending on whether we use the Old Style or the New Style calendar.

To make matters even more complicated, since the time of the emperor Charlemagne, around 800 C.E. we in the West have used the birth of Christ as the marker for reckoning dates. This system, called Anno Domini (A.D.), "in the year of our Lord," was started by Dionysius Exiguus, a monk living in Rome in the early part of the sixth century C.E. Unfortunately, he miscalculated the birth of Christ by four to eight years, making Christ born several years Before Christ (B.C.)! He also did not include a year 0. Historians now often replace the terms B.C. and A.D. with B.C.E. "before the Common Era," and C.E. "the Common Era," but the base year when the counting begins is the same one calculated by Dionysius. As a result of all of these considerations, the absolute dating for events and individuals prior to fairly recent times is very tricky, and the further back we go, especially for the ancient history of China, Egypt, and Mesopotamia, it is nearly impossible. The dates used in this volume are suggested by leading scholars—many dates are fairly certain, others are highly disputed, and others are most certainly possible. Often times relative chronology, that one thing happened before or after something else, is as important as determining a precise date.

Sources

In this text students are asked to explore historical events and trends by analyzing the writing of both contemporary observers and formally trained scholars. Historians call these texts *sources*. The sources in this book have been chosen because they relate to what historians do: Historians use these materials as evidence to reconstruct what happened in the past and to attempt to explain why it happened that way rather than some other way.

Historians interpret the past using a variety of sources including written texts, archaeological and scientific data, oral histories such as songs and stories, and images such as paintings and photographs. In this volume we deal mainly, although not exclusively, with written sources. Some of these are **primary sources:** official documents, letters, diaries, records, chronicles, and other accounts written or recounted by people who experienced or witnessed the events being studied. Historians use these sources as evidence in writing books and articles that seek to interpret the past. These books and articles are in turn called **secondary sources.** Together, the primary and secondary sources form a body of knowledge that other scholars and historians can consult. Previous generations of historians often saw the two types of sources as being very different. They believed that historical (primary) sources were more subject to the biases and perspectives of the author than secondary sources by professional historians, whom they saw as being subject to scientific and factual rules. In this book we do not distinguish between the two types of sources for two reasons. First, many sources are both primary and secondary. For example, some of the most powerful depictions of the ancient world were written by historians who based their work on the accounts of others but whose work we read also as evidence of their attitudes and ideas as citizens of past societies. Second, we now know that the work of all historians, like all other authors, is affected by their perspectives and biases. Thus the distinction between the two types of sources often (although not always) confuses matters more than it simplifies them.

Through this textbook, the student becomes the historian. Students are given the sources, as well as accompanying text intended to introduce the subject, to guide investigations and to aid in the evaluation of the arguments and ideas put forth by the sources. These are the tools needed to answer the questions posed in each chapter and unit. It will quickly become evident that none of the sources is definitive. Rather, they are all part of debates between scholars, observers, and other commentators on the human past. Thus the sources and scholars in this book disagree with or contradict each other at times. Sometimes these debates are obvious within a *chapter* in which the analyses of scholars are presented alongside some of the evidence used in their work. Sometimes they are evident within the larger structure of the *part*, made up of several chapters, in which a period of world history is addressed. Finally, some debates appear in sequential parts in which scholars discuss similar themes for different periods of time.

Our hope is that students will see in this textbook part of the process that historians use to write history and explain the past. This process usually begins with primary sources. An important historian of the twentieth century, Marc Bloch commented that "the past does not change; but our knowledge of the past is constantly being transformed and perfected." New sources, whether written or archaeological, are always being discovered. Old sources are constantly being reinterpreted, often by asking new questions and applying new analytical techniques to materials that have been around for millennia. Historians thus make a number of choices in interpreting source material. First, from all of the materials available, historians choose certain documents and certain details from those documents to include in their analyses. Second, historians sometimes reject information in a document as either inaccurate or wrong—this is part of the art of source criticism. And third, historians not only reject information they consider to be in error but also gather meanings that are not specifically stated in a document. Indeed, part of the task of the historian is to make reasoned deductions from information within a given source. In the end, documents contain a great deal of interesting material that is often organized in very unhelpful ways. The historian takes this information, subjects it to criticism and analysis, and then reorganizes it to present a particular understanding of the past. The end result is a new history and the continuation of a debate that is age old. History is not actually the past itself, but it is our understanding of that past. As Marc Bloch suggests, that understanding changes with each individual and each generation.

The principal goal of this textbook is to present theories and evidence that attempt to explain and make sense of some of the major developments of human experiences in the past. This textbook does not seek to impose a single interpretation of history or to guide the student toward a perception of the "truth." Rather, through *questions* that connect different sources, chapters, and periods of time, this textbook will help students evaluate the very notion of historical truth. This textbook also does not claim to be a complete human record. The sources have been selected to inform and to enable a deeper understanding of a few major questions, rather than to superficially survey many different facets of the human experience.

The sources have also been chosen to specifically engage discussion on how humans interact with each other and the environment. As a result, an effort has been made to represent the widest possible range of experiences across time and around the world. The reality, however, is that we have very few written sources from certain periods in some regions. Thus, for example, southern Africa, northern Europe and Asia, Oceania, and certain parts of the Americas are underrepresented in the first parts of the text. Hopefully, this will change in future editions of this text as new sources become available.

In reading the primary and secondary sources in the following chapters, keep in mind both the perspectives of each author and the information available to him or her. Both primary and secondary sources should be read with equal skepticism. Even with the benefit of hindsight, historians have a great deal of difficulty interpreting the past. Interpretations are even more difficult for participants in an event who do not have the benefit of time, distance, and retrospect. Frequently, their information is not complete. They may also feel passionately about the events, which can lead to bias in their observations. For historians as well, it is difficult to place objective evaluation before personal ideology and perspective. History is colored by perspective—the perspective of the writer and the perspective of the audience. Our job, as historians, is to understand and account for that perspective as we seek a more accurate approximation of the past. Consequently, by looking at history from the viewpoint of the author, we can better understand the meaning of a document.

Understanding perspective is also an important tool in evaluating sources for historical accuracy. In the questions contained in each chapter, the student is frequently asked to compare theories and accounts, and then interpret their meaning as well as to assess their precision. Only infrequently will an account be entirely convincing. Often, students may decide that conflicting arguments either all have value or all have flaws. This will give students the opportunity to construct their own theories, based on the evidence in the sources. Through this process, students will come to understand history as debate, as perspective, and as a body of knowledge. That is the first step toward becoming an historian.

Themes in Premodern World History

At the heart of world history is an understanding of how human societies share many traits and at the same time are distinct and unique sets of people and experiences. In many ways, world historians celebrate the diversity of cultures and models of societies in the world. At the same time, both comparative analyses and studies of societal interaction reveal similarities between societies that are in contact with each other as well as those around the world from each other. In studying societies in history, a number of **themes** emerge.

The first theme is the necessity for food. Food gathering or production has many implications. Hunting parties require cooperation. The preservation or cooking of foodstuffs drives the development of certain technologies. Shifts in food production are especially important: When societies transition to cultivation, for example, it's not just food production that changes. The labor requirements of clearing fields and building irrigation systems, for example, necessitate the development of political organization and specialization of labor. The need to distribute food among workers spurs record-keeping techniques. The new relationship with the land helps to shift peoples' spiritual conceptions.

The development of cultivation is a precondition for the development of urban areas, a key transformation in human history. Cities and towns are made possible when there is a food surplus that allows some members of society to specialize as nonfood producers. Some might become artisans, artists, and scholars such as leatherworkers, poets, and astronomers. Others might become priests, soldiers, scribes, or even rulers. The concentration of these specialists in one area facilitates innovations, and the concentration of wealth in cities facilitates commerce. However, while the city is an important innovation in early human history, it is important to note that for the period studied in this volume, most humans remained rural dwellers, largely either as farmers, herders, or foragers. Some of these populations were nomadic. Others—most farmers, for example—were sedentary. However, war, famine, and political problems at home or better opportunities elsewhere sometimes forced even farmers to give up their sedentary lifestyle and move. The migration of these populations both in large groups and as individuals or families is an important theme in human history as well.

All people, whether sedentary or nomadic, develop social and cultural systems over time. They come to share certain values and senses of aesthetics and morality within their groups because they are constantly sharing with each other. This often results in the development of shared languages, spiritual and religious rituals and ethics, and views of the world. They pass these traits on to their children, who may or may not entirely accept them, as no society is entirely stagnant. Values and traits may also be shared with neighboring peoples, although often less completely. Thus the boundaries between societies are often fuzzy. A similar trend can be seen in **material culture**—the useful and decorated goods that societies produce. Often, neighboring groups produce similar technologies and techniques of design, which societies interpret as proof of the diffusion of ideas and skills among population groups.

Societies small enough that they encompass only a single extended family are usually managed by the elders of the kin-group. However, when a society grows larger than the extended family, its population finds it necessary to develop a political system such as a state, with laws, officials, and boundaries. The state historically took many forms, from small and sometimes relatively democratic city-states that encompassed only a few thousand people to large, centralized empires to diffuse confederacies of allied cities, tribes, or kin-groups. Each system was generally adopted because it was found to best suit the local environment and culture of the people. However, states were also a reflection of power within society and sometimes suited the needs of powerful groups and individuals more than the needs of the majority of the population. This was sometimes reflected in a social system that was stratified by class, with wealthy or powerful leaders at the top and relatively powerless peasants at the bottom. All of these possibilities merely hint at the enormous variation of governments and states found across societies.

States were and still are closely intertwined with economic systems. Economic exchanges have historically taken many forms. Some, like barter systems in which individuals or groups exchange resources with each other, are largely decentralized. Others, like tribute and tax systems in which the state receives money in recognition of its right to rule or as an indication of the people's submission, are highly centralized. One major innovation that occurred repeatedly in human history was the development and recognition of high-value, easily portable currency—either metal coins or other—that made possible systems of banking, interest, and insurance as well as facilitating trade. Often, barter, tribute, and currency exchange could be found within a single society at the same time.

One trait that is shared by all humans is the need to establish one's own identity within the complex mishmash of states, cities, families, religions, languages, and occupations of the wider world. This is true today and was true historically. For most of the period covered in this textbook, humans identified themselves mostly by their language affiliation, family group, and religion. Occupation was important as well, as was social class. In a few really successful states, the government managed to instill a sense of national identity across the population, but this was relatively rare. One factor that was not present in the ancient world as we know it today was race. Although many societies distinguished between themselves and "others" and sometimes even developed a sense of "ethnicity," there was no unified or codified sense of superiority based on skin color across the world.

Unlike the concept of race, understandings of gender are of enormous importance for the societies represented in this book. Throughout history, men and women have built human societies together, and gender has helped to shape the individual's experience in a society. Women and men were often assigned different roles in food production and controlled different spheres of politics, economics, and culture, but in many cases there was a great deal of overlap, and gender roles could be changed by the actions of members of both genders. The relationships between men and women, and among people of the same gender, helped to define the way societies were organized through shared concepts like honor and virtue. Historically, there has been a great diversity in the roles of women in different societies: In politics, for example, in some places and times powerful queens ruled while in others women were almost entirely excluded from the political sphere. In no case, however, was gender unimportant.

All of these themes—food production, political organization, society and culture, economics, identity formation, and gender—are underpinned by three sets of relationships that unify the human experience. These are the relationships among humans, the relationships between humans and their environment, and the relationships between societies and the challenges that they face. History, with the aid of the social sciences, helps us to identify and understand these commonalities better.

World history is, in some ways, a rejection of previous views of history that drew solid lines between different groups of humans. The crudest of these views were racial theories that suggested there are several different "races" of humans, each with different traits. Proponents of this theory often believed that some groups of humans were superior to others, and their work was used to uphold some of the worst actions in human history—slavery, racism, and genocide. Other scholars, as we shall see, believed that the world was firmly divided into different *civilizations,* cultures, or states, and that the inhabitants of each acted entirely differently. World historians tend to view history somewhat differently, believing that human societies learn from each other and trade and share with each other. Humans can change or expand their membership into new societies by moving, converting, or assimilating. Moreover, humans from different societies often have children together, thus creating large groups of people with multiple heritages. All of these relationships underline a fundamental sameness in the human experience. Societies—no matter where, no matter when—face similar challenges, threats, and opportunities. They all react to these changing conditions with the objective of surviving and thriving. Their strategies may diverge, but underneath there are certain commonalities.

But if humans everywhere share certain characteristics, why do they employ different strategies? In part, the answer is that different societies in place and time live in different environments. This means not only that they inhabit unique ecologies and geographical locations but also that they have unique sets of neighbors, unique cultures and sociopolitical organizations, and unique histories. Their unique environments, therefore, largely shape their responses to challenges and opportunities.

Civilization: A Student's Introduction

In this book, we often use the term **societies** to describe cohesive communities of humans that identify themselves as sharing values and social and political institutions. However, we also use the term **civilization** to mean essentially the same thing. As you will see, many of the scholars whose work we excerpt in this volume prefer to use civilization. The idea of a civilization and civilizations is one of the most complex and important to master in world history. As a word, civilization not only describes societies being studied but also lets us understand the way scholars and other authors think about historical worlds. Words have meaning and sometimes, as in the case of *civilization,* words have multiple meanings. In the short selections that follow, we show how four historians understand the term *civilization* from the perspective of four different continents.

In the first source, the forefather of world history Fernand Braudel describes how the term *civilization* first appeared in early eighteenth-century France. It was used by French writers—and later other Europeans—to celebrate the "advanced" state of development of their own society. Rather rapidly, Europeans came to juxtapose their own "civilized" state with the supposed "barbarism" of non-Europeans—especially the inhabitants of the Americas, Oceania, and Africa. In this sense, civilization was laden with value judgments: Civilized western Europeans were assumed to be better or to have progressed further than noncivilized inhabitants of other regions. This idea continued into the twentieth century, but was challenged by thinkers from other regions, like the great West African scholar Cheikh Anta Diop, who argued that Europeans had never been uniquely civilized.

Meanwhile, in the nineteenth century the term *civilization* took on a new meaning. Rather than only representing a certain state of sophistication or stage of development, it came to be used in the plural to describe different large groups of people living largely separate lives. Thus scholars developed the idea of many coexisting civilizations, each somehow intrinsically different from the others. This strand of thought, also described by Braudel, has been very powerful in recent years. Politicians like the American Samuel Huntington, for example, suggest that the world is divided into a certain number of great civilizations (eight in his case), all of which compete with each other.

There are problems with both of these conceptions of civilizations. In the first place, the idea that societies strive to evolve from barbarism to civilization suggests that there is only one model of progress—the European model. As we show in this text, however, there are many different models of development in different societies, and not all have to become like modern western Europe to "succeed." In the second place, many world historians such as Andre Gunder Frank (who lived in Latin America, Europe, and the United States) argue that the world is not divided into rigidly defined civilizations that compete with each other. Instead, history tells us that different groups of people trade, collaborate, and share, and often meld with each other. While differences may seem great at times, and competition or even war may seem to predominate, at other times the frontiers between societies are blurred and a great deal of interaction takes place. This does not mean that the term *civilization* is useless, but rather that it must be used with care. (Users of both volumes of this reader will note that this discussion is matched by a debate over notions of civilization in the early twenty-first century in Chapter 25 of Volume 2).

The Evolution of the Term *Civilization*

Fernand Braudel can be described as one of the first "world historians." His work on the Mediterranean Ocean and surrounding African, Asian, and European societies pioneered the study of interaction between wide regions. He especially focused on the role of geography in shaping culture and on economic exchange. In this important text, translated into English by Richard Mayne, Braudel describes the evolution of the word civilization *from a French term used to describe desirable ways of acting into a value ascribed to various societies and finally into a way to differentiate among different groups.*

>> 1. A History of Civilizations
FERNAND BRAUDEL [1963]

1. Changing Vocabulary

The word 'civilization'—a neologism—emerged late, and unobtrusively, in eighteenth-century France. It was formed from 'civilized' and 'to civilize', which had long existed and were in general use in the sixteenth century. In about 1732, 'civilization' was still only a term in jurisprudence: it denoted an act of justice or a judgement which turned a criminal trial into civil proceedings. Its modern meaning, 'the process of becoming civilized', appeared later, in 1752, from the pen of the French statesman and economist Anne Robert Jacques Turgot, who was then preparing a universal history, although he did not publish it himself. The official début of the word in print occurred in 1756, in a work entitled *A Treatise on Population* by Victor Riqueti, Marquis of Mirabeau, the father of the celebrated revolutionary Honoré, Count Mirabeau. He referred to 'the scope of civilization' and even 'the luxury of a false civilization'. [...]

Source: Fernand Braudel, *A History of Civilizations* (New York: Penguin Press, 1994), 3–4, 6–7. Originally published in French, 1963.

In its new sense, civilization meant broadly the opposite of barbarism. On one side were the civilized peoples: on the other, primitive savages or barbarians. Even the 'noble savage' dear to Jean-Jacques Rousseau and his disciples in the eighteenth century was not regarded as *civilized*. Without a doubt, the French at the end of the reign of Louis XV were pleased to see in this new word the image of their own society—which at a distance may still appeal to us even today. At all events, the word appeared because it was needed. Until then, *poli* (polite), *policé* (organized), *civil* and *civilizé* had no corresponding nouns. The word *police* rather connoted social order—which distanced it somewhat from the adjective *polite,* defined in Furetière's 1690 *Universal Dictionary* as follows: 'Used figuratively in ethics to mean civilized. To civilize: to polish the manners, make civil and sociable . . . Nothing is more apt to civilize a young man than the conversation of ladies.' […]

In about 1819 the word 'civilization', hitherto singular, began to be used in the plural. From then onwards, it 'tended to assume a new *and quite different* meaning: i.e., the characteristics common to the collective life of a period or a group'. Thus one might speak of the civilization of fifth-century Athens or French civilization in the century of Louis XIV. This distinction between singular and plural, properly considered, raises a further substantial complication.

In the twentieth century, in fact, the plural of the word predominates, and is closest to our personal experience. Museums transport us in time, plunging us more or less completely into past civilizations. Actual travelling is more instructive still. To cross the Channel or the Rhine, to go south to the Mediterranean: these are clear and memorable experiences, all of which underline the plural nature of civilizations. Each, undeniably, is distinct.

If we were asked, now, to define civilization in the singular, we should certainly be more hesitant. The use of the plural signifies, in fact, the gradual decline of a concept—the typically eighteenth-century notion that there was such a thing as civilization, coupled with faith in progress and confined to a few privileged peoples or groups, humanity's 'élite'. The twentieth century, happily, has abandoned a certain number of such value-judgements, and would be hard put to it to decide—and on what criteria—which civilization was the best.

This being so, civilization in the singular has lost some of its cachet. It no longer represents the supreme moral and intellectual value that it seemed to embody in the eighteenth century. Today, for example, we more naturally tend to call some abominable misdeed 'a crime against *humanity*' rather than against *civilization,* although both mean much the same thing. We feel somewhat uneasy about using the word *civilization* in its old sense, connoting human excellence or superiority.

The "Clash of Civilizations"

In 1993, Samuel P. Huntington, a political scientist who had served several White House administrations, made the argument that the importance of the nation-state is fading as humans align themselves into eight great civilizations that compete with each other on a global stage. He identifies these as the "Western, Confucian, Japanese, Islamic, Hindu, Slavic-Orthodox, Latin American, and possibly African civilizations." These civilizations have existed for some time, he argues, but are now rising to even greater prominence than before. In this short excerpt, Huntington gives a definition of civilizations as he understands them.

Source: Samuel P. Huntington, "The Clash of Civilizations?" *Foreign Affairs* 72 (Summer 1993): 22–36.

>> 2. "The Clash of Civilizations?"

SAMUEL P. HUNTINGTON [1993]

What do we mean when we talk of a civilization? A civilization is a cultural entity. Villages, regions, ethnic groups, nationalities, religious groups, all have distinct cultures at different levels of cultural heterogeneity. The culture of a village in southern Italy may be different from that of a village in northern Italy, but both will share in a common Italian culture that distinguishes them from German villages. European communities, in turn, will share cultural features that distinguish them from Arab or Chinese communities. Arabs, Chinese and Westerners, however, are not part of any broader cultural entity. They constitute civilizations. A civilization is thus the highest cultural grouping of people and the broadest level of cultural identity people have short of that which distinguishes humans from other species. It is defined both by common objective elements, such as language, history, religion, customs, institutions, and by the subjective self-identification of people.

An Afrocentric Critique of Civilization Theory

The notion of multiple coexisting civilizations was widely accepted in the mid-twentieth century, as was the concept of civilization as an advanced stage of human development. It was generally accepted by Western scholars, at least, that human civilization began in Greece and reached its height in Europe. However, after the Second World War (1939–1945) a number of critics began to question this idea. Among them were the Afrocentrists like the great Senegalese social scientist Cheikh Anta Diop, who argued that the African regions of Egypt and Ethiopia were the originators of civilized lifestyles. In doing so, they pointed out that the term civilization *was not applied scientifically or objectively by scholars, but rather reflected certain biases. Ironically, this was true of both the Eurocentric, Greek-centered views of the origins of civilization and their own Afrocentric, Egypt-centered views. Thus they set the foundation for later critiques of civilization theories.*

>> 3. The African Origin of Civilization: Myth or Reality

CHEIKH ANTA DIOP [1955]

Contribution of Ethiopia-Nubia and Egypt

According to the unanimous testimony of the Ancients, first the Ethiopians and then the Egyptians created and raised to an extraordinary stage of development all the elements of civilization, while other peoples especially the Eurasians, were still in barbarism. The explanation for this must be sought in the material conditions in which the accident of geography had placed them at the beginning of time. For man to adapt, these conditions required the invention of sciences complemented by the creation of arts and religion.

It is impossible to stress all that the world, particularly the Hellenistic world, owed to the Egyptians. The Greeks merely continued and developed, sometimes partially, what the Egyptians had invented. By virtue of their materialistic tendencies, the Greeks stripped those inventions of the religious, idealistic shell in which the Egyptians had enveloped them. On

Source: Cheikh Anta Diop, *The African Origin of Civilization: Myth or Reality* (Chicago: Lawrence Hill, 1974), 230–5. Originally published in French, 1955.

the one hand, the rugged life on the Eurasian plains apparently intensified the materialistic instinct of the peoples living there; on the other hand, it forged moral values diametrically opposite to Egyptian moral values, which stemmed from a collective, sedentary, relatively easy, peaceful life, once it had been regulated by a few social laws.

To the extent that the Egyptians were horrified by theft, nomadism, and war, to the same extent these practices were deemed highly moral on the Eurasian plains. Only a warrior killed on the battlefield could enter Valhalla, the Germanic paradise. Among the Egyptians, no felicity was possible except for the deceased who could prove, at the Tribunal of Osiris, that he had been charitable to the poor and had never sinned. This was the antithesis of the spirit of rapine and conquest that generally characterized the peoples of the north, driven, in a sense, away from a country unfavored by Nature. In contrast, existence was so easy in the valley of the Nile, a veritable Garden of Eden, between two deserts, that the Egyptians tended to believe that Nature's benefits poured down from the sky. They finally adored it in the form of an Omnipotent Being, Creator of All that Exists and Dispenser of Blessings. Their early materialism— in other words, their vitalism—would henceforth become a materialism transposed to the sky, a metaphysical materialism, if one may call it that.

On the contrary, the horizons of the Greek were never to pass beyond material, visible man, the conqueror of hostile Nature. On the earth, everything gravitated around him; the supreme objective of art was to reproduce his exact likeness. In the "heavens," paradoxically, he alone was to be found, with his earthly faults and weaknesses, beneath the shell of gods distinguished from ordinary mortals only by physical strength. Thus, when the Greek borrowed the Egyptian god, a real god in the full sense of the word, provided with all the moral perfections that stem from sedentary life, he could understand that deity only by reducing him to the level of man. Consequently, the adoptive Pantheon of the Greek was merely another humanity. This anthropomorphism, in this particular case, was but an acute materialism; it was

characteristic of the Greek mind. Strictly speaking, the Greek miracle does not exist, for if we try to analyze the process of adapting Egyptian values to Greece, there is obviously nothing miraculous about it, in the intellectual sense of the term. At most we can say that this trend toward materialism, that was to characterize the West, was favorable to scientific development.

Once they had borrowed Egyptian values, the wordly genius of the Greeks, emanating basically from the Eurasian plains and from their religious indifference, favored the existence of a secular, worldly science. Taught publicly by equally worldly philosophers, this science was no longer a monopoly of a priestly group to be jealously guarded and kept from the people, lest it be lost in social upheavals:

The power and prestige of the mind which, everywhere else, exercised their invisible empire, alongside of military force, were not in the hands of the priests, nor of government officials among the Greeks, but in the hands of the researcher and the thinker. As was already visibly the case with Thales, Pythagoras, and Empedocles, the intellectual could become the center of a circle in a school, an academy, or the living community of an order, drawing nearer first to one, then to the other, setting scientific, moral, and political goals, and tying it all together to form a philosophical tradition.

Scientific, philosophical teaching was dispensed by laymen distinguished from the common people only by their intellectual level or social status. No saintly halo encompassed them. In "Isis and Osiris," Plutrach reported that, according to the testimony of all Greek scholars and philosophers taught by the Egyptians, the latter were careful about secularizing their knowledge. Solon, Thales, Plato, Lycurgus, Pythagoras encountered difficulty before being accepted as students by the Egyptians. Still according to Plutarch, the Egyptians preferred Pythagoras because of his mystical temperament. Reciprocally, Pythagoras was one of the Greeks who most revered the Egyptians. The foregoing is the conclusion of a passage in which Plutarch explains the esoteric significance of the name *Amon:* that which is hidden invisible.

As Amélineau observes, it is strange that we do not place more stress on the Egyptian contribution to civilization:

I then realized, and realized clearly, that the most famous Greek systems, notably those of Plato and Aristotle, had originated in Egypt. I also realized that the lofty genius of the Greeks had been able to present Egyptian ideas incomparably, especially in Plato but I thought that what we loved in the Greeks, we should not scorn or simply disdain in the Egyptians. Today, when two authors collaborate, the credit for their work in common is shared equally by each. I fail to see why ancient Greece should reap all the honor for ideas she borrowed from Egypt.

Amélineau also points out that if certain of Plato's ideas have become obscure, it is because we fail to place them in the context of their Egyptian source. This is the case, for example, with Plato's ideas on the creation of the world by the Demiurge. We know, moreover, that Pythagoras, Thales, Solon, Archimedes, and Eratosthenes, among others, were trained in Egypt. Egypt was indeed the classic land where two-thirds of the Greek scholars went to study. In reality, it can be said that, during the Hellenistic epoch, Alexandria was the intellectual center of the world. Assembled there were all the Greek scholars we talk about today. The fact that they were trained outside of Greece, in Egypt, could never be overemphasized.

Even Greek architecture has its roots in Egypt. As early as the Twelfth Dynasty, proto-Doric columns are round (Egyptian cliff tombs of Beni Hasan). Greco-Roman monuments are mere miniatures as compared with Egyptian monuments. Notre-Dame Cathedral in Paris, with all its towers, could easily be placed in the hypostyle hall of the temple of Karnak; the Greek Parthenon could fit into those walls even more easily.

The typically Negro—or Kushite, as Lenormant writes—kind of fable, with animals as characters, was introduced into Greece by the Egyptian Negro, Aesop, who was to inspire the fables of the Frenchman La Fontaine. Edgar Allan Poe, in "Some Words with a Mummy," presents a symbolic idea of the scope of scientific and technical knowledge in ancient Egypt.

From Egyptian priests, Herodotus had received information revealing the basic mathematical data on the Great Pyramid of Cheops. Several mathematicians and astronomers have produced works on that pyramid; their sensational revelations have not failed to unleash a flood of arguments which, as expected, are not expressed in the form of a coherent, scientific account. Without venturing into what might be considered excessive pyramidology, we can cite the following:

Astronomers have noted in the Great Pyramid indication of the sidereal year, the anomalistic year, the precessions of the equinoxes "for 6,000 years; whereas modern astronomy knows them for only about 400 years." Mathematicians have detected in it the exact value of "pi," the exact average distance between the sun and the earth, the polar diameter of the earth, and so on.

We could prolong the list by citing even more impressive statistics. Could this result from mere chance? As Matila C. Ghyka writes, that would be inconceivable:

Any single one of these items could be a coincidence; for them all to be fortuitous would be almost as unlikely as a temporary revision of the second principle of thermodynamics (water freezing over fire) imagined by physicists, or the miracle of typewriting monkeys . . . Nevertheless, thus completed and perfected, thanks to the research of Dieulatoy, E. Male, and Lun, the hypothesis of Viollet-le-Due on the transmission of certain Egyptian diagrams to the Arabs, then to the Clunisians; through the intermediary of the Greco-Nestorian school of Alexandria, is quite plausible. Astronomically, the Great Pyramid can be the "gnomon of the Great Year," as well as the "metronome" whose harmony, often misunderstood, echoes throughout Greek art, Gothic architecture, the first Renaissance, and in any art that rediscovers the "divine proportion" and the pulsation of life.

The author also quotes Abbé Moreux's opinion that the Great Pyramid does not represent the "groping beginnings of Egyptian civilization and science, but rather the crowning of a culture that had attained its apogee and, before disappearing, probably wished to leave future generations a proud testimonial of its superiority."

This astronomical and mathematical knowledge, instead of completely vanishing from Black Africa, has left traces that Marcel Griaule was perceptive enough to detect among the Dogon, however astounding that may seem today.

On numerous occasions, reference has been made to the fact that the Greeks borrowed their gods from Egypt; here is the proof: "Almost all the names of the gods came into Greece from Egypt. My inquiries prove that they were all derived from a foreign source, and my opinion is that Egypt furnished the greater number"

Since the Egyptian origin of civilization and the extensive borrowing of the Greeks from the Egyptians are historically evident, we may well wonder with Amélineau why, despite those facts, most people stress the role played by Greece while overlooking that of Egypt. The reason for this attitude can be detected merely by recalling the root of the question. As Egypt is a Negro country, with a civilization created by Blacks, any thesis tending to prove the contrary would have no future. The protagonists of such theories are not unaware of this. So it is wiser and safer to strip Egypt, simply and most discreetly, of all its creations in favor of a really White nation (Greece). This false attribution to Greece of the values of a so-called White Egypt reveals a profound contradiction that is not the least important proof of Egypt's Negro origin.

Notwithstanding the opinion of André Siegfried, the Black is clearly capable of creating technique. He is the very one who first created it at a time when all the white races, steeped in barbarism, were barely fit for civilization. When we say that the ancestors of the Blacks, who today live mainly in Black Africa, were the first to invent mathematics, astronomy, the calendar, sciences in general, arts, religion, agriculture, social organization, medicine, writing, technique, architecture; that they were the first to erect buildings out of 6 million tons of stone (the Great Pyramid) as architects and engineers—not simply as unskilled laborers; that they built the immense temple of Karnak, that forest of columns with its famed hypostyle hall large enough to hold Notre-Dame and its towers; that they sculpted the first colossal statues (Colossi of Memnon, etc.)—when we say all that we are merely expressing the plain unvarnished truth that no one today can refute by arguments worthy of the name.

Consequently, the Black man must become able to restore the continuity of his national historic past, to draw from it the moral advantage needed to reconquer his place in the modern world, without falling into the excesses of a Nazism in reverse for, insofar as one can speak of a race, the civilization that is his might have been created by any other human race placed in so favorable and so unique a setting.

A Transnational Critique of Civilization Theory

The late Andre Gunder Frank is celebrated as one of the most provocative and controversial world historians. Balancing economic and anthropological approaches to history, Frank challenged many of the dominant ideas of earlier generations of scholars. He was also well known for engaging in passionate disputes with ideological opponents, often on the H-World list-serv. In this post from H-World that evolved from a paper given at a United Nations Conference, Frank rejects the very idea of separate civilizations as contrary to the realities of human existence.

>> 4. Toward Humano- and Eco-centrism: Unity in Diversity, Not Clash of Civilizations

ANDRE GUNDER FRANK [2001]

[1] To begin with, there is no way to identify any boundary between such larger civilizational, and even less among any smaller component or other social units nor therefore to tell where or when one begins and the other ends. [2] All of these alleged civilizations / societies / cultures / nations / ethnicities and also religions experience transformation over time, that is change from one time to another. Like a river flowing under a bridge, it is never the same from one moment to the next. Moreover even more than over rivers, bridges over any such cultural "unit" would have to be built and rebuilt continuously as it changes its width and course. Like the Yellow river, "China" and its millennial "civilization" itself—or rather themselves!—has continuously changed its course and breadth and sometimes radically so during very short periods of time. [3] Like rivers also only much more so, the extent, shape and content of all of these imagined separate or individual "units" has been and still is the—only temporary and even changing!—result of contact and mutual influence among each other. Not only the various past and present streams of confluence, but also the content of all socio-cultural "units" are mixed up not only by seepage but also by interconnecting relations among them at any and all time. As significant as it is neglected is the mutual dependence and contribution of Central Asian "barbarian nomads" and "civilized settlers" across the Inner Asian Frontiers as Owen Lattimore called them in the "Chinese" [and Manchurian, Korean, etc.] East Asia. But the same was equally important in the formation and transformation of civilization/s in South Asia, West Asia, Siberian and Russian North Asia, not to mention their marginal peninsular appendage in Europe.

[4] The very socio-cultural "identity," much more so than that of streams, rivers and lakes or even of civilizational oceans, is more defined FOR us by others, especially by our neighbors, than it is BY us ourselves. In forming—and reforming!—our identities, we in very large part shape and reshape our identities in reaction to those imposed on us by others. Then we re-evaluate the often negative cast of the identity that was thrust upon us by others and re-cast it for ourselves in a more positive light with which we then try shine near and far. That is particularly the case when military or other political oppression generates responses that take nationalist or ethnic forms as a result of especially of increased oppression. That in turn is mostly the result the attempt or success in increasing economic benefits for some at increased cost to others. Even more so is that the case when shrinking economic pie diminishes the absolute amount available to all and generates conflicts over the remaining shares.

Source: Andre Gunder Frank, "Toward Humano- and Eco-centrism: Unity in Diversity, Not Clash of Civilizations" (www.h-net.org/~world) 22 October, 2001. Paper originally presented at United Nations Conference on Dialogue of Civilizations, 31 July–3 August, 2001.

>> Mastering the Material

1. Consider the several definitions of the word *civilization* as given by Braudel and Huntington, as well as the criticisms made by Diop and Frank. To what extent is the term a useful one? What are its limitations?

Terms to Know

cultivation   *(P. 3)*

pastoralism   *(P. 3)*

sedentary   *(P. 3)*

periodization   *(P. 3)*

archaic   *(P. 3)*

primary sources   *(P. 5)*

secondary sources   *(P. 5)*

themes   *(P. 7)*

material culture   *(P. 8)*

societies   *(P. 10)*

civilization   *(P. 10)*

Part 1

Interrogating the Origins and Development of Civilization and City-State Societies (c. 8000–600 B.C.E.)

The great pyramids on the plateau above Giza were already over 3,700 years old when the Sultans in the thirteenth century C.E. began to strip them of their fine limestone casing in order to build their mosques and palaces in medieval Cairo. Still, today those immense monuments to the power and wealth of the pharaohs lend a timelessness to the land of Egypt, even as the modern city begins to crowd around the eastern side of those ancient structures. Yet the engineering skills of the Egyptians, though the most visible of their achievements, are surpassed by the ability of the Fourth Dynasty pharaohs to organize, supply, and feed such a massive workforce for the more than six decades it took to build the pyramids. Historians' studies of the distant past, however, reveal more than simply how the Egyptians managed to achieve such great heights; they teach us about our own societies as well. As Barry Kemp, a contemporary Egyptologist, wrote in *Ancient Egypt: The Anatomy of a Civilization,* "the study of ancient history exposes" the "bedrock of modern life" itself. This part examines some of that ancient bedrock on a global basis, beginning around the ninth millennium B.C.E.

One of the founders of the new world history, Fernand Braudel, suggests that history actually consists of the interaction of three separate levels, or planes, over time. The first plane is geographical, that timeless level in which human beings interact with their natural environment. Humans always attempt to reshape what their environment presents to them. But this interaction with geography, this reshaping of the environment, produces a worldview or outlook that is very long lasting. The second plane, Braudel suggests, is social in nature—formed by human beings living in groups. This plane is slightly faster paced and includes the creation of the underlying structures of humans' interactions among themselves. This level includes how societies are organized and how, as a group, individuals within society conceive of what Braudel and others call their "collective destinies." And finally, the third plane is political in nature—this is the fast-paced story of individuals and events, of battles and elections. In the end, the totality of these interacting levels produces what we call "history." In Part 1, we will take a closer look at Braudel's first two planes; in future parts we explore more closely the third.

We begin with that most fundamental plane of human activity—interaction between societies and their physical environments. The geography and climate of each region of the globe, together with the region's plants and animals, present both an opportunity and a limit to human beings. Ecological conditions, imperfect as they are, require humans to shape their world in one way or another to flourish. Some historians, like Arnold Toynbee, call this the "challenge-and-response" approach to nature and cultural creation. Toynbee argues that all societies face challenges, and the responses to these challenges vary considerably from place to place. But commonalities exist between societies as well, and despite ecological differences, human beings often develop comparable strategies when faced with similar challenges and opportunities. Additionally, the environment and the human response to it produce something more important than simply a mechanism for survival: It produces a set of attitudes about life and the universe that not only changes little over time but also helps to define some of the basic characteristics of that culture. How people see their physical world affects how they react to both daily needs and unforeseen crises. As historians, we need to understand a society's physical environment and its perception of that environment in order to comprehend and explain its past. Two primary examples of the relationship of geography to human beings can be seen in ancient Iraq (Mesopotamia) and Egypt. Though their physical environment was quite similar in some ways, it was vastly different in other. As a result, each society coped with the physical demands of their natural world differently, and each developed a mentality about life and the universe that was nearly the opposite of the other.

As important as geography is in cultural and social development, events also shape long-term developments and mental attitudes. One such event was the invention of agriculture in the ninth millennium B.C.E. in what scholars call the **Neolithic Revolution.** Around this time, in what is now southern Turkey and northern Iraq and Syria, novice farmers domesticated plants and animals for the first time. The agriculture they developed eventually produced a better diet, a larger population, and a settled way of life for its practitioners. For people living in villages and towns, agriculture created its own long-enduring, almost timeless rhythms of life, rhythms that were closely tied to climate, seasonal cycles, and land use. With these rhythms also came mental structures and new ways of looking at the world and the forces at work within it. This agricultural way of life, complete with its social structures and worldview, has persisted into the contemporary world. Even in the 1930s, 80 percent of all Egyptians were farmers, working their land in ways similar to those of their ancestors thousands of years earlier. Human beings invented agriculture elsewhere as well—the domestication of cereals in east Asia and the Americas replicated what took place in west Asia. The invention of agriculture, with its consequences of a food surplus and settled way of life, eventually led to cultural advances that would otherwise have not been possible.

A second culture-shifting event distantly followed the invention of agriculture: the emergence of cities. Scholars invariably connect "civilization" with the development of cities and an urban way of life beginning in about 3000 B.C.E. Both agriculture and cities transformed the very physical environment that human beings moved in—even now the great temples of the Maya pierce the jungle canopy in Tikal, and the temple mounds of Ur and other long-vanished Mesopotamian cities dot the arid landscape of southern Iraq. Both agriculture and cities created a set of attitudes about the universe and fellow human beings that were long lasting. But cities relied for their very existence on farmers and their produce. Food surpluses freed some individuals to pursue nonagricultural activities, both cultural and economic, permitting cities to create a level of civilization and specialization that had not yet been known. Thus cities became centers for innovations, including writing. Conversely, urban environments were notoriously unhealthy in

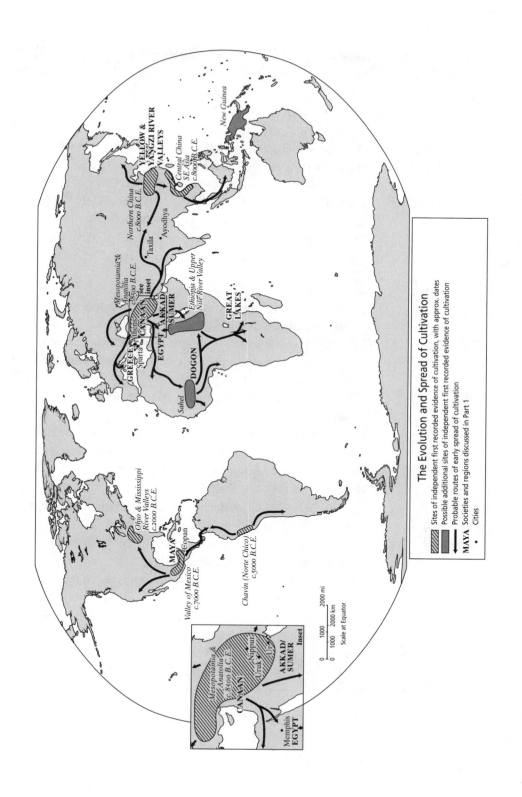

The Evolution and Spread of Cultivation

Sites of independent first recorded evidence of cultivation, with approx. dates

Possible additional sites of independent first recorded evidence of cultivation

Probable routes of early spread of cultivation

MAYA Societies and regions discussed in Part 1

• Cities

Yellow & Yangzi River Valleys

Central China SE Asia c.8000 B.C.E.

New Guinea

Northern China c.8000 B.C.E.

Taxila

Ayodhya

Mesopotamia & Anatolia c.8500 B.C.E. see inset

AKKAD/ SUMER

Ethiopia & Upper Nile River Valley

GREAT LAKES

GREECE Athens Sparta

CANAAN

EGYPT

DOGON

Sahel

Ohio & Mississippi River Valleys c.2000 B.C.E.

MAYA

Copan

Valley of Mexico c.7000 B.C.E.

Chavin (Norte Chico) c.5000 B.C.E.

Scale at Equator

0   1000   2000 km
0   1000   2000 mi

Inset

Mesopotamia & Anatolia c.8500 B.C.E.

CANAAN

Nippur

Uruk

AKKAD/ SUMER

Memphis

EGYPT

21

Part I Timeline

c. 9000 B.C.E.	The first human domestication of plants and animals, in the northern part of the Fertile Crescent; it will soon spread out.
c. 8500–8000 B.C.E.	The independent domestication of millet and rice in China.
c. 4500–3500 B.C.E.	The domestication and development of corn (maize) in the Tehuacan valley southeast of Mexico City.
c. 3100 B.C.E.	The unification of most of the Nile Valley and Delta by the pharaoh Narmer (or Menes) through conquest.
c. 3000 B.C.E.	The transition from towns to the earliest urban developments and city states in Sumer in the Tigris-Euphrates Valley.
c. 2500 B.C.E.	Indus River Valley cities emerge.
2350 B.C.E.	Sargon establishes the dynasty of Akkad, controlling all of southern Mesopotamia.
c. 2000 B.C.E.	Sahelian West African societies possess a full spectrum of domesticated food crops including millet, sorghum, and finger millet.
1792 B.C.E.	The accession of Hammurabi, the Amorite king of Babylon.
c. 1650 B.C.E.	The second temporary collapse of a unified Egypt, and its partial occupation for the first time by foreign invaders (the Hyksos from southwest Asia).
c. 1550 B.C.E.	Beginning of the New Kingdom in Egypt.
c. 1500 B.C.E.	The rise of walled cities during the Shang Dynasty, the first historic kings of China.
c. 1400 B.C.E.	Suggested date for the arrival of the Hebrew patriarch Jacob and his sons in Canaan.
c. 800 B.C.E.	The beginning of Maya complex state societies in the Petén area of Guatemala.
c. 800 B.C.E.	The development of the first Greek city-states (the *polis*) toward the end of the Greek Dark Age.
c. 700–600 B.C.E.	Emergence of cities in northern India; they become the basis for both small kingdoms and "republics."

antiquity and the Middle Ages—cities relied on constant immigration from the countryside to replenish the ranks of city dwellers thinned by disease. Nevertheless cities, with their individual architectural structures, urban plans, and lifestyles, developed in Eurasia from China to Greece and beyond, in West Africa, and in the New World from the Valley of Mexico to Peru.

Cities, however, are more than simply large agglomerations of people. Historians point out how cities produce a specific kind of identity that distinguishes the urbanite from not only the rural population but also urban dwellers in other cities. Pride in a city produced a political identity and particularism that we call the city-state. City-state systems arose in Mesopotamia, Greece, Mesoamerica, and India, first in the Indus Valley, and again later and separately in the Ganges plain. Because city-states were so fiercely independent, any form of large political union among them was either difficult, as in Mesopotamia, or impossible, as in Greece and Mesoamerica. But paradoxically, city-states helped produce a common culture shared by all urban dwellers in the region, and they exported this culture as a standard of civilization to other areas by trade or colonization. The presence of cities, however, did not inevitably mean the absence of larger political units in antiquity. In both Egypt and China, for different reasons, cities did not impede the creation of larger states.

Finally, cities were subject to problems, many of which are familiar to us today. Internal harmony was always precarious. The law codes of kings and shared societal norms promoted cooperation and outlawed or shamed criminals, thus preserving the type of internal stability necessary for any society—especially an urban society—to survive and flourish. But outside pressures were as much of a threat to cities as internal ones. City-states were constantly at war with one another, and even success in battle could ruin a city financially. The results of a loss were more dramatic: diminished monetary and human resources, lost territory, or in extreme cases total annihilation. Cities also ran the risk of attack by kingdoms, or, even more menacingly, from nomadic or seminomadic peoples on the fringes of their world. Fear of the barbarian, the uncivilized hordes, at the gate is as old as cities and is reproduced in written texts over and over. By contrast, nomadic peoples' views of city dwellers are less frequently preserved, although some, like the Hebrews, left records of their clashes with urbanized peoples. For them as nomadic pastoralists, cities were both an attraction and a danger. Urbanization, as it turns out, was a two-way street, and negotiating that street could mean the end of a way of life for either the nomad or the city dweller.

Chapter 1

The Natural Environment and Human Beings

Constraints and Advantages

"Egypt," the Greek historian Herodotus wrote in the fifth century B.C.E., "is the gift of the Nile." Observing that no other place in the world produced food so effortlessly and bountifully as did this already ancient land, Herodotus correctly identified the Nile, which the ancient Egyptians themselves simply called "The River," as the most important geographic feature of Egypt. The Nile is the only real river in the whole of North Africa, a phenomenon that gave the inhabitants of that valley a great advantage over all the other peoples west of them. As the source of life-giving water and fertile silt, the Nile presented to ingenious and hard-working human beings the possibility of great agricultural wealth.

In this chapter you will learn how the environment, and the ability to transform it, are important elements in human history and its study. Geography, with its physical features and climate, its native plants and animals, presents to any society a great challenge—geographic characteristics help to define the potential limits of any one group while at the same time providing a series of resources and attributes to be exploited in aid of society. In any given landscape, human beings use and transform what nature has provided, often creating the most extraordinary civilizations out of what are sometimes the harshest of environments. Machu Picchu on a peak in the high Andes, and the great jungle temples of Angkor Wat are triumphs of human skill and effort by the Inca and the Khmer, respectively. Because of these constraints and advantages, historians have come to see geography as an ever-present force in human experience. As Fernand Braudel argues in Reading 1, the physical environment helps to write the very script from which human dramas are played. Similarly, J. N. Postgate in Reading 2 indicates how geography is integral to understanding of the history of any particular part of the world, such as ancient Mesopotamia.

Periodically an obvious feature of the landscape is overlooked by historians. Egypt, for instance, is more than the Nile. The valley is well insulated from the outside by a series of natural barriers. To the east and west, Egypt was shielded from invasion by harsh deserts, often called "the Red Land" because of the color of the sand. Even with the might of modern military technology behind him, German Field Marshall Erwin von Rommel found Egypt's Western Desert to be a formidable barrier in World War II. To the north and south, the population was protected respectively by the Mediterranean Sea and a swampy delta and by a large set of rapids, the First Cataract. Thus the very narrow, 700-mile long land of Egypt is defined by both its core, the Nile River, and its boundaries, the natural barriers that protect it from invasions. This geographic reality had a profound impact on Egypt's history. Politically, the Egyptians enjoyed more than 1,000 years of history with no foreign incursions. This security allowed them to create social and political institutions that lasted thousands of years and contributed to a sense that the universe was well ordered and just. And from a cultural point of view, the isolating, yet fertile, physical environment led Egyptian society to be predominately inwardly focused. The Egyptians did not readily partake of the Mediterranean world or southwest Asia, and this is sometimes reflected in Egyptian culture. Sea trade, for example, was sometimes specifically rejected, as we will see in the selection "Hymn to Hapy"—it was seen as an activity that interferes with the harvest. And even their contacts further south into the neighboring African region of Nubia, as we will see in Part II, were episodic in nature. These realities reflect both Egypt's geography and richness in resources. Except for a ready supply of wood, the Egyptians wanted for very little. This self-sufficiency and geographic insulation allowed them to develop a culture that was largely separate from their neighbors. For them, the Nile Valley, the Land of Egypt, was perfect, and they viewed everything outside that valley with grave suspicion and mistrust.

Finally, the physical environment has a strong impact on a people's worldview—how they see the universe and their role within it. The plants and animals within each society's world inhabit the popular imagination, and climate and spatial contours are reflected in their stories. In *The Epic of Gilgamesh* the cedar forests are contrasted with the rolling steppe land, and in *Popol Vuh* bats and monkeys play a central role in the events that unfold within the story. In ancient writings variations in weather such as violent storms and floods are a central motif, even if the storms' meanings vary from culture to culture. But more significantly, the environment plays a key role in attitudes toward life and the world. In Readings 6, 8, and 9, we see how the environmental characteristics of Mesopotamia, Egypt, and Mesoamerica placed physical limits on these societies, but also offered unique opportunities: We learn how individuals took advantage of these opportunities, and we see how each environment helped shape overall attitudes toward life and life's experiences. For example, the people of ancient Iraq approached their world very pessimistically, in response to the harshness of their environment. But the Egyptians were the opposite—their physical environment, with its annual inundation and its resulting great potential for agriculture as well as the natural barriers from invasion, was kind and benign enough to give the Egyptian population a very positive outlook on life. Of the three places, Mesoamerica had the harshest environment in many ways, producing a worldview that life is difficult but can be understandable and even productive in light of the cycle of birth, death, and rebirth that was part of a universal pattern.

The Importance of Geography in History

Until the twentieth century, historians rarely took geography and the physical environment into consideration when analyzing historical events. That changed after the First World War with the development of a school of historical thinking that moved beyond the political and the military. Beginning in France, this new approach to the past has come to be known as "Annales history" because of the name of its journal, Annales: Economies, Sociétés, Civilizations. *Historians of the* Annales *school emphasized what they called "total history," employing all of the social sciences in their attempt to understand the past in a more comprehensive manner than ever before. Fernand Braudel was one of the main exponents of this new style of history, and geography was one of the primary social sciences that he used in his analyses. In the following passage, he sets out clearly the importance of the physical environment in human affairs; geography, he argues, presents not only opportunities and advantages but also limits and challenges. Human beings exploit what is offered to them, while simultaneously attempting to alter the landscape to suit their needs better. Thus geography "is the stage on which humanity's endless dramas are played out," and the geography of any given area determines in part "their story lines and explains their nature." Without a sense of the physical environment in which a society acts, we cannot understand fully the historical events in that part of the world.*

>> 5. A History of Civilizations

FERNAND BRAUDEL [1963]

The Study of Civilization Involves All the Social Sciences

Civilizations as Geographical Areas

Civilizations, vast or otherwise, can always be located on a map. An essential part of their character depends on the constraints or advantages of their geographical situation.

This, of course, will have been affected for centuries or even millennia by human effort. Every landscape bears the traces of this continuous and cumulative labour, generation after generation contributing to the whole. So doing, humanity itself has been transformed by what the French historian Jules Michelet called 'the decisive shaping of self by self', or (as Karl Marx put it) 'the production of people by people'.

To discuss civilization is to discuss space, land and its contours, climate, vegetation, animal species and natural or other advantages. It is also to discuss what humanity has made of these basic conditions: agriculture, stock-breeding, food, shelter, clothing, communications, industry and so on.

The stage on which humanity's endless dramas are played out partly determines their story-line and explains their nature. The cast will alter, but the set remains broadly the same.

For the expert on India, Hermann Goetz, there are two essential Indias. One is humid, with heavy rainfall, lakes, marshes, forests and jungles, aquatic plants and flowers—the land of people with dark skins. It contrasts with the dryer India of the Indo-Gangetic plain, plus the Deccan plateau—the home of lighter-skinned people, many of them war-like. India is a whole, in Goetz's view, is a debate and a tug-of-war between these two contrasting areas and peoples.

Source: Fernand Braudel, *A History of Civilizations* (New York: Penguin Press, 1994), 9–11. Originally published in French, 1963.

The natural and man-made environment, of course, cannot predetermine everything. It is not all-powerful. But it greatly affects the inherent or acquired advantages of any given situation.

To take inherent advantages, every civilization is born of immediate opportunities, rapidly exploited. Thus in the dawn of time, river civilizations flourished in the old world: Chinese civilization along the Yellow River; pre-Indian along the Indus; Sumerian, Babylonian and Assyrian on the Euphrates and the Tigris; Egyptian on the Nile. A similar group of vigorous civilizations developed in Northern Europe, around the Baltic and the North Sea—not to mention the Atlantic Ocean itself. Much of the West and its dependencies today, in fact, are grouped around that ocean, rather as the Roman world of former times was grouped around the Mediterranean.

These classic instances reveal above all the prime importance of communications. No civilization can survive without mobility: all are enriched by trade and the stimulating impact of strangers. Islam, for instance, is inconceivable without the movement of its caravans across the 'dry seas' of its deserts and steppes, without its expeditions in the Mediterranean and across the Indian Ocean as far as Malacca and China.

Mentioning these achievements has already led us beyond the natural and immediate advantages which supposedly gave rise to civilizations. To overcome the hostility of the desert or the sudden squalls of the Mediterranean, to exploit the steady winds of the Indian Ocean, or to dam a river—all that needed human effort, to enjoy advantages, or rather to create them.

But why were some people capable of such achievements, but not others, in some places but not others, for generations on end?

Arnold Toynbee offered a tempting theory. All human achievement, he thought, involved challenge and response. Nature had to present itself as a difficulty to be overcome. If human beings took up the challenge, their response would lay the foundations of civilization.

But if this theory were carried to the limit, would it imply that the greater the challenge from Nature, the stronger humanity's response? It seems doubtful. In the twentieth century, civilized men and women have taken up the forbidding challenge of the deserts, the polar regions and the equator. Yet, despite the material interests involved, such as gold or oil, they have not yet settled and multiplied in those areas and founded true civilizations there. A challenge, yes, and also a response: but civilization does not always follow—at least until improved technology makes the response more adequate.

Every civilization, then, is based on an area with more or less fixed limits. Each has its own geography with its own opportunities and constraints, some virtually permanent and quite different from one civilization to another. The result? A variegated world, whose maps can indicate which areas have houses built of wood, and which of clay, bamboo, paper, bricks or stone; which areas use wool or cotton or silk for textiles; which areas grow various food crops—rice, maize, wheat, etc. The challenge varies: so does the response.

The Physical Environment of Early Mesopotamia

In this selection, the historian J. N. Postgate applies Braudel's general assertions to the specific environment of ancient Mesopotamia, now modern Iraq. The history of Mesopotamia, especially the south, the area of ancient Sumer and Akkad, can only be understood in terms of the constraints and opportunities presented to its inhabitants by its physical environment, from climate to landforms. Even though human beings first developed agriculture in the rolling hills of northern Iraq, urban life first developed in the south under harsh conditions. On the surface, the physical environment of southern Iraq seems very beneficial: year-round water in two major rivers, the Tigris and Euphrates, a fertile floodplain and delta, and rich soil deposited by annual floods. In reality, however, conditions are harsher. The flooding of the Tigris and Euphrates Rivers was often disastrous. The floods were irregular and unpredictable; they tended to bring too much water all at once, and in the wrong season to be helpful for agriculture. The floods also brought less nutrient-laden silt than rivers in other parts of the world, and they failed to effectively wash the salts from the soil. Thus over time salt deposits built up in the soil, rendering agriculture impossible, and some places had to be abandoned even in antiquity. Southern Mesopotamia is also very flat and perilously close to sea level; this made irrigation easy but drainage difficult. The lack of natural barriers also invited invasions off the steppe land to the west and from the mountains in the east. As a result, there was constant tension between the urban dwellers of Mesopotamia and their less sedentary neighbors. But the two rivers also supplied a very important geographic element for human development: a means of easy transportation and thus communication from south to north. Because the original cities of southern Mesopotamia lacked many natural resources, the Tigris and the Euphrates served as pathways for trade and cultural diffusion. And finally, as Postgate hints, the ease of transportation provided by the rivers and flat flood plain promoted a common culture and lifestyle throughout Mesopotamia.

>> 6. Early Mesopotamia: Society and Economy at the Dawn of History

J. N. POSTGATE [1992]

Mesopotamia: The Land and the Life

The name 'Mesopotamia', coined for a Roman province, is now used for the land between the rivers Tigris and Euphrates, and in many general books it features as the eastern horn of the 'fertile crescent'. The Mesopotamian heartland was a strip of land wrested by human vigilance from adverse climatic conditions. Its geography is essential to the understanding of its history: it defines the lifestyle of the agricultural community, and thereby of the city. It preordains the location of settlements and of the routes between them. Extremes of temperature and abrupt changes in landscape divide the area into very distinct environments, which can be blocked out on a map much more clearly than in most temperate parts of the world. The different zones favour or impose different lifestyles, which have often coincided with ethnic and political divisions and so have a direct impact on history. Sometimes it is the physical conformation of the country that has an obvious effect on its human geography: mountain ranges act as barriers to communication, plains enable it and rivers channel it. Major political units grow up in areas of easy communication, whether in the South or North Mesopotamian plain—Sumer, Babylon, Assyria—or on the Iranian or Anatolian plateaux—Elam, the Hittite Empire, Urartu; the intervening mountain ridges and valleys of the Taurus and Zagros, like so many mountainous areas in the world, foster

Source: J. N. Postgate, *Early Mesopotamia: Society and Economy at the Dawn of History* (New York: Routledge, 1992), 3.

local independence and discourage the rise of larger groupings, political, ethnic and linguistic. Here there were never major centres of cultural diffusion, and it was on the plains of North and South Mesopotamia that social and political developments were forged.

Gilgamesh and the Great Flood

As we have discussed, geography has a great impact on how individuals view the world around them. The inhabitants of ancient Iraq formed a set of attitudes about life and the universe that reflected the difficult and precarious physical conditions in which they lived. The harsh environment of southern Iraq, along with the often destructive flooding of the Tigris and Euphrates Rivers, produced a worldview that was generally pessimistic and negative. We can see this pessimism most clearly in the great poem, The Epic of Gilgamesh. *The story of Gilgamesh goes back to third millennium B.C.E. Sumer, but the version that we have today was written in the Semitic language of Akkadian, probably around 2000 B.C.E. The story describes the constant danger of flooding that the lower reaches of the Tigris and the Eurphrates were prone to. In the course of his adventures and eventual search for everlasting life, the hero Gilgamesh met Utnapishtim, the Mesopotamian version of the biblical Noah, who told the hero of a great flood that had once destroyed almost all of humankind. Unlike the God of the ancient Hebrews, who punished human beings for wickedness and disobedience, the gods in the poem are irrational and vengeful, bringing destruction to humanity for frivolous reasons. For example, Enlil, a primal deity who was the ruler of the gods, disliked the noise that humans were making. Thus Adad, the storm god, helped cause a flood so terrible that even the gods themselves cowered in fear like dogs. The storm and terrible flood in* The Epic of Gilgamesh *are reflections of the tough and unpredictable world in which the inhabitants of Sumer and Akkad lived.*

Despite the prevailing pessimism of this episode, the passage also reveals some of the opportunities and advantages that this same environment provided. The rivers and fertile plain allowed the people of ancient Iraq to grow wheat, graze sheep and cattle, and make wine; the rivers also provided reeds for everyday needs and fish and water fowl for consumption. Moreover, the people of Sumer and Akkad had not only fairly easy access to wood—especially local tamarisk, various species of date palm, and pine—but also a variety of petroleum products, all of which they used in ship building. The poem, in fact, shows that contact by boat with areas like the nearby Persian Gulf was a normal rather than an unusual event. And finally, from a political perspective, the flood plain of the Tigris and the Euphrates was divided among largely independent city-states, like Shurrupak and Uruk, the cities of Utnapishtim and Gilgamesh, respectively. Although agriculture was the mainstay of Mesopotamian life, it was not idealized—rural life was secondary to the great urban establishments that we will see later in Part I. Thus the particular climate, plant species, soil conditions, and rivers of ancient Iraq helped to produce a civilization and history that was unique.

>> 7. The Epic of Gilgamesh

[THIRD MILLENNIUM B.C.E. (SUMERIAN TALE);
SECOND MILLENNIUM B.C.E. (WRITTEN
AKKADIAN VERSION)]

The Story of the Flood

'You know the city Shurrupak, it stands on the banks of Euphrates? That city grew old and the gods that were in it were old. There was Anu, lord of the firmament, their father, and warrior Enlil their counsellor, Ninurta the helper, and Ennugi watcher over canals; and with them also was Ea. In those days the world teemed, the people multiplied, the world bellowed like a wild bull, and the great god was aroused by the clamour. Enlil heard the clamour and he said to the gods in council, "The uproar of mankind is intolerable and sleep is no longer possible by reason of the babel." So the gods agreed to exterminate mankind. Enlil did this, but Ea because of his oath warned me in a dream. He whispered their words to my house of reeds, "Reed-house, reed-house! Wall, O wall, hearken reed-house, wall reflect; O man of Shurrupak, son of Ubara-Tutu; tear down your house and build a boat, abandon possessions and look for life, despise worldly goods and save your soul alive. Tear down your house, I say, and build a boat. These are the measurements of the barque as you shall build her: let her beam equal her length, let her deck be roofed like the vault that covers the abyss; then take up into the boat the seed of all living creatures."

'When I had understood I said to my lord, "Behold, what you have commanded I will honour and perform, but how shall I answer the people, the city, the elders?" Then Ea opened his mouth and said to me, his servant, "Tell them this: I have learnt that Enlil is wrathful against me, I dare no longer walk in his land nor live in his city; I will go down to the Gulf to dwell with Ea my lord. But on you he will rain down

abundance, rare fish and shy wild-fowl, a rich harvest-tide. In the evening the rider of the storm will bring you wheat in torrents."

'In the first light of dawn all my household gathered round me, the children brought pitch and the men whatever was necessary. On the fifth day I laid the keel and the ribs, then I made fast the planking. The ground-space was one acre, each side of the deck measured one hundred and twenty cubits, making a square. I built six decks below, seven in all, I divided them into nine sections with bulkheads between. I drove in wedges where needed, I saw to the punt-poles, and laid in supplies. The carriers brought oil in baskets, I poured pitch into the furnace and asphalt and oil; more oil was consumed in caulking, and more again the master of the boat took into his stores. I slaughtered bullocks for the people and every day I killed sheep. I gave the shipwrights wine to drink as though it were river water, raw wine and red wine and oil and white wine. There was feasting then as there is at the time of the New Year's festival; I myself anointed my head. On the seventh day the boat was complete.

'Then was the launching full of difficulty; there was shifting of ballast above and below till two thirds was submerged. I loaded into her all that I had of gold and of living things, my family, my kin, the beast of the field both wild and tame, and all the craftsmen. I sent them on board, for the time that Shamash had ordained was already fulfilled when he said, "In the evening, when the rider of the storm sends down the destroying rain, enter the boat and batten her down." The time was fulfilled, the evening came, the rider of the storm sent down the rain. I looked out at the weather and it was terrible, so I too boarded the boat and battened her down. All was now complete, the battening and the caulking; so I handed the tiller to Puzur-Amurri the steersman, with the navigation and the care of the whole boat.

Source: N. K. Sandars, trans., *The Epic of Gilgamesh* (New York: Penguin Press, 1972), 108–111.

'With the first light of dawn a black cloud came from the horizon; it thundered within where Adad, lord of the storm was riding. In front over hill and plain Shullat and Hanish, heralds of the storm, led on. Then the gods of the abyss rose up; Nergal pulled out the dams of the nether waters, Ninurta the war-lord threw down the dykes, and the seven judges of hell, the Annunaki, raised their torches, lighting the land with their livid flame. A stupor of despair went up to heaven when the god of the storm turned daylight to darkness, when he smashed the land like a cup. One whole day the tempest raged, gathering fury as it went, it poured over the people like the tides of battle; a man could not see his brother nor the people be seen from heaven. Even the gods were terrified at the flood, they fled to the highest heaven, the firmament of Anu; they crouched against the walls, cowering like curs. Then Ishtar the sweet-voiced Queen of Heaven cried out like a woman in travail: "Alas the days of old are turned to dust because I commanded evil; why did I command this evil in the council of all the gods? I commanded wars to destroy the people, but are they not my people, for I brought them forth? Now like the spawn of fish they float in the ocean." The great gods of heaven and hell wept, they covered their mouths.

'For six days and six nights the winds blew, torrent and tempest and flood overwhelmed the world, tempest and flood raged together like warring hosts. When the seventh day dawned the storm from the south subsided, the sea grew calm, the flood was stilled; I looked at the face of the world and there was silence, all mankind was turned to clay. The surface of the sea stretched as flat as a roof-top; I opened a hatch and the light fell on my face. Then I bowed low, I sat down and I wept, the tears streamed down my face, for on every side was the waste of water. I looked for land in vain, but fourteen leagues distant there appeared a mountain, and there the boat grounded; on the mountain of Nisir the boat held fast, she held fast and did not budge. One day she held, and a second day on the mountain of Nisir she held fast and did not budge. A third day, and a fourth day she held fast on the mountain and did not budge; a fifth day and sixth day she held fast on the mountain. When the seventh day dawned I loosed a dove and let her go. She flew away, but finding no resting-place she returned. Then I loosed a swallow, and she flew away but finding no resting-place she returned. I loosed a raven, she saw that the waters had retreated, she ate, she flew around, she cawed, and she did not come back. Then I threw everything open to the four winds, I made a sacrifice and poured out a libation on the mountain top. Seven and again seven cauldrons I set up on their stands, I heaped up wood and cane and cedar and myrtle. When the gods smelled the sweet savour, they gathered like flies over the sacrifice.

Hymn to Hapy

As Herodotus was keenly aware, the geography of Egypt produced an environment that was conducive to human survival and development, and one of the central features of that physical environment was the Nile River itself. The Nile, with its flood plain and natural basins, provided year-round water and ready food in the form of various plants and animals. But the river has an additional characteristic that the Tigris and the Euphrates do not have: an annual, predictable flood, or inundation, whose quality benefited the inhabitants of the Nile Valley in a way that is nearly unique in the world. Beginning in July, the flood came at exactly the right time for growing crops. Likewise, it washed the salt out of the soil and deposited a thick layer of extremely fertile silt from Ethiopia in central Africa—the dark color of the earth gave Egypt the epithet of "the Black Land."

The consequences of this kind physical environment can be seen in the "Hymn to Hapy," the god of the flood, or inundation. Unlike Mesopotamia, there are no unpleasant storm gods in the almost stormless Egypt. Instead, the annual flood—a physical event—is itself turned into a beneficent deity who brings life and prosperity to the land of Egypt. The god, though a male, is portrayed with female breasts to show his nurturing qualities, and from his head sprouts various water plants that symbolize the Nile Valley and the delta. In the gendered natural world of the Egyptians, male and female characteristics often blurred— male gods could produce life out of their bodies and they could nurture all of humankind.

The "Hymn to Hapy" reveals much about the relationship between geography and the ancient Egyptians. First, from a practical point of view, the Hymn indicates what the Nile allowed the Egyptians to grow, including a variety of grains, to eat naturally, like fish and fowl, and to use, either through cultivation (like flax for linen) or naturally (like papyrus for books). But the Nile also allowed the raising of cattle in great numbers. Unlike the more arid conditions that prevail in the rest of the Mediterranean basin, Egypt was able to support large herds of cattle, a feat that amazed its visitors. The end result of this physical environment, and the human manipulation of it through agriculture, was that the people of Egypt, as the Hymn points out, did not go hungry: To be well fed was the normal state of affairs.

Second, this particular physical environment had an enormously positive impact on the Egyptians' psychological outlook on the world. Unlike their Mesopotamian counter-parts, the Egyptians believed their gods and the cosmos to be largely benevolent toward human beings. The endless repetitive and predictable cycles of nature promoted a sense of well-being and optimism. The Egyptians viewed their everyday world of agriculture so positively that their conception of the afterlife was not of a better place, but exactly the same place with some minor adjustments. The cult of the dead, with its mummies, tomb goods, and devotion to Osiris—simultaneously a god of grain, resurrection, and the Underworld—was meant to replicate for all eternity the peaceful agricultural life that was experienced while living. The agricultural world of the Nile Valley was as close to para-dise as a human could come. The Egyptians idealized this rural world in a way that was only possible due to the positive physical environment in which they lived.

>> 8. Hymn to Hapy

[MIDDLE KINGDOM COMPOSITION; SURVIVES IN PAPYRI FROM EIGHTEENTH DYNASTY (c. 1550–1305)]

(xi, 6) Adoration of Hapy:
Hail to you, Hapy,
Sprung from earth,
Come to nourish Egypt!
Of secret ways,
A darkness by day,

To whom his followers sing!
Who floods the fields that Re has made,
To nourish all who thirst;
Lets drink the waterless desert,
His dew descending from the sky.

Friend of Geb, lord of Nepri,
Promoter of the arts of Ptah.
Lord of the fishes,
He makes fowl stream south,
No bird falling down from heat.

Source: "Hymn to Hapy," in *Ancient Egyptian Literature: A Book of Readings*, v. 1: *The Old and Middle Kingdoms*, edited by Miriam Lichtheim (Berkeley: University of California Press, 1975), 205–209.

Maker of barley, creator of emmer,
He lets the temples celebrate.

When he is sluggish (xii, i) noses clog,
Everyone is poor;
As the sacred loaves are pared,
A million perish among men.
When he plunders, the whole land rages,
Great and small roar;
People change according to his coming,
When Khnum has fashioned him.
When he floods, earth rejoices,
Every belly jubilates,
Every jawbone takes on laughter,
Every tooth is bared.

Food provider, bounty maker,
Who creates all that is good!
Lord of awe, sweetly fragrant,
Gracious when he comes.
Who makes herbage for the herds,
Gives (5) sacrifice for every god.
Dwelling in the netherworld,
He controls both sky and earth.
Conqueror of the Two Lands,
He fills the stores,
Makes bulge the burns,
Gives bounty to the poor.

Grower of all delightful trees—
He has no revenue;
Barges exist by his might—
He is not hewn in stone.
Mountains cleave by his surge—
One sees no workmen, no leader,
He carries off in secrecy.
No one knows the place he's in,
His cavern is not found in books.

He has no shrines, no portions,
No service of his choice;
But youths, his children, hail him,
One greets him like a king.
Lawful, timely, he comes forth,
Filling Egypt, South and North;
(xiii, 1) As one drinks, all eyes are on him,
Who makes his bounty overflow.

He who grieved goes out in joy,
Every heart rejoices;
Sobk, Neith's child, bares his teeth,
The Nine Gods exult.
As he spouts, makes drink the fields,
Everyone grows vigorous.
Rich because another toils,
One has no quarrel with him;
Maker of food he's not defied,
One sets no limits for him.

Light-maker who comes from dark,
Fattener of herds,
Might that fashions all,
None can live without him.
People are clothed (5) with the flax of his fields,
For he made Hedj-hotep serve him;
He made anointing with his unguents,
For he is the like of Ptah.
All kinds of crafts exist through him,
All books of godly words,
His produce from the sedges.

Entering the cavern,
Coming out above,
He wants his coming secret.
If he is heavy, the people dwindle,
A year's food supply is lost.
The rich man looks concerned,

Everyone is seen with weapons,
Friend does not attend to friend.
Cloth is wanting for one's clothes,
Noble children lack their finery;
There's no eye-paint to be had,
No one is anointed.

This truth is fixed in people's hearts:
Want is followed by deceit.
He who consorts with the sea,
Does not (xiv, I) harvest grain.
Though one praises all the gods,
Birds will not come down to deserts.
No one beats his hand with gold,
No man can get drunk on silver,
One can not eat lapis lazuli,
Barley is foremost and strong!

Songs to the harp are made for you,
One sings to you with clapping hands;
The youths, your children hail you,
Crowds adorn themselves for you,
Who comes with riches, decks the land,
Makes flourish every body;
Sustains the pregnant woman's heart,
And loves a multitude of herds.

When he rises at the residence,
Men feast on the meadows' gifts,
(5) Decked with lotus for the nose,
And all the things that sprout from earth.

Children's hands are filled with herbs,
They forget to eat.
Good things are strewn about the houses,
The whole land leaps for joy.

When you overflow, O Hapy,
Sacrifice is made for you;
Oxen are slaughtered for you,
A great oblation is made to you.
Fowl is fattened for you,
Desert game snared for you,
As one repays your bounty.
One offers to all the gods
Of that which Hapy has provided,
Choice incense, oxen, goats,
And birds in holocaust.

Mighty is Hapy in his cavern,
His name unknown to those below,
For the gods do not reveal it.
You people who extol the gods,
Respect the awe his son has made,
The All-Lord who sustains the shores!
  Oh joy when you come!
  Oh joy when you come, O Hapy,
  Oh joy when you come!
  You who feed men and herds
  With your meadow gifts!
  Oh joy when you come!
  Oh joy when you come, O Hapy,
  Oh joy when you come!

The Physical Environment of Mesoamerica

Due to the systematic destruction of Maya texts by the Spanish, almost no written documents from Mesoamerica survive today. In the middle of the sixteenth century, however, Quiché speakers in the highlands of Guatemala used the newly acquired Roman alphabet to write down, in their own language, a version of the ancient Popol Vuh, *or* Council Book. *This remarkable prose work tells the story of the Quiché Maya from before the beginning of time through to the Spanish Conquest. As with most foundation myths, the* Popol Vuh *reveals much about the relationship between the physical environment and human beings. The physical conditions of this part of the Maya world, and attitudes toward them, are clear throughout the work. The two passages from the selection below tell about the origin of human beings. In the course of the story, the gods make four attempts to create humans, the first three of which were unsuccessful. In the third attempt, the gods formed creatures out of wood, but because they did not worship the gods properly, they were destroyed in a great flood—which also included a rain of burning pine resin. The gods were successful in their fourth attempt, however, creating the first four human beings, each of whom served as a* **protoancestor,** *"our first mother-fathers," of the four Quiché lineages (extended families). Significantly, these first humans were made out of the most important foodstuff of the Maya, ground yellow and white corn (maize), mixed with water, like some sort of giant tamale. This connected humans as well to the powerful maize god, who was both a god of creation and of resurrection.*

The story, however, hints at a geography that presented more challenges than opportunities, especially when compared to Mesopotamia and Egypt. The soil is almost universally poor, whether in the lowlands of the Petén and Yucatán or the highlands of Guatemala. Likewise the climate is harsh in much of the region. Yet despite this difficult environment, the Popol Vuh *suggests that a wide range of food was available to the Maya, either by foraging or through cultivation. And while the environment produced inhospitable creatures like jaguars and poisonous snakes, the Maya believed these animals also had a positive divine quality that could be beneficial to human beings. Theirs was a hard world in which the gods could be nurturing and life-giving, as in Egypt, or destructive, as in Mesopotamia, though never for frivolous reasons. As we will see in Part II, this harsh environment of Mesoamerica produced a concept of demanding gods that occasionally required human sacrifice so that the community might thrive. But the various episodes in the* Popol Vuh *are as much about hope and rebirth as they are about death and destruction. The* Popol Vuh *shows how the world might be a dangerous place for human beings, but it also can be an understandable one with inevitable cycles that could be productive for humans.*

>> 9. Popol Vuh

[ANCIENT TALE WRITTEN DOWN IN THE ROMAN ALPHABET IN THE MID-SIXTEENTH CENTURY C.E.]

Again there comes a humiliation, destruction, and demolition. The manikins, woodcarvings were killed when the Heart of Sky devised a flood for them. A great flood was made; it came down on the heads of the manikins, woodcarvings.

The man's body was carved from the wood of the coral tree by the Maker. Modeler. And as for the woman, the Maker, Modeler needed the hearts of bulrushes for the woman's body. They were not competent, nor did they speak before the builder and sculptor who made them and brought them forth, and so they were killed, done in by a flood:

There came a rain of resin from the sky.

There came the one named Gouger of Faces: he gouged out their eyeballs.

There came Sudden Bloodletter: he snapped off their heads.

There came Crunching Jaguar: he ate their flesh.

There came Tearing Jaguar: he tore them open.

Source: Dennis Tedlock, trans., *Popol Vuh: The Mayan Book of the Dawn of Life* (New York: Touchstone, 1996), 71–73, 145–147.

They were pounded down to the bones and tendons, smashed and pulverized even to the bones. Their faces were smashed because they were incompetent before their mother and their father, the Heart of Sky, named Hurricane. The earth was blackened because of this; the black rainstorm began, rain all day and rain all night. Into their houses came the animals, small and great. Their faces were crushed by things of wood and stone. Everything spoke: their water jars, their tortilla griddles, their plates, their cooking pots, their dogs, their grinding stones, each and every thing crushed their faces. Their dogs and turkeys told them:

"You caused us pain, you ate us, but now it is *you* whom *we* shall eat." And this is the grinding stone:

"[...] We were undone because of you.

And here is the beginning of the conception of humans, and of the search for the ingredients of the human body. So they spoke, the Bearer, Begetter, the Makers, Modelers named Sovereign Plumed Serpent:

"The dawn has approached, preparations have been made, and morning has come for the provider, nurturer, born in the light, begotten in the light. Morning has come for humankind, for the people of the face of the earth," they said. It all came together as they went on thinking in the darkness, in the night, as they searched and they sifted, they thought and they wondered.

And here their thoughts came out in clear light. They sought and discovered what was needed for human flesh. It was only a short while before the sun, moon, and stars were to appear above the Makers and Modelers. Split Place, Bitter Water Place is the name: the yellow corn, white corn came from there.

And these are the names of the animals who brought the food: fox, coyote, parrot, crow. There were four animals who brought the news of the ears of yellow corn and white corn. They were coming from over there at Split Place, they showed the way to the split.

And this was when they found the staple foods.

And these were the ingredients for the flesh of the human work, the human design, and the water was for the blood. It became human blood, and corn was also used by the Bearer, Begetter.

And so they were happy over the provisions of the good mountain, filled with sweet things, thick with yellow corn, white corn, and thick with pataxte and cacao, countless zapotes, anonas, jocotes, nances, matasanos, sweets—the rich foods filling up the citadel named Split Place, Bitter Water Place. All the edible fruits were there: small staples, great staples, small plants, great plants. The way was shown by the animals.

And then the yellow corn and white corn were ground, and Xmucane did the grinding nine times. Food was used, along with the water she rinsed her hands with, for the creation of grease; it became human fat when it was worked by the Bearer, Begetter, Sovereign Plumed Serpent, as they are called.

After that, they put it into words:

the making, the modeling of our first mother-
    father,
with yellow corn, white corn alone for the flesh,
food alone for the human legs and arms,
for our first fathers, the four human works.

It was staples alone that made up their flesh.

These are the names of the first people who were made and modeled.

This is the first person: Jaguar Quitze.
And now the second: Jaguar Night.
And now the third: Not Right Now.
And the fourth: Dark Jaguar.

And these are the names of our first mother-fathers. They were simply made and modeled, it is said; they had no mother and no father. We have named the men by themselves. No woman gave birth to them, nor were they begotten by the builder, sculptor, Bearer, Begetter. By sacrifice alone, by genius alone they were made, they were modeled by the Maker, Modeler, Bearer, Begetter, Sovereign Plumed Serpent. And when they came to fruition, they came out human:

They talked and they made words.

They looked and they listened.

They walked, they worked.

They were good people, handsome, with looks of the male kind. Thoughts came into existence and they gazed; their vision came all at once. Perfectly they saw, perfectly they knew everything under the sky, whenever they looked. The moment they turned around and looked around in the sky, on the earth, everything was seen without any obstruction. They didn't have to walk around before they could see what was under the sky; they just stayed where they were.

As they looked, their knowledge became intense. Their sight passed through trees, through rocks, through lakes, through seas, through mountains, through plains. Jaguar Quitze, Jaguar Night, Not Right Now, and Dark Jaguar were truly gifted people.

And then they were asked by the builder and mason:

"What do you know about your being? Don't you look, don't you listen? Isn't your speech good, and your walk? So you must look, to see out under the sky. Don't you see the mountain-plain clearly? So try it," they were told.

And then they saw everything under the sky perfectly. After that, they thanked the Maker, Modeler:

"Truly now,

double thanks, triple thanks

that we've been formed, we've been given

our mouths, our faces,

we speak, we listen,

we wonder, we move,

our knowledge is good, we've understood

what is far and near,

and we've seen what is great and small

under the sky, on the earth.

Thanks to you we've been formed,

we've come to be made and modeled,

our grandmother, our grandfather,"

they said when they gave thanks for having been made and modeled.

>> Mastering the Material

1. Why does Fernand Braudel think that the study of geography is important for the study of history? What does he see as the connection between the physical environment and history?

2. How is J. N. Postgate's description of the environment and geography of Mesopotamia and its impact on Mesopotamian societies reflected in *The Epic of Gilgamesh*?

3. What do *The Epic of Gilgamesh* and the "Hymn to Hapy" reveal about the attitudes and worldviews of the people of Mesopotamia and Egypt, respectively?

4. Floods—some devastating, others benign—figure into a variety of cultures worldwide. How do the various flood stories in this chapter differ from one another? What do these differences tell us about the cultures involved?

Chapter 2

The Origins of Agriculture and Civilization

In *The Satyricon,* Petronius, a Roman writer under the emperor Nero, describes a fantastic banquet given by Trimalchio, a very rich former slave living on the Bay of Naples. Trimalchio's feast included everything from humble olives and figs to an elaborate dish that included sow's udders, lobsters, and tarts made of the finest flour. All of this food was not by accident. Some of it, like the oysters and red mullet, came from the Mediterranean Sea. The boar had been hunted locally. Most of these foodstuffs, however, had been cultivated by farmers in Italy and around the Mediterranean Basin. Bountiful displays like this are revealing for several reasons. Scholars argue, for instance, that literary motifs of banquets and gorging almost always indicate a world in which the diet is not extravagant, and even possibly sparse. Literature often presents a fantasy world of what people would like to eat, but do not. Even in the second century C.E., at the height of the Roman Empire, peasants in some parts of the Mediterranean had to supplement their food supplies by foraging and hunting. But foods like those described by Petronius did exist. All of the agricultural products on Trimalchio's table emerged from the Neolithic Revolution in the ninth millennium B.C.E., and to those first farmers. Indeed, the attempt to provide for some sort of long-term and sustainable food supply is one thread connecting human societies across space and through time. In this chapter you will learn about the origins, nature, and consequences of the invention of agriculture.

The transition from hunter-gatherer to food cultivation and production is called the Neolithic Revolution. This revolution is perhaps the single most important event in human history. Without a plentiful and reliable food supply, the human population could not expand and civilization as we understand it could not exist. Food surpluses and population growth allowed for a greater differentiation and specialization of labor in society and for leisure time to do activities other than mere survival. A lack of sustained food sets limits on the cultural activities of any group, but the freedom from hunger permits human beings to develop in ways that they cannot do while continually searching for nourishment.

The agricultural revolution first took place in what we call the "Fertile Crescent," a large arc that runs from eastern Iraq at the edge of the Zagros Mountains north to southern Turkey and northern Syria, and then south toward Damascus. Scholars have various explanations for why these incipient farmers first decided to domesticate plants and animals, but none of them are entirely satisfactory. What is clear, however, is that several favorable conditions came together in the same place and time: a set of wild plants and animals that could be domesticated fairly easily, fertile soil, an arc of dependable rainfall of about one inch at exactly the right time of year, and a human population willing and able to exploit these natural resources in new ways. Some evidence suggests that animals such as sheep and goats were domesticated before plants, but soon both went hand in hand. Evidence also suggests that domestication occurred independently at different locations in the Fertile Crescent at about the same time. With agriculture humans began a more sedentary, settled life, moving from a strictly foraging way of life to a mixed system that included **horticulture,** and ending with permanent settlements and burgeoning towns. Moreover, knowledge of agriculture became diffused to more and more populations over time. Jared Diamond summarizes the birth and diffusion of agriculture in Reading 10, contrasting the Fertile Crescent to other parts of the world, especially the Americas.

But agriculture, a sedentary way of life, and civilization based on an urban lifestyle developed in places other than the Fertile Crescent, and often at around the same time. In the New World critical and staple crops were developed almost as early as in Eurasia. Corn (maize) may have been domesticated in the Tehuacán Valley south of Mexico City in the seventh millennium B.C.E. Further south, potatoes were domesticated around 5000 B.C.E., and quinoa, an important seed crop, was cultivated by 4000 B.C.E. Sometimes the domestication of local crops and the diffusion of crops from elsewhere went hand in hand. Pre-Inca cultures in Peru, like the Chavin (around 1000 to 200 B.C.E.), cultivated primarily potatoes and quinoa, but the diffusion of maize into South America had already taken place by then as well. A similar story comes from the Far East. Millet, an important cereal found throughout the Old World, may very well have been domesticated in northern China at about the same time that barley and wheat were being domesticated in northern Iraq and southern Turkey. And Francesca Bray suggests that early farmers domesticated rice somewhere in the plains of southeast Asia.

Along with the domestication of plants and animals came a host of agricultural techniques. Farming could not spread or be improved without continued developments in technology that permitted a surplus. In northern China, millet and wheat were grown in the same fields but at different times of the year—this allowed for crop rotation, which rehabilitated the soil, and a double harvest of cereals. Likewise, the development of irrigation systems allowed for higher productivity and an expansion of crops into arable land that would otherwise not be cultivated. Egypt was luckier than most other places. After the annual Nile floodwaters had receded, and the barley and emmer wheat had been planted, the crop did not need to be irrigated—farmers simply waited until the cereals were ready for harvest. Only gardens and fruit trees required artificial irrigation. In Asia, however, irrigation systems were necessary for successful agriculture. Although cereals in northern Iraq needed no irrigation, those in southern Iraq, in Mesopotamia itself, did. Early farmers began to build a series of canals from the Tigris and the Euphrates in order to facilitate the watering of fields. Farmers also created irrigation systems in China. This situation led Karl Wittfogel, a historian of China, to theorize about what he called "hydraulic societies." In this theory, Wittfogel argues that in order to build large-scale irrigation, Asian societies especially had to develop strong, if not authoritarian, governments. His *Oriental Despotism* (1957), a classroom standard for many years, has now been generally discredited. In its place, Bray (Reading 12) has shown how irrigation systems in places like China and Mesopotamia did not require highly centralized or despotic political systems to work. And John Henderson (Reading 13) goes even further in arguing that elaborate "hydraulic societies" were not at all necessary for the rise of civilization. Irrigation, for instance, was far more crucial to growing rice than millet, and the political center of ancient China was in the millet-producing north.

The division of the world's population into categories of hunter-gatherers and agriculturalists is something of a false dichotomy. Other patterns of food production exist as well. *Pastoral* societies, for example, rely on the domestication of animals brought about by the agricultural revolution, but they are nomadic in nature, traveling with their herds to new pastures as the seasons change. This practice is what we call *transhumance*, and these nomadic cultures are not, strictly speaking, agriculturalist. Some scholars have also identified societies engaged in a complex mix of food production that included the more intermediary step of horticulture: gardening. Anthropologists observe that gardening is a distinctly different kind of activity from either foraging or farming, yet it can have aspects of both. Horticulturalists practice a simpler form of plant cultivation, and this may or may not evolve into agriculture. Many tribal societies, especially in tropical forests in places like New Guinea, remain horticulturalists to this day. Lastly, other societies, past and present, engaged (or continue to engage) in a system that combined at least three of these basic food systems. Two examples are the Maya and some sub-Saharan African peoples.

Different cultures remember the origins of agriculture differently. Some cultures, like Vedic India or the ancient Hebrews, looked down on agriculture and farming. Both groups had their origins as pastoralists, and so farming and farmers were suspect. In India, the top two castes were actually forbidden to engage in agriculture. But this reaction is unusual. The Romans, for instance, held that the only honorable pursuit for a citizen was farming. Most often agriculture was connected with the gods or with great heroes of the mythic past. In ancient Greece, grain and bread were the gifts of the great goddess Demeter. Among the Maya, the divine twins, Hunahpu and Xbalanque, cultivated gardens on behalf of their divine mother and grandmother. In the passages that follow, sources from the Dogon in Mali and the Chinese connected the learning of agriculture to culture heroes of a distant past, heroes who were in one way or another connected to the divine.

The First Farmers

The importance of food production for human history cannot be gainsaid. In an article written just prior to his best-selling environmental history Guns, Germs, and Steel, *the scientist-turned-historian Jared Diamond succinctly summarizes the whole of the Neolithic Revolution, explaining how it happened and what its important consequences were: The domestication of plants and animals after 9000 B.C.E. and the subsequent diffusion of critical knowledge outward were essential for the development of human society and culture. He also points out another important feature: The wild plants available to the incipient farmers were relatively easy to domesticate and highly nutritious for human beings. One critical crop was einkorn, a particular species of wheat. But some plants, including einkorn, do not necessarily grow well outside of their native habitats. The other cereals domesticated in the Fertile Crescent, emmer wheat and barley, were more adaptable to other climates and became the cereal staples for both Mesopotamia and Egypt. The population growth that resulted from cultivating these crops promoted increased trade between these regions. Neolithic-period Jericho had a relatively large population of some 2,000 inhabitants, and the primary source of its success was trade. But cultivation, pastoralism, and trade have their downsides. Living in such close proximity to livestock meant that humans sometimes contracted the diseases of their animals. Eventually, humans developed immunities to most diseases, but before that happened the effects were often disasterous. Moreover, through trade, diseases were spread throughout Eurasia and large parts of Africa, traveling from one population to another. Eventually, as Diamond points out, these diseases would spread to the Americas with devastating consequences.*

>> 10. Location, Location, Location: The First Farmers

JARED DIAMOND [1997]

Human history's most important event since the last Ice Age was the first rise of agriculture in Southwest Asia's Fertile Crescent. The origin of agriculture triggered a long train of economic, political, and technological developments, which began there and spread outward. As one example, this wave of changes explains why this journal, published in a land originally inhabited by Native Americans, is nevertheless written in a language of the Indo-European language family that arose 10,000 years earlier and 10,000 miles distant, in or near the crescent. Why did agriculture first develop in the narrow swath of hills extending only from southeast Turkey to western Iran [...]? A report on page 1312 of this issue (1) helps answer that question by pinpointing the site of domestication for einkorn wheat, one of eight so-called "founder crops" that launched crescent agriculture around 9000 B.C (2).

Botanists already knew that cultivated einkorn's ancestor was a very similar wild cereal that still grows in natural habitats in the crescent (3). It was unknown, however, where within the crescent wild einkorn was first taken into cultivation. Heun *et al.* (1) analyzed DNA from 68 lines of cultivated einkorn, plus 261 wild einkorn lines sampled over the crescent's whole expanse as well as outside the crescent.

Among those wild lines, the most distinct genetically proved to be a group of 11 from the Karacadağ mountains of southeast Turkey. Those 11 also turned out to be the ones genetically most similar to cultivated einkorn, and so presumably the crop's immediate ancestors. This discovery is compatible with previous nonmolecular evidence. The Karacadağ mountains were already known to support stands of wild einkorn so dense and extensive that they were being harvested by hunter-gatherers even before einkorn's domestication. Nearby archeological sites contain remains of both wild and cultivated einkorn and are among the crescent's oldest farming sites.

What are some of the broad implications of these findings? Genetically and morphologically, cultivated einkorn is quite similar to wild einkorn in general. Now that the specific wild ancestral line has been identified as being even more similar to the crop, we can better appreciate why einkorn's domestication was so easy and quick. The crescent's archeological record shows that at most a few centuries were required for the transition from hunter-gatherer villages harvesting wild plants to farming villages planting fully domesticated crops.

Source: Jared Diamond, "Location, Location, Location: The First Farmers," *Science* 278 (Nov. 1997); 1243–1244.

For einkorn (and probably for the other founder crops as well), that transition required changes in only a few genetic loci, which account for the few morphological changes distinguishing the crop from wild einkorn (1).

But those few changes were of great value to the earliest farmers. They included heavier seeds and denser seed masses (yielding a crop even more productive than its wild ancestor), plus a firm stalk making seeds more easily harvestable by preventing them from dropping to the ground. Repeated cycles of sowing, growing, and harvesting wild einkorn would have selected automatically for those mutations (3). The first cultivators could have had no conscious intent to produce a crop, and no way of anticipating how radically agriculture would change their societies.

These few, simple changes during einkorn's domestication contrast sharply with the drastic biological reorganization required for the domestication of Native Americans' leading cereal, maize, from its wild ancestor, teosinte. This difference alone helps explain why densely populated agricultural societies arose so much earlier and developed so much more rapidly in the crescent than in the New World.

Can we attach any significant to the new finding that, within the crescent, einkorn was domesticated specifically in southeast Turkey rather than at some other site? Here we find another clue to the early rapid rise of crescent agriculture. In different parts of the crescent lived wild species ancestral to some of the world's earliest and most useful species of crops and livestock. With the discovery by Heun *et al. (1)*, we can pinpoint the origins of three of the crescent's eight founder crops (chickpea, bitter vetch, and now einkorn) to eastern Turkey. Grapes and olives were domesticated nearby to the south; sheep, pigs, goats, and cattle close by in possibly the central, north central, eastern, and western crescent, respectively; and barley, emmer wheat, peas, lentils, and flax in still-to- be-identified parts of the crescent. Only slightly to the northeast of the crescent, on the shores of the Caspian Sea, grows the wild grass *Aegilops squarrosa*. When it

hybridized with cultivated emmer wheat spreading east from the crescent, the result was bread wheat, the most valuable single crop in the modern world. Thus, the crescent's diversity of useful wild plant and animal species, living in close proximity to each other, enabled the crescent's first farmers quickly to assemble a balanced package of domesticates meeting all of humanity's basic needs: carbohydrates, protein, oil, milk, animal transport and traction, and vegetable and animal fiber for rope and clothing (3, 4).

That valuable package spread rapidly through and beyond the crescent [...], not only outcompeting hunter-gatherer economies in productivity, but also preempting alternative sequences of plant and animal domestication that might otherwise have arisen elsewhere in western Eurasia. The spread was accelerated by the west-east axis of the whole Eurasian continent as well as of the crescent itself, permitting crops, livestock, and people to expand at the same latitude without having to adapt to new day lengths, climates, and diseases. Cultivated einkorn's rapid diffusion from the Karacadağ mountains preempted possible independent domestications of einkorn elsewhere in its wild range. The rapid diffusion of both einkorn and emmer in turn preempted widespread cultivation of other related domesticable wild grasses, such as Timopheev's wheat. In contrast, the New World's north-south axis required domesticates to adapt to changes of latitude as they spread. The resulting slow spread of crops within Native America permitted numerous independent domestications of the same crop or of related crops (for example, squashes and cottons) in different areas. Within less than 2000 years of the beginnings of domestication in the crescent, its results had been carried east and west to launch the origins of food production over a huge swath of Eurasia [...], from Pakistan to the Balkans (3). Food production's expansion over the Americas, Africa, and the Indian subcontinent was much slower because of the north-south axes of those landmasses (4).

In short, einkorn domestication in the Karacadağ mountains exemplifies the enormous head start that western Eurasian societies gained from Fertile Crescent biogeography. For history's broad patterns, as for real estate investment, location is almost everything. Plant and animal domestication was prerequisite to the growth of large, dense, sedentary human populations, in which the food-producing activities of part of the population yielded storable food surpluses to feed non–food-producing parts of the population. Hence, food production triggered the emergence of kings, bureaucrats, scribes, professional soldiers, and metal-workers and other full-time crafts-people (4). Literacy, metallurgy, stratified societies, advanced weapons, and empires rested on food production. In addition, smallpox and the other crowd epidemic diseases of Eurasia could evolve only in those dense, sedentary human populations living in close contact with domesticated animals, whose own pathogens evolved into those special-ized pathogens afflicting us (4). Thus, a long straight line runs through world history, from those first domesticates at the Karacadağ mountains and

elsewhere in the Fertile Crescent, to the "guns, germs, and steel" by which European colonists in modern times destroyed so many native societies of other continents.

References and Notes

1. M. Heun *et al. Science* 278, 1312 (1997).
2. All dates that I cite are so-called calibrated radiocarbon dates, which are corrected for temporal fluctuations in atmospheric carbon isotope ratios and thus correspond to approximate calendar years. The dates in (1) are younger because they instead are uncalibrated dates.
3. D. Zohary and M. Hopf, *Domestication of Plants in the Old World* (Oxford Univ. Press, Oxford, ed. 2, 1993).
4. J. Diamond, *Guns, Germs and Steel: The Fates of Human Societies* (Norton, New York, 1997).

The Eloquent Peasant

The diffusion of agriculture into Egypt is the subject of some controversy. While some scholars argue for an Ethiopian origin of some domesticated plants, most agree that the source of Egyptian agriculture was through southwest Asia. In the "Hymn to Hapy" we have already seen many of the agricultural products that the Egyptians grew in the Nile Valley, such as flax and barley, both of which originated in the Fertile Crescent. The Middle Kingdom (about 2040–1650 B.C.E.) story of "The Eloquent Peasant" adds some important details to the agricultural story. The business of Egypt was agriculture, and its importance in the Nile Valley and nearby oases make a common theme in Egyptian tales. In this story a peasant from the closest oasis to Egypt, the Wadi Natrun (Salt-Field), brings various products—both imported into his own oasis from further afield, like staves from the Farafra Oasis and leopard skins from even further away, and his own produce—to the lower stretches of the Nile Valley for trad-ing. In the course of his journey he is robbed of his donkey and goods, and he seeks justice from a royal official. Two of the most important farm items that the peasant possessed were barley, which was cultivated not only on the banks of the Nile but also in all of the oases west of the valley, and his donkey. The Egyptians used barley for bread, some of which they ate and some of which they fermented into the beer men-tioned in the tale. The peasant presented his case most effectively, and at the end of the story the royal official orders Nemynakht to give the peasant not only the goods that he had seized but also his own pigs, cattle, donkeys, emmer wheat, and barley. All of these animals and plants had diffused into Egypt from Asia. Finally, the natron mentioned in the story was a salt used by the Egyptians in the preparation of mummies for the tomb and was an important trade item. Some of the plants, animals, and objects listed for trade are unknown to us.

>> 11. The Eloquent Peasant
[c. 2040–1650 B.C.E.]

(R1) There was a man named Khun-Anup, a peasant of Salt-Field. He had a wife whose name was [Ma]rye. This peasant said to his wife: "Look here, I am going down to Egypt to bring food from there for my children. Go, measure for me the barley which is in the barn, what is left of [last year's] barley." Then she measured for him [twenty-six] gallons of barley. (5) This peasant said to his wife: "Look, you have twenty gallons of barley as food for you and your children. Now make for me these six gallons of barley into bread and beer for every day in which [I shall travel]."

This peasant went down to Egypt. He had loaded his donkeys with rushes, *rdmt*-grass, (10) natron, salt, sticks of — — —, staves from Cattle-Country, leopard skins, (15) wolf skins, *ns3*-plants, '*nw*-stones, *tnm*-plants, *hprwr*-plants, (20) *s3hwt, s3skwt, miswt*-plants, *snt*-stones, '*b3w*-stones, (25) *ibs3*-plants, *inbi*-plants, pidgeons, *n'rw*-birds, *wgs*-birds, (30) *wbn*-plants, *tbsw*-plants, *gngnt*, earth-hair, and *inst*; (35) in sum, all the good products of Salt-Field. This peasant went south toward Hnes. He arrived in the district of Perfefi, north of Medenyt. There he met a man standing on the riverbank whose name was Nemtynakht. He was the son of a man (40) named Isri and subordinate of the high steward Rensi, the son of Meru.

This Nemtynakht said, when he saw this peasant's donkeys which tempted his heart: "If only I had a potent divine image through which I could seize this peasant's goods!" Now the house of this Nemtynakht was at the beginning (45) of a path which was narrow, not so wide as to exceed the width of a shawl. And one side of it was under water, the other under barley. This Nemtynakht said to his servant: "Go, bring me a sheet from my house." It was brought to him straightway. He spread it out on the beginning of the path, (50) so that its fringe touched the water, its hem the barley.

Now this peasant came along the public road. (Bl, I) Then this Nemtynakht said: "Be careful, peasant; don't step on my clothes! This peasant said: "I'll do as you wish, my course is a good one." So he went up higher. This Nemtynakht said: (5) "Will you have my barley for a path?" This peasant said: "My course is a good one. The riverbank is steep and our way is under barley, for you block the path with your clothes. Will you then not let us pass on the road?"

Just then one of the donkeys filled (10) its mouth with a wisp of barley. This Nemtynakht said: "Now I shall seize your donkey, peasant, for eating my barley. It shall tread out grain for its offense!" This peasant said: "My course is a good one. Only one (wisp) is destroyed. Could I buy my donkey for its value, if you seize it (15) for filling its mouth with a wisp of barley? But I know the lord of this domain; it belongs to the high steward Rensi, the son of Meru. He punishes every robber in this whole land. Shall I be robbed in his domain?" This Nemtynakht said: "Is this the saying people say: (20) 'A poor man's name is pronounced for his master's sake'. It is I who speak to you, and you invoke the high steward!"

Then he took a stick of green tamarisk to him and trashed all his limbs with it, seized his donkeys, drove them to his domain. Then this peasant (25) wept very loudly for the pain of that which was done to him. This Nemtynakht said: "Don't raise your voice, peasant. Look, you are bound for the abode of the Lord of Silence!" This

Source: "The Eloquent Peasant," in *Ancient Egyptian Literature: A Book of Readings*, v. 1: *The Old and Middle Kingdoms*, edited by Miriam Lichtheim (Berkeley: University of California Press, 1975), 170–171, 182.

peasant said: "You beat me, you steal my goods, and now you take the complaint from my mouth! O Lord of Silence, give me back (30) my things, so that I can stop crying to your dreadedness!" [...]

Then the high steward Rensi, the son of Meru, sent two guards [to bring Nemtynakht].

(135) He was brought and a report was made of [all his property] — — — his wheat, his barley, his donkeys, — — —, his pigs, his small cattle — — —. — — — of this Nemtynakht [was given] to this peasant — — —.

Colophon: It is finished — — —.

Agriculture

China is as important for the development of agriculture in east Asia as the Fertile Crescent is for west Asia. Here, as elsewhere, controversies dominate the discussion. The important transition from hunter-gatherer to sedentary farmer by the ninth millennium B.C.E. is very poorly understood. Likewise the dates and places where incipient farmers first domesticated the critical cereals millet and rice are the subject of an ongoing debate. Millet was almost certainly domesticated in northern China rather than brought in from elsewhere, but the origin of rice is more problematic. In her survey of agriculture in China, Francesca Bray raises two critical issues: Karl Wittfogel's theory of "hydraulic civilizations" and "oriental despotism," and the origin of domesticated rice. Her critique of Wittfogel is well founded. The increased production of cereals in northern China and the rise of a centralized state under the Qin and Han are unconnected. The same is true for the south of China. Irrigation systems in China did not require an elaborate state bureaucracy to produce or run them. The problem of rice domestication is more difficult. In this reading, Bray provides a concise look at the arguments and evidence for various points of view, showing how important it is for historians to be cautious when promoting a particular theory. More recent archaeological work, however, seems to suggest that incipient farmers domesticated rice around 8000 B.C.E. in the mid-Yangzi River valley.

>> 12. Agriculture

FRANCESCA BRAY [1984]

Grandiose irrigation schemes were established in Northern China in Han times and even earlier, supplying water to farmers in a series of channels, flumes and ditches described in idealized form in the *Chou Kuan* [Zhouguan]. The water was used by northern farmers for their wheat and millet crops, but it did not actually stand in the fields, and little or no wet rice was grown in the North. [...] The irrigation systems of the south were very different. They were not dependent on the centralized control of rivers and canals, for in the south water was generally abundant. Individuals or small groups of farmers could tap the sources by leading a small channel off a stream, digging a tank, or setting up a swape or a square-pallet chain-pump where their fields bordered the river. Ever since Wittfogel (9) propounded his theory of 'hydraulic civilisations' the presence of irrigation works in China and other Asiatic societies has been assumed by many people to imply elaborate bureaucratic control, but in fact even comparatively complex irrigation works, given favourable natural conditions, can be constructed and maintained by small autonomous groups. D. & J. Oates (I) suggest that even the great hydraulic networks of Mesopotamia originated in local networks constructed independently by farming communities,

Source: Francesca Bray, "Agriculture," in *Science and Civilisation in China*, v. 6, edited by Joseph Needham (Cambridge: Cambridge University Press, 1984) 108–109, 481, 487.

while the famous Balinese *subaks* were all initiated and maintained by small groups of peasant farmers.[1] Twitchett (6) points out that in the Tang dynasty much of the routine maintenance of irrigation canals was carried out locally by small groups; only in emergencies was labour organised on a large scale by the country authorities.[2] [...]

The Origins of Domesticated Rice in Asia

De Candolle, taking as literal the tradition that one of the cereals grown by the legendary emperor Shen Nung [Shen Nong] was rice, concluded that rice had been domesticated in China by −2800, long prior to its use in India.[3] This was undoubtedly unreliable evidence. The only archeological support for de Candolle's hypothesis until recently was the identification in the early 1920s, by two Swedish botanists, of imprints on a pottery jar from the neolithic site of Yang-shao [Yangshao] in Honan [Henan]; these imprints, they believed, were made by cultivated rice.[4] But until recently the Yang-shao [Yangshao] culture was supposed to have flourished rather late, *c.* −2000, and in any case doubt was cast on the identification of the imprints. Subsequent botanical investigations identified the chief area of distribution of wild *Oryza* species as the Eastern Himalayas and mountainous zones of mainland Southeast Asia, while archaeological remains of

domesticated rice were discovered at Harappan and other Indian sites which were presumed to predate any of the finds of rice in China.[5] [...]

Neither the archaeological, the botanical, nor the linguistic evidence define a centre of domestication more precisely than the piedmont zone of Southeast Asia described above; the uncertainty as to the exact pedigree of *O. sativa* compounds the problem. Few would disagree with the eminent geneticist T. T. Chang's view that both Asian and African domesticated rice are descended from a common Gondwanaland ancestor, but more recent developments are impossible to establish with any degree of certainty: 'Cytogenetic evidence has been well established on the relatively close affinity among the wild perennial, wild annual, and cultivated annual forms of rice in Asia, but it is impossible to critically compare [sic] the affinity between any two members with that of the others because of the deficiencies in describing and designating the parents used in interspecific crosses.'[6] Even archaeological evidence can only be suggestive, not conclusive, when it comes to the history of domestication. Benedict and Ting Ying (2) propose a South Chinese origin for Asian domesticated rice, Solheim and the Southeast Asianists a Northern Thai origin, Liu Tze-ming (1) believes it originated in the Yunnan plateau and spread thence to South China, Southeast Asia

---

[1] Liefrinck (I).

[2] It is not easy to see where the dividing line lies between irrigation systems that can be managed individually or cooperatively and those that must be centrally organised. Generally speaking if the water supply is sparse or irregular, conflicts will arise more often, and the area that can be managed by cooperation will be smaller, than in irrigation systems where water is freely available: 'There is a threshold of complexity in irrigation systems at which cooperation must give way to coordination; at which those served by the systems relinquish their decision-making power and their direct role in settling disputes. Authority and responsibility for these vital functions are then transferred to managerial structures of one sort or another. This is not to say that cooperation is then absent, but rather that it is no longer the dominant pattern of operation. The transfer to managerial coordination is not simply dependent on the size of the irrigated area. It is also—and more directly—dependent on the number of farmers drawing water *from a single source*' (B. Pasternak (3), p. 194).

[3] (I), p. 385.

[4] Anderssen (I), p. 366.

[5] Vishnu-Mittre (2), especially p. 572. These have subsequently proved to be misidentifications of impressions of wheat; Charles A. Reed (4), p. 918.

[6] T. T. Chang (2), p. 429.

and India, while Watanabe Tadayo (*I*) thinks domesticated rice had its origin in Assam and spread from there to Yunnan and points East. As a Chinese ethnographer, himself a member of a national minority, said when we were discussing the problem in the National Minorities Institute in Kunming, the debate really seems to hinge as much on national pride as on any scientific exactitude. So although we shall henceforward conform to the Chinese usage in distinguishing between *keng* and *hsien* rather than *indica* and *japonica*, we do this for purposes of convenience, not because we are convinced that Asian domesticated rice is Chinese in its origins.

Complex Food Systems in Mesoamerica

Food production among the Maya was a complex operation that does not fit the usual models used by some historians. In the course of his book The World of the Ancient Maya, *historian John Henderson highlights the problem of how not only to define agriculture but also to recognize it archaeologically. He cautions us not to "oversimplify or distort a wide range of very complex developmental processes." At the same time he describes for us how foraging for food and horticulturalist practices were as important for the Maya as what we would label as agriculture. When the divine twins, Hunahpu and Xbalanque, gave food to the rat in the* Popol Vuh, *they were the products of the garden and orchard, corn seeds, squash seeds, chili, beans, and two species of cacao. These products, including most species of beans, are native to the New World.*

   Henderson, like other scholars, is a strong critic of Wittfogel's theories on agriculture and civilization. He is even more critical of the dismissive approach to the New World by V. Gordon Childe, one of the most important scholars of early human history and the one who actually coined the phrase "Neolithic Revolution." Henderson makes us aware of the many different ways in which societies collected and produced foodstuffs historically.

>> 13. The World of the Ancient Maya

JOHN S. HENDERSON 1997

The problems of defining civilization and explaining its rise have preoccupied some of the best minds in archeology. Maya civilization, unusual in its setting and its form, makes a crucial contribution to our understanding of the general processes involved in the origins of civilization. The general public and theorists alike almost universally view civilizations as urban phenomena and focus on cities as their most prominent feature. Theories that purport to account for the origins of civilization are often in fact explanations for the beginnings of urban life. Maya civilization was organized around great civic centers that were seats of power and hubs of social, religious, economic, and political affairs, but those centers were noticeably different from cities as they are usually defined. Only a few Maya cities ever approached the density of population usually associated with urbanism, and even that growth occurred centuries after the essential features of Maya civilization had emerged. No theory that focuses on demographic aspects of the rise of cities can account for Maya development.

Source: John S. Henderson, *The World of the Ancient Maya*, 2nd edition (Ithaca: Cornell University Press, 1997), 2–3, 67–69.

With few exceptions, the earliest civilizations arose and flourished in great temperate or semiarid river valleys and in environmentally varied highland regions. Only in Mesoamerica and Southeast Asia were lowland tropical forests their cradle. Most explanations for the rise of civilization are tailored to fit very different environmental circumstances and are of dubious relevance to the Maya case. The ideas of Karl Wittfogel illustrate the problem well. Wittfogel, among the most influential of the theorists to consider the beginnings of civilization, was most familiar with the river-valley civilizations of China and the Near East. Reduced to its most simplistic form, his argument places the stimulus for civilization in the development of large-scale irrigation facilities needed to feed expanding populations. Such facilities, he claims, have heavy and continuous managerial requirements that can be met only by a highly organized bureaucracy. In effect, the need for complex hydraulic works calls centralized, often despotic, states into existence. Without substantial modification, the theory of hydraulic civilization cannot account for the appearance and florescence of civilization in the tropical lowlands of Mesoamerica, where irrigation makes little sense as a farming strategy. The theory is also open to criticism when it is applied to the areas from which Wittfogel derived the data for its initial formulations, but it has been extremely influential.

Similar ideas have been invoked to explain the rise of civilization in the highlands of central Mexico. Here theorists have also sought to tie civilization to cities, and much of their discussion has been directed toward the beginnings of urbanism. Some scholars are inclined to play down the complexity of lowland Mesoamerican societies, particularly the Olmec; a related view treats the Maya as a derivative civilization, whose complexity was a result of heavy influence from highland urban civilizations. The most extreme solution to the problems posed by lowland Mesoamerican civilizations must be credited to V. Gordon Childe, probably the most influential of all archeological theorists. Childe simply eliminated the entire New World as an arena of interesting ancient cultural development, remarking, "Never been there—peripheral and highly suspect."

For reasons that should become increasingly evident as we explore the problem, these approaches are not satisfactory. In many ways Maya culture is the most complex ever to arise in the New World. The Maya are, for example, the only Native American people to develop a full-fledged writing system, and their complex of astronomical, mathematical, and calendrical thought is sophisticated from any perspective. [...]

Much of the problem stems from the supposed link between settled life and agriculture. Earlier generations of archaeologists believed that the relationship was clear-cut and absolute: sedentism is a "better" way of life and one that was naturally adopted everywhere when the development of agriculture increased productivity to such an extent that people could afford to give up nomadic ways. In an alternative formulation: agriculture is such an obviously superior mode of subsistence that, once it developed, people naturally chose the sedentary life it demanded. Recent archeological and anthropological thought calls these links into question. Archaeological and ethnographic cases show clearly that nonagricultural peoples in resource-rich environments have led fully sedentary lives. In some parts of Mesoamerica, varied environmental zones are closely spaced. A wealth of plants, small animals, fish, shellfish, and other wild foods provided the economic foundation for several early village communities. The notion that a settled agricultural life is superior and desirable reflects the values of farming societies. Nonfarmers have very different value systems revolving around mobile, foraging lifestyles. They have often puzzled Westerners with their "irrational" refusal to convert to settled farming. [...]

The relationship between settled life and agriculture is by no means a simple one. Nor was it always and everywhere the same. In some instances, agriculture and a settled way of life developed very gradually in tandem. [...]

Agriculture is hard to define and harder still to recognize archaeologically. Mesoamerican peoples of the conquest period produced most of their food by means of a complex series of activities: preparing and clearing plots, planting crops, protecting them from other plants and animals, and often using more elaborate techniques as well. It is perfectly reasonable to call these practices "agriculture." Even today, though, native Mesoamericans do not rely solely on farming for their food: they hunt; they fish; they gather insects, mollusks, and other animals; they acquire plant foods in a variety of ways besides cultivating crops and collecting wild plants. People often protect fruit trees that they regard as their own, even though they have not planted them. They may plant trees but not tend them. They may clear unwanted plant competitors from berry patches or from around medicinal herbs. They may alter the distribution of any of these plants by dispersing their seeds—scattering berries near houses, for example—and the new locations may foster more intensive tending. In addition to obvious crops, most groups cultivate or otherwise encourage a wide range of other useful plants. These activities are not agricultural in the strict sense, but they can have similar functions. They provide important foods and medicines, and they have similar effects on plant populations. Modern ethnographers, like the Spanish colonists and conquistadores before them, have been distracted by those aspects of native subsistence which are most like modern farming. No outsider has produced a truly comprehensive description of native Mesoamerican plant use.

Archaeological remains never include the complete roster of useful plants, and there is seldom any way to judge what proportion they do represent. At best, when preservation is exceptionally good, fragments of some of the plants used by a prehistoric group survive along with some of the tools used in processing them. Such incomplete evidence does not always show whether plants were cultivated. Agriculture may produce physical changes in the crop plants themselves, such as increased seed size, but not in every instance. Simpler kinds of cultivation can also produce similar alterations. Affected plant parts do not always survive. Even if there were some way of determining the relative contribution of strictly agricultural activities to prehistoric diets, what proportion would define an "agricultural" way of life? The data will always be incomplete, and assigning early subsistence systems to such categories as "agriculture" and "hunting and gathering" will always be arbitrary and misleading.

Complex Food Systems in Africa

Food production in ancient sub-Saharan Africa is as complicated as Mesoamerica, with agriculture and foraging techniques differing widely across this large and diverse continent. In the following article excerpt, David Schoenbrun analyzes what he calls the "eclectic food system" that developed over the course of centuries in central Africa. The four main societies that Schoenbrun examines practiced a wide variety of food systems, from cereal production to herding, despite the fact that they were located quite close to each other. His article points out two other features of African agriculture as well, features that can be seen elsewhere in the world. First, the diffusion of different food production technologies is a critical element in the varied food systems of the Great Lakes area. And second, social consequences result from the type of food production undertaken. Schoenbrun comments on something long discussed by anthropologists: Societies that are primarily horticulturalist very often practice **matrilineality** *and* **matrilocality**—*that is, descent is reckoned principally through the mother's side, and upon marriage, the groom moves into* *his wife's household. Moreover, the tending of gardens in horticulturalist societies was—and in some cases still is—the work of women, but this is by no means universal. By comparison, in the agricultural world of ancient Greece, women were involved in all aspects of farming except plowing. Schoenbrun reminds us that there is no one pattern for human behavior, whether it be in food production or social organization.*

>> 14. We Are What We Eat:
Ancient Agriculture between the Great Lakes

DAVID L. SCHOENBRUN [1993]

Introduction: An Old Story

Nearly three millennia ago, between eastern Africa's Great Lakes, a long period during which food-producing communities settled largely environmentally distinct zones drew to a close with the arrival of Eastern Highlands Bantu-speaking farmers. Around 500 B.C. this earlier era of specialized foodways gave way to widespread contacts among the different communities, with Bantu-speaking peoples incorporating the technical agricultural knowledge of their predecessors in the region. In the centuries before A.D. 500, after more than 700 years of this complex Lakes Bantu synthesis, a period of consolidation set in. Lakes Bantu-speaking communities then spread fully through the region, possessed of a rich and diverse agricultural synthesis that supported population growth, shaped and responded to environmental changes and engendered unique regional variants.

These vital changes in food systems began in the Neolithic and drove the elaboration of the Early Iron age. After the turn of the Christian Era, environmental change, population growth and settlement expansion all induced the creation and colonization of microenvironments best exploited by increasingly complex crop rotations and mixed farming using both wooden and iron implements. The broadly similar but a really differing foodways undergirded the growth of the regional cultural identities depicted in the famous corpus of Lakes oral histories. The agricultural past of the Kivu Rift provided the states in Rwanda, Buha and Kivu with the productive basis for struggles over their formation, organization and survival. And, the peoples who lived between the Rift and Victoria Nyanza developed the horticultural and pastoral base used during the eras recalled in oral traditions as the times of the Aba Tembuzi and AbaCwezi in ancient Kitara. [...]

Conclusion

The roots of the modern social, economic, environmental and political formations in the Lakes region lie in the earliest periods of Lakes history, even before the advent of iron and pottery. Developed and diverse food systems preceded the emergence of the Early Iron Age but flowered during the roughly thousand years after 500 B.C. The varied cultural contexts matched the diversity of this florescence. People speaking several different languages were herding cattle, sowing grains, planting root crops, fishing and hunting all across the area. No fewer than three such groups lived in the central grasslands near the Kagera bend; archeologists should search there for early evidence of cattle-keeping and cereal raising.

In the earliest periods, beginning well before 3000 years ago, the first food producers settled in the western parts of the region. Their food systems, different enough in their requirements of rainfall and soils, produced a sort of patchwork pattern of settlement. Mixed-farming Sog Eastern Sudanic peoples and the primarily pastoral Tale Southern Cushites settled side by side between

Source: David Schoenbrun, "We Are What We Eat: Ancient Agriculture between the Great Lakes," *The Journal of African History* 34 (1993): 1–2, 27–28.

the Victoria Nyanza littoral and the Western Rift highlands. The mainly root-cropping and fishing Eastern Highlands Bantu and the cereal and stock raising Central Sudanic peoples settled amidst one other, divided primarily by the high moisture and warm temperature requirements of the Bantu crop complex. These farmers may have been partly responsible for the earliest constrictions of forests in the western Lakes region. Their technology may have been neolithic, but iron before 500 B.C. cannot be ruled out.

The environmental specificity of this settlement pattern led to longstanding interaction among the various agricultural traditions. Agricultural practices also shaped and responded to environmental changes such as receding forest cover and shrinking rainfall amounts, respectively. The Eastern Highlands Bantu took up cereal farming and one of their descendant groups, the Great Lakes Bantu, later developed large stock-raising, presumably in order to expand their settlement options and to increase the productivity of their food systems. They probably learned about the new food ways through intermarriage, cooperative hunting parties and trade relations linking the products unique to each environmental region and historical tradition. For example, Eastern Highlands Bantu peoples may have exchanged dried fish and yarn flour for sheep or cattle with Sudanic communities. Or Tale Southern Cushites may have given bulls to Great Lakes Bantu peoples in return for iron implements.

The story told in this paper employs large-scale environmental, demographic and technological explanations of historical change, resting as it does on a narrow range of linguistic evidence in these semantic fields. But more than instrumental processes lay at the heart of the Eastern Bantu agricultural synthesis. If further study on the historical transformations of Bantu kinship systems bears anticipated fruit, we may soon be in a position to offer sociological hypotheses to explain the apparent dissolution into Great Lakes Bantu societies of Sudanic and Cushitic ones. The kernel of the argument resides in Eastern Highlands Bantu

society having been a matrilineal and a matrilocal one, wherein women superintended and carried out agricultural production and outsider males were easily incorporated. Two implications follow from this formulation, Either non-Bantu men married into Eastern Highlands Bantu and, later, Great Lakes Bantu families in order to join their productive expertise to their new wife's and her sisters' (also ensuring that their children would come to speak as a first language a Bantu tongue). Or Bantu-speaking women married into Sudanic and Cushite societies, maintained strong ties to their natal homesteads and raised bilingual children. A number of as yet unsubstantiated assumptions leave these explanations of the rise to prominence of Great Lakes Bantu-speaking society no more than speculative. We do not yet know for certain if Eastern Highlands Bantu society was, indeed, matrilineal. And, if it was, had women control over all the main features of agricultural practice? Furthermore, it seems from linguistic and ethnographic evidence that, at least in Great Lakes Bantu societies, during the period of the Early Iron Age and the early florescence of Bantu-speakers as cattle-users, their kinship system was already becoming patrilineal, as are nearly all modern Lakes societies. For now, though, these suggestions must remain tentative. [. . .]

The 500 to 700 years after 500 B.C. marked the heyday of the Early Iron Age, during which Great Lakes Bantu communities developed their economic power and left a lasting impression on the landscape. Though food, environment and technology were closely linked during that time, I believe that the demands on land, labor and technical expertise made by the farmers and herders who undertook the agricultural developments, charted here as a blending of historical traditions, characterize more appropriately a period in the African past too often linked only to technology. The Early Iron Age in the Lakes region was as much an age of cultural contact and economic development as it was a period of metallurgical advance.

Conversations with Ogotemêli

In the mid-twentieth century, two French anthropologists, Marcel Griaule and Germaine Dieterlen, wrote down the sacred stories of the Dogon, an ethnic group living predominately in Mali. These stories are part of an oral tradition that undoubtedly went back many, many centuries, reflecting the practices and worldview of the Dogon from very early times. One story talks about the divine spirit Nummo and the first human being Lébé. Critical to the narrative is how the Dogon learned how to grow millet, a staple in Africa just as it was in northern China. Equally significantly, it was a blacksmith who taught the Dogon "the art of sowing." Developments in metallurgy and agriculture often went hand in hand in early history, and as we will see in Part II, the smith had a special, if not sacred, place in many cultures of sub-Saharan Africa.

>> 15. Conversations with Ogotemmêli: An Introduction to Dogon Religious Ideas

MARCEL GRIAULE [ORAL HISTORY WRITTEN DOWN C. 1963]

Eighth Day: The Third Word and the Work of Redemption

The millet harvest had long been over. Between the two Ogols, in the Hogon's field, the dry stalks rustled in the slightest breath of wind. The earth had to wait through a whole season of wind and sun before it would be opened up again. Not for a long time would the peasants begin to reckon the crop by its height, anxiously watching its growth in the meantime and assisting it by sacrifices of fowls, by unremitting prayer and complicated precautions. It would be months before the first appearance of the young stalks would be hailed as 'nose tips', or the first sign of the leaves bending to the wind as 'cock's tails', or before the earth, disappearing under a carpet of green

growth, would be described as 'hidden mounds' or the expression 'swallow the beasts' would indicate that the stalks were high enough to hide a sheep from view.

The European walked along the raised tracks above the harvested fields in which the baobabs stood out pinkish-green against the rising sun. He knew the names of all those in the Ogol country and the chronological order of their planting for twenty years back. He admired from a distance the eighth on the list, Adama, the largest of them all. Nine men with linked arms would hardly be able to encircle its trunk. Adama was larger than the Gravel baobab, whose seeds were like sand, larger than the Ropy baobab, whose fruit yielded a cream running like cheese, larger too than the Tall one, or gnarled Ancestor, or Small Seeds, High Bosom, Little Bulk or Plac-Plac, whose fragile fruits burst as they fall. Then, as he made his way into the narrow streets and took up his position in Ogotemmêli's courtyard, he cast a glance at the topmost branches, visible above

Source: Marcel Griaule, *Conversations with Ogotemmêli: An Introduction to Dogon Religious Ideas* (London: Oxford University Press, 1965), 56–57.

the roofs, of the tree known simply as *the Baobab*, without further qualification, the ancestor of all these monster growths.

'The old man whom the seventh Nummo ate,' said Ogotemmêli, 'was called Lébé. The stones which all priests wear round their necks are his bones.' But men had no knowledge of the subterranean resurrections at the time when they occurred. They did not acquire the treasure of the stones immediately after they had been placed there. They did not know what caused the rains which now began to fall and were the signal for the clearing of the field marked out by the smith.

These first rains indeed were for the purpose of purification. The seventh Nummo, a pure spirit, in swallowing the old man, had assimilated defiled human nature and the lapsed second Word. When he vomited to the rhythm of the blows on the anvil, there was ejected, with the pure covenant stones, a liquid which carried away the impurity. This liquid spread out into stagnant pools and flowing rivers, carving out valleys and flooding hollows. It had to be swept away and replaced by water which was pure and beneficent. This was done by the rain, which the Great Nummo in Heaven sent to help the seventh Nummo in his labours.

But this water from Heaven did not merely drive back the flood of the rivers; it also watered the primal field, and thus made it possible for the smith to teach the art of sowing.

It was much later, according to some, that men learnt of the prodigious events which had taken place underground. The land became too small for their needs, and they decided to emigrate *en masse*. Wishing, however, to keep their links with the past, and to have the same soil under their feet, they opened Lébé's grave, intending to take the bones and the earth with them when they went. It was then that they discovered the arrangement of stones thrown up by the seventh Nummo and the Spirit himself in the form of a serpent.

According to others, they made this discovery in the first year of cultivation, when the time came to give the field its first dressing.

Others again say that they buried Lébé and sowed the seed the same day. It was at the harvest that they opened the grave, thinking the old man had risen again like the millet.

Cultural Heroes and the Origins of Agriculture

Both crafts and the arts of civilization are attributed to different deities or heroes, depending on the culture involved. The Sumerians gave the god Enki credit for everything from agriculture to civilization itself. Prometheus, a Titan, taught the Greeks the basics of civilization, and the god Dionysus gave them the gift of wine. The Chinese ascribed a variety of gifts provided to human beings, from fire to town walls, to a group of legendary kings and culture heroes of the third millennium B.C.E. Ban Gu, who wrote in the first century C.E., mentions some of those mythic heroes in the following passage. ShenNong, the "Divine Farmer," began the process by teaching the Chinese how to plow and weed, as well as identify important medicinal plants. Other ancient texts also credit ShenNong with the very invention of agriculture itself. His successors continued to contribute to China's agricultural well-being. The importance of agriculture, especially as a source of wealth and social stability, pervades this and other similar ancient Chinese writings.

>> 16. Han Shu 24

[FIRST CENTURY C.E.]

Shih-huo Chih [Zhi Shihan]: "Treatise on Food and Money" Economic History of China up to A.D. 25

Introduction: Subject of Treatise—Food and Money; Food and Its Distribution Essential

Of the eight [objects of] government in the "Great Plan," the *Hung-fan* [Hongfan] [of the Book of History], the first was called *Shih* [Shi], "Food" [for the people]; and the second, *Huo*, "Media of Exchange." The former may be said to be the excellent grains and [other] edibles produced by the agriculturalists. The latter may be defined as textiles, woven of vegetable fibers and of silk, of which wearing apparel can be made; as well as metals, knife [money], tortoise shells, cowries [et cetera], with which wealth may be divided, benefits distributed, and [what the people] have exchanged for [what they have not]. The two [objects of government] are fundamental for the maintenance of the people.

Pre-1000 B.C.: Invention of Plow; Supply and Demand Met through Markets

It was in the generation of Shen-nung [ShenNong] that [the wood of] a tree was first fashioned into a plowshare, and a tree [limb or trunk] was bent by the application of the heat of fire into a plow-handle. The advantages of plowing and weeding were then taught to all under Heaven, and thus food was sufficient. Markets were set up at noontime and people were called to them from all the surrounding country, and [in them] commodities for exchange were gathered from all parts of [their] world. [The people] exchanged [their goods] and returned [home]. Each obtained what he [wanted], and thus commodities were circulated. With food enough [for everyone], and commodities in general circulation, it followed that the state was replete [in resources], and the people

were rich. Consequently the instruction [and fostering of the people] was successfully undertaken.

Pre-1000 B.C.: Implements and Media of Exchange Developed: Court Scholars Advise on Seasons: Ministry of Agriculture Foremost Function of Government

Huang-ti [Huangdi] (The Yellow Emperor) and his successors made changes according to the needs of the time, causing the people never to grow weary [of their occupations]. Yao ordered the Four Scholars to deliver respectfully [their calculations of] the seasons to the people. Shun appointed [the prince Ch'i [Qi] as] Minister of Agriculture because many people were for the first time suffering from famine. [With his appointment] this [ministry of agriculture] was made the first of the [eight] objects of government.

Pre-1000 B.C.: Government Control of Drainage; Nine Units; Diversified Crops; Taxation; Equitable Distribution

Yü [the Great] caused the floods to recede, and defined the *chiu-chou* [jiuzhou] (nine geographical units for governmental administration). He instituted [methods of control] for the land [the arable parts being made] into fields. Each [of the units] according to that which it could produce whether distant from or near to [the capital] was taxed *fu*, and [was ordered to] present articles of tribute *kung*, [some in] baskets. He encouraged [the people] to exchange what they had for what they had not; and the ten thousand states were brought under good rule. [. . .]

Pre-700 B.C.: Settlement of the Four Classifications among the People Other Than Those with Government Posts and/or Honorary Rank

Wherefore, the Holy Kings brought the people within territorial boundaries erected walled [cities with] suburban enclosures that they should

Source: Nancy Lee Swann, trans., *Han Shu* 24 (Princeton: Princeton University Press, 1950), 109–116.

dwell therein. [Outside the settlements] they had cottages and fields instituted that [the people] might share equitably [in division of the land]. They opened markets with booths to let the people have [commercial] intercourse, and they established schools, both high and low, in order to give them instruction.

Scholars, farmers, craftsmen, and merchants, the four [classifications among the] people, had their [respective] occupations. Those who learned in order to hold official positions were the scholars; those who cultivated the land and produced grains were the farmers; those who devised and made utensils [and implements] were the craftsmen, and those who circulated wealth and sold commodities were the merchants. The Holy Kings on measuring personal capacity assigned duties; the four [classifications] among the people by showing their ability received their tasks. Therefore, there were no neglected offices *Kuan* [Guan] at court; no [idle] people roaming about in settlements and no uncultivated fields in the land.

>> Mastering the Materials

1. What does Diamond see as the most important feature of the development of agriculture in the Fertile Crescent? How does he contrast the Fertile Crescent to what happened in the New World?

2. How do the "The Eloquent Peasant" and the "Hymn to Hapy" present a fairly complete agricultural picture of ancient Egypt?

3. How many ways of producing and securing food are there? How are these different foodways exhibited in various parts of the ancient world?

4. How do the Dogon and Chinese remember the origins of agriculture? What does this tell us about their respective cultures?

>> Making Connections

1. Agriculture seems to have arisen first in regions that were amenable to cultivation because of the natural resources, climate, and local ecology. What do you think are the connections between the environment of places like Egypt and Mesopotamia (Chapter 1) and the early introduction of cultivation in these regions?

2. Agriculture seems to have been independently "invented" only a handful of times in human history. How do you think other populations around the world came to possess agricultural technology?

Chapter 3

The City

Its Origins and Nature

Over the course of history human beings have organized themselves in a variety of ways. While we in the twenty-first century take the nation-state, with its fixed boundaries and elaborate governmental structures, for granted, it is, in fact, a very recent invention only several centuries old. An early form of social and political organization is what we sometimes call a "tribe." The tribe is based on kinship and common ancestry, and identity is more closely linked to the members of kin groups rather than to a specific territory. This group usually has a common language, or dialect, and possesses a shared culture. In ancient Greece, the Thessalians constituted a "tribe," or *ethnos*, that was loosely organized even after they settled into cities. Ancient Egypt, however, provides a different form of organization and identity. The Egyptians from around 3000 B.C.E. on created a social and political system that was defined by a region, by geography, the Nile Valley and delta—the Two Lands. The hallmark of Egypt was an elaborate agricultural system under a god–king, the pharaoh. This identification with the land of Egypt itself is the closest thing that we have to a nation-state in antiquity. But human beings devised an alternative to either the tribe or the larger territorial agrarian state: the city and the city-state. In this chapter you will see how scholars characterize cities and city-states in different parts of the world and why urban dwellers took such pride in their cities.

Cities and urbanized populations constitute a kind of paradox. Cities and city-states often produce the most sophisticated of cultural systems possible, setting a standard for centuries if not millennia to come. The **city-state** culture created in Mesopotamia, for instance, would be the model of civilization in western Asia for thousands of years. Even in the period after Alexander the Great, the ancient method of writing—cuneiform—and Mesopotamian art styles were the norm throughout much of the region. Moreover, part of this cultural brilliance is due to trade and contact with others. Unlike Egypt, Mesopotamian city-states were always involved in trade and commerce. But there is a contradiction here. City-state systems, wherever and whenever they occurred, even when creating cultural uniformity, always promoted particularism, a certain exclusivity, rather than political unification or inclusiveness. Large-scale political union was periodically achieved by force, but was invariably short lived. The inhabitants of city-states preferred to identify with their own city rather than with a larger state or polity. What distinguished urban dwellers from village or town dwellers was a strong identity to the city itself. This strong identity could not be overcome by mere conquest, but persisted under the most adverse conditions.

The origin and development of cities is more problematic than it might first appear. It is difficult to say, for instance, why and at what point a large agrarian town becomes a "city." Much of this is a question of definition, though not entirely so: At one point a settlement ceased to be a "town" and became a "city." While pinpointing causes and origins may be impossible, two features of urban life are clear. First, all urban systems seem to have evolved gradually over time, whether in the New World or Old—each new phase of a settlement was based on what came before; continuity with the past is a common feature of urban development. This does not mean that there might not be a strong impetus to transform a farming community into a city. The Etruscans, for example, introduced urban forms to central Italy about 600 B.C.E.—Rome, a not very distinguished Iron Age settlement, was one of the places so transformed. But an influence from the outside was not necessary, as in ancient Iraq or Mesoamerica. And second, cities possess certain characteristics that set them apart from towns. Historians usually consider population growth to be a critical benchmark for the transition from town to city, but a demographic change is insufficient in itself: Population growth must be accompanied by strong social and economic differentiation. Similarly, cities often experience a shift in political culture to strong rulers, coinciding with the development of a sophisticated culture, complete with monumental architecture and usually, but not always, literacy. What had been large agricultural establishments become, over time, economic, cultural, political, and religious centers that dominate the local territory and villages within it. But there is also an intangible quality to urbanization: Inhabitants of a city possess an identity, a pride that transcends but does not entirely replace family loyalty and social ties. This psychological factor is as important as population numbers and institutional and cultural sophistication for the determination of whether or not a settlement has become a "city."

Until recently scholars doubted whether urbanization was as much a part of the New World experience as it was the Old. Calling the great monuments of Mesoamerica exclusively ceremonial centers and depicting them as partially inhabited or only periodically visited, scholars dismissed the possibility that the Americas had cities like those of Mesopotamia. We now know that the Maya and others built great urban complexes in the New World, and that the history of these resulting city-states, or polities, paralleled in many ways the history of city-states elsewhere in the world. But getting at this history has been difficult. Possessing few written records, historians have had to rely on the detailed work of archaeologists to reconstruct the origin and growth of cities in Mesoamerica. But not all sites have been fully excavated, and some areas, like the Mirador basin in the Petén of Guatemala, have not even been fully surveyed and mapped. As a result, the dating for cities and their rise changes frequently. Two of the passages in this chapter look at Mesoamerican urbanization from a perspective different from that usually employed by historians, two museum exhibits. Through their reviews of these exhibits, Octavio Paz, as well as Richard Leventhal and Charles Howarth not only discuss the urban culture of Mesoamerica but also provide insights into some of the problems of doing history. They also give us a sense of some of the tools that historians need to make sense out of the past.

The urban phenomenon of Mesopotamia and Mesoamerica had its counterpart in Europe as well with the development of the Greek city-state, the *polis*. Greek history, however, diverges from some of the more familiar patterns seen elsewhere in the world—instead of continuity, Greek history is periodically punctuated with discontinuities. Over the course of the Middle and Late Bronze Age, from about 2000 to about 1200 B.C.E., the Greek landscape became dominated by large palace complexes. The focal point for most individuals was their agricultural village, but the village itself was carefully controlled by powerful kings. Although the Greeks developed a sophisticated culture in the Late Bronze Age, their civilization was strictly rural rather than urban in nature. The brilliant world that the Greeks had created collapsed at the end of the Bronze Age, along with the destruction of the other civilizations of the eastern Mediterranean. After a lengthy period that scholars like to call "The Dark Age," Greek life began over again between 900 and 800 B.C.E. By then the Bronze Age past was but a distant and garbled memory. This time, in lieu of palaces and kings, a radically new form of organization emerged to become the focal point of the Greeks—the *polis*, or city-state. While not all Greeks came to live in city-states, the *polis* was extremely popular—more than 700 *poleis* existed in antiquity—and helped to define the Greeks as Greeks. Aristotle wrote that human beings were *polis* animals, and by that he meant that for individuals to reach their full potential as human beings, they had to live in a Greek-type city. The last three passages in this chapter discuss how the Greek *polis* came into being and how the Greeks themselves characterized this new political organization.

Early Mesopotamian Cities

Some of the earliest cities in the world are found in southern Mesopotamia, in the land of Sumer. The origins of the Sumerians are as yet unclear, but we do know that they began to inhabit that region continuously from about 5000 B.C.E. on. Two thousand years later, around 3000 B.C.E., the Sumerians transformed their increasingly larger agricultural and market towns into proper cities. A type of physical absorption of local villages by the larger towns occurred: In the area around Uruk, one of the most ancient cities in Sumer, the number of villages drops by almost 75 percent as the number of acres that formed the urban core of the emerging city-state increased 200 times. In analyzing this phenomenon of city formation, J. N. Postgate observes that three major interconnected cultural characteristics help to define early Mesopotamia: complex social organization, literacy, and urbanization. In addition to the city as a political and economic center, he stresses that it was also a ceremonial center. In an earlier chapter he pointed out the importance of the relationship between urban identity and religious structures: "Strong local identities [are] expressed in their allegiance to a city god and their pride in the temple." The chief deity is at the heart of any urban establishment and identity, both physically and politically: The city belonged to the god, and his or her temple was a monument to the power of that deity and the city. The king, in turn, was the primary representative of the god on earth. The city was the standard against which everything else was measured in Mesopotamia, and this way of life was duplicated from the Persian Gulf all the way up the Tigris and Euphrates Rivers and across the Fertile Crescent to places such as Ebla in western Syria.

>> 17. Early Mesopotamia: Society and Economy at the Dawn of History

J.N. POSTGATE [1992]

City and Countryside

While its true singularity may lie deeper in the complexity of social organization, the two most striking characteristics of early Mesopotamia are its literacy and it urbanization. Just as we need to appreciate the nature of the written record to use its messages, we must be aware that all our documentary and archeological evidence derives from the city, and so be conscious of the inherent biases which result from this. Perhaps we would in any case have chosen to approach Mesopotamian civilization through its cities, since it is there that everything most special to it is concentrated, but in fact we have no choice. Although we have some insights into the rural scene, this is only by courtesy of documents which were themselves generated within the city. It is only those aspects of the countryside with which the city-dweller was involved that the texts will illumine, and at present the only archeological evidence is the distribution of settlements. Fortunately there was a very close relationship between the early cities and their hinterland, so that the texts are more informative than we might expect. The links fall into legal relationships, the contractual bonds between landlord and tenant, palace and dependant, recruiting officer and recruit, and the political movements

exposed by state correspondence from Mari and elsewhere, from which great shafts of light have transformed our picture of the nomads in the ancient Near East.

Defining a City

Usually the first question asked about an ancient city is how big it was. A simple answer to this is to quote the size of the ancient mounds, and, although this simplicity conceals a host of technical and procedural problems, at one level it has a certain validity. Archeological surveys can distinguish a hierarchy of settlement size even before the Uruk period, and Adams' work in particular shows that during the fourth millennium a separate class of larger settlement—or 'city'—can be differentiated from the smaller sites or 'villages.' It must be stressed that the transition from one settlement class to another may be drawn at different points on the absolute scale in different periods, since the classification depends not on absolute size, but on the relative position within a hierarchy. If our classes have any significance, they will correspond to the function of the settlement within that hierarchy. We have already seen how the ceremonial role of the city as the home of the central shrine of a district follows from the literary compositions of Early Dynastic times, and this gives us a solid criterion on which to isolate a class of major settlement, recognized as such by the people of the time [...]. We can also assume with confidence that most of these also functioned as economic and political centres, and that their functional differences from other

Source: J. N. Postgate, *Early Mesopotamia: Society and Economy at the Dawn of History* (New York: Routledge, 1992), 73–74.

settlements should be detectable in the archeological record.

The Outward Form

The range of city size is well illustrated in the Early Dynastic period by the cases of Uruk and Abu Salabikh [...]. At the beginning of the Epic of Gilgamesh we are exhorted to admire the size of his city Uruk, in particular the wall he built round it [...], and indeed at Uruk the city wall dates to the ED period and is 9 km in length.

Uruk, a Mesopotamian City

The evidence that Postgate and other historians use to understand Mesopotamian urbanization comes from archaeology and different types of written documents. One of the most important literary sources to have survived the millennia is The Epic of Gilgamesh. *The following passage reveals several important facets of urbanization already noted by Postgate. Initially, we can see the great pride that the people of ancient Uruk took in their main temple, Eanna. Temples, called ziggurats in Akkadian, served as focal points for the inhabitants of Mesopotamian cities. This particular temple was dedicated to both Ishtar (the Sumerian Inanna), the goddess of love and fertility, and Anu (the Sumerian An), the father of Ishtar and all the other gods. The city belonged to the chief deities, and the people of Uruk closely identified themselves with these deities. They built these great monuments to the deities in the city's center—part of the exterior of the temple was so polished that it shone like copper; in his pride, the poet even invites the listener to touch the very entry way of the temple. But he speaks with equal pride of the great wall that surrounded the city, defining its urban core. The wall is not built out of cut stone, which is too distant to be practical, nor out of sun-baked clay brick, which was plentiful and cheap but impermanent. Instead the people of Uruk made it out of burnt brick, which is labor-intensive and expensive. The fired clay bricks, however, gave the wall permanence and stature—these walls were impressive to look at, and the remnants of them remain so today. At the end of the poem, Gilgamesh instructs the mythic boatman who ferries the dead to the Underworld to examine the magnificent burnt brick walls of Uruk. The hero adds as well that this wall not only surrounded the urban core, with its great temple to Ishtar, but also included gardens and fields as two-thirds of the whole. Finally, each city-state had a chief ruler. Kingship, the very right to rule, came from the king of the gods, Enlil, and kings like Gilgamesh, who was two-thirds god and one-third man, were charged with acting as the god's steward on earth. The poet instructs Gilgamesh in his role as king—he was to lead his armies to victory and rule the people of Uruk justly. To help him in his rule, the poet shows how Gilgamesh had at his disposal a wide variety of individuals, from his concubine and jester, to his servants and stewards, all of whom lived in his palace. The palace and the temple, one with its public officials and bureaucrats, the other with its many priests, priestesses, and musicians, were the chief focal points of ancient Mesopotamian cities—these were monumental structures that went beyond local shrines and village headmen's houses. A city was a quantitative and qualitative leap in culture, and thus urbanization, as Postgate points out, is one of the defining characteristics of Mesopotamian civilization.*

>> 18. The Epic of Gilgamesh

[THIRD MILLENNIUM B.C.E. (SUMERIAN TALE); SECOND MILLENNIUM B.C.E. (WRITTEN AKKADIAN VERSION)]

I will proclaim to the world the deeds of Gilgamesh. This was the man to whom all things were known; this was the king who knew the countries of the world. He was wise, he saw mysteries and knew secret things, he brought us a tale of the days before the flood. He went on a long journey, was weary, worn-out with labour, returning he rested, he engraved on a stone the whole story.

When the gods created Gilgamesh they gave him a perfect body. Shamash the glorious sun endowed him with beauty, Adad the god of the storm endowed him with courage, the great gods made his beauty perfect, surpassing all others, terrifying like a great wild bull. Two thirds they made him god and one third man.

In Uruk he built walls, a great rampart, and the temple of blessed Eanna for the god of the firmament Anu, and for Ishtar the goddess of love. Look at it still today: the outer wall where the cornice runs, it shines with the brilliance of copper; and the inner wall, it has no equal. Touch the threshold, it is ancient. Approach Eanna the dwelling of Ishtar, our lady of love and war, the like of which no latter-day king, no man alive can equal. Climb upon the wall of Uruk; walk along it, I say; regard the foundation terrace and examine the masonry: is it not burnt brick and good? The seven sages laid the foundations. [...]

The Death of Gilgamesh

The destiny was fulfilled which the father of the gods, Enlil of the mountain, had decreed for Gilgamesh: 'In nether-earth the darkness will show him a light: of mankind, all that are known, none will leave a monument for generations to come to compare with his. The heroes, the wise men, like the new moon have their waxing and waning. Men will say, "Who has ever ruled with might and with power like him?" As in the dark month, the month of shadows, so without him there is no light. O Gilgamesh, this was the meaning of your dream. You were given the kingship, such was your destiny, everlasting life was not your destiny. Because of this do not be sad at heart, do not be grieved or oppressed; he has given you power to bind and to loose, to be the darkness and the light of mankind. He has given unexampled supremacy over the people, victory in battle from which no fugitive returns, in forays and assaults from which there is no going back. But do not abuse this power, deal justly with your servants in the palace, deal justly before the face of the Sun.'

The king has laid himself down and will not rise again,

The Lord of Kullab will not rise again;

He overcame evil, he will not come again;

Though he was strong of arm he will not rise again;

He had wisdom and a comely face, he will not come again;

He is gone into the mountain, he will not come again;

On the bed of fate he lies, he will not rise again,

From the couch of many colours he will not come again.

The people of the city, great and small, are not silent; they lift up the lament, all men of flesh and blood lift up the lament. Fate has spoken; like a hooked fish he lies stretched on the bed, like a gazelle that is caught in a noose. Inhuman Namtar is heavy upon him, Namtar that has neither hand or foot, that drinks no water and eats no meat.

For Gilgamesh, son of Ninsun, they weighed out their offerings; his dear wife, his son, his concubine, his musicians, his jester, and all his household; his servants, his stewards, all who lived in the palace weighed out their offerings for

---

Source: N. K. Sandars, trans., *The Epic of Gilgamesh* (New York: Penguin Press, 1972), 61, 118–119.

Gilgamesh the son of Ninsun, the heart of Uruk. They weighed out their offerings to Ereshkigal, the Queen of Death, and all the gods of the dead. To Namtar, who is fate, they weighed out the offering. Bread for Neti the Keeper of the Gate, bread for Ningizzida the god of the serpent, the lord of the Tree of Life; for Dumuzi also, the young shepherd, for Enki and Ninki, for Endukugga and Nindukugga, for Emmul and Nimmul, all the ancestral gods, forbears of Enlil. A feast for Shulpae the god of feasting. For Samuqan, god of the herds, for the mother Ninhursag, and the gods of creation in the place of creation, for the host of heaven, priest and priestess weighed out the offering of the dead.

Gilgamesh, the son of Ninsun, lies in the tomb. At the place of offerings he weighed the bread-offering, at the place of libation he poured out the wine. In those days the lord Gilgamesh departed, the son of Ninsun, the king, peerless, without an equal among men, who did not neglect Enlil his master. O Gilgamesh, lord of Kullab, great is thy praise.

Cities in Mesoamerica

Historians require many different tools to reconstruct and understand the past in a meaningful way. When John Lloyd Stevens visited the Maya ruins in the late 1830s and early 1840s, he described them as a work of a "powerful and mysterious people" whose "hieroglyphics," which he could not read, undoubtedly explained much of what he saw. We have progressed a long way since his journey into the jungles of Mesoamerica with Frederick Catherwood. The two museum exhibitions reviewed in the next two passages explore the difficulties that face the historian and suggest different ways of overcoming those problems. Each author sees different problems when examining the material remains of the great Maya urban complexes. For Octavio Paz, the 1990 Nobel Prize–winning poet and author, the key problem concerns the use of Maya inscriptions for understanding the past. While scholars originally depicted the ancient Maya as peaceful astronomers gazing at the heavens, the partial decipherment of their system of writing has altered that picture enormously. Dynasties and war dominate the written record of the Maya in the same way that they do in Mesopotamia. But Paz suggests that the new information must be tempered with what he calls "more complex realities." The material world displayed in the museum exhibitions in Fort Worth and Cleveland permits the scholar to place society, economics, and politics into the context of religion and religious beliefs. By doing this, Paz argues, we get a more nuanced picture of the Mesoamerican city-state. The passage by Leventhal and Howarth adds another dimension. The main problem that concerned them was how a large site like Copan could have been provisioned adequately with food given its meager resources. Some scholars working in the region before them had relied on sixteenth and twentieth century **ethnographies***—observations and studies of living local populations by outsiders—for understanding what had happened centuries earlier. These writers had generally concluded from observing contemporary rural populations in the area that Maya city-states must have been relatively small. Leventhal and Howarth criticize this methodology and suggest that recent archaeology and NASA photographs reveal that Maya complexes like Copan were densely populated and well-fed city-states. Ethnography can be a valuable tool for the historian, but it must be used very cautiously and in conjunction with other information and sciences.*

>> 19. Food of the Gods

OCTAVIO PAZ [1987]

Schele and Miller emphasize the centrality of the institution of monarchy among the Maya, and the dynastic character of their history. Most of the inscriptions present facts about the rulers; similarly, many of the figures that appear on the reliefs of the monuments and stelae are stylized representations of the kings, their wives and retinues. It is a dynastic art close to that of the Egyptian pharaohs and the rajahs of ancient Cambodia. One also recalls the absolute monarchs of Europe, like the Sun King of France, in the seventeenth century. Was the city of Palenque Pacal's Versailles? Yes and no. The Maya cities were more than the residences of the king and his court. Of course a monarchy implies a court, and the Maya kings were the center of an aristocratic and refined society composed of high dignitaries, their wives and relatives. There is no doubt that these courtiers were mainly warriors, a common feature of all the monarchies of history. Common too in this type of society is the existence of military and semireligous brotherhoods composed of aristocrats. The marvelous mural paintings in the sanctuary-fort of Cacaxtla, clearly of Maya execution, depict the two military orders, the Jaguar and the Eagle warriors. The continuous presence of representations of these two orders, in various sites and in monuments from different eras, is an indication that they formed a permanent element in the Mesoamerican societies.

Once we accept the vision of the Maya world proposed by the new historians, we must revise it. Their purely dynastic and warlike model has obvious limitations. Carried away by the legitimate enthusiasm of discovery, Schele and Miller at times tend to minimize, in their remarkable and revolutionary book, certain aspects of Maya culture that seem to me no less important. Their picture of the Maya world is an inversion of the image presented by Thompson and Morley. For the latter, the true Maya history was that of the sky; down here, under the rule of the "peaceful theocracies," nothing happened. In the new conception of Schele and Miller, history descends from the sky and returns to earth; and a great deal happens down here. But it is always the same thing: kings who ascend to the throne, battle to triumph or defeat, and die. One generalization has been replaced with another. Certainly the image that Schele and Miller present is a true one, but it requires more complex realities. The subtitle of their book, after all, is *Dynasty and Ritual in Maya Art*. The dynastic element entered into the ritual; in turn the ritual derived from a cosmogony, and was its symbolic representation.

Until recently it was believed that the Mesoamerican cities were not cities at all, but rather ceremonial centers inhabited solely by priests and a few functionaries. Today we know that they were indeed true cities, centers of economic, political, military, and religious activity. One of the most important of these recent discoveries is the existence of an intensive agriculture, without which the survival of the urban centers would have been impossible. And alongside intensive agriculture there were artisanal production and commerce. René Dilon, in his work on Teotihuacán, has shown that the city was a major manufacturing and commercial center, with sections composed of foreign artisans and artists whose products, from ceramics to arms and finely carved stones, were distributed throughout Mesoamerica. [...]

What we know of the Mesoamerican religions allows us to say that, despite the diversity of the names of the gods and other differences, all of them are variations of the same cosmogonic myths and of the same theology. The common religious base for all of the Mesoamerican cultures is a basic myth according to which the gods sacrificed themselves to create the world; the mission of mankind is to preserve universal life, including one's own, by feeding the gods with divine substance: blood.

Source: Octavio Paz, "Food of the Gods," *The New York Review of Books* (26 February 1987): 3–4.

This myth explains the central place of sacrifice in Mesoamerican civilization. War not only had a political and economic dimension for the city-states, but also a religious one. War and trade were politics, and at the same time a rite.

One can draw a triangle: merchants, warriors, and priests. In the center of the triangle: the monarch. The king is a warrior, a priest, and in certain moments of the rites, a god. Ignacio Bernal has written, "In Tula and in Tenochtitlan there was a continual symbiosis between the ruler, the priest and the warrior." And Schele and Miller note that the Maya kings always appear with the attributes and signs of the gods.

>> 20. "Copan: Ancient City of the Maya"

RICHARD M. LEVENTHAL AND CHARLES H. HOWARTH, JR. [1981]

But was Copan a city? How was it organized socially and politically? What were its local long-distance trade connections? What was the composition of a Maya household? These and many other questions have dominated Maya archeology for the past 50 years and are addressed in this exhibit. Ceramic vessels, stone and shell artifacts and stone sculpture, recovered by the first Peabody Museum expedition to Copan in the 1890's, are all part of this show and have been assembled to help answer some of these question. Plaster casts made in the 1890's of several stelae and altars, including the famous Stele A, create a general impression of the city.

Copan presents a perfect example of the Late Classic Maya urban organization. Located on the floor of a small valley, the center of the city is divided into two main areas: the flat "Great Plaza" and the towering "Acropolis." The Great Plaza area, dotted with stelae and altars, is bounded by long platforms on three sides and a small temple on the south. The low parallel structures of the

In sum: the city brings us to trade, trade to politics and war, war to religion, religion to sacrifice. In the Mesoamerican myth of the creation, the double nature of the sacrifice appears with absolute clarity: the gods, in order to create the world, shed their blood; men, in order to maintain the world, must in turn shed their own blood, which is the food of the gods. The figure of the god-king is the visible manifestation of the duality of the sacrifice: the king is both a warrior (who sacrifices prisoners) and a god (who sheds his own blood). The sacrifice of the others is performed in the "flowering war," self-sacrifice in the ascetic practices of the monarchs.

"Ballcourt" mark the transition from the flat plaza to the huge Acropolis. On the edge of the Acropolis rose a 30-meter-high pyramid ascended by the magnificent Hieroglyphic Stairway, not only a masterpiece of artistic achievement, but most important, an historical record of Copan's rulers. The Copan Acropolis, consisting of two raised courtyards surrounded by temples and palaces, was apparently the most important area of the city, and this central section is surrounded by a dense ring of houses. Another area of extreme density extends to the east of the center into the "Sepultura" region where many of the elite lived. This is connected to the main center by an ancient roadway, called a *sacbe*. Further from the center, density decreases, although there are pockets of heavy concentration throughout some sections of the valley.

Ethnographic Evidence

How did this view of Copan and other Maya sites as urban centers develop? Evidence from sixteenth-century ethnohistoric sources and modern ethnographic studies at first seemed to indicate that Copan, Tikal, Seibal, Palenque and other ancient Maya sites were merely empty

Source: Richard M. Leventhal and Charles H. Howarth, Jr., "Copan: Ancient City of the Maya," *Archaeology* (July/August 1981): 53–55.

ceremonial centers inhabited by only a few priests while the populace was scattered throughout the surrounding countryside. This view was supported by the belief that the Classic Maya practiced slash-and-burn agriculture, as their sixteenth century counterparts did and modern descendants do. [...]

The situation is much more complicated; the organization and customs of today simply do not reflect those of the ancient Maya. Even the sixteenth-century Maya were already far removed from their ancestral past. The Classic Maya collapse of A.D. 900, the gradual changes during the Postclassic period (A.D. 900–1518) and the infiltration of Old World customs and attitudes after the Spanish arrival in 1518, have all irrevocably changed the makeup of this society. Ethnographic and historic accounts may help us develop ideas about the ancient Maya, but they must be continually tested and reexamined.

Changing Views

[T]he empty ceremonial center surrounded by slash-and-burn farming areas was firmly set in the minds of archaeologists, leading to the very low population estimates proposed for the surrounding areas. During the 1950's and 1960's excavations provided a slightly different view of the Maya lowlands. Exploration along the Belize River by Gordon R. Willey and at Tikal by William R. Coe and William Haviland of the University of Pennsylvania revealed a rather dense occupation of house structures. Intensive examination of these small domestic structures indicated that they were simultaneously occupied. By 1970, the Tikal survey had been completed and indicated a population estimate of close to 70,000 people. Archeological evidence also revealed that the central area of Tikal was probably heavily occupied by the ruling elite, priests and their retainers, all non-food producers. This substantial population combined with the dense occupation of the center itself pointed to a definite urban environment.

Yet, the problem of food and how it could be supplied to such a large population continued to baffle archaeologists. At one point, the estimates on how much food the slash-and-burn system could produce were elevated, although they were still not high enough to support the large population concentrations around the central Maya lowland region. Another theory stated that the central cities of the lowlands had enough power to import great quantities of foodstuffs. Basically, archeologists were grasping at solutions.

It finally became clear that perhaps the ethnohistoric and ethnographic information on the cultivation process had misled archaeologists. Today, there is firm archaeological evidence that the Maya utilized a variety of intensive agricultural methods to provide the necessary food, although slash-and-burn techniques were probably used. They terraced hillsides to diminish the problem of erosion and leaching. In large swampy areas the Maya constructed a raised field system. This consisted of canals dug on a grid; the dirt from the canals was placed onto square plots thus creating artificial farmland. Recently, this method has been identified throughout the lowlands with the help of NASA satellite pictures and new radar systems.

During the past 20 years, the view of the ancient Maya social organization has drastically changed. These were not backward people living in the jungle at the very edge of existence. It is clear from recent archaeological work that their technological expertise allowed them to overcome most of the problems posed by the tropical environment. Our knowledge of the Maya continues to expand as more sites are discovered and excavated and new theories are developed. This new exhibit at Boston's Museum of Science presents the most recent thinking on the Maya as exemplified at Copan. The objects in the show are not simply exhibited as magnificent art pieces but rather are utilized to help present as complete a picture as possible of the Maya, one of the most advanced and important ancient civilizations in the world.

The Origins of the *Polis*

The Greek Archaic Period, approximately the ninth through the sixth centuries B.C.E., was marked by a series of revolutions and creative experimentations. One of the most important shifts in Greek life in this period came with the invention of a new form of community, a new form of political organization itself—the polis, or city-state. In this selection, archaeologist Anthony Snodgrass highlights several important aspects of this cultural and political development. First, he argues that the new system has two primary characteristics, each of which is markedly different from the past. On the one hand, the new city-state has a unique external identity. Each polis is politically independent from every other polis. And on the other hand, each new city-state has an internal identity: No distinction was made between those who lived in the urban core and those who resided in the countryside as they all now shared a common identity and loyalty to the polis. The Greeks soon came to call this internal identity "citizenship," something that distinguished the Greek urban phenomenon from that of Mesopotamia. In Reading 22, Thucydides provides a good example of this very kind of identity. Second, Snodgrass argues that the main dynamic of Greek history from this point on concerned the internal struggle over who comprised the citizen body and what the various rights and duties, benefits and services accrued to citizens within that body. Integral to the polis is a shared sense of a common life, whether in the form of religious celebrations or decision making. Aristotle, in Reading 23, provides a sense of the complexity of this shared community experience. As Snodgrass observes, the Greek city-states soon abolished their monarchies or, in the case of Sparta, limited them. Subsequently, authority became more widely dispersed within the community itself. Permission for change within the city-state was sought from the gods, especially the oracle at Delphi, but the authority to wield power came from below, at first from the top social class, and eventually, in places like Athens, from all social classes. As we will see later in Part II, while women's political role in the polis was limited, they were nevertheless considered to be an integral and important part of the city-state

>> 21. Archaic Greece: The Age of Experiment

ANTHONY SNODGRASS [1980]

There may be ways in which a tribal system could accommodate a soaring rise in population without disintegrating. But in the event the more advanced communities in Greece adopted a different solution, one which led to urbanization, but only by an indirect route. The distribution of these more developed states coincides fairly well with that of the more advanced areas of Mycenaean culture, where towns had once existed. Memory of the names of the former towns, though not always their location, certainly survived. But the new system was to be no more re-establishment of the old. The towns were to be quite different physically and, above all, they were to form part of a quite different political system. We know that in the Mycenaean world a kingdom normally included a number of towns all subject to the king's rule, and we suspect a very marked discrimination between town and country. These were features that were not to be revived in the new states.

Source: Anthony Snodgrass, *Archaic Greece: The Age of Experiment* (Berkeley: University of California Press, 1980), 28–29, 85–86.

As so often happens, the name adopted for the new institution was a well-worn term with many meanings besides the one now intended. "Polis', since the time when it outgrew its earlier meaning of 'citadel' or 'stronghold', had probably meant merely a conurbation of a certain minimum size. Now, in its strictest usage, it came to mean a settlement with two essential and new qualities: first, political independence (not always unqualified) from its neighbors; second, political unity with a tract of country surrounding it, this time entirely unqualified, in that no formal distinction was normally made between the inhabitants of the countryside and the inhabitants of the main settlement. Although in one or two cases the institution of monarchy survived into the lifetime of the new system, and although it later proved possible to reconcile the two in the rather different régime of the Archaic tyrannies, the growth of the polis coincided with the general disappearance of hereditary monarchies. The idea of a king ruling over a single town and its territory had perhaps not been quite unknown in Mycenaean times; but we do not find it in the *Catalogue of Ships,* the place in Homer where above all we should expect it to occur if it were a regular Mycenaean feature and its appearances elsewhere in the poems are few and controversial. Appropriately enough in the cases where hereditary monarchy still lingered on in the eighth century and later, the word now used for 'king', *basileus,* had in Mycenaean Greek apparently signified a mere nobleman or petty chieftain. [...]

The Just City?

By the seventh century BC, most of the decisive steps that were to shape Greek civilization had already been taken. After the tremendous structural changes of the later eighth century, several generations were needed to absorb their full implications; but because it was this process of absorption which carried Greek civilization visibly ahead of its rivals and into uncharted territory, its period is often styled the 'Age of Revolution'. The facts seem hardly to support such a description, which should embrace as a central feature the idea of *political* revolution; and that we do not really find in Archaic Greece. Experiment rather than revolution is what distinguishes these years; for all their undoubted vitality and originality, the developments took place within certain accepted norms.

Of these last, one is of paramount importance: the fact that the forms of state in Greece were now accepted. The implications of this were wide. The state was the whole basis of society, the society which in turn created every aspect of the Greek achievement. Henceforward, few questioned that the proper medium for true civilization was a network of small independent states, and few could yet envisage the notion of a Panhellenic culture. Once the multifarious pattern of polis and ethnos came into being—the numbers ran into hundreds in Greece and the Aegean alone, not counting colonies—then relatively little occurred to alter it during the Archaic period. Occasionally a small polis was swallowed up by a more powerful neighbor, or a town within an ethnos would aspire to the status of an independent polis, or even to the subordination of its fellow-nationals; but as a whole the framework remained at least formally secure, down to and beyond the end of Archaic times. The early developments, the differences and the struggles took place almost entirely within this framework; they concerned the form of government, not the form of state. Of course there was interstate warfare as well; but its aim was much more often that of an advantage, an ascendancy, even a hegemony for one's own state, rather than the complete eclipse of another one. Attempts in this latter direction, as for example by Corinth against Megara and later Epidauros [...], usually ended in failure. It is significant that the biggest successful war of outright conquest of Greek by Greek was fought just before the general acceptance of this political pattern: the Spartan conquest of Messenia, which may even have resembled a traditional tribal conquest, in that the later traditions about it show a certain lack of geographical concentration, and make vague references to feuds and cattle-rustling. Most other cases of the conquest, destruction or merging of independent states, by contrast, belong not to the Archaic but to the Classical period.

There can be no doubt that much of the variety and richness of Greek civilization arose from just this multiplicity of political units. There were many different directions in which a state and its constitution could develop and in Archaic Greece the choice between these rested with the citizen-body, independent of outside pressure; probably no two states followed exactly the same path. But who composed the citizen-body? This was the first critical question, one so fundamental that it seems reasonable to make it the basis of any classification of Archaic states. Already there were many different answers to it in the different states; but it should be frankly admitted that the largest group consists of those for whom we have no reliable evidence at all.

The *Polis* of Athens

In a famous passage in his history, Thucydides described the evolution of Athens from a humble monarchy into a polis *of considerable size. He ascribes the process of the unification of Athens with the surrounding Attic countryside, villages, and even other small* poleis, *to Theseus, a hero who would have lived in the Late Bronze Age. The process of creating what was the largest unitary* polis *in the Greek world was called synoecism, or a "living together." It included the abolition of local governments and the centralization of political power in the urban core. Equally importantly (and unlike the Mesopotamian city-states), all of the inhabitants of the* polis, *whether they lived in downtown Athens or in villages and towns further away (such as Marathon, some twenty-six miles distant), were citizens of the same "city"—all were "Athenians." This sense of a common citizenship invariably led to struggles in all the city-states over defining citizen rights and obligations. The process that Thucydides describes was duplicated throughout mainland Greece and nearby islands. When the Greeks subsequently founded new city-states in other parts of the Mediterranean Basin and Black Sea area, they did so on the basis of their experiences within Greece itself.*

>> 22. History of the Peloponnesian War

THUCYDIDES [LAST THIRD OF THE FIFTH CENTURY B.C.E.]

Indeed, from very early times this way of life had been especially characteristic of the Athenians. From the time of Cecrops and the first kings down to the time of Theseus the inhabitants of Attica had always lived in independent cities, each with its own town hall and its own government. Only in times of danger did they meet together and consult the King at Athens; for the rest of the time each state looked after its own affairs and made its own decisions. There were actually occasions when some of the states made war on Athens, as Eleusis under Eumolpus did against King Erechtheus. But when Theseus became King he showed himself as intelligent as he was powerful. In his reorganization of the country one of the most important things he did was to abolish the separate councils and governments of the small cities and to bring them all together into the present city of Athens, making one deliberative assembly and one seat of government foe all. Individuals could look after their own property

Source: Thucydides, *History of the Peloponnesian War*, translated by Rex Warner (New York: Penguin Books, 1954), 134–135.

just as before, but Theseus compelled them to have only one centre for their political life—namely, Athens—and, as they all became Athenian citizens, it was a great city that Theseus handed down to those who came after him. From him dates the feast of the Union of Attica which the Athenians still hold today in honour of Athene and pay for out of public funds. Before this time the city consisted of the present Acropolis and the part below it facing southwards.

Evidence for this is to be found in the fact that in the Acropolis itself are the temples of the other gods as well as of Athene; and the temples outside the Acropolis are, in the main, situated in this part of the city—for instance, the temple of Olympian Zeus, of Pythian Apollo, of Earth, and of Dionysus in the Marsh, in whose honour the more ancient Dionysia are still held in the month of Anthesterion, a custom which is also preserved up to the present day by the Ionians who came from Athens. Other ancient temples also are in this part of the city. Then there is the spring of water which is now called 'The Nine Fountains', since the tyrants had the fountains made, but used to be called Callirhoe or 'Fair Stream' when the water came straight out of the earth. The people in those days used to use this spring for all purposes since it was so close to them, and, from this ancient habit of theirs is derived the custom of using it for ceremonies before marriage and in other religious ceremonies. Then, too, the Acropolis is still called 'the city' by the Athenians. This is because they used to live there in the past.

For a long time, therefore, the Athenians had lived in independent communities throughout Attica. And even after the unification of Attica the old habits were retained, most Athenians, both in earlier generations and right down to the time of this present war, being born and bred in the country.

Humans as *Polis* Dwellers

Aristotle, the future tutor of Alexander the Great, was born in the northern Greek polis of Stagira in 384 B.C.E. In his Politics, *the philosopher explains the nature of the polis and how humans need to live in a polis to be fulfilled completely. In the course of his discussion he also indicates the exclusivity of the Greek city-state: The polis is, in part, an association of families and households, rather than of individuals. It is a whole social fabric that encompasses religion and marriage, almost always within the group itself, as well as politics and culture. To become a member, a citizen, of a city-state different from that into which you were born was almost impossible. Citizenship was the most important form of status differentiation in the Greek world, and the acquisition of a different citizenship was almost unheard of. Immigrants to Athens, for instance, almost always remained resident aliens, so-called* metics, *for their whole lives. Moreover, not all urban entities qualified as a polis—a polis was more than a place with a wall around it, like Uruk. Babylon for Aristotle may have been a great urban complex, but it most certainly was not a polis. As a result, Babylonians could not reach their full potential as human beings. Thus the Greek city-state, with its membership and particular institutions, was a way that the Greeks distinguished themselves from non-Greeks as well as from other Greeks.*

Source: Aristotle, *The Politics of Aristotle*, translated by Ernest Barker (New York: Oxford University Press, 1962), 4–5, 98–99.

>> 23. The Politics of Aristotle

ARISTOTLE [MOST LIKELY BETWEEN 335 AND 322 B.C.E.]

§ 8. When we come to the final and perfect association, formed from a number of villages, we have already reached the polis—an association which may be said to have reached the height of full self-sufficiency; or rather [to speak more exactly] we may say that while it *grows* for the sake of mere life [and is so far, and at that stage, still short of full self-sufficiency], it *exists* [when once it is fully grown] for the sake of a good life [and is therefore fully self-sufficient].

Because it is the completion of associations existing by nature, every polis exists by nature, having itself the same quality as the earlier associations from which it grew. It is the end or consummation to which those associations move, and the 'nature' of things consists in their end or consummation; for what each thing is when its growth is completed we call the nature of that thing, whether it be a man or a horse or a family. **1253 a** § 9. Again [and this is a second reason for regarding the state as natural] the end, or final cause, is the best. Now self-sufficiency [which it is the object of the state to bring about] is the end, and so is the best; [and on this it follows that the state brings about the best, and is therefore natural, since nature always aims at bringing about the best].

From these considerations it is evident that the polis belongs to the class of things that exist by nature, and that man is by nature an animal intended to live in a polis. He who is without a polis, by reason of his own nature and not of some accident, is either a poor sort of being, or a being higher than man: he is like the man of whom Homer wrote in denunciation:

'Clanless and lawless and heartless is he.'

§ 10. The man who is such by nature [i.e. unable to join in the society of a polis] at once plunges into a passion for war; he is in the position of a [...] solitary advanced piece in a game of draughts.

§ 5. The identity of a polis is not constituted by its walls. It would be possible to surround the whole of the Peloponnese by a single wall: [but would that make it a single polis?]. Babylon (which, it is said, had been captured for three whole days before some of its inhabitants knew of the fact) may perhaps be counted a polis of this dubious nature: so, too, might any polis which had the dimensions of a people [*ethnos*] rather than those of a city. § 6. But it will be better to reserve the consideration of this question [i.e. how large a polis can be and yet remain a single polis] for some other occasion. To determine the size of a polis—to settle how large it can properly be, and whether it ought to consist of the members of one people or of several—is a duty incumbent on the statesman. [It is, therefore, a matter to be considered in connexion [sic] with the art of statesmanship, rather than in connexion [sic] with the theory of the identity of the polis].

>> Mastering the Materials

1. After reading the modern scholars in this chapter, how would you define a city? What are its chief characteristics?

2. Why is Gilgamesh so proud of his city Uruk? What does this tell us about the Mesopotamian urban experience and landscape?

3. How does Aristotle characterize the Greek city-state, the *polis*? Based on your reading of Snodgrass and Aristotle, describe how the Greek *polis* differs from other city-state experiences.

>> Making Connections

1. Historians use many different types of evidence to reconstruct and explain the past. How many different kinds of evidence have you seen in Part I? What are both the value and limitations of each form of evidence? How is archaeology particularly useful to the historian, especially when it comes to the origin and development of cities?

2. Cities seem only to arise in agricultural societies. Why do you think this is? Based on the evidence from this and the last two chapters, what do you think is the connection between cultivation and urbanization?

3. Some scholars think that the term *civilization* is roughly equivalent to *urbanization*—that when societies develop to the degree that they have sedentary, urbanized populations, they have become "civilized." Based on the sources in this chapter and the discussion in the introduction, do you think this definition of the term *civilization* should be adopted? Why or why not?

Chapter 4

Consolidation and Fragmentation of Power

The Urban Context

With the development of cities and urban structures, a new chapter in human history began—life and culture would never be the same again. The impact of cities was not limited to the development of city-states. Some cities remain just that, cities. Thus, you will learn about two basic phenomena in this chapter, each of which has the city at its core. First, in some instances the existence of cities did not impede the creation of political entities on a larger scale. Egypt and China are two good examples. Second, and in contrast, cities did prevent political consolidation elsewhere, even when rulers attempted to extend their authority to encompass areas beyond their city-states. Mesopotamia is the prime example.

Civilization in the Nile Valley is approximately as old as that of Mesopotamia. Yet despite many similarities, their cultural and political histories diverged greatly from one another. Like southern Iraq, Egypt would seem to have all the prerequisites for urbanization and competing city-states: Agricultural towns began to develop into dense population centers, often surrounded by thick walls; each community had local deities with whom the population strongly identified; and an elite exerted control over local resources, agricultural and human. But the city-state was not the route that the inhabitants of the Nile Valley took. While initially creating what Barry Kemp calls "incipient city-states," the Egyptians ended up by forging a unified political unit running the entire length of the Nile River to the Mediterranean Sea under the rule of one man, the pharaoh. The pharaonic state emerged rapidly when Narmer, also called Menes, the ruler of the expanding city of Hierakonpolis (Nekhen), unified most of the valley and the delta into a single political unit around 3000 B.C.E. The physical conquest of the Nile Valley and delta was solidified by the creation of a remarkable set of institutions, symbols, and myths, all of which reinforced the same idea that the normal state of affairs was unity, and that the wholeness of the land was properly expressed in the very person of the pharaoh himself. One important document, the "Memphite Theology," reveals the religious context for the king of Egypt as the living god, Horus himself. Every pharaoh became Horus upon his coronation, and thus became the embodiment of Egypt itself. This strong monarchical political system was the hallmark of Egyptian history for millennia, and even after native Egyptians had ceased to be its kings, rulers—including the Roman emperors—still portrayed themselves as pharaoh.

The development of Chinese political authority mirrors in some ways that of Egypt. While large walled towns arose early, cities themselves seem not to have emerged on the Yellow River until around 1500 B.C.E. Despite the development of cities during the Shang dynasty, the urban foundations did not lead to political fragmentation. The Shang kings did not rule a particularly large area of the Yellow River, but this territory became the core of a larger state many centuries later. Lineages and clans were important in early China, and the leaders of large clans managed to take over other clans that were each centered in their own cities. Thus some urban centers became subordinated to others, and individual rulers came to exert great power, both by means of mobilizing a large number of men into an army and by monopolizing certain religious practices. Anthropologists observe that political leadership is always connected to religion in one way or another—leaders claim to be not only favored by the gods but also able to manipulate divine forces for the good of the community. During the Shang dynasty, one of the most important religious practices controlled by the kings was a form of divination, a way of seeking the will of the gods by means of oracle bones. These Shang kings, though not nearly as strong as those of later dynasties, nonetheless contributed certain important elements that were always a part of political rule in China, including a connection between themselves and the divine powers of the universe. In addition to the ancestor worship practiced by the Shang kings, later Chinese rulers also claimed exclusive right to worship Heaven, a supernatural moral authority that granted them the Mandate to rule.

In other areas of the world, by contrast, the development of urban entities entailed the creation of independent city-states that rarely, if ever, came together in larger political units. The three major city-state systems that we surveyed in Chapter 3—Mesopotamia, Mesoamerica, and Greece—shared certain characteristics of development. Each, for example, maintained strong urban identities that prevented easy political unification. Similarly, each system, despite its political fragmentation, produced a common culture that all of the cities shared in and that became a standard for others to copy. Nevertheless, each also developed societies, institutions, and cultures that were radically different from one another. On the surface, the history of Mesopotamia might suggest one of consistent political consolidation—Hammurabi, the powerful Amorite king, might seem to be the natural successor of earlier kings like Shulgi of Third Dynasty Ur. Yet even though kings like Shulgi and Hammurabi did control the whole of southern Iraq, they ruled by force, and the disintegration of their states into fragments was commonplace. The Maya and the Greeks, by contrast, never even attempted to create larger consolidated political units, the very idea of the larger polity being antithetical to their understanding of the nature of the city-state itself. Despite their similarities, however, we see two very different internal dynamics taking place within their two city-state systems, internal dynamics that helped to shape unique cultural and political developments.

A final example of the development of city-states comes from the Indian subcontinent. Although the urban life of the Harappa culture in the Indus Valley was almost as old as that of Mesopotamia, by about 1700 B.C.E. the main urban centers of this region had largely disappeared. Cities reemerged again around the seventh century B.C.E., but this time in northern India in the Ganges plain and the foothills of the Himalayas. In this region, tribal structures gave way to the kind of urban life seen in ancient Iraq or Greece. Scholars relate how some of these city-states were monarchies, but others were what we could call republics. These cities played an important role in the economic and cultural life of northern India, and the great religious developments that took place in India happened within the context of these cities. Not surprisingly, a prince of one of these cities, Rama, is the hero of one of the greatest of all Sanskrit epic poems, *The Rāmāyaṇa* of Vālmīkī. Reading 31 provides a somewhat idealized image of one of the great urban centers on the Gangetic plain, Ayodhyā.

The Unification of Egypt

Urbanization did not invariably mean the foundation of city-states. In Egypt, what could have been city-states never fully came into being. Instead, as historian Barry Kemp discusses, two or three urban centers began to take over their neighbors, and eventually the ruler of one of these centers, Narmer, emerged as the head of the entire Nile Valley and delta region. His god, Horus, the falcon god, became a national god, and Narmer, in turn, became an incarnation of that god himself. Yet in the process of unification, local sensibilities were not crushed but were instead incorporated into the larger almost national identity of "the Two Lands," that is, the Nile Valley and the delta. Local cities became the chief place for administrative districts, which the Greeks—and current Egyptologists—called "nomes," and local gods were incorporated into a national pantheon. Similarly, the pharaoh himself was called "He who belongs to the Sedge and the Bee," referring to Upper and Lower Egypt: The whole of the land was constantly reinforced by remembering its various parts. The word pharaoh *itself comes from* per-o, *or "Great House" (the palace), and disguises the important political and religious duality of the ruler's position. In turn, each of the two parts of Egypt was represented by a different color, plant, goddess, and crown, all of which were repeated endlessly in different ways, and all of which were connected with the pharaoh himself. Periodically, as Kemp observes, local identities reasserted themselves, but this state of affairs was rare and generally short lived. The natural order was always the unity of the Two Lands.*

>> 24. Ancient Egypt: Anatomy of a Civilization

BARRY J. KEMP [1989]

We are entitled to ask: what was the source of the disorder that made itself felt at this time? It is a common sensation for the people of a settled society to feel surrounded and threatened by a turbulent and hostile outside world [...]. For the small political units of late Predynastic Egypt the settings were parochial: the alien deserts and neighbouring communities not too far away along the Nile. But the more successful of these communities, the incipient city-states, had become engaged in more organized conflicts over territory, the conflicts which were to lead to the birth of the Egyptian state. The urgent reality of conflict involving attacks on walled settlements and the horrors of the battlefield were sometimes translated into pictorial scenes of actual combat [...], although the essence of conflict, of disequilibrium, was still

Source: Barry J. Kemp, *Ancient Egypt: Anatomy of a Civilization* (London: Routledge, 1989), 50, 52.

viewed in generalized allegorical terms. From the experience of disorder and struggle, the shattering of an earlier equilibrium, arose the perception of a world in conflict, real or potential, between chaos and order. This was to remain a theme of intellectual concern for the rest of Egyptian history, as did the notion that containment (though not ultimate defeat) of disorder and unrule was possible through the rule of kings and the benign presence of a supreme divine force [...].

The myth of Horus and Seth is not a reflection of how the Egyptian state emerged politically. The details of the period of internal warfare among the incipient city-states of the Nile Valley are unlikely ever to be known, but we can safely assume that it was not a simple epic struggle between two protagonists. The myth of the state in historic times was a clever adaption of an earlier, more generalized statement of an ideal world originating in Upper Egypt. It combined the old concept of an ultimate harmony through balanced opposites with the newly perceived need for a single superior force. It was created as part of the great codification of court culture. It drew upon local mythology, which in the case of both Horus and Seth was centred in Upper Egypt. It became part of the long active interest which the Egyptians maintained in symbolic geography; in effect, a process of internal colonization at an intellectual level.

One further observation needs to be made. The 1st Dynasty began as a state which was territorially as large as most which were to occupy the lower Nile Valley until modern times. There was no long process of growth from a spread of city states, a common early political form which had a thriving history in, for example, Mesopotamia. We have already used the term 'incipient city-state' for territories in southern Upper Egypt centred on Hierakonpolis and Nagada. 'Incipient' seems an appropriate word since they cannot have matched the complexity of contemporary city states in other parts of the Near East. We can be fairly sure of two, and we can suspect that there were others either already in existence (e.g. one based on Thinis) or still at an even earlier stage of formation (perhaps at Maadi and Buto in the Delta, Abadiya in Upper Egypt, and Qustul in Lower Nubia). The internal warfare pursued most vigorously from the south terminated this polycentric period of political growth, but as states everywhere discover sooner or later, regional assertion remains a powerful force even when its centres are submerged within a larger polity. The game goes on. The Pharaonic state was remarkably successful, through the mechanism of symbolic geography, in creating an ideology with numerous provincial ramifications. We can speak of a national framework of myth. Yet submerged local identities remained. The one we see most clearly in the later historic periods (from 6th Dynasty onward) is a submerged city-state of Thebes.

The Memphite Theology

One of the most important documents from Egypt's Old Kingdom, about 2650 to 2135 B.C.E., is a treatise that scholars call the "Memphite Theology." This treatise contains the myth of how the god Horus, the nephew of the wicked Seth and son of the murdered Osiris, became the first king, or pharaoh, of Egypt. The story relates the religious principles for and justification of how the pharaoh, as Horus incarnate, came to rule the Two Lands. The political order in Egypt was divinely ordained, and each new king became Horus, the ruler of Egypt, at the same time that the dead king became Osiris, the ruler of the Underworld. This endless cycle of kings, like the cycles of day to night and of flood to growing, were, in fact, all one and the same, and all timeless. But the story relates a very important historical event as well: the actual unification of Egypt by Narmer. This story is set at a city that Narmer built, alternately called "White Walls" and Menne(u)fer,

"Beauty Endures," which the Greeks heard as Memphis, and which also recalls Narmer's other name, Menes, *"He who endures."* The symbolic importance of this new city is critical for understanding the new political order that Narmer created. This city was built as a military, administrative, and religious center. Sacred to Ptah, the chief temple was called Hikuptah, *"Temple of the ka [soul] of Ptah,"* which the Greeks heard as Aigyptos, and from which we get Egypt. Ptah was one of several creator gods, and his role in establishing the divine monarchy was crucial. Similarly, Memphis was called "the balance [or fulcrum] of the Two Lands"—geographically and politically it sits at the boundary between the Nile Valley and the delta. Just south of modern Cairo, Memphis was also called the place that "unites the Two Lands," and appropriately enough, it was where pharaohs came to be crowned. "The Memphite Theology" presented the ideology of kingship in a way that united Egypt under the banner of its god–king. While Egypt would periodically disintegrate into local units, that was the exception rather than the rule.

>> 25. Memphite Theology

[OLD KINGDOM (2650–2135 B.C.E.) TEXT
REINSCRIBED AROUND 710 B.C.E.]

(13c) Then Horus stood over the land. He is the uniter of this land, proclaimed in the great name: Ta-tenen, South-of-his-Wall, Lord of Eternity. Then sprouted (14c) the two Great Magicians upon his head. He is Horus who arose as king of Upper and Lower Egypt, who united the Two Lands in the Nome of the Wall, the place in which the Two Lands were united.

(I5c) Reed and papyrus were placed on the double door of the House of Ptah. That means Horus and Seth, pacified and united. They fraternized so as to cease quarreling (16c), in whatever place they might be, being united in the House of Ptah, the "Balance of the Two Lands" in which Upper and Lower Egypt had been weighed.

This is the land (17c)———the burial of Osiris in the House of Sokar. (18c)———Isis and Nephthys without delay, (19) for Osiris had drowned in his water. Isis [and Nephthys] looked out, [beheld him and attended to him]. (20a) Horus speaks to Isis and Nephthys: "Hurry, grasp

him———." (21a) Isis and Nephthys speak to Osiris: "We come, we take you———."

(20b)———[They heeded in time] and brought him to (21b) [land. He entered the hidden portals in the glory of the lords of eternity].——— [Thus Osiris came into] the earth (22) at the royal fortress, to the north of [the land to which he had come. And his son Horus arose as king of Upper Egypt, arose as king of Lower Egypt, in the embrace of his father Osiris and of the gods in front of him and behind him.]

(23) There was built the royal fortress [at the command of Geb———]. [...]

Memphis the Royal City

The Great Throne that gives joy to the heart of the gods in the House of Ptah is the granary of Ta-tenen, the mistress of all life, through which the sustenance of the Two Lands is provided, (62) owing to the fact that Osiris was drowned in his water. Isis and Nephthys looked out, beheld him, and attended to him. Horus quickly commanded Isis and Nephthys to grasp Osiris and prevent his drowning (i.e. his submerging). (63) They heeded in time and

Source: "Memphite Theology," in *Ancient Egyptian Literature: A Book of Readings*, v. 1: *The Old and Middle Kingdoms*, edited by Miriam Lichtheim (Berkeley: University of California Press, 1975), 53, 55–56.

brought him to land. He entered the hidden portals in the glory of the lords of eternity, in the steps of him who rises in the horizon, on the ways of Re at the Great Throne. (64) He entered the palace and joined the gods of Ta-tenen Ptah, lord of years.

Thus Osiris came into earth at the Royal Fortress, to the north of the land to which he had come. His son Horus arose as king of Upper Egypt, arose as king of Lower Egypt, in the embrace of his father Osiris and of the gods in front of him and behind him.

Shang Oracle Bones

One of the oldest historical sources that we have for ancient China are oracle bones, over 200,000 of which have been found. After the tortoise shells and shoulder blades of cattle were cracked by the application of high heat, diviners would interpret what the cracks meant, and from this the king would make predictions for the future and seek approval for taking certain actions in the present. These meanings and decisions were then inscribed on the bones themselves. From the inscriptions we learn a great deal about the activities—ritual, military, economic, and administrative—of the Shang royal court (about 1570–1045 B.C.E., but traditionally dated to 1600–1027 B.C.E.). The range of information on the bones is extensive, even if brief in any one instance, and their content and subject matter changed over time. The bones David Keightley describes in this passage illustrate sacrifices as a part of ancestor worship, the mobilization of a large military force, and predictions of either a good or poor harvest of millet, the chief crop of northern China at this time. Questions about childbirth, dream interpretation, and the building of settlements were also asked. Prominent historians like Keightley and J. K. Fairbank conclude from evidence like this that the Shang state was a "patrimonial theocracy," and they argue that remnants of Shang ritual and ancestor worship, of family and patriarchy, persisted into much later times.

>> 26. Shang Oracle-Bone Inscriptions

DAVID N. KEIGHTLEY [c.1570–1075 B.C.E.]

Sacrifices and Rituals

(*Preface:*) Divined: (*Charge:*) "(We) should offer to Xiang Jia, Father Geng, and Father Xin, one cow."

(*Preface:*) Divined: (*Charge:*) "(We) should not offer to Xiang Jia, Father Geng, and Father Xin, one cow." (I. Bin) (*Yibian* 7767 [S532.3] = *Heji* 6647 front [Y1420.2]; Fig. 4)

Mobilizations

(*Preface:*) Crack-making on *dingyou* (day 34), Que divined: (*Charge:*) "This season, the king raises men, 5,000 (of them), to compaign against the Tufang; he will receive assistance in this case." (*Postface:*) Third moon. (I. Bin) (*Houbian* 1.31.5 [S1.1, but recorded as 1.31.6] = *Heji* 6409 [Y1.1]) [...]

Agriculture

(*Preface:*) Crack-making on [*bing-*]*chen* (day 53), Que divined: (*Charge:*) "We will receive millet harvest."

Source: David N. Keightley, "Shang Oracle-Bone Inscriptions," in *New Sources of Early Chinese History*, edited by Edward Shaughnessy (Berkeley: The Society for the Study of Early China, 1997), 31–33, 38–39.

(*Preface*:) Crack-making on *bingchen* (day 53), Que divined: (*Charge*:) "We may not receive millet harvest." (*Postface*:) Fourth moon. (*Bingbian* 8.1–2 [S197.2] = *Heji* 9950 front [Y536.2]; Fig. 1a) (*Prognostication*:) The king read the cracks and said: "Auspicious. We will receive this harvest." (I. Bin) (*Bingbian* 9 [S196.3] = *Heji* 9950 back [Y535.1]; Fig. 1b) [...]

Childbirth

(*Preface*:) Crack-making on *jiashen* (day 21), Que divined: (*Charge*:) "Lady Hao will give birth and it will be good."[35] (*Prognostication*:) The king read the cracks and said: "(Expecting it to be =) If it be on a ding day that she gives birth, it will be good. (Expecting it to be =) If it be on a *geng* day that she give birth, it will be prolonged auspiciousness." (*Verification*:) (After) thirty-one days, on *jiayin* (day 51), she gave birth. It was not good. It was a girl. [...]

Dreams

Crack-making on *jichou* (day 26), Que divined: "The king's dream was due to Ancestor Yi (the twelfth Shang king)". [...]

Settlement Building

Crack-making on *renzi* (day 49), Zheng divined: "(Expecting to =) If we build a settlement, Di (the high god of Shang) will not obstruct (?) (but) approve." Third moon.

The King of the Road

The political situation in ancient Mesopotamia was often confused. In the course of the third millennium B.C.E. a new Semitic-speaking group settled in the area just north of Sumer, a region soon to be called the Land of Akkad, after its chief city. Before Sargon (the founder and king of Akkad), rulers from one city or another attempted to exert hegemony over all the others. Generally the kings of the Sumerian cities were called ensi, *the "Steward [of the god]." But some rulers were called* lugal, *"Big Man," which to scholars suggests that they ruled over several cities. The situation in southern Iraq, however, was almost always fragmented. Historians like Postgate argue that the people of the various city-states seemed to feel that they belonged to a common land, and that they even recognized the primacy of one city above the others. Nevertheless, the chief city changed periodically, and the ruler of any chief city rarely exercised authority in the other city-states. Sometimes nominal suzerainty over the fragmented region was replaced by actual conquest and control, especially after about 2350 B.C.E., when kings tried to replicate Sargon's achievements and create larger political units with themselves at the center. One such example is Shulgi, the second king of Third Dynasty Ur (r. about 2095–2047 B.C.E.). He called himself the "King of Sumer and Akkad," that is, of the whole of southern Iraq, and the "King of the Four Corners [of the Universe]." In his self-proclaimed universal dominion he even took the unusual step of asserting his divine status, something that another king was the first to have done some 200 years earlier. Shulgi boasts of his relationship with the gods and of his warrior prowess, and at the end of his hymn we can see the physical symbols of his political power. But this dynasty's control over southern Mesopotamia did not last to the end of the century, and it was replaced with the usual state of affairs, fragmentation into smaller units once more.*

>> 27. "The King of the Road": A Self-Laudatory Shulgi Hymn

[FIRST HALF OF THE TWENTY-FIRST CENTURY B.C.E.]

I, the king, a hero from the (mother's) womb am I,   (1)

I, Shulgi, a mighty man from (the day) I was born am I,

A fierce-eyed lion, born of the *ushumgal* am I,

King of the four corners (of the universe) am I,

Herdsman, shepherd of the blackheads am I,

The trustworthy, the god of all the lands am I,

The son born on Ninsun am I,

Called to the heart of holy An am I,

He who was blessed by Enlil am I,

Shulgi, the beloved of Ninlil am I,   (10)

Faithfully nurtured by Nintu am I,

Endowed with wisdom by Enki am I,

The mighty king of Nanna am I,

The open-jawed lion of Utu am I,

Shulgi chosen for the vulva of Inanna am I,

A princely donkey all set for the road am I,

A horse that swings (his) tail on the highway am I,

A noble donkey of Sumugan eager for the course am I,

The wise scribe of Nidaba am I.

Like my heroship, like my might,   (20)

I am accomplished in wisdom (as well),

I *vie* with its (wisdom's) true word,

I love justice,

I do not love evil,

I hate the evil word,

I, Shulgi, a mighty king, supreme am I.

Because I am a powerful man rejoining in his "loins,"

I *enlarged* the footpaths, straightened the highways of the land,

I made secure travel, built there "big houses,"

Planted gardens alongside of them,
   established resting-places,   (30)

Settled there friendly folk,

(So that) who comes from below, who come from above,

Might refresh themselves in its cool (shade),

The wayfarer who travels the highway a night,

Might find refuge there like in a well-built city.

That my name be established unto distant days that it leave not the mouth (of men),

That my praise be spread wide in the land,

That I be *eulogized* in all the lands,

I, the runner, rose in my strength, *all set* for the course,

(And) from Nippur to Ur,   (40)

I resolved to traverse as if it were (but a [...] distance) of one *danna*.

With valiant Uru my brother and friend,

I drank strong drink in the palace founded by An,   (80)

My minstrels sang for me the seven *tigi*-songs.

By the side of my spouse, the maid Inanna, the Qun, the "vulva" of heaven (and) earth,

I sat at its (the palace's) banquet.

Source: "The King of the Road: A Self-Laudatory Shulgi Hymn," in *The Ancient Near East: An Anthology of Texts and Pictures*, v. 2, edited by James B. Pritchard (Princeton: Princeton University Press, 1975), 132–133, 135.

She spoke not my *judgment* as a (final)
    judgment,

Wheresoever I lift my eyes, thither I go,

Wheresoever my heart moves me,
    thither I proceed.

An set the holy crown upon my head,

Made me take the scepter in the
    "lapis-lazuli" Ekur,

On the radiant dais, he raised heaven high
    the firmly founded throne,

He exalted there the power of (my)
    kingship.   (90)

I bent low all the lands, made secure the people,

The four-corners of the universe, the people in
    unison, call my name,

Chant holy songs,

Pronounce my exaltation (saying):

"He that is nurtured by the exalted power of
    kingship,

Presented by Sin, out of the Ekishnugal,

With heroship, might, and a good life,

Endowed with lofty power by Nunamnir,

Shulgi, the destroyer of all the foreign lands,
    who makes all the people secure,

Who in accordance with the *me* of
    the universe,   (100)

Shulgi, cherished by the trusted son of An (Sin)!"

Oh, Nidaba, praise!

Lordship in Mesoamerica

The city-state experience in the Americas among the Maya has characteristics of both Mesopotamia and Greece. Like the inhabitants of ancient Iraq, the Maya believed that rulership, that legitimate authority over the members of the community, came from somewhere outside the community itself. Part of royal authority derived from religion. Kings claimed divine ancestry—predecessors almost always became gods upon death—but only rarely did they assume divine status while living. Moreover, in the Mayan Popol Vuh *the actual right to rule came from the legendary Nacxit, "the great lord and sole judge over a populous domain." Nacxit exercised his authority somewhere east of Guatemala in the Yucatán. Like Shulgi, the author of the* Popol Vuh *carefully lists the various emblems denoting power and authority that the first ruler received, from a canopy and throne to egret and parrot feathers. But unlike Shulgi, the leaders of the Quiché Maya did not claim a control over other cities or the entire world. The Keeper of the Mat was the primary ruler of the Quiché, and once he and a lesser lord received the symbols of their authority, they established a city of their own lineages in the highlands, which they named after their chief deity, Hacauitz. But, as the story relates, their population grew and they abandoned the place only to establish new cities. The Maya city-states were fiercely independent, and like the Greeks, they were usually able to maintain their independent status. Some kings sought to control nearby cities by trade, intermarriage, or treaty, but they did not attempt to create larger political units. Individual identity as linked to their social structure and their chief god made each city-state unique and incapable of incorporating others into the system. Strong city-state loyalties, as expressed through kings, lineages, and the gods, insured that the political world of the Maya always remained fragmented.*

>> 28. Popol Vuh: The Mayan Book of the Dawn of Life

[ANCIENT TALE WRITTEN DOWN IN THE ROMAN ALPHABET IN THE MID-SIXTEENTH CENTURY C.E.]

And then they came before the lord named Nacxit, the great lord and sole judge over a populous domain.

And he was the one who gave out the signs of lordship, all the emblems; the signs of the Keeper of the Mat and the Keeper of the Reception House Mat were set forth.

And when the signs of the splendor and lordship of the Keeper of the Mat and Keeper of the Reception House Mat were set forth, Nacxit gave a complete set of emblems of lordship. Here are their names:

Canopy, throne.

Bone flute, bird whistle.

Sparkling powder, yellow ocher.

Puma's paw, jaguar's paw.

Head and hoof of deer.

Leather armband, snail-shell rattle.

Tobacco gourd, food bowl.

Parrot feathers, egret feathers.

So they came away bringing all of these. Then, from beside the sea, they brought back the writing of Tulan, the writing of Zuyua. They spoke of their investiture in their signs, in their words.

Also, after they had reached their citadel, named Hacauitz, all the Tams and Ilocs gathered there. All the tribes gathered themselves together; they were happy. When Noble Two, Noble Acutec, and Noble Lord came back, they resumed their lordship over the tribes. The Rabinals, the Cakchiquels, and those of Bird House were happy. Only the signs of the greatness of lordship were revealed before them. Now the lords became great in their very being; when they had displayed their lordship previously, it was incomplete.

This was when they were at Hacauitz. The only ones with them were all those who had originally come from the east. And they spent a long time there on that mountain. Now they were all numerous.

And the wives of Jaguar Quitze, Jaguar Night, and Not Right Now died there. Then they came away, they left their mountain place behind. They sought another mountain where they could settle. They settled countless mountains, giving them epithets and names: Our first mothers and our first fathers multiplied and gained strength at those places, according to what the people of ancient times said when they told about the abandonment of their first citadel, named Hacauitz.

Citizenship in Ancient Greece

No human institution, including cities, remains unchanged for long. One of the most remarkable changes for the Greek city-states revolved around the evolution of citizenship. In this selection, archaeologist Anthony Snodgrass reiterates that the most important event, intellectually and politically, in early Greek history was the idea of the independent city-state, or polis. But along with this political independence—something that was common to city-states in Mesopotamia and Mesoamerica as well—came the notion of belonging, of citizenship. The idea that members of the community have a shared sense of a common life that included political and legal rights was Greek. From the eighth century B.C.E. on, Snodgrass comments that political innovations and refinements in the nature of citizenship occurred with some

Source: Dennis Tedlock, trans., *Popol Vuh: The Mayan Book of the Dawn of Life* (New York: Touchstone, 1996), 179–180.

speed. Citizenship was more than just an idle phrase or catchword—it had a specific content of mutual rights, benefits, and obligations. These citizen rights and benefits became more extensive over time because of the relative security of the Greek city-states internally and externally: No one Greek polis, *even the militarily powerful Sparta, could dominate many, let alone all, of the Greek city-states, and no external power threatened to overwhelm the city-states until the rise of Persia over the course of the sixth century* B.C.E. *As a result, various* poleis *underwent different internal changes with fairly little interference from the outside. Each* polis *guarded its independence and its citizenship closely, which led to problems when a concerted effort was required against a common enemy like Persia, but also fostered a richness of cultural forms and experiments that continued for a very long period of time.*

>> 29. Archaic Greece: The Age of Experiment

ANTHONY SNODGRASS [1980]

That some similar process worked itself out in the last generation of the Archaic period is likely enough, though impossible to prove. The invasion of Xerxes was, after all, simply a further act in a drama which had been inaugurated in the 540s when the Persians reached Ionia, and which had been approaching a climax since the outbreak of the Ionian Revolt in 499. Many Greeks, artists among them, will have felt that a supreme crisis was shortly to be upon them, and their thoughts may have turned more strongly in the direction of change. But I have not laboured this point at such length merely in order to establish a detail of relative chronology. If we modify the original hypothesis, made at the beginning of this chapter, from one of a final Greek deafeat in the Persian Wars to one in which the final confrontation had not occurred at all—once again, a far from inconceivable eventuality historically—then the inference will become clear. It is that, irrespective of the great military events of 480 and 479, the society of Archaic Greece (and especially of Archaic Athens) was embarked on a course which would certainly have generated major political and cultural developments, and possibly ones essentially similar to those which, in the event, did take place. I am not for one moment disputing the fact that the onset of the Persians, once we remember that it was a process

covering two generations, was the catalyst which brought Archaic Greece to its highest pitch of achievement. But the decision of the thirty-one states to march and sail against a people whose empire already stretched from the Indus to Cyrenaica, and whose soldiers had been seen far up the Nile and north of the Danube, was a decision as important in its antecedents as in its sequel. It was the culmination of a long process of ferment among the Greeks, resulting in the conclusion that it was worth almost anything to be able to carry on following their own ways and serving their own values.

We cannot know that such thoughts went through the minds of the participants. But I hope that at least the foregoing chapters have made clear what some of these ways and values might have been. Looking back over the generations which had contributed to them, I still find that the most remarkable developments are the initial ones, and that the 'structural revolution' of the later eighth century was the greatest turning-point in Greece's earlier history. It was a greater step to conceive of the small independent state than to let it develop along its own course. The idea of citizenship, of the free members of such a state having certain inalienable rights, led naturally to the extension of those rights. Yet the independence of the state was also a guarantee of the many variations in the speed of developments, allowing one state to learn from the example and the experience of others. Together, these ideas were almost a prescription for political innovation, so long as the precarious balance of

Source: Anthony Snodgrass, *Archaic Greece: The Age of Experiment* (Berkeley: University of California Press, 1980), 213–214.

power within Greece, and the equally precarious immunity from external interference, were maintained. It was Greece's good fortune that, for over two centuries, these conditions were permitted to exist; by the end, it was clear to most Greeks that the gains that they had made were worth fighting for.

Constitution of the Athenians

The content of citizenship varied from polis *to* polis, *and even within a single* polis *changes took place. As is often the case for ancient Greece, we are best informed about Athens, for which we have many sources. The Greek philosopher Aristotle, in his* Constitution of Athens, *traces the development of Athenian political institutions and citizen rights from the origins of the city-state until his own day in the fourth century* B.C.E. *One of the biggest shifts for the Athenians came with the reforms of Solon in the sixth century* B.C.E. *While the dates and exact context for Solon's reforms are the subject of historical controversy, his importance is not. It was Solon who first gave real meaning to what it meant to be a citizen of Athens. In this section of Aristotle's* Constitution of Athens *certain features stand out in particular. First, Solon enrolled all the Athenians into one of four different traditional economic classes. In itself, this was not particularly radical. But what he did was to allot to the members of each economic class some political rights. Prior to his time, political rights were based on wealth and birth; now they were based solely on wealth, something an individual could potentially change. Second, he abolished debt bondage—no Athenian could be reduced to slavery or other forms of dependent labor due to debts. Third, all citizens, even women, had the right to a trial by jury, and all male citizens, regardless of the economic status, had the right to be a part of that jury. And finally, he set up copies of his laws in the main market square of Athens, the* agora. *The law ought not to be the secret knowledge of the few, but should be public. The law, its enforcement, and its knowledge, was now an affair for the entire community, not just a part of it. Thus, to be an Athenian citizen actually meant something: It meant that citizens had both political and legal rights, that they were free in their person, and that the law had to be publicly known and publicly executed. Over the course of the next century and a half the content of Athenian citizenship continued to expand, in the end producing democracy, a phenomenon that we will see in Part II.*

>> 30. Aristotle's Constitution of Athens and Related Texts

ARISTOTLE [LAST HALF OF THE FOURTH CENTURY B.C.E.]

7. Solon set up a constitution and also made other laws. After that, the Athenians ceased to make use of the laws of Draco with the exception of those relating to murder. The laws were inscribed on the Kyrbeis[1] and placed in the portico of the King, and all swore to observe them. The nine Archons, however, regularly affirmed by an oath at the Stone[2] that they would dedicate a golden statue if they ever should be found to have transgressed one of the laws; and they still swear in the same fashion down to the present day. He made the laws unalterable for one hundred years and set up the political order in the following way:

Source: Aristotle, *Aristotle's Constitution of Athens and Related Texts*, translated by Kurt von Fritz and Ernst Kapp (New York: Hafner Publishing, 1950), 74–75, 77.

[1]Wooden tablets set up on pillars revolving around an axis.

[2]This stone is also mentioned and described in Chapter 55.

He divided the population, according to property qualifications, into four classes as they had been divided before—namely, Pentacosiomedimni, Knights, Zeugitae, and Thetes.[1] He distributed the higher offices, namely, those of the nine Archons, the Treasurers, The Poletae,[2] the Eleven,[3] and the Colacretae[4] so that they were to be held by men taken from the Pentacosiomedimni, the Knights, and the Zeugitae, and assigned the offices to them in proportion to their property qualifications. To those who belonged to the census of the Thetes, he gave only a share in the Assembly of the People and in the law courts. A person belonged to the census of the Pentacosiomedimni if he obtained from his own property a return of five hundred measures of dry and liquid produce, both of them reckoned together. If he had an income of three hundred measures, or, as others say, if he was able to keep horses, he was rated a Knight; and as confirmation of the latter explanation they adduce the name of the class ["Knights"] as being derived from the fact mentioned, and some ancient votive offerings. For on the Acropolis there is a statue of Diphilus with the following inscription:

Anthemion, the son of Diphilus, has dedicated this statue to the Gods, when from the status of a Thes he had been raised to the status of a Knight.

And a horse stands beside him in testimony of the fact that the status of a Knight means this [that is, the ability to keep a horse].

In spite of this, it is more probable that this class also, like that of the Pentacosiomedimni, was distinguished by measures. To the census of the Zeugitae[5] belonged those who had an income of two hundred measures (liquid or dry). The rest belonged to the census of the Thetes and had no share in the magistracies. Consequently, even today when the superintending officer asks a man who is about to draw the lot for an office to what census class he belongs, nobody would ever say that […] he is a Thes.

9. This, then, was the order established by Solon in regard to the public offices. The three most democratic features of his constitution appear to be following: first, and most important, the law that nobody could contract a loan secured on his person; secondly, the rule that anyone who wished to do so could claim redress on behalf of a person who had been wronged; thirdly (and, according to the prevailing opinion, this more than anything else has increased the political power of the common people), the right of appeal to a jury court. For when the people have a right to vote in the courts, they become the masters of the state. Moreover, since the laws are not written down in clear and simple terms, but are like the one about inheritances and heiresses, disputes over interpretation will inevitably arise, and the court has the decision in all affairs, both public and private. Some people believe that Solon deliberately made the laws obscure so that the people would be masters of the decision. But this is not likely. The reason is rather that he was not able to formulate the best principle in general terms. It is not fair to interpret his intentions on the basis of what is happening in the present;[6] it should be done on the basis of the general character of his constitution.

---

[1] These terms are explained a little below in the present chapter.

[2] Officials who farmed out public revenues, sold confiscated property, and drew up all public contracts. See also Chapter 47.

[3] The superintendents of the State Prison.

[4] A very ancient office connected with the administration of finances. The specific duties assigned to the Colacretae seem to have changed again and again in the course of time. They are still mentioned in the last decade of the fifth century. But there is no evidence of the existence of the office after the restoration of democracy in 403 B.C.

[5] The word "Zeugites" is derived from *zeugos*, which means a yoke, in this case probably a team of oxen.

[6] Namely, when the unclear wording of the laws on inheritances and heiresses caused innumerable lawsuits.

A North Indian city

The primary version of The Rāmāyaṇa probably dates from the fifth century B.C.E. or shortly thereafter. In the course of Rama's adventures, the poet describes the important and ancient northern Indian city of Ayodhyā. Like Gilgamesh's Uruk, the people of Rama's Ayodhyā claimed great antiquity for their city, asserting that its foundations were established by none other than the mythical ruler Manu himself. The well-fortified city, the poet tells us, was laid out in a grid plan with broad avenues and was dotted with parks and markets. Artisans and actresses, bards and charioteers, merchants and priests, all inhabited Ayodhyā and contributed to its success as a major cultural and urban center in the north. Although Ayodhyā may have been one of the most spectacular of Indian cities in the eyes of the poet, it was not the only one. Cities like it stretched all across the north, as far west as Taxila, an important urban center in the Indus Valley. Ayodhyā retained its prominence well into the Gupta period, about 300 to 700 C.E

>> 31. The Rāmāyaṇa of Vālmīki: An Epic of Ancient India

[FIFTH CENTURY B.C.E.]

1-3. This great tale, known as *Rāmāyaṇa*, concerns itself with the dynasty of the great and victorious kings, the Ikṣvākus, descendants of Brahmā, lord of creatures, and those to whom this whole earth first of all belonged. Among them was Sagara, who caused the ocean to be dug and who had sixty thousand sons to form his entourage when he went abroad.

4. I will recite it from the beginning in its entirety, omitting nothing. It is in keeping with the goals of righteousness, profit, and pleasure, and should be listened to with faith.

5. There is a great, happy, and prosperous country called Kosala, situated on the banks of the Sarayū river and rich in abundance of wealth and grain.

6. There was situated the world-famous city of Ayodhyā, a city built by Manu himself, lord of men.

7. It was a great and majestic city, twelve leagues long and three wide, with well-ordered avenues.

8. It was adorned with a great and well-ordered royal highway, always strewn with loose blossoms and constantly sprinkled with water.

9. King Daśdaratha, who had expanded a realm already great, dwelt in that city, like the lord of the gods in heaven.

10. It was provided with doors and gates, and its markets had well-ordered interiors. It contained every implement and weapon, and was the resort of every artisan.

11. It was majestic, unequaled in splendor, and thronged with bards and rhapsodists. It had pennants on its tall towers and bristled with hundreds of "hundred-slayers."

12. It was a great city filled with troops of actresses everywhere, dotted with parks and mango groves, and girdled by ramparts.

13. It was a fortress with a deep moat impossible to cross, was unassailable by its enemies, and was filled with horses, elephants, cows, camels, and donkeys.

14. Filled with crowds of neighboring kings come to pay tribute, it was likewise adorned with merchants of many different lands.

Source: Robert P. Goldman, trans., *The Rāmāyaṇa of Vālmīki: An Epic of Ancient India*, v. 1 (Princeton: Princeton University Press, 1984), 134–5.

15. It was splendid with hills and palaces fashioned of jewels. Bristling with its rooftop turrets, it resembled Indra's Amarāvatī.

16. Colorful, laid out like a chessboard, and crowded with hosts of the most beautiful women, it was filled with every kind of jewel and adorned with palatial buildings.

17. Situated on level ground, its houses were built in close proximity to one another, without the slightest gap between them. It held plentiful stores of *śāli* rice, and its water was like the juice of sugar cane.

18. Loudly resounding with drums and stringed instruments—*dundubhis*, *mṛdaṅgas*, lutes, and *paṇovas*—it was truly unsurpassed on earth.

19. The outer walls of its dwellings were well constructed, and it was filled with good men.

Indeed, it was like a palace in the sky that perfected beings had gained through austerities.

20-22. King Daśaratha had populated the entire city with thousands of great chariot warriors, both skillful and dexterous—men who would never loose their arrows upon a foe who was isolated from his comrades, the sole support of his family, in hiding, or in flight, but who slew with their sharp weapons, or even the strength of their bare hands, lions, tigers, and boars, bellowing with rage in the forest.

23. But the king also peopled the city with great brahmans who tended the sacred fires and had mastered the *vedas* with their six adjunct sciences—men who were devoted to truth, and gave away thousands in charity—and with prominent seers, like the great seers themselves.

>> Mastering the Material

1. What does evidence from the "Memphite Theology" and the Shang oracle bones tell us about their respective political cultures? All things considered, why might larger consolidated states arise in a place like Egypt or China?

2. What is it about city-state systems that inhibit the growth of larger polities?

3. Why did the notion of citizenship arise first among the populations of the Greek city-states rather than elsewhere?

4. What was the real meaning of the differences between city-states and the larger political units for the inhabitants of each? In what ways did these systems fundamentally differ?

5. According to the ancient sources, what do the city-state systems of Mesoamerica, Greece, and Mesopotamia have in common? What might distinguish them from each other?

>> Making Connections

1. How do you think the particular environment and geography of Egypt (Chapter 1) contributed to the development of Egypt as a single, unified state in this period?

2. Look at a physical map of Greece and China and locate the various major cities on that map. How might their respective geographies have played a role in their development of either independent city-states or a single large polity?

3. How would you characterize the Indian city of Ayodhyā, and how does it compare with the other city-states that we have looked at in this and the previous chapter?

Chapter 5

Order and Chaos

Threats to Cities and Civilization

In the course of the twelfth dynasty (around 1990–1785 B.C.E.), an unknown Egyptian writer produced *The Admonitions of Ipuwer.* The author paints a picture of Egypt in chaos and disorder: Gangs roamed the countryside; towns are devastated; the desert encroached on arable land; society was turned upside-down; and nomads looked hungrily upon Egypt. Although most likely fiction, this piece presents an Egyptian's worst nightmare—the very collapse of civilization itself. Ancient societies always existed on the brink of continuous disaster, whether natural or human-made. And city-states no less than their modern counterpart—the nation-state—faced grave dangers to their well-being and very existence. Historians, sometimes equating the threat to city life with a threat to human "civilization" itself, have long examined the factors that threatened the stability of city-states and urban life in antiquity. While some historians focus particularly on social causes, another, Chester Starr, takes a slightly different approach, looking at what he calls "the price of civilization." As we will see, his analysis is useful for all students of history in that he identifies some of the major causes of disastrous stress on urban life.

All societies, whether urbanized or not, have internal tensions that can, under certain conditions, lead to the disintegration of that society. In the highly differentiated social system of the city-states of either the Old or New World, the potential for conflicts arose due to the unequal distribution of resources and power. In conditions like this, the strong often take advantage of their position, and latent tension might turn to violence and change. Aristotle wrote that tyranny arose in the Greek city-states due to a deviation from justice. The tyrants, from families that had been excluded from power by traditional aristocracies, used civil unrest to promote themselves as populist leaders against an entrenched aristocracy. In Mesopotamia, by contrast, kings stepped into the breach by providing law codes that attempted to improve social and economic conditions, and generally to formalize existing custom into a system acceptable to the majority of inhabitants. The laws of Mesopotamian kings like Ur-Nammu and Hammurabi were written to promote justice and protect the weak. The mediating force of the law, as we will see in Part II, was essential in China at a point when it too was undergoing great political and social changes in the Warring States period. Another practical side of law codes in antiquity is that they limited the amount of retribution that one individual, and his family, could take for wrongs and crimes committed by another individual. Without such a limit, a society could fall apart, especially in the case of crimes like murder and their resulting blood feuds.

The tension between the individual and society at large can also have drastic consequences for community. Societies in this period had a very definite sense of what was proper and attempted to devise mechanisms to prevent individuals from acting against the social norms. In ancient Egypt the threatened punishment for those who deviated from societal standards was the loss of an afterlife. *The Book of the Dead* is an almost unique piece of evidence that provides great detail on what the Egyptians considered to be good behavior. In the section entitled "The Declaration of Innocence," the deceased read out all of those wrongs that they claimed not to have committed. Ancient Egypt had no law codes as we understand them, and the ethical depictions in the Declaration served as a kind of touchstone of social responsibility that was essential for the maintenance of order in Egyptian life. While the Egyptians were the most extreme in outlining what a good Egyptian must do while living, other cultures did the same thing, sometimes explicitly, as in India's *The Laws of Manu,* and other times implicitly.

Although internal tensions have always had the potential for tearing apart city-states and other forms of polities, outside attack was an even greater threat. Few cities of this period experienced revolutions, but many were severely damaged or utterly destroyed in the course of warfare. The danger of war came from several directions. First, every city-state system in antiquity was prone to constant internecine war. In Mesopotamia, Mesoamerica, and Greece, city-states constantly competed with each other in battle. Defeat in war might entail the loss of financial or human resources—the payment of stiff reparations or the enslavement of part of the population. In Mesoamerica the *Popol Vuh* records how defeated warriors and kings were offered as human sacrifices to the gods of the winner. But the consequences of defeat might also include the sacking of the city and its extinction. The utter destruction of the city of Carthage in 146 B.C.E. after the Third Punic War was a Roman attempt to eradicate the cultural and political identity of a defeated enemy.

Second, the conquest of cities by others in an attempt to build up larger political entities also posed a big threat. Various Akkadian and Sumerian kings periodically conquered their neighboring city-states. While the kingdoms that they created did not last very long, the conquered city-states temporarily lost much of their political independence and financial wherewithal. These same cities could even be pillaged by a successor, as Naram-Sin did to Nippur. What is striking about his sack of Nippur and its temple to Enlil is that this city was regarded as the source of sovereignty over the whole of the land of Sumer and Akkad. Its violation by Naram-Sin was considered to be an outrage remembered by later generations.

Additionally, cities and city life were always tempting targets for nomadic and semi-nomadic peoples on the fringes of the urbanized world. The Egyptians, with such a long territory to defend, often referred to these feared nomads with generic titles such as the sand-dwellers and horizon-dwellers. Both Mesopotamia and China faced repeated invasions of nomadic peoples throughout their history, and these nomads occasionally took over the state and ruled it. However, nomadic peoples often saw cities not just as something to be plundered, but as places that were corrupting and dangerous. The biblical story of Dinah, the daughter of Jacob, illustrates how nomads viewed city dwellers and urban life.

Rise and Fall of the Ancient World

The rise of the city-state in Mesopotamia was not, as Chester Starr argues, without its price. The inhabitants of cities were in a continuous struggle in one form or another against either the elements or one another. Cities were always threatened by various forms of tensions and chaos, and order was sometimes maintained by a very tenuous thread. Although Starr's discussion concerns ancient Iraq, he identifies three major threats to urban civilization that apply to all ancient political and social systems, including the city-state: the unjust exploitation of the weaker members of society by the stronger; the tension between the desires of the individual and the community at large; and the effects of both war and invasion on the city-state. Each of these threats had the potential of destroying or severely weakening city-states and urban life in one way or another. The dangers to civilization are surprisingly similar from culture to culture, as are the attempts to maintain order against potential chaos, either internal or external.

>> 32. The Rise and Fall of the Ancient World

CHESTER STARR [1960]

That the ordinary Babylonian clearly understood why his society had a gloomy cast one may doubt, but it was not difficult for him to see some other parts of the price which he and his fellows had to pay for civilization.

Mesopotamian farmers and artisans produced a considerable surplus of products beyond their own personal requirements. They were not, however, able to keep this surplus, for the temples and the king channeled it off in each state in the form of rent, taxes, and gifts. These managers invested part of the savings of the whole state in canals, temples, walls, and other socially useful capital structures, and some of the food was also returned to the citizens in the months preceding a new harvest. The priests and king also utilized an appreciable fraction of this surplus to enhance their own comfort, even luxury; the tomb of one queen of Ur astounded the modern world with its wealth of delicate jewelry, harps, and sacrificed servants.

To conclude that the upper classes of Babylonian society were simply parasites would

be unjust, for the priests and the king held together the state, harbored its reserves, and expanded its strength. Nevertheless, it is true that, in emerging from agricultural villages, men gave up the relative equality of that stage. Some became the managers of society; most worked to support themselves and the managers; in the course of wars and economic distress, unfortunate men even found themselves enslaved or forced to sell themselves or their children into slavery. Throughout ancient civilization, slaves were rarely used in agriculture. They lived in cities, where they were domestic servants and artisans, and they might rise to freedom through hard work. The Marxist argument that early civilizations rested on slavery is far from correct.

Still, the inhabitants of a Sumerian city were stratified into upper classes, lower classes, and chattels, that is slaves. It may be noted, too, that of the two sexes women were now definitely subordinated in the processes of law and government. Although their positions still fairly high in Sumerian days, it tended rather to sink than to rise; a fine example of the masculine arrogance of the lawmakers is the provision in some Assyrian laws of the twelfth century B.C. that "when she

Source: Chester G. Starr, *Rise and Fall of the Ancient World* (Chicago: Rand McNally, 1960), 28–30.

deserves it, a man may pull out the hair of his wife, mutilate or twist her ears, with no liability attaching to him."

The inevitable product of the differentiation of classes was a chain of exploitation, unrest, and attempts at reform. Already in the third millennium B.C., king Urukagina of Lagash (c. 2375) boasted that he took away the prerogatives of the foremen and officials and contracted with the city god "that he would not deliver up the orphan and the widow to the powerful man." A further fruit was the promulgation of law code after law code to set the rules of society so that all classes might know their duties and their rights, especially with respect to property, wages, and criminal assaults; for the latter, punishment varied according to the class of the culprit. [...]

Another form of tension in civilization, of which men are well aware today, is the relation between the individual and the society within which he lives. To what extent, that is, can a man lead his life as *he* wills, and to what extent must he yield his independence of mind, of property, even of body to the state and other social groupings?

This problem was not consciously perceived in early Babylonia, but it existed. The Sumerian city was a highly regimented organization. Above the city stood the gods whom all must serve. The ordinary human being had so little view of his own personal importance that he had only the barest idea of an afterlife. Yet a central theme in the epic of Gilgamesh is that of the hero who gained fame for himself and so assured himself the only true immortality that this age knew. [...]

In the history most civilized states there is an oscillation between tight communal organization and relatively greater individual freedom of action. This oscillation may be detected in early Babylonia as well; "breakdowns" of society occurred, in which strong men grasped what they could. The common results were famine and external invasion, and the reassertion of communal ties; civilization cannot be based on anarchy. Overall, however, the slow drift of Mesopotamian history was toward somewhat greater independence of individual action within the confines of social organization. One mark is the fact that by the time of Hammurabi, individuals held their land as vassals of the king or even enjoyed ownership. Another indication is the reluctance of men to rely entirely upon the state religious machinery to protect them as a group; men now inclined to feel that they each had a personal protector among the gods, to whom they could appeal for aid in individual problems.

A very obvious result of the appearance of civilization was the emergence of war. In earlier times, packs of food-gatherers probably had had only occasional contacts. Even in villages, men had been relatively self-sufficient and had clashed with each other rarely. The first cities, however, set the stage for a type of conflict which subsequent civilizations have rarely been able to overcome.

Civilization required the crystallization of a large mass of men into a definitely organized state. Bound to each other closely and attached to patron deities, the citizens of each Babylonian city felt themselves to be to some degree unique. Nonetheless, no city was culturally or economically independent of its fellow states and the outside world.

Sumerian culture was the culture of an entire area, not of one city; and all of the small political units needed timber, metals, stone, spices, and other products brought by water and by caravans of asses. Foreign trade brought foreign ideas, which at once stimulated and disturbed the cultural patterns of any one city. Foreign trade also brought unceasing economic rivalry. Add to this witches' brew the egotism of kings and some hunger for land, and one can understand why the records of Mesopotamian civilization are studied with long, bitter wars.

Generally, victory in war brought acknowledgment of the superiority of one city's god over another, the exaction of tribute and slaves for the temples of the victors, and perhaps a coveted piece of land. Now and then some able king went further and united several states under his sway.

The Laws of Ur-Nammu

One of the greatest internal threats to the stability of a city-state was the perceived and real unjust exploitation by the powerful against the weak. To provide justice and equity in Mesopotamia, and in an attempt to limit uncontrolled vengeance exacted by individuals for various wrongs, kings promulgated law codes that established not only the proper legal relationships between individuals, but also the appropriate fines and punishments for injuries and crimes. The most famous of these codes was that of the Babylonian king Hammurabi (r. about 1728–1686 B.C.E.). On the inscription containing his code, the king, as the servant of the gods, is shown receiving the law from Shamash, the god of the Sun and Justice. The gods mentioned in the inscription instruct Hammurabi to destroy the wicked, to establish justice, and to protect the widow and the orphan. Hammurabi, however, was not the first to publish such a law code, nor are the sentiments expressed in the code unique to him. The earliest law code that we have in history is that of Ur-Nammu (r. 2112–2095 B.C.E.), the first king of Third Dynasty Ur. Similar to the god's instructions to Hammurabi centuries later, the Sumerian Sun god, Utu, and the Moon god, Nanna, ordered Ur-Nammu to "establish equity in the land," part of which meant protecting widows and orphans. Critical in the code is a set of fines for wrongs done to individuals. To prevent social chaos by unlimited vengeance, the king provided a set of monetary compensations for possible wrongs, from loss of limbs to bride price. Sometimes called the lex talionis, *"the law of retaliation in kind," an individual was not permitted to exact more than what was appropriate for the injury sustained. This helped ancient society from spiraling out of control by ever-greater exactions of retribution.*

As state institutions became stronger and the need for self-help to redress wrongs diminished, law codes like this one helped to provide guidelines for what was acceptable behavior and punishment. They also tell us what a society thought was important enough to enshrine in the law and thus reveal much about the roles of women and men in society. While women are often protected in codes like this, punishment for similar crimes and misconduct vary by gender and by social class. Thus a woman who seduces a man is subject to the death penalty, but a free man who rapes a virgin slave woman is only subject to a monetary fine.

>> 33. Laws of Ur-Nammu

[AROUND 2100 B.C.E., PRESERVED IN COPIES FROM AROUND 1800–1700 B.C.E.]

Then did Ur-Nammu, the mighty warrior, king of Ur, king of Sumer and Akkad, by the might of Nanna, lord of the city (of Ur), and in accordance with the true word of Utu, establish equity in the land (114–116) (and) he banished malediction, violence and strife. (117–122) *By granting immunity in Akkad to the maritime trade the seafarers' overseer, to the herdsman from the "oxen-taker," the "sheep-taker," and the "donkey-taker," he* (123–124) set Sumer and Akkad *free.* [...]

(143–144) He fashioned the bronze *silá*-measure, (145–149) he standardized the one *mina*

Source: "The Laws of Ur-Nammu," in *The Ancient Near East: An Anthology of Texts and Pictures,* v. 2, edited by James B. Pritchard (Princeton: Princeton University Press, 1975), 31–33.

weight, (and) standardized the stone-weight of a shekel of silver *in relation to* one mina.

(150−152) At that time, the bank of the Tigris, the bank of the Euphrates…(153−160 destroyed)…(161) the king (or "owner") provided a head gardener.

(162−168) The orphan was not delivered up to the rich man; the widow was not delivered up to the mighty man; the man of one shekel was not delivered up to the man of one mina. […]

If the wife of a man, *by employing her charms,* followed after another man and he slept with her, they (i.e., the authorities) shall slay that woman, but that male (i.e. the other man) shall be set free.

5: (223−239 = B § 2). If a man proceeded by force, and defollowered the virgin (lit.: "undeflowered") slave-woman of another man, that man must pay five shekels of silver.

6: (app. 240−244 = B § 3). If a man divorces his primary wife, he must pay (her) one mina of silver.

7: (app. 245−249 = B § 4). If it is a (former) widow (whom) he divorces, he must pay (her) one-half mina of silver.

8: (250−255 = B § 5). If (however) the man had slept with the widow without there having

been any marriage contract, he need not pay (her) any silver. […]

11: (281−290 = B § 10). If a man accused the wife of a man of fornication, and the river (-ordeal) proved her innocent, then the man who had accused her must pay one-third of a mina of silver.

12: (291−301 = B § 11). If a (prospective) son-in-law entered the house of his (prospective) father-in-law, but his father-in-law later gave [his daughter (i.e., the prospective bride) to] another man, he (the father-in-law) shall return to him (i.e., the rejected son-in-law) *two-fold* the amount of bridal presents he had brought. […]

15: (324−330 = B § 13 + § 21). If a [man…] cut off the foot (var.: limb) of [another man *with his…*], he shall pay ten shekels of silver.

16: (331−338, omitted in B). If a man, in the course of a scuffle, smashed the limb of another man with a club, he shall pay one mina of silver.

17: (339−344 = B § 22). If someone severed the nose of another man with a *copper knife,* he must pay two-thirds of a mina of silver.

Justice in the City

Like the inhabitants of Mesopotamia, most Greek city-states established law codes as well. When Athens was on the verge of civil war and collapse in the sixth century, Solon, an aristocratic politician, was chosen as a lawgiver to bring peace and tranquility to Athenian life. Ancient Greeks credited Solon with establishing the first comprehensive law code for the Athenians. Proclaiming his intention to promote justice, Solon had his laws put on wooden tablets and set up in the agora, *the central market of Athens, for all to read.*

Perhaps the best statement on law and justice in a general sense came from the philosopher Protagoras in the fifth century B.C.E. Protagoras in Plato's dialogue of the same name pointed out to his audience that what makes a city-state survive is a "sense of justice." Both justice and a respect for others must be shared by all members of the polis if a city is to flourish. In his story of the evolution of human society from barbarism to urbanized life, Protagoras said that Zeus, the king of the gods, commanded Hermes to distribute justice and respect for others to all members of the community, not just to a select few. "The art of politics," he said, required civic virtue, which was itself a product of both justice and mutual respect, for without that virtue, humans would simply devour one another like animals. Protagoras's concerns were not merely philosophical musings. During the Peloponnesian War (431–404 B.C.E.), polis after polis fell into factional fighting and destroyed themselves through civil war. The city-state was a fragile institution, and the fabric of civilized life could be torn by the stress brought on by war.

>> 34. Protagoras and Meno

PLATO [SETTING OF DIALOGUE 430S B.C.E.;
COMPOSITION 390S B.C.E.]

'Once upon a time, there existed gods but no mortal creatures. When the appointed time came for these also to be born, the gods formed them within the earth out of a mixture of earth and fire and the substances which are compounded from earth and fire. And when they were ready to bring them to the light, they charged Prometheus and Epimetheus with the task of equipping them and allotting suitable powers to each kind. [. . .]

'Since, then, man had a share in the portion of gods, in the first place because of his divine kinship he alone among the living creatures believed in gods, and set to work to erect altars, and images of them. Secondly, by the art which they possessed, men soon discovered articulate speech and names, and invented houses and clothes and shoes and beddings and got food from the earth.

'Thus provided for, they lived at first in scattered groups; there were no cities. Consequently they were devoured by wild beasts, since they were in every respect the weaker, and their technical skill, though a sufficient aid to their nurture, did not extend to making war on the beasts, for they had not the art of politics, of which the art of war is a part. They sought therefore to save themselves by coming together and founding fortified cities, but when they gathered in communities they injured one another for want of political skill, and so scattered again and continued to be devoured. Zeus therefore, fearing the total destruction of our race, sent Hermes to impart to men the qualities of respect for others and a sense of justice, so as to bring order into our cities and create a bond of friendship and union. Hermes asked Zeus in what manner he was to bestow these gifts on men. "Shall I distribute them as the arts were distributed—that is, on the principle that one trained doctor suffices for many laymen, and so with the other experts? Shall I distribute justice and respect for their fellows in this way, or to all alike?" "To all" said Zeus. "Let all have their share. There could never be cities if only a few shared in these virtues, as in the arts. Moreover, you must lay it down as my law that if any one in incapable of acquiring his share of these two virtues he shall be put to death as a plague to the city."

'Thus it is, Socrates, and from this cause, that in a debate involving skill of building, or in any other craft, the Athenians, like other men, believe that few are capable of giving advice, and if someone outside those few volunteers to advise them, then as you say, they do not tolerate it—rightly so, in my submission. But when the subject of their counsel involves political wisdom, which must always follow the path of justice and moderation, they listen to every man's opinion, for they think that everyone must share in this kind of virtue; otherwise the state could not exist. That, Socrates, is the reason for this.

'Here is another proof that I am not deceiving you in saying that all men do in fact believe that everyone shares a sense of justice and civic virtue. In specialized skills, as you say, if a man claims to be good at the flute or at some other art when he is not, people either laugh at him or are annoyed, and his family restrain him as if he were crazy. But

Source: Plato, *Protagoras and Meno*, translated by W. K. C. Guthrie (New York: Penguin Press, 1956), 52–55.

when it comes to justice and civic virtue as a whole, even if someone is known to be wicked, yet if he publicly tells the truth about himself, his truthfulness, which in the other case was counted a virtue, is here considered madness. Everyone, it is said, ought to say he is good, whether he is or not, and whoever does not make such a claim is out of his mind; for a man cannot be without some share in justice, or he would not be human.

'So much then for the point that men rightly take all alike into their counsels concerning virtue of this sort, because they believe that all have a share in it. I shall next try to demonstrate to you that they do not regard it as innate or automatic, but as acquired by instruction and taking thought. No one is angered by the faults which are believed to be due to nature or chance, nor do people rebuke or teach or punish those who exhibit them, in the hope of curing them: they simply pity them. Who would be so foolish as to treat in that way the ugly or dwarfish or weak? Everyone knows that it is nature or chance which gives this kind of characteristics to a man, both the good and the bad. But it is otherwise with the good qualities which are thought to be acquired through care and practice and instruction. It is the absence of these, surely, and the presence of the corresponding vices, that call forth indignation and punishment and admonition. Among these faults are to be put injustice and irreligion and in general everything that is contrary to civic virtue.

The Judgment of the Dead

In addition to justice and the law, Chester Starr pointed out that individuals in the ancient world had societal standards to which they had to conform as well. Individuals were not entirely free to do as they wished because a violation of these standards could jeopardize the entire community. These standards are instructive as they tell us what a society as a collective unit thought proper behavior consisted of. One important source of our understanding of the code of personal conduct in ancient Egypt derives from The Book of the Dead. *At death, the deceased appeared before Thoth and Anubis in the Hall of the Two Truths: There the heart of the deceased was placed on a scale opposite the feather of Ma'at, Justice and Truth. If one had done wrong in life, the heart would bear witness to that fact, and the scale would sink—the heart was then fed to the monstrous goddess Ammut, who had a crocodile's head, ending all hope for eternal life. To protect the dead person from such a horrible fate, the deceased carried into death* The Book of the Dead, *through whose magical spells innocence was proclaimed. The following section from that scroll, two declarations from "The Judgment of the Dead," presents the ethical standards by which good Egyptians based their lives. Similar in some ways to the shorter Ten Commandments of the Hebrews, this is a long list of wrongful deeds, from taking milk from children and harming cattle to sexual improprieties, which the deceased claimed not to have done. From this list we can see what was important for the Egyptians. This set of offenses to the gods generally applied to both sexes, but when necessary, it was adapted to suit the gender of the deceased. The biggest differences in these scrolls were at the very beginning: women, to maintain propriety, were not shown with their husbands, but the reverse was not true for men, and men were often shown harvesting grain, an activity not performed by women. On many levels* The Book of the Dead *offers a rare glimpse into the world of social harmony as well as the threats to that harmony.*

>> 35. The Judgment of the Dead

[c.1550–1080 b.c.e.]

The Judgment of the Dead: The Declaration of Innocence

(1) To be said on reaching the Hall of the Two Truths so as to purge N of any sins committed and to see the face of every god:

Hail to you, great God, Lord of the
    Two Truths!

I have come to you, my Lord,

I was brought to see your beauty.

I know you, I know the names of the forty-two
    gods,

Who are with you in the Hall of the Two Truths,

Who live by warding off evildoers,

Who drink of their blood,

On that day (5) of judging characters before
    Wennofer.

Lo, your name is "He-of-Two-Daughters,"

(And) "He-of-Maat's-Two-Eyes."

Lo, I come before you,

Bringing Maat to you,

Having repelled evil for you.

I have not done crimes against people,

I have not mistreated cattle,

I have not sinned in the Place of Truth.

I have not known what should not be known,

I have not done any harm.

I did not begin a day by exacting more than
    my due,

My name did not reach the bark of the
    mighty ruler.

I have not blasphemed (10) a god,

I have not robbed the poor.

I have not done what the god abhors,

I have not maligned a servant to his master.

I have not caused pain,

I have not cause tears.

I have not killed,

I have not ordered to kill,

I have not made anyone suffer.

I have not damaged the offerings in the temples,

I have not depleted the loaves of the gods,

I have not stolen (15) the cakes of the dead.

I have not copulated nor defiled myself.

I have not increased nor reduced the measure,

I have not diminished the arura,

I have not cheated in the fields.

I have not added to the weight of the balance,

I have not falsified the plummet of the scales.

I have not taken milk from the mouth of children,

I have not deprived cattle of their pasture.

I have not snared birds in the reeds of the gods,

I have not caught fish in their ponds.

I have not held back water in its season,

I have not dammed a flowing stream,

I have not quenched a needed (20) fire.

I have not neglected the days of meat offerings,

I have not detained cattle belonging to the god,

I have not stopped a god in his procession.

I am pure, I am pure, I am pure, I am pure!

I am pure as is pure that great heron in Hnes.

I am truly the nose of the Lord of Breath,

Who sustains all the people,

On the day of completing the Eye in On,

In the second month of winter, last day,

In the presence of the lord of this land.

I have seen the completion of the Eye in On!

Source: "The Judgment of the Dead," in *Ancient Egyptian Literature: A Book of Readings v. 2: The New Kingdom,* edited by Miriam Lichtheim (Berkeley: University of California Press, 1976), 124–126.

No evil shall befall me in this land,
In this Hall of the Two Truths;
For I know the names of the gods in it,
The followers of the great God!

The Declaration to the Forty-two Gods

O wide-of-stride who comes from On: I have not done evil.

O Flame-grasper who comes from Kheraha: I have not robbed.

O Long-nosed who comes from Khnum: I have not coveted.

O Shadow-eater who comes from the cave: I have not stolen.

O Savage-faced who comes from Rostau: I have not killed people.

O Lion-Twins who come from heaven: I have not trimmed the measure.

O Flint-eyed who comes from Khem: I have not cheated.

O Fiery-one who comes backward: I have not stolen a god's property.

O Bone-smasher who comes from Hnes: I have not told lies.

O Flame-thrower who comes from Memphis: I have not seized food.

O Cave-dweller who comes from the west: I have not sulked.

O White-toothed who comes from Lakeland: I have not trespassed.

O Blood-eater who comes from slaughterplace: I have not slain sacred cattle.

O Entrail-eater who comes from the tribunal: I have not extorted.

O Lord of Maat who comes from Maaty: I have not stolen bread rations.

O Wanderer who comes from Bubastis: I have not spied.

O Pale-one who comes form On: I have not prattled.

O Villain who comes from Anjdty: I have contended only for my goods.

Warfare and Human Sacrifice

Warfare is not unique to any one area of the world or to any single time period. Competition for resources, coupled with an almost universal ideology of the leader as warrior, has meant that humans have waged wars against one another from time immemorial. While scholars occasionally identify one group or another as a "warrior society," all polities throughout time have engaged in war. For city-states, war was a constant threat to their independence if not their very survival. In Mesoamerica archaeologists have shown how armed conflict between city-states was part of a way of life for kings. This same theme, with the same consequences, is repeated in the Popol Vuh. *The following passage relates how several cities of the Quiché Maya came to be founded and how war broke out amongst them. In an attempt to gain control of the Quiché stronghold called Bearded Place, the Ilocs, a rival group of lineages, attacked in full force but were repulsed. The cost of this "tumult and war" was heavy for the losing side: Some of the Ilocs were tortured and then sacrificed to the gods, while others became "slaves and serfs." Warring among the city-states, with an ever-grander display of human sacrifice, increased in parts of Mesoamerica as time went on. Some scholars have speculated that some wars were undertaken simply for the purpose of acquiring war captives for human sacrifices. Such sacrifices proclaimed the power of the king, while simultaneously nourishing the gods and maintaining the natural order of the universe. But in the extreme, such warfare threatened the very existence of the losing polity.*

>> 36. Popol Vuh: The Mayan Book of the Dawn of Life

[ANCIENT TALE WRITTEN DOWN IN THE
ROMAN ALPHABET IN THE
MID-SIXTEENTH CENTURY C.E.]

And Bearded Place is the name of the mountain of their citadel. They stayed there and they settled down there.

And they tested their fiery splendor there. They ground their gypsum, their plaster, in the fourth generation of lords. It was said that Noble Rooftree ruled when Nine Deer was the Lord Minister, and then the lords named Noble Sweatbath and Iztayul reigned as Keeper of the Mat and Keeper of the Reception House Mat. They reigned there at Beared Place. It was through their works that it became an excellent citadel.

The number of great houses only reached three, there at Bearded Place. There were not yet a score and four great houses, but only three of them:

Just one Cauec great house.

And just one great house for the Greathouses.

And finally, just one for the Lord Quichés.

But the three were housed in just two buildings, one in each of the two divisions of the citadel.

This is the way it was when they were at Bearded Place:

They were of just one mind: there was no evil for them, nor were there difficulties.

Their reign was all in calm: there were no quarrels for them, and no disturbances.

Their hearts were filled with a steady light: there was nothing of stupidity and nothing of envy in what they did.

Their splendor was modest: they caused no amazement, nor had they grown great.

And then they tested themselves. They excelled in the Shield Dance, there at Bearded Place. They did it as a sign of their sovereignty. It was a sign of their fiery splendor and a sign of their greatness.

When it was seen by the Ilocs, the Ilocs began to foment war. It was their desire that the Lord Noble Sweatbath be murdered, and that the other lord be allied with them. It was Lord Iztayul they wanted to persuade; the Ilocs wanted him as their disciple in committing murder. But their jealous plotting behind the back of the Lord Noble Sweatbath failed to work out. They just wanted it over with, but the lord wasn't killed by the Ilocs on the first try.

Such were the roots of disturbances, of tumult and war. First they invaded the citadel, the killers were on the move. What they wanted was to obliterate the very identity of the Quichés. Only then, they thought, could they alone have sovereignty, and it was for this alone that they came to kill. They were captured and they were made prisoners. Not many of them ever got their freedom again.

And then began the cutting of flesh. They cut the Ilocs open before the gods. This was in payment for their wrongs against Lord Noble Sweatbath. And many others went into bondage; they were made into slaves and serfs. They had simply given themselves up in defeat by fomenting war against the lord and against the canyon and the citadel. What their hearts had desired was the destruction and disintegration of the very identity of the Quiché lord, but it did not come to pass.

In this way it came about that people were cut open before the gods. The shields of war were made then; it was the very beginning of the fortification of the citadel at Bearded Place. The root of fiery splendor was implanted there, and because of it the reign of the Quiché lords was truly great. They were lords of singular genius. There was nothing to humble them; nothing happened to make fools of them or to ruin the greatness of their reign, which took root there at Bearded Place.

The penance done for the gods increased there, striking terror again, and all the tribes were terrified, small tribes and great tribes. They witnessed the arrival of people captured in war, who

Source: Dennis Tedlock, trans., *Popol Vuh: The Mayan Book of the Dawn of Life* (New York: Touchstone, 1996), 181–183.

were cut open and killed for the splendor and majesty of Lord Noble Sweatbath and Lord Iztayul, along with the Greathouses and the Lord Quichés. There were only three branches of kin there at the citadel named Bearded Place.

And it was also there that they began feasting and drinking over the blossoming of their daughters. This was the way the ones they named the "Three Great Houses" stayed together. They drank their drinks there and ate their corn there, the payment for their sisters, payment for their daughters. There was only happiness in their hearts when they did it. They ate, they feasted inside their palaces.

The Curse of Agade

Over the centuries Mesopotamia was subjected to repeated wars and invasions. This twin threat to the city-states of the region is highlighted in a poem written about 2000 B.C.E. to denounce Naram-Sin, a powerful Akkadian king. Naram-Sin, whose capital was Agade, had followed in the footsteps of his warrior grandfather, Sargon. Sargon had conquered and then unified all of the cities of Sumer and Akkad into one large kingdom. His grandson, however, went one step further by declaring himself to be divine. In the course of his reign, Naram-Sin went so far as to plunder and destroy the Ekur, the Temple of Enlil (king of the gods) at Nippur (an ancient Sumerian city). Not content with plundering the temple, he despoiled the city of Nippur itself. To punish the house of Naram-Sin, Enlil called down a curse on the city of Agade. He brought down the Gutians, wild men from the Zagros Mountains to the east, to plunder the cities of the plain. At the same time, we know that the Semitic-speaking Amorites swept into Mesopotamia from the steppes in the west.

The following poem relates this incident, which demonstrates the precarious situation of the Mesopotamian city-state. Periodically these city-states were threatened with conquest by various powerful local Sumerian or Akkadian kings, some of whom, like Naram-Sin, might destroy them. And equally, they were threatened by the menace of nomadic invasions from the mountains to the east or the steppe lands to the west. These invaders, like the Gutians, not only destroyed but occasionally took over the cities themselves. War, invasion, and occupation had a potentially devastating effect on urban life, but in most instances the cities rebounded over time.

>> 37. The Curse of Agade
[c. 2000 B.C.E.]

(Then) Naram-Sin in a vision . . . ,

He kept it to himself, put it not in speech, spoke with nobody about it,

Because of the Ekur, he dressed in sackcloth,

Covered his chariot with a boat-covering mat,

Loaded not his boat with . . . ,

Gave away everything desirable for Kingship.

Seven years Naram-Sin remained firm,

Who had ever seen that a king should "put hand on head for seven years!"

(But then) seeking an oracle at the house,

Source: "The Curse of Agade," in *The Ancient Near East: An Anthology of Texts and Pictures,* v. 2, edited by James B. Pritchard (Princeton: Princeton University Press, 1975), 208–211.

In the "built" house there was no oracle,

Seeking an oracle a second time at the house,

In the "built" house there was no oracle.

(Whereupon) changing his line of *action,*

He defied the word of Enlil,

Crushed those who had submitted to him (Enlil),

Mobilized his troops,

Like a mighty man *accustomed* to high-handed (action),

He put a restraining hand on the Ekur.

Like a runner *contemptuous* of (his body's) strength,

He treated the *giguna* like thirty shekels.

Like a bandit who plunders a city,

He erected large ladders against the house.

To destroy the Ekur like a huge boat,

To turn it into dust like a mountain mined for silver,

To cut it to pieces like a mountain of lapis lazuli,

To prostrate it like a city, ravaged by Ishkur,

Against the house that was not a mountain where cedar was felled,

He forged great axes,

Sharpened double-edged "axes of destruction,"

Fixed copper *spikes* at the bottom of it,

Levelled it down to the "foundation" of the land,

Fixed axes at the top of it,

The house lay stretched "neck to ground," like a man who had been killed (in battle).

He tore up its *mes*-trees,

The raining dust rose sky high.

He struck down its doorposts, cut off the vitality of the land,

At the "Gate of no Grain Cutting," he cut grain,

Grain was cut off from the "hand" of the land.

Its "Gate of Peace" he broke down with the pickaxe,

Peace was estranged from the lands,

(And) from the "noble" fields (and) acres of the wide . . . . [...]

(Although all these) were not the possessions of an attacking city,

He docked large boats at the quay by the house,

Docked large boats at the quay by the house of Enlil,

Carried off the possessions from the city,

(But with) the carrying off the possessions of the city,

Counsel departed from the city,

As the boats *took off* from the quay, the good sense of Agade turned to folly,

The . . . storm that . . . ,

The rampant Flood who knows no rival,

Enlil, because his beloved Ekur had been attacked, what destruction he wrought!

He lifted his eyes to the . . . -mountain,

Mustered the "wide" mountain as one.

The unsubmissive people, the land (whose people) is without number,

Gutium, the land that brooks no control,

Whose understanding is human, (but) whose form (and) *stuttering* words are that of a dog,

Enlil brought down from the mountain.

In vast numbers, like locusts, they covered the earth,

Their "arm" stretched out for him in the steppe like an *animal-trap,*

Nothing escaped their "arm,"

No one *eluded* their "arm."

The herald took not to the road,

The (sea)-rider sailed not his boat along the river.

The . . . -goats of Enlil that broke out of their sheep-fold—their shepherd made them follow him,

The cows that broke out of their stalls, their cowherd made them follow him.

On the *trees* of the *(river)-banks* watches were set up,

Brigands dwelt on the road.

In the gates of the land the doors stood (deep) in dust,

All the lands raised a bitter cry on their city walls

Furrows embedded the cities although (their) inside was not a steppe, (their) outside was not wide (open land).

After the cities had been built, after they had been struck down,

The large fields (and) acres produced no grain,

The flooded acres produced no fish,

The watered gardens produced no honey (and) wine,

The heavy *clouds* brought not rain, there grew no *mashgur*-tree.

Nomads from the Steppes

China, like Mesopotamia, was subject to the constant threat of attack by nomads off the steppes. During the Zhou Dynasty the northern frontier was periodically raided by a group called the Xianyun. In a collection of poetry called the Shi jing, *the poem* Cai Qi *("Gathering the Sow Thistle") praises the great victory of Fang Shu against "savage tribes" who had attempted a raid at harvest time. The first incursion of these steppe nomads was in 840 B.C.E., but it was by no means the last. Although some scholars suggest that the Xianyun forces were horse-mounted cavalry, others argue that they fought in the same manner as the Zhou armies, with war chariots and "well disciplined warriors." The menace of the nomads against the fields and cities of China is a continuous theme in Chinese history, and eventually the mounted warrior became a frightening reality that rulers and generals alike had to deal with.*

>> 38. Shi jing 178

[c. 770–700 B.C.E.]

178. Cai Qi

They were gathering the white millet,

In those new fields,

And in these acres brought only one year under cultivation,

When Fang Shu came to take the command.

His chariots were three thousand,

With a host of well-disciplined warriors.

Fang Shu led them on,

In his carriage drawn by four piebalds,

Four piebalds orderly moving.

Red shone his grand carriage,

With its chequered bamboo screen, and seal-skin quivers,

With the hooks for the trappings of the breast-bands, and the rein-ends.

They were gathering the white millet,

In those new fields,

And all about these villages,

When Fang Shu came to take the command.

His chariots were three thousand;

Source: *Shi jing* 178, from the University of Virginia Chinese Text Initiative. Permanent URL http://etext.lib.virginia.edu/chinese/shijing/AnoShih.html.

His banners, with their blazonry of dragons, and
    of serpents and tortoises, fluttered gaily.

Fang Shu led them on,

The naves of his wheels bound with leather, and
    his yoke ornamented.

Tinkle-tinkle went the eight bells at the horses' bits.

He wore the robes conferred [by the king];

His red knee-covers were resplendent,

And the gems of his girdle-pendant sounding.

Rapid is the flight of the hawk,

Soaring in the heavens,

And again descending and settling in its place.

Fang Shu came to take the command.

His chariots were three thousand,

With a host of well disciplined warriors.

Fang Shu led them on.

With his jinglers and drummers,

He marshalled his hosts and addressed them.

Intelligent and true is Fang Shu,

Deep rolled the sound of his drums;

With a lighter sound he led the troops back.

Foolish were the savage tribes of King,

Presuming to oppose our great region.

Fang Shu is of great age,

But full of vigour were his plans.

He led his army on,

Seized [the chiefs] for the question, and made
    captives of a crowd [besides].

Numerous were his war chariots,

Numerous and in grand array,

Like the clap or the roll of thunder their onset.

Intelligent and true is Fang Shu.

He had gone and smitten the Xianyun,

And the tribes of King came, awed by his majesty.

The Nomadic Point of View— The Case of Dinah

Civilization has not always been thought of positively, even by those who might seem to be major contributors to it. The Roman historian Tacitus, for example, decried the fact that the Britons were taking up Roman customs and habits, including urban life. All of this, he lamented, was just another form of their enslavement. Unfortunately we rarely have the nomadic perspective on urban life—usually we have only the city dwellers' comments on and fears about nonsedentary groups. In the biblical book of Genesis, *however, we have the point of view of the Hebrew nomads as they grazed their flocks in the shadows of the city walls of Canaan. From their vantage point, the Hebrews saw urban life and even farming itself negatively: Cain, the first farmer, murdered his shepherd brother, Abel; the Tower of Babel and the cities of Sodom and Gomorrah were urban examples of rebellion against God and were punished. City dwellers from the nomadic perspective were corrupting and evil—they stole your livestock, they raped your sisters, and they abused your laws of hospitality. A good example of urban abuse and the nomadic response is the story of Dinah. When Dinah had gone into the city to visit with the women of the town, she was raped by Shechem, a prince of that place. In revenge for the rape, Dinah's brothers murdered all the men of the city, enslaved the women and children, and plundered the city's goods and livestock. Jacob, Dinah's father, was worried about reprisals and moved his family and flock to new pastures. When the cities organized to pursue Jacob and his sons, God caused them to panic, thereby ending their pursuit.*

In addition to providing the nomads' perception of urban dwellers and city life, the story of Dinah suggests something equally important about honor and status, both of which are linked to gender. Some scholars consider this episode to represent the beginning of the critical social attitudes of honor and shame so prevalent in the Mediterranean in antiquity and today. Male honor consisted primarily in how a man was seen in the eyes of other men in society—it concerned his personal status and power. Female honor, however, closely connected as it was to the family, involved maintaining the sexual purity of the women in one's kin group. The rape of Dinah brought shame and dishonor on both her family and herself, along with a loss of honor and status to her brothers: It had to be avenged. From the perspective of Dinah's brothers, the urbanites got what they deserved. For the city dwellers, it was an example of the treachery and danger posed by the nomads in their midst.

>> 39. Genesis 34

[TALE FROM THE FIFTEENTH OR FOURTEENTH CENTURY B.C.E.; CANONIZATION OF THE TORAH BY FIFTH CENTURY B.C.E.]

Now Dinah the daughter of Leah, whom she had borne to Jacob, went out to visit the women of the region. When Shechem son of Hamor the Hivite, prince of the region, saw her, he seized her and lay with her by force. And his soul was drawn to Dinah daughter of Jacob; he loved the girl, and spoke tenderly to her. So Shechem spoke to his father Hamor, saying, "Get me this girl to be my wife."

Now Jacob heard that Shechem had defiled his daughter Dinah; but his sons were with his cattle in the field, so Jacob held his peace until they came. And Hamor the father of Shechem went out to Jacob to speak with him, just as the sons of Jacob came in from the field. When they heard of it, the men were indignant and very angry, because he had committed an outrage in Israel by lying with Jacob's daughter, for such a thing ought not to be done.

But Hamor spoke with them, saying, "The heart of my son Shechem longs for your daughter; please give her to him in marriage. Make marriages with us; give your daughters to us, and take our daughters for yourselves. You shall live with us; and the land shall be open to you; live and trade in it, and get property in it." Shechem also said to her father and to her brothers, "Let me find favor with you, and whatever you say to me I will give. Put the marriage present and gift as high as you like, and I will give whatever you ask me; only give me the girl to be my wife."

The sons of Jacob answered Shechem and his father Hamor deceitfully, because he had defiled their sister Dinah. They said to them, "We cannot do this thing, to give our sister to one who is uncircumcised, for that would be a disgrace to us. Only on this condition will we consent to you: that you will become as we are and every male among you be circumcised. Then we will give our daughters to you, and we will take your daughters for ourselves, and we will live among you and become one people. But if you will not listen to us and be circumcised, then we will take our daughter and be gone."

Their words pleased Hamor and Hamor's son Shechem. And the young man did not delay to do the thing, because he was delighted with Jacob's daughter. Now he was the most honored of all his family. So Hamor and his son Shechem came to the gate of their city and spoke to the men of their city, saying: "These people are friendly with us; let them live in the land and trade in it, for the land is large

Source: Genesis 34, *The New Oxford Annotated Bible* (Oxford: Oxford University Press), 44–45.

enough for them; let us take their daughters in marriage, and let us give them our daughters. Only on this condition will they agree to live among us, to become one people: that every male among us be circumcised as they are circumcised. Will not their livestock, their property, and all their animals be ours? Only let us agree with them and they will live among us." And all who went out of the city gate heeded Hamor and his son Shechem; and every male was circumcised, all who went out of the gate of his city.

On the third day, when they were still in pain, two of the sons of Jacob, Simeon and Levi, Dinah's brothers, took their swords and came against the city unawares, and killed all the males. They killed Hamor and his son Shechem with the sword, and took Dinah out of Shechem's house, and went away. And the other sons of Jacob came upon the slain, and plundered the city, because their sister had been defiled. They took their flocks and their herds, their donkeys, and whatever was in the city and in the field. All their wealth, all their little ones and their wives, all that was in the houses, they captured and made their prey. Then Jacob said to Simeon and Levi, "You have brought trouble on me by making me odious to the inhabitants of the land, the Canaanites and the Perizzites; my numbers are few, and if they gather themselves against me and attack me, I shall be destroyed, both I and my household." But they said, "Should our sister be treated like a whore?"

>> Mastering the Material

1. What do scholars like Chester Starr see as the "price of civilization"? How is his analysis reflected in our ancient sources?

2. Based on this chapter's sources, what were the major threats to the stability and safety of ancient cities and states?

3. One major challenge for ancient societies was making sure that their members adhered to the society's norms. What different strategies for achieving this goal are embodied in Plato's *Protagoras*, the *Laws of Ur-Nammu*, and the "Declaration of Innocence"?

4. Green and Habicht hold very different views of the development of the Greek *polis* following the rise of Macedonia. Based on their arguments, with whom do you agree more, and why?

5. How did nomadic peoples view cities and urban dwellers, and how did city folk view nomads?

>> Making Connections

1. Agricultural societies, and especially cities, developed very sophisticated legal and moral codes in this period. Why do you think this was so?

2. As we saw in Chapter 1, geography and the physical environment both create possibilities and set limits for cultures and societies. How are these possibilities and limits manifested in this current chapter?

Part 1 Conclusion

On the middle stretch of the Euphrates River, where the borders of modern Syria and Iraq come together, sit the imposing ruins of Dura Europos. Founded by Alexander the Great's Seleucid successors between 300 and 280 B.C.E., Dura was a commercial and military center of some importance until the Sasanid Persians destroyed it in 256 C.E. But of even greater importance for historians of early antiquity is Dura Europos' nearby predecessor, the ancient Mesopotamian city of Mari. Originally founded in the early third millennium B.C.E., Mari has a complex cultural and political history that spans more than 1,000 years. The city had several periods of great prosperity, the last being under its powerful Amorite king, Zimri-Lim (about 1775–1760 B.C.E.). His large palace complex contains an extensive royal archive, and its unique frescoes—now housed in Paris at the Louvre Museum—bespeak the king's wealth and the city's cultural prominence. Mari's history epitomizes the major themes of Part I.

Central to human history is the very physical world in which we all move and act. The natural world always presents conditions that individuals can exploit, as well as limits beyond which they cannot expand. Mari's geographical location on the Euphrates presented a variety of possibilities but also some challenges to its earliest inhabitants. Their location allowed them to take advantage of the diffusion of the agricultural revolution that had originated further north and that had already diffused south of them. The land here is fertile, but the region is arid and rainfall scarce. Moreover, the river's annual floods, even though potentially devastating down river, were never high enough in this area to deposit additional layers of fertile silt. The Euphrates, however, presented the means for productive cereal farming if used effectively. Archaeologists have found that the inhabitants of Mari constructed elaborate channels from the Euphrates to water their crops and to control what rain did fall. Even as late as the second millennium B.C.E., the kings of Mari boasted of their canal-building activities and of the agricultural abundance that they, the kings and the canals, provided to the kingdom's inhabitants. The royal archives show that this was not idle bragging— the storerooms of the king were filled with cereals and produce from the rich farmland that he controlled. Pastoralism, another product of the agricultural revolution, was also important in this part of the Middle East. Archaeological finds indicate that wool was used for clothing and that the animals provided victims for sacrificial rites and food for the well off.

Mari's position on the middle Euphrates meant that its agricultural opportunities were more limited than those of the cities of the alluvial plain of southern Iraq, but was ideal for trade. From the very beginning, Mari's inhabitants established extensive trading networks up and down the river, as well as overland, especially to the west and the Mediterranean Sea. The geographic location of Mari put it at the hub of trade routes that extended as far east as the Indus Valley, and eventually as far west as the island of Crete. This same geography undoubtedly influenced the worldview of Mari's inhabitants, although we are poorly informed in this area. Since the earliest population of this city was part of the land of Sumer and Akkad, they would have had the same mental outlook on the universe as those who lived further south. Similarly, when nomadic rulers seized Mari in later generations, they would have brought with them many of the outward trappings and attitudes of a herding society.

Mari's history also typifies the urbanization that was a major theme of the ancient world. Although founded a little later than other cities in Mesopotamia, it was an urban establishment of great importance from the very beginning. A city similar in most ways to those in southern Iraq, Mari was the northern-most urban expression of Mesopotamian civilization. Its language and material culture were identical to that of the cities of the alluvial plain, and its kings even appear on lists that indicate that they too once held sovereignty over the whole land of Sumer and Akkad. Also like the cities of the south, a main focal point for the people of Mari were its temples, especially to Ishtar early in its history, and then to Shamash after about 2000 B.C.E. Another focal point of this and every Mesopotamian city was the royal palace. The palace of Zimri-Lim, large parts of which still stand today, was constructed on the foundation of previous royal residences. The palace was the center of Mari's economic and political activity, and its enormous archives tell of an elaborate bureaucratic system that was present in other Mesopotamian cities as well.

Despite its wealth and sophistication, however, Mari ultimately suffered a fate similar to that of other great cities of antiquity, whether here, in Mesoamerica, or on the Gangetic plain. The threats to Mari were identical to those of cities everywhere around the globe. On some occasions Mari was taken over by another Mesopotamian city, serving as an outpost for that regime. The kings of Third Dynasty Ur, for example, ended the independence of Mari and ruled it through governors in the late third millennium B.C.E. On other occasions, Mari engaged in battles with neighbors like Ebla, an important city further west, and lost—this time, however, Mari suffered only diminished financial resources through the loss of a dependency that it had controlled up to that time. Sometimes Mari was not so fortunate: Mesopotamian kings sacked the city and its temples on at least one occasion. An Akkadian king, possibly the powerful Sargon (around 2371–2316 B.C.E.), plundered the city mercilessly. Mari, however, proved resilient, and rose again to prominence.

In addition to ambitious kings of other city-states, Mari had to contend with the nomadic peoples of the region. The most feared of these pastoral nomads were the Amorites, described in ancient documents as "tent dwellers...who eat raw meat," and as "a ravaging people...which does not know grain." The Amorites moved into Mesopotamia in the late third millennium B.C.E., establishing their own rule over the various city-states of Sumer and Akkad. For Mari these new kings actually meant a new period of independence and great prosperity. The Amorites assimilated quickly into Mesopotamian culture and life, and acted much like all of the kings before them—they fought, allied, and traded with neighboring nomads and rival city-states. Alliances, however, could be short lived, and the erstwhile ally of Zimri-Lin, Hammurabi, the great Amorite king of Babylon, waged war against Mari. In his victory in 1759 B.C.E., Hammurabi destroyed the city utterly. This time Mari would not recover.

Throughout antiquity, cities and civilizations rose and fell, but the basic structures of ancient history, that bedrock mentioned by Kemp, continued. At its center were daily lives and worldviews that resulted from human interaction with the environment, from agriculture with its own particular patterns and rhythms, and from cities with their complex cultures, social structures, and political institutions. Upon these local and global stages, the subsequent events of history took place.

Further Reading

Various scholarly works by the new generation of world historians relate to many of the themes in Part I. One of the newest in this area is Felipe Fernández-Arnesto, *Pathfinders: A Global History of Exploration* (Oxford: Oxford University Press, 2006). This thought-provoking volume concerns many of the issues raised throughout this and subsequent parts. While historians and archaeologists have written much on the origins and significance of the Agricultural Revolution, in his *The Emergence of Civilization: From Hunting and Gathering to Agriculture, Cities, and the State in the Near East* (New York: Routledge, 1990) Charles K. Maisels has written an excellent synthetic work that discusses both the techniques used by scholars of early history and the results that they have achieved. An excellent look at the whole of the Eastern Mediterranean is William Stiebing, *Ancient Near Eastern History and Culture* (New York: Longman, 2003). For a more detailed look at the development in this and later periods in some of the regions covered in this volume, see, for example, Christopher Ehret, *The Civilizations of Africa: A History to 1800* (Charlottesville: University of Virginia Press, 2002), and Norman Hammond, *Ancient Maya Civilization* (New Brunswick: Rutgers University Press, 1982).

Terms to Know

Neolithic Revolution
  (P. 20)

protoancestor *(P. 35)*

horticulture *(P. 39)*

matrilineality *(P. 49)*

matrilocality *(P. 49)*

ethnographies *(P. 62)*

Transition and Transformation

From Islands of Culture to Regional "World Systems" (600 B.C.E.–300 C.E.)

"History," Marc Bloch argued in *The Historian's Craft*, "is the science of men in time." And time, he went on to observe, was a question of perpetual change. The period of time covered here in Part 2, 600 B.C.E. to 300 C.E., was one of not only perpetual but also massive change on a nearly global scale. More than ever before, developments occurred that had influence beyond any one society or group, and changes within societies often owed as much to the importation of ideas as to internal innovations. Although the invention of agriculture and advancements in metallurgical skills had had global consequences very early on, the world after 600 B.C.E. became far more interconnected as goods, people, and ideas flowed with unprecedented rapidity between societies. Realizing the interconnection of "the whole of the inhabited world," Greek historians made their first attempt at writing a "universal history" in the fourth century B.C.E. Yet even these writers were only dimly aware of the great changes taking place in the Mediterranean basin, let alone worldwide. This part explores three particularly widespread phenomena from this period: an intellectual revolution that spanned the whole of Eurasia; the rise for the first time of successful multicultural large state systems; and the diffusion of skills, technology, and art on a wide scale.

Underpinning these radical transformations was an intellectual shift exemplified not by politics or social organization, but rather by religion. Religion and religious expressions serve as the background against which new ways of thinking arose. Thus, an understanding of that background is central to understanding the changes that took place. Scholars suggest that religion provided ancient peoples with a way of looking at themselves and the universe, as we saw in Part 1. Thus on a community level, religion provided a unifying force for the population: In Egypt, the pharaoh was a god-king by whose commands the entire nation prospered; and the city-states of Mesopotamia, Mesoamerica, and Greece possessed a religious identity that centered on the worship of a common set of deities. Moreover, religion also affected mental constructs and attitudes. Religious beliefs helped to shape worldviews at the same time that they provided explanatory models of how that universe worked, and why events in the life of an individual or community, whether war or disease, occurred. Religion was a central approach to everyday experience, and because of that it reflects human beings' relationship to the universe as well as to one another. But religion provided more than an explanation; it also provided a mechanism for dealing with the world and each other. The insightful work of Yehezkel Kaufmann helps us to understand the religious context for the entire ancient world, bridging for us the old and the new ways of looking at and interpreting the universe.

Although the basic religious outlook of the people of Egypt and Mesopotamia did not change in the period Part 2 covers, that was not the case for the rest of Eurasia. Beginning around 600 B.C.E. an intellectual revolution started that challenged old perceptions and ways of thinking, providing at the same time new visions for existing societies. These radical new approaches to knowledge and action constitute what could be called the first global phenomenon in human history. Karl Jaspers, a mid-twentieth-century German philosopher, observed that a revolution in thought happened simultaneously, and independently, from Greece to China. He called this intellectual explosion "The Axial Period," or "**Axial Age**"—that which came before was replaced by bold new ways of conceptualizing the universe and human beings. After Jaspers had propounded his ideas, historians like Arnaldo Momigliano refined them and then applied them more thoroughly to their own studies. Chapter 7 presents Jaspers, Momigliano, and some of the evidence for the intellectual transformations from 600 to 200 B.C.E.

The second global phenomenon explored in Part 2 followed immediately upon the Axial Age: the rise of successful large state systems like the Chinese and Roman empires. The Axial Age, of course, had repercussions in all aspects of life and culture. In Athens, for instance, playwrights adapted, secularized, and then reintegrated the old stories of the heroes and gods into a new intellectual form: tragic theater. Rather than simply abandoning the material from an earlier age, they used the old stories to discuss the human condition in ways that had never been done before. However, one of the most important effects of the new thinking and new vision was in the political world. Again in Athens, the rise of debate and speculative thought that was central to the Greek intellectual revolution helped to create a democratic system. And in India, the powerful ruler Aśoka recast his kingdom along Buddhist lines. On an even larger political scale, the effects of the Axial Age were profound. For over a thousand years states had come and gone. But these states, even the mightiest, were ephemeral in nature. Such was not to be the case for China and Rome. It is no coincidence that these two successful empires follow upon the Axial Age. The intellectual achievements of that process influenced both the creation and cohesiveness of these larger political units. Without this intellectual basis, it is doubtful that either would have been any more successful than their predecessors in Egypt or the Middle East. In Chapter 8 we will see how China after its unification and Rome following Caesar Augustus managed to bring together successfully various groups into multicultural empires that the leaders of each claimed encompassed the whole of the inhabited world. Yet despite the many similarities between Rome and China, their individual experiences within the Axial Age resulted in different systems of government and different patterns of thought and culture in the period that followed.

The emergence of large-scale diffusion constitutes the third global phenomenon covered in Part 2. Archaeologists can document the cultural contacts between various peoples from many millennia before this era: Such things as pottery, artistic motifs, animals, and technologies were exchanged from the very beginning of human social development. What makes this period different from those before, however, was the extensive nature of these contacts, especially in the Old World. Archaeologists studying this period have found dyed Roman cloth in China and Chinese silks in Rome. Likewise, sub-Saharan goods made their way into the Mediterranean, and iron-smelting technology expanded south into central Africa. In the New World, exchanges took place between peoples over a wide distance. The passages in this part examine both the source of cultural change—independent invention as opposed to diffusion—and three of the basic mechanisms of diffusion and exchange: trade, individual migration, and conquest. Each method of contact brought its own cultural changes, some small and others enormous. Between 600 B.C.E. and 300 C.E., the world became far more connected than ever before; contacts between far-flung groups became increasingly more extensive.

Part 2 Timeline

1365 B.C.E.	Accession of The Egyptian Pharaoh Amenhotep IV (Akhenaten), who would develop a henotheistic cult out of traditional Egyptian religion.
c. 1250 B.C.E.	One of the traditional dates for the birth of Moses.
585 B.C.E.	Thales of Miletus predicts an eclipse of the sun; the beginning of the Ionian Intellectual Revolution and the Axial Age in Greece.
c. 563 B.C.E.	The birth of the Buddha, one of several new thinkers in Axial Age India.
551 B.C.E.	The birth of Confucius, an intellectual leader of the One Hundred Schools of Thought in China.
540 B.C.E.	Composition of the Second Book of Isaiah and the beginning of the Axial Age in Judah.
c. 503 B.C.E.	Cleisthenes introduces democratic reforms in Athens.
323 B.C.E.	The death of Alexander the Great and the beginning of the Hellenistic world.
273 B.C.E.	Accession of Aśoka, one of the most powerful rulers of ancient India; he would unite most of the Indian subcontinent and convert to Buddhism.
221 B.C.E.	The king of Qin takes a new title to become the First Emperor of Qin.
206 B.C.E.	The beginning of the Han Dynasty in China.

(Continued)

c. 200–100 B.C.E.	Discovery and first use of the monsoonal winds to and from India by the Greeks and other Mediterranean mariners.
31 B.C.E.	Octavian, the future Caesar Augustus, defeats Marc Antony at Actium. The beginning of the Roman Empire.
c. 90–160 C.E.	Iron-smelting techniques developed in West Africa and Nubia reach Angola, the south-westernmost point of the Bantu diffusion.
c. 100–150 C.E.	The beginning of figurative representations of the Buddha in northern India; the representations are done in the Greek style of art.
212 C.E.	The Roman emperor Caracalla extends citizenship to all free inhabitants of the Roman Empire, ending a process of integration begun by the emperor Claudius.
c. 200–250 C.E.	Latest date for the beginning of the "Classic Period" in Mesoamerica.
c. 400 C.E.	Jenne-Jeno, a settlement on the Niger River, reaches approximately 7,000 inhabitants, making it the earliest known West African city.

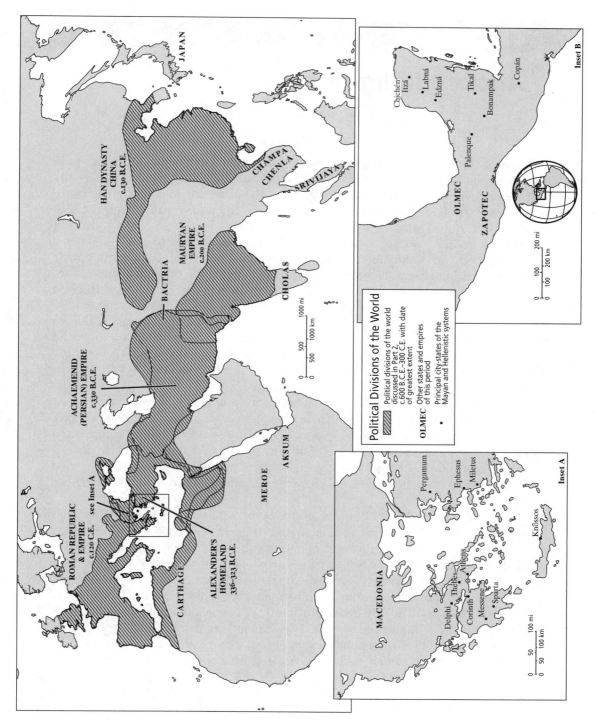

Political Divisions of the World

Political divisions of the world discussed in Part 2, c.600 B.C.E.–300 C.E. with date of greatest extent

OLMEC   Other states and empires of this period

•   Principal city-states of the Mayan and Hellenistic systems

JAPAN

HAN DYNASTY CHINA c.130 B.C.E.

CHAMPA

CHENLA

SRIVIJAYA

MAURYAN EMPIRE c.200 B.C.E.

BACTRIA

CHOLAS

ACHAEMENID (PERSIAN) EMPIRE c.330 B.C.E.

MEROE

AKSUM

ROMAN REPUBLIC & EMPIRE c.120 C.E.

see Inset A

ALEXANDER'S HOMELAND 336–323 B.C.E.

CARTHAGE

0   500   1000 mi

0   500   1000 km

Inset B

Chichén Itzá

Labná

Edzná

Tikal

Bonampak

Copán

Palenque

OLMEC

ZAPOTEC

0   100   200 mi

0   100   200 km

Inset A

MACEDONIA

Pergamum

Ephesus

Miletus

Delphi

Thebes

Athens

Corinth

Messene

Sparta

Knossos

0   50   100 mi

0   50   100 km

Chapter 6

Ancient Religions

Cosmology, Cosmogony, and Right Ritual

In 365 B.C.E. the Roman historian Livy reports that a devastating plague broke out in Rome, continuing well into the next year. The cause of the epidemic was clear—the gods were angry and had to be appeased. When the usual religious ceremonies were of no avail, the Roman authorities imported new rituals from their neighbors in the hope of restoring what they called the *Pax Deorum,* the "peace of the gods." But the Roman people panicked when these new ceremonies were themselves washed out by the flooding of the Tiber: Clearly the gods had not been appeased, and their anger continued unabated. The centrality of religion in the life of the Romans cannot be gainsaid—they conceived of life as a series of ritual acts that had to be performed in specific ritual places. Religion and religious forms and expressions are common to all cultures in all time periods. Similarly, as a foundation that reflects and influences every aspect of life, religion tends to change very slowly in its form and outlook, and as such tells us a great deal about the hopes and aspirations of individuals and groups. The great intellectual and political transformations that are explored in Part 2 are in part a challenge to the religious systems of their day.

In the ancient world itself, religion and religious practices were very much a part of communal obligations, affecting in one way or another all human institutions: social, political, economic, and cultural. We can learn a great deal about ancient cultures and about how individuals in these cultures think and change over time by looking at their basic religious system. Livy, for example, dubs these practices as "superstitious," and his skepticism is one indication of the growing sophistication and changes in religious outlook of his time.

In this chapter we will learn how scholars have organized, systematized, and characterized ancient and modern religious systems. In general they have identified two basic forms of cosmology, each of which is the exact opposite of the other: polytheism and monotheism. **Polytheism** ostensibly is the belief in many gods—the Egyptian *Book of the Dead,* for instance, lists some 480 deities; Hinduism counts more than 300,000,000. In contrast, **monotheism**—as embodied, for example, in Judaism, Christianity, and Islam—is the belief in one God. But this scholarly division of the religious world is deceptive. Yehezkel Kaufmann, the first author featured in this chapter, points out that the difference between polytheism and monotheism is *not* the number of gods within each system. When all of the gods in a polytheistic system are reduced to one god, what results is not monotheism but **henotheism.** The pharaoh Akhenaten did precisely this when he created his cult to the Aten, or Sun Disk, as demonstrated in the last passage in this chapter. Rather, Kaufmann argues that the difference between polytheism and monotheism has to do with the very nature and shape of the universe within each system. Reducing the number of gods does not change the actual nature of how the universe itself works or functions. Instead, the number of gods in each system results from how the universe works. Kaufmann's analysis provides us with a good tool for understanding the beliefs and practices of peoples ancient and modern. Polytheism remains as an important belief system to this day and is practiced by millions, whether in the highlands of Guatemala or the subcontinent of India. Understanding as clearly as possible how polytheism differs from monotheism helps us to understand both differing worldviews and differing responses to a similar event in the lives of individuals from two different cultures, one monotheistic, the other polytheistic.

While modern religion tends to emphasize personal ethics and morality, ancient religion placed great emphasis on rites and rituals as the core of religious expression. Ethics and morality were important to ancient peoples as well, but the sources of both varied greatly from society to society. In Vedic India, prior to 200 B.C.E., the connection between actions and religion was stronger than in most other ancient religions and cultures, yet even here ethical relations were often defined in more philosophical terms. In all of these societies, it was believed that the community could not survive unless the right rituals were carried out and without the avoidance of spiritual pollution. In Part 1 we saw how the Egyptians believed that their gods disapproved of a wide variety of actions, and that the commission of those acts could deprive one of the afterlife. Yet the Egyptian gods themselves did not reveal right conduct from wrong, as Yahweh did to Moses. Moreover, by carrying out the appropriate rituals, one could hide from the gods the wrongs committed in one's life. Generally speaking, in ancient society, custom and tradition rather than the gods dictated ethics and morality. Deities like the Greek Zeus and Babylonian Shamash were very concerned that justice be maintained, but they did not prescribe what constituted moral or ethical behavior. For the Romans, for instance, adultery was a great social wrong that could result in the death of an adulterer. But adultery was not a crime against the gods, who themselves committed adultery, nor, until Caesar Augustus, was it a crime against the state.

All polytheistic societies have a variety of stories that explain the birth of the universe (**cosmogony**) and the birth of the gods (**theogony**), and these stories in turn explain how the universe looks and functions (**cosmology**). Hesiod's *Theogony* is a classic version by a Greek writer of how the gods and goddesses came into being. Similar accounts are related by the Maya in the *Popol Vuh* and by the Indians in the Vedic period. The epic poem *The Ramayana*, like the poems of Homer, also reveals much about the nature of the gods and how the universe works. These same sources also show how human beings cope with a universe that worked this way, from practices like divination—the seeking out of the will of the gods and of Fate— to prayer and sacrifice. In every instance, human beings not only mimic the actions of the gods themselves, as in the Maya ball game or Vedic sacrifices, but also hope to produce certain common results—to please the gods and to keep demonic forces at bay. Through religious practices, human beings are instrumental in helping the gods keep chaos at a distance, as well as cosmic order and harmony in place. The major communal festivals are meant to keep the cosmos orderly—the maintaining of the *Pax Deorum,* or the Peace of the Gods.

The Nature of Polytheism

In his seminal work on the origins, development, and distinctiveness of monotheism in ancient Israel, Yehezkel Kaufmann provides a critical analysis of the nature of polytheism. He argues that the differences between polytheism and monotheism derive from how practitioners within each system conceive of the cosmos—the universe—rather than the number of gods in the system. He notes that the reduction of the number of gods in polytheism does not in itself create a new category of religion because the basic ideas about how the universe is structured and works remain unchanged. Similarly, he suggests that the scholarly focus on the plurality of gods misses the very premise of polytheism itself: something existed before the gods themselves came into being. He calls that which came before the gods themselves "the primordial" or "metadivine" realm. This realm is often conceived of as watery and chaotic, usually as consisting of one or more superannuated deities, and as full of power. The primordial realm is the source of Fate, and in its generative forces, it is the source of the gods themselves. Thus, the various parts of the cosmos come into being from this primordial realm, through sexual intercourse in one form or another. The plurality of gods, with all of their limits and functions, is the result of the nature of a universe that is structured in this fashion. Finally, all of the boundaries within the cosmos itself are ambiguous and blurred, from divinity to gender. Monotheism as practiced by the Israelites, Kaufmann argues, is the precise opposite. Nothing existed prior to Yahweh, for He always was. Likewise, the cosmos and its various parts did not come into being through sexual intercourse, but through the speech of God Himself—He is unlimited in his powers, sharing them with no one. And finally, a gulf exists between the Creator and the created. In the end, Kaufmann provides a useful model for understanding religion and religious phenomena, ancient and modern.

>> 40. The Religion of Israel:
From Its Beginnings to the Babylonian Exile

YEHEZKEL KAUFMANN [1972]

We designate as pagan all the religions of mankind from the beginnings of recorded history to the present, excepting Israelite religion and its derivatives, Christianity and Islam. This distinction assumes that, on the one hand, there is something unique about Israelite religion that sets is off from all the rest, and on the other, that there is an essential common aspect to all other religions which gives them their pagan character. What is that common essence?

Paganism has embodied itself in an enormous variety of forms: in deification of the animate and the inanimate, in belief in spirits and

---

Source: Yehezkel Kaufmann, *The Religion of Israel: From Its Beginnings to the Babylonian Exile*, translated by Moshe Greenberg (Chicago: University of Chicago Press, 1960; Schocken Books, 1972), 21–2, 24–5, 31–2, 35.

demons, in magic and incantations. It knows lofty cosmic gods and has produced the longing for knowledge of and communion with the "world soul." It evolved profound religious systems which sought to comprehend the secrets of existence, of life and death, of the destiny of man and the universe. It envisioned the triumph of good over evil at the end of days. Paganism bore such exotic fruit as the religion of the Australian aborigines, and that of the tribes of Africa and America; such delicate flowers as Greek thought; and the speculations of Babylon and Egypt, India, China, and Persia, with all their complex ramifications.

Yet all these embodiments involve one idea which is the distinguishing mark of pagan thought: the idea that there exists a realm of being prior to the gods and above them, upon which the gods depend, and whose decrees they must obey. Deity belongs to, and is derived from, a primordial realm. This realm is conceived of variously—as darkness, water, spirit, earth, sky, and so forth—but always as the womb in which the seeds of all being are contained. Alternatively, this idea appears as a belief in a primordial realm beside the gods, as independent and primary as the gods themselves. Not being subject to the gods, it necessarily limits them. The first conception, however, is the fundamental one. This is to say that in the pagan view, the gods are not the source of all that is, nor do they transcend the universe. They are, rather, part of a realm precedent to and independent of them. They are rooted in this realm, are bound by its nature, are subservient to its laws. To be sure, paganism has personal gods who create and govern the world of men. But a divine will, sovereign and absolute, which governs all and is the cause of all being—such a conception is unknown. There are heads of pantheons, there are creators and maintainers of the cosmos; but transcending them is the primordial realm, with its pre-existent, autonomous forces. This is the radical dichotomy of paganism; from it spring both mythology and magic.

Myth is the tale of the life of the gods. In myth the gods appear not only as actors, but as acted upon. At the heart of myth is the tension between the gods and other forces that shape their destinies. Myth describes the unfolding destiny of the gods, giving expression to the idea that besides the will of the gods there are other, independent forces that wholly or in part determine their destinies. Fate, says myth, apportions lots to the gods as well as to men. This is a great symbol of paganism's fundamental idea: the existence of a realm of power to which the gods themselves are subject.

The limitation of divine powers finds its source in the theogonies that are part of every mythology. The gods emerge out of the primordial substance, having been generated by its boundless fertility. It is not the gods and their will that exist at first, but the primordial realm with its inherent forces. Whether this realm is conceived of as original chaos, or as a kind of primal god, is immaterial. What is decisive is that the gods are born out of it by the natural, involuntary process of procreation. Even the "primal god" is thought of as no more than "father" of the gods and the world, engendering these out of his seed or his substance with no more control over their nature and destiny than a human father has over the nature and destiny of his offspring. His "paternity" does not involve universal rule and power. Indeed, it is typical of the ruling gods that they are usually of the second or third generation. The son who dethrones or murders his father, or rescues him from distress, and thus rises above him, is a feature of pagan mythologies. [...]

The following features are characteristic of pagan cosmogonies: a primordial realm which harbors the seeds of all being; a theogony telling of the birth of gods who are sexually differentiated and who procreate; the creation of the cosmos out of the primordial stuff—the same out of which the gods emerged, or from some "divine" substance. Also prevalent is the idea of several divine acts of creation; i.e., creation is not a single act, it has several divine "roots." [...]

Egyptian cosmogonies speak of the primeval waters, Nun, within which the first god, Atum, was formed. Atum engendered upon himself twins, Shu and Tefnet, from whom were born Geb (earth) and his wife, Nut (sky). Shu lifted Nut off her husband, thus creating the world. From these pairs the gods were born. But there are several accounts of creation. Re, Ptah, Neith, Amon, and others are each, at one time or another, represented as creators. Thus, Re, the sun-god, is also said to be the primal god who fathered Nut; yet Nut is his mother, who gives birth to him daily. In Memphis, Ptah was regarded as the first god, as Nun, out of whom the gods emerged. But Ptah himself was divided into the male Ptah-Nun and the female Ptah-Naunet. Another version speaks of a lotus plant that grew out of the primeval waters in which the sun-god was sitting as a child. Yet another has the sun-god emerge from an egg that lay on a hill that rose out of the water. All these stories speak in terms of birth and procreation and derive the gods from a primordial realm. [...]

Although the will of the gods plays a significant part in the cosmogonies, there is something that transcends it: the power of matter, the innate nature of the primordial order. The gods are conceived in the world-stuff, emerge out it, and are subject to its nature.

The god has a potent mana, inherited from the primordial stuff through which he acts. But this power is regarded as inhering in the substance of the god, not in his will or spirit. This becomes evident from myths in which the god remains potent even after his death—i.e., after he has ceased being a willing being and has become mere lifeless substance. The various stories of creation out of the corpses of gods and the widespread cult of the graves of the gods are rooted in this concept. Moreover, the god's mana belongs to everything given off by his body; his tears, his spittle, his blood, his mutilated members, his dung—all are represented as sources of life and creation.

The dependence of the gods upon what lies outside them is embodied in the common notion that they are in need of food and drink.

Corresponding to the theogony which tells how they were born out of the primeval substance, this makes their continued existence dependent upon the external matter they take in. It is a kind of permanent "theogony." Child-gods imbibe vigor from the breasts of goddesses. Certain substances are often specified as the sources of divine vitality: the Indian soma, the Germanic mead, the Greek nectar and ambrosia. At times the gods have recourse to magical foods and drinks that endow them with special powers, that heal them of sickness, that protect them against evil magic, that rejuvenate them, that act as aphrodisiacs, and so forth. [...]

The outcome of the pagan view that the gods originate in the world stuff is to remove any fixed bounds between them and the world of men and other creatures. For there is a common womb out of which both the gods and all the phenomena of nature have sprung. This confusion of realms manifests itself both in mythology and the cult.

Thus, we find no clear-cut distinction between worship of nature and worship of the gods of nature. What began as worship of natural phenomena, developed into the cult of nature-gods. Even in the theistic stage, however, the worship of nature itself, as the embodiment of the life processes of the gods, lingers on. In one way or another the sun, moon, stars, waters, fire, etc., were always worshiped, even after the myth-markers had created a universe full of gods of whom these were but symbols.

But it is not only the larger phenomena of nature that are deified and sanctified. Various substances—fetishes thought to be charged with mana or viewed as housing gods or spirits—are treated as divinities. The cult of sacred stones, sacred trees, or sacred animals is an important element of paganism. A typical expression of this idea is found in totemism, in which animals or inanimate objects are considered bearers of divine power or lodgings of spirit and gods who are the kin of the tribe. Here we find an actual kinship relation between the god and the world.

A Greek Account of the Birth of the Gods

Hesiod, a near contemporary of Homer, composed his version of the origins of the cosmos close to 700 B.C.E. While the fifth century B.C.E. Greek historian Herodotus asserted that both Homer and Hesiod invented all of the tales about the gods and goddesses, Hesiod has undoubtedly put into verse stories and beliefs that were almost as old as the Greeks themselves. In this section of Theogony, *or* The Birth of the Gods, *Hesiod presents many of the principles of polytheism set out by Kaufmann: a primordial realm in existence before the gods themselves, embodied in this case by the likes of Chaos; the sexual nature of the cosmos—the various deities come into being by birth and intercourse; and Fate, that basic law of the primordial realm itself, pervading the universe, limiting even the gods themselves. Thus, neither Chronos nor Zeus could evade what was fated for them. And finally we see a blurring of boundaries and realms, including gender: Zeus gave birth to Athena, and would later give birth to Dionysus from his "male womb." What Hesiod's poem shows is that everything in the universe is connected to everything else, and it all goes back to that original primordial realm.*

>> 41. Theogony

HESIOD [C. 700 B.C.E.]

Hail, then, children of Zeus:
  grant me lovely singing.

Now sound out the holy stock
  of the everlasting immortals
who came into being out of Gaia
  and starry Ouranos
and gloomy Night, whom Pontos, the salt sea,
  brought to maturity;
and tell, how at the first the gods
  and the earth were begotten
and rivers, and the boundless sea,
  raging in its swell,
the blazing stars, and the wide sky above all,
  tell of

the gods, bestowers of blessings,
  who were begotten of all these,
and how they divided their riches
  and distributed their privileges,
and how they first took possession
  of many-folded Olympos,
tell me all this, you Muses
  who have your homes on Olympos,
from the beginning, and tell who was first
  to come forth among them.
    First of all there came Chaos,
    and after him came
Gaia of the broad breast,
  to be the unshakable foundation
of all the immortals who keep the crests
  of snowy Olympos,
and Tartaros the foggy in the pit
  of the wide-wayed earth,

Source: Hesiod, *Theogony*, translated by Richmond Lattimore (Ann Arbor: The University of Michigan Press, 1959), 129–31, 150–1, 176–9.

and Eros, who is love, handsomest among all
   the immortals,
who breaks the limbs' strength,
   who in all gods, in all human beings
overpowers the intelligence in the breast,
   and all their shrewd planning.
From Chaos was born Erebos, the dark,
   and black Night,
and from Night again Aither and Hemera,
   the day, were begotten,
for she lay in love with Erebos
   and conceived and bore these two.
But Gaia's first born was one
   who matched her every dimension,
Ouranos, the starry sky,
   to cover her all over,
to be an unshakable standing-place
   for the blessed immortals.
Then she brought forth the tall Hills,
   those wild haunts that are beloved
by the goddess Nymphs who live on the hills
   and in their forests.
Without any sweet act of love
   she produced the barren
sea, Pontos, seething in his fury of waves,
   and after this
she lay with Ouranos, and bore him
   deep-swirling Okeanos
the ocean-stream. [. . .]

Rheia, submissive in love to Kronos,
   bore glorious children,
Histia and Demeter,
   Hera of the golden sandals,
and strong Hades, who under the ground
   lives in his palace

and has a heart without pity;
   the deep-thunderous Earthshaker,
and Zeus of the counsels,
   who is the father of gods and of mortals,
and underneath whose thunder
   the whole wide earth shudders;
but, as each of these children
   came from the womb of its mother
to her knees, great Kronos swallowed it down,
   with the intention
that no other of the proud children
   of the line of Ouranos
should ever hold the king's position
   among the immortals.
For he had heard, from Gaia
   and from starry Ouranos,
that it had been ordained for him,
   for all his great strength,
to be beaten by his son,
   and through the designs of great Zeus.
Therefore he kept watch, and did not sleep,
   but waited
for his children, and swallowed them,
   and Rheia's sorrow was beyond forgetting.
But when she was about to bear Zeus,
   the father of mortals
and gods, then Rheia went
   and entreated her own dear parents,
and these were Gaia and starry Ouranos,
   to think of some plan
by which, when she gave birth to her
   dear son,
   the thing might not
be known, and the fury of revenge
   be on devious-devising Kronos
the great, for his father,

and his own children whom he
  had swallowed.
They listened gladly
  to their beloved daughter, and consented,
and explained to her
  all that had been appointed to happen
concerning Kronos, who was King, and his son,
  of the powerful
spirit, and sent her to Lyktos,
  in the fertile countryside of Crete
at that time when she was to bring forth
  the youngest of her children,
great Zeus; and the Earth, gigantic Gaia,
  took him inside her. [. . .]

Zeus, as King of the gods,
  took as his first wife Metis,
and she knew more than all the gods
  or mortal people.
But when she was about to be delivered
  of the goddess, gray-eyed
Athene, then Zeus, deceiving her perception
  by treachery
and by slippery speeches,
  put her away inside his own belly.
This was by the advices of Gaia,
  and starry Ouranos,
for so they counseled,
  in order that no other everlasting
god, beside Zeus, should ever be given
  the kingly position.
For it had been arranged that, from her,
  children surpassing in wisdom
should be born, first the gray-eyed girl,
  the Tritogeneia
Athene; and she is the equal of her father

in wise counsel
and strength; but then a son to be King
  over gods and mortals
was to be born of her, and his heart
  would be overmastering:
but before this, Zeus put her away
  inside his own belly
so that this goddess should think for him,
  for good and for evil.
    Next Zeus took to himself Themis,
  the shining, who bore him the Seasons,
Lawfulness, and Justice,
  and prospering Peacetime: these
are concerned to oversee the actions
  of mortal people;
and the Fates, to whom Zeus of the counsels
  gave the highest position:
    Last of all, Zeus took Hera
  to be his fresh consort,
and she, lying in the arms
  of the father of gods and mortals,
conceived and bore Hebe to him,
  and Ares,
  and Eileithyia.
    Then from his head, by himself,
  he produced Athene of the gray eyes,
great goddess, weariless,
  waker of battle noise, leader of armies,
a goddess queen who delights in war cries,
  onslaughts, and battles,
while Hera, without any act of love,
  brought forth glorious
Hephaistos, for she was angered
  and quarreling with her husband;
and Hephaistos in arts and crafts
  surpassed all the Ouranians.

A Mayan Account of the Birth of the Universe

The basic attitudes and concepts embedded in Hesiod's poem are present cross-culturally in all cosmogonies. The Maya account can be seen in the Popol Vuh, *technically* The Council Book, *but alternatively* The Dawn of Life. *The* Popol Vuh *explains how the universe came into being and how things came to be the way they are today. In the* Popol Vuh *three primordial deities existed before the gods themselves came into being—the Sovereign Plumed Serpent, who acted as Maker and Modeler, Bearer and Begetter; and Xpiyacoc and Xmucane, the divine Grandparents of all that came to be. Like the Egyptian god Ptah, part of these deities' creative act is through speech, and part is by "sowing" their seed. Not only are these divinities the mother and father of everything that is, but they are also "the Great Knowers," and the source of Fate. They are called the "day keepers," "setting out the days" for the universe. Divination, the practice of finding out the will of the gods and of Fate itself, was an act done by other gods themselvess and by human beings mimicking the gods. It consists of "running their hands over the corn kernels, over the coral seeds." The shaman in the Guatemalan highlands still practices this form of sacred knowledge.*

>> 42. Popol Vuh: The Mayan Book of the Dawn of Life

[ANCIENT TALE WRITTEN DOWN IN THE ROMAN ALPHABET IN THE MID-SIXTEENTH CENTURY C.E.]

This is the beginning of the Ancient Word, here in this place called Quiché. Here we shall inscribe, we shall implant the Ancient Word, the potential and source for everything done in the citadel of Quiché, in the nation of Quiché people.

And here we shall take up the demonstration, revelation, and account of how things were put in shadow and brought to light by

the Maker, Modeler,
named Bearer, Begetter,
Hunahpu Possum, Nunahpu Coyote,
Great White Peccary, Coati,
Sovereign Plumed Serpent,
Heart of the Lake, Heart of the Sea,

plate shaper, bowl shaper, as they are called,
also named, also described as
the midwife matchmaker
named Xpiyacoc, Xmucane,
defender, protector,
twice a midwife, twice a matchmaker,

as is said in the words of Quiché. They accounted for everything—and did it, too—as enlightened beings, in enlightened words. We shall write about this now amid the preaching of God, in Christendom now. We shall bring it out because there is no longer

a place to see it, a Council Book,
a place to see "The Light That Came from
    Beside the Sea,"
the account of "Our Place in the Shadows,"
a place to see "The Dawn of Life,"

Source: Dennis Tedlock, trans. *Popol Vuh: The Mayan Book of the Dawn of Life* (New York: Touchstone, 1996), 63–5, 69–70.

as it called. There is the original book and ancient writing, but the one who reads and assesses it has a hidden identity. It takes a long performance and account to complete the lighting of all the sky-earth:

the fourfold siding, fourfold cornering,

measuring, fourfold staking,

halving the cord, stretching the cord

in the sky, on the earth,

the four sides, the four corners, as it is said,

by the Maker, Modeler,

mother-father of life, of humankind,

giver of breath, giver of heart,

bearer, upbringer in the light that lasts

of those born in the light, begotten in the light;

worrier, knower of everything, whatever there is:

sky-earth, lake-sea.

This is the account, here it is:

Now it still ripples, now it still murmurs, ripples, it still sighs, still hums, and it is empty under the sky.

Here follow the first words, the first eloquence:

There is not yet one person, one animal, bird, fish, crab, tree, rock, hollow, canyon, meadow, forest. Only the sky alone is there; the face of the earth is not clear. Only the sea alone is pooled under all the sky; there is nothing whatever gathered together. It is at rest; not a single thing stirs. It is held back, kept at rest under the sky.

Whatever there is that might be is simply not there: only the pooled water, only the calm sea, only it alone is pooled.

Whatever might be is simply not there: only murmurs, ripples, in the dark, in the night. Only the Maker, Modeler alone, Sovereign Plumed Serpent, the Bearers, Begetters are in the water, a glittering light. They are there, they are enclosed in quetzal feathers, in blue-green.

Thus the name, "Plumed Serpent." They are great knowers, great thinkers in their very being.

And of course there is the sky, and there is also the Heart of Sky. This is the name of the god, as it is spoken.

And then came his word, he came here to the Sovereign Plumed Serpent, here in the blackness, in the early dawn. He spoke with the Sovereign Plumed Serpent, and they talked, then they thought, then they worried. They agreed with each other, they joined their words, their thoughts. Then it was clear, then they reached accord in the light, and then humanity was clear, when they conceived the growth, the generation of trees, of bushes, and the growth of life, of humankind, in the blackness, in the early dawn, all because of the Heart of Sky, named Hurricane. Thunderbolt Hurricane comes first, the second is Newborn Thunderbolt, and the third is Sudden Thunderbolt.

So there were three of them, as Heart of Sky, who came to the Sovereign Plumed Serpent, when the dawn of life was conceived:

"How should the sowing be, and the dawning? Who is to be the provider, nurturer?"

"Let it be this way, think about it: this water should be removed, emptied out for the formation of the earth's own plate and platform, then should come the sowing, the dawning of the sky-earth. But there will be no high days and no bright praise for our work, our design, until the rise of the human work, the human design," they said. [. . .]

Then comes the naming of those who are the midmost seers: the "Grandmother of Day, Grandmother of Light," as the Maker, Modeler called them. These are names of Xpiyacoc and Xmucane.

When Hurricane had spoken with the Sovereign Plumed Serpent, they invoked the daykeepers, diviners, the midmost seers:

"There is yet to find, yet to discover how we are to model a person, construct a person again, a provider, nurturer, so that we are called upon and we are recognized: our recompense is in words.

Midwife, matchmaker,

our grandmother, our grandfather,

Xpiyacoc, Xmucane,

let there be planting, let there be the dawning

of our invocation, our sustenance, our recognition by the human work, the human design, the human figure, the human form. So be it, fulfill your names: Hunahpu Possum, Hunahpu Coyote, Bearer twice over, Begetter twice over, Great Peccary, Great Coati, lapidary, jeweler, sawyer, carpenter, plate shaper, bowl shaper, incense maker, master craftsman, Grandmother of Day, Grandmother of Light.

You have been called upon because of our work, our design. Run your hands over the kernels of corn, over the seeds of the coral tree, just get it done, just let it come out whether we should carve and gouge a mouth, a face in wood," they told the daykeepers.

And then comes the borrowing, the counting of days; the hand is moved over the corn kernels, over the coral seeds, the days, the lots.

Then they spoke to them, one of them a grandmother, the other a grandfather.

This is the grandfather, this is the master of the coral seeds: Xpiyacoc is his name.

And this is the grandmother, the daykeeper, diviner who stands behind others: Xmucane is her name.

And they said, as they set out the days:

"Just let it be found, just let it be discovered, say it, our ear is listening, may you talk, may you speak, just find the wood for the carving and sculpting by the builder, sculptor. Is this to be the provider, the nurturer when it comes to the planting, the dawning? You corn kernels, you coral seeds, you days, you lots: may you succeed, may you be accurate,"

they said to the corn kernels, coral seeds, days, lots. "Have shame, you up there, Heart of Sky: attempt no deception before the mouth and face of Sovereign Plumed Serpent," they said.

Vedic Understandings of the Cosmic System

In India, Vedic religion provides a cosmology similar to that of the Greeks and the Maya. The passages here add some new details about the nature of the universe while reemphasizing those that we have already seen. According to The Laws of Manu, *the primordial deity before all gods was "The Lord who is self-existent," a phrase used in Egyptian cosmologies as well. From his own body he emitted water and then impregnated it with his own semen. From this union was born Brahmā, "the grandfather of all people." In this cosmogony we see not only the generative power of the primordial realm, but also its physicality—it consists of primordial "stuff," and all that comes into being is ultimately connected to that realm. Everything, from gods to rocks, ends up having a "soul" or "life force," because everything is ultimately composed of and connected to that metadivine realm. The consequences of this interconnectedness are revealed in a short section from* The Ramayana: *The gods are not only limited in various ways—they compete with one another, they require sustenance, they are subject to Fate—but they are also in battle with demonic forces. In his own fight with Mahabali, the* asura *(demon) king, Vishnu transcends his divinity to become a human being. This blurring of boundaries between god and man is common to all polytheistic systems, as is this constant struggle against the demonic forces within the cosmos. In the following sequence, the gods themselves perform sacrifices, and Vishnu succeeds in vanquishing Mahabali, forcing him into the Underworld.*

>> 43. The Laws of Manu

[ANCIENT TRADITIONS WRITTEN DOWN IN THE FIRST TWO CENTURIES C.E.]

Chapter 1

[*1*] The great sages approached Manu when he was seated in single-minded concentration; they exchanged mutual salutations in the proper manner and then they said this to him: [*2*] 'Sir, please tell us, properly and in order, the duties of all (four) classes and also of the people who are born between (two classes). [*3*] For you, lord, are the only one who knows the true meaning of what is to be done in this whole system made by the Self-existent one, that cannot be imagined and cannot be measured.'

[*4*] When the great and great-souled sages had properly asked him this, Manu, whose energy was boundless, honoured them and replied,

Listen! [*5*] Once upon a time this (universe) was made of darkness, without anything that could be discerned, without any distinguishing marks, impossible to know through reasoning or understanding; it seemed to be entirely asleep. [*6*] Then the Lord who is Self-existent, himself unmanifest, caused this (universe) to become manifest; putting his energy into the great elements and everything else, he became visible and dispelled the darkness. [*7*] The one who can be grasped only by what is beyond the sensory powers, who is subtle, unmanifest, eternal, unimaginable, he of whom all creatures are made—he is the one who actually appeared.

[*8*] He thought deeply, for he wished to emit various sorts of creatures from his own body; first he emitted the waters, and then he emitted his semen in them. [*9*] That (semen) became a golden egg, as bright as the sun with his thousand rays; Brahmā himself, the grandfather of all people, was born in that (egg). [*10*] 'The waters are born of man,' so it is said; indeed, the waters are the children of the (primordial) man. And since they were his resting place in ancient time, therefore he is traditionally known as Nārāyana ('Resting on those born of man'). [*11*] The one who is the first cause, unmanifest, eternal, the essence of what is real and unreal, emitted the Man, who is known in the world as Brahmā.

[*12*] The Lord dwelt in that egg for a whole year, and then just by thinking he himself divided the egg into two. [*13*] Out of the two fragments he made the sky and the earth, and the atmosphere in the middle, and the eight cardinal directions, and the eternal place of the waters. [*14*] And out of himself he grew the mind-and-heart, the essence of what is real and unreal, and from mind-and-heart came the sense of 'I', the controlling consciousness of self, [*15*] and the great one which is the self, and all (material things that have) the three qualities, and, one by one, the five sensory powers that grasp the sensory objects.

Source: Wendy Doniger, trans., *The Laws of Manu* (New York: Penguin Press, 1991), 3–5.

>> 44. The Ramayana

[FIFTH CENTURY B.C.E.]

Mahabali's Story

This is consecrated ground where Vishnu once sat in meditation. (Although Rama was Vishnu, his human incarnation made him unaware of his identity at the moment.) While Vishnu was thus engaged, Mahabali seized the earth and heaven and brought them under his subjection. He celebrated his victory by performing a great yagna, and used this occasion to invite and honour all learned men. All the gods who had suffered in their encounter with Mahabali arrived in a body at the spot where Vishnu was in meditation and begged him to help them regain their kingdoms. In response to their appeals, Vishnu took birth in a brahmin family as a person of tiny proportions; within this diminutive personality was packed a great deal of power and learning. Mahabali was quick to sense his greatness when this dawrfish man presented himself at the palace gate. Mahabali received the visitor warmly and respectfully.

The visitor said, "I have come from afar after hearing of your greatness. My ambition in life has been to have a glimpse of one who is renowned alike for his valour and generosity. Now, after meeting you, I have attained my life's ambition. Achievements such as yours cannot be measured. When a poor man like me has a glimpse of your divinity, a part of it comes to me also."

"Oh great one, do not praise me," Mahabali replied. "I am after all a fighter and conqueror—base qualities when compared to the learning and special attainments of one like you. I am not easily led by appearances. I can know how great you must be. I shall be happy if you will accept a gift in return for the honour you have done in visiting me."

"I want nothing. I need no gift other than your goodwill."

"No, please don't go, ask for something, mention anything you want. It will please me to grant it."

"If you insist, then give me a piece of land."

"Yes, choose it wherever you like."

"Not more than what would be measured in three strides of my feet..."

Bali laughed, looked him up and down, and said, "Is that all?"

"Yes."

"I shall now...," began Mahabali, but before he could complete his sentence, his guru Sukracharya interrupted to warn, "King, do not be rash. The small figure you see is a deception: he is minute, but this microcosm..."

"Oh, stop! I know my responsibility. To give while one can is the right time, and to prevent a gift is an unholy act, unworthy of you. He who is selfish is never worse than the one who stays the hand that is about to give. Don't stop me," he said; and poured out a little water from a vessel on the upturned palm of the little man to seal his promise. (It is found in some texts that at this moment Sukracharya assumed the size of a bee and flew into the spout of the vessel in order to block the flow of water and thus prevent the oath being given. The dwarf, sensing this, took a sharp *dharba* grass and thrust it in to clear the obstruction and it pricked the eye of Sukracharya, who thereafter came to be known as the one-eyed savant.) Pouring this oblation of water, Bali said to the little man, "Now measure and take your three steps of earth."

The moment the water fell on his hand, this person, who was a figure of fun even to his parents till then, assumed a majestic stature spanning the earth and the sky. With the first step he measured the entire earth, with the second he covered the heavens. No more space was left in the whole universe, and he asked Mahabali, "Where shall I place the third step?"

Mahabali, overawed, knelt, bowed, and said, "Here on my head, if no other space is available." Vishnu raised his foot, placed it on Mahabali's head, and pressed him down to the netherworld. "You may stay there," he said, and thus disposed of the tormentor of the worlds.

Source: R. K. Narayan, trans., *The Ramayana* (New York: Penguin Press, 1972), 14–6.

Humans and the Cosmos

Religion—that critical set of rites, rituals, and ceremonies—was the mechanism by which ancient peoples sought to cope with a universe that looked and functioned in this manner. The Laws of Manu *state the importance of Veda, "sacred knowledge," in the form of rites and sacrifices; all good humans within that society had to live lives according to the prescriptions of religion, and those who did not were appropriately punished. In this way the Greeks who settled in India after the conquest of Alexander the Great and who had been enrolled in the highest caste were ultimately reduced to the bottom of society because of their inability to perform the necessary rites and rituals required of them* (The Laws of Manu *10.44). Cult, a system of religious ceremonies and divine worship, is a central feature of all polytheistic religions, not just Hinduism. In the* Popol Vuh, *two forms of cult are explained: the origins of the famous Maya ball games—the recreation of the triumph of the Twins over the demonic forces of the Lords of Xibalba (the Underworld)—and human sacrifice. In this way cult celebrates the events in the lives of the gods, and mimics, as we have already seen with divination and sacrifice, what the gods themselves do. The following passage also includes another form of blood sacrifice, genital mutilation. But in addition to pleasing the gods and to helping the gods in their function of preserving cosmic order, human beings practice religion to get something from the gods—prayer and sacrifice serve as a contract between the offerer and the divinity. For the Maya, human sacrifice sustains both the gods and human beings by defeating the Lords of Death. In another example, the simplest Roman prayer says "I give [to you, god,] so that you might give [to me.]" What is largely missing from this equation was morality and ethics, and this was the great criticism of Plato. In his* Euthyphro *Plato characterizes Greek religion as the science of asking and giving, "of how to say and do, in prayer and in sacrifice, what is pleasing to the gods." His characterization, while exaggerated, is true of ancient polytheism in general.*

>> 45. The Laws of Manu

[ANCIENT TRADITIONS WRITTEN DOWN IN THE FIRST TWO CENTURIES C.E.]

Chapter 2

[*1*] Learn the religion that is constantly followed and assented to in the heart by learned men, good men who have neither hatred nor passion.

[*2*] Acting out of desire is not approved of, but here on earth there is no such thing as no desire; for even studying the Veda and engaging in the rituals enjoined in the Veda are based upon desire. [*3*] Desire is the very root of the conception of a definite intention, and sacrifices are the result of that intention; all the vows and the duties of restriction are traditionally said to come from the conception of a definite intention. [*4*] Not a single rite is ever performed here on earth by a man without desire; for each and every thing that he does is motivated by the desire for precisely that thing. [*5*] The man who is properly occupied in these (desires) goes to the world of the immortals, and here on earth he achieves all the desires for which he has conceived an intention.

[*6*] The root of religion is the entire Veda, and (then) the tradition and customs of those who know

---

Source: Wendy Doniger, trans., *The Laws of Manu* (New York: Penguin Press, 1991), 17–8.

(the Veda), and the conduct of virtuous people, and what is satisfactory to oneself. [7] Whatever duty Manu proclaimed for whatever person, all of that was declared in the Veda, for it contains all knowledge. [8] So when a learned man has looked thoroughly at all of this with the eye of knowledge, he should devote himself to his own duty in accordance with the authority of the revealed canon. [9] For the human being who fulfils the duty declared in the revealed canon and in tradition wins renown here on earth and unsurpassable happiness after death. [10] The Veda should be known as the revealed canon, and the teachings of religion as the tradition. These two are indisputable in all matters, for religion arose out of the two of them. [11] Any twice-born man who disregards these two roots (of religion) because he relies on the teachings of logic should be excommunicated by virtuous people as an atheist and a reviler of the Veda.

[12] The Veda, tradition, the conduct of good people, and what is pleasing to oneself—they say that this is the four-fold mark of religion, right before one's eyes. [13] The knowledge of religion is prescribed for those who are not attached to profit and pleasure; the revealed canon is the supreme authority for those who wish to understand religion. [14] But where the revealed canon is divided, both (views) are traditionally regarded as law; for wise men say that both of them are valid laws. [15] (For example), the sacrifice is performed at all times—when the sun has risen, when it has not risen, and at the very juncture of daybreak: this is what the revealed Vedic canon says. [16] The man whose ritual life, beginning with the infusion (of semen) and ending with cremation, is dictated by Vedic verses should be recognized as entitled to (study) this teaching, but not anyone else.

>> 46. Popol Vuh: The Mayan Book of the Dawn of Life

[ANCIENT TALE WRITTEN DOWN IN
THE ROMAN ALPHABET IN THE
MID-SIXTEENTH CENTURY C.E.]

Happy now, they went to play ball at the court. So they played ball at a distance, all by themselves. They swept out the court of their fathers.

And the it came into the hearing of the lords of Xibalba:

"Who's begun a game again up there, over our heads? Don't they have any shame, stomping around this way? Didn't One and Seven Hunahpu die trying to magnify themselves in front of us? So, you must deliver another summons," They said as before, One and Seven Death, all the lords.

"They are hereby summoned," they told their messengers. "You are to say, on reaching them:

' "They must come," say the lords, "We would play ball with them here. In seven days we'll have

a game," say the lords,' you will say when you arrive," the messengers were told.

And then they came along a wide roadway, the road to the house of the boys, which actually ended at their house, so that the messengers came directly to their grandmother. As for the boys, they were away playing ball when the messengers of Xinalba got there.

" 'Truly, they are to come,' say the lords," said the messengers of Xibalba. So then and there the day was specified by the messengers of Xibalba:

" 'In seven days our game will take place,' " Xmucane was told there.

"Very well. They'll go when the day comes, messengers," said the grandmother, and the messengers left. They went back. [...]

And there they tried to force them into a game:

"Here, let's jump over our drink four times, clear across, one of us after the other, boys," they were told by One Death.

"You'll never put that one over on us. Don't we know what our death is, you lords? Watch!"

Source: Dennis Tedlock, trans., *Popol Vuh: The Mayan Book of the Dawn of Life* (New York: Touchstone, 1996), 112–3, 131–2, 135–8, 163–5.

they said, then they faced each other. They grabbed each other by the hands and went head first into the oven.

And there they died, together, and now all the Xibalbans were happy, raising their shouts, raising their cheers. [...]

And on the fifth day they reappeared. They were seen in the water by the people. The two of them looked like catfish when their faces were seen by Xibalba. And having germinated in the waters, they appeared the day after that as two vagabonds, with rags before and rags behind, and rags all over too. They seemed unrefined when they were examined by Xibalba; they acted differently now. [...]

Next they would sacrifice themselves, one of them dying for the other, stretched out as if in death. First they would kill themselves, but then they would suddenly look alive again. The Xibalbans could only admire what they did. Everything they did now was already the groundwork for their defeat of Xibalba. [...]

And then they were asked by the lord:

"You have yet to kill a person! Make a sacrifice without death!" they were told.

"Very well," they said.

And then they took hold of a human sacrifice.

And they held up a human heart on high.

And they showed its roundness to the lords.

And now One and Seven Death admired it, and now that person was brought right back to life. His heart was overjoyed when he came back to life, and the lords were amazed:

"Sacrifice yet again, even do it to yourselves! Let's see it! At heart, that's the dance we really want from you," the lords said now.

"Very well, lord," they replied, and then they sacrificed themselves.

And this is the sacrifice of little Hunahpu by Xbalanque. One by one his legs, his arms were spread wide. His head came off, rolled far away outside. His heart, dug out, was smothered in a leaf, and all the Xibalbans went crazy at the sight.

So now, only one of them was dancing there: Xbalanque.

"Get up!" he said, and Hunahpu came back to life. The two of them were overjoyed at this—and likewise the lords rejoiced, as if they were doing it themselves. One and Seven Death were as glad at heart as if they themselves were actually doing the dance.

And then the hearts of the lords were filled with longing, with yearning for the dance of little Hunahpu and Xbalanque, so then came these words from One and Seven Death"

"Do it to us! Sacrifice us!" they said. "Sacrifice both of us!" said One and Seven Death to little Hunahpu and Xbalanque.

"Very well. You ought to come back to life. What is death to you? And aren't we making you happy, along with the vassals of your domain?" they told the lords.

And this one was the first to be sacrificed: the lord at the very top, the one whose name is One Death, the ruler of Xibalba.

And with One Death dead, the next to be taken was Seven Death. They did not come back to life. [...]

And here they burn their copal, and here also is the origin of the masking of Tohil.

And when they went before Tohil and Auilix, they went to visit them and keep their day. Now they gave thanks before them for the dawning, and now they bowed low before their stones, there in the forest. Now it was only a manifestation of his genius that spoke when the penitents and sacrificers came before Tohil, and what they brought and burned was not great. All they burned before their gods was resin, just bits of pitchy bark, along with marigolds.

And when Tohil spoke now it was only his genius. When the gods taught procedures to the penitents and sacrificers, they said this when they spoke:

"This very place has become our mountain, our plain. Now that we are yours, our day and our birth have become great, because all the peoples are yours, all the tribes. And since we are still your companions, even in your citadel, we shall give you procedures:

"Do not reveal us to the tribes when they burn with envy over us. They are truly numerous now, so don't you let us be hunted down, but rather give the creatures of the grasses and grains to us, such as the female deer and female birds. Please come give us a little of their blood, take pity on us. And set the pelts of the deer aside, save them. These are for disguises, for deception. They will become deerskin bundles, and they will also serve as our surrogates before the tribes. When you are asked:

'Where is Tohil?' then you will show them the deerskin bundle, yet you won't be giving yourselves away. And there is still more for you to do. You will become great in your very being. Defeat all the tribes. They must bring blood and lymph before us, they must come to embrace us. They belong to us already," said Tohil, Auilix, and Hacauitz. They had a youthful appearance when they saw them, when they came to burn offerings before them.

So then began the hunting of the young of all the birds and deer; they were taken in the hunt by the penitents and sacrificers.

And when they got hold of the birds and fawns, they would then go to anoint the mouth of the stone of Tohil or Auilix with the blood of the deer or bird. And the bloody drink was drunk by the gods. The stone would speak at once when the penitents and sacrificers arrived, when they went to make their burnt offerings.

They did the very same thing before the deerskin bundles: they burned resin, and they also burned marigolds and stevia. There was a deerskin bundle for each of the gods, which was displayed there on the mountain.

They didn't occupy their houses during the day, but just walked in the mountains. And this was their food: just the larva of the yellow jacket, the larva of the wasp, and the larva of the bee, which they hunted. As yet there wasn't anything good to eat or good to drink. Also, it wasn't obvious how to get to their houses, nor was it obvious where their wives stayed.

And the tribes were already densely packed, settling down one by one, with each division of a tribe gathering itself together. Now they were crowding the roads; already their roadways were obvious.

As for Jaguar Quitze, Jaguar Night, Not Right Now, and Dark Jaguar, it wasn't obvious where they were. When they saw the people of the tribes passing by on the roads, that was when they would get up on the mountain peaks, just crying out with the cry of the coyote and the cry of the fox. And they would make the cries of the puma and jaguar, whenever they saw the tribes out walking in numbers. The tribes were saying:

"It's just a coyote crying out," and "Just a fox."

"Just a puma. Just a jaguar."

In the minds of all the tribes, it was as if humans weren't involved. They did it just as a way of decoying the tribes; that was what their hearts desired. They did it so that the tribes wouldn't get really frightened just yet; that was what they intended when they cried out with the cry of the puma and the cry of the jaguar. And then, when they saw just one or two people out walking, they intended to overwhelm them.

Each day, when they came back to their houses and wives, they brought just the same things—yellow jacket larvae, wasp larvae, and bee larvae—and gave them to their wives, each day. And when they went before Tohil, Auilix, and Hacauitz, they thought to themselves:

"They are Tohil, Auilix, and Hacauitz, yet we only give them the blood of deer and birds, we only take stitches in our ears and our elbows when we ask for our strength and our manhood from Tohil, Auilix, and Hacauitz. Who will take care of the death of the tribes? Should we just kill them one by one?" they said among themselves.

And when they went before Tohil, Auilix, and Hacauitz, they took stitches in their ears and their elbows in front of the gods. They spilled their blood, they poured gourdfuls into the mouths of the stones. But these weren't really stones: each one became like a boy when they arrived, happy once again over the blood.

And then came a further sign as to what the penitents and sacrificers should do:

"You must win a great many victories. Your right to do this came from over there at Tulan, when you brought us here," they were told. Then the matter of the suckling was set forth, at the place called Stagger, and the blood that would result from it, the rainstorm of blood, also became a gift for Tohil, along with Auilix and Hacauitz.

Now here begins the abduction of the people of the tribes by Jaguar Quitze, Jaguar Night, Not Right Now, and Dark Jaguar.

Contrasting Monotheism and Henotheism

Some scholars have argued that the Egyptian pharaoh, Amenhotep IV, also known as Akhenaten, was the first monotheist, and that his cult to the Sun Disk, or Aten, was a monotheistic expression. Some have even argued that the cult to the Aten might have been an inspiration to Moses. These scholars point to Psalm 104 as proof of the connection between the two religion expressions. But Akhenaten was not a monotheist, nor was his cult monotheistic—it is a form of henotheism. Most polytheistic religions have a henotheistic phenomenon in which one god is stressed over the others, or the other gods become aspects of the one god. In Hinduism, Shiva Sharabha is a henotheistic manifestation. But in henotheism, though the number of gods is reduced to one, the cosmos and its functioning remain unchanged. Moreover, Akhenaten always worshipped his father as a god, and considered himself to be a god as well. But that aside, the Aten and his universe remain unchanged from what had gone on before. "The Great Hymn to the Aten," for example, reveals a cosmic system that functions as it always had: The Aten has his daily cycles of rising and sleeping; when he sleeps, the forces of the demonic are unleashed; he gets tired; he is the physical sun itself; the Aten is an integral part of nature; other gods are mentioned in the hymn as well, like Hapy and Ma'at. As some Egyptologists point out, the cult of the Aten, which had been developing for some time, was a natural development out of Egyptian religion, rather than a new religion itself. The contrast of this hymn to the Hebrew Psalm 104 is striking. In this Psalm God is not a part of nature, but above it; God made the sun and he controls all that is in the world itself; God has no physical needs, including sleep; there are no demonic forces—everything that He made is good, including the creatures of the night, all of which worship Him. This evidence supports Kaufmann's argument that monotheism presents a worldview that is the exact opposite of polytheism, even polytheism reduced to one main god.

>> 47. The Great Hymn to the Aten

[c. 1370–1360 B.C.E.]

(1) Adoration of *Re-Harakhti-who-rejoices-in-lightland In-his-name-Shu-who-is-Aten,* living forever; the great living Aten who is in jubilee, the lord of all that the Disk encircles, lord of sky, lord of earth, lord of the house-of-Aten in Akhet-Aten; (and of) the King of Upper and Lower Egypt, who lives by Maat, the Lord of the Two Lands, *Neferkheprure, Sole-one-of-Re;* the Son of Re who lives by Maat, the Lord of Crowns, *Akhenaten,* great in his lifetime; (and) his beloved great Queen, the Lady of the Two Lands, *Nefernefru-Aten Nefertiti,* who lives in health and youth

---

Source: "The Great Hymn to the Aten," in *Ancient Egyptian literature: A Book of Readings,* v. 2: *The New Kingdom,* edited by Miriam Lichtheim (Berkeley: University of California Press, 1976), 96–9.

forever. The Vizier, the Fanbearer on the right of the King, — — —[Ay]; he says:

Splendid you rise in heaven's lightland,
O living Aten, creator of life!
When you have dawned in eastern lightland,
You fill every land with your beauty.
You are beauteous, great, radiant,
High over every land;
Your rays embrace the lands,
To the limit of all that you made.
Being Re, you reach their limits,
You bend them <for> the son whom you love;
Though you are far, your rays are on earth,
Though one sees you, you strides are unseen.

When you set in western lightland,
Earth is in darkness as if in death;
One sleeps in chambers, heads covered,
One eye does not see another.
Were they robbed of their goods,
That are under their heads,
People would not remark it.
Every lion comes from its den,
All the serpents bite;
Darkness hovers, earth is silent,
As their maker rests in lightland.

Earth brightens when you dawn in lightland,
When you shine as Aten of daytime;
As you dispel the dark,
As you cast your rays,
The Two Lands are in festivity.
Awake they stand on their feet,
You have roused them;
Bodies cleansed, (5) clothed,

Their arms adore your appearance.
The entire land sets out to work,
All beasts browse on their herbs;
Trees, herbs are sprouting,
Birds fly from their nests,
Their wings greeting your *ka*.
All flocks frisk on their feet,
All that fly up and alight,
They live when you dawn for them.
Ships fare north, fare south as well,
Roads lie open when you rise;
The fish in the river dart before you,
Your rays are in the midst of the sea.

Who makes seed grow in women,
Who creates people from sperm;
Who feeds the son in his mother's womb,
Who soothes him to still his tears.
Nurse in the womb,
Giver of breath,
To nourish all that he made.
When he comes from the womb to breathe,
On the day of his birth,
You open wide his mouth,
You supply his needs.
When the chick in the egg speaks in the shell,
You give him breath within to sustain him;
When you have made him complete,
To break out from the egg,
He comes out from the egg,
To announce his completion,
Walking on his legs he comes from it.

How many are your deeds,
Though hidden from sight,
O Sole God beside whom there is none!

You made the earth as you wished, you alone,
All peoples, herds, and flocks;
All upon earth that walk on legs,
All on high that fly on wings,
The lands of Khor and Kush,
The land of Egypt.
You set every man in his place,
You supply their needs;
Everyone has his food,
His lifetime is counted.
Their tongues differ in speech,
Their characters likewise;
Their skins are distinct,
For you distinguished the peoples.

You made Hapy in *dat*,
You bring him when you will,
To nourish the people,
For you made them for yourself.
Lord of all who toils for them,
Lord of all lands who shines for them,
Aten of daytime, great in glory!
All distant lands, you make them live,
You made a heavenly Hapy descend for them;
(10) He makes waves on the mountains like
  the sea,
To drench their fields and their towns.
How excellent are your ways, O Lord of eternity!
A Hapy from heaven for foreign peoples,
And all lands' creatures that walk on legs,
For Egypt the Hapy who comes from *dat*.

Your rays nurse all fields,
When you shine they live, they grow for you;
You made the seasons to foster all that you
  made,
Winter to cool them, heat that they taste you.
You made the far sky to shine therein,
To behold all that you made;
You alone, shining in your form of living Aten,
Risen, radiant, distant, near.
You made millions of forms from yourself alone,
Towns, villages, fields, the river's course;
All eyes observe you upon them,
For you are the Aten of daytime on high.
. . . . . . — — —. . .

You are in my heart,
There is no other who knows you,
Only your son, *Neferkheprure, Sole-one-of-Re,*
Whom you have taught your ways and your
  might.
<Those on> earth come from your hand as you
  made them,
When you have dawned they live,
When you set they die;
You yourself are lifetime, one lives by you.
All eyes are on <your> beauty until you set,
All labor ceases when you rest in the west;
When you rise you stir [everyone] for the King,
Every leg is on the move since you founded
  the earth.
You rouse them for your son who came from
  your body,
The King who lives by Maat, the Lord of the
  Two Lands,
Neferkheprure, Sole-one-of-Re,
The Son of Re who lives by Maat, the Lord of
  crowns,
Akhenaten, great in his lifetime;
(And) the great Queen whom he loves, the Lady
  of the Two Lands,
Nefer-nefru-Aten Nefertiti, living forever.

>> 48. Psalm 104

[ANCIENT HYMN; FINAL ARRANGEMENT IN
SIXTH CENTURY B.C.E.]

Psalm 104

1   Bless the LORD, O my soul.

O LORD my God, you are very great.

You are clothed with honor and majesty,

2   wrapped in light as with a garment.

You stretch out the heavens like a tent,

3   you set the beams of your chambers on the
waters,

you make the clouds your chariot,

you ride on the wings of the wind,

4   you make the winds your messengers,

fire and flame your ministers.

5   You set the earth on its foundations,

so that it shall never be shaken.

6   You cover it with the deep as with a garment;

the waters stood above the mountains.

7   At your rebuke they flee;

at the sound of your thunder they take
to flight.

8   They rose up to the mountains, ran down to
the valleys

to the place that you appointed for them.

9   You set a boundary that they may not pass,

so that they might not again cover the
earth.

10   You make springs gush forth in the valleys;

they flow between the hills,

11   giving drink to every wild animal;

the wild asses quench their thirst.

12   By the streams the birds of the air have their
habitation;

they sing among the branches.

13   From your lofty abode you water the
mountains;

the earth is satisfied with the fruit of your
work.

14   You cause the grass to grow for the cattle,

and plants for people to use,

to bring forth food from the earth,

15   and wine to gladden the human heart,

oil to make the face shine,

and bread to strengthen the human heart.

16   The trees of the LORD are watered
abundantly,

the cedars of Lebanon that he planted.

17   In them the birds build their nests;

the stork has its home in the fir trees.

18   The high mountains are for the wild goats;

the rocks are a refuge for the coneys.

19   You have made the moon to mark the
seasons;

the sun knows its time for setting.

20   You make darkness, and it is night,

when all the animals of the forest come
creeping out.

21   The young lions roar for their prey,

seeking their food from God.

22   When the sun rises, they withdraw

and lie down in their dens.

23   People go out to their work

and to their labor until the evening.

24   O LORD, how manifold are your works!

In wisdom you have made them all;

the earth is full of your creatures.

25   Yonder is the sea, great and wide,

creeping things innumerable are there,

Source: Psalm 104, *The New Oxford Annotated Bible,* (Oxford: Oxford University Press), 762–4.

living things both small and great.

26 There go the ships,

and Leviathan that you formed to sport in it.

27 These all look to you

to give them their food in due season;

28 when you give to them, they gather it up;

when you open your hand, they are filled with good things.

29 When you hide your face, they are dismayed;

when you take away their breath, they die and return to their dust.

30 When you send forth your spirit, they are created;

and you renew the face of the ground.

31 May the glory of the LORD endure forever;

may the LORD rejoice in his works—

32 who looks on the earth and it trembles,

who touches the mountains and they smoke.

33 I will sing to the LORD as long as I live;

I will sing praise to my God while I have being.

34 May my meditation be pleasing to him,

for I rejoice in the LORD.

35 Let sinners be consumed from the earth,

and let the wicked be on more.

Bless the LORD, O my soul.

Praise the LORD!

>> Mastering the Material

1. Yehezkel Kaufmann argues that the essence of polytheism has nothing to do with the plurality of gods. What does Kaufmann identify as the critical feature that characterizes the polytheistic universe? What other characteristics does he see?

2. How does the evidence from Hesiod, the *Popol Vuh,* and ancient India illustrate the key points of Kaufmann's analysis? From these sources, how would you characterize the nature and functioning of the polytheistic universe?

3. Does Plato's characterization of ancient polytheistic religion in the *Euthyphro* coincide with Kaufmann's analysis?

4. Compare and contrast the attitudes toward the universe in the "Hymn to the Aten" and Psalm 104. Can the religion of Akhenaten be considered monotheistic? Why or why not?

>> Making Connections

1. In Part 1 you read many ancient texts that concerned the gods and religion. How do these texts help illustrate Kaufmann's main points concerning polytheism and the polytheistic universe?

2. The gods and religion came up frequently in the ancient sources that you read on the city-states and other forms of polity in Part 1. Think about the material in Chapter 6: Why was religion so important to ancient peoples and rulers? What was the connection between religion and the political order? What was the connection between religion and society?

Chapter 7

The Axial Age

New Reflections on Society, Religion, and Knowledge

One of the principal features of the past that historians study is the way societies change over time. When changes are rapid and radical, we call them "revolutions." While we usually think of modern political revolutions, revolutionary changes occurred in the premodern world as well. The Neolithic agricultural revolution discussed in Part 1 was a radical change that affected a large part of the globe. Another significant revolution in antiquity was the sudden spurt of intellectual creativity and development across a region that stretched from Greece in the west to China in the east. Rivaling the later Enlightenment and the Age of Reason in its significance, these changes were collectively labeled the "Axial Period," or "Axial Age" by philosopher Karl Jaspers. In this chapter we explore the Axial Age in Eurasia alongside analogous intellectual developments in the New World. Through the sources, we see how individuals in each of several societies in this period provided intellectual alternatives to the existing systems of thought.

Jaspers observed that between about 600 and 200 B.C.E. parallel but totally independent cultural and intellectual transformations swept Eurasia. Thinkers arose in four, possibly five, societies who not only openly challenged the old ways of thought and action but also provided new visions to replace those old ways. In Greece, China, India, Israel, and arguably Persia, these critics and visionaries promoted new points of view that helped to redefine their own cultures and civilizations for all time. Central to their critique was a challenge to the polytheistic way of structuring and explaining the universe. The old orthodoxies, the old order—whether embodied in priests and ritual, or in religiously sanctioned steel-fisted political and social hierarchies—were both questioned and reimagined. Despite political tensions and antagonism, these new visions contributed to the intellectual foundation for the new politics that were coming into being.

Around 585 B.C.E. in the *polis* of Miletus on the Ionian coast, the philosopher Thales predicted an eclipse of the sun. In so doing he began what historians call the Ionian Intellectual Revolution, a revolution that marks one of the most important cultural shifts in Western history. While Thales and other Ionian thinkers did not attack the gods or religion itself, they did question and challenge the polytheistic notion of the universe. Natural phenomena, like eclipses, lightning, or plagues, were not caused by Zeus or Apollo, they suggested, but occurred according to natural laws. They argued that the universe was orderly and rational, and that it could be understood and explained by reason and observation. By setting aside supernatural explanations and unquestioned traditional authority, a new method of thinking and discourse evolved over the course of the sixth century and beyond. Since no one now had a monopoly on wisdom, new groups emerged in Greek society with alternative points of view to present for discussion to a wider audience—the word often used for this contending of ideas was *agōn,* or "struggle," "athletic contest." In this context speculative philosophers emerged to explain both ethics and the natural world. With them came the birth of Western philosophy and science, as well as the teaching profession. Likewise the medical doctor, in rejecting the divine origin of disease, laid the foundation for Western medicine. And finally, the historian challenged the role of the gods in human affairs, and so replaced the epic poet to explain the past; the historian provided a secular rather than divine explanation for human actions and events. Thucydides, a leading Athenian politician and historian, exemplifies the new rational spirit in exploring and understanding human events. Not all Greeks, however, would follow the new thinking. In 413 B.C.E., during the Peloponnesian War, Athenian panic over an eclipse of the moon, coupled with dire warnings from the soothsayers, resulted in a disastrous decision to delay evacuation from Sicily and contributed to their total defeat there at the hands of the Syracusans. Nevertheless, the intellectual revolution that started in Ionia at the beginning of the sixth century continued for centuries, laying the groundwork for thought and development in the region.

China underwent a similar intellectual transformation in the same period. Within the context of the disintegration of the Zhou Dynasty over the course of the Spring and Autumn Period (770–481 B.C.E.) and then China's collapse into violence and chaos in the Warring States Period (around 403–221 B.C.E.), a group of thinkers arose akin to those found in Greece: the "Hundred Schools" of philosophers. As in the Ionian Intellectual Revolution and its aftermath, a burst of creative energy swept China. In response to political change, social upheaval, and violence across the region, individuals sought new meanings and new explanations to the world around them. **Daoism,** with its philosophy of withdrawal from the world, and **Legalism,** with what some considered a rigid if not inhumane adherence to laws and their execution, are two of the approaches that emerged at this time. Confucius, our example of the Axial Age in East Asia, responded even differently to the changing political conditions and intellectual currents of his age. All of these thinkers would profoundly affect Chinese civilization, establishing, as the eminent historian of China John Fairbank notes, the very basis of thought for China from that point on.

Like Greece and China, the Indian subcontinent experienced its intellectual flowering in the Axial Age as well. While the philosophers of China were responding to a culture in transition, if not collapse, the response in India was quite different. The migrations of Aryan speakers into India in the second millennium B.C.E. brought a new religion and a new social structure and hierarchy into the subcontinent. Vedic religion—with its elaborate set of rites and sacrifices, a powerful Brahmin priesthood, and the caste system—dominated much of Indian life for centuries. But economic and social conditions were changing here, too. The existing orthodoxy was attacked from within and without, often in very subtle ways. Such works as the *Upanishads* provided a new understanding of life and religion, introducing philosophy into Vedic religion in a way that the Greeks never did. While the thinking in the *Upanishads* largely complemented the existing religious understanding, other schools of thought directly challenged that system of values. Mahavira (the founder of the Jain sect) and the Buddha propounded an even stronger alternative to the existing system of thought and set forth the greatest challenge to the polytheistic ordering of the cosmos.

And finally, new thinkers also arose in the Middle East. While Mesopotamia, as Jaspers notes, was largely absent from the sweeping intellectual changes occurring elsewhere in the Axial Age, cultures on either side of it were not. To the east, in Persia, it is quite possible that Zoroaster began to preach his new religion. But the dates of this teacher and the very translations of the early texts are the subject of great scholarly dispute. Moreover, it is not entirely clear whether Cyrus (r. 557–530 B.C.E.) and his successors followed Zoroastrian teachings exclusively. And to the west, in the former kingdom of Judah, a new Jerusalem was rebuilt after the Exile, and a new prophetic vision was proclaimed in works like *Isaiah*.

The Axial Age Defined

Shortly after the Second World War, the German philosopher Karl Jaspers published The Origin and Goal of History. *In this work he put forward a model for understanding the nature and consequences of an intellectual revolution that swept Eurasia from around 600 to 200 B.C.E., which he dubbed the "Axial Period," or "Axial Age." While there are some serious flaws in his analysis, his overall observations and thesis about the nature and scope of the changes that took place have been widely accepted by scholars of both regional and world history. Jaspers' ideas are useful for conceptualizing and understanding some of the biggest intellectual changes ever to occur simultaneously on this landmass. Similarly, while this burst of imagination and vision happened independently in each culture, it nonetheless represents one of the first truly "world events" in history. In this passage Jaspers emphasizes some of the salient characteristics of this intellectual revolution, noting the role of speculative thought and reason over myth. Moreover, he posits that the philosophers and the prophets, both of whom emerged at this time, stressed a new kind of spirituality and emphasized justice over religious form and ritual. In their critique of the existing way of viewing the world, these new thinkers, Jaspers argues, created new cultural systems that helped redefine their respective societies.*

>> 49. The Origin and Goal of History

KARL JASPERS [1953]

The most extraordinary events are concentrated in this period. Confucius and Lao-tse were living in China, all the schools of Chinese philosophy came into being, including those of Mo-ti, Chuang-tse, Lieh-tsu and a host of others; India produced the Upanishads and Buddha and, like China, ran the whole gamut of philosophical possibilities down to scepticism, to materialism, sophism and nihilism; in Iran Zarathustra taught a challenging view of the world as a struggle between good

Source: Karl Jaspers, *The Origin and Goal of History,* translated by Michael Bullock (New Haven: Yale University Press, 1953), 2–3, 6–7.

and evil; in Palestine the prophets made their appearance, from Elijah, by way of Isaiah and Jeremiah to Deutero-Isaiah; Greece witnessed the appearance of Homer, of the philosophers—Parmenides, Heraclitus and Plato—of the tragedians, Thucydides and Archimedes. Everything implied by these names developed during these few centuries almost simultaneously in China, India, and the West, without any one of these regions knowing of the others.

What is new about this age, in all three areas of the world, is that man becomes conscious of Being as a whole, of himself and his limitations. He experiences the terror of the world and his own powerlessness. He asks radical questions. Face to face with the void he strives for liberation and redemption. By consciously recognising his limits he sets himself the highest goals. He experiences absoluteness in the depth of selfhood and in the lucidity of transcendence.

All this took place in reflection. Consciousness became once more conscious of itself, thinking became its own object. Spiritual conflicts arose, accompanied by attempts to convince others through the communication of thoughts, reasons and experiences. The most contradictory possibilities were essayed. Discussion, the formation of parties and the division of the spiritual realm into opposites which nonetheless remained related to one another, created unrest and movement to the very brink of spiritual chaos.

In this age were born the fundamental categories within which we still think today, and the beginnings of the world religions, by which human beings still live, were created. The step into universality was taken in every sense.

As a result of this process, hitherto unconsciously accepted ideas, customs and conditions were subjected to examination, questioned and liquidated. Everything was swept into the vortex. In so far as the traditional substance still possessed vitality and reality, its manifestations were clarified and thereby transmuted.

The *Mythical Age,* with its tranquility and self-evidence, was at an end. The Greeks, Indian and Chinese philosophers were unmythical in their decisive insights, as were the prophets in their ideas of God. Rationality and rationally clarified experience launched a struggle against the myth (*logos* against *mythos*); a further struggle developed for the transcendence of the One God against non-existent demons, and finally an ethical rebellion took place against the unreal figures of the gods. Religion was rendered ethical, and the majesty of the deity thereby increased. The myth, on the other hand, became the material of a language which expressed by it something very different from what it had originally signified: it was turned into parable. Myths were remoulded, were understood at a new depth during this transition, which was myth-creating after a new fashion, at the very moment when the myth as a whole was destroyed. The old mythical world slowly sank into oblivion, but remained as a background to the whole through the continued belief of the mass of the people (and was subsequently able to gain the upper hand over the wide areas).

This overall modification of humanity may be termed *spiritualisation.* The unquestioned grasp on life is loosened, the calm of polarities becomes the disquiet of opposites and antinomies. Man is no longer enclosed within himself. He becomes uncertain of himself and thereby open to new and boundless possibilities. He can hear and understand what no one had hitherto asked or proclaimed. The unheard-of becomes manifest. Together with his world and his own self, Being becomes sensible to man, but not with finality: the question remains.

For the first time *philosophers* appeared. Human beings dared to rely on themselves as individuals. Hermits and wandering thinkers in China, ascetics in India, philosophers in Greece and prophets in Israel all belong together, however much they may differ from each other in their beliefs, the contents of their thought and their inner dispositions. Man proved capable of contrasting himself inwardly with the entire universe. He discovered within himself the origin from which to raise himself above his own self and the world.

In *speculative thought* he lifts himself up towards Being itself, which is apprehended without duality in the disappearance of subject and object, in the coincidence of opposites. That which is experienced in the loftiest flights of the spirit as a coming-to-oneself within Being, or as *unio mystica*, as becoming one with the Godhead, or as becoming a tool for the will of God is expressed in an ambiguous and easily misunderstood form in objectifying speculative thought. [...]

Assuming this view of the Axial Period to be correct, it would seem to throw a light upon the entire history of the world, in such a way as to reveal something like a structure of world history. Let me endeavor to adumbrate this structure:

(1) The *thousands of years old ancient civilisations* are everywhere brought to an end by the Axial Period, which melts them down, assimilates them or causes them to sink from view, irrespective of whether it was the same peoples or others that became the bearers of the new cultural forms. Pre-Axial cultures, like those of Babylon, Egypt, the Indus valley and the aboriginal culture of China, may have been magnificent in their own way, but they appear in some manner unawakened. The ancient cultures only persist in those elements which enter the Axial Period and become part of the new beginning.

Measured against the lucid humanity of the Axial Period, a strange veil seems to lie over the most ancient cultures preceding it, as though man had not yet really come to himself. This fact is not obscured by isolated beginnings, moving in themselves, but without effect on the whole or on what followed (such as the Egyptian discourse of a man tired of life with his soul, the Babylonian psalms of repentance and the Gilgamesh). The monumental element in religion and religious art, and the extensive State-formations and juridical creations corresponding to it, are objects of awe and admiration to the consciousness of the Axial Period; they are even taken as models (by Confucius and Plato, for instance), but they are seen in a new light that transmutes their meaning.

Thus the imperial idea, which gains new force toward the end of the Axial Period and terminates this era in the political domain, was a heritage from the ancient civilisations. But whereas it originally constituted a culture-creating principle, it now becomes the means by which a declining culture is stabilised by being laid in its coffin. It is as though the principle that once bore mankind upward, despite its factually depotic nature, had broken through afresh in the form of conscious despotism, but this time merely to preserve a culture in icy rigidity.

The Axial Age Refined

The Roman historian Arnaldo Momigliano refines Jasper's thesis further, both simplifying it and adding another critical element. He suggests that all societies that were a part of this "age of criticism" had some things in common: a degree of literacy, elaborate urban planning, advanced economic development, and a cosmopolitan or international aspect to their society. The visions of the new thinkers, he argues, are more universal and more abstract than any that came before, and were often at odds with the contemporary political and religious authorities. That Confucius never received a much-desired court appointment is no mystery, nor are the attacks on the Buddha a surprise. Critiques and alternatives to existing modes of religious and political reality are rarely appreciated by those in authority, whether in the ancient world or later, during the Enlightenment of the Early Modern Period.

>> 50. Alien Wisdom: The Limits of Hellenization

Arnaldo Momigliano [1975]

The novelty of such a situation will be more apparent if we compare with it what can be called the classical situation of the ancient world between 600 and 300 B.C. It has become a commonplace, after Karl Jaspers' *Vom Ursprung und Ziel der Geschichte*—the first original book on history to appear in post-war Germany in 1949—to speak of the *Archsenzeit,* of the axial age, which included the China of Confucius and Lao-Tse, the India of Buddha, the Iran of Zoroaster, the Palestine of the Prophets and the Greece of the philosophers, the tragedians and the historians. There is a very real element of truth in this formulation. All these civilizations display literacy, a complex political organization combining central government and local authorities, elaborate town-planning, advanced metal technology and the practice of international diplomacy. In all these civilizations there is a profound tension between political powers and intellectual movements. Everywhere one notices attempts to introduce greater purity, greater justice, greater perfection and a more universal explanation of things. New models of reality, either mystically or prophetically or rationally apprehended, are propounded as a criticism of, and alternative to, the prevailing models. We are in the age of criticism—and social criticism transpires even from the involuted imagery of Zoroaster's Gathas. The personality of the critics is bound to emerge: they are the masters whose thoughts still count today and whose names we remember.

It is not for me here to try to account for the common features of movements so different in nature as those we have mentioned. What matters to us is that they were independent of each other and, to the best of our knowledge, ignored each other.

The Birth of History in Greece

The invention and writing of history—the systematic examination of the past—was one of the greatest products of the Ionian Intellectual Revolution. The historian challenged the role of the gods in human affairs. Herodotus, sometimes called "The Father of History," began his examination of the Persian Wars by saying, "This is the exposition of the research ("historia") of Herodotus of Halicarnasus ..." In a single moment Herodotus invented a method for exploring the past as well as a whole new prose genre. He also created a new explanation for the events in the life of the community: It was not the gods but history that explained what happened and why. By taking the gods out of human affairs, he, like the Ionian philosophers before him, challenged the traditional system of thinking about how and why events happened in the lives of human beings. Thucydides, a near contemporary of Herodotus, exemplifies this new rational spirit at the beginning of his history of the Peloponnesian War when he explains his basic method and approach. He rejected the explanations of the epic poets like Homer, the chroniclers, and, implicitly, even Herodotus himself, whom Thucydides considered to be still too closely associated with the mythic and the fabulous. Thucydides specifically rejected omens and the gods, instead looking to human causes for the disastrous events that befell the Athenians and the other Greeks. History, as a secular, desacralized examination of the past is a rare cultural artifact

Source: Arnaldo Momigliano, *Alien Wisdom: The Limits of Hellenization* (Cambridge: Cambridge University Press, 1975), 8–9.

in antiquity. Although the Chinese chronicler Sima Qian came very close to inventing "history," as the Court Astrologer he remained too closely tied to the existing theories and methods of looking at time and events to chart a totally new way of explaining the past. Despite his ambivalence about supernatural explanations of the victor's justice—he looked at tragic heroes as victims of both their own personal flaws and the (not always fair) Mandate of Heaven—Sima Qian continued the traditional methods of chronicling and accounting for past events within the context of cosmic astrological cycles in his Shi Ji (Records of the Grant Astrologer-Chronicler). *Herodotus represents a strong break with the previous way of looking at past generations, while at the same time providing the basis for a whole new approach. In China, that break with the tradition had to wait until 710 c.e., when a complete rejection of supernatural interpretations of history was proposed by Liu Zhiji (661–621 c.e.) in his* Shi Tong (Comprehensive history).

>> 51. History of the Peloponnesian War

THUCYDIDES [LAST THIRD OF THE FIFTH CENTURY B.C.E.]

Thucydides the Athenian wrote the history of the war fought between Athens and Sparta, beginning the account at the very outbreak of the war, in the belief that it was going to be a great war and more worth writing about than any of those which had taken place in the past. My belief was based on the fact that the two sides were at the very height of their power and preparedness, and I saw, too, that the rest of the Hellenic world was committed to one side or the other; even those who were not immediately engaged were deliberating on the courses which they were to take later. This was the greatest disturbance in the history of the Hellenes, affecting also a large part of the non-Hellenic world, and indeed, I might almost say, the whole of mankind. For though I have found it impossible, because of its remoteness in time, to acquire a really precise knowledge of the distant past or even of the history preceding our own period, yet, after looking back into it as far as I can, all the evidence leads me to conclude that these periods were not great periods either in warfare or in anything else. [...]

However, I do not think that one will be far wrong in accepting the conclusions I have reached from the evidence which I have put forward. It is better evidence than that of the poets, who exaggerate the importance of their themes, or of the prose chroniclers, who are less interested in telling the truth than in catching the attention of their public, whose authorities cannot be checked, and whose subject-matter, owing to the passage of time, is mostly lost in the unreliable streams of mythology. We may claim instead to have used only the plainest evidence and to have reached conclusions which are reasonably accurate, considering that we have been dealing with ancient history. As for this present war, even though people are apt to think that the war in which they are fighting is the greatest of all wars and, when it is over, to relapse again into their admiration of the past, nevertheless, if one looks at the facts themselves, one will see that this was the greatest war of all.

In this history I have made use of set speeches some of which were delivered just before and others during the war. I have found it difficult to remember the precise words used in the speeches which I listened to myself and my various informants have experienced the same difficulty; so my method has been, while keeping

Source: Thucydides, *History of the Peloponnesian War*, translated by Rex Warner (Baltimore: Penguin Press, 1972), 35, 47–9.

as closely as possible to the general sense of the words that were actually used, to make the speakers say what, in my opinion, was called for by each situation.

And with regard to my factual reporting of the events of the war I have made it a principle not to write down the first story that came my way, and not even to be guided by my own general impressions; either I was present myself at the events which I have described or else I heard of them from eye-witnesses whose reports I have checked with as much thoroughness as possible. Not that even so the truth was easy to discover: different eye-witnesses give different accounts of the same events, speaking out of partiality for one side or the other or else from imperfect memories. And it may well be that my history will seem less easy to read because of the absence in it of a romantic element. It will be enough for me, however, if these words of mine are judged useful by those who want to understand clearly the events which happened in the past and which (human nature being what it is) will, at some time or other and in much the same ways, be repeated in the future. My work is not a piece of writing designed to meet the taste of an immediate public, but was done to last forever.

The greatest war in the past was the Persian War; yet in this war the decision was reached quickly as a result of two naval battles and two battles on land. The Peloponnesian War, on the other hand, not only lasted for a long time, but throughout its course brought with it unprecedented suffering for Hellas. Never before had so many cities been captured and then devastated, whether by foreign armies or by Hellenic powers themselves (some of these cities, after capture, were resettled with new inhabitants); never had there been so many exiles; never such loss of life—both in the actual warfare and in internal revolutions. Old stories of past prodigies, which had not found much confirmation in recent experience, now became credible. Wide areas, for instance, were affected by violent earthquakes; there were more frequent eclipses of the sun than had ever been recorded before; in various parts of the country there were extensive droughts followed by famine; and there was the plague which did more harm and destroyed more life than almost any other single factor. All these calamities fell together upon the Hellenes after the outbreak of war.

War began when the Athenians and Peloponnesians broke the Thirty Years Truce which had been made after the capture of Euboea. As to the reasons why they broke the truce, I propose first to give an account of the causes of complaint which they had against each other and of the specific instances where their interests clashed: this is in order that there should be no doubt in anyone's mind about what led to this great war falling upon the Hellenes. But the real reason for the war is, in my opinion, most likely to be disguised by such an argument. What made war inevitable was the growth of Athenian power and the fear which this caused in Sparta. As for the reasons for breaking the truce and declaring war which were openly expressed by each side, are as follows.

The Birth of Philosophy in China

Jaspers cogently argues that China was as much a part of the Axial Age as Greece or India. The "Hundred Schools" of philosophers produced a wide range of philosophic discourse in this period. One important school of thought was Legalism. *During the violence and chaos of the Warring States Period, the Legalist philosophers arose to assert the primacy of the law and its execution over any other consideration. They maintained that the law had to be applied to all—except the king—equally, regardless of status, and that its application must be uniform and consistent, without regard to any mitigating circumstances. The rigid, formulaic execution of laws, and the often unreasonably harsh penalties that went with them, worked well to establish order, but fell short of what many thinkers considered to be justice and virtue. Preceding the Legalists in the Spring and Autumn Period was another school of thinking initiated by one of the greatest Chinese philosophers of all time, Confucius (551–479 B.C.E.). The revolutionary quality and consequences of his thought would help to transform Chinese culture over the course of many centuries. But Confucius presents a paradox—his ostensible social and religious conservatism belie his critique and his vision. Like many of the Greek philosophers, Confucius refused to be drawn into discussions of the nature of religion and the afterlife (The Analects 3.11; 11.12). Like those philosophers, he asserted that everyone was obliged to perform right ritual, but unlike them he sometimes used that occasion to critique his contemporaries on social rather than religious grounds (The Analects 3.1). Moreover, like the Greek sophists, he stressed education and ethics, making them the foundation for good government and a virtuous life. His stress on humanity, justice, and the intellect was a direct attack on those in power, many of whom he considered to be usurpers and no better than bandits. Although Confucius looks back to a Golden Age of the Zhou Dynasty, he attacked the very basis of what current historians sometimes call the "feudal order" that had emerged in China: Hereditary privilege and a monopoly of violence did not bring virtue. His stress on education and reason as well as his belief in the perfectability of the human being brings Confucius to conclusions similar to those of Protagoras and other Greek philosophers, despite their separation by thousands of miles. Confucius' observations and comments were remembered and collected by his followers, and were compiled by them approximately seventy-five years after his death.*

>> 52. The Analects of Confucius

CONFUCIUS [AROUND 551–479 B.C.E.; COMPILED AROUND 400 B.C.E.]

4.1. The Master said: "It is beautiful to live amidst humanity. To choose a dwelling place destitute of humanity is hardly wise."

4.2. The Master said: "A man without humanity cannot long bear adversity and cannot long know joy. A good man rests in his humanity, a wise man profits from his humanity."

4.3. The Master said: "Only a good man can love people and hate people."

4.4. The Master said: "Seeking to achieve humanity leaves no room for evil."

4.5. The Master said: "Riches and rank are what every man craves; yet if the only way to obtain them goes against his principles, he should desist from such a pursuit. Poverty and obscurity are what every man hates; yet if the only escape from them goes against his principles, he should accept his lot. If a gentleman forsakes humanity, how can he make a name for himself? Never for a moment does a gentleman part from humanity; he clings to it through trials, he clings to it through tribulations." [...]

4.9. The Master said: "A scholar sets his heart on the Way; if he is ashamed of the shabby clothes and coarse food, he is not worth listening to." [...]

Source: Confucius, *The Analects of Confucius*, translated by Simon Leys (New York: W. W. Norton, 1997), 15–7, 30–1, 50, 60–1, 66, 75, 86–7.

4.14. The Master said: "Do not worry if you are without a position; worry lest you do not deserve a position. Do not worry if you are not famous; worry lest you do not deserve to be famous." [...]

4.16. The Master said: "A gentleman considers what is just; a small man considers what is expedient."

4.17. The Master said: "When you see a worthy man, seek to emulate him. When you see an unworthy man, examine yourself." [...]

7.8. The Master said: "I enlighten only the enthusiastic; I guide only the fervent. After I have lifted up one corner of a question, if the student cannot discover the other three, I do not repeat." [...]

7.12. The Master said: "If seeking wealth were a decent pursuit, I too would seek it, even if I had to work as a janitor. As it is, I'd rather follow my inclinations." [...]

7.16. The Master said: "Even though you have only coarse grain for food, water for drink, and your bent arm for a pillow, you may still be happy. Riches and honors without justice are to me as fleeting clouds." [...]

7.19. The Governor of She asked Zilu about Confucius. Zilu did not reply. The Master said: "Why did you not say 'He is the sort of man who, in his enthusiasm, forgets to eat, in his joy forgets to worry, and who ignores the approach of old age?"

7.20. The Master said: "For my part, I am not endowed with innate knowledge. I am simply a man who loves the past and who is diligent in investigating it."

7.21. The Master never talked of: miracles, violence, disorders, spirits. [...]

11.12. Zilu asked how to serve the spirits and gods. The Master said: "You are not yet able to serve men, how could you serve the spirits?"

Zilu said: "May I ask you about death?" The Master said: "You do not yet know life, how could you know death?" [...]

13.3. Zilu asked: "If the ruler of Wei were to entrust you with the government of the country, what would be your first initiative?" The Master said: "It would certainly be to rectify the names." Zilu said: "Really? Isn't this a little farfetched? What is this rectification for?" The Master said: "How boorish can you get! Whereupon a gentleman is incompetent, thereupon he should remain silent. If the names are not correct, language is without an object. When language is without an object, no affair can be effected. When no affair can be effected, rites and music wither. When rites and music wither, punishments and penalties miss their target. When punishments and penalties miss their target, the people do not know where they stand. Therefore, whatever a gentleman conceives of, he must be able to say [...]

13.4. Fan Chi asked Confucius to teach him agronomy. The Master said: "Better ask an old farmer." Fan Chi asked to be taught gardening. The Master said: "Better ask an old gardener."

Fan Chi left. The Master said: "What a vulgar man! If their betters cultivate the rites, the people will not dare to be disrespectful. If their betters cultivate justice, the people will not dare to be disobedient. If their betters cultivate good faith, the people will not dare to be mendacious. To such a country, people would flock from everywhere with their babies strapped to their backs. What is the use of agronomy?" [...]

14.2. The Master said: "A scholar who cares for his material comfort does not deserve to be called a scholar." [...]

15.8. The Master said: "When dealing with a man who is capable of understanding your teaching, if you do not teach him, you waste the man. When dealing with a man who is incapable of understanding your teaching, if you do teach him, you waste your teaching. A wise teacher wastes no man and wastes no teaching."

15.9. The Master said: "A righteous man, a man attached to humanity, does not seek life at the expense of his humanity; there are instances where he will give his life in order to fulfill his humanity."

15.10. Zigong asked how to practice humanity. The Master said: "A craftman who wishes to do good work must first sharpen his tools. In whatever country you may settle, offer your services to the most virtuous ministers and befriend those gentlemen who cultivate humanity." [...]

17.6 Zizhang asked Confucius about humanity. The Master said: "Whoever could spread the five practices everywhere in the world would implement humanity." "And what are these?" "Courtesy, tolerance, good faith, diligence, generosity. Courtesy wards off insults; tolerance wins all hearts; good faith inspires the trust of others; diligence ensures success; generosity confers authority upon others." [...]

17.8. The Master said: "Zilu, have you heard of the six qualities and their six perversions?" — "No." — "Sit down, I will tell you. The love of humanity without the love of learning degenerates into silliness. The love of intelligence without the love of learning degenerates into frivolity. The love of chivalry without the love of learning degenerates into banditry. The love of frankness without the love of learning degenerates into brutality. The love of valor without the love of learning degenerates into violence. The love of force without love of learning degenerates into anarchy."

A New Vision of Righteous Living from South Asia

Over the centuries the inhabitants of the subcontinent of India had developed elaborate social, political, intellectual, and religious systems. As we saw in The Laws of Manu, *these systems were closely tied to a polytheistic notion of the universe and to religious sanctions: The social order and the religious order were two sides of the same coin. But as times changed, and individuals and groups became unhappy with their place within this system, challenges were mounted. Some individuals sought a solution by withdrawing from the world to become ascetics. But the Buddha, who initially tried this approach, came to confront the reality of his society head on: His attack on the religious and social system of his time was both subtle and revolutionary. He ignored the caste system, the Brahmin priests with their sacrifices and rituals, and even the gods themselves, deeming all of these things to be unimportant and ultimately irrelevant to human happiness and fulfillment. While Confucius and even Socrates maintained the traditional religious systems of their respective societies, the Buddha struck at the very core of Vedic religion by eliminating priests, rituals, sacrifices, and the entire polytheistic worldview. By advocating what he called the "middle road" to right living, he put forth an alternative vision for human life and action. In his first sermon, "The Setting in Motion of the Wheel of the Law (Dharma)," the Buddha established what in many ways was an uncomplicated path to wisdom, and, at the same time, provided a statement of what he saw as fundamental truths. Rejecting both ascetic harshness and overindulgent hedonism, the Buddha provided a set of egalitarian teachings that required neither Vedic religion and priests nor the caste system. Even women became an integral part of the Buddhist movement. The present form of the Buddha's sermon was written down by his followers many generations after its delivery. Like many ancient philosophers, the Buddha did not write his teachings down, but these were passed down orally from student to student until finally committed to writing. The Buddha's philosophy, at first confined to a few, became, like Christianity and Islam later on, a worldwide movement, with missionaries spreading his teachings to central and eastern Asia, and with pilgrims visiting northern India to see sites associated with the Founder.*

>> 53. Buddha's First Sermon

[MID-SIXTH CENTURY B.C.E. SERMON;
WRITTEN DOWN SEVERAL GENERATIONS
LATER]

The Middle Path (c. 6th Century BCE)

Setting in Motion the Wheel of the Law

And the Blessed one thus addressed the five Bhikkhus [monks]. "There are two extremes, O Bhikkhus, which he who has given up the world, ought to avoid. What are these two extremes? a life given to pleasures, devoted to pleasures and lusts: this is degrading, sensual, vulgar, ignoble, and profitless; and a life given to mortifications: this is painful, ignoble, and profitless. By avoiding these two extremes, O Bhikkhus, the Tathagata [a title of Buddha meaning perhaps "he who has arrived at truth"] has gained the knowledge of the Middle Path which leads to insight, which leads to wisdom which conduces to calm, to knowledge, to the Sambodhi [total enlightenment], to Nirvana [state of release from samsara, the cycle of existence and rebirth].

The Eightfold Path

"Which, O Bhikkhus, is this Middle Path the knowledge of which the Tathagata has gained, which leads to insight, which leads to wisdom, which conduces to calm, to knowledge, to the Sambodhi, to Nirvana? It is the Holy Eightfold Path, namely,

Right Belief [understanding the truth about the universality of suffering and knowing the path to its extinction],

Right Aspiration [a mind free of ill will, sensuous desire and cruelty],

Right Speech [abstaining from lying, harsh language and gossip],

Right Conduct [avoiding killing, stealing and unlawful sexual intercourse],

Right Means of Livelihood [avoiding any occupation that brings harm directly or indirectly to any other living being],

Right Endeavor [avoiding unwholesome and evil things],

Right Memory [awareness in contemplation],

Right Meditation [concentration that ultimately reaches the level of a trance],

This, O Bhikkhus, is the Middle Path the knowledge of which the Tathagata has gained, which leads to insight, which leads to wisdom, which conduces to calm, to knowledge, to the Sambodhi, to Nirvana.

The Four Noble Truths

"This, O Bhikkhus, is the Noble Truth of Suffering: Birth is suffering; decay is suffering; illness is suffering; death is suffering. Presence of objects we hate, is suffering; Separation from objects we love, is suffering; not to obtain what we desire, is suffering. Briefly, . . . clinging to existence is suffering.

"This, O Bhikkhus, is the Noble Truth of Cause of suffering Thirst, which leads to rebirth, accompanied by pleasure and lust, finding its delight here and there. This thirst is threefold, namely, thirst for pleasure, thirst for existence, thirst for prosperity.

"This, O Bhikkhus, is the Noble Truth of the Cessation of suffering: it ceases with the complete cessation of this thirst,—a cessation which consists in the absence of every passion with the abandoning of this thirst, with doing away with it, with the deliverance from it, with the destruction of desire.

"This, O Bhikkhus, is the Noble Truth of the Path which leads to the cessation of suffering: that Holy Eightfold Path, that is to say, Right Belief, Right Aspiration, Right Speech, Right Conduct, Right Means of Livelihood, Right Endeavor, Right Memory, Right Meditation.

"As long, O Bhikkhus, as I did not possess with perfect purity this true knowledge and insight into these four Noble Truths...so long, O Bhikkhus, I knew that I had not yet obtained the highest, absolute Sambodhi in the world of men and gods....

"But since I possessed, O Bhikkhus, with perfect purity this true knowledge and insight

Source: "Buddha's First Sermon," version produced by Maitreya Sangha, permanent URL http://sangha.net/messengers/buddha.htm.

into these four Noble Truths...then I knew, O Bhikkhus, that I had obtained the highest, universal Sambodhi....

"And this knowledge and insight arose in my mind: "The emancipation of my mind cannot be lost; this is my last birth; hence I shall not be born again!"

The New Jerusalem

In 588 B.C.E. the king of Babylon attacked Jerusalem, the capital of the Hebrew kingdom of Judah. The city finally fell in 586 B.C.E., and with the destruction of both the Temple and the city itself, the population was deported to Babylonia. Almost half a century later Babylon itself fell to Cyrus the Great, king of Persia. This change of fortunes ultimately resulted in the return of the Jews from exile. Upon the reestablishment of Jerusalem, the kind of intellectual ferment that we saw in Greece, China, and India occurred in Judah as well. Nehemiah, *written about a century after the return, reflects the reestablishment of not only the physical city with its walls and gates but also both the religious and civic community, complete with new rules and definitions for membership within that community. While the reestablishment of the Temple and "the Law" were critical to the refounding of the Jewish nation, post-exilic Jerusalem also produced a reshaping of Judaism. The prophetic vision put forward in what biblical scholars call the* Second Isaiah *proclaims Yahweh as a universal God for all people to worship. Scholars argue that these passages show a revolutionary emphasis on ethical monotheism over ritual monotheism, on justice over temple sacrifices. A similar theme can be seen in* Zechariah *as well.*

>> 54. Nehemiah 3:1–7; 8:1–8; 13:1–27 and Isaiah 43; 44:28–45:22; and 66

[AROUND 450 B.C.E. AND AROUND 539 B.C.E.]

Nehemiah 3

Then the high priest Eliashib set to work with his fellow priests and rebuilt the Sheep Gate. They consecrated it and set up its doors; they consecrated it as far as the Tower of the Hundred and as far as the Tower of Hananel. And the men of Jericho built next to him. And next to them Zaccur son of Imri built.

The sons of Hassenaah built the Fish gate; they laid its beams and set up its doors, its bolts, and its bars. Next to them Meremoth son of Uriah son of Hakkoz made repairs. Next to them

Meshullam son of Berechiah son of Meshezabel made repairs. Next to them Zadok son of Baana made repairs. Next to them the Tekoites made repairs; but their nobles would not put their shoulders to the work of their Lord.

Joiada son of Paseah and Meshullam son of Besodeiah repaired the Old Gate; they laid its beams and set up its doors, its bolts, and its bars. Next to them repairs were made by Melatiah the Gibeonite and Jadon the Meronothite—the men of Gibeon and of Mizpah—who were under the jurisdiction of the governor of the province Beyond the River. [...]

Nehemiah 8

When the seventh month came—the people of Israel being settled in their towns—all the people gathered together into the square before the Water

Source: Nehemiah 3:1–27; 8:1–8; 13:1–27 and Isaiah 43; 44:28–45:22; and 66, *The New Oxford Annotated Bible* (Oxford: Oxford University Press), 596–7, 602–3, 609–10, 923–5, 927–9, 957–9.

Gate. They told the scribe Ezra to bring the book of the law of Moses, which the LORD had given to Israel. Accordingly, the priest Ezra brought the law before the assembly, both men and women and all who could hear with understanding. This was on the first day of the seventh month. He read from it facing the square before the Water Gate from early morning until midday, in the presence of the men and the women and those who could understand; and the ears of all the people were attentive to the book of law. The scribe Ezra stood on a wooden platform that had been made for the purpose; and beside him stood Mattithiah, Shema, Anaiah, Uriah, Hilkiah, and Maaseiah on his right hand; and Pedaiah, Mishael, Malchijah, Hashum, Hashbaddanah, Zechariah, and Meshullam on his left hand. And Ezra opened the book in the sight of all the people, for he was standing above all the people; and when he opened it, all the people stood up. Then Ezra blessed the LORD, the great God, and all the people answered, "Amen, Amen," lifting up their hands. Then they bowed their heads and worshiped the LORD with their faces to the ground. Also Jeshua, Bani, Sherebiah, Jamin, Akkub, Shabbethai, Hodiah, Maaseiah, Kelita, Azariah, Jozabad, Hannan, Pelaiah, the Levites, helped the people to understand the law, while the people remained in their places. So they read from the book, from the law of God, with interpretation. They gave the sense, so that the people understood the reading. [...]

Nehemiah 13

On that day they read from the book of Moses in the hearing of the people; and in it was found written that no Ammonite or Moabite should ever enter the assembly of God, because they did not meet the Israelites with bread and water, but hired Balaam against them to curse them—yet our God turned the curse into a blessing. When the people heard the law, they separated from Israel all those of foreign descent.

Now before this, the priest Eliashib, who was appointed over the chambers of the house of our God, and who was related to Tobiah, prepared for Tobiah a large room where they had previously put the grain offering, the frankincense, the vessels, and the tithes of grain, wine, and oil, which were given by commandment to the Levites, singers, and gatekeepers, and the contributions for the priests. While this was taking place I was not in Jerusalem, for in the thirty-second year of King Artaxerxes of Babylon I went to the king. After some time I asked leave of the king and returned to Jerusalem. I then discovered the wrong that Eliashib had done on behalf of Tobiah, preparing a room for him in the courts of the house of God. And I was very angry, and I threw all the household furniture of Tobiah out of the room. Then I gave orders and they cleansed the chambers, and I brought back the vessels of the house of God, with the grain offering and the frankincense.

I also found out that the portions of the Levites had not been given to them; so that the Levites and the singers, who had conducted the service, had gone back to their fields. So I remonstrated with the officials and said, "Why is the house of God forsaken?" And I gathered them together and set them in their stations. Then all Judah brought the tithe of the grain, wine, and oil into the storehouses. And I appointed as treasurers over the storehouses the priest Shelemiah, the scribe Zadok, and Pedaiah of the Levites, and as their assistant Hanan son of Zaccur son of Matteniah, for they were considered faithful; and their duty was to distribute to their associates. Remember me, O my God, concerning this, and do not wipe out my good deeds that I have done for the house of my God and for his service.

In those days I saw in Judah people treading wine presses on the sabbath, and bringing in heaps of grain and loading them on donkeys; and also wine, grapes, figs, and all kinds of burdens, which they brought into Jerusalem on the sabbath day; and I warned them at that time against selling food. Tyrians also, who lived in the city, brought in fish and all kinds of merchandise and sold them on the sabbath to the people of Judah, and in Jerusalem. Then I remonstrated with the nobles of Judah and said to them, "What is this evil thing that you are doing, profaning the sabbath day? Did not your ancestors act in this way, and did not our God bring all this disaster on us and on this city? Yet you bring more wrath on Israel by profaning the sabbath." [. . .]

In those days also I saw Jews who had married women of Ashdod, Ammon and Moab; and half of their children spoke the language of Ashdod, and they could not speak the language of Judah, but spoke the language of various peoples. And I contended with them and cursed them and beat some of them and pulled out their hair; and I made them take an oath in the name of God saying, "You shall not give your daughters to their sons, or take their daughters for your sons or for yourselves. Did not King Solomon of Israel sin on account of such women? Among the man's nations there was no king like him, and he was beloved by his God, and God made him king over all Israel; nevertheless, foreign women made even him to sin. Shall we then listen to you and do all this great evil and act treacherously against our God by marrying foreign women?" [. . .]

Isaiah 43

But now thus says the LORD,
  he who created you, O Jacob,
  he who formed you, O Israel:
Do not fear, for I have redeemed
    you;
  I have called you by name, you
    are mine.
When you pass through the
    waters, I will be with you;
  and through the rivers, they
    shall not overwhelm you;
  when you walk through fire you
    shall not be burned,
  and the flame shall not
    consume you.
For I am the LORD, your God,
  the Holy One of Israel, your
    Savior.

I give Egypt as your ransom,
  Ethiopia and Seba in exchange
    for you.
Because you are precious in
    my sight,
  and honored, and I love you,
I give people in return for you,
  nations in exchange for your
    life.
Do not fear, for I am with you;
  I will bring your offspring from
    the east;
  and from the west I will
    gather you;
I will say to the north, "Give
    them up,"
  and to the south, "Do not withhold,
bring my sons from far away
  and my daughters from the end
    of the earth—
everyone who is called by my
    name,
  whom I created for my glory,
  whom I formed and made."
Bring forth the people who are
    blind, yet have eyes,
  who are deaf, yet have ears!
Let all the nations gather together,
  and let the peoples assemble.
Who among them declared this,
  and foretold to us the former
    things?
Let them bring their witnesses to
    justify them,
  and let them hear and say, "It
    is true."

You are my witnesses, says the
LORD,
and my servant whom I have
chosen,
so that you may know and
believe me
and understand that I am he.
Before me no god was formed,
nor shall there be any after me.
I, I am the LORD,
and besides me there is no
savior.
I declared and saved and
proclaimed,
when there was no strange god
among you;
and you are my witnesses, says
the LORD.
I am God, and also henceforth I
am He;
there is no one who can deliver
from my hand;
I work and who can hinder it?
Thus says the LORD,
your Redeemer, the Holy One
of Israel;
For your sake I will send to
Babylon
and break down all the bars,
and the shouting of the
Chaldeans will be turned to
Lamentation.
I am the LORD, your Holy One,
the Creator of Israel, your king. [. . .]

Isaiah 44

[W]ho says of Cyrus, "He is my
shepherd,

and he shall carry out all my
purpose";
and who says of Jerusalem, "It
shall be rebuilt,"
and of the temple, "Your
foundation shall be laid."

Isaiah 45

Thus says the LORD to his
anointed, to Cyrus,
whose right hand I have grasped
to subdue nations before him
and strip kings of their robes,
to open doors before him —
and the gates shall not be closed:
I will go before you
and level the mountains,
I will break in pieces the doors
of bronze
and cut through the bars of
iron,
I will give you the treasures of
darkness
and riches hidden in secret
places,
so that you may know that it is, I
the LORD,
the God of Israel, who call you
by your name.
For the sake of my servant Jacob,
and Israel my chosen,
I call you by your name,
I surname you, though you do
not know me.
I am the LORD, and there is
no other;
besides me there is no god.

I arm you, though you do not
    know me,
so that they may know, from the
    rising of the sun
    and from the west, that there is
    no one besides me;
    I am the LORD, and there is
    no other.
I form light and create darkness,
    I make weal and create woe;
    I the LORD do all these things.

Shower, O heavens, from above,
    and let the skies rain down
    righteousness;
let the earth open, that salvation
    may spring up,"
    and let it cause righteousness to
    sprout up also;
    I the LORD have created it. [. . .]
I have aroused Cyrus in
    righteousness,
    and I will make all his paths
    straight;
he shall build my city
    and set my exiles free,
not for price or reward,
    says the LORD of hosts.
Thus says the LORD:
The wealth of Egypt and the
    merchandise of Ethiopia,
    and the Sabeans, tall of stature,
shall come over to you and
    be yours,
    they shall follow you;
    they shall come over in chains
    and bow down to you.
They will make supplication to
    you, saying,

"God is with you alone, and
    there is no other;
    there is no god besides him."
Truly, you are a God who hides
    himself,
    O God of Israel, the Savior.
All of them are put to shame and
    confounded,
    the makers of idols go in
    confusion together.
But Israel is saved by the LORD
    with everlasting salvation;
you shall not be put to shame or
    confounded
    to all eternity. [. . .]
Assemble yourselves and come
    together,
    draw near, you survivors of the
    nations!
They have no knowledge—
    those who carry about their
    wooden idols,
and keep on praying to a god
    that cannot save.
Declare and present your case;
    let them take counsel together!
Who told this long ago?
    Who declared it of old?
Was it not I, the LORD?
    There is no other god besides
    me,
a righteous God and a Savior;
    there is no one besides me.

Turn to me and be saved,
    all the ends of the earth!
    For I am God, and there is
    no other. [. . .]

Isaiah 66

Thus says the LORD:
Heaven is my throne
   and the earth is my footstool;
what is the house that you would
   build for me,
   and what is my resting place?
All these things my hand has
   made,
   and so all these things
    are mine,
     says the LORD.
But this is the one to whom I will
   look,
   to the humble and contrite
    in spirit,
   who trembles at my word.

Whoever slaughters an ox is like
   one who kills a human
   being;
   whoever sacrifices a lamb, like
   one who breaks a dog's
   neck;
whoever presents a grain offering,
   like one who offers swine's
   blood;
   whoever makes a memorial
   offering of frankincense,
   like one who blesses an
   idol.
These have chosen their own
   ways,
   and in their abominations they
   take delight;
I also will choose to mock them,
   and bring upon them what
   they fear;

because, when I called, no one
   answered,
   when I spoke, they did not
   listen;
but they did what was evil in
   my sight,
   and chose what did not
   please me.
Hear the word of the LORD,
   you who tremble at his word:
Your own people who hate you
   and reject you for my name's
   sake
have said, "Let the LORD be
   glorified,
   so that we may see your joy";
   but it is they who shall be put
   to shame.

Listen, an uproar from the city!
   A voice from the temple!
The voice of the LORD,
   dealing retribution to his
   enemies!
Before she was in labor
   she gave birth;
before her pain came upon her
   she delivered a son.
Who has heard of such a thing?
   Who has seen such things?
Shall a land be born in one day?
   Shall a nation be delivered in
   one moment?
Yet as soon as Zion was in labor
   she delivered her children.
Shall I open the womb and not
   deliver?
   says the LORD;

shall I, the one who delivers, shut
    the womb?
  says your God.

Rejoice with Jerusalem, and be
    glad for her,
  all you who love her;
rejoice with her in joy,
  all you who mourn over her—
that you may nurse and be
    satisfied
  from her consoling breast;
that you may drink deeply with
    delight
  from her glorious bosom.

For thus says the LORD:
I will extend prosperity to her like
    a river,
  and the wealth of the nations
    like an overflowing stream;
and you shall nurse and be carried
    on her arm,
  and dandled on her knees.
As a mother comforts her child,
  so I will comfort you;
  you shall be comforted in
    Jerusalem.
You shall see, and your heart shall
    rejoice;
  your bodies shall flourish like
    the grass;
and it shall be known that the
    hand of the LORD is with
    his servants,
  and his indignation is against
    his enemies.

For the LORD will come in fire,
  and his chariots like the
    whirlwind,
to pay back his anger in fury,
  and his rebuke in flames of fire.
For by fire will the LORD execute
    judgment,
  and by his sword, on all flesh;
  and those slain by the LORD
    shall be many.

Those who sanctify and purify themselves to go into the gardens, following the one in the center, eating the flesh of pigs, vermin, and rodents, shall come to an end together, says the LORD.

For I know their works and their thoughts, and I am coming to gather all nations and tongues; and they shall come and shall see my glory, and I will set a sign among them. From them I will send survivors to the nations, to Tarshish, Put, and Lud—which draw the bow—to Tubal and Javan, to the coastlands far away that have not heard of my fame or seen my glory; and they shall declare my glory among the nations. They shall bring all your kindred from all the nations as an offering to the LORD, on horses, and in chariots, and in litters, and on mules, and on dromedaries, to my holy mountain Jerusalem, says the LORD, just as the Israelites bring a grain offering in a clean vessel to the house of the LORD. And I will also take some of them as priests and as Levites, says the LORD.

For as the new heavens and the
    new earth,
  which I will make,
shall remain before me, says
    the LORD;
  so shall your descendants and
    your name remain.

From new moon to new moon,
  and from sabbath to sabbath,
all flesh shall come to worship
    before me,
says the LORD.

And they shall go out and look at the dead bodies of the people who have rebelled against me; for their worm shall not die, their fire shall not be quenched, and they shall be an abhorrence to all flesh.

A Mesoamerican Axial Age

Mesoamerica is always absent from the discussion of the Axial Age—aside from kings, no great names are known, and, aside from the Popol Vuh, *no great works of thinking have been recovered or discovered. Adding to the complication are difficulties in chronology. Nonetheless, change took place in the world of the Maya that was no less profound than the changes in Eurasia. The great urban centers of the "Classic Period" arose, with their fine art and architecture dominating the landscape as never before. These sophisticated urban forms were made possible in part by a new kind of ruler, kings who proclaimed divine ancestry and occasionally divinity itself. For example, the king of Palenque, Pakal, identified himself with the Maize God. These "holy lords" helped to shape the urban culture of their city-states and in an essential way made themselves the center of that universe. These city-states have all the prerequisites Momigliano noted for intellectual ferment and change, and these kings, as reimagined, became the new vision for their societies. David Drew in* The Lost Chronicles of the Maya Kings *gives some sense of this transition from an archaic to a more cosmopolitan world dominated by very powerful kings, kings whose bloody ceremonies and very existence kept their universe in order and their kingdom on top. While these kings, and their priesthoods, did not reject the polytheistic cosmos, they did transform it into an intellectual system in which they were at the center. An expression of the intellectual life of these cities, Drew suggests that the* Popol Vuh *may have had its beginning at this time: here we see another side of the Maya ball game and human sacrifice that we read about in Chapter 6.*

>> 55. The Lost Chronicles of the Maya Kings

DAVID DREW [1999]

The Early Classic

The term 'Classic Period' was introduced earlier this century to describe the Maya at the height of their powers and prosperity. It was perceived as a period of extraordinarily original achievement, of intellectual and artistic accomplishment unmatched in any other part of Mesoamerica, all seemingly contained within a period of six centuries between about AD 300 and AD 900. Today the lustre of that Golden Age remains undimmed. Yet we now know the tenor of those times to have been very different from the arcadian image that scholars once contrived. Competition and conflict, burgeoning populations stretching agricultural ingenuity and the carrying capacity of the forest environment—such were the pressures, ultimately to become the stresses, that formed the background to the brilliance and creativity of the period.

Source: David Drew, *The Lost Chronicles of the Maya Kings* (Berkeley: University of California Press, 1999), 181, 314–5, 320–1.

It is also apparent today [...] that many of the essential ingredients of Maya civilization were already in place by the beginning of the Classic Period: urban centres, great building projects, intensive agriculture, the emergence of a powerful ruling élite, such details as the use of the corbel vault in architecture and fine painted ceramics. The difference, which still justifies the use of the term, is that during the Classic period all these elements came together throughout the Southern Lowlands. In particular, the anonymous rulers of the Preclassic became *k'ul ahaws* or Holy Lords. The Classic was, supremely, the time of kings in Maya society, individuals who assumed power over their city state through that institutionalized royal succession advertised in the inscriptions on their monuments. [...]

Religion and the State

Human sacrifice was a public spectacle, a collective experience. The softening up and torturing may have gone on in more private, exclusive surroundings, but for the final dispatch on the chosen ritual occasion crowds would have pressed into the plazas of Maya cities. The victim met his end either in the ball-court or at the top of a pyramid, the lifeless body quite possibly cast down the stairs on a symbolic tumble to the Underworld. Sacrifice represented the recycling of sacred energy, the blood that was shed bringing divine power into the immediate world to make the crops grow and bring prosperity to the community at large. Of course the whole procedure also bestowed enormous power on the small number who organized it all, who mediated between humans and the gods, in other words, Maya kings. The drama of human sacrifice was but one element in the display of their religious and political authority, which were indivisible.

Rulers referred to themselves on their monuments as *k'ul ahaw*, translated as 'holy lord' but more commonly rendered as 'divine king'. What this actually meant to Maya themselves, the kind of awe with which a loin-clothed farmer gazed up at the magnificent figure of his ruler emerging from a distant temple, is impossible to gauge. Was he looking at a man or a god? Perhaps both. For our more clear-cut concepts of divinity are not particularly helpful, as we have seen. In a world where gods and men were thought to inhabit the same all-inclusive existence and regularly communicated with each other, and where all things shared in a sliding scale of a sacred, possessing differing degrees of *k'ulel,* the difference between humans and divine beings was perhaps more quantitative than qualitative. In fact gods themselves revealed very human frailties. They could grow old and die, and could be outwitted and vanquished by mortals, as the saga of the Hero Twins showed. As mythic protagonists, the latter occupy a characteristically ambivalent position as heroes of an amorphous in-between time before the present creation. Represented as proto-humans, they served to demonstrate how certain outstanding and particularly resourceful individuals could hold their own amongst the gods, overcome the forces of death and destruction and achieve resurrection as powerful celestial beings. This was the perfect pattern for Maya rulers—people who were more powerful and 'sacred' than anyone else in their community while they were alive and at their death took their place in the divine firmament. At least that appears to be how Maya kings saw it. For of course the myth of the Hero Twins was their own creation, which they used to help justify their right to rule. All we are able to do is follow, in images and texts, their own projections of themselves.

It is no coincidence that the Hero Twins first appear in Maya art in the Late Preclassic period, at the time when Maya kingship was taking shape. By the Late Classic it is easier to identify them as the role models for kings, who on important ceremonial occasions would assume their guise. The ballcourt, the original place of sacrifice and confrontation with the gods, with its sloping side walls conceived as a great crack in the earth and point of contact with the Underworld, was the key arena for performance of this kind. At the time of creation the Maize God was brought back to life by his sons. Although resurrected, he seems to have been perceived as remaining in the earth, staying on beneath the ballcourt of the Underworld; in effect, he was still there just under the ground in the ballcourt of every Maya city. And so, taking on the identity of the Hero Twins in a renewed struggle against the forces of darkness, Maya kings, through the ritualized execution of captives, were seen to dispatch the Lords of Death and revive the Maize God, providing him with sustenance in the form of sacrificial blood and thus ensuring the future fertility of the earth.

Kings portrayed themselves with the aspects of a number of different deities and, dressed in masks and elaborate costume, they took on their powers and 'became' these gods for a while. [...]

The ball-court, as we have seen, was a crevice in the earth, the point of communication with the Underworld. Stelae were perceived as trees, the Maya phrase used to describe them being literally *te tun* or 'stone tree'. These in effect grew out of the Underworld and the trampled sacrificial victims often seen at their base were thus neatly positioned close to their destination at death. The standing figure upon the stela, the living ruler who had planted it, was the trunk, king as tree once more, the central pillar of his society. To complete this world view embodied in the stela, deified ancestors were often carved at the very top, above the king, floating in the celestial realms. If plazas were water on the surface of the Underworld and stelae were trees, pyramids, the most imposing features of the city centre, were mountains—where contact was made between the earth and the heavens, which were associated with creation in the Popol Vuh— and contained the tombs of kings. Thus the stacks of pyramids one on top of the other at Copán, for example, or Tikal, were perceived as ancestral mountain ranges, reflecting the very ancient idea, which survives among the Maya today, of hills as places inhabited by the spirits of the dead.

Thus the *k'ul ahaw* or holy Maya lord strode, or more likely was borne on a litter dressed as a god, through an extraordinary artificial landscape, a mirror of the world order that he maintained. Against the back-drop of brightly painted temples and pyramids that served as awesome hoardings to advertise the power of kings, he re-enacted in elaborate ritual, in music and dance, the myths of creation and the histories of his ancestors. From this distance it is natural for us, too, to be over-awed by the power and divinity that hedged a Maya king, where religion did not simply serve to explain the human condition and the secrets of the universe but presented the ruler as the most important secret of all, the exclusive channel of communication with the gods, upon whom the lives and livelihoods of all Maya people depended. [...]

The institution of 'divine' kingship, as it had become refined by the Late Classic, was the product of many centuries of development. It could not have evolved so successfully through coercion, but because it was based on broadly shared interests and common understandings held throughout Maya society. The management of the supernatural was a vital, practical aspect of Maya life, and had always been so. The services the king provided as broker with the divine would have been seen as essential by the community at large and, although a body of royal mythology had been superimposed upon them, the most fundamental of religious beliefs, in the gods as the powers of nature personified, had changed little since the days when communication with the spirit world was the responsibility of the village shaman. Above all, of course, the system endured for the simple reason that most sections of Maya society prospered. If that prosperity faltered and sections of the population ceased to benefit, it might be a different matter entirely.

>> Mastering the Material

1. How do Karl Jaspers and Arnaldo Momigliano define the "Axial Age"? Why do they see this historical and intellectual phenomenon as central to the development of human history?

2. In what ways do the thinkers in Greece, China, and India undermine the nature of the polytheistic universe and challenge the polytheistic explanation for why things happen? How is this also a challenge, either implicitly or explicitly, of the existing political and social orders of the time?

3. In challenging the existing order—religious, political, and social—how do the thinkers of the Axial Age provide alternatives to their respective cultures?

4. How do the thinkers in China, India, Israel, and Greece help to define, or in some cases redefine, their own cultures?

5. How might the developments in Mesoamerica described by David Drew be seen to parallel those in Eurasia during this period?

>> Making Connections

1. What happened in the time period covered in Part 1 that permitted something like the Axial Age to take place? What are the preconditions for the Axial Age?

2. Jaspers and Momigliano argue that the Axial Age failed to take place in Egypt and Mesopotamia. Taking into consideration your readings in Part 1, why do you think that Egypt and Mesopotamia did not experience the Axial Age?

Chapter 8

The New Politics and Culture

The Consequences of the New Vision

Before the sixteenth century C.E. very few successful large state systems, or **empires,** emerged. The source of this lack of success is not hard to find: Early empires tended to be held together by sheer violence and terror, like the Assyrian Empire. Even the Persian Empire, which was more successful than most, lasted only about two centuries and was subject to frequent rebellions. When it passed, it left very little imprint, cultural or otherwise, on the peoples west of the Iranian plateau that had been a part of that enormous empire. In antiquity, only two empires end up being effective political units over a long time period—China, beginning with the Qin and Han Dynasties, and its contemporary, the Roman Empire. These two large state systems had something in common: policies of inclusion. Both China and Rome found ways to include and accept the different peoples who were a part of their empires, rather than to exclude and suppress. While the Chinese and Romans created sophisticated and inclusive governmental systems, the longevity of their empires was the result of more than politics itself. In both civilizations we see the creation of a common culture to which all people could belong and with which all people could identify. This common identity and culture meant continuity over long periods of time, despite the vicissitudes of occasional political ineptness and periodic civil wars and invasions. In each case, we have a complex system over a large territory that long survived its creator, the First Emperor of Qin in China and Caesar Augustus in Rome. In this chapter we will learn about the contributions of Axial Age thinking in the creation of three great empires, China, Rome, and India.

The creation of the Chinese empire was one of the greatest achievements of the post–Axial Age period. This achievement, however, was made possible because of a series of critical revolutions, from technological changes to social transformations. Of these revolutions, two stand out in particular. On the one hand, the intellectual revolution of the "Hundred Schools," especially with Confucianism and Legalism, had powerful political and social implications. These two schools of thought attacked the social and political basis of power while at the same time provided alternatives to the existing order. On the other hand, the political chaos of the Warring States Period brought on a political revolution, a revolution with its own social and political consequences. By 221 B.C.E. Chinese leaders consciously created the first centralized state for a newly unified China. Sima Qian outlines the course of this dual revolution, from the emergence of a centralized state of Qin in 325 B.C.E., to the unification of China itself about a century later by Ying Zheng, the king of Qin. Zheng, as ruler of "all under Heaven" and harkening back to the cultural heroes Three August Ones (*san hang*) and Five Lords (*wu di*) *Huang Di,* took a new title, *Shihuangdi,* "The First August Lord," or, more commonly, the First Emperor of Qin. While this first imperial dynasty was short lived, the principles and practices of centralization it developed would continue into the next dynasty, the Han. The Han tempered the harsh Legalism of the Qin with the milder Confucian principles, simultaneously building skillfully upon the Qin centralizing structures—this dynasty created the basis for a system of government that would last two millennia. Cho-yun Hsu carefully sets out the successful efforts of the Han, while at the same time examining the problems they faced, especially with local elites.

The Mediterranean basin followed a different political pattern than that of China. In the west, the Ionian Intellectual Revolution and its continuation into the fifth and fourth centuries B.C.E. profoundly affected many aspects of Greek life and culture. One area particularly influenced by the new rational modes of thinking was politics. With the Ionian Intellectual Revolution, individuals within the *polis* became more willing to engage in dialogue with one another, as well as to think in terms of alternatives when presented with a particular political problem. The end result was explosive: the invention of democracy itself. One Athenian politician, Cleisthenes, managed to conjure up a whole new political order that the Athenians proudly called "*isonomia,*" or "equality before the law," but which their enemies disparagingly dubbed "*democratia,*" or "rule by the people." By shifting power away from the aristocracy, Cleisthenes, according to Aristotle, "delivered the constitution of the *polis* over to the masses." Argument, discussion, and civic discourse replaced appeals to superior authorities or violence in the conduct of the affairs of the *polis*. Thucydides presents the basis and ideals of democratic Athens in his "Funeral Speech of Pericles." Despite the occasional formation of Leagues of various sorts, however, the type of city-state particularism that we saw in Part 1 prevented the Greeks from ever embarking on large state ventures.

This cozy world of the Greek city-state might have gone on indefinitely had it not been for one individual: Alexander the Great. Alexander changed forever the face of the eastern Mediterranean basin and the Middle East. At first glance it might appear that Alexander and his successors created as successful an empire as the First Emperor of Qin and the Han, but that is not the case. Alexander's empire died with him. While no scholar disputes the political fragmentation of Alexander's empire, the new scholarship, as we will see with Alan Samuel, argues against any cultural unity as well.

In the end, it was left to the Romans to do what the Greeks, including Alexander the Great, seemed incapable of doing—creating a universal political order. But the Roman Empire is something of a paradox. Like the Greeks, the Romans had a strong belief in the city-state as the key to human and political success. As the selection from Greg Woolf shows, the Romans considered the city-state the very foundation of human civilization. Yet they also developed a notion of community that transcended territory and city-state particularism. Moreover, despite acquiring a massive amount of land over time, the Romans did not develop a highly centralized government similar to that of China. Instead, scholars always contrast Rome and China, pointing out the paucity of Roman officials at the height of the Roman Empire—only about 180 for the whole of

Rome. The very success of the Roman Empire lay elsewhere: The Romans created political unity by creating a universal people with a universal culture. In his diary, Marcus Aurelius, the last great emperor of the second century C.E., exulted in being part of what he calls a "cosmopolis"—a "world city" that embraced all human beings on the basis of their reason and common humanity. Woolf analyzes the complicated process of culture formation in the Roman Empire, and Aelius Aristides, a contemporary of Marcus Aurelius, illustrates the effects of this process on the Empire itself.

In addition to China and Rome, another great empire arose in the post–Axial Age, this time in the Indian subcontinent. Alexander's incursions east of the old Persian Empire had the unlikely consequence of bringing together two major cultural strands, even if tenuously. Political and commercial relations between India and the Mediterranean now became standard, as we shall see in Chapter 9. On the political front the Maurya Dynasty emerged following the death of Alexander the Great. This was the most powerful dynasty of the Indian subcontinent to date. Commencing with Chandragupta, they extended their power and authority over most of India, from what is now eastern Afghanistan and the Himalayas to Mysore, in the far south of the peninsula. The Hellenistic king Seleucus I ceded to Chandragupta any claims that he had to lands in the northwest and Indus Valley, and in return received critical help from the Indian ruler in the form of 500 war elephants, the tank of ancient warfare. Intermarriage and diplomacy between the Seleucids and the Mauryans also took place. But it was Aśoka, the grandson of Chandragupta, who extended the Mauryan empire to its greatest height. In the course of his bloody conquests, Aśoka converted to Buddhism and, as a consequence of that conversion, placed his empire on a footing different from that which preceded him. His "Rock Edicts" in this chapter are an example of his new basis for rule. But this empire, though based on policies of inclusion and respect, did not outlast Aśoka. At his death the Mauryan empire was plagued by internal strife and external invasions that prevented its successful continuation.

The Unification of China

The Han Court Astrologer and Chronicler, Sima Qian, outlines the centralizing activities of Zheng, the king of Qin who became the first emperor of China and assumed the dynastic name Qin Shihuangdi. After defeating the various kings, Zheng concentrated as well as he could both military and political power into his own hands. In addition to reorganizing the territory under his command, the First Emperor of Qin created a common system of laws and their execution, of weights and measures, and of writing, abolishing regional customs and local scripts. Like French Revolutionaries millennia later, Shihuangdi created a common political and even intellectual culture for his realm. The First Emperor also attempted the continuing transformation of society, establishing the primacy of farmers and farming in China. Finally, Sima Qian also describes the various intellectual influences on Shihuangdi, ranging from Legalism to the occult.

While the activities of the Qin emperor were praised by some Confucian scholars, others, as Sima Qian explains, opposed him, resulting in a backlash against his policies.

Not surprisingly, a rebellion arose during the brief reign of his son, in the course of which a new dynasty—the Han—emerged victorious. The Qin, however, had provided two important legacies for the future: proof that Legalism itself was an insufficient basis for good rule and the centralization of authority in China in the hands of one man, the Emperor. Although they did not reject Legalism completely, the Han added Confucian principles to their government, transforming the latter into what is sometimes called "Imperial Confucianism." Likewise the Han emperors expanded upon the centralized structure of the Qin, refining it into a more powerful and efficient governmental and military system whose outlines would survive until the twentieth century. Excerpts from an article by historian Cho-yun Hsu highlight important aspects of the world that the Han Dynasty created.

>> 56. Historical Records

Sima Qian [109–91 b.c.e.]

Chief Minister Wang Wan, Imperial Secretary Feng Jie, Superintendent of Trials Li Si, and others all said: 'In days of old the territory of the Five Emperors was 1,000 *li* square, and beyond this was the territory of the feudal princes and of the barbarians. Some of the feudal princes came to court and some did not, for the Son of Heaven was unable to exercise control. Now Your Majesty has raised a righteous army to punish the oppressors and bring peace and order to all under Heaven, so that everywhere within the seas has become our provinces and districts and the laws and ordinances have as a result become unified. This is something which has never once existed from remote antiquity onwards, and which the Five Emperors did not attain. Your servants have carefully discussed this with the scholars of broad learning and, as in antiquity there was the Heavenly August, the Earthly August, and the Supreme August, and the Supreme August was the most highly honoured, so your servants, risking death, submit a venerable title, and propose that the King should become "the Supreme August". His commands should be "edicts", his orders should be "decrees", and the Son of Heaven should refer to himself as "the mysterious one"'. The King said: 'Omit the word "supreme" and write "august" and pick out the title of "emperor" used from remote

antiquity, so that the title will be "August Emperor". The rest shall be as you suggest.' And an edict was issued saying that it should be done. King Zhuangxiang was to be posthumously honoured as 'the Supreme August on High'.

The following edict was issued: 'We have heard that in high antiquity there were titles but no posthumous names. In middle antiquity there were titles, but when people died they were provided with posthumous names in accordance with their conduct. If this is so, then it is a case of the son passing judgement on the father and the subject passing judgement on the ruler. This is quite pointless, and We will not adopt this practice in such matters. Hemnceforward the law on posthumous names is abolished. We are the First August Emperor and later generations will be numbered in accordance with this system, Second Generation, Third Generation, right down to Ten Thousandth Generation, and this tradition will continue without end.'

To continue the succession of the Five Powers the First Emperor considered that, as Zhou had got the Power of Fire and Qin was replacing the Zhou power, it should adopt what fire does not overcome, so it was precisely at this moment that the Power of Water started. The beginning of the year was changed, and the court celebrations all started at the beginning of the tenth month. In all garments, flags, and pennants

Source: Sima Qian, *Historical Records*, translated by Raymond Dawson (Oxford: Oxford University Press, 1994), 64–7, 69.

black was made predominant. And as far as number was concerned they took six as the basis of calculation, so that tallies and law caps were 6 inches, carriages were 6 feet wide, 6 feet equalled a 'pace', and imperial carriages had six horses. The Yellow River was renamed 'the Powerful Water' to inaugurate the Power of Water. Repression was intensive and matters were all decided by the law, for only through harsh treatment and the abandonment of humaneness, kindness, harmony, and righteousness could he accord with the destiny of the Five Powers. And so the law was made rigorous, and for a long time no amnesty was declared.

The Chief Minister Wang Wan and others said: 'The states are newly defeated and the territories of Yan, Qi, and Chu are distant, so if we do not establish kings for them there will be no means of bringing order to them. We beg to set up your sons in authority, but it is up to the Supreme One alone to favour us with his agreement.' The First Emperor handed down their suggestion to the ministers, and they all thought this would be expedient. But the Superintendent of Trials Li Si advised: 'Only after an extremely large number of sons and younger brothers and people of the same surname had been enfeoffed by King Wen and King Wu did they win the adherence of the distant, and then they attacked and smote each other and behaved like enemies. And when the feudal states wrought vengeance on each other more and more, the Zhou Son of Heaven was incapable of preventing them. Now all within the seas has been unified thanks to Your Majesty's divine power, and everywhere has been turned into provinces and districts. And if your sons and the successful officials are richly rewarded from the public revenues, that will be quite sufficient to secure easy control. If there is no dissension throughout the Empire, then this is the technique for securing tranquility. To establish feudal states would not be expedient.' The First Emperor said: it is because of the existence of marquises and kings that all under Heaven has shared in suffering from unceasing

hostilities. When, thanks to the ancestral temples, all under Heaven has for the first time been brought to order, if states are reintroduced, this will mean the establishment of armies, and it would surely be difficult to seek peace in those places. The advice of the Superintendent of Trials is right.'

So the Empire was divided into thirty-six provinces, and a governor and army commander and an inspector were established for each. The people were renamed 'the black-headed people', and there were great celebrations. The weapons from all under Heaven were gathered in and collected together at Xianyang and were melted down to make bells and stands and twelve statues of men made of metal, each 1,000 piculs in weight, to be set up in the courts and palaces. All weights and measures were placed under a unified system, and the axle length of carriages was standardized. For writings they standardized the characters.

The land to the east stretched as far as the sea and Chaoxian, to the west as far as Lintao and Qiangzhong, to the south as far as the land where the doors face north, and in the north they constructed defences along the Yellow River to form the frontier, and along the Yin Mountains as far as Liaodong. One hundred and twenty thousand powerful and wealthy households from all under Heaven were transferred to Xianyang. All the temples together with Zhangtai and Shanglin were to the south of the Wei. Every time Qin destroyed a feudal state, a replica of its palaces and mansions was produced and it was created on the slope north of Xianyang, overlooking the Wei to the south, while eastwards from Yongmen as far as the Jing and Wei there was a series of mansions, connecting walkways, and pavilions. The beautiful women, bells, and drums which they had obtained from the various states were installed there to fill them.

In the twenty-seventh year the First Emperor toured Longxi and Beidi, went out via Jitou Mountain and passed Huizhong. Then he built the Xin palace south of the Wei, and subsequently it was renamed the Temple of the Apex, to represent the Apex of Heaven. From the Temple of the Apex a roadway went through to Mount Li, and the front hall of the Ganquan palace was built, and they built a walled roadway from Xianyang to connect with it. This year one degree of promotion was bestowed and express roads were constructed.

In the twenty-eighth year the First Emperor traveled eastwards through his provinces and districts and ascended Mount Zouyi. He set up a stone tablet, and after discussion with the various Confucian scholars of Lu an inscription was carved on the stone extolling the virtue of Qin. They also discussed the matter of the *feng* and *shan* sacrifices and the sacrifices to mountains and rivers. So next he ascended Mount Tai, set up a stone tablet, and made the *feng* sacrifice. [...]

In his twenty-eighth year, the August Emperor makes a beginning.

Laws and standards are corrected and adjusted, as a means of recording the myriad things.

Thus he clarified human affairs, and brings concord to father and son.

With sagacity, wisdom, humaneness, and righteousness, he has made manifest all principles.

In the east he has pacified the eastern lands, and thus he has inspected officers and men.

When this task had been magnificently accomplished, he then turned towards the sea.

Through the achievements of the August Emperor, the basic tasks are diligently worked on.

Farming is put first and non-essentials are abolished, and it is the black-headed people who are made wealthy.

All people under Heaven, have heart and mind in unison.

Implements are given a uniform measure, and the characters used in writing are standardized. [...]

Feeling sorrow for the black-headed people, he relaxes not morning or evening.

Removing doubt he fixes the laws, so that all understand what they are forbidden to do.

The regional earls have their separate duties, and all government is regulated and made easy.

>> 57. The Changing Relationship between Local Society and the Central Political Power in the Former Han: 206 B.C.–8 A.D.

Cho-Yun Hsu [1965]

The consolidation of China did not come immediately with China's unification. It was not fully accomplished until the middle of the Former (Western) Han. The monolithic nature of the political powers and a group of local elite were then forming. And the bureaucracy, becoming much elaborated during this era, served to link the two. The elite group functioned, on the one hand as the reservoir of candidates to officialdom, and on the other hand, as the leading element with education, prestige, and often wealth, in the community. Based on these concepts, this paper ventures to present the formation of the local elite group through the changing social base of political power during Western Han. The problems are threefold: the changing nature of the political power in different periods, the community order, and the local government structure, which provided the local elite group with certain circumstances favorable to its taking root. [...]

Source: Cho-Yun Hsu, "The Changing Relationship between Local Society and the Central Political Power in the Former Han: 206 B.C.–8 A.D.," *Comparative Studies in Society and History* 7 (1965), 358–9, 361, 369–70.

During the first period, the attitude of the Han court at Ch'ang-an [Chang'an] toward the provinces was not quite that of a central government towards its unified parts. There was a dualism, it may be said, between the capital area on the one hand and the provinces and principalities on the East Plain on the other. The passes between the capital area (present Shensi [Shaanxi] province) and the eastern regions were carefully guarded, and passports were required of all travelers. Even horses of specified heights and ages produced in the western regions were banned from exportation to the eastern provinces.

Suspicion towards principalities in the East, ruled by brothers and cousins of the emperor, was of course especially strong. Subjects of certain principalities were not allowed to serve as imperial court attendants. As late as the end of the Western Han Dynasty, people still recalled an old injunction that no citizen of any principality should take office at the capital in spite of his ability. [...]

The social order in local communities was not dramatically altered until 127 B.C. under Emperor Wu, when rich men, ranking officials, and "local elite" were compulsorily moved from the provinces to the capital area.

Uprooting leaders or potential leaders of local communities and transplanting them to the capital area were not novel measures. Both Ch'in Shih-Huang-ti [Qin Shihuangdi] and Kao-tsu [Gaozu] had done the same long ago. In fact, it was a common saying that there had been seven waves of population movement. Each time an emperor passed away, around his tomb there was established a new country to be settled with people from the provinces, who were selected according to three categories: rich men, families of ranking officials, and local elite—in order to "guard the deceased monarch". [...]

Thus, the local elite consisted of three elements, a sort of power trinity: the local administrative staffs including the district chiefs directly over the community people, the valiant-type leaders, and

those recommended to enter the central officialdom. This pattern remained throughout the subsequent history of China without drastic changes. And the local elite evolved during later centuries into what has been called, in an all-inclusive and hence confused way, the "gentry".

It is common for "in-groups" who control power to do their best in keeping the privilege in the family and for their posterity. In the Han period, after the reign of Emperor Chao [Zhao], powerful families began to form and expand at the local level. In one case, during the reign of Emperor Hsüan [Xuan], five brothers were serving in the same local administration, including one recommended to the central government. Yet another, from whom the tax collector did not venture to collect, was engaged in trade. This may serve to illustrate the functioning as well as the influence of the local elite. One capable mayor of the capital during the reigns of Emperors Chao [Zhao] and Hsüan [Xuan] definitely preferred to recruit young men from the families of the local elite, because of their resourcefulness, he said; perhaps it would be nearer to the truth to say because of their influence in the community.

The local elites soon had such a firm grip in their home provinces, as well as a fairly strong voice at the imperial court, that to move them once again to the capital area as had been done with their predecessors in the reign of Emperor Wu, could hardly be possible or successful. This, perhaps, might be the real reason why establishing new settlements around the imperial tomb was given up in 40 B.C. and again in 15 B.C.

By the end of the former Han period, local lineages, an associated phenomenon of elite power structure, did become important enough to oppose Wang Mang. They gathered people either to rebel with political aspirations or build fortresses for self-defense. Almost everywhere, they played a role as the core of a snowball of resistance. Yü Ying-shih, in an outstanding paper, has listed eighty-eight rebel groups, of which fifty-six are classifiable as "distinguished clans" or "notable families". These local lineages formed the social base of the Eastern Han regime, a point made by L.S. Yang a quarter of a century ago. It seems safe to add that they had already been in the process of becoming the social base of political power toward the end of the former Han.

The Invention of Greek Democracy

Cleisthenes, an aristocratic Athenian politician of the late sixth century B.C.E., invented a complex democratic system that included social engineering coupled with elaborate political innovations. He came up with his complicated system in order to solve a particular political problem that followed from the ousting of the Athenian tyrant, Hippias. The new politics caught on quickly. Over the course of the fifth century, Athenian political institutions became increasingly democratic, and came to signify a whole way of life. The most eloquent defense of democracy and a democratic way of life against its detractors came from Pericles in his "Funeral Oration" in 431–0 as recorded by Thucydides. In this speech the Athenian leader presented to his audience the basis of their government, and in so doing was one of the first Greeks to use the word "democracy" positively. Pericles, while emphasizing respect for one another as citizens, suggested that one of the most critical features of Athenian democracy was the centrality of debate and discussion—reason rather than fear had to be the basis of action in the polis. And, as he notes, this reasoned debate was open to all the adult male members of the community. While some modern scholars have doubted the democratic nature of Athenian government, the ancients did not. Aristotle in his Politics identifies five types of democracies, from the mildly democratic to the radical: Athens is his example of the most extreme form.

Pericles' speech, however, ends with another reality of Athenian democracy, the exclusion of citizen women from the political process. This was a gender-segregated world in which the public sphere, from shopping in the markets to participation in politics, was almost exclusively reserved for males. Nevertheless women were an essential part of the polis, as Aristotle points out, comprising half of the adult citizen population. Aristotle criticized what he considered to be the excessive freedom allowed Spartan women, but even in Athens citizen women had occasional outdoor public functions, especially in various civic and religious festivals.

>> 58. History of the Peloponnesian War

THUCYDIDES [LAST THIRD OF THE FIFTH CENTURY B.C.E.]

'I have no wish to make a long speech on subjects familiar to you all: so I shall say nothing about the warlike deeds by which we acquired our power or the battles in which we or our fathers gallantly resisted our enemies, Greek or foreign. What I want to do is, in the first place, to discuss the spirit in which we faced our trials and also our constitution and the way of life which has made us great. After that I shall speak in praise of the dead, believing that this kind of speech is not inappropriate to the

Source: Thucydides, *History of the Peloponnesian War*, translated by Rex Warner (Baltimore: Penguin Press, 1972), 145–7, 150–1.

present occasion, and that this whole assembly, of citizens and foreigners, may listen to it with advantage.

'Let me say that our system of government does not copy the institutions of our neighbours. It is more the case of our being a model to others, than of our imitating anyone else. Our constitution is called a democracy because power is in the hands not of a minority but of the whole people. When it is a question of settling private disputes, everyone is equal before the law; when it is a question of putting one person before another in positions of public responsibility, what counts is not membership of a particular class, but the actual ability which the man possesses. No one, so long as he has it in him to be of service to the state, is kept in political obscurity because of poverty. And, just as our political life is free and open, so is our day-to-day life in our relations with each other. We do not get into a state with our next-door neighbour if he enjoys himself in his own way, nor do we give him the kind of black looks which, though they do no real harm, still do hurt people's feelings. We are free and tolerant in our private lives; but in public affairs we keep to the law. This is because it commands our deep respect.

'We give our obedience to those whom we put in positions of authority, and we obey the laws themselves, especially those which are for the protection of the oppressed, and those unwritten laws which it is an acknowledged shame to break.

'And here is another point. When our work is over, we are in a position to enjoy all kinds of recreation for our spirits. There are various kinds of contests and sacrifices regularly throughout the year; in our own homes we find a beauty and a good taste which delight us every day and which drive away our cares. Then the greatness of our city brings it about that all the good things from all over the world flow in to us, so that to us seems just as natural to enjoy foreign goods as our own local products.

'Then there is a great difference between us and our opponents, in our attitude towards military security. Here are some examples: Our city is open to the world, and we have no periodical deportations in order to prevent people observing or finding out secrets which might be of military advantage to the enemy. This is because we rely, not on secret weapons, but on our own real courage and loyalty. There is a difference, too, in our educational systems. The Spartans, from their earliest boyhood, are submitted to the most laborious training in courage; we pass our lives without all these restrictions, and yet are just as ready to face the same dangers as they are. Here is a proof of this: When the Spartans invade our land, they do not come by themselves, but bring all their allies with them; whereas we, when we launch an attack abroad, do the job by ourselves, and, though fighting on foreign soil, do not often fail to defeat opponents who are fighting for their own hearths and homes. [...] We do not have to spend our time practicing to meet sufferings which are still in the future; and when they are actually upon us we show ourselves just as brave as these others who are always in strict training. This is one point in which, I think, our city deserves to be admired. There are also others:

'Our love of what is beautiful does not lead to extravagance; our love of the things of the mind does not make us soft. We regard wealth as something to be properly used, rather than as something to boast about. As for poverty, no one need be ashamed to admit it: the real shame is in not taking practical measures to escape from it. Here each individual is interested not only in his own affairs but in the affairs of the state as well: even those who are mostly occupied with their own business are extremely well-informed on general politics — this is a peculiarity of ours: we do not say that a man who takes no interest in politics is a man who minds his own business; we say that he has no business here at all. We Athenians, in our own person, take our decisions on policy or submit them to proper discussions: for we do not think that there is an incompatibility between words and deeds; the worst thing is to rush into action before the consequences have been properly debated. And this is another point where we differ from other people. We are capable at the same time of taking risks and of estimating them beforehand. Others are brave out of ignorance; and, when they stop to think, they begin to fear. But the man who can most truly be accounted brave is he who best knows the meaning of what is sweet in life and of what is terrible, and then goes out undeterred to meet what is to come.

'Again, in questions of general good feeling there is a great contrast between us and most other people. We make friends by doing good to others, not by receiving good from them. This makes our friendship all the more reliable, since we want to keep alive the gratitude of those who are in our debt by showing continued goodwill to them: whereas the feelings of one who owes us something lack the same enthusiasm, since he knows that, when he repays our kindness, it will be more like paying back a debt than giving something spontaneously. We are unique in this. When we do kindnesses to others, we do not do them out of any calculations of profit or loss: we do them without afterthought, relying on our free liberality. Taking everything together then, I declare that our city is an education to Greece, and I declare that in my opinion each single one of our citizens, in all the manifold aspects of life, is able to show himself the rightful lord and owner of his own person, and do this, moreover, with exceptional grace and freedom depends on being courageous. Let there be no relaxation in face of the perils of the war. [...]

'Perhaps I should say a word or two on the duties of women to those among you who are now widowed. I can say all I have to say in a short word of advice. Your great glory is not to be inferior to what God has made you, and the greatest glory of a woman is to be least talked about by men, whether they are praising you or criticizing you. I have now, as the law demanded, said what I had to say. For the time being our offerings to the dead have been made, and for the future their children will be supported at the public expense by the city, until they come of age. This is the crown and prize which she offers, both to the dead and to their children, for the ordeals which they have faced. Where the rewards of valour are the greatest, there you will find also the best and bravest spirits among the people. And now, when you have mourned for your dear ones, you must depart.'

>> 59. The Politics of Aristotle

ARISTOTLE [c. 335–322 B.C.E.]

Every household is a part of a polis. The society of husband and wife, and that of parents and children, are parts of the household. The goodness of every part must be considered with reference to the goodness of the whole. We must therefore consider the government [of the whole polis] before we proceed to deal with the training of children and women—at any rate if we hold that the goodness of children and women makes any difference to the goodness of the polis. § 16. And it *must* make a difference. Women are a half of the free population: children grow up to be partners in the government of the state.

Source: Aristotle, *The Politics of Aristotle*, translated by Ernest Barker (New York: Oxford University Press, 1962), 37–8.

The Limits of Hellenism

Despite the death of Alexander the Great in 323 B.C.E., many of the Macedonians and Greeks he brought eastward remained in the Middle East and Egypt. Their population was augmented by other Greek immigrants for the next 100 years, many of whom remained connected to their homeland and to each other. To describe the new interconnected world that they created after Alexander's death, the German historian Johann Droysen coined the word "Hellenismus," or **Hellenism**, *in the nineteenth century. From that point on scholars have debated the essential characteristics of the Hellenistic world, often focusing on culture. In much of the twentieth century scholars wrote about a new cosmopolitan civilization from the Indus Valley to the Mediterranean that was a fusion of Greek and indigenous cultures.*

However, this idealized view of the Hellenistic world has had many critics. While all scholars recognize the extraordinary intellectual and cultural achievements that took place during the Hellenistic period, particularly in Alexandria, some contend that rather than a fusion and intermingling of cultures, these achievements are still primarily Greek in nature. Alan Samuel presents one of the clearest expositions of this new view. He argues against fusion and syncretism, stressing instead that in each of the new Hellenistic kingdoms two separate and isolated communities lived side by side. This apartness, or separation, was not ordained by law but rather developed from the cultural conservatism of both newcomers and natives alike. This absence of cultural integration is particularly noteworthy in a place like Egypt, where immigrant soldiers were billeted in the homes of Egyptians. For Samuel there was no fusion in Egypt—there were only "two solitudes."

>> 60. The Shifting Sands of History: Interpretations of Ptolemaic Egypt

ALAN E. SAMUEL [1989]

Recent work shows that the consensus which gave the period after Alexander coherence and meaning for the flow of history in antiquity has thoroughly broken up. No longer can we assert confidently that the world which Alexander opened to the Greeks provided an opportunity for Hellenism to blend with many local cultures to create a new and universal culture for the Mediterranean. The idea that the amalgamation of religious ideas fertilized the ground to make people ready for the Christian message, a notion which could be adopted happily by evangelical Christians and rationalist atheists alike, no longer seems to have so much validity. In other areas, the evidence now suggests a greater diversity of culture and cultures among the peoples of the Mediterranean, a diversity which can be understood as leading into the multicultural community which was the Roman Empire. The survival of the many languages, religious traditions, cultural communities and even political separatism which seems to have continued despite the Augustan unification of

Source: Alan E. Samuel, *The Shifting Sands of History: Interpretations of Ptolemaic Egypt* (Lanham, MD: University Press of America, 1989), 10, 45–8.

the Mediterranean has attracted attention in recent years, again, perhaps due to a greater toleration of genuine diversity in the modern world. In the same way, writers about the period before Rome gained political supremacy have been willing to approach different areas without attempting to fit them into a unified picture of the history of the period. [...]

As I emphasized a few years ago, the Greeks maintained their culture in Egypt in almost complete separation from the surrounding milieu, preferring even Greek literature of pre-Alexandrian time to the local and contemporary productions of Alexandria. Much the same was true for religion. While the notion of "syncretism" of Greek and oriental themes in religion is hard a-dying, the evidence goes very much against it, at least in any significant sense. While Greeks accepted the divinities they encountered in the East (as they had always been willing to worship newly found deities), their conceptualization and cult practices remained entirely Hellenic. This conservative quality of Hellenism is now more and more being recognized, and the changing perspective of the impulses which drove Greek culture in Egypt in the three centuries of Ptolemaic rule call for reassessments of many aspects of the culture. [...]

The same fidelity to its traditions shows on the Egyptian side. As the art and architecture of Egyptian temples remained almost untouched by Hellenic influences, so the Egyptians kept cult and religious practice insulated from Greek. It is well known that priestly service is almost complete separated on ethnic lines, Greeks serving as priests in Greek cult but almost never in Egyptian, Egyptians in turn rarely crossing out of their tradition into Greek. [...]

We will be able to support with conviction or to refute what appears to be true from the evidence currently available, that the Egyptians—even upper class Egyptians—were not much touched by Greek culture, even though in a general way, some writers in Egyptian were aware of themes in other literatures of the Near East. We will be able much better to see whether indeed the two dominant peoples of Egypt, the Greeks and the natives, remained in their two solitudes for the long period of Ptolemaic rule.

The Universal Cities of the Roman Empire

The success of the Roman Empire did not lay in the strength of its armies or even in the wisdom of its first Emperor, Caesar Augustus (r. 31 B.C.E.–14 C.E.). Rather, the Romans succeeded in creating a grand, expansive state where others in the west had failed because of their ability to create a universal cultural and political system that was inclusive rather than exclusive. Over time, from the late fourth century B.C.E. to the height of the Roman Empire, Rome became an idea as much as it remained a place. Key to this inclusiveness were two interrelated phenomena, the extension of citizenship to others and urbanization. In 381 B.C.E. the Romans did something that no Greek city-state could have conceived of doing: They extended their citizenship to their neighbors, the people of Tusculum. The process of enfranchising individuals and communities ended in 212 C.E. when Emperor Caracalla gave Roman citizenship to the few remaining people in the empire who did not yet possess it. Citizenship was the only universally recognized form of status in the ancient world, and, as Woolf points out, enfranchisement meant being brought into the Roman community itself, both politically and religiously. But, as he also points out, one could not receive citizenship if one was not "fully civilized." In the Roman understanding, cities and urbanization made one civilized, and these constitute the cement of the whole system. The Roman

Empire was an empire of cities rather than of peoples or territories, and these cities stretched from what is now Scotland to the banks of the Tigris and Euphrates rivers. Cities helped to create what could be called a collective Roman identity in two ways. First, urbanization provided a basis for a degree of legal uniformity. Each city in the empire was a self-governing political unit with a charter of Roman-type free institutions. This encouraged a shared sense of political and civic values from one end of the empire to the other. And second, as Woolf carefully points out, cities and urbanization provided a flexible yet cohesive cultural system—there was a commonality of shared urban experiences from Syria to Britain, and from the Rhine to the Sahara.

The political success of the Roman Empire rested on the creation of a new cultural idiom, a cultural idiom that embraced regional diversity at the same time that it expressed Romanness. To be Roman, as Woolf points out, was not just one thing—there was not just one standard of what was or was not "Roman." In the end, the Romans created a common civilization that assumed regional cultural diversity, as well as a common citizenship that assumed a local identity. The unity of the Roman Empire, as Marcus Aurelius pointed out in his diary, was expressed by its diversity and multiplicity.

Aelius Aristides, a Roman citizen from Mysia in Asia Minor, visited Rome in 144 C.E. On that occasion he delivered a somewhat exaggerated speech called "To Rome." Despite the exaggerated nature that is characteristic of speeches like this, Aelius Aristides expresses very well the dual aspect of the new Roman identity and civilization, the generous extension of citizenship to many throughout the Roman world, and the critical role of cities.

>> 61. Becoming Roman: The Origins of Provincial Civilization in Gaul

GREG WOOLF [1998]

Besides, there was no standard Roman civilization against which provincial cultures might be measured. The city of Rome was a cultural melting pot and Italy experienced similar changes to the provinces. Nor did Romanization culminate in cultural uniformity throughout the empire. Eumenius' grandfather would not have felt culturally disoriented in Autun, but he would have been perfectly aware of its differences from Athens or Rome, and regional variations are apparent to archaeologist in every sphere of material culture. Contrasts between capital and provinces, East and West, rich and poor, city and countryside are themselves a major feature of Roman imperial culture. Romanization may have been 'the process by which the inhabitants come to be, and to think of themselves as, Romans', but there was more than one kind of Roman, and studies of provincial culture need to account for the cultural diversity, as well as the unity, of the empire.

Romanization has often been used as an umbrella term to conceal a multitude of separate processes. Some regard that as a major drawback of the concept, others see is as its

Source: Greg Woolf, *Becoming Roman: The Origins of Provincial Civilization in Gaul* (Cambridge: Cambridge University Press, 1998), 7, 59, 248–9.

most attractive feature. Romanization has no explanatory potential, because it was not an active force, the course of which can be traced through a variety of indices, and the level of which can be measured. But used descriptively, Romanization is a convenient shorthand for the series of cultural changes that created an imperial civilization, within which both differences and similarities came to form a coherent pattern. [...]

Romans could not define themselves purely in contradistinction to barbarians, since not all civilized men were Romans. Civilization remained a necessary but not a sufficient precondition of full integration. To become a Roman one also had to be enfranchised, received, that is, into the political and religious community of the *populous Romanus*. But culture remained an important criterion. *Humanitas* in its highest form was represented by a series of intellectual and moral accomplishments and qualities that, in a Western context, were the exclusive property of a narrow elite of Roman citizens. Yet *humanitas* was also quintessentially human, the fulfillment of the potential of the *genus humanum*. Barbarism in its lowest form was the absence of these qualities, and as a result barbarians were imperfect humans. [...]

The problem, then, is to understand why Roman identity remained so attractive to those within the empire, yet failed to enchant those beyond it. One starting point is provided by the comparison already drawn with Hellenism, Judaism and Christianity. The seductiveness of those cultural movements did not derive from any material rewards open to those who adopted Greek, Jewish or Christian identities, but rather from the content and organization of those cultural systems. Roman culture equally demands to be treated in terms of its content and structure as well as of any pragmatic advantages Roman identity offered to adherents. This is an area where cultural analysis is underdeveloped, but it is helpful to return to the notion of culture as organized around symbolic centres, points in an interconnected symbol system which are less open to negotiation and change than others, values which operate as points of reference in relation to which other values may be calculated, concepts which articulate the symbol systems, spaghetti junctions in a semantic field through which all travelers pass frequently and where chains of significance meet, intersect and depart again. Symbolic centres do not all occur in the same area of culture. For Greeks of the Roman period, for instance, language, cults and mythology through which religion was linked to descent, often via the Homeric poems, were central to cultural definition, while for Jews, religion was central but language less so. The stress Romans placed on customs (*mores*) and the central articulating function acquired by the notion of civilization (*humanitas*) have already been discussed. One explanation for the limits of Roman culture would be to posit a similar centrality for the relationship conceived between Roman civilization and the Roman empire, between being Roman in a cultural sense and being a member of the Roman political community. Such a notion might be contrasted with the weaker association of cultural and political identity in the case of the Greeks, for whom panhellenism rarely provided the basis for common political action. Roman identity, on the other hand, had not been formulated in conditions of political pluralism, and at least since the late Republic, political dissidents had been represented as culturally deviant, whether barbarizing like Sertorius or hellenizing like Anthony, or flirting with both as in the case of Catiline. *Humanitas* may have been formulated as a universalizing concept, but Roman identity was perhaps more jealously guarded and closely defined, to the extent that it was simply not available beyond the limits of the empire. That intimate relationship between Roman civilization and Roman empire is also a reminder of the centrality of imperialism in the Roman culture of the principate.

>> 62. To Rome

AELIUS ARISTIDES [144 C.E.]

Most noteworthy by far and most marvelous of all is the grandeur of your concept of citizenship[?]. There is nothing on earth like it.

For you have divided all the people of the Empire—when I say that, I mean the whole world—in two classes: the more cultured, better born, and more influential everywhere you have declared Roman citizens and even of the same stock; the rest vassals and subject. Neither sea nor any intervening distance on the land excludes one from citizenship. No distinction is made between Asia and Europe in this respect. Everything lies open to everybody; and no one fit for office or a position of trust is an alien. There exists a universal democracy under one man, the best *princeps* and administrator....

You have not made Rome a world's conceit, by letting nobody else share in it. No, you have sought out the complement of citizens it deserves. You have made the word "Roman" apply not to a city but to a universal people—and, at that, not just one of all the peoples there are, but equivalent to all the rest. You no longer classify peoples as Greek or barbarian....You have redivided mankind into Romans and non-Romans. So far have you extended the name of your city. Under this classification there are many in each city who are no less fellow citizens of yours than of those of their own stock, though some of them have never seen this city. You have no need to garrison their citadels; the biggest and most influential men everywhere keep watch over their own native places for you. You have a double hold upon those cities—from right here and through the Roman citizens in each.

No envy sets foot in your Empire. You have set an example in being free from envy yourselves, by throwing open all doors and offering to qualified men the opportunity to play in turn a ruler's part no less than a subject's. No hatred creeps in either from those who fail to qualify. Since the state is universal and like one city, magistrates naturally treat the governed not as aliens but as their own. Besides, the state imparts to all peoples security from the men in power among them. If these men presume to do anything irregular, your wrath and punishment will promptly catch up with them.

So, of course, things as they are satisfy and benefit both poor and rich. No other way of life remains. There is one pattern of government, embracing all. Under you, what was formerly thought incapable of conjunction has been united, rule of an Empire at once strong and humane, mild rule without oppression [?]. Thus towns are free of garrisons, whole provinces are adequately guarded by battalions and cavalry companies, which are not stationed in force in the various cities of each people but scattered through the countryside among a multitude of the population, so that many provinces do not know where their garrison is.

But if a city anywhere, through excessive bigness, has outgrown its capacity to use self-restraint, you do not withhold from such the men needed to take charge of and watch over it.

Moreover, all people are happier to send in their tribute to you than anyone would be to collect it for himself from others....

Instead of quarreling over empire and primacy, through which all wars formerly broke out, some of your subjects...relax in utmost delight, content to be released from troubles and miseries, and aware that they were formerly engaged in aimless shadow-boxing. Others do not know or remember what territory they once ruled....But they accepted your leadership fully, and in a flash revived. How they came to this they cannot say; they know nothing, except to look with awe upon the present state of affairs....Whether there ever were wars is now doubted; most people hear of them in the category of empty legends. Whenever they occurred somewhere along the frontiers, as is natural in a vast, measureless empire...then just

Source: Aelius Aristides, "To Rome," in *Roman Civilization, Sourcebook II: The Empire,* edited by N. Lewis and M. Reinhold (New York: Harper & Row, 1966), 135–7.

like legends the wars passed by quickly and so did talk of them. Such profound peace has come to you, although war is your ancestral way of life....

Were there ever so many cities, inland and maritime? Were they ever so thoroughly modernized? Could a person in the past travel thus, counting up the cities by the number of days on the road, sometimes even going past two or three of them...?

The upshot is that not only were former empires so inferior at the top, but also the peoples whom they ruled were none of them on a par, in numbers or in caliber, with those same peoples under you. You may contrast the tribe of the past with the city there today. Indeed, it may be said that they were virtually kings of wilderness and fortresses, while you alone govern cities.

Now under you all the Greek cities emerge. All the monuments, works of art and adornments in them mean glory for you, the same as an adornment in your suburbs. Seashore and interior are filled with cities, some founded and others enlarged under you and by you. Ionia, the great prize, is rid of garrisons and satraps, and stands out as a model of elegance to the world. She now outstrips her old self by as much as she was formerly reputed to be ahead of other peoples in taste and refinement.

A Buddhist Empire in South Asia

Aśoka's conquests in South and Central Asia are eclipsed by his subsequent governmental and administrative reforms, which were on a par with those of the Qin and Han emperors. But most striking of all his actions are his edicts and their contents, some carved on rock faces and others on pillars. Published in local languages from one end of his realm to the other, these edicts spell out a remarkable program of individual responsibility to society at large. In his reconceptualization of ethical relations, Aśoka proclaims that Dhamma (Dharma) consisted of righteous and good behavior toward others. The effects of Aśoka's conversion to Buddhism are evident throughout his edicts—the edicts themselves present a Buddhist basis for good government and proper personal behavior. This particular set of edicts describes Aśoka's conversion from warfare, violence, and bloodshed to internal peace, domestic tranquility, and foreign diplomacy. Eschewing almost all blood sacrifices and even ritual and ceremonies, Aśoka counsels ethical behavior, from respect to not only one's parents but also other religions to kindness to prisoners, the poor, and the aged. By following his prescripts of restraint and responsibility in one's personal life, a new philosophical conquest is achieved, a conquest that results in joy in this world and the next.

>> 63. Rock Edicts

Aśoka [Third century b.c.e.]

Beloved-of-the-Gods, King Piyadasi, has caused this Dhamma edict to be written. [1] Here (in my domain) no living beings are to be slaughtered or offered in sacrifice. Nor should festivals be held, for Beloved-of-the-Gods, King Piyadasi, sees much to object to in such festivals, although there are some festivals that Beloved-of-the-Gods, King Piyadasi, does approve of.

Formerly, in the kitchen of Beloved-of-the-Gods, King Piyadasi, hundreds of thousands of animals were killed every day to make curry. But now with the writing of this Dhamma edict only three creatures, two peacocks and a deer are killed, and the deer not always. And in time, not even these three creatures will be killed.

Source: Aśoka, "Rock Edicts," rendered by Ven. S. Dhammika, permanent URL http://www.cs. colostate.edu/~malaiya/ashoka.html.

2 Everywhere [2] within Beloved-of-the-Gods, King Piyadasi's domain, and among the people beyond the borders, the Cholas, the Pandyas, the Satiyaputras, the Keralaputras, as far as Tamraparni and where the Greek king Antiochos rules, and among the kings who are neighbors of Antiochos, [3] everywhere has Beloved-of-the-Gods, King Piyadasi, made provision for two types of medical treatment: medical treatment for humans and medical treatment for animals. Wherever medical herbs suitable for humans or animals are not available, I have had them imported and grown. Wherever medical roots or fruits are not available I have had them imported and grown. Along roads I have had wells dug and trees planted for the benefit of humans and animals. [4]

3 Beloved-of-the-Gods, King Piyadasi, speaks thus: [5] Twelve years after my coronation this has been ordered—Everywhere in my domain the Yuktas, the Rajjukas and the Pradesikas shall go on inspection tours every five years for the purpose of Dhamma instruction and also to conduct other business. [6] Respect for mother and father is good, generosity to friends, acquaintances, relatives, Brahmans and ascetics is good, not killing living beings is good, moderation in spending and moderation in saving is good. The Council shall notify the Yuktas about the observance of these instructions in these very words.

4 In the past, for many hundreds of years, killing or harming living beings and improper behavior towards relatives, and improper behavior towards Brahmans and ascetics has increased. [7] But now due to Beloved-of-the-Gods, King Piyadasi's Dhamma practice, the sound of the drum has been replaced by the sound of the Dhamma. [8] The sighting of heavenly cars, auspicious elephants, bodies of fire and other divine sightings has not happened for many hundreds of years. But now because Beloved-of-the-Gods, King Piyadasi promotes restraint in the killing and harming of living beings, proper behavior towards relatives, Brahmans and ascetics, and respect for mother, father and elders, such sightings have increased. [9]

These and many other kinds of Dhamma practice have been encouraged by Beloved-of-the-Gods, King Piyadasi, and he will continue to promote Dhamma practice. And the sons, grandsons and great-grandsons of Beloved-of-the-Gods, King Piyadasi, too will continue to promote Dhamma practice until the end of time; living by Dhamma and virtue, they will instruct in Dhamma. Truly, this is the highest work, to instruct in Dhamma. But practicing the Dhamma cannot be done by one who is devoid of virtue and therefore its promotion and growth is commendable.

This edict has been written so that it may please my successors to devote themselves to promoting these things and not allow them to decline. Beloved-of-the-Gods, King Piyadasi, has had this written twelve years after his coronation.

5 Beloved-of-the-Gods, King Piyadasi, speaks thus: [10] To do good is difficult. One who does good first does something hard to do. I have done many good deeds, and, if my sons, grandsons and their descendants up to the end of the world act in like manner, they too will do much good. But whoever amongst them neglects this, they will do evil. Truly, it is easy to do evil. [11]

In the past there were no Dhamma Mahamatras but such officers were appointed by me thirteen years after my coronation. Now they work among all religions for the establishment of Dhamma, for the promotion of Dhamma, and for the welfare and happiness of all who are devoted to Dhamma. They work among the Greeks, the Kambojas, the Gandharas, the Rastrikas, the Pitinikas and other peoples on the western borders. [12] They work among soldiers, chiefs, Brahmans, householders, the poor, the aged and those devoted to Dhamma—for their welfare and happiness—so that they may be free from harassment. They (Dhamma Mahamatras) work for the proper treatment of prisoners, towards their unfettering, and if the Mahamatras think, "This one has a family to support," "That one has been bewitched," "This one is old," then they work for the release of such prisoners. They work here, in outlying towns, in the women's quarters belonging to my brothers and sisters, and among my other relatives. They are occupied everywhere. These Dhamma Mahamatras are occupied in my domain among people devoted to Dhamma to determine who is devoted to Dhamma, who is established in Dhamma, and who is generous.

This Dhamma edict has been written on stone so that it might endure long and that my descendants might act in conformity with it. [...]

7 Beloved-of-the-Gods, King Piyadasi, desires that all religions should reside everywhere, for all of them desire self-control and purity of heart. [14] But people have various desires and various passions, and they may practice all of what they should or only a part of it. But one who receives great gifts yet is lacking in self-control, purity of heart, gratitude and firm devotion, such a person is mean. [...]

9 Beloved-of-the-Gods, King Piyadasi, speaks thus: [17] In times of sickness, for the marriage of sons and daughters, at the birth of children, before embarking on a journey, on these and other occasions, people perform various ceremonies. Women in particular perform many vulgar and worthless ceremonies. These types of ceremonies can be performed by all means, but they bear little fruit. What does bear great fruit, however, is the ceremony of the Dhamma. This involves proper behavior towards servants and employees, respect for teachers, restraint towards living beings, and generosity towards ascetics and Brahmans. These and other things constitute the ceremony of the Dhamma. Therefore a father, a son, a brother, a master, a friend, a companion, and even a neighbor should say: "This is good, this is the ceremony that should be performed until its purpose is fulfilled, this I shall do." [18] Other ceremonies are of doubtful fruit, for they may achieve their purpose, or they may not, and even if they do, it is only in this world. But the ceremony of the Dhamma is timeless. Even if it does not achieve its purpose in this world, it produces great merit in the next, whereas if it does achieve its purpose in this world, one gets great merit both here and there through the ceremony of the Dhamma. [...]

12 Beloved-of-the-Gods, King Piyadasi, honors both ascetics and the householders of all religions, and he honors them with gifts and honors of various kinds. [22] But Beloved-of-the-Gods, King Piyadasi, does not value gifts and honors as much as he values this—that there should be growth in the essentials of all religions. [23] Growth in essentials can be done in different ways, but all of them have as their root restraint in speech, that is, not praising one's own religion, or condemning the religion of others without good cause. And if there is cause for criticism, it should be done in a mild way. But it is better to honor other religions for this reason. By so doing, one's own religion benefits, and so do other religions, while doing otherwise harms one's own religion and the religions of others. Whoever praises his own religion, due to excessive devotion, and condemns others with the thought "Let me glorify my own religion," only harms his own religion. Therefore contact (between religions) is good. [24] One should listen to and respect the doctrines professed by others. Beloved-of-the-Gods, King Piyadasi, desires that all should be well-learned in the good doctrines of other religions.

Those who are content with their own religion should be told this: Beloved-of-the-Gods, King Piyadasi, does not value gifts and honors as much as he values that there should be growth in the essentials of all religions. And to this end many are working—Dhamma Mahamatras, Mahamatras in charge of the women's quarters, officers in charge of outlying areas, and other such officers. And the fruit of this is that one's own religion grows and the Dhamma is illuminated also.

13 Beloved-of-the-Gods, King Piyadasi, conquered the Kalingas eight years after his coronation. [25] One hundred and fifty thousand were deported, one hundred thousand were killed and many more died (from other causes). After the Kalingas had been conquered, Beloved-of-the-Gods came to feel a strong inclination towards the Dhamma, a love for the Dhamma and for instruction in Dhamma. Now

Beloved-of-the-Gods feels deep remorse for having conquered the Kalingas.

Indeed, Beloved-of-the-Gods is deeply pained by the killing, dying and deportation that take place when an unconquered country is conquered. But Beloved-of-the-Gods is pained even more by this—that Brahmans, ascetics, and householders of different religions who live in those countries, and who are respectful to superiors, to mother and father, to elders, and who behave properly and have strong loyalty towards friends, acquaintances, companions, relatives, servants and employees—that they are injured, killed or separated from their loved ones. Even those who are not affected (by all this) suffer when they see friends, acquaintances, companions and relatives affected. These misfortunes befall all (as a result of war), and this pains Beloved-of-the-Gods.

There is no country, except among the Greeks, where these two groups, Brahmans and ascetics, are not found, and there is no country where people are not devoted to one or another religion.[26] Therefore the killing, death or deportation of a hundredth, or even a thousandth part of those who died during the conquest of Kalinga now pains Beloved-of-the-Gods. Now Beloved-of-the-Gods thinks that even those who do wrong should be forgiven where forgiveness is possible.

Even the forest people, who live in Beloved-of-the-Gods' domain, are entreated and reasoned with to act properly. They are told that despite his remorse Beloved-of-the-Gods has the power to punish them if necessary, so that they should be ashamed of their wrong and not be killed. Truly, Beloved-of-the-Gods desires non-injury, restraint and impartiality to all beings, even where wrong has been done.

Now it is conquest by Dhamma that Beloved-of-the-Gods considers to be the best conquest. [27] And it (conquest by Dhamma) has been won here, on the borders, even six hundred yojanas away, where the Greek king Antiochos rules, beyond there where the four kings named Ptolemy, Antigonos, Magas and Alexander rule, likewise in the south among the Cholas, the Pandyas, and as far as Tamraparni. [28] Here in the king's domain among the Greeks, the Kambojas, the Nabhakas, the Nabhapamkits, the Bhojas, the Pitinikas, the Andhras and the Palidas, everywhere people are following Beloved-of-the-Gods' instructions in Dhamma. Even where Beloved-of-the-Gods' envoys have not been, these people too, having heard of the practice of Dhamma and the ordinances and instructions in Dhamma given by Beloved-of-the-Gods, are following it and will continue to do so. This conquest has been won everywhere, and it gives great joy—the joy which only conquest by Dhamma can give. But even this joy is of little consequence. Beloved-of-the-Gods considers the great fruit to be experienced in the next world to be more important.

I have had this Dhamma edict written so that my sons and great-grandsons may not consider making new conquests, or that if military conquests are made, that they be done with forbearance and light punishment, or better still, that they consider making conquest by Dhamma only, for that bears fruit in this world and the next. May all their intense devotion be given to this which has a result in this world and the next.

>> Mastering the Materials

1. Read the "Funeral Speech of Pericles" in Thucydides carefully. What is the connection between the development of democracy and the principles of thinking developed in the Ionian Intellectual Revolution?

2. To what might you attribute the success of empires like that of China, beginning with the Qin and Han Dynasties, and of Rome, beginning with Caesar Augustus? What does an orator like Aelius Aristides, for example, see as the greatest achievement of the Romans?

3. How did culture help to create a common identity in both China and Rome? What are some of the other consequences for China and Rome of this creation of a common identity and common culture?

4. How are the policies of Aśoka influenced by the intellectual developments of the Axial Age?

>> Making Connections

1. How did the Axial Age thinkers contribute to later political developments in India, China, and Greece? What kind of political systems emerge in these places?

2. Despite the intellectual advances of the Axial Age, why could the Greeks never think beyond their individual *polis*? In thinking about this, remember the material in Part 1. What might have limited their ability to create larger political units, even after Alexander the Great's conquests?

3. How would you compare the political developments of this chapter with what took place politically in the period covered in Part 1?

Chapter 9

Carriers of Exchange

Toward the end of the *Odyssey,* Homer has the main hero tell the story of a visit by Phoenician seamen to Ithaca. Odysseus' father traded his cattle for their manufactured trinkets and, perhaps surprisingly, a gold necklace strung with Baltic amber. Homer was witness to the mutual commercial and cultural exchanges between the Middle East and southeast Europe that had resumed in the course of the ninth century B.C.E. after nearly a three-century break. Despite the importance of these exchanges, they remained on a fairly limited scale at first. In the period discussed in Part 2, however, interaction increased immensely. This intermingling, and its cultural consequences, closely approximates a kind of "globalization" that the world had never seen before. In this chapter we discuss some of the processes and mechanisms of cross-cultural exchange and development from 600 B.C.E. to 300 C.E.

Although cultures change as a result of independent invention and can even develop unique structures in relative isolation, as in early Mesoamerica and much of pharaonic Egypt, contact between peoples is perhaps the greater source of change. Even in the New World, although isolated from Africa and Eurasia, exchanges took place among the various groups that inhabited North and South America. The diffusion of goods, technologies, and ideas often stimulates transformations more extensively and quickly than invention itself. But the importation of an object is far different than the acquisition of a technology or technical skill, as in the transmission of the alphabet from the Middle East to the Greeks. As explored in Reading 65 by Walter Burkert, this transfer involved intimate contact between the Greeks and the Phoenicians themselves. The picture, however, is not always clear in its fine details, even when the results of diffusion itself are. Often the written record and literary sources are inadequate to explain fully—or even partially—what has taken place. As a result, another science is critical for historians: archaeology. The work of both Elizabeth Isichei and William Watson illustrate the use of archaeology to study the diffusion of technology and art in sub-Saharan Africa and China, respectively.

The methods and mechanisms of exchange are as important and as interesting as the exchange itself. One of the most important modes of cultural diffusion and interaction is through trade. The changing patterns of commerce in this period are well represented by the experience of Egypt and surrounding regions of Northeast Africa. While trade into and out of the Nile Valley had gone on since predynastic times, the Egyptians in the pharaonic period did not develop a large, well-defined merchant class of the type seen in China and Mesopotamia. Trade, an almost exclusive monopoly of the pharaoh's court, often had all the appearances of a raid rather than a true commercial venture, as seen in the exploits of Harkhuf, a high official in the Sixth Dynasty. By the Roman period, however, *The Periplus of the Erythraean Sea* reveals the development of a merchant class in Egypt that was at the hub of an extensive trading network that stretched from Italy to India, and from Alexandria up the Nile by caravan to Axum in Ethiopia. Overland caravans also stretched from the Mediterranean to China, with Palmyra in Syria representing a way station on that route.

In addition to trade, small-scale immigration is another mechanism of cultural diffusion. Individual Greeks settled in central Italy in the seventh century B.C.E., bringing with them a variety of technical skills. Later, intellectuals from Ionia fled from advancing Persian armies, and in so doing helped to spread the new thinking of the Axial Age west to mainland Greece and Italy. Sima Qian presents a striking example of the important effects of immigration in China. The episode in Reading 71 relates how the king of Qin sought to expel all aliens from his kingdom, regardless of their contributions or merit.

A final mechanism of exchange consists of the movement of large numbers of people, either as conquerors or settlers, or both, of new territories. We have already seen in this volume the effects of the migrations of groups like the Amorites into Mesopotamia and of Aryan speakers into northern India. Sometimes, however, the cultural effects of a conquest can take place years, if not centuries, after the invading armies have left. Despite the brief Achaemenid suzerainty over the Indus Valley, Aśoka followed the lead of the Persian kings with his great rock inscriptions and his artistic and architectural motifs. Similarly, although Alexander stayed but a little while in the Indus Valley, and the Greeks but a short time longer, the first iconic images of the Buddha are taken from Hellenistic models beginning in the first century C.E. by invading kings who converted to Buddhism.

Cultural Exchange in Mesoamerica

Octavio Paz examines the originality of ancient Mexican art which, he suggests, derived from its complete isolation from Old World cultures and civilizations. Although independent invention occurred often enough in the Old World, the diffusion of objects, ideas, and technologies tended to be the rule rather than the exception. That was not as much the case in the New World. The inhabitants of the Americas had to invent for themselves agriculture and monumental architecture, art and writing, urban forms and political systems, and they did all of these things without the influence of far-flung peoples and cultures. The positive result of this relative isolation, Paz argues, included the development of a brilliant civilization that was unique from that found in the rest of the world. While scholars take exception to his notion that this cultural isolation was also the primary cause for the collapse of their world when Europeans first came to their shores, his observations on the unique qualities of the culture in the Americas still holds. Yet despite the exceptional originality of Mesoamerican culture, even Octavio Paz notes that the diverse peoples of that region shared a common civilization. This commonality was made possible by the diffusion of objects and skills from one group to another throughout the whole of antiquity. In addition to migration and conquest, trade was probably the most common mechanism of cultural diffusion in the New World.

>> 64. The Power of Ancient Mexican Art

OCTAVIO PAZ [1990]

As the new lands gradually revealed themselves to the eyes of the Europeans, it could be seen that they were products of history as well as nature. The Indian societies were seen by the first Spanish missionaries as a theological mystery. The *General History of the Things of New Spain* is an extraordinary book, one of the founding works of the science of anthropology. Yet the author, Bernardino de Sahagún, always believed that the ancient Mexican religion was one of Satan's ploys and that it had to be eradicated from the soul of the Indian. This theological mystery later became a historical problem. What changed was the mental viewpoint but not the conceptual difficulty. Unlike the cases of Persia, Egypt, or Babylonia, the American civilizations were no older than the civilization of Europe. They were simply different, yet this difference was radical: it constituted a real "otherness."

No matter how isolated the centers of civilization of the Old World may have been, there were always contacts and links between the Mediterranean cultures and those of the Near East, and between the latter and those of India and the Far East. Persians and Greeks were in India, while Buddhism spread from India into China, Korea, and Japan. On the other hand, although we cannot rule out entirely the possibility of contacts between the civilizations of Asia and America, it seems obvious that America experienced nothing comparable to these transfusions of ideas, styles, techniques, and religions that revitalized the societies of the Old World. In pre-Columbian America there were no external influences as important as those of Babylonian astronomy in the Mediterranean, Persian and Greek art in

Buddhist India, Mahayana Buddhism in China, or Chinese ideograms and Confucian thought in Japan. It seems that there was some rather limited contact between the Mesoamerican and Andean regions, yet these two societies owe nothing or very little to extraneous influences. In economic practices and artistic forms, in social organization and cosmological and ethical concepts, the two great civilizations of America were original in the broad sense of the word: their origin was internal.

It was precisely this originality that was one of the causes, and perhaps the decisive one, of their destruction. Originality is also a synonym for "otherness" and both terms point to isolation. Neither of the two civilizations of America had an experience that was common and constant among the societies of the Old World: the presence of the other, the intrusion of alien civilizations and cultures. This is why they saw the Spaniards as beings from another world, as gods. The reason for their defeat is to be found not so much in their technical inferiority as in their historical isolation. Their mental universe included the belief in another world and its gods, but not the idea of another civilization and its inhabitants.

From the beginning, the European historical mind came face to face with the hermetic civilizations of America. From the second half of the sixteenth century there were multiple attempts to suppress the differences that seemed to deny the unity of the human race. Some claimed that the ancient Mexicans were one of the lost tribes of Israel; others attributed a Phoenician or Carthaginian origin to them; others, like the Mexican scholar Sigüenza y Góngora, thought that the similarities between certain Christian ceremonies and some of the ritual practices of ancient Mexico were a distorted echo of the sermon of the Gospel by the apostle Saint Thomas, known among the

Source: Octavio Paz, "The Power of Ancient Mexican Art," *The New York Review of Books,* 6 December 1990, 18–20.

Indians by the name of Quetzalcóatl (Sigüenza also believed that Neptune had been a leader of civilizations and the founding father of Mexicans). The Jesuit Athanasius Kircher, a walking encyclopedia with a craze for everything Egyptian, argued that the pyramids and other pieces of evidence were ample proof that Mexican civilization was an overseas version of Egyptian civilization, an opinion that must have delighted one of his readers and admirers, Sor Juana Inés de la Cruz.... Each one of these exercises in concealment was followed by a resurgence of American "otherness." It was unavoidable. At the and of the eighteenth century the recognition of this difference marked the beginning of true understanding. Yet this recognition entailed a paradox: the link between ourselves and the other depends not on resemblance but on difference. We are united not by a bridge but be an abyss. Man is a plurality: men.

I have mentioned the distinguishing features of Mesoamerican civilization as originality, isolation, and something I have had to call "otherness." I should also add two more features: spatial homogeneity and temporal continuity. In the territory of Mesoamerica—a rugged land of contrasts in which every climate and every landscape coexists—several cultures arose whose frontiers more or less coincided with geographical boundaries: the northwest, the high central plateau, the Gulf of Mexico coast, the Valley of Oaxaca, Yucatán, and the low-lying regions of the southeast that extend to Guatemala and Honduras. The diversity of cultures, languages, and artistic styles does not fracture the essential unity of this civilization. Although it is not easy to mistake a Mayan work for one from Teotihuacán—the two poles or extremities of Mesoamerica—in each of the great cultures there are certain common denominators.

The Orientalizing Revolution in Greece

Over the course of the eighth century B.C.E., *Greek contact with others radically transformed Hellenic culture. After centuries of isolation, the Greeks began to trade overseas, the most important destinations being those along the eastern seaboard of the Mediterranean Sea. Here they came into contact with a wide variety of peoples and cultures, from inland Urartia (what is now eastern Turkey) to coastal Phoenicia. Because of this contact with the east, scholars have come to call this the "Orientalizing Revolution." And a revolution it was: metallurgical skills, artistic motifs, sculpture, and possibly even literary and religious ideas were diffused from east to west. In the course of explaining the changes that took place in Greece as a result of this contact, Walter Burkert shows how the Greeks always did more than simply borrow an object. They also learned techniques and skills from individuals like the Phoenicians, while simultaneously transforming what they had learned and borrowed into something that was uniquely theirs. In other words, cultural diffusion between these two worlds was both intimate and complex. The example included here is how the Greeks came to borrow and even learn how to teach to their children the Phoenician way of writing. Our alphabet derives from the Greek system by way of the Etruscans, from whom the Romans learned how to write.*

>> 65. The Orientalizing Revolution: Near Eastern Influence on Greek Culture in the Early Archaic Age

WALTER BURKERT [1992]

This is not to preclude more subtle interpretations of Greek achievements as a consequence. Yet in the period at about the middle of the eighth century, when direct contact had been established between the Assyrians and the Greeks, Greek culture must have been much less self-conscious and therefore much more malleable and open to foreign influence than it became in subsequent generations. It is the formative epoch of Greek civilization that experienced the orientalizing revolution. [...]

For the manner in which the transmission of writing occurred there is an invaluable clue, even if it is often overlooked: the Greek names of the letters (*alpha, beta, gamma,* and so on) with their unalterable order. These are Semitic words—bull, house, and so on—which have no sense at all in Greek. They were preserved for one particular reason: All teaching of reading and writing began with learning this sequence by heart. This explains also why much earlier the standardized sequence appears in two completely different Semitic alphabetic scripts, in the Ugaritic cuneiform alphabet attested in the thirteenth century and in the "Phoenician" alphabet, evidence of which has now been uncovered from as early as the twelfth century. Even across language barriers, the same mnemonic sequence was learned by rote in the same way. With the alphabetic script, for the first time a system of writing had come into being which was so simple that it could be used by all people of normal intelligence even outside the circles of learned professional scribes; they need to be taught for only a short time and to get some practice in handwriting. We may form some picture of the teaching of writing in the Syro-Palestinian region. When much later we read in Josephus that "of all those who dealt with the Greeks, the Phoenicians used writing the most, for private business as well as for their public affairs," he was referring to a school tradition going back a thousand years. The inference is that the "inventor" who first used these letters for the notation of the Greek language had participated in at least one school lesson, whether of the Aramaic or the Phoenician type, whether in Syria or on Cyprus, perhaps even somewhere else with some emigrant who had received an elementary education. This gives cause to reflect on the sheer coincidence that rules the evidence available to us: The Semitic letter names *alpha, beta,* and so on occur in Greek literature in the fifth century at the earliest, but they must have been in current use ever since the eighth century, as they had been adopted along with the original alphabet; that those meaningless word patterns should have been introduced into Greek at any later time is quite impossible. [...]

Thus it is clear that the adoption of the Phoenician script by the Greeks was more than the copying of letter forms: it included the transmission of the technique of teaching and learning how to read and write. This presupposes a certain intimacy of contacts, as is also indicated by those objects which almost never show up in the archaeological documentation and yet are much more significant for the tradition of writing than individual graffiti: writing tablets and leather scrolls together with the appropriate writing tools. These indeed must have accompanied the use of the Greek script from the start. The writing tablet, *deltos* in Greek, has even kept its Semitic name, *daltu—daleth* in Hebrew—together with the name of the special wax with which it is covered, *malthe. Daltu* originally means door but is used for a writing tablet already in thirteenth-century Ugarit, as it is in Hebrew later on.

Source: Walter Burkert, *The Orientalizing Revolution: Near Eastern Influence on Greek Culture in the Early Archaic Age,* translated by Margaret E. Pinder and Walter Burkert (Cambridge, MA: Harvard University Press, 1992), 8, 28–30.

Cultural Diffusion in China and Africa

The spread of metallurgy, especially iron working, throughout sub-Saharan Africa in premodern times is the subject of great scholarly controversy. Elizabeth Isichei suggests that while iron smelting might possibly have been an independent development, she doubts that it was. Instead she argues that this technology came from north to south by one of several possible routes. What makes the study of this topic so frustrating is that the exact method of diffusion remains unclear. Bantu speakers, for instance, seem to have brought this technology with them as they settled in new places, but exactly how and under what conditions they acquired this skill, and who might be responsible for passing it on to others further afield is uncertain. Archaeology, however, indicates the range of the spread of iron working so that by 1400 C.E. we know that "the Ages of Metals was almost universal" in sub-Saharan Africa.

The process of diffusion, technological and artistic, often occurs on the fringes of the more urbanized world. The Thracians, for example, adopted and adapted many aspects of Greek art. So too on the fringes of the Chinese world, cultural and economic exchanges took place. William Watson explores the complex relationship between the Chinese and their northern nomadic neighbors. While previous scholarship emphasized the movement of nomadic influences into China, using archaeology Watson shows that the reverse is also true. He shows how certain weapon technologies and artistic motifs were adopted by groups on the other side of the Chinese frontier.

>> 66. A History of African Societies to 1870

ELIZABETH ISICHEI [1997]

The Beginnings of Iron Working

The most puzzling aspect of the history of iron working in Africa is the fact that it seems to have begun in northern Africa and south of the Sahara at about the same time.

Iron first became important in Egypt under the Saite kings (663–525 BCE). The first evidence of iron smelting in Meroe (on the Nile, north of modern Khartoum) dates from the sixth century BCE, but the great slag heaps which led to the misleading epithet 'the Birmingham of Africa' were produced early in the Christian era. Iron working in Aksum, in northern Ethiopia, is thought to date from much the same time. There

is no direct, but much indirect, evidence for iron smelting in Carthage (another mystery), but since the Phoenicians came from the heartland of ancient metallurgy, it is generally assumed that it was present from the city's foundation, traditionally 813.

Remarkably, the earliest attested instances of iron working in sub-Saharan Africa are contemporary with those in northern Africa, or even earlier. Most of the evidence clusters around the sixth century BCE, though some studies suggest dates as much as three centuries earlier. The beginning of iron working at Taruga, in central Nigeria, is firmly dated to the sixth century BCE. At KatsinaAla, which, like Taruga, is part of the Nok cultural complex, iron working began in the fourth century BCE. For a long time, these central Nigerian dates stood in

Source: Elizabeth Isichei, *A History of African Societies to 1870* (Cambridge: Cambridge University Press, 1997), 70–3.

puzzling isolation, but there is now increasing evidence of the spread of iron in modern Ghana towards the end of the first millennium BCE. There is also a seventh-century BCE date for iron working in Niger. It is increasingly clear that Nok iron working was not a mysterious unique phenomenon, but one manifestation among many of a widely diffused Early Iron Age from *c.* 600 BCE on.

Schmidt's research in Buhaya in East Africa revealed a sophisticated iron technology flourishing from *c.* 500 BCE on, and perhaps earlier, associated with the fine pottery, with incised decoration, known as Urewe were. At first, the scholarly community hesitated to accept this, but it appears to be confirmed by similar dates from Rwanda and Burundi. There is evidence of iron working in Cameroun from the fourth century BCE, and in Gabon at the same time, if not earlier.

Iron working reached southern Africa with great rapidity, and was established in Natal by *c.* 300 CE—a phenomenon which, as we have seen, is often associated with 'Bantu expansion'.

With its associated and distinct but related pottery, the complex described above is generally called the Early Iron Age. It bypassed western Kenya altogether, probably because prospective Bantu settlers were discouraged by the arid zones to the west and south, so that this region went straight from the Pastoral Neolithic to the Later Iron Age. In the history of pyrotechnology, as in the history of pastoralism and agriculture, researchers struggle to fit together the sometimes apparently mutually inconsistent evidence of archaeology and language. The ever earlier dates suggested for metal working are consistent with the fact that proto-Southern Nilotic, dated at least two thousand years ago, includes words for iron and forging. Proto-Bantu lacked words for iron working, but both Eastern and Western Bantu languages share a common vocabulary for metal working—'ore', 'anvil', 'hammer', 'forging', 'charcoal'—which has been taken to imply diffusion from a single centre. […]

Patterns of Diffusion

Not surprisingly, the question of how iron working spread in Africa has attracted a vast amount of attention. Trade in iron objects is, of course, quite distinct from the transfer of technology, and iron smelting, in particular, has often been surrounded by a secrecy which makes its rapid diffusion all the more striking. It was once thought that iron working diffused throughout sub-Saharan Africa from Meroe, but it has long been realised that this is improbable, since smelting in sub-Saharan Africa was roughly contemporaneous. Archaeological work in the Southern Sudan, which has yielded no evidence of iron working before 500 CE, confirms this.

Did iron working spread from Carthage, via Libyan intermediaries? Was it independently invented in Africa? Scholars have been, on the whole, resistant to the latter idea, partly because the extremely high temperatures required make a chance discovery unlikely, and partly because until recently there was thought to be no intermediate copper/bronze age. I originally supported it, on the grounds that meticulous excavations in Borno and Hausaland, which are both north or north-east of the Nok culture, suggest that iron smelting developed there as much as a thousand years later. This seems inconsistent with the advent of iron technology from the vicinity of the Nile or from the Mediterranean world. New evidence about the Saharan Copper Age makes it seem more probable that pyrotechnology did indeed reach West Africa from the north. It is likely that knowledge of iron smelting travelled along a variety of routes. Some believe that it reached the interlacustrine area from West Africa, and others, despite the problems of dating, from Meroe. An independent invention there is a real possibility. The mapping of furnace types might be expected to provide a clue to the pattern of pyrotechnology's diffusion, but they often survive only in fragments, and there is no general agreement on their categorisation. […]

It is likely that pyrotechnology, like the control of scarce resources such as salt, contributed to the enlargement of political scale and the growth of social stratification. The paradox here, is that the inputs—iron ore, charcoal and clay for furnace construction—were so widely available. The craft of smelting was usually a secret, passed on from father to son. If it was practised in the dry season, and the smelters farmed during the rains, they were likely to become richer than their neighbours. In some cases, control of iron technology may have led to the creation of states, or to the seizing of power by blacksmiths within them. This is a theme developed in the next chapter.

The crucial innovation was iron smelting, not blacksmithing, for the production of steel from the furnace meant that the latter, crucially significant in Asian and European pyrotechnology, was relatively unimportant in Africa. Yet it is blacksmithing which is the primary source of political symbolism. Smelting, conducted in secret, was often symbolically identified with gestation and birth; smithing was part of the public domain.

>> 67. The Chinese Contribution to Eastern Nomad Culture in the Pre-Han and Early Han Periods

WILLIAM WATSON [1972]

The involvement of China with nomadic peoples inhabiting territories on her northwestern frontier, a fruitful theme for both political and cultural historians, has hitherto sadly lacked the precisions which archaeological research can supply. The traditional Chinese picture, based largely on the experience of the last few pre-Christian centuries, has been one of invading barbarian hordes held at bay, more or less, along the line of the Great Wall, which was completed by the first emperor of Ch'in [Qin] at the end of the second century B.C. This ideology of exclusive offence and defence was projected into earlier periods, so that such a prime event as the move of the Chou [Zhou] dynasts' capital from the north-west into the central plain in 771 B.C. is ascribed to a barbarian irruption. But even in the brief outlines which it at present furnishes, the archaeological record indicates a more complex interpretation of economic and cultural factors. [...]

From the time of the oracle sentences of the late Shang period, in the thirteenth to eleventh centuries B.C., the Chinese have referred to the foreign peoples on her borders by terms which appear to designate regions rather than ethnic identity. A thousand years later it is clear that the empire of the Hsiung-nu [Xionghu] included under its sway peoples of race as diverse as any to be found in the eastern steppes, probably not excluding Iranic elements. Rather than reflecting mere indifference to the character of exotic peoples the ancient Chinese nomenclature recognizes the transcending importance of alliances into which a variety of ethnically diverse but economically similar communities might be drawn, and which over long periods, in spite of local shifts of territory and political relations, presented a fairly uniform field for territorial exploitation by the Chinese, or a uniform threat to the Chinese oecumene. Cultural exchange between China and Siberia and later between China and the eastern steppes originated, on the Chinese side, less from the centre of the Chinese state on the Middle Yellow River than from a broad zone crossing Inner Mongolia, northern Shensi [Shaanxi] and Shansi [Shanxi], where contact with the economic and cultural continuum of the steppes was first made and Chinese forms and ideas were selected and adapted. It has been well argued that the turbulence of the nomads of this 'Northern Zone' was caused no less by the pressure of Chinese expansion, with its settlement of agricultural population and tax-collecting

Source: William Watson, "The Chinese Contribution to Eastern Nomad Culture in the Pre-Han and Early Han Periods," *World Archaeology* 4 (1972), 139, 141–2.

propensity, than by marauding enterprise of the barbarians (Lattimore 1940, chaps. ix, x).

In the eight century B.C. the central Chinese state of Chin [Jin] attacked the non-Chinese inhabitants of the uplands of Shansi [Shanxi] and drove them eastwards beyond the north–south running T'ai-hang [Taihang] range. In the following century it carried out a similar operation to the west, expelling the Ti [Di] tribes beyond the northward bend of the Yellow River on to the edge of the Ordos territory. Thereafter expeditions were mounted by the Jung [Rong] and Red Ti [Di] tribes inhabitating the regions on the western and eastern slopes of the T'ai-hang [Taihang] mountains. Their assaults southwards reached a part of China through which much of the trade conducted with the barbarians must have passed. It touched on the boundaries of the Ch'i [Qi] state, whose growing commercial power, starting with trade in salt, increasingly enabled it to intervene in Chinese feudal politics (Ma 1962). One recalls that at about the same time, in the far west, the famous Scythian raid into Western Asia reached a nodal point of trade at Lake Urmia.

From this time, in the northern region of China, a boundary discernible between ethnic groups can be shown to correspond to an important cultural division deducible from burial methods,

from bronze weapons and other materials. The Western Ti [Di] and the Eastern Jung [Rong] divided along the line of the T'ai-hang [Taihang] shan, and their differentiation appears to have been more particular than the politico-regional distinction general in Chinese nomenclature. The same mountain line marks the limit of the eastward extension of the nomad culture in the typical form which it assumed in the eastern steppes from the fifth century B.C. To the west of the line occur the triad of nomadic traits: short sword, three-bladed arrow and animal-style bronzes; to the east of the line, progressively impoverished to the shores of the Japan sea, stretches a vast province of the slab-grave culture. In the latter region population was sparse indeed, bone and multiple-microlith tools taking the place of bronze, and hunting combining with limited agriculture (Mikami 1961: 97–166; Watson 1971: 125–38). The slab-graves themselves, which in China proper reach into Hopei [Hebei], are an aspect of the *mayaki* (beacons), tombs associated with remains of both earlier phases of the south Siberian Tagar culture and covering approximately the first two-thirds of the first millennium. In north-east China they survive as a legacy of the northern orientation of China's external relations which preceded the establishment of the characteristic nomad culture of the steppes and the ensuing westerly contacts.

Changing North-East African Trade Patterns

Archaeology indicates that the Egyptians already imported wine from southwest Asia in early pharaonic times, and literary sources relate how cedar wood from Lebanon was always a critical commodity for kings and priests alike. However, a well-defined merchant or trading class remains absent from most of the available records. Instead, a good example of the kind of "trade" that went on in early times is found in funeral inscriptions like that of Harkhuf, a royal official to several pharaohs around 2200 B.C.E. Like other royal officials, Harkhuf went overland along caravan routes into Nubia in order to bring back luxury items like ebony, incense, and elephant tusks. On one occasion Harkhuf brought back for the pharaoh cattle and goats, and another time, a dwarf from the Land of Punt. All of his activities constituted trade in only the broadest sense of the word. Some of these exchanges are described as gift giving, while others hint at military force and plundering. But this simple form of trade made its cultural impact: The Egyptians brought in goods from abroad, for which they exchanged small luxury items like fig-urines and carved ivory. As a result, Egyptian objects, artistic motifs, and architectural styles can be found all the way up the Nile and along the eastern coast of the Mediterranean Sea.

All of this changed, however, in Greco-Roman Egypt. The most significant change involved the development of extensive sea trade. Several limited seafaring expeditions were undertaken down the coast of east Africa in earlier periods, the most famous being that of the pharaoh Hatshepsut to the fabled Land of Punt. But aside from expeditions like hers, the Egyptians did not engage in much trade in the Red Sea. The discovery of how to use the seasonal monsoons from Africa to India, and vice versa, in the Roman period transformed everything, however. Overland caravans continued, but sea trading became safer, faster, and more profitable than the traditional land routes. In the first century C.E. in The Periplus (Circumnavigation) of the Erythræan (Red) Sea, *the author details the exchange of manufactured and processed goods from Egypt and the Mediterranean basin to sub-Saharan Africa, Arabia, and India. In return, merchants brought back such varied items as ivory, spices, Indian cotton, and steel. This work even shows how traders distinguished goods meant for either royalty or common people. Archaeologists have also found Roman manufactured items, like glass, in Afghanistan and India, and Roman coins as far east as Vietnam. In this expanded, and almost global, network historians argue the likelihood of an exchange of ideas as well as goods between east and west.*

>> 68. The Autobiography of Harkhuf

[c. 2200 B.C.E.]

(I) The count, Sole Companion, Lector-priest, Chamberlain, Warden of Nekhen, Mayor of Nekheb, Royal Seal-bearer, Chief of scouts, Privy-councillor of all affairs of Upper Egypt, favorite of his lord, Harkhuf.

The Royal Seal-bearer, Sole Companion, Lector-priest, Chief of scouts, who brings the produce of all foreign lands to his lord, who brings gifts to the Royal Ornament, Governor of all mountainlands belonging to the southern region, who casts the dread of Horus into the foreign lands, who does what his lord praises; the Royal Seal-bearer, Sole Companion, Lector-priest, Chief of scouts, honored by Sokar, Harkhuf, says:

The majestry of Mernere, my lord, sent me together with my father, the sole companion and lector-priest, Iri, to Yam, to open the way to that country. (5) I did it in seven months; I brought from it all kinds of beautiful and rare gifts, and was praised for it very greatly.

His majesty sent me a second time alone. I went up on the Yebu road and came down via Mekher, Terers, and Irtjetj (which are in) Irtjet in the space of eight months. I came down bringing gifts from that country in great quantity, the likes of which had never before been brought back to this land. I came down through the region of the house of the chief of Setju and Irtjet, I explored those foreign lands. I have not found it done by any companion and chief of scouts who went to Yam (10) previously. [...]

Source: "The Autobiography of Harkhuf" in *Ancient Egyptian Literature: A Book of Readings, vol. 1, The Old and Middle Kingdoms,* edited by Miriam Lichtheim (Berkeley: University of California Press, 1975), 25–6.

I came down with three hundred donkeys laden with incense, ebony, *hknw*-oil, *s3t*, (5) panther skins, elephant's-tusks, throw sticks, and all sorts of good products. Now when the ruler of Irtjet, Setju, and Wawat saw how strong and numerous the troop from Yam was which came down with me to the residence together with the army that had been sent with me, this ruler escorted me, gave me cattle and goats, and led me on the mountain paths of Irtjet—because of the excellence of the vigilance I had employed beyond that of any companion and chief of scouts who had been sent to Yam before. [...]

(I) The King's own seal: Year 2, third month of the first season, day 15. The King's decree to the Sole companion, Lector-priest, Chief of scouts, Harkhuf. Notice has been taken of this dispatch of yours which you made for the King at the Palace, to let one know that you have come down in safety from Yam with the army that was with you. You have said in this dispatch of yours that you have brought (5) all kinds of great and beautiful gifts, which Hathor mistress of Imaau has given to the *ka* of King Neferkare, who lives forever. You have said in this dispatch of yours that you have brought a pygmy of the god's dances from the land of the horizon-dwellers, like the pygmy whom the god's seal-bearer Bawerded brought from Punt in the time of King Isesi. You have said to my majesty that his like has never been brought by anyone who did Yam previously.

>> 69. The Periplus of the Erythræan Sea

[FIRST CENTURY C.E.]

The Voyage around the Erythræan Sea

1. Of the designated ports on the Erythræan Sea, and the market-towns around it, the first is the Egyptian port of Mussel Harbor. To those sailing down from that place, on the right hand, after eighteen hundred stadia, there is Berenice. The harbors of both are at the boundary of Egypt, and are bays opening from the Erythræan Sea.

2. On the right-hand coast next below Berenice is the country of the Berbers. Along the shore are the Fish-Eaters, living in scattered caves in the narrow valleys. Further inland are the Berbers, and beyond them the Wild-flesh-Eaters and Calf-Eaters, each tribe governed by its chief; and behind them, further inland, in the country toward the west, there lies a city called Meroe.

3. Below the Calf-Eaters there is a little market-town on the shore after sailing about four thousand stadia from Berenice, called Ptolemais of the Hunts, from which the hunters started for the interior under the dynasty of the Ptolemies. This market-town has the true land-tortoise in small quantity; it is white and smaller in the shells. And here also is found a little ivory, like that of Adulis. But the place has no harbor and is reached only by small boats.

4. Below Ptolemais of the Hunts, at a distance of about three thousand stadia, there is Adulis, a port established by law, lying at the inner end of a bay that runs in toward the south. Before the harbor lies the so-called Mountain Island, about two hundred stadia seaward from the very head of the bay, with the shores of the mainland close to it on both sides. Ships bound for this port now anchor here because of attacks from the land. They used formerly to anchor at the very head of the bay, by an island called Diodorus, close to the shore, which could be reached on foot from the land; by which means the barbarous natives attacked the island. Opposite Mountain Island, on the mainland twenty stadia from shore, lies Adulis, a fair-sized village,

Source: Lionel Casson, trans., *The Periplus of the Erythræan Sea* (Princeton: Princeton University Press, 1989), 22–5.

from which there is a three-days' journey to Coloe, an inland town and the first market for ivory. From that place to the city of the people called Auxumites there is a five days' journey more; to that place all the ivory is brought from the country beyond the Nile through the district called Cyeneum, and thence to Adulis. Practically the whole number of elephants and rhinoceros that are killed live in the places inland, although at rare intervals they are hunted on the seacoast even near Adulis. Before the harbor of that market-town, out at sea on the right hand, there lie a great many little sandy islands called Alalæi, yielding tortoise-shell, which is brought to market there by the Fish-Eaters. [...]

6. There are imported into these places, undressed cloth made in Egypt for the Berbers; robes from Arsinoe; cloaks of poor quality dyed in colors; double-fringed linen mantles; many articles of flint glass, and others of murrhine, made in Diospolis; and brass, which is used for ornament and in cut pieces instead of coin; sheets of soft copper, used for cooking-utensils and cut up for bracelets and anklets for the women; iron, which is made into spears used against the elephants and other wild beasts, and in their wars. Besides these, small axes are imported, and adzes and swords; copper drinking-cups, round and large; a little coin for those coming to the market; wine of Laodicea and Italy, not much; olive oil, nor much; for the king, gold and silver plate made after the fashion of the country, and for clothing, military cloaks, and thin coats of skin, of no great value. Likewise from the district of Ariaca across this sea, there are imported Indian iron, and steel, and Indian cotton cloth; the broad cloth called *monachê* and that called *sagmatogênê*, and girdles, and coats of skin and mallow-colored cloth, and a few muslins, and colored lac. There are exported from these places ivory, and tortoise-shell and rhinoceros-horn. The most from Egypt is brought to this market from the month of January to September, that is, from Tybi to Thoth; but seasonably they put to sea about the month of September.

7. From this place the Arabian Gulf trends toward the east and becomes narrowest just before the Gulf of Avalites. [...] There are imported into this place, flint glass, assorted; juice of sour grapes from Diospolis; dressed cloth, assorted, made for the Berbers; wheat, wine, and a little tin. There are exported from the same place, and sometimes by the Berbers themselves crossing on rafts to Ocelis and Muza on the opposite shore, spices, a little ivory, tortoise-shell, and a very little myrrh, but better than the rest. And the Berbers who live in the place are very unruly.

8. After Avalites there is another market-town, better than this, called Malao, distant a sail of about eight hundred stadia. The anchorage is an open roadstead, sheltered by a spit running out from the east. Here the natives are more peaceable. There are imported into this place the things already mentioned, and many tunics, cloaks from Arsinoe, dressed and dyed; drinking-cups, sheets of soft copper in small quantity, iron, and gold and silver coin, not much. There are exported from these places myrrh, a little frankincense, (that known as far-side), the harder cinnamon, *duaca*, Indian copal and *macir*, which are imported into Arabia; and slaves, but rarely.

Palmyra Caravan Tariffs

Caravans evoke images of camels plying enormous stretches of sand dunes, carrying exotic goods from one end of Eurasia to the other. In antiquity, however, the most common beast of burden was the donkey, and exchanges between east and west always went through a series of intermediaries. One of the most interesting stops on the caravan route was Palmyra, a vast city in the Syrian Desert half way between Damascus and the Euphrates River. The main streets of this oasis town were unpaved so as to protect the feet of the camels, and on its southeastern edge the Palmyrans built a large market and Tariff Court—all goods coming into and out of the city were taxed before their journey continued. From the list of duties recorded on the walls of the Tariff Court, we learn what items were being imported and exported, and how valuable various commodities were. Imported from the very bottom of the Arabian Peninsula, myrrh, used for perfumes and as incense, was taxed more heavily than an individual slave. Some critical points are not mentioned in the inscription itself, at least directly. For example, the taxed purple cloth from the Mediterranean coast ended up in China. Similarly, the culture of Palmyra itself was greatly influenced by its position on the trade routes. Occupying the critical space between the Greco-Roman and Mesopotamian worlds, Palmyra was richly endowed with the culture of both, something that can be seen in its many public and religious monuments. Palmyra was a link in the transfer of goods and ideas, something that was replicated all the way to China. Further east, for instance, cities like Samarkand served as cultural intermediaries between east and west; scholars note that Persian traders introduced Zoroastrianism into Samarkand, and from there, Sogdian traders introduced it into China.

>> 70. Palmyra Caravan Tariffs

[137 C.E.]

The Customs Regulations of the Customs District of Hadriana Palmyra and of the Wells of Caesar

From those who import slaves into Palmyra or within its borders the tax farmer is to exact 22 *denarii* per head…; for a slave [who is sold in the town and is not to be?] exported, 12 *denarii*; for a slave of more than one year's service who is for sale, 10 *denarii*; for exported… slaves, 12 *denarii* per head.

Furthermore, in the case of a camel-load of dried products, the tax farmer shall exact 3 *denarii* for each camel-load imported, 3 *denarii* for one camel-load exported, 2 *denarii* for one donkey-load imported or exported.

In the case of purple wool he shall exact 8 *asses* for each fleece imported and also for each exported.

For each camel-load of myrrh imported in alabaster vessels he shall exact 25 *denarii*; for each load of myrrh[?] exported, 13 *denarii*. For each camel-load of myrrh imported in goatskins he shall exact 13 *denarii*; and for each load exported 7 *denarii*. For each donkey-load of myrrh imported in alabaster vessels he shall exact 13 *denarii*, and for each load exported 7 *denarii*. For each donkey-load of myrrh imported in goatskins he shall exact 7 *denarii*, and for each load exported 4 *denarii*.

For each camel-load of olive oil imported in four goatskins, [he shall exact] 13 *denarii*, and for each load exported 13 *denarii*. For each camel-load of olive oil imported in two goatskins he shall exact 7 *denarii*, and for each load exported

Source: "Palmyra Caravan Tariffs," in *Roman Civilization, Sourcebook II: The Empire*, edited by N. Lewis and M. Reinhold (New York: Harper & Row, 1966), 330–2.

7 *denarii*. For each donkey-load of olive oil imported he shall exact 7 *denarii*, and for each load exported 7 *denarii*. . . .

Furthermore, the tax farmer shall exact on each woman who receives 1 *denarius* or more 1 *denarius* per woman, and on each woman who receives 8 *asses*, he shall exact 8 *asses*, and on each woman who receives 6 *asses*, he shall exact 6 *asses*.

Furthermore, the tax farmer shall exact from the workshops as follows: from the leather shops . . . according to custom, 1 *denarius* per month per shop; from the importers and merchants of hides he shall take 2 *asses* per hide. Similarly, the clothing merchants and retailers who sell in the city shall pay the tax farmer the appropriate sum.

For the use of the two springs of the town, 800 *denarii* per annum.

The tax farmer shall exact 1 *denarius* for every load of grain, wine, fodder, and all similar commodities, that is, for each camel-load each trip.

For each camel brought in without a load he shall exact 1 *denarius,* as was exacted by Cilix, imperial freedman. . . . [. . .]

I decree that [the tax farmer] shall exact 1 *denarius* for a load of foodstuffs according to the regulation for import from outside the frontier or export; but those who transport produce to and from the villages [of the territory of Palmyra] are to be exempt in accordance with the concession made to them. With respect to pine cones and similar products which are imported for the market, it is decreed that the duty shall be assessed as for dried products, as is done in the other cities.

With respect to camels, whether they are brought in from outside the frontiers without loads or loaded, 1 *denarius* is due for each according to the regulation, as also Corbulo, *vir clarissimus,* sanctioned in the letter to Barbarus. As concerns camel skins, no duty is to be exacted, and in the case of vegetable fodder . . . it is decided that it is subject to duty because it is salable. [The rest is here omitted.]

Immigrants as a Cultural Force in China

Sima Qian records that the king, and later First Emperor, of Qin wished to expel all aliens from his imperial court—the king considered these immigrants from other states of the preunification China to be a disruptive influence in his government. Li Si, an immigrant but also a Legalist scholar and high court official, wrote a reasoned and powerful memorial against the proposed policy. He pointed out how immigrants had made considerable contributions to Qin from very early times. So-called barbarians, he notes, had been employed as civil servants, and had helped expand Qin. And Shang Yang, one of the greatest minds of the Legalist school and an immigrant, had been a Chancellor for Xiao, the Duke of Qin. Li Si also describes the important trading connections of the kingdom and the many products brought in from abroad. He argued against the mindless deportation of immigrants, suggesting that those individuals who were of the greatest value to the king of Qin would now bring their skills and talents to his enemies. Convinced, the king rescinded his order. This selection illustrates two important strands in Chinese history: that the culture and politics of China were shaped in significant ways by people outside of the emperor's place of origin and outside of his inner circle, and that political authorities were sometimes suspicious, if not hostile, to new people and new ways of doing things.

>> 71. Historical Records

SIMA QIAN [109–91 B.C.E.]

Just at that time Zheng Guo, a man of Han, came to cause dissension in Qin through the construction of drainage and irrigation channels. After the work had been done he was found out. Members of the Qin royal house and important officials all told the King of Qin: 'People from the feudal states who come to serve Qin in general merely travel here to cause dissension in Qin on behalf of their own rulers. We request the complete expulsion of aliens.' There was discussion whether Li Si should also be included among those expelled, so he submitted a memorial saying:

Your servant has heard officials discussing the expulsion of aliens, and humbly considers it to be a mistake. In earlier times, when Duke Mu was in search of public servants, he obtained You Yu from the Rong barbarians in the west and got Baili Xi from Yuan in the east. He welcomed Jian Shu from Song, and attracted Pi Bao and Gongsun Zhi from Jin. These five gentlemen were not brought up by Qin, but Duke Mu employed them, and he annexed twenty states and subsequently became overlord of the Western Rong. Making use of Shang Yang's system of law, Duke Xiao transformed the customs and usages, and the people consequently prospered and the state consequently grew rich and powerful. The common people were delighted to be employed and feudal lords became friendly and offered allegiance. He captured the Chu and Wei armies, and took 1,000 li of territory, so that right up to the present Qin is well governed and strong. [...] He nibbled away at the feudal states and enabled Qin to complete the imperial heritage. These four rulers all made use of the achievements of aliens. Looking at it from this point of view, surely
aliens have not been ignored by Qin! Yet supposing these four rulers had rejected aliens and not admitted them, kept such public servants at a distance and not given them employment, this would have meant that the state would be without the reality of wealth and profit and that Qin would lack the reputation for strength and greatness.

At present Your Majesty has jade from the Kun Mountains brought to him and possesses the treasure of Sui and He. From your girdle hang pearls as bright as the moon, and you wear the Taia sword. You drive horses like Xianli, put up banners adorned with green phoenixes, and set up drums made from the hide of the divine alligator. Qin does not produce one among these various treasures, so why does Your Majesty take pleasure in them? If they must be what the Qin state produces before they are acceptable, then these night-brightening jade ornaments would not embellish the court and vessels of rhinoceros-horn and ivory would not serve as your playthings, and women from Zheng and Wei would not fill the rear quarters of your palace, and fine coursers would not occupy the outer stables, the bronze and tin of Jiangnan would not be made into useful objects, and the cinnabar and blue of western Shu would not be made into paint. If the means of adorning the rear quarters of the palace and filling the lower ranks of the concubines, of giving pleasure to the heart and mind and delighting the ears and eyes, must derive from Qin before they are acceptable, then these hairpins with Yuan pearls, these ear-ornaments with long pearls attached, these silk garments from Donga, and these embroidered adornments would not come into your presence, nor would the fashionable, elegant, fascinating, and charming women of Zhao stand at your side. Now striking earthenware jugs and banging jars,

---

Source: Sima Qian, *Historical Records*, translated by Raymond Dawson (Oxford: Oxford University Press, 1994), 27–9.

strumming the zithern and smiting the thigh while singing 'Wu! Wu!' to delight the ear is truly the sound of Qin; while Zheng, Wei, Sangjian, Zhao, Yu, Wu, and Xiang are the music of different states. If you now abandon striking jugs and banging on jars and go over to the Zheng and Wei, and if you give up strumming the zithern and accept the Zhao and Yu, why is it that you behave like this? What pleases our ideas we have to have in our presence. It simply suits our senses. Now when it comes to selecting men, you do not do likewise. You do not question whether they are acceptable or not and you do not discuss whether they are crooked or straight. Those who are not from Qin are got rid of, and those who are aliens are expelled. If that is so, then what these people take seriously consists of sexual attraction, music, pearls, and jade, and what they take lightly consists of people. This is not a method with which to bestride all within the seas or control the feudal states. [...]

This is the reason why the Five Emperors and the Three Kings were without enemies. Now in fact you are getting rid of the black-headed people so as to provide a resource for enemy countries, and you expel aliens so as to build up the strength of the feudal states. You are causing public servants from all under Heaven to hold back and not venture to turn their faces towards the west, to halt their feet and not enter Qin. This is what is called 'contributing weapons to brigands and presenting provisions to robbers'.

Now articles which are valuable although not produced by Qin are many, and public servants who wish to show their loyalty although not brought up by Qin are numerous. If you now expel aliens so as to provide a resource for enemy states and reduce your people so as to increase your foes, then you will not only be making yourself empty at home but also sowing the seeds of resentment in the feudal states. If you aim for the state to be free of dangers, this cannot be achieved.

Accordingly the King of Qin rescinded the order for the expulsion of aliens and restored Li Si to office, and ultimately he made use of his plans and stratagems.

The Lion Capital

One of the most sacred spots in Buddhism is Sarnath: Here the Buddha delivered his first sermon in the Deer Park, and here, centuries later, Aśoka built a stupa to house relics of the Buddha and erected a large column to commemorate the events that had taken place here. One of the most important pieces of early Indian art is Aśoka's Lion capital now housed in the Archaeological Museum. Once part of his enormous pillar, the bell-shaped inverted lotus—the flower suggesting birth and enlightenment—was inspired by Persian capitals and became a standard for Indian architecture from this time on. Likewise the four lions on the top of the capital derive from Persian and Mesopotamian models. Some scholars argue that the very idea of a sculptural piece like this is Greek inspired. On the abacus itself are carved four sacred Vedic animals: a bull, an elephant, a horse, and a lion, each representing the cardinal points of the compass and each separated by a Buddhist Wheel of the Law. Though now lost, the capital was surmounted by a large Wheel of the Law. Aśoka's artists ended up combining some of the major cultural elements—Persian, Vedic, Buddhist, and possibly Greek—in Indian life in a single monument. Chinese pilgrims to Sarnath in the seventh century C.E. still marveled at the beauty of this monument, and the capital is currently the symbol of the Republic of India.

>> 72. The Aśoka Capital
[THIRD CENTURY B.C.E.]

सत्यमेव जयते

The Diffusion of Greek Art in the Ancient World

Until the first century C.E. the Buddha had always been portrayed without an image. Instead, symbols from the main events in his life represented him, like the Wheel of the Law for his first sermon, or the pipal tree for his enlightenment. All of that changed when the Kushan invaders entered Afghanistan and India from the north. For whatever reason, the Kushan kings wished to portray the Buddha in a formal image—when they did so, on coins and in stone, they used as their model Hellenistic, and to a lesser degree Roman, art. In the following passage, John Boardman explains the substance and nature of the diffusion of Greek art into the Buddhist artistic

Source: The Aśoka Capital, Sarnath, India, http://en.wikipedia.org/wiki/Image:Emblem_of_India.svg.

tradition. The Buddha's name appears in Greek on their coins, his image is that of a kind of Apollo, and the reliefs of religious and pseudo-historic themes sport Corinthian capitals and erotes, or cherub-like creatures. Kushan artists also produced reliefs of Greek figures and styles such as Tritons, Atlantids, and votive swags. Boardman's final point is critical to note: The inspiration for portraying the Buddha in a Greek fashion was in part the result of the continued presence of Greek artistic traditions in that region long after the Greeks had vanished, but the actual success of these works came from "the skilful choice by Indian artists of what could serve them." In a later period, Buddhist missionaries—themselves a mechanism of exchange—spread this Greco-Buddhist, or Indo-Corinthian, art north and east into China and Japan, and southeast as far as Java. Art historians and archaeologists make an important point about cultural diffusion that is often overlooked by political historians: Individuals only borrow those items, physical or intellectual, from others that they can and choose to fit into their own intellectual and cultural systems. Thus, later in this volume, we will see how Buddhism could be adapted into Chinese worldviews much more effectively and fully than Islam.

>> 73. The Diffusion of Classical Art in Antiquity

JOHN BOARDMAN [1993]

Much of the discussion over the last century about Greek influence on Indian art has centred on the creation of the sculptural type for the Buddha. He had at first been represented only by symbols—a footprint, tree or throne—thus at Bharhut, and elsewhere in north India. The creation of a figure type (expressly forbidden under early Buddhism) seems to have happened in the first century AD, either in Gandhara or in the Mathura region to the south, which we have found not altogether immune to western influence. We are concerned with the standing Buddha rather than the seated figure, long established in the east for princes and sages. One might regard the classical influence as including the general idea of representing a man-god in this purely human form, which was of course well familiar in the west, and it is very likely that

the example of westerner's treatment of their gods was indeed an important factor in the innovation. Seated figures adopt an eastern pose, but the monumental standing ones soon take a lightly relaxed stance, of which we see an early example on the gold casket from Bimaran. This is closer to classical contrapposto than to the almost boneless treatment especially of female figures in Indian art, as at Sanchi, or the rather wooden, four-square studies of *yaksas* from the same general area, that appear to be the earliest examples of monumental stone free-standing statuary in India [...], and are only precursors to standing figures of the Buddha. More significant probably is the rendering of dress. We have already observed in the Parthian world the linear adaptation of naturalistic Greek dress. This is apparent also on the Buddhas, but combined with a far more realistic treatment of the fall of folds and on some even a hint of modelled volume that characterizes the best Greek work [...]. This is Classical or Hellenistic Greek, not

Source: John Boardman, *The Diffusion of Classical Art in Antiquity* (Princeton: Princeton University Press, 1994), 126, 144–5. Images are from Wikicommons.

archaizing Greek transmitted by Persia or Bactria, nor distinctively Roman. The *usnisa,* a topknot which characterizes the Buddha, is translated into a Hellenistic coiffure of wavy hair. To define the classical sources for the figure more closely is difficult. In a way they are implicit in most Greek divine and even athlete images created since the fifth century BC and were familiar in miniature on coins. There was nothing in earlier Indian statuary to suggest such a treatment of form or dress, and the Hindu pantheon provided no adequate model for an aristocratic and wholly human deity.

Gandharan relief sculpture is more varied and brings us back closer to Hellenistic forms than do the Buddhas, and certainly to earlier years, pre-Kanishka. It is useful now to bear in mind the Greek poses and dress of the figures on the early stone palettes, and the standing figures carved in high relief on the ivory rhyta from Nisa, as [...] isolated yet engaged with each other by gesture or pose. In Gandhara there are several series of small frieze reliefs, often identified as stair-risers, but which perhaps served as thresholds to niches on Buddhist monuments. The earliest stylistically carry figures of men and women in Greek dress and poses, often couples regaling each other with cups, and sometimes pouring from wineskins into cups or mixing bowls in the Greek manner. [...]

It would be impossible to hold that the sculptural style of north India owed a great deal to anything other than native inspiration and tradition. But what classical there was proved influential and may even have determined the direction in which the arts of Gandhara were to move. It produced some striking individual studies and persistent motifs, a stock-in-trade for artists whose own traditions could not readily answer the needs of Buddhism, but who found in classical art a responsive and easily assimilated idiom. It was, moreover, continuously accessible, from the Indo-Greek and Bactrian heritage and through new intercourse with the west. The Buddha, the man-god, is in many ways far more like a Greek god than any other eastern deity, no less for the narrative cycle of his story and appearance of his standing figure than for his humanity. As a result Buddhist art carried the subtle stamp of the classical for centuries and over thousands of miles. But the monumental arts of the Kushan courts and of later Buddhist and Hindu temples absorbed and obliterated (for all but the most keen-sighted) the occident far more effectively than Greece had done the arts of the east, until its own Classical period. It would be perverse to think that Greek art was the undoing of native Indian art; it contributed to its richness and development in the way that many foreign arts had worked long before on Greek art. Its message lingered in forms long abandoned in the west. We observed this with the Hadda figures [...] and it is no less apparent in many late statues of Boddhisattva, such as the head [...], whose classicizing style and excellence of carving would be hard to match in the contemporary Mediterranean world.

The tenets and practice of Buddhism are so unlike those of the classical world that it is surprising that classical art could play any role at all in visual interpretation of the eastern religion. The cosmological and mythological content of Buddhism, largely derived from the Hindu, was if anything more grotesque than the Olympian Greek. Classical art may have helped devise expression of the essentially human and peaceable aspects of the Buddha's life and teaching, but not through any shared view of man's place in the world. Buddhist practice transcended the almost mindless cruelty of the classical world: the difference, it may be, between encouraging man to aspire to immortal *nirvana,* and making immortals behave like mere men. The success of classical art in Gandhara was probably largely the result of the earlier infiltration of Greek art into India, and of the skilful choice by Indian artists of what could serve them. Beyond and after Gandhara it was only the trappings of classical art that survived—but survive they did, and tenaciously.

>> 74. Greco-Buddhist art

[THIRD CENTURY B.C.E.–FIRST
MILLENNIUM C.E.]

>> Image of the Buddha with the Greek demigod
Herakles, c. first century C.E.

>> Greek-style Ichthyo-Centaur (seahorse-man) from Gandhara,
Pakistan, c. second century C.E.

#1: http://commons.wikimedia.org/wiki/Image:Buddha-Vajrapani-Herakles.jpg.

#2: http://commons.wikimedia.org/wiki/Image:Ichthyo-Centaur.jpg.

>> Indo-Corinthian Kushan frieze with the Hindu gods Indra and Brahma in Greek style, second century C.E.

>> Buddha of Gandhara, Afghanistan, in the Greek Style, c. second century C.E.

#3: http://commons.wikimedia.org/wiki/Image:Kushan%2C_Brahma%2C_Indra%2C_Indian.jpg.
#4: http://commons.wikimedia.org/wiki/Image:Buddha_Gandhara.jpg.

>> Mastering the Materials

1. What does Octavio Paz see as the greatest strength of Mesoamerican civilization?

2. Despite its isolation from the Old World, how do Paz and Drew see diffusion as a factor in creating a common culture and civilization in Mesoamerica?

3. What is the role of diffusion in places like sub-Saharan Africa, Greece, and China? What is actually being exchanged?

4. Compare and contrast trade in the "Autobiography of Harkhuf" with what takes place in *The Periplus of the Erythraean Sea*. In what ways might the methods, articles, and results of trade be considered similar? What are their biggest differences, and to what would you attribute these differences?

5. How important do you think trade is in Eurasia? What are some of the consequences of trade?

6. What is the role of the movement of people—either in very small groups, or as armies, or in vast migrations—in cultural, social, and political change? What examples can you find in this chapter's sources?

7. How are we to understand the portrayal of the Buddha and his followers in a Greek manner long after the Greeks had lived in that area? What might this suggest about diffusion?

>> Making Connections

1. In what ways are the Axial Age, the creation of large empires, and vast trading networks "global" phenomena?

2. How do the events in the Americas also fit into this same pattern, even if on a more limited scale?

3. The diffusion of objects, skills, and ideas is a central feature of human exchange throughout all periods of history. How many examples of diffusion can you find in Parts 1 and 2? How many mechanisms of diffusion can you identify?

Part 2 Conclusion

During the thirty-fourth year of his reign, the King of the State of Qin (later Shihuangdi, the First Emperor of Qin) held an elaborate state banquet at his enormous palace in Xianyang, his capital. In the course of wishing the emperor a long life, two of his ministers, one a Confucian scholar and the other a Legalist, engaged in a heated debate over the value of past precedent as against the current centralizing activities of the emperor. This implicit criticism of Shihuangdi's actions by the Confucian scholar led the angry and fearful ruler to burn the books of the "Hundred Schools" and supposedly to execute 460 leading scholars in the following year. In his growing agitation, the First Emperor also sent out magicians to find the magic fungus and elixirs meant to achieve immortality. Not only did the magicians return empty handed, but a meteor—always a bad omen—fell shortly thereafter, causing the emperor to consult the oracle of the tortoise shell. Although these episodes may have been added to Sima Qian's *Shi ji* by Han Dynasty scholars—who had a motive for making the previous dynasty look bad—they illustrate clearly the main themes of this unit.

Initially, we see the importance of religion in antiquity, despite any changes that might have taken place politically or intellectually. The First Emperor of Qin may have had at his disposal an Academy of hundreds of scholars, but he continued to perform the ancient sacrifices, to consult traditional oracles, and to interpret and understand natural phenomena in a manner that was probably little changed from earliest times. The same attitudes can be found everywhere in the period covered in this unit. In Rome, the death of the emperor Commodus—the sometimes gladiator son of Marcus Aurelius—was heralded by a series of bad omens, including a comet. Nevertheless the world had changed, and ancient religion forms part of the context for the nearly global transformations that occurred between 600 B.C.E. and 300 C.E.

Equally importantly, these incidents spotlight three major nearly global phenomena that characterize the period under consideration in Part 2. First, this set of events only took place as a result of that great burst of creative energy in the Axial Age that produced philosophic innovations and communities that could not be erased. Thus, although Shihuangdi's Chief Minister attempted to stifle disagreement and multiple points of view by burning books and killing scholars, he was unsuccessful: The philosophers of the Axial Age had built a foundation for their respective cultures that has lasted even into the twenty-first century. These thinkers challenged the older religious models for understanding the universe while providing an alternative vision for their societies. Second, the Axial Age with its reasoned critique helped bring about another phenomenon of global significance, at least for the Old World—the creation of successful empires, or large state systems. Ironically, it was the "Hundred Schools," with its Confucian and Legalist thinkers, that allowed the king of Qin to build an empire, at the same time that they created an atmosphere for continued criticism and discussion. The Qin Dynasty was short lived, but the First Emperor and his immediate successors in the Han Dynasty established the outlines of the Chinese empire that lasted until the beginning of the twentieth century. This same political unity was replicated in the west with the Roman Empire. Even though individual rulers were sometimes prone to excess and violence, what kept these two empires together were common cultural systems that diverse populations belonged to and identified with, even in the midst of occasional turmoil and chaos. And finally, we see in this time period a world that was interconnected as never before. The two ministers debating at the First Emperor's banquet were immigrants who had brought their knowledge and skills into the "Qin" imperial court. One of the expeditions that the First Emperor sent to find the elusive elixirs most probably went beyond China's border to Japan. Under the Han Dynasty, China was at the center of an extensive trading network that went west and south. Merchants and emissaries from other societies came to China as well. In 166 C.E., the Chinese record the first traders from the Roman Empire to reach China itself. Migration and trade are but two of the important mechanisms of cultural diffusion and change, and, by the end of this period, both were global enterprises extending across the entire Old World, including sub-Saharan Africa and the far north of Europe.

With the intellectual advances of the Axial Age, the creation of large successful empires, and the network of connections created by trade and movement of individuals and larger groups, the Old World would never be the same again. The foundations of and direction for Marc Bloch's perpetual changes had been set. And even in the New World, communities were not isolated from one another. In this same period, great cities with elaborate and sophisticated cultures were born, and contact among groups was commonplace. The emergence of a unified cultural system in Mesoamerica is, in many respects, analogous to what went on in the Old World. And like the Old World, this cultural system not only helped to define the remainder of pre-Columbian America, but also has lasted, to one degree or another, to this day.

Further Reading

A great number of historians, social anthropologists, and archaeologists have written about the issues and topics raised in Part 2. Ancient religion, always a controversial subject, is no different. One of the most interesting works in this field combines gender and religion, anthropology and history, polytheism and monotheism: Judith Ochshorn, *The Female Experience and the Nature of the Divine* (Bloomington: Indiana University Press, 1981). Several area studies also make significant contributions to our understanding of the development of key cultures before, during, and immediately after the Axial Age. For China, see the magisterial work by John King Fairbank, *China: A New History* (Cambridge, MA: Harvard University Press, 1992). For India, the best standard volume remains Romila Thapar's *A History of India,* volume 1 (New York: Penguin Press, 1966). One of the most important developments in Part 2 revolves around culture formation in the empires that resulted from the Axial Age. In addition to John

Fairbank's monograph on China, see Richard Hingley, *Globalizing of Roman Culture* (New York: Routledge, 2005), in which he argues that the Roman Empire is the first truly "global culture." And finally, we discussed the various mechanisms of exchange and encounter. One of these mechanisms is colonization. For one of the most interesting and comprehensive examinations of cross-cultural colonization and its cultural consequences, see the edited volume by Gil J. Stein, *The Archaeology of Colonial Encounters: Comparative Perspectives* (Santa Fe, NM: School of American Research Press, 2004).

Terms to Know

Axial Age *(p. 108)*

polytheism *(p. 112)*

monotheism *(p. 112)*

henotheism *(p. 112)*

comogony *(p. 113)*

theogony *(p. 113)*

cosmology *(p. 113)*

Daoism *(p. 135)*

Legalism *(p. 135)*

empire *(p. 157)*

isonomia *(p. 158)*

democratia *(p. 158)*

Hellenism *(p. 167)*

dharma *(p. 172)*

The Transformation and Rebirth of World Systems (200 C.E.–1000 C.E.)

Introduction

In the second century C.E., the Roman Emperor Hadrian could travel from Britain to Mesopotamia in modern day Iraq without leaving Roman imperial borders; the vast Roman Empire ruled over the Mediterranean basin, much of Europe, and large parts of western Asia. Arriving in Mesopotamia, Hadrian could gaze east and contemplate the Parthian Empire of Persia: wealthy, urbane, and with a history that was old and rich, even by Roman standards. Beyond Persia, farther to the east, lay the sophisticated empire of the Han Dynasty of China with power and influence that extended from central to southeast Asia. In India, the Gupta Empire dominated much of the Asian subcontinent. Outside of this Eurasian axis, the situation was much the same. The Kingdom of Aksum, centered in Ethiopia, controlled large regions of northeastern Africa and the Arabian Peninsula.

A similar pattern of dominant empires was also evident in the Americas as the powerful city of Teotihuacan and the states of the Maya held sway over much of Mesoamerica. In short, empires controlled much of the world in the early centuries of the first millennium. The sources that follow will take a closer look at these empires as they declined and collapsed, and as their remains were transformed into new polities. This process of decline, collapse, and transformation is an intrinsically important one for historians to study as it not only informs about why states fail, but what happens afterward. How was imperial authority replaced and how did new states evolve after the collapse of the empire? How did newcomers and their customs, technologies, and traditions interact with imperial residents? And how did the fall of empires limit or accelerate exchanges between human societies? Such questions will be addressed in the sources in Part 3.

Empires were complex political organizations claiming sovereignty over large areas and diverse peoples. Imperial strength helped to create cultural, linguistic, and religious uniformity among diverse peoples who may have had little in common with one another before they became imperial subjects. Domestic peace and good internal communications eased the movement of people and the diffusion of ideas, which further aided in leveling differences among subject populations. At the peak of their power, the influence of these empires extended beyond their borders as their culture, religion, and other elements of their societies were carried abroad by merchants, missionaries, and soldiers, among others. Their military power based on large populations, technological superiority, and economic strength was often enough to keep their smaller neighbors subdued and their larger neighbors in check while their wealth could buy peace from those who they could not defeat. Secure in their power, empires reigned supreme over much of the world's population.

Empires, like other political entities, experience periods of growth, stability, crisis, decline, and eventually collapse or transformation into a polity that is quantifiably different. It is this last phase of collapse or transformation that serves as the focus for the sources in this part. The decline of an empire, followed by its eventual end, was typically the result of numerous reasons, as the readings in Chapter 10 show. Empires did not fall apart under the weight of a single calamity. It often took multiple crises emanating from several quarters to create a rift in the imperial fabric. These disasters often built on one another, with each new difficulty accentuating previous ones and creating a cycle of crisis and deterioration that eventually made the empire unable to respond to additional challenges. This process sometimes took decades, sometimes centuries. As new problems emerged, imperial authorities would deal with them, but each time with an ever-smaller margin of error. Eventually, the empire's capacity to react was simply overwhelmed, and its political power collapsed.

The fall of an entire imperial system often led to a period of chaos and readjustment but also created new opportunities for those ambitious enough to take advantage. As the political power of an empire weakened, so too did its hold on its subject peoples within and outside the empire. Weak central governments had a difficult time controlling unruly nobles and other internal dissenters. At the same time, the breakdown of political boundaries and the deterioration of the armies and fortifications that maintained them allowed for a freer movement of people and ideas. Thus, these shifts in political power and political readjustment resulted in periods of massive migrations. This is the focus of Chapter 11. In Europe, for example, the decline of Roman power led to a large influx of Germanic people from Northern and Eastern Europe into regions previously dominated by the Romans. Similar processes occurred in China, Persia, and Mesoamerica.

Imperial citizens regarded these newcomers as "barbarians": ferocious, uncouth, possessing outlandish customs, and a threat to the existence of their civilized society. Some modern historians have not treated them much better, typically viewing them through the lens of imperial narrators and considering them to be little more than a marauding destructive force. Others have romanticized them as noble savages, ruled by representative councils and with a deep connection to the environment around them. Both of these representations fall short of the truth. More recently, scholars have begun to give more nuance to these barbarians and to study them in their own right. These people were not merely destroyers, but builders and innovators as well. Their cultures melded with the cultures of settled peoples to create fusions that were the basis of new societies. As the readings in Chapter 12 illustrate, these people became the heirs of the former empires and the founders of the polities that emerged in the absence of imperial power.

Finally, in Chapter 13 an important consequence of these massive migrations and political upheavals emerges: the diffusion of culture, ideas, and innovations. In Eurasia, Africa, and the Americas the movement of peoples brought new ideas and technologies to the populations of diverse regions and joined with them to create new ethnic and sociocultural groupings. This union of barbarian and imperial societies led to remarkable changes amidst all the conflict engendered by their meetings. The years that followed imperial collapse were often marked by widespread disruption, plunging many regions into "Dark Ages." In some places, states as an institution completely disappeared. In others, political fragmentation became common as individual empires were dismembered into countless small kingdoms. Yet, all was not lost. The new people that came in the migrations brought with them innovative ideas for governing; novel forms of administration and law; original cultural contributions; and new languages, religions, and technology. As they assimilated into their new environments and survived the chaotic early years, they began the long process of rebuilding and transforming their new societies.

Part 3 Timeline

c. 65 C.E.	Latest date for the arrival of Buddhism in China.
117–138 C.E.	Reign of Roman Emperor Hadrian.
220 C.E.	Han Dynasty rule ends in China.
410 C.E.	Rome sacked by Visigoths.
445–453 C.E.	Reign of Attila the Hun.
476 C.E.	Deposition of the last Western Roman Emperor.
c. 500–530 C.E.	Decline of the Indian Gupta Empire.
c. 570–632 C.E.	Life of the Prophet Muhammad.
581–618 C.E.	Sui Dynasty rules China.
597 C.E.	Arrival of Roman Christianity in England.
604 C.E.	Publication of the Seventeen Article Constitution in Japan.
637 C.E.	Collapse of the Persian Sassanian Empire.
c. 650–750 C.E.	Fire and destruction of Teotihuacan.
c. 660–700 C.E.	Decline and collapse of Aksum.
711 C.E.	Muslim conquest of Spain.
768–814 C.E.	Reign of Charlemagne.
c. 800–840 C.E.	Probable dates for the collapse of the principal Maya city-states.

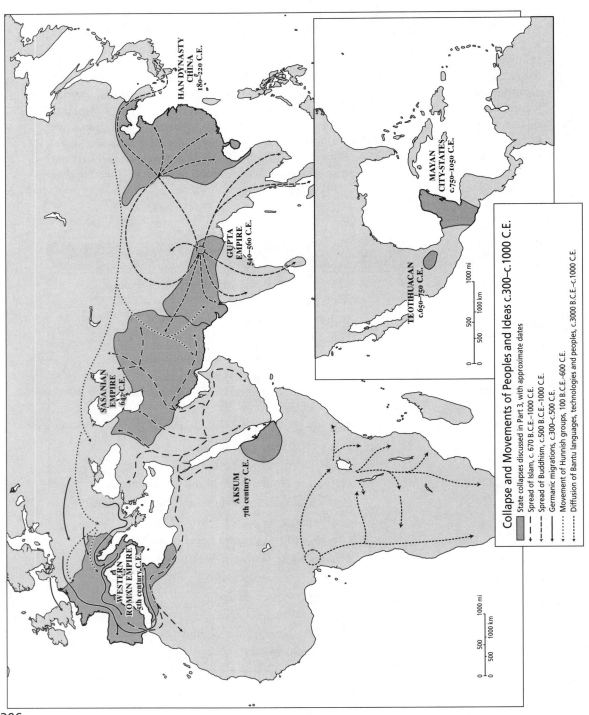

Collapse and Movements of Peoples and Ideas c.300–c.1000 C.E.

State collapses discussed in Part 3, with approximate dates

- – – Spread of Islam, c. 670 B.C.E.–1000 C.E.
- → Spread of Buddhism, c.500 B.C.E.–1000 C.E.
- → Germanic migrations, c.300–c.500 C.E.
- ⋯⋯ Movement of Hunnish groups, 100 B.C.E.–600 C.E.
- ⋯⋯ Diffusion of Bantu languages, technologies and peoples, c.3000 B.C.E.–c.1000 C.E.

HAN DYNASTY CHINA
180–220 C.E.

GUPTA EMPIRE
540–560 C.E.

SASANIAN EMPIRE
642 C.E.

AKSUM
7th century C.E.

WESTERN ROMAN EMPIRE
5th century C.E.

TEOTIHUACAN
c.650–750 C.E.

MAYAN CITY-STATES
c.750–1050 C.E.

1000 mi

500   1000 km

500

0

1000 mi

500   1000 km

500

0

Chapter 10

The Fall of Empires

Over the course of a few hundred years, between 200 C.E. and 800 C.E., the empire-dominated world underwent a radical transformation. The Romans, Parthians, Han, Gupta, Maya, and others saw their imperial systems fall into civil wars, their borders overrun, and their armies defeated. Even the land on which they lived turned against them as environmental deterioration limited their ability to respond to challenges. The very strengths that had made these empires possible and had sustained them during their prime became sources of weakness and conflict. The large empires became difficult to administer from centrally located capitals, and regions in the periphery drifted in and out of imperial control or became hotbeds of civil war and political dissatisfaction, as was the case with the Romans, Persians, Han, and possibly Aksum. Imperial prosperity created economic disparity and resentment against the ruling classes, a possible cause for the decline of Han China and perhaps Teotihuacan. Wealth in material goods and culture sometimes attracted the prying eyes of outsiders who desired the affluence and security that empires offered and who were occasionally willing to take what they wanted by force. Barbarians overrunning imperial borders in search of gold, land, and stability became a common theme in the decline of many empires including the Han, Gupta, and Romans. A decay of government institutions, economic problems that affected the ability of the government to pay its soldiers, and failed wars that damaged morale, drained the treasury, and killed soldiers hamstrung the armies that were supposed to stop such barbarian incursions. Even the security and stability that empires provided and that promoted population growth created problems as an ever-larger number of citizens outgrew and exhausted the ecological resources that sustained them.

Since ancient times, historians have been trying to explain why powerful empires collapse. The Greek historian Polybius, one of the earliest to deal with this issue, thought that collapse was inevitable since, in his view, empires were organisms that had to pass through a natural process of birth, maturity, and finally decay. This biological view of empires has remained popular with some historians up to the present. The first modern historian to attempt a methodical study on the decline of an empire was the Englishman Edward Gibbon (1737–1794) with *The Decline and Fall of the Roman Empire.* In seventy-one chapters and citing over 8,000 sources, Gibbon was able to pinpoint close to two dozen factors that contributed to the collapse of the Roman Empire. The work was clearly a masterpiece of historical scholarship and became a critical success when it was published between 1776 and 1788. However, it also attracted significant criticism for Gibbon's thinly veiled attacks on Christianity, to which he assigned a large share of the blame for Roman decline. Moreover, in spite of Gibbon's mastery of his topic, the book still has factual mistakes, inaccuracies, and inconsistent arguments. Contemporary historians have challenged and refuted many of Gibbon's central points.

Today, most historians would agree with Gibbon that empires collapse for multiple reasons, not due to single factors. The bigger debates come when historians try to reach a consensus as to what the specific reasons were and how all of the factors interacted to slow down or accelerate decline. The selections in this chapter attempt to capture some of this variety as they highlight the range of factors that weakened imperial power. The first selection by Andre Gunder Frank and Barry Gills serves to orient some of the topics raised in later selections. Their main theme is connectivity, as Frank and Gills see the political fortunes of the great Eurasian empires (Rome, Han China, Gupta India, and Persia) to be directly linked. When one domino in this imperial chain toppled, it had repercussions on its neighbors. The next two selections by Augustine, bishop of Hippo, and the Muslim scholar Ibn Khaldûn present the views of two premodern historians on the problem of decline. In the brief essay by Jared Diamond, he discusses the ecological problems that can also contribute to decline. Diamond's essay is rich in its comparative approach as he considers societies from all over the world including Easter Island, the Maya, and Rome. Each of the remaining sources in this chapter attempts to explain the decline of a specific empire—Roman, Sâsânian Persia, Teotihuacan, Maya, and Aksum. All of these sources support the notion that imperial collapse had many causes including barbarian invasions, economic problems, class struggles, civil wars, ethnic discontent, and ecological deterioration. In short, the dominant theme that emerges is that empires, for all their power, were fragile polities always facing the prospect of weakness, decline, and eventual collapse.

Eurasian Collapse—A Continental Crisis

The theme of imperial decline and collapse is the focus of the selection by Barry Gills and Andre Gunder Frank. Gills and Frank have been pioneers in the study of world history, notably in the study of the connections between societies. Because most scholars who study interconnections between societies concentrate on the recent past, less attention has been given to connecting the decline of empires across the Ancient World. Instead, most ancient historians have focused on regional and internal interpretations of imperial decline and collapse. Gills and Frank suggest that this approach is flawed; they see a Eurasia in the second century that was intensely connected. Economic troubles and revolts in China reverberated all the way to Rome and vice versa—and affected everyone in between. In their larger argument, Gills and Frank argue that an interconnected world system has existed not for 500 years but for 5,000, especially as it applies to Eurasia.

>> 75. World System Cycles, Crises and Hegemonic Shifts, 1700 B.C. to 1700 A.D.

BARRY K. GILLS AND ANDRE GUNDER FRANK [1993]

From the third through the fifth centuries AD, the previous period of expansion and consolidating hegemonies was followed by a major world systemic crisis on a Pan-Eurasian scale. During this world systemic crisis the Han and Roman, as well as the intermediary Kushan and Parthian hegemonic structures simultaneously disintegrated. Frederick Teggart examined international political economic linkages through Central Asia for the Roman period.

When war occurred on the routes in the Tarim Basis [in which is now China's western Xinjian region] disturbances broke out in Parthia and either in Armenia or on the border of Syria. Evidently then, war in the Tarim occasioned an interruption of traffic on the silk route, and this interruption aroused hostilities at points along the route as far west as the Euphrates.

Teggart correlated and compared the timing of wars and barbarian invasions in Rome and China and concluded that

Thus the effects of wars which arose out of interruptions of the great "silk route" through Persia are plainly visible in the internal history of Rome.... Seemingly there could be no better illustration of interdependence of nations than the consideration that a decision of the Chinese government should have been responsible for a financial panic in the capital of the Roman empire.

However, even Teggart seems to have considered wars and other political disturbances more as the *cause* of interruptions of trade, rather than the other way around. Yet, it may also be argued with equal or greater reason that many uprisings, wars, alliances, and other political developments were themselves stimulated if not caused by changing local, regional, or even system-wide economic conditions and interests.

Thus first the *rise* and then again the *decline* of Han China (and their Central Asian Xiongnu neighbors), Kushan India, Parthian Persia, and western imperial Rome occurred at very much the same time. The political-economic decline of these empires was also manifested in the notable simultaneous decline of Central Asian and maritime trade among them. The fourth and fifth centuries AD seem to have been a period of major Eurasian (system) wide economic and political decline, indeed. This apparently interrelated series of declines is another important instance of what we see as a major world system wide crisis. Therefore, we wish however briefly to examine some of its regional manifestations in greater detail.

The hegemonic disintegration of the Han preceded that of Rome, becoming acute by the late second century AD. The third and fourth centuries in China were a period of economic retrogression, with a significant decline in internal and external trade and demonetization of the economy. Many cities disappeared altogether and the monetary economy practically collapsed. The political center of gravity shifted from the former capital of Chang'an to Louyang, and the economic center of gravity from the Guanzhong region to the Henan region, and thereafter to the Yangtse (Yangzi) Valley. Nevertheless, cities linked to the Eurasian trade continued to exist and prosper, such as the centers in the western

Source: Barry K. Gills and Andre Gunder Frank, "World System Cycles, Crises, and Hegemonic Shifts, 1700 B.C. to 1700 A.D.," in *The World System: Five Hundred Years or Five Thousand?* edited by A. G. Frank and B. K. Gills (London: Routledge, 1993), 167–171.

Hexi area (the modern Gansu corridor). Wealthy merchant houses existed in this period of general urban decline and the Northern Wei dynasty seems to have been particularly favorable toward merchant activity up until the early sixth century.

The Kushan empire in north India and Central Asia disintegrated, and India's political center of gravity shifted back to the middle-Ganges plain during the Gupta period (c. 300–500 AD). The Gupta empire in north India rose in the fourth century, and was destroyed by the White Huns in the sixth century. During the Gupta period landed property gained value and land grants by the king increased in significance, while the urban economy in general showed clear signs of decline. Nonetheless, during the Gupta period some trade between India and China and between India and the west continued. The Ujjain region in the Gupta period prospered from international trade and Barygaza was still an active port. However, this trade was diverted.

It seems reasonable to conclude that even when north India suffered a general urban decline in the Gupta period, certain cities along the trade route from Kashmir to the north Indian plain prospered…political changes in the post-Kushan period disturbed the Eurasian commercial network from the Roman empire to China but did not destroy it. A major shift took place in the north-west, where the route through Kashmir connecting India to Central Asia gained importance. As the seaports in western India continued to flourish the new Kashmir route brought both western India and the Ganges plain closer to China.

Liu maintains that from the third to fourth centuries a series of political changes in Asia and Europe disturbed the trade network connecting China and the West through the west-north-western Indian routes. These upheavals appeared across all of Eurasia: China was divided for three centuries after the disintegration of the Han empire (220 AD), except for a brief unification of north China under the Qin (280–316 AD). The Kushan empire (which controlled Kashmir, Bactria, Kabul, and north-west India) collapsed under the weight of White Hun deprivations in the fourth century. As a result, many urban centres in Central Asia declined or became depopulated during the fourth and fifth centuries. Major cities like Bactra and Taxila and many lesser ones experienced significant decline, "became desolate" and ended up "all in ruins." Bactria "might have temporarily lost its nodal function because of the pressure of Sassanians, and subsequent damage done by the Hephthalites or White Huns." The Roman empire disintegrated and led to the establishment of the eastern Byzantine empire (395 AD).

It is noteworthy that the Gupta empire rose to power and privilege at the expense of regional predecessors during a period of generalized economic crisis, which had weakened its predecessors in the Indian region.

At about the same time, this was true too of the Sassanians, who replaced the Parthians in Persia. For in the third century also the Sassanian empire took control of the former domains of the Parthians and the Kushan in Persia and Central Asia. However Sassanian power also was in ascendancy, as Roman and Han power declined. The Gupta perhaps less, and the Sassanians perhaps more, successfully managed to retain some power as sort of super-accumulating monopoly rent from their positions along the way while other economic and political powers had already waned or went under in the generalized world system economic and political crisis. However, neither Gupta nor Sassanian power lasted very long. Perhaps that was not only because they suffered from repeated batterings by the White Huns in the fourth–sixth centuries. Perhaps Gupta and Sassanian power was also a sort of flash in the pan, precisely because they were only able to take advantage of their rivals' economic and political decline in a period of economic downswing; which would also limit and ultimately destroy their own capabilities.

Returning to the third and fourth centuries, they were a period of significant economic contraction in the Roman empire. This included contraction in the market and currency devaluation (even demonetization), and reversal of urbanization, especially in the western provinces of the empire. Childe argues that by AD 150 the "frontiers of the civilized world" had been reached and that the external market could expand no more. Thus, "Unable to expand the whole system began to contract... by 250 AD all semblance of prosperity vanished." The hegemonic disintegration forces of the third century were severe, but the empire was formally kept together. Huge quantities of bullion flowed to the east to make up for Rome's chronic structural deficit on its trade in luxury goods with Asia, thus increasing the pressure on the Roman treasury to debase the coinage. The aristocratic ruling class was discouraged by its own ideology from investing in industry, and preferred for reasons of status to invest in land and commerce. The competition of slave labor with free labor depressed wages in the latter and thus depressed the expansion of the market.

Western Europe suffered perhaps more than any other region in the world system from the economic retrogression effected by this world systemic crisis. Moreover, many centuries passed before western Europe recovered, and then only partially. A unique amalgamation of late Roman and Germanic institutions took form in the west-European provinces of the Roman empire. The institutions of feudalism were in place by the time of the death of Charlemagne in 814, and western Europe declined into the "Dark Ages." However, we agree with the evidence and arguments of scholars like Dopsch [...] and Lombard [...] to the effect that even in Europe, trade and markets never declined as much as the more dominant tradition of Max Weber and Henri Pirenne had taught us. Nonetheless, western Europe became an economic backwater in the world system, with concomitantly backward and primitive political institutions. Thus, it would be largely bypassed by the next world economic upturn, which began in the sixth century. When it finally did begin to recover, it was as part of a process of reintegration into the world economy whose center was then located in the East.

The Sack of Rome

One of the earliest thinkers to comment on the decline of an empire was the Christian theologian and philosopher Augustine, Bishop of Hippo. In 410, the Visigoths, a Germanic tribe that had settled inside the borders of the Roman Empire, captured and pillaged the city of Rome. Although the Visigoths only stayed in the city for three days before departing, the sacking of Rome had deep psychological and political ramifications. Some blamed Christianity—the official religion of the Empire by the fifth century—and its God for the plundering. This letter from Augustine to Marcellinus, a Christian imperial official in Carthage, addresses those charges. Note how Augustine makes use of historical knowledge to discredit the charges and goes on the offensive by arguing that not only is Christianity blameless in the recent catastrophes, but that it has, in fact, saved the Empire from an earlier collapse. Augustine finishes the letter (not included in this fragment) by promising Marcellinus that he would respond to other questions in additional letters or a book. Augustine chose the latter and wrote The City of God, *his most famous and influential work.*

>> 76. Letter 138, to Marcellinus

AUGUSTINE OF HIPPO [412 C.E.]

But what am I to reply to those who say that many evils have befallen the Roman state at the hands of Christian emperors? This is sweeping complaint and a tricky one. For, if I were to relate frankly certain facts about past emperors, I could detail similar things, or perhaps even worse ones, about the non-Christian emperors, and so they would understand either that the fault was in the men, not in the teaching, or that it was not in the emperors but in those other men without whom emperors cannot get anything done. Their own literature speaks plainly of the time when the Roman state began to decline; long before the name of Christ had shed light upon the earth this was said: 'O mercenary city and ripe for the plucking if it could find a buyer! And in the book on the war with Catiline, which was certainly written before the coming of Christ, this most famous of their historians does not pass over in silence the time when 'first the army of the Roman people began to become adept in making love; in drinking; in admiring statues, pictures, engraved vases; in looting these privately and publicly; in ravaging shrines; in defiling everything both sacred and common. Therefore, when the avarice and greed of corrupt and abandoned morals ceased to spare even those men whom they considered gods, at that moment the much-praised glory and even the survival of the state began to be endangered. It would take too long to tell the outcome of those worst of vices, and of the decline of human fortunes brought on by the increase in wickedness. Let them listen to their own satirist babbling the truth: 'Modest fortune kept the Latin women chaste in the old times, and these things kept their humble homes safe from the touch of vice: toil and brief sleep, and hands hardened and roughened by carding the Tuscan fleece, and Hannibal's approach to the city, and their husbands' having to stand guard on the Colline rampart. But now we suffer the evil effects of long-continued peace; luxury, more cruel than warfare, weighs upon us and takes vengeance of our conquered city. No crime, no deed of lust has been alien to us since Roman poverty perished. How, then, can you expect me to exaggerate the great misfortunes brought on by an immorality carried aloft by its successful onset, when they themselves, though taking a more moderate view, saw that loss of poverty at Rome, rather than of wealth, was a subject of mourning? For, by the former their purity of morals was preserved, but by the latter a dread wickedness, worse than any enemy, invaded, not the walls of the city, but the minds of the citizens.

Thanks to the Lord our God, who has sent us a sovereign help against those evils! Where would that stream of the repulsive malice of the human race not have carried us, who would not have been swept along with it, in what depths would it not have overwhelmed us, if the cross of Christ had not been planted, firm and high, in the great rock of authority, so that we might take hold of its strength and be steadied, and might not be drawn under the vast current of the ruined world by listening to evil advisers, urging us to evil? For, in the midst of that faith of depraved morals, and of an ancient decadent learning, it was eminently right for a heavenly authority to come and to bring relief by counseling voluntary poverty, chastity, kindness, justice, concord, true filial love, and those other virtues which are the light and strength of life, not only to make us lead this life with the utmost regard for honor, nor only for the sake of making the society of the earthly city as united as possible, but also that we may attain salvation and reach that heavenly and divine country, whose peoples

Source: Augustine of Hippo, "Letter 138, to Marcellinus," in *Saint Augustine: Letters, Volume III (131–164)* translated by Wilfrid Parsons (New York: Fathers of the Church, Inc., 1953), 48–50.

are immortal. Faith, hope, and charity enroll us as citizens in that country, but, as long as we voyage far from it, we are to bear with those—if we cannot bring about their amendment—who told that without punishing vice that state can survive, that state which the first Romans founded and increased by their virtues. For, although they did preserve a certain characteristic uprightness, sufficient to found, increase, and preserve an earthly city. God showed in the rich and far-famed Roman Empire how much can be achieved by natural virtues without true religion, so that we might understand how, with this added, men can become citizens of another state whose king is truth, whose law is love, whose measure is eternity.

Luxuries and Decline

Almost 1,000 years after Augustine, another North African, the Muslim scholar and statesman Ibn Khaldûn, tackled the challenge of understanding why civilizations declined. Ibn Khaldûn was one of the monumental figures of his age. He was born in Tunis in 1332 to a prominent family with a long history of government service. He spent much of his early adult life in public service and later took up an academic career as a law professor and judge. It was during this time that he wrote the Kitab al-'Ibar, *his universal history. The* Muqaddimah *is the introduction to this impressive work. In applying a critical methodology rarely seen at this time, Ibn Khaldûn helped lay the ground work for modern and objective historical scholarship. He was not so much interested in the facts about the past as he was in the patterns and forces that shaped civilizations. According to his findings, the history of civilizations is one of cycles. As one civilization or dynasty declines, another one is ready to take its place and begin the cycle anew. In this selection, Ibn Khaldûn discusses why dynasties, which are so strong when they first come on the scene, can be so quickly seduced by comfort and luxury, ultimately leading to their demise.*

>> 77. The Muqaddimah: An Introduction to History

IBN KHALDÛN [C. 1375 C.E.]

II When the natural tendencies of royal authority to claim all glory for itself and to acquire luxury and tranquility have been firmly established, the dynasty approaches senility

This can be explained in several ways.

First: As we have stated, (royal authority), by its very nature, must claim all glory for itself. As long as glory was the common (property) of the group, and all members of the group made an identical effort, their aspirations to gain the upper hand over others and to defend their own possessions were expressed in exemplary unruliness and lack of restraint. They all aimed at fame. Therefore, they considered death encountered in pursuit of glory, sweet, and they preferred annihilation to the loss of (glory). Now, however, when one of them claims all glory for himself, he treats the others severely and holds them in check. Further, he excludes them from possessing property and appropriates if for himself. People, thus, become too lazy to care for fame. They become dispirited and come to love humbleness and servitude.

Source: Ibn Khaldûn, *The Muqaddimah: An Introduction to History*, edited by N. J. Dawood, translated by F. Rosenthal (Princeton: Princeton University Press, 1989), 133–136.

The next generation grows up in this (condition). They consider their allowances the government's payment to them for military service and support. No other thought occurs to them, (but) a person would rarely hire himself out to sacrifice his life. This (situation) debilitates the dynasty and undermines its strength. Its group feeling decays because the people who represent the group feeling have lost their energy. As a result, the dynasty progresses toward weakness and senility.

Second: As we have said before, royal authority by its very nature requires luxury. People get accustomed to a great number of things. Their expenses are higher than their allowances and their income is not sufficient to pay for their expenditure. Those who are poor perish. Spendthrifts squander their income on luxuries. This (condition) becomes aggravated in the later generations. Eventually, all their income cannot pay for the luxuries and other things they have become used to. They grow needy. When their rulers urge them to defray the costs of raids and wars, they cannot get around it. Therefore, (the rulers) impose penalties on the (people) and deprive many of them of their property, either by appropriating it for themselves or by handing it over to their own children and supporters in the dynasty. In that way, they make the people too weak to keep their own affairs going, and their weakness the recoils upon the ruler and weakens him.

Also, when luxury increases in a dynasty and people's income becomes insufficient for their needs and expenses, the ruler, that is, the government, must increase their allowances in order to tide them over and remedy their unsound condition. The amount of tax revenue, however, is a fixed one. It neither increases nor decreases. When it is increased by new customs duties, the amount to be collected as a result of the increase has fixed limits (and cannot be increased again). And when the tax revenues must go to pay for recently increased allowances that had to be increased for everybody in view of new luxuries and great expenditure, the militia decreases in number from what it had been before the increase in allowances.[1]

Luxury, meanwhile, is still on the increase. As a result, allowances become larger, and the militia decreases in number. This happens a third and a fourth time. Eventually, the army is reduced to the smallest possible size. The result is that the military defense of the dynasty is weakened and the power of the dynasty declines. Neighbouring dynasties, or groups and tribes under the control of the dynasty itself, become bold and attack it, and God permits it to suffer the destruction that He has destined for His creatures.

Furthermore, luxury corrupts the character, through luxury the soul acquiring diverse kinds of evil and sophisticated customs, as will be mentioned in the section of sedentary culture. People lose the good qualities that were a sign and indication of royal authority. They adopt the contrary bad qualities. This points toward retrogression and ruin, according to the way God (has planned) for His creatures in his connection. The dynasty shows symptoms of dissolution and disintegration. It becomes affected by the chronic diseases of senility and finally dies.

Third: As we have mentioned, royal authority, by its very nature, requires tranquility. When people become accustomed to tranquility and rest and adopt them as character traits, they become part of their nature. This is the case with all the things to which one grows accustomed.

The new generations grow up in comfort and the ease of luxury and tranquility. The trait of savagery (that former generations had possessed) undergoes transformation. They forget the customs of desert life that enabled them to achieve

---

[1]That is, since the allowances to be paid are higher than before, and the tax income has not increased, fewer men can be hired.

royal authority, such as great energy, the habit of rapacity, and the ability to travel in the wilderness and find one's way in waste regions. No difference remains between them and ordinary city dwellers, except for their fighting skill and emblems. Their military defense weakens, their energy is lost, and their strength is undermined. The evil effects of this situation on the dynasty show themselves in the form of senility.

People, meanwhile, continue to adopt ever newer forms of luxury and sedentary culture and of peace, tranquility, and softens in all their conditions, and to sink ever deeper into them. They thus become estranged from desert life and desert toughness. Gradually, they lose more and more of the old virtues. They forget the quality of bravery that was their protection and defense. Eventually, they come to depend upon some other militia, if they have one.

An example of this is the nations whose history is available in the books you have. What I said will be found to be correct and admitting of no doubt.

In a dynasty affected by senility as the result of luxury and rest, it sometimes happens that the ruler chooses helpers and partisans from groups not related to the ruling dynasty but used to toughness. He uses them as an army which will be better able to suffer the hardships of wars, hunger, and privation. This could prove a cure for the senility of the dynasty when it comes, but only until God permits His command regarding the dynasty to be executed.

That was what happened to the Turkish dynasty in the East. Most members of its army were Turkish clients. The rulers then chose horsemen and soldiers from among the white slave (Mamelukes) who were brought to them. They were more eager to fight and better able to suffer privations than the children of the earlier white slaves who had grown up in easy circumstances as a ruling class in the shadow of the government.

The same was the case with the Almohad dynasty in Ifriqiyah. Their rulers often selected their armies from the Zanâtah and the Arabs. They used many of them, and disregarded their own people who had become used to luxury. Thus, the dynasty obtained another, new life, unaffected by senility.

Ecological Collapse

Modern people tend to think that environmental problems are a new concern. Indeed, global warming, greenhouse gases, and industrial pollution are largely by-products of our highly industrialized world. However, the abuse of the environment and its subsequent deterioration have been bedeviling human societies since the origins of human history. For ancient people lacking modern agricultural techniques, easy movement of goods, and reliable assistance from government, the environment may have been even more important than it is to the citizens of modern societies. Crop failures caused by soils that had become exhausted from continuous planting; the salination of agricultural lands, which rendered them useless for farming; or insufficient irrigation due to lack of rain often meant death for a large number of people. In the most acute cases, persistent environmental problems brought even the mightiest empires to their knees. In this selection, Jared Diamond focuses on the catastrophic effects that environmental problems have had on some human societies.

>> 78. Ecological Collapses of Past Civilizations

JARED DIAMOND [1994]

A justification frequently offered for studying history is that it gives us the opportunity to learn from human errors in the past. Until recently, though, it appeared that we had nothing to learn from the past about how to avoid the environmental predicament in which all human societies now find themselves. The greatest risk to humanity in coming decades is that we may continue to damage our environment to a degree where our current standard of living or even our existence becomes impossible. That dilemma has seemed a unique one in human history, a consequence of our uniquely high modern numbers coupled with our uniquely destructive modern technology.

However, it is now being realized that many past societies did collapse through destroying their environmental underpinnings, and that we thus do have environmental lessons to learn from our past. This is burgeoning area of paleontology and archeology, with most of the compelling evidence having been gathered only within the last 12 years. [...]

The clearest examples involve Polynesian societies on remote Pacific islands [...]. Polynesia was settled by canoe voyagers, originating ultimately from Bismarck Archipelago and islands north of New Guinea, in two waves of colonization around 1600 B.C. and around 300–1000 A.D. Many Polynesian islands lie hundreds or even thousands of miles from the nearest island. Therefore many Polynesian societies, once founded by overwater colonists, lost contact with their ancestral source population and became totally cut off from contact with other human societies for a thousand years or more. We can thus be certain that their fates were not due to influences of neighbors.

Among such isolated Polynesian societies, different ones underwent very different fates. Some, such as Tongan society, are socially stratified kingdoms that have persisted uninterruptedly for 3,600 years from their founding until the present, without any signs of a marked decline in population or complexity. Some, such as the societies of Easter Island and New Zealand's South Island, did decline drastically in numbers and complexity but continued to exist. A dozen others, including the societies of Henderson and Necker, collapsed so completely that no people remained alive.

The most spectacular collapse is also the one best documented archaeologically [...]. Easter Island, the most remote habitable scrap of land in the world, is famous for its hundreds of giant stone statues. Those statues were carved, dragged miles overland, and erected on platforms by a Stone Age people without power sources except for their own muscles. When Europeans "discovered" Easter in 1722, the carving of statues had already ceased, and Easter was already descending into an orgy of cannibalism and starvation. But the ultimate cause of that collapse, which inspired an expedition by Thor Heyerdahl and much speculation by others, has long been in doubt.

The ecological origins of Easter's collapse began to emerge only 15 years ago, when palynological evidence for Easter's former vegetation was uncovered. That evidence has now been fleshed out by archeological and paleontological excavations, which are still on-going. The following picture of Easter's history has emerged.

Today Easter is barren, eroded, devoid of native trees, devoid of native land birds, and with breeding seabirds confined to offshore rock stacks. When Polynesians discovered it around 300 A.D., Easter was covered with tropical forest. The first Polynesian settlers began to clear the forest for agriculture. They used the trees to build

Source: Jared Diamond, "Ecological Collapses of Past Civilizations," in *Proceedings of the American Philosophical Society* 138 (1994): 363–365, 367–368.

canoes with which they went to sea to hunt porpoises and deep-water fish. They ate native land birds, seabirds, and palm fruits and also used the palm trees as rollers and levers to transport and erect their giant statues.

In this initially rich environment, Easter's human population exploded and came to surpass a density of 150 people per square mile. Eventually, the forest was cleared so completely that the tree species themselves became extinct, and so did all the land birds and many of the seabirds. Without tree cover, topsoil eroded, agricultural yields fell, and fuel sources other than weeds and crop wastes disappeared. Without canoes, deep-sea fishing became impossible. The sole remaining large source of protein was other humans. Without logs as rollers and levers, the transporting and erecting of statues became impossible. The extinctions eliminated much of Easter's resource base and left no possibility of rebuilding Easter society. While humans did not become extinct on Easter, three-quarters of the human population did die out along with a possibly indigenous system of writing. What had been one of the world's most remarkable civilization fell apart. [...]

There remain many familiar collapses of ancient civilizations for which ecological interpretations are not as obviously applicable. They include the falls of Classic Lowland Maya civilization [...], Angkor Wat, and Harappan (Indus) Valley civilization, as well as the most debated fall of all, that of the Roman Empire.

All four of these collapses are confounded by effects of militaristic neighbors. Rome was sacked by barbarians from the north and east, Angkor Wat was sacked by the Thais, Indo-Europeans equipped with cavalry took over the Indus Valley, and Mexicans may have intruded on the Maya.

Yet it remains unclear whether these ultimately military defeats were just the last straw for an already weakened society. Had those societies been on Pacific Islands, they might have gone on to decline in isolation, as did Easter island society. One still has to explain why Angkor Wat finally succumbed to the Thais, and Rome to barbarians, after resisting those enemies successfully for so long. Military explanations seem especially questionable for the fall of Harappan civilization, since it may have preceded Indo-European arrivals, and for the Mayan collapse, since evidence of Mexican intruders is very local in the Maya realm.

Contributions from ecological factors suggest themselves for all four of these cases. For example, there is a detailed record of deforestation for the Mayan valley of Copan [...], indicating that the city of Copan may have exhausted accessible sources of timber and fuel, as did the Anasazi city at Chaco Canyon. An east-to-west wave of rise of civilization, rise of human numbers, and consequent destruction of Mediterranean habitats began in the Fertile Crescent, where agriculture itself arose. The wave spread westwards with agriculture to Greece, where deforestation and erosion are well documented from late-Mycenaean times. From there it spread to the western Mediterranean [...]. For example, Rome depended significantly on Morocco for timber and on Tunisia for grain, but those countries are now heavily degraded and no longer wood or grain exporters.

Much more paleobotanical evidence will be required to compare the relative importance of ecological factors, military factors, and social/economic/political factors in these familiar collapses.

The Fall of the Roman Empire

The Roman Empire may have been the most powerful empire of the ancient world. However, as early as the third century, the empire began to experience severe problems that sapped its strength. A series of reforms by the emperors Diocletian (r. 284–305) and Constantine (r. 306–337) slowed the decline but did not stop it altogether. In 395, after the death of Emperor Theodosius I, the Roman Empire was split into an eastern and a western half. The Romans had been splitting their empire since the third century in order to govern the vast empire better. Every now and again a powerful emperor such as Theodosius would rejoin the two halves, only to have it split again after his death. After the death of Theodosius, the empire was divided between his two sons, never to be united again. This final split had disastrous consequences for the poorer and weaker western half. Lacking demographic, military, and economic resources to assure its survival and beset by domestic conflicts, the Western Empire finally collapsed politically in 476 due to its own internal weaknesses and massive Germanic invasions. The following selection by A. H. M. Jones is a recent and highly regarded attempt to explain the reasons for the political fall of Rome in the west.

>> 79. The Decline of the Ancient World

A. H. M. JONES [1966]

Why Did the Western Empire Fall?

The causes of the fall of the western empire in the fifth century have been endlessly debated since Augustine's day, but those who have debated the question have all been westerners, and have tended to forget that the eastern empire did not fall till many centuries later. Many of the causes alleged for the fall of the west were common to the east, and therefore cannot be complete and self-sufficient causes. If, as the pagans said in 410, it was the gods, incensed by the apostasy of the empire, who struck it down, why did they not strike down the equally Christian eastern parts? If, as Salvian argues, it was God who sent the barbarians to chastize the sinful Romans, why did He not send barbarians to chastize the equally sinful Constantinopolitans? If Christianity, as Gibbon thought, sapped the empire's morale and weakened it by internal schisms, why did not the more Christian east, with its much more virulent theological disputes, fall first?

We must look then for points in which the two halves of the empire differed. In the first place the western provinces were much more exposed to barbarian attack. The western emperor had to guard the long fronts of the Rhine and the upper Danube, the eastern emperor only the lower Danube. For on the eastern front his neighbor was the Persian empire, a civilized power which was not on the whole aggressive and kept its treaties. If a Persian war broke out, it was a more serious affair than a barbarian invasion, but wars were rare until the sixth century, and they then tested the Roman empire very severely. Moreover, if the western emperor failed to hold any part of the Rhine and Danube fronts, he had no second line of defence; the invaders could penetrate straight into Italy and Gaul, and even into Spain. The eastern emperor, if he failed, as he often did, to hold the lower Danube, only lost control temporarily of the European dioceses; for no enemy could force the Bosphorus and the Hellespont, guarded by Constantinople itself. Asia Minor, Syria and Egypt thus remained sealed off from invasion.

The barbarian invaders soon grasped the strategical position and, even if they first crossed the lower Danube and ravaged Thrace and Illyricum, soon tired of these exhausted lands and, unable to penetrate into the rich lands of Asia Minor, trekked westwards to Italy. This path was successively followed by the

Source: A. H. M. Jones, *The Decline of the Ancient World* (New York: Holt, Rinehart and Winston, 1966), 362–367.

Visigoths under Alaric and the Ostrogoths under Theoderic.

In the second place the eastern parts were probably more populous, more intensively cultivated and richer than the western. This is hard to prove and difficult to believe nowadays, when the Balkans, Asia Minor and Syria are poor and thinly peopled, and only Egypt is rich and populous, whereas in the west Italy, France, Britain and the Low Countries are wealthy and densely populated, and only north Africa is poor. But many lines of argument suggest that the reverse was true in Roman times. The population of Egypt was about 8 million, that of Gaul (which included besides modern France the Low Countries and Germany west of the Rhine) can be estimated at about $2\frac{1}{2}$ million. The diocese of Egypt yielded perhaps three times as much revenue as that of Africa. Archaeological evidence proves that many areas now desert or waste in Syria and Asia Minor were inhabited and cultivated in late Roman times, and suggest that much of the most fertile soil in northern Gaul and Britain was still uncleared forest. It is moreover possible to estimate the wealth of different areas in the Roman empire from the number and scale of the public buildings of the cities, since the rich put much of their surplus wealth into such buildings. On this test the Mediterranean lands, eastern and southern Spain, southern Gaul, Italy, Africa, the southern Balkans, Asia Minor, Syria and Egypt were all wealthy, and Asia Minor and Syria the wealthiest of all, whereas Britain, northern Gaul and the Danubian lands were miserably poor. This analysis is borne out by literary testimonies. In the west Sardinia, Sicily and above all Africa, were regarded as the richest provinces, the granaries of the empire, and Aquitania as more fertile than northern Gaul. This implies that the potential fertility of the northern plains had not yet been exploited to the full.

In some other ways the east was superior to the west. It enjoyed much greater political stability and less of its resources were wasted in civil wars. From the accession of Diocletian in 284 to the death of Maurice in 602 there were only five attempted usurpations, those of Domitus Domitianus under Diocletian, of Procopius under Valens, of Basiliscus, Marcian and Leontius under Zeno, and all were quickly subdued without many casualties. In the west there were rebellions or usurpations by Carausius, Maxentius, Alexander, Magnentius, Firmus, Magnus Maximus, Gildo, Constantine, Jovinus and John, most of which involved heavy fighting, and after the death of Valentinian III a succession of ephemeral emperors.

The social and economic structure of the east was healthier than that of the west. In the east more of the land was owned by peasant proprietors, who paid taxes only, and thus a larger proportion of the total yield of agriculture went to the peasantry. In the west a much higher proportion of the land was owned by great landlords, whose tenants had to pay rents in excess of their taxes, and the general condition of the peasantry was therefore poorer. This is reflected in the recurrent revolts of the Bacaudae in Gaul and Spain, which at times contained troops urgently needed elsewhere.

Another result of this difference in social structure was that the landed aristocracy in the west obtained a stranglehold of the administration, with two deleterious results. They were inefficient administrators, and allowed the bureaucracy to add a very appreciable sum to the burden of taxation by their exorbitant fees. They were over-indulgent to their own class, and slack in curbing grants of immunity and reductions and remissions of taxes. In the east the administrative machine remained in the hands of men of middle-class origin, who owed their advancement to the imperial government; they kept the expenses of tax collection down to a very reasonable figure, and periodically cancelled reductions of tax granted to landowners. A higher proportion of the total yield of agriculture thus reached the imperial treasury, and less was absorbed by the bureaucracy and by landlords.

Another question may be asked. When the western empire had stood firm for two-and-a-half centuries from the reign of Augustus, and had surmounted the crisis of the mid-thirdcentury, and, recognized by Diocletian, had maintained itself intact for another three generations, why did it so rapidly collapse in the fifth century? Was the collapse primarily due to increased outside pressure or to internal decay or to a mixture of both?

One can only approximately gauge the external pressure on the empire. If one compares two historians who wrote on a similar scale of the first and of the fourth centuries A.D., Tacitus and Ammianus, one gains the impression that in the former period there was no heavy pressure on the frontiers, but in general peace, with only occasional border wars, whereas in the latter the emperors were constantly engaged in checking a breakthrough here and another breakthrough there.

The first serious attack on the Roman frontier was under Marcus Aurelius, and in the mid-third century the migrations of the Goths and other German tribes set up a general movement along the Danube, while the west German tribes grouped in the Frankish and Alamannic federation became more aggressive. The emperors of the late third century managed to restore the line, but it was henceforth held with far more effort than before. In the third quarter of the fourth century the westward movement of the Huns set all the German tribes in motion, and their pressure on the empire was redoubled. The tremendous losses incurred by the western Roman army during this period, amounting it would seem to two-thirds of its effectives, are striking evidence of the severity of the barbarian attacks.

One cause of weakness to the western parts was their administrative separation from the east. Formerly the emperors had been able to draw freely on the wealth of the east to finance the defence of the west. From the time of Diocletian the relatively poor western parts had to make do on their own resources with only occasional aid from the east.

To meet the increased barbarian pressure both halves of the empire enormously increased their armed forces, probably doubling their numbers. How far the high standard of military efficiency established in the principate was kept up, it is difficult to say, but it is unlikely that there was any significant decline. As any reader of Tacitus knows, the army of the early principate was not perfect. In peaceful times discipline became very slack, and the men spent their days on their private avocations and rarely attended a parade. Troops could get out of hand and plunder the provinces they were supposed to protect, and could panic in the face of the enemy. The officers were not professional soldiers and were often incompetent. These and other weaknesses appear in the later Roman empire, but the officers were on the whole of better quality, being experienced professionals. Small bodies of Roman troops still could and did defeat very much larger barbarian hordes in the fourth, fifth and sixth centuries.

The heavy economic burden imposed by the increased size of the army overstrained the resources of the empire and produced a number of weaknesses. It may seem an exaggeration to say that the resources of so large an area as the Roman empire could be overstrained by feeding, clothing and arming an extra 300,000 men, but it must be remembered that the empire was technologically even more backward than Europe of the Middle Ages. With primitive methods of agriculture, industrial production and transport it took very many more man-hours than today to produce the food for rations, to weave the fabrics for uniforms, to hammer out the arms and armour and to transport all this material by barge and wagon to the frontiers. Taxation had to be enormously increased, and to assess and collect the increased taxes, the civil service had to be expanded, thus increasing the taxation load again.

The heavy burden of taxation was probably the root cause of the economic decline of the empire. Marginal lands, which could not yield a profit to the landlord over and above the taxes, ceased to be cultivated. The population seems also to have shrunk. This is a highly disputable point, but there are distinct signs of a chronic shortage of agricultural manpower, notably the reluctance of landlords to surrender their tenants as recruits, the legislation tying tenants to their farms, the constant attempts of landlords to filch tenants from their neighbors, and the large-scale settlement of barbarians on the land. The shortage was not due to a flight from the land to the towns—the movement was rather in the opposite direction. It was exacerbated by the demands of conscription, but it is difficult to resist the suggestion that the peasant population failed to maintain its numbers. The decline in the cultivated area, though not primarily due to manpower shortage, implies that the rural population did decline. The reason for this was that the peasantry, after paying their taxes, and the tenants their rent, did not retain enough food to rear large families, and many died of malnutrition or of actual starvation in bad seasons or after enemy devastations.

Ideally speaking the empire could of course have reduced the economic burden by rigid efficiency and drastic pruning of superfluities. It maintained large numbers of idle or nominal soldiers and sinecurist civil servants. According to old custom it fed 120,000 citizens of Rome, and added to these 80,000 citizens of Constantinople. These were a direct burden on the treasury. It also tolerated, and indeed encouraged, the growth of other classes of idle mouths, notably the clergy. Paganism had cost very little, its priests, except in Egypt, receiving no remuneration except portions of sacrifices. The churches, with their many thousands of clergy, maintained from agricultural rents and first fruits, constituted a new and substantial burden on the economy. The emperors moreover did nothing to curb the growth of the official aristocracy in numbers and wealth, and thus tolerated and encouraged the increase of another unproductive class.

The basic cause of the economic decline of the empire was in fact the increasing number of (economically speaking) idle mouths—senators with their vast households, decurions, civil servants, lawyers, soldiers, clergy, citizens of the capitals—as compared with the number of producers. The resultant burden of taxation and rents proved too much for the peasantry, who slowly dwindled in numbers.

It has been argued that the empire was weakened by the decay of its trade and industry. It is in fact very doubtful if trade and industry did decay; the production and distribution of high-grade and luxury goods for the rich certainly continued to flourish down to the sixth century, and the bulk of industrial and commercial activity had probably always been devoted to such goods. In any event industry and trade had at all times made so small a contribution to the national income that their decay, if it did occur, was economically unimportant.

This economic pressure was, it must be remembered, as severe in the eastern as in the western parts. The east maintained as large an army and a civil service, and had an even larger and richer body of clergy, if a less wealthy aristocracy, than the west. Its rate of taxation was very high, its marginal lands fell out of cultivation, and its population probably sank. But it had greater reserves of agricultural wealth and manpower on which to draw.

The Conquest of the Sâsânian Empire

After the fall of the Western Roman Empire, the Eastern Empire, also known as the Byzantine Empire, recovered rapidly and vibrantly. By the middle of the sixth century the Byzantines had recovered most of North Africa as well as parts of Italy and Spain and were at war with the Persians, now ruled by the Sâsânian Dynasty, successors to the Parthians. The war with Persia continued intermittently for almost a century, but by 628 the Byzantines had captured the Persian capital of Ctesiphon and a peace treaty was signed with both sides exhausted. As they fought, moreover, a new power had been growing in the Arabian Peninsula. Sometime around 610 an Arab merchant by the name of

Muhammad Ibn Abdallah began to receive revelations that he interpreted to come from God. By the time he died in 632, Mohammad had established a powerful alliance of Arab tribes under his leadership who were faithful to the new religion he had founded, Islam. With the neighboring Byzantines and Persians weak from their long struggle, the Muslims, as the followers of Islam are called, were able to bring most of western Asia and North Africa under their control. Marshall Hodgson describes the Muslims' rapid neutralization of the Byzantines, whom Hodgson refers to as Romans, and their conquest of the Persian Empire under Umar, the second Caliph, or successor to Muhammad. In Persia, they found a weakened giant; the wars with the Byzantines and the civil wars that followed had severely destabilized the Sâsânian Dynasty. Ecological problems with their economic consequences and a large disaffected minority population also limited the Persians' ability to react effectively.

>> 80. The Venture of Islam:
Conscience and History in a World Civilization

MARSHALL G. S. HODGSON [1974]

In 634, two years after Muhammad, his lieutenant Abû-Bakr had died, leaving 'Umar as his acknowledged successor. 'Umar may have been responsible for the decision to occupy the agricultural provinces; in any case, he carried it out systematically. Some initial successes in 635, especially in Syria where even Damascus was occupied for a time, may have been due to the force of surprise. In 636 the Roman army in Syria—not the main army of the empire, of course—was destroyed at a point well chosen by the Muslims on the Yarmûk river; the Arab auxiliaries, forming a major portion of the Roman army, having gone over to the Muslims at a crucial point. Most of the Syrian cities then capitulated with little struggle. This encouraged the Muslims to make a more concerted and highly organized effort against the Iraq. In 637 the main army of the Sâsânians was destroyed at Qâdisiyyah, guarding the Euphrates. Presumably it was after this battle that the Sâsânian Arab auxiliaries went over to the Muslims. Most of the cities of the Iraq the capitulated. In the Iraq, among the

cities surrendered was the capital of the empire, Ctesiphon, where little resistance was offered. By 641, when the Roman emperor Heraclius died, practically all of the Aramaic-speaking lowlands had been occupied, including the Jazîrah (Mesopotamia proper) in the north and the Kârûn (Dujayl) valley in Khûzistân.

The Roman provincial power in Syria and the central Sâsânian power in the Iraq seem to have lost all morale and to have collapsed without serious attempts at internal co-operation or regrouping. In Syria, at least, this appears to have resulted from the apathy not only of the peasants but even of the urban populations, who in the Agrarian Age participated somewhat in the privileges of rule and would normally obstruct usurpation by an alien group. [...] When the imperial army was broken, the city populations accepted individual treaties with the Muslims (stipulating a lower rate of taxation) and received them in friendliness. The Greek-speaking landlord class withdrew to the Anatolian highlands and never came back.

In the long run, the collapse of the Sâsânians in the Iraq was still more decisive. Especially since Nûshîrvân, a large part of the Mesopotamian alluvial plain had become virtually a state farm, in the 'Sawâd', where the revenues were not allowed

---

Source: Marshall G. S. Hodgson, *The Venture of Islam: Conscience and History in a World Civilization*, vol. 1 (Chicago: University of Chicago Press, 1974), 200–304.

to be diverted to private landholders. It was maintained by a massive irrigation system which was no longer manageable on a piecemeal basis as irrigation there once had been and still was, to some degree, even in earlier Sâsânian times. This had formed the physical basis for the centralized army and hence for the centralized, bureaucratic empire. Now, only close and continuous central administration could keep it in order at all. A central collapse would mean ruin throughout large agricultural tracts—and must confirm the disaster to the central treasury. But following the Sâsânian defeat in the last war with Rome, several years had passed in political chaos as various claimants to the throne and factions in the army fought for the prize of power; different Sâsânian provinces were run almost in independence by the generals. A major shift in the Tigris bed seems to have created permanent swamps in the lower Iraq and ruined much farmland there even before the war was concluded. It is just possible that the changes in land formation were already beginning which eventually made much of the alluvial plain inherently harder to irrigate than it was earlier. But the political disruption alone was enough to account for unprecedented disaster conditions in the Iraq. This disaster, in turn, made it more difficult for the winner in the civil wars […] to impose his authority. Nûshîrvân's policies had ended, at least for the moment, in collapse.

Even apart from the disorders, the population of the plain could have little interest in holding the state lands for one government rather than another. The majority of people there were Christian and Jewish, or Manichean, and had suffered disabilities under the Mazdean hierarchy. The Sâsânian upper agrarian classes did not have a personal interest—or following—in the plain; they seem to have been based chiefly on the Iranian highlands. The most important part of the Sâsânian soldiery with a local interest in the Iraq were Arabs—some of them having been lately deprived of their autonomy. When the Sâsânian forces made a strategic withdrawal to the highlands, then, the Sâsânian nobility went with them; the Sâsânian Arab soldiery went over to the independent Arabs; and neither the peasantry nor the urban populations that remained offered resistance to the new military masters.

When Arab possessions of the Fertile Crescent had been assured, a wholesale migration of tribes from all parts of Arabia poured in, men bringing their families along, to join the victorious armies. These soon provided enormous army potential. The families were lodged in military bases quickly built on the edge of the desert, and armies were sent into all neighboring lands. The first expedition beyond the Aramaic lowlands began late in 639 into Egypt, well known to the Meccans for its wealth. In Egypt, the Coptic inhabitants had likewise resisted the Greek imperial church in the name of a Monophysite Christian creed and had been most bitterly persecuted since the evacuation of the Sâsânians. During 641, most of the country was occupied, and in 642 even Alexandria, the local Roman capital. Within a few years, Egypt was supplying the Hijâz with tribute grain as it had been supplying Byzantium.

In 641 began the advance into the Roman and Sâsânian highlands. Despite some initial reverses, Mu'âwiyah (son of Abû-Sufyân, former leader of the Quraysh), as governor of Syria, was able in the next few years to raid not only into Cilicia (southeast of the Taurus mountains) but far into the Anatolian peninsula, reaching Amorium by 646; but he was unable to occupy much territory beyond Melitene permanently, and by 647 was reduced to destroying fortresses in Roman territory which, for the time being, he could not expect to hold.

But the most important advances were into Sâsânian territory from Baṣrah and especially Kûfah. It was to these centres that the bulk of the new Arab immigration came, swamping the older, more city-disciplined, elements that had known Sâsânian rule and Sâsânian service from the time of the Lakhmids of Ḥîrah; whereas the corresponding older elements continued to predominate in Syria. The army sent into Irâq 'Ajamî, the main plateau area of western Iran, overcame a major Sâsânian army at Nihâvand in 641; by 643 the main cities of the province had capitulated. Deprived of their capital and of the state income from the alluvial plain, the Sâsânians seem to have been unable to concert their forces. In contrast to the Byzantines, whose main reserves and administrative headquarters were intact at distinct Constantinople, the Sâsânians were thereafter reduced to piecemeal resistance on a provincial basis. Eventually, their whole empire was overrun and the Arabs inherited their major resources and political potentialities. In this way, the Arabs' success in the Iraq made it possible for them to form an enduring new empire despite their ultimate failure to overcome the Byzantines in the latters' homelands.

The Fall of Teotihuacan

Not all empires collapsed due to outside invasions. The fall of Teotihuacan in Mexico suggests that it was insiders who brought it down. Teotihuacan was the principal city in the central Mexican highlands, dominating most of the region and extending its influence into modern-day Central America. Unfortunately for modern historians, the Teotihuacanos left no written records; we must instead decipher their civilization from their impressive archaeological remains. The city of Teotihuacan was quite large, especially by New World standards, covering over nine square miles and arranged in a grid pattern, very much like modern cities. Sometime around 650—but perhaps as late as 750—fire swept through sections of the city, ending Teotihuacan's domination. Its impact on Mexican civilization was long lasting; myths and stories of Teotihuacan's grandeur were still common at the time of the Spanish arrival. In this selection, René Millon, one of the foremost scholars of the city, attempts to reconstruct what happened during the fateful fire. He suggests that it was the Teotihuacanos themselves who destroyed the city, perhaps in an act of revolution against the city's leaders and the temples with which they were so closely associated. Other scholars have challenged Millon's arguments, positing instead that foreign invaders were responsible for the destruction of the city. It is a debate with little hope of definitive resolution unless new sources emerge.

>> 81. Last Years of Teotihuacan Dominance

RENÉ MILLON [1988]

Destruction by Fire

The end of Teotihuacan as a major power was fiery and cataclysmic. The fire was very selective. Violent destruction and burning were confined largely to monumental architecture on the "Street of the Dead" and to temples and associated buildings in the rest of the city. Our initial mapping survey recorded a high concentration of evidence for burning in the center and little of it elsewhere in the city. Because of the importance of this question, between 1974 and 1979 we systematically resurveyed major parts of the city specifically for such evidence, both the structures along the "Street of the Dead" and the permanent structures in eleven of the remaining eighteen square kilometers of construction, including close to a thousand apartment compounds (42 percent of the total). On the "Street of the Dead" and for varying distances

---

Source: René Millon, "Last Years of Teotihuacan Dominance," in *The Collapse of Ancient States and Civilizations*, edited by Norman Yoffee and George L. Cowgill (Tucson: University of Arizona Press, 1988), 149–150, 155–156.

on either side of it unequivocal evidence of burning was found on 147 buildings, with an additional 31 possibly burned. This includes virtually all the buildings on the "Street of the Dead" on which judgment was possible, excluding only those so completely reconstructed or otherwise altered that no basis for judgment existed. In the rest of the city, of a total of 68 temples examined specifically for evidences of burning, 28 were burned and 8 were possibly burned, for a total of 53 percent, whereas 22 showed no signs of burning (32 percent), and 10 were so altered that no judgment was possible. Of a total of 965 apartment compounds similarly examined, 45 showed clear evidence of burning (5 percent), 85 others were possibly burned (9 percent), for a total of 14 percent as opposed to 53 percent for temples. It is clear that the principal targets of burning were temples, pyramids, and public buildings.

What were the circumstances immediately preceding this deliberately planned systematic destruction? What we now know of the city's last years does not seem to prepare us for it. In 1981 I speculated on the immediate antecedents of the city's violent end in the following passage:

Accumulating problems and conflicts, internal and external, may have been met by more exercise of force than customary, exacerbating existing tensions and creating new ones, and precipitating rapid, convulsive social and economic deterioration—so rapid that it is not manifest in what we see. For Teotihuacan to have been destroyed as it was, the state apparatus must have been in a condition of near impotence. Except for one possible reference by Leopoldo Batres [...], there is no evidence that the city's inhabitants were slaughtered. The data available imply that the destruction was relatively bloodless, whether carried out from within or by invaders. This must mean that it occurred at a time of internal crisis. In the face of growing crisis, a split may have developed within the hierarchy over how to meet it. The ensuing factional dispute could have grown so deep and bitter as gradually to paralyze the power of the state and render it unable to act effectively when the onslaught came, from within or without. [...]

The location and intensity of the fires along the "Street of the Dead" point to an organized, planned campaign of ritual destruction. Destruction most frequently took the form of burning in front of and on both sides of staircases and on the tops of temple platforms. In the Ciudadela all temples have visible evidence of burning with one equivocal exception [...]. The same is true of most of the other structures, including the two palaces [...]. The sides of the Ciudadela temple platforms fronting the "Street of the Dead" were intensely burned in addition to the fronts and sides of their staircases. Across the street in the Great Compound all but three of the apartment compounds that have not been heavily altered by modern land leveling show evidence of burning. [...]

Those who carried out the destruction were so successful that the new Teotihuacan that later grew up around the ruins of the old never again approached the greatness of its predecessor. Its importance remained localized. It never again was a major religious center. The "Street of the Dead" would have been for the first time an apt description, and it remained so for hundreds of years. No longer did any of its temples function; no longer was it the pilgrimage center it had been. Most of the buildings on the "Street of the Dead" were never used again. Where reuse occurred, it appears primarily to have been sporadic, with some exceptions six or seven hundred years later in Aztec times.

The measure of the importance of religion and ideology in the rise to dominance of Teotihuacan is apparent in the form taken by its destruction. To destroy Teotihuacan and prevent it from ever again rising to a position of dominance, it was necessary to destroy all its sacred buildings and desacralize their sites through ritual destruction by fire. The religion of Teotihuacan must have been inextricably tied to place, either because this is where the world had been created and where time began, or because of similar if less cosmically elemental beliefs. The totality, scale, and intensity of the destruction must have been such that it no longer was possible to reconstitute in any viable form the belief system that had been shattered—either at Teotihuacan itself or elsewhere.

Who Did It?

Since 1976 I have been trying with little success to resolve the problem of who was responsible for the destruction of the center of Teotihuacan. The 1980–1982 work by Instituto Nacional de Antropología e Historia (INAH) investigators has added immeasurably to our knowledge about the attack. But evidence for the identity of the attackers is largely negative. No exotic or foreign persons or artifacts have been associated with it. No bodies other than those discussed earlier have been found (they may have been removed by the survivors, of course). The enigma remains. Nevertheless, it seems worthwhile briefly to reexamine the question, even though most of what I have to say is speculative.

It now seems to me more likely that Teotihuacanos rather than outsiders were responsible. I say this not only because of the recent discoveries in the Ciudadela, but also because the scale, intensity, duration, and sheer excessiveness of the destruction imply a sustained motivation and dedication that seems more likely to be the consequence of explosive internal pressures than of actions carried out by outsiders. The latter cannot be excluded, of course, nor can a combination of the two. Obviously, we are far from understanding how and why a sufficient number of Teotihuacanos might have reached the point of embarking on the destructive course that was to end forever the city's preeminence. If the impetus for the destruction was internal, it is at least possible that the evidence we seek may exist in the city itself, if we are able to recognize it.

Environmental Problems: Aksum and the Maya

The ecological problems highlighted by Jared Diamond (in Reading 78) get a fuller treatment in the next two selections. In the first, Stuart Hay examines the difficulties faced by the Kingdom of Aksum in Ethiopia. At the peak of its power between the third and fifth centuries, Aksum's supremacy extended over much of the Horn of Africa and into the Arabian Peninsula. But by the late 600s Aksum was declining under a series of internal political problems and possibly revolts by subject people. These troubles were made worse by a failing ecological system that the Aksumites had eroded during their period of political and demographic growth. In the second selection, T. Patrick Culbert examines the collapse of the Maya in Central America and southern Mexico, which largely remains a mystery. The archaeological records document a civilization at the height of its power in the eighth century followed a few decades later by a complete cessation of building projects and a drastic drop in population. Historians and archaeologists have advanced numerous reasons for this decline including foreign invasions, disease, social revolution, and, as with Aksum, environmental collapse. The real culprit is likely to have been a combination of several of these causes. However, Culbert argues that only environmental problems can explain the rapid loss of population even if other causes helped to accelerate the end of the Maya.

>> 82. Aksum: An African Civilisation in Late Antiquity

STUART MUNRO HAY [1991]

The long period of occupation of the city of Aksum evidently had a profound effect on the surrounding countryside, from which it drew the materials of subsistence. Some of the processes set in train can be inferred from the present state of the land, and consideration of the various factors involved. The local industries, including the manufacture of glass, faience, brick and pottery, and metal-working, all needed wood or charcoal for their furnaces. Charcoal was probably in further demand for cooking, and heating when necessary, and wood was used for furniture and other equipment as well as house-building. These activities slowly robbed the surrounding hills of their covering trees [...] and exposed their topsoil to degradation and erosion. The expansion of the population, probably adequately coped with at first by enlarging the food catchment areas by improved roads and transport facilities for goods into the city, and more intensive cultivation on the surrounding lands, eventually subjected these to overcropping. The pressure on the land would have shortened the rotation period of the crops, land which should have lain fallow for longer being pressed into use too soon. The subsequent lowering of the fertility level of the land again resulted in degradation and erosion, leaving an exhausted soil in the proximity of the city and the immediate countryside. Difficulties in maintaining the food-supplies may have been a significant factor in removing the capital elsewhere. A certain amount of recovery may have [been] possible in some areas around the town, since the fertility of the hinterland of the much smaller town of later times was noted by travelers a thousand or so years later. [...]

The work of the geomorphologist Karl Butzer [...] has suggested that the climate of northern Ethiopia may have changed for the worse just after the Aksumite period. The measurement of the Nile flood levels, recorded in Egypt, indicates that after a long period of excellent rainfall, more erratic precipitation ensued; this seems to have been after the abandonment of the city. However, if the land had reached a state of advanced degradation during the late Aksumite period, even the heavier rains, though theoretically ideal for the growth of the crops, would have contributed to the erosion on the slopes above the city and in the surrounding fields. What had been an advantage before had become another element in the vicious circle of the decay of the resources. It was the material brought down by the run-off caused by the rains from the hillsides that began to cover the buildings in the town as they were abandoned and fell into ruin. Butzer's figures suggest that until about 750 AD floods were high in Egypt, then poorer with very low levels from the mid-tenth to late eleventh centuries, the period when the kingdom, after the invasion of the queen of the Bani al-Hamwiyya, had decayed almost to the point when the Zagwé dynasty could take over [...]. The low-water levels after 730, in part following the spring rains in the Aksumite region, were already averaging below normal. It may be going too far to say that insufficient "little" rains (the March to May rains) combined with erosion caused by the action of strong June-September rains on the denuded land both to shorten the growing season and remove the topsoil. Nevertheless, climatic factors may have had their part to play in the abandonment of Aksum.

There are several hints that things began to go wrong in the Aksumite state in the later sixth and the early seventh century. Kaleb seems to have lost both prestige and an expensive war during his contretemps with Abreha, though after his death some sort of peace was patched up. The invasion may have been too costly a gesture for Aksum at the time, and the outlay in men and money must have had a deleterious effect on Aksumite power at

Source: Stuart Munro Hay, *Aksum: An African Civilisation in Late Antiquity* (Edinburgh: Edinburgh University Press, 1991), 258–260.

home. Possibly the great plague of the 540s [...], said to have emerged from Pelusium in Egypt, also had some effect on Aksum, as it did on the Roman world from the Mesopotamian provinces to Gaul, and across to Persia. The general political and commercial climate after first the Yemen and then Jerusalem and Alexandria fell to the Persians must have much damaged Ethiopia's trade in the Red Sea, and accordingly its prosperity.

To an unknown extent, troubles at the centre must have generated the hope in the outlying parts of the kingdom that it was time to essay another trial of strength with the Aksumite rulers, and revolts may have occurred which further weakened the kingdom by cutting off certain internal resources and routes [...]. For example, the Beja tribes, some of which had been crushed by Ezana long ago, later became independent of the *najashis* [...] and may have caused trouble to their theoretical overlords for some time before. The Agaw who later came to power with the Zagwé dynasty may also have been involved in the unrest.

>> 83. The Collapse of Classic Maya Civilization

T. PATRICK CULBERT [1988]

Agricultural Stress and the Maya Collapse

Research in the Maya lowlands since 1970 seems to me to indicate more strongly than ever the potential dangers in the population-subsistence balance in the Late Classic period. All available data show that populations in the southern lowlands rose rapidly to a Late Classic peak. Not only was the population unusually dense for a preindustrial civilization (200 persons/km^2), but it covered an area too large to allow adjustment through relocation or emigration. At the time of the Maya collapse, population fell dramatically, even allowing for the pockets of population known to have persisted into the Postclassic. The magnitude of the population loss between A.D 800 and 1000 was such that I do not believe that social malfunction alone can account for it. Consequently, any explanation of the collapse that does not include subsistence failure seems unsatisfactory.

Maya agriculture became increasingly intensive as the population rose, and the scale of the substance economy was much larger than previously realized. Both terrace and raised-field systems in some parts of the lowlands covered territories of great size. The support systems of the largest sites probably involved transportation of large volumes of foodstuffs from substantial distances (50 to 100 km). I believe that large-scale intensification occurred late, probably as a response to population growth. In the short term the system was successful enough to maintain dense populations for a century or two before the collapse.

The scale of the subsistence system, however, was such that it may not have had much potential for long-term stability. To continue functioning effectively, it would have needed management to ensure that farmers did not relax their efforts in any of the labor-intensive routines. But there is no evidence [...], that the Maya made any change in a management system that had developed in a time of considerably less complexity. Manpower demands for agriculture must have been very high, perhaps even high enough to stress the large population pool of the Late Classic. Nevertheless,

Source: T. Patrick Culbert, "The Collapse of Classic Maya Civilization," in *The Collapse of Ancient States and Civilizations,* edited by Norman Yoffee and George L. Cowgill (Tucson: University of Arizona Press, 1988), 99–100.

the lavish use of labor for public construction continued until the point of the collapse. In addition, military competition between sites may have been a drain upon manpower, and there is increasing evidence that the southern lowland Maya have been under military pressure from the north. Finally, agricultural risks must have been greatly increased by intensification. These would have included both short-term risks such as year-to-year climatic variation, insects, and plant disease , and cumulative long-term effects such as erosion and declining soil fertility. The Late Classic Maya, in other words, had committed themselves to an agricultural system whose long-range results and security were unknown.

Given the tight interconnections of all these factors and the paucity of precise data, one could construct almost any scenario of agricultural failure that suited one's fancy. I prefer to emphasize long-term environmental degradation as a critical factor. It seems quite possible that even had the Maya turned to more adaptive management and labor policies, they might still have faced disaster. The Maya system of intensification may be one in which short-term productive increase may simply be incompatible with long-range ecological stability.

>> Mastering the Material

1. What are some of the causes that bring about imperial decline? Which of these would you consider most significant? Why?

2. Gills and Frank suggest that the interconnections between the Eurasian empires played a role in their demise. Based on the other sources that you have read, how accurate do you think Gills and Frank are?

3. Augustine and Ibn Khaldûn both blame a taste for luxuries as a major cause in imperial weakness. To what degree do you think they are right?

4. Based on this chapter's sources, how critical is the environment to imperial survival? How responsible is ecological deterioration for the decline of empire?

5. Why do empires need strong and effective governments and administrations to survive?

>> Making Connections

1. Consider the sources in this chapter, as well as those in Parts 1 and 2. What are the advantages and drawbacks of using archaeological sources to reconstruct historical events?

2. How do the challenges faced by classical societies differ from those faced by early cities (Chapter 5), and how are they similar?

Chapter 11

Migrations of the First Millennium

As the great empires declined, collapsed, or were transformed, the political ramifications extended far beyond their own borders. In Eurasia, where societies were closely interconnected, problems in China affected Rome long after. The two empires were the bookends of the continent and when one end was pushed, the other end undoubtedly felt it. The "books" in this Eurasian bookshelf—to exhaust the metaphor completely—were barbarian nomadic tribes native to the Central Asian steppes. The problems experienced by the Han Empire in the early third century forced power struggles in Central Asia as these tribes fought one another for supremacy. A similar situation seems to have occurred in the Americas, where the decline of Teotihuacan had an impact on the Maya as well as on their barbarian neighbors to the north. One result of all this conflict was migration on a massive scale inside former imperial borders.

The newcomers did not have a very good reputation from the point of view of imperial citizens. Early Chinese sources declared that some of their barbarian neighbors were violent and warlike by nature and possessed horses that sweated blood. Indian sources noted the rough nature of people who lived outside their empire—they dressed in skins, ate wild things, and lived in caves. They also made numerous comments on the short stature and alien facial features of those peoples. The Roman historian Ammianus Marcellinus also commented on how different some barbarians were from imperial citizens, but finally admitted that "their shape, however disagreeable, is human."

Contempt and hostility against outsiders has, in many ways, been inherited by many modern historians who pay attention to the barbarians only when they come in contact with the empires. This is partly understandable, as barbarian tribes rarely produced written sources, leaving modern scholars to understand them through the biased words of their imperial observers. Approached like this, as Lester Little explains in Reading 89, barbarian societies never get considered in their own right as vibrant and constructive entities, making significant contributions of their own. Instead, they are doomed to adorn the pages of history books as wild men and women whose chief historical role has been to destroy their more civilized neighbors. It is only recently that scholars have begun to study barbarian societies independent of the empires, allowing their own archaeological and other native sources to speak for themselves.

In the Eurasian context, the Huns were one of the most important of these barbarian tribes. Their perambulations offer a good example of the migrations and their consequences. Historians have devoted significant efforts to linking the Huns with other nomadic groups from the steppes including the Hsiung-nu, whose raids into China were a major problem for the Han Dynasty, and the Huna or White Huns whose impact in India is discussed by Romila Thapar, but these efforts have yielded inconclusive results. Much of what we know about the Huns comes from the writings of the Roman historian Ammianus Marcellinus, who paints an image of merciless ferocity. He describes the Huns as they marched west subjugating the Alans, another steppe tribe, forcefully incorporating them into their federation. The Huns then turned on the Goths, a Germanic people possibly native to Scandinavia, who, unable to defend themselves, sought refuge inside the borders of the Roman Empire in 376. By the 440s, the Huns—under the leadership of Attila—were openly at war with the rapidly weakening Romans and had penetrated into France, where a coalition of Roman and Gothic forces stopped further incursions. Attila then turned his attention against Italy, the very heart of the Roman Empire. There, he had limited success against the walled cities. By 453, Attila was dead. His many sons divided his empire among themselves and many of his followers melted back into the Eurasian steppe lands to be assimilated by other steppe peoples.

The westward push of the Huns had additional consequences for the Roman Empire. The Romans had allowed the Goths, specifically the Visigoths or Western Goths, to settle inside their borders, but treated them rather cruelly. This eventually put the Visigoths on the warpath, and in 378 they destroyed a Roman army at Adrianople. Although relations between the two peoples improved as the fourth century closed, by the early 400s they were at war again and the Visigoths were threatening Italy itself, a threat that would culminate with the sacking of Rome in 410. To defend against this menace, the western emperor recalled legions from other parts of the empire to defend Italy. The bulk of these troops came from Britain and the Rhine River frontier outposts, leaving both of these areas vulnerable. Soon thereafter, hordes of Germanic tribesmen rushed over the frozen Rhine and made their way into the interior sections of the Empire. Britain enjoyed a few more decades with no full-fledged invasions, but it was still the target of recurring raids from Germanic tribesmen. In Reading 86 Bede, an English monk writing in the eighth century, describes the early arrival of the island's future conquerors.

These migratory invasions were a common theme in the troubles experienced by the empires—even the American empires seem to have had their share of barbarian incursions. Just as China and Rome were connected in a pan-Eurasian world system, so too were the Mesoamerican empires linked by a pan-American system. What this means is that the fall of Teotihuacan likely had consequences for the Maya. In this case, the impact may have been commercial as other Mexican tribes moved into the power vacuum created by the empire's fall. These newcomers likely competed economically with the Maya, and the pressures they placed on Maya society in both economic and demographic terms may have contributed to the eventual Maya political collapse. As the selection by Michael Coe in this chapter suggests, some of these immigrants did more than just compete economically with the people of Mesoamerica. Invasions by people from the north added to the increasingly chaotic situation that followed the collapse of the classic civilizations between the eighth and ninth centuries.

The expansion of the Bantu-speaking peoples of sub-Saharan Africa provides us with a counterexample to the migration by conquest model seen in Eurasia and the Americas. The Bantu language group originates in western Africa, specifically the grasslands of

Cameroon. However, over a period of several millennia these related languages spread across the trunk of Africa and far to the south. Historians, linguists, and archaeologists believe that Bantu technology—iron, cultivation, and pastoralism—spread along with language. There is a great deal of debate about how this package of culture and technology moved. To some degree innovations can move by themselves as people adopt their neighbor's technology and share their own expertise. However, it seems likely that the movement of Bantu farmers and herders into new regions played a role as well. The Bantu probably owe their expansion to their rapid population growth when compared with that of their neighbors. With larger numbers they were able to expand more quickly. This does not mean that there were no conquests, but it may suggest that Bantu success may owe more to the population pressures they applied on their neighbors than to any large-scale warfare or massive disruption. A leading researcher of the Bantu diffusion, Christopher Ehret, has detailed the way this process might have occurred in some parts of Africa.

The Huns

Ammianus Marcellinus was a staff officer in the Roman Army in the second half of the fourth century and a witness to many of the critical events of his lifetime. He traveled the width of the Empire from Gaul (France) to the borders with Persia and was an active participant in numerous military campaigns against the enemies of Rome. Late in his life he wrote a history of the Roman Empire in 31 books. Unfortunately, only books 14–31, covering the years 354–378, have survived. During Ammianus's lifetime, the Roman Empire came under increasing pressure on its frontier from the Persians and from independent tribes that lived outside imperial borders. Among the most troublesome and terrifying to the Romans were the Huns. In the following selection Ammianus describes an alien people who were beyond anything that Ammianus considered civilized. The account reveals as much about the Huns as it does about Ammianus and the Roman society of which he was a part. In the last part of the selection, Ammianus describes the Huns' push to the west, driving the Goths (Greuthungi) in those regions ahead of them and eventually into the borders of the Roman Empire.

>> 84. The Later Roman Empire

AMMIANUS MARCELLINUS [LATE FOURTH CENTURY C.E.]

The Nature of the Huns and Alans

The seed-bed and origin of all this destruction and of the various calamities inflicted by the wrath of Mars, which raged everywhere with unusual fury, I find to be this. The people of Huns, who are mentioned only cursorily in ancient writers and who dwell beyond the Sea of Azov (Palus Maeotis) near the frozen ocean, are quite abnormally savage. From the moment of birth they make deep gashes in their children's cheeks, so that when in due course hair appears its growth is checked by the wrinkled scars; as

Source: Ammianus Marcellinus, *The Later Roman Empire (A.D. 354–378)*, edited and translated by Walter Hamilton (London: Penguin Books, 1986), 411–412, 414–416.

they grow older this gives them the unlovely appearance of beardless eunuchs. They have squat bodies, strong limbs, and thick necks, and are so prodigiously ugly and bent that they might be two-legged animals, or the figures crudely carved from stumps which are seen on the parapets of bridges. Still, their shape, however disagreeable, is human; but their way of life is so rough that they have no use for fire or seasoned food, but live on the roots of wild plants and the half-raw flesh of any sort of animal, which they warm a little by placing in between their thighs and the backs of their horses. They have no buildings to shelter them, but avoid anything of the kind as carefully as we avoid living in the neighborhood of tombs; not so much as a hut thatched with reeds is to be found among them. They roam at large over mountains and forests, and are inured from the cradle to cold, hunger, and thirst. On foreign soil only extreme necessity can persuade them to come under a roof, since they believe that it is not safe for them to do so. They wear garments of linen or of the skins of field-mice stitched together, and there is no difference between their clothing whether they are at home or abroad. Once they have put their necks into some dingy shirt they never take it off or change it till it rots and falls to pieces from incessant wear. They have round caps of fur on their heads, and protect their hairy legs with goatskins. Their shapeless shoes are not made on a last and make it hard to walk easily. In consequence they are ill-fitted to fight on foot, and remain glued to their horses, hardy but ugly beasts, on which they sometimes sit like women to perform their everyday business. Buying or selling, eating or drinking, are all done by day or night on horseback, and they even bow forward over their beasts' narrow necks to enjoy a deep and dreamy sleep. When they need to debate some important matter they conduct their conference in the same posture. They are not subject to the authority of any king, but break through any obstacle in their path under the improvised command of their chief men.

They sometimes fight *by challenging their foes to single combat,* but when they join battle they advance in packs, uttering their various warcries. Being lightly equipped and very sudden in their movements they can deliberately scatter and gallop about at random, inflicting tremendous slaughter; their extreme nimbleness enables them to force a rampart or pillage an enemy's camp before one catches sight of them. What makes them the most formidable of all warriors is that they shoot from a distance arrows tipped with sharp splinters of bone instead of the usual heads; these are joined the shafts with wonderful skill. At close quarters they fight without regard for their lives, and while their opponents are guarding against sword-thrusts they catch their limbs in lassos of twisted cloth which make it impossible for them to ride or walk. None of them ploughs or ever touches a plough-handle. They have no fixed abode, no home or law or settled manner of life, but wander like refugees with the wagons in which they live. In these their wives weave their filthy clothing, mate with their husbands, give birth to their children, and rear them to the age of puberty. No one if asked can tell where he comes from, having been conceived in one place, born somewhere else, and reared even further off. You cannot make a truce with them, because they are quite unreliable and easily swayed by any breath of rumour which promises advantage; like unreasoning beasts they are entirely at the mercy of the maddest impulses. They are totally ignorant of the distinction between right and wrong, their speech is shifty and obscure, and they are under no restraint from religion or superstition. Their greed for gold is prodigious, and they are so fickle and prone to anger that often in a single day they will quarrel with their allies without any provocation, and then make it up again without anyone attempting to reconcile them.

This wild race, moving without encumbrances and consumed by a savage passion to pillage the property of others, advanced robbing and slaughtering over the lands of their neighbors till they reached the Alans. [...]

The Huns and Alans Expel the Goths from Their Homes

The Huns, overrunning the territory of those Alans who border on the Greuthungi and are commonly called the Don Alans, killed and stripped many of them, and made a pact of friendship with the survivors. This success emboldened them to make a sudden inroad on the rich and extensive realm of Ermenrich, a warlike king whose many heroic exploits had made him a terror to his neighbors. Ermenrich was hard hit by the violence of this unexpected storm. For some time he endeavored to stand his ground, but exaggerated reports circulated of the dreadful fate which awaited him, and he found release from his fears by taking his own life. He was succeeded as king by Vithimir, who resisted the Alans for a time, relying on the help of other Huns whom he had hired to support him. But after many defeats he was overwhelmed by superior force and lost his life in battle. The guardianship of his young son Videric was undertaken by Alatheus and Saphrax, experienced commanders of proved courage, but their plans were frustrated by circumstances, and they had to abandon any hope of successful resistance. So they prudently withdrew to the line of the river Dniester (Danastius), which waters the wide plains between the Danube and the Dnieper (Borysthenes).

Athanaric the chief of the Thervingi, against whom, as I have already said, Valens had recently taken the field to punish him for sending help to Procopius, heard of these unexpected events and attempted to maintain his ground, being resolved to put forth all his strength if he should be attacked like the rest. Accordingly he took up his position in a good spot near the banks of the Dniester but some distance from the defensive works of the Greuthungi, and sent Munderic, who later commanded of the Arabian frontier, together with Lagariman and some other notables twenty miles ahead to watch for the approach of the enemy, while he himself marshaled his army undisturbed. But things turned out very differently from what he expected. The Huns, who are good guessers, suspected that there was a larger force further off. So they paid no attention to the troops they had seen, who had lain down the rest as if they had no enemy near them. Then the Huns forded the river by moonlight, and took what was undoubtedly the best course. They forestalled the possibility of any warning reaching the enemy by making a rapid assault on Athanaric himself, and before he could recover from the surprise of their first onset drove him with some losses on their own part to take refuge in rugged mountain country. This new situation and the fear that there was worse to follow constrained him to erect a high rampart extending from the Pruth (Gerasus) to the Danube and striking the territory of the Taifali. He believed that this hastily but carefully constructed barrier would ensure his security. But while he was pushing on this important work he was hard pressed by the rapid advance of the Huns, who would have overwhelmed him if the weight of booty they were carrying had not forced them to desist.

A report, however, now spread widely among the other Gothic tribes that a hitherto unknown race of men had approached from some remote corner of the earth, uprooting and destroying everything in its path like a whirlwind descending from high mountains. Weakened by lack of the necessities of life the greater part of the people abandoned Athanaric, and looked for a dwelling far from all knowledge of the barbarians. After much debate where to settle they fixed upon Thrace as the most eligible refuge for two reasons, first, because of its fertility, and second, because it is separated by the broad stream of the Danube from the regions exposed to the thunderbolts of the Alien Mars. This decision met with unanimous support.

The Huna in India

Some historians associate the Huns with another barbarian group that invaded the Gupta Empire in India. This association between the two groups is far from clear and remains a matter of debate. Whether there was a relationship or not, it is clear that barbarians (mleccha) invaded India sometime in the mid-400s. These invaders of India, known variously as the Huna, White Huns, or Hephthalites, were partly responsible for hastening the end of the Gupta Empire in the early sixth century. Their stay in India was short lived, however, as a local coalition, which included remnants of the Gupta, drove them out in 528. In the following selection Romila Thapar embraces the Hun/Huna relationship and discusses their impact on Indian society.

>> 85. The Image of the Barbarian in Early India

ROMILA THAPAR [1971]

The coming of the Huns was not a traumatic event in the history of India. Its impact has perhaps been exaggerated owing to its continual comparison with the arrival of the Huns in Europe. Even the parallel which is frequently drawn between the Huns dealing a death blow to the Roman empire and the Hūṇas doing the same to the Gupta empire (fourth–fifth centuries A.D.) is not strictly comparable since the nature of the two empires was different as also the cause of their decline. Northern India was by now familiar with foreign invasions and government under *mleccha* dynasties. The Hūṇas were known to inhabit the northern regions and are sometimes mentioned together with the Cīna (Chinese). The close of the fifth century A.D. saw the Hūṇa invasions of India under their chief Toramāna. The location of his inscription at Eran (Madhya Pradesh) and the discovery of his seals at Kauśāmbī (Uttar Pradesh) point to his having controlled a substantial part of *ārya-varta*. Hence the problem of living in a region overrun by the *mleccha* referred to earlier. Toramāna's son Mihirakula lived up to the conventional image of the Hun. He is particularly remembered for his cruelty which has become a part of northern Indian folklore. His violence however was directed mainly against the Buddhists and the Jainas, whose literature is replete with complaints about him. He was however forced back from the Ganges valley and the Hūṇa kingdom after him was reduced to a small area of northern India. The Hūṇa invasion itself did not produce any major changes in the life of northern India, except at the topmost political level. Epigraphical evidence suggests that the feudatories of the Gupta kings continued as the local governors under Hūṇa rule. Hūṇas used Sanskrit as their official language and patronized Hindu cults and sects.

The impact of the Huns was greater in other spheres. Hun activities in central Asia affected north Indian trade which had close links with central Asia. Furthermore in the wake of the Huns came a number of other tribes and peoples from central Asia jostling for land and occupation in northern India. This led to a migration of peoples in these parts which in turn upset one of the stabilizing factors of the caste structure, the inter-relationship between caste and locality. Some of these movements of peoples from the north southwards can be traced in the place names and the caste names, as in the case of the Gurjaras and Ābhīras.

Source: Romila Thapar, "The Image of the Barbarian in Early India," *Comparative Studies in Society and History* 13 (1971): 425–426.

The Angles and Saxons Come to Britain

By the time the Huns reached western Europe in the middle of the fifth century under the leadership of their king Attila, most of the Western Roman Empire was in disarray. Britain was in particularly bad shape. In 410, the last Roman troops were withdrawn to stop the advance of Germanic tribes in other parts of the Empire. The Romano-Britons who lived on the island were left to their own devices. In order to stop the raids of the Picts (the inhabitants of ancient Scotland) and other raiders, the Romano-Britons allied themselves with other barbarian tribes—the Angles, Saxons, and Jutes—to defend the island. This was nothing new; the Romans had a long tradition of allying themselves with some barbarian tribes against others. In the case of England, however, the alliance did little to secure the safety of the Romano-British population as the Angles, Saxons, and Jutes quickly turned from protectors to conquerors. Seeing the island bereft of defenses they began its conquest aided by additional migration of their kinsmen from the European mainland. Within a century, they had most of Britain under their control. In the following selection, Bede—the great historian of Anglo-Saxon England— describes the arrival of the earliest Angles, Saxons, and Jutes and the depredations to which they subjected the native population.

>> 86. Ecclesiastical History of the English People

BEDE [C. 731 C.E.]

In the year of our Lord 449, Martian became Emperor with Valentinian, the forty-sixth in succession from Augustus, ruling for seven years. In his time the Angles or Saxons came to Britain at the invitation of King Vortigern in three long-ships, and were granted lands in the eastern part of the island on condition that they protected the country: nevertheless, their real intention was to subdue it. They engaged the enemy advancing from the north, and having defeated them, sent back news of their success to their homeland, adding that the country was fertile and the Britons cowardly. Whereupon a larger fleet quickly came over with a great body of warriors, which, when joined to the original forces, constituted an invincible army.

These also received from the Britons grants of land where they could settle among them on condition that they maintained the peace and security of the island against all enemies in return for regular pay.

These new-comers were from the three most formidable races of Germany, the Saxons, Angles, and Jutes. From the Jutes are descended the people of Kent and the Isle of Wight and those in the province of the West Saxons opposite the Isle of Wight who are called Jutes this day. From Saxons—that is, the country now known as the land of the Old Saxons—came the East, South and West Saxons. And from the Angles—that is, the country known as Angulus, which lies between the provinces of the Jutes and Saxons and is said to remain unpopulated to this day— are descended the East and Middle Angles, the Mercians, all the Northumbrian stock (that is, those people living north of the river Humber), and the other English peoples. Their first chieftains are said to have been the brothers Hengist and Horsa. The latter was subsequently killed in battle against the Britons, and was buried in east

---

Source: Bede, *Ecclesiastical History of the English People with Bede's Letter to Egbert and Cuthbert's Letter on the Death of Bede* (London: Penguin Books, 1990), 62–64.

Kent, where the monument bearing his name still stands. They were the sons of Wictgils, whose father was Witta, whose father was Wecta, son of Woden, from whose stock sprang the royal house of many provinces.

It was not long before such hordes of these alien peoples vied together to crowd into the island that the natives who had invited them began to live in terror. Then all of a sudden the Angles made an alliance with the Picts, whom by this time they had driven some distance away, and began to turn their arms against their allies. They began by demanding a greater supply of provisions; then, seeking to provoke a quarrel, threatened that unless larger supplies were forthcoming, they would terminate their treaty and ravage the whole island. Nor were they slow to carry out their threats. In short, the fires kindled by the pagans proved to be God's just punishment on the sins of the nation, just as the fires once kindled by the

Chaldeans destroyed the walls and buildings of Jerusalem. For, as the just Judge ordained, these heathen conquerors devastated the surrounding cities and countryside, extended the conflagration from the eastern to the western shores without opposition and established a stronghold over nearly all the doomed island. Public and private buildings were razed; priests were slain at the altar; bishops and people alike, regardless of rank, were destroyed with fire and sword, and none remained to bury those who had suffered a cruel death. A few wretched survivors captured in the hills were butchered wholesale, and others, desperate with hunger, came out and surrendered to the enemy for food, although they were doomed to lifelong slavery even if they escaped instant massacre. Some fled overseas in their misery; others, clinging to their homeland, eked out a wretched and fearful existence among the mountains, forests, and crags, ever on the alert for danger.

Barbarians in Mesoamerica

The place of the barbarians in the political collapse of Mesoamerican civilizations is harder to establish than that of Eurasian empires. Whereas it is clear that Huns, Goths, Vandals, and Alans played an important part in the deterioration of Roman rule, we can not reach the same conclusion about any American counterparts. The collapse of Teotihuacan and the Maya appear to have been mostly the result of internal forces. Even when outsiders contributed to this decline, their part appears to have been relatively minor. Michael Coe suggests that the main impact of such foreigners came after the disappearance of Teotihuacano and Maya power. With these two stabilizing forces gone, Mesoamerica entered a rather chaotic phase that was worsened by the arrival of these newcomers.

>> 87. Mexico

MICHAEL D. COE [1984]

Following in the wake of the widespread disturbances which brought to a close the civilizations of the Classic around the end of the ninth century BC was an entirely new mode of organized life. The silent characteristic of this age, the

Post-Classic, was a heightened emphasis on militarism, in fact, a glorification of war in all its aspects. The intellectual hierarchy of the older cultures had now either disappeared or was relegated to inferior status. In its place was an upstart class of tough professional warriors, grouped into military orders which took their names from the animals from which they may have claimed a

Source: Michael D. Coe, *Mexico* (London: Thames and Hudson, 1984), 121–123.

kind of totemic descent: coyote, jaguar, and eagle. Wars were the rule of the day, those unfortunate enough to be captured destined for sacrifice to gods who were now hungry for the taste of human blood. As a result, for the first time in Mexico there was a widespread need for the construction of strongpoints and the fortification of towns.

Throughout Mexico, this was a time which saw a great deal of confusion and movement of peoples, amalgamating to form small, aggressive, conquest states, and splitting up with as much speed as they had risen. Even tribes of distinctly different speech sometimes came together to form a single state—as we know from their annals, for we have entered the realm of history. [...]

It was not only internal pressure brought by new conquest states that disturbed Mexico. Probably more far-reaching in their long-range effects were the great migrations into Mexico by barbaric tribes inhabiting the wastelands beyond the northern limits of Mesoamerican farming. The Aztecs called all the northerners beyond the pale of civilized life 'Chichimeca', a name meaning something like 'lineage of the dog', not a term of opprobrium since several ruling dynasties in the Valley of Mexico were proud to claim Chichimec ancestry. These barbarians were nomadic hunters who carried their bows and arrows everywhere with them and knew not how to cultivate the land. In the account recorded by Father Sahagún, wildest of all were the 'Teochichimeca', the 'real' Chichimeca, who lived in caves and clothed themselves in animal skins and yucca-fiber sandals, subsisting on wild fruits, roots and seeds and on the meat of humble animals like the rabbit. Between them and the civilized peoples were the 'Tamime', Chichimeca who had picked up a smattering of the customs and speech of their more advanced neighbors to the south; they wore the cast-off rags of civilization and did a little farming to supplement their wild diet.

Who in fact were the Chichimesa? The inner plateau of northern Mexico is a vast rocky desert bordered on the west and east by the two Sierra Madre ranges. Here lived until recent times primitive tribes like the Uto-Aztecan speaking Zacateca and Tepehuan, the Guachichil of unknown affiliation, and the Pame. These peoples were, then, exactly what the Aztecs meant by 'Teochichimeca'. The heirs of the old 'Desert Culture', forbidden tillage of the soil because of low rainfall, they were mainly collectors of mesquite seeds and hunters of rabbits, which were caught in communal drives. Being perforce semi-nomadic, they traveled in small bands under the leadership of a headman and lived, like the Chichimeca, in either caves or else dome-shaped brush shelters. Lacking from their simple religions were temples, idols, and priests. Most were unfamiliar with pottery or the loom. Easily recognizable here is a mode of existence shared with desert-living Indians as far north as Oregon and one recalling the Archaic backgrounds of Mexican civilization.

Dependent upon fluctuations in rainfall, the northern border of Mesoamerica actually wavered back and forth over the centuries, as farmers moved north or were forced back by drought. One long, narrow band of cultivators extended along the most eastern slopes of the Sierra Madre Occidental almost to the American Southwest; another lay to the west of these mountains, on the coast of western Mexico to the Gulf of California. The peoples of these two strips were not particularly advanced. On the contrary, their position as farmers was rather precarious and they of necessity possessed some of the characteristics of the nomads, just as the frontiersmen of the American West adopted Indian customs as their own. In other words, they were 'semi-Chichimeca' like those Tamime described by Sahagún.

In general, the northerners, like all Desert Culture tribes, were quite peaceful. This was especially so when desert conditions were relatively good; then, increased precipitation brought in farmers from the south and the frontiers marched forward. When, however, the reverse was true, the wild nomads, driven to desperation by drought and starvation, pushed south into regions that were formerly occupied by tillers of the soil, raiding the outposts of civilization. Then, even the part-farmers of the north were pushed backs. This would account for the great Chichimec invasions which took place in the Post-Classic period.

The Expansion of the Bantu

The migrations of people across the Eurasian continent, especially those that came into contact with the Romans, is fairly well documented. The same cannot be said for other parts of the world, where a lack of written sources has left modern scholars unable to document precisely how and when large numbers of people moved around. In these cases, scholars have had to rely on less traditional sources—such as linguistic evidence and archaeology—to determine the mass movement of certain groups. This research has increasingly yielded some very promising results, with Christopher Ehret's selection on the expansion of the Bantu-speaking people of sub-Saharan Africa being one of the most interesting and sophisticated case studies. The Bantu arrived in the African Great Lakes region around 1000 B.C.E. There they adopted and developed iron working as well as new systems of agricultural production that allowed their population to swell. Their large population, especially in comparison to their neighbors, may have been the primary reason their expansion was so far reaching.

>> 88. An African Classical Age: Eastern and Southern Africa in World History, 1000 B.C. to A.D. 400

CHRISTOPHER EHRET [1998]

Over the early and middle centuries of the last millennium B.C., then, the Mashariki societies built up their numbers and gradually expanded their territories. During the same period, they began to gain acquaintance as well, through their contacts with the Central Sudanians and Eastern Sahelians, with new kinds of agricultural production, especially the cultivation of African grain crops. For a long time they made little use themselves of this knowledge. But by the last three or four centuries of the era, it has been proposed here, Mashariki farmers had settled throughout the warmer, lower-lying forested areas that extended from the Western Rift valley to Lake Nyanza and from the Kivu Basin southward to the southwestern side of Lake Tanganyika, and they had begun to reach a kind of critical population density across those regions. It would have been a density that, in absolute terms, was still extremely low in comparison with modern agricultural population densities across many of those same areas. But with respect to the expectations of the time, it would have been felt by the people themselves as a critical pressure on the viability of their very long-fallow type of agriculture.

The reaching of this demographic stage can be proposed to have had two kinds of consequences. First, it triggered off a series of expansions out of many parts of the Lake Mashariki lands, each population movement seeking out new areas farther afield where their

Source: Christopher Ehret, *An African Classical Age: Eastern and Southern Africa in World History, 1000 B.C. to A.D. 400* (Charlottesville: University Press of Virginia, 1998), 106–107.

accustomed livelihood might be carried on. These movements surely did not all begin at the same point in time, but probably developed over a period of a few centuries, toward the close of the millennium, as the perceived pressure of population growth began to make itself felt in different areas. And second, it led to the fuller putting into practice of that knowledge of grain cultivating technology which the cultural interactions of the earlier centuries of the last millennium B.C. bequeathed to the Mashariki societies. This second consequence allowed a continuing growth and expansion of the Lakes Bantu populations who remained in the Nyanza Basin itself, and it allowed the Bantu communities who left the region to resettle in a variety of environments, especially in east-central and southeastern Africa, where grain cultivation often was essential to farmers' survival. What is argued here, in other words, is that the fundamental factors that explain the vast expansion of Bantu peoples at the turn of the era lie not, as scholars have often argued, in the emergence of ironworking technology, but in the long-term developments of agricultural history.

The growth of the Bantu societies may have had unexpected consequences also for the expansion of another people, the Tale Southern Cushites. Rather than the impetus for expansion being generated by developments within Tale Southern Cushitic society itself, it may well have been the clearing of forest and brush for cultivation by Lakes communities on the east of Lake Nyanza, and by Southern Nyanza peoples around the south and southwest of the lake, that allowed the Tale to spread eastward, with their cattle, during the second half of the last millennium B.C. Cattle keeping may thus, in the last few centuries B.C., have increased greatly in importance among both the Lake and Southern-Nyanza peoples [...] primarily because of the efforts that these Bantu communities made on behalf of their own nonpastoral agriculture. The Tale moved in as opportunity provided by Bantu farmers allowed and became in the process the major contributors of the new knowledge and expertise in animal husbandry.

Challenging the Master Narrative

*Lester Little challenges much of the current historical treatment of the European "barbarians" from the point of view of the master narrative. The **master narrative** is the storyline that historians have assembled to teach the history of a particular region to their students. For European history this narrative begins with Egypt and Mesopotamia and then moves on to Greece, Rome, and the Middle Ages. The problem with this approach is that it does not begin to focus on the native peoples of non-Mediterranean Europe until the latter years of the Roman Empire. Little argues that any narrative that focuses on Greece and Rome is flawed because it views the Germanic and Celtic people of Europe as barbarian outsiders whose main contribution was the destruction of the Roman world. In such a narrative, Germans and Celts do not get the recognition due to them for their arts, language, religion, settlements, and other contributions. Instead, Little would have us make northern Europe the center of our studies, pushing the Romans to the periphery and making them the outsiders. Some historians welcome this approach to history as a way of understanding those people who lived outside imperial borders on their own terms and not those of the empires with which they interacted.*

>> 89. Cypress Beams, Kufic Script, and Cut Stone: Rebuilding the Master Narrative of European History

LESTER K. LITTLE [2004]

This familiar narrative may be the part of our professional experience that we medievalists have most in common. And since it has been so unchanging for so long, it seems surely to be what we in turn have most in common both with our teachers and with our students. The particular version that I consumed and virtually memorized a half century ago was *A Survey of European Civilization* by Wallace K. Ferguson and Geoffrey Brunn, a textbook first published in 1936, but that I was reading in its second edition, dated 1952.[1]

The organization of the first section of this book contains no surprises; indeed we could all cite the usual succession of topics, if not of actual chapter titles: "Prehistoric Man"; "The Mediterranean World, c. 5000 to c. 500 B.C." (with subchapters on the Land of the Two Rivers and on Egypt, the "Gift of the Nile"); "The Greek City-states" (with a subchapter on "the Persian threat"); "The Hellenistic Age"; "The Roman Republic"; "The Roman World in the First Two Centuries"; "The Decline of the Roman Empire"; "The Christian Church in the Roman Empire"; "The Barbarian Invasion of the Empire"; "The Eastern Empire Becomes Byzantine"; "The Rise of Islam and the Expansion of the Mohammedan Empire"; and finally, our destination for the moment, a chapter on the Franks, the Lombards, and the papacy. The Carolingian rise to power,

the assumption of first the royal and then the imperial title, and the "Carolingian Renaissance" are all woven seamlessly into the long tale.

Such a "survey of European civilization" is unabashedly teleological and clearly privileges politics and high culture. It is the story of powerful, well-organized groups that succeeded in subjecting other peoples and imposing on them their own ideas, institutions, and methods. Told this way, however, it is seriously out of kilter with the scholarly developments of the last several decades, which have so dramatically expanded our knowledge and understanding of the various subdivisions of medieval studies, now hardly recognizable as akin to the field as it was a half century ago, when the very concept of medieval studies itself was not in use. And yet, we have not been nearly so inventive in reconfiguring the master narrative of early European history to reflect these advances. The textbooks of recent years, while in their detailed parts impressively sophisticated and up-to-date, differ very little in their overall schemes from their predecessors of decades past, particularly in the way they continue to begin, in one way or another, with the Roman Empire. [...]

Any narrative of European history that begins with the ancient near East and then moves on to Greece and Rome is fatally flawed. Indeed, any account of the Middle Ages that starts off with the Roman Empire is beyond redemption. To begin in such a way is to set a standard against which all that follows will be measured: measured against Roman government, law, administration, engineering, architecture, and military might, as well as against Latin literature and the Christian

---

Source: Lester K. Little, "Cypress Beams, Kufic Script, and Cut Stone: Rebuilding the Master Narrative of European History," *Speculum* 79 (2004): 914–915, 918–919.

[1]Wallace K. Ferguson and Geoffrey Brunn, *A Survey of European Civilization*, 2nd ed. (Cambridge Mass., 1952).

religion. "All that follows" will inevitably be seen as decline, destruction, or deviation.[1]

The narrative should instead begin with the topography of Europe and the peoples who inhabited it, principally the Celts and the Germans, and those who occupied the Mediterranean lands south of where the Celts reached. The full range of Celtic settlement; their tools and weapons; their social and political organization; their myths, gods, druids, religious practices, and their language all merit inclusion, since they are all relevant for what follows. On the southern fringe of all this, there were the Etruscans, the Latins, and others. Ferguson and Brunn, by the way, while generous in the quantity of references they made to the Egyptians, the Persians, and the Germans, make no mention whatever of the Celts.[2]

This Europe, the Europe of these speakers of Celtic and Germanic languages, lived for centuries in the shadow of the Roman Republic and then was subjected to massive efforts, not all successful, at expansion, conquest, and colonial domination by the Romans. Roman rule meant mainly military and administrative control. Otherwise the conquered peoples were left largely alone. Then came the moment of the Germans, the abandonment of Britain by the Romans, and the creation of a Germanic layer over that of the Celts. And while the armies of the Roman Empire never returned to claim the territories north of the Alps, starting in the late sixth century there took place what Erich Auerbach referred to as a second Roman conquest, this time of missionaries bringing the Christian religion, inextricably tied by them to Roman culture. These missionaries, first sent by a Roman pope who styled himself "Consul of God," were literate, well disciplined, and loyal to the papacy. The effects of their labors, written of approvingly by Christopher Dawson in a famous and influential book of 1932, far outlasted those of the Roman armies.[3]

In spite of these multiple takeovers, there is no reason to imagine that the peoples of Europe gave up their indigenous cultures. Acculturation is a matter of selecting and rejecting, of borrowing and adapting, and it is never unidirectional. The result of studying it dispassionately will not yield a linear narrative of the transmission of a particular cultural tradition, or set of traditions, but a study of the cultures of the indigenous peoples of the territory in which we are ostensibly interested and of the dialogues between them and the purveyors of the powerful cultural messages emanating from the Mediterranean edge of the territory. It is into such a context that we are challenged to incorporate what we have been

---

[1]Much very productive work is being done under the aegis of the scientific program of the European Science Foundation called the Transformation of the Roman World, an excellent project except perhaps for the name, which itself perpetuates the grand narrative. See Frans Theuws, "Introduction: Rituals in Transforming Societies," in *Rituals of Power: From Late Antiquity to the Early Middle Ages,* ed. Frans Theuws and Janet L. Nelson, Transformation of the Roman World 8 (Leiden, 2000), pp. 1–13; and Ian Wood, "Report: The European Science Foundation's Programme on the Transformation of the Roman World," *Early Medieval Europe 6 (1997),* 217–27.

[2]Barry Cunliffe, *The Ancient Celts* (Oxford, 1997); H. D. Rankin, *Celts and the Classical World* (London, 1987); Barry Cunliffe, *Rome and the Barbarians* (New York, 1975); Thomas S. Burns, *Rome and the Barbarians, 100 B.C–A.D. 400* (Baltimore, 2003); Peter S. Wells, *The Barbarians Speak: How the Conquered Peoples Shaped Roman Europe* (Princeton, N.J., 1999).

[3]Erich Auerbach, *Mimesis: The Representation of Reality in Western Literature,* trans. Willard Trask (Garden City, N.Y., 1957), pp. 80–81. "Here lies the difference between the Christian and the original Roman conquest: the agents of Christianity do not simply organize an administration from above, leaving everything else to its natural development; they are duty bound to take an interest in the specific detail of everyday incidents; Christianization is directly concerned with and concerns the individual person and the individual event." Christopher Dawson argued that Catholic Christianity was the key element in the construction of Europe in *The Making of Europe: An Introduction to the History of European Unity* (London, 1932).

learning about, among other subjects, religion and women.

No one could argue seriously that the history of Latin America should begin in Spain or Portugal, any more than that of Iberia itself should start in Mecca. The birthplace of Japan is neither China nor India, just as that of North America is not England. So let us allow the history of Europe to begin where in fact it did begin, not in the Fertile Crescent, but in Europe.

>> Mastering the Materials

1. Based on the sources in this chapter, do you believe the barbarian migrations were a cause or a side effect of imperial decline?

2. What do Ammianus Marcellinus and other writers who describe barbarians reveal about their own societies?

3. Why did residents of the empires fear barbarians? What did the barbarians represent?

4. Why are political instability and migration so closely connected?

5. How does the periphery of an empire figure in its post-imperial history? Does it tend to become more or less important? Why?

>> Making Connections

1. Why is it important to study societies by using sources associated with that society? What danger do we run when we study a society using sources produced by outsiders?

Chapter 12

The Heirs of Empires

Rebuilding the State System

The fall of empires such as the Han, the Persians, the Maya, and the Romans completely altered the world. The stability and experienced government that these polities possessed often deteriorated after the imperial period. It was up to their successors to rebuild them. In almost every case this was an uphill battle. In some cases, as in Mesoamerica, a period of chaos ensued during which the Mayan and Teotihuacano states disappeared as an institution. In other regions the major hurdle was **political fragmentation** and weakness as the single empire was carved into numerous miniscule **successor states.** China, for example, had disintegrated into sixteen kingdoms by 384. The Germanic conquerors of the Roman Empire split western Europe into dozens of small kingdoms. These small polities lacked the resources of their oversized predecessors and adopted generally simpler political and bureaucratic structures. They were also engaged in a struggle to survive. Yet, perhaps surprisingly, they also undertook projects aimed at rebuilding what was lost. Long regarded as "dark periods," the era following imperial disintegration can conversely be seen as one of exchange, experimentation, and innovation.

Amidst all this conflict, these little kingdoms had to restore at least a measure of effective government and administration and establish some legitimacy for their right to rule. In these situations the new rulers often turned to the conquered native populations and to indigenous institutions to keep themselves in power and to enhance their ability to govern. The Arabs, after their conquest of the Sâsânian and parts of the Roman Empire, often turned to Roman and Persian tax collectors to gather revenue. They also employed local languages, mostly Greek, and local aristocrats for low level government help while keeping central administration firmly in Arab hands. In Europe, new Germanic rulers relied extensively on the expertise and support of the Roman senatorial and bureaucratic classes. Moreover, the Germans lacked many of the complex institutions needed to govern even their small kingdoms and in such cases they again turned to Roman practices and administrators as discussed by Patrick Geary in the first essay of this chapter. A similar situation occurred in China. Arthur Wright shows in Reading 92 how the Sui Dynasty in China used previous dynastic models to learn how to rule effectively and when the Tang Dynasty replaced the Sui, it kept many of the reforms and advances in government made by the latter and added to them by, for example, ensuring that imperial heirs followed in the footsteps of their fathers as shown in Reading 93.

Legitimacy was harder to achieve for those who conquered by force, but it was by no means impossible. In the fourth century, after the Hsiung-nu [Xiongnu] captured parts of China their king declared that he was restoring the Han Dynasty and placed himself in the role of the new Han ruler. This was almost a century after the Han had lost power! And as Reading 91 shows, some of these new dynasties created a mythological history for themselves that tied them by blood to the former rulers. In this example, the Franks claimed descent from the Trojans who just happened to also be the ancestors of the Romans. This tactic proved convenient and effective as it gave Frankish kings a claim to rule that was based on blood, even if it had been diluted by centuries of separation.

The readings on Japan provide an alternative model for state building. Japan does not fit well into the model of empire/successor state that has been the focus of our discussion so far. Japan was an isolated part of Asia until at least the fourth century, falling beyond the limits of Chinese territorial ambitions. There was no empire in Japan before its period of state formation when foreign invaders arrived and began to take over the island. Instead, these invaders found a politically fragmented island with hundreds of kingdoms and few native institutions that they could use to build an effective state. Undeterred, these new arrivals turned to China for inspiration and adopted numerous customs and institutions from China including models of state building, language, and religion. This became an increasingly common process in East Asia as the smaller states that surrounded China aspired to emulate Chinese culture, society, and government. By the eighth century, a host of sovereign satellite states, including Japan, which acknowledged Chinese superiority and admired its civilization, surrounded China. These surrounding states became the heirs of China, not in terms of taking over Chinese territory, but in that they became the beneficiaries of centuries of accumulated Chinese culture.

The fact that the heirs and conquerors of the empires embraced, adapted to, and altered numerous elements of imperial cultures raises the question of whether these empires collapsed or not. One way historians define historical periods is by the number of continuities and discontinuities that they find within such periods. Continuities are simply elements of a civilization—institutions, religions, languages, and cultural movements, among others—that persist from one period to another, while discontinuities are elements that come to an end. When discontinuities outweigh continuities in a particular society, historians can say that a period has ended and another has begun. The problem with this approach is that traditionally scholars have given more weight to political events than to occurrences in other quarters. As a result, the division between historical periods is often associated with an important event, especially political ones: the overthrow of the last Roman Emperor (476), the ascension of the Tang Dynasty (618), or the foundation of the Muslim Empire (632). But human societies do not only define themselves in terms of political historical events. Simply because the Tang Dynasty replaced the Sui Dynasty in 618 does not mean that everything in China changed immediately. Continuities in culture, religion, and language, for example, persisted from one period to another, blurring the line between two historical periods. To be sure, things would change in time, but certainly these changes did not occur overnight. This does not mean that important historical events are meaningless; they matter a great deal. However, by looking at other, less obvious occurrences that do not have the resonance of an emperor dying, a new dynasty taking over, or the beginnings of a new religious system, we are forced to look at the many elements that go into making a vibrant society and in so doing gain a clearer image of the past.

Europe after Rome

After the fall of the last western Roman Emperors, western Europe entered a period of political fragmentation as numerous Germanic tribes carved out kingdoms for themselves from the remnants of the empire. The Visigoths, after sacking Rome, kept moving west and ended up with lordship over southern Gaul (modern France) and much of Spain; the Burgundians took over parts of western France and Switzerland; the Angles, Saxons, and Jutes had England. The Ostrogoths with their king Theodoric ruled in Italy, where they uneasily shared power with the Eastern Roman or Byzantine Emperor Justinian who harbored dreams of recapturing the West and reuniting the Roman Empire under his authority. Finally, the Franks, one of the smaller Germanic tribes, held sway over most of modern Belgium and northern France. In this selection, Patrick Geary highlights the efforts of Clovis, king of the Franks from 481 to 511, and his dynasty, the Merovingians, to govern their kingdom by extensively merging Roman practices with Germanic ones. This fusion of customs and institutions was responsible for much Merovingian success. Yet, as Geary points out, it may also be responsible for the practice of dividing the kingdom whenever a king died, often leaving the heirs with years of civil war on their hands as they fought one another until one emerged supreme and united the kingdom once again. After two centuries of this dynastic instability, the Merovingians were spent, and the Carolingians, a noble family, overthrew them.

>> 90. Before France and Germany: The Creation and Transformation of the Merovingian World

PATRICK J. GEARY [1988]

The image most commonly held of Clovis's control over his vast conquests is a lordship established and maintained by personal charisma and fear. Gregory's descriptions of Clovis's elimination of his kinsmen and of his brutal retaliation for an affront made by a Frankish warrior who dared dispute his share of booty captured at Soissons reinforce this image of the barbarian conqueror, quick to lie and quicker to kill. Such qualities he may well have possessed, although they were not particularly barbarian—they can also characterize late Roman emperors. However these traits alone would hardly have made possible not only

his conquests but the creation of a kingdom which, although weakened and divided upon his death, was visible enough to be passed on to his successors. The very heterogeneity of the lands and peoples he conquered provided multiple, complementary systems of political, social, and religious control on which to establish continuity and stability. Unlike most barbarian conquerors, including Atilla and even Theodoric, Clovis's kingdom and his family endured for centuries.

The failure of Atilla to establish a dynasty was hardly surprising. The rise and fall of such charismatic rulers was common enough in antiquity. The fate of Theodoric's Gothic kingdom deserves more consideration. His brilliant achievement suffered from two fatal weaknesses. First, he never attempted a synthesis of Roman and Gothic societies, thus bequeathing an unstable situation to his successors. Second and more fundamentally, Italy

Source: Patrick J. Geary, *Before France and Germany: The Creation and Transformation of the Merovingian World* (New York: Oxford University Press, 1988), 88–95.

was simply too close to Constantinople and the center of Roman interests to be allowed to go its own way.

Theodoric had attempted to preserve virtually intact two traditions, that of his orthodox Christian Roman population and that of the Arian Gothic army settled largely around Ravenna, Verona, and Pavia. The attraction of Roman tradition and culture was, however, too seductive for members of his own family, and after his death in 526 the next generation of Amals found themselves alienated from the more traditional Gothic aristocracy and bitterly divided among themselves. Ultimately Amalasuntha, the widow of Theodoric's son and regent for her minor son Athalaric (516–534), was driven to plan to secretly deliver Italy to Emperor Justinian. Her murder in 535 gave Justinian the opportunity to declare war on the Goths, and the ensuing twenty years of bloody conflict annihilated the Ostrogoths and left Italy prostrate.

In contrast to Theodoric's brilliant and doomed political structure in Italy, Clovis's kingdom from the beginning experienced a much more thorough mixture of Frankish and Roman traditions. Moreover, Gaul and Germany were simply too peripheral to Byzantine concerns to attract more than the cursory interest of Justinian and his successors. Thus the Franks were left to work out the implications of their success in relative peace.

The charisma conveyed by the long hair and mythic origins of Clovis's ancestors, and his ability in convincing others that he was the only channel through which this charisma might be transmitted to future generations, may no doubt be credited with some of his success. Too much can be made of this, however. More important for the establishment of continuity and effectiveness in rule was the dual Roman heritage of both conquerors and conquered.

The indigenous population both of the north and especially of Aquitaine, the region south of the Loire that had been part of the Visigothic kingdom, had preserved the late Roman infrastructure virtually intact. Not only did Latin letters and language continue to be cultivated and vulgar Roman law continue to order people's lives, but Roman fiscal and agricultural structures, the network of Roman roads, towns, and commercial systems, although greatly privatized, had nevertheless survived without serious interruption. All of this was inherited by the Franks, along with the remains of the Roman bureaucracy that continued to operate them. After their victory, Clovis's Franks, accustomed to working closely with Romans, were in an ideal position to absorb them into the administration.

The Franks themselves were likewise deeply Romanized. [...] Generations of Roman service had taught the Franks much about Roman organization and control. This heritage is even visible in that supposedly most Frankish tradition, the Salic Law. Sometime between 508 and 511 Clovis issued what is known as the *Pactus Legis Salicae,* a capital and controversial text which we shall be mentioning often in our discussion of Frankish society. The *Pactus,* in its oldest extant form, consists of sixty-five chapters and is, after the Visigothic Law, the oldest example of a written code for a barbarian kingdom. Written law was certainly not a barbarian tradition; the very act of codifying traditional custom, in whatever haphazard manner, could only originate under the influence of Roman law and could have been done only by persons trained in that tradition. The text is in Latin, and scholars have long abandoned the hypothesis that the Latin was a translation of a now-lost Frankish version. Concepts of Roman law and Roman legal organization appear in the very form of the text. In issuing the text, Clovis was acting not as a barbarian king but as the legitimate ruler of a section of the Romanized world. Moreover, the *Pactus* applies not simply to Franks. It is intended for all the *barbari* in his realm. [...]

The Franks of Clovis's time were accustomed to Roman traditions of law. They were equally accustomed, or soon made themselves so, to the use of Roman administration. As we have seen, even before his defeat of Syagrius, Clovis had been recognized by Bishop Remigius as a legitimate Roman governor, and after his victories over internal and external rivals, Roman and barbarian alike, his legitimacy had been acknowledged by the emperor. Thus the court of Clovis and his successors included not only the traditional officers of a Frankish aristocrat's household, here elevated to royal prominence—the king's *antrustiones,* or personal following, which enjoyed particular royal factor, headed by his *maior domus* or mayor of the palace, the constable, chamberlain, and the like—but Roman officers as well. Although no royal documents from Merovingian kings prior to 528 have survived, the form of later diplomas indicates that the kings had absorbed the secretaries (*scrinarii*) and chancellors (*referendarii*) of the late Roman administration.[...]

In the early sixth century, the duality of the heritage was most clearly in evidence in local administration. Our sources are extraordinarily meager, but apparently Gallo-Roman bishops continued to represent their communities, and the remains of local judicial and fiscal administration were left intact. The primary change was that *comes* or count, personally connected to the king and thus in some sense Frankish, was assigned along with perhaps a small garrison to major towns. His responsibilities were largely military and judicial. He raised the levy from the area and enforced royal law as it applied to Franks when he could. Without the cooperation of the bishop and other Gallo-Romans he could accomplish little, but this cooperation was usually forthcoming provided he did not attempt to increase the burden of taxation or interfere in the sphere of influence created by the local elites. In fact, he often seems to have married into these elites, particularly in remote areas of the kingdom where Franks were few. We shall see more of this process in subsequent chapters.

At the top of the political spectrum, the dual heritage was seen in a decision that had far-reaching implications for Francia: the division of Clovis's kingdom upon his death in 511.[...]

The solution of dividing the kingdoms among his four sons seems less a Frankish than a Roman one. Clovis's territories were divided along roughly Roman political boundaries, and each brother was established with his own court and (no doubt Roman) advisors centered in a major city. The divisions reflect less the Roman imperial tradition than the particularist traditions of the Gallo-Roman aristocracy; they did not respect the integrity of Roman provinces but rather that of the smaller Roman *civitates,* which had become the focal points of Gallo-Roman interest. Thus Theuderic, whose court was in Reims, received in addition the areas centered in Trier, Mainz, Cologne, Basel, and Châlons, as well as the recently subdued lands on the right bank of the Rhine. Chlothar received the old Salic heartlands between the Charbonnière forest and the Somme River along with Noyon, Soissons, his capital, and Laon. Childebert's portion included the coastal regions from the Somme to Brittany, probably including, along with Paris, his capital, Amiens, Beauvias, Rouen, Meaux, Le Mans, and Rennes. The last brother, Chlodomer, reigned from Orléans over Tours, Sens, and probably Troyes, Auxerre, Chartres, Angers, and Nantes.

Just how these portions were determined is unknown. Certainly they must have been devised by Romans with a knowledge of fiscal receipts from each region as well as an eye to maintaining the integrity of their own power bases. Even in this most central question of the fate of the Frankish kingdom, it is most likely that decisions were made by Franks and Romans working in close harmony.

The Propaganda of Lineage

The Frankish quest to gain legitimacy as rightful heirs of the Roman emperors did not stop with the adoption of Roman customs and institutions. As the following source suggests, the Franks set about creating historical myths about their origins that linked them by blood to the Romans. As this chronicler claims, with no basis in fact, the Franks were actually the descendants of the survivors of Troy. The Romans themselves claimed to be the descendants of the Trojan hero Aeneas. This writer is cleverly making the Trojans the common ancestor of both Romans and Franks, which would in fact make Romans and Franks long-lost relatives. What he leaves unsaid, but which his audience is likely to have understood, is that the Franks as blood relatives of the Romans were the rightful heirs to the Roman Empire.

>> 91. Liber Historiae Francorum

[c. 727 c.e.]

Concerning the Origin and Deeds of the Franks and Their Frequent Struggles

Let us set out the beginnings of the kings of the Franks and their origin and also the origins of the people and its deeds. There is in Asia the city of the Trojans in the region called Illium. This is where Aeneas reigned. The Trojans were a strong and brave people, the men were warriors and very difficult to discipline. They provoked conflict and stormy contention and fought successfully on their surrounding borders. But the kings of the Greeks rose up against Aeneas with a very large army and fought against Aeneas and there was a great deal of slaughter. Many Trojans fell in the battle and therefore Aeneas fled and shut himself up in the city of Illium. The Greeks besieged the city for ten years and when the city was conquered, the tyrant Aeneas fled to Italy to obtain men to carry on the fighting. Priam and Antenor, two of the other Trojan princes, embarked on ships with twelve thousand of the men remaining from the Trojan army. They departed and came to the banks of the Tanais [Don] river. They sailed into the Maeotian swamps [of the Sea of Azov], penetrated the frontiers of the Pannonias which were near the Maeotian swamps and began to build a city as their memorial. They called it Sicambria and lived there many years growing into a great people.

The Unification of China

The Han Dynasty ruled China in its various guises from 206 b.c.e. to 220 c.e. Its decline had some strong similarities to that of the Western Roman Empire as both empires endured years of dynastic instability and invasions by barbarians. Likewise, there were many similarities in the way their respective regions recovered, with both exhibiting a fusion of imperial and foreign elements. The collapse of the Han in 220 led to a period of political fragmentation that lasted until 581. This division ended when the Sui Dynasty unified China once again. Wen-ti [Wendi] (r. 581–601), the founder of the dynasty, represented many of the foreign influences that had penetrated Chinese society since the fall of the Han. He was of mixed Turkic-Chinese origin and was raised as a Buddhist, a religion native to India. The period during which the Sui ruled was one of intense developments in law, culture, military campaigns, and even matters of infrastructure. The primary challenge to the Sui was the unification and government of an empire that had not been effectively united in over 350 years. In the following selection, Yale sinologist

Source: *Liber Historiae Francorum,* edited and translated by Bernard S. Bachrach (Lawrence, KS: Coronado Press, 1973), 23.

Arthur Wright explains the difficulties faced by the Sui and the historical models they had at their disposal to overcome them. In keeping with the similarities with the Roman world, Wright goes on to compare the troubles as well as the solutions of the Sui with those of Charlemagne, the Carolingian ruler who unified most of Europe under his authority in the late eighth and early ninth centuries.

>> 92. The Sui Dynasty

ARTHUR F. WRIGHT [1978]

The Sui leaders were aware of the challenges that faced them. They knew the vast and rugged land; they knew about the repeated failures of efforts at reunification during the three centuries that preceded them. But they also knew a great deal about the first dynasties that succeeded in establishing a unified and centralized empire in the third and second centuries B.C. These were the dynasties of Ch'in [Qin] (221–207 B.C.) and of Western Han (206–6 B.C.). The Ch'in [Qin], they knew, had, by the relentless use of the military force and terror, destroyed what was left of the old order: its system of independent states, its great families, and the local networks of power and loyalties that supported them. Once in unchallenged control, the Ch'in [Qin] had taken the most draconian measures to consolidate their power. They had torn the leading families from their local bases of power and transported them to the Ch'in [Qin] capital in the west; they had destroyed the city walls in every part of their new empire and, abolishing ancient state boundaries, had put the empire under a rational system of local administration, staffed by Ch'in [Qin]-appointed bureaucrats. They had proscribed ancient traditions of thought, outlawed those who spread such traditions, and destroyed their books. They made laws of the empire supreme, and they terrorized their subjects by decreeing brutal punishments for even minor infractions. The men of Sui knew that the Ch'in [Qin] had brought the period of the Warring States to an end and established the First Sovereign Emperor to rule over "all under Heaven." But they also knew that the Ch'in [Qin] had gone too far too fast too ruthlessly and that their empire exploded into rebellion shortly after the death of the First Emperor. Thus the accomplishments of the Ch'in [Qin] undoubtedly excited their admiration while that dynasty's short life and violent end made it a dubious model for those seeking to reunify the empire seven centuries later. The model they took was rather the Former or Western Han, which was beneficiary of the Ch'in [Qin] unification, the Han that subtly incorporated many useful Ch'in [Qin] innovations while allowing local cultures to revive and thinking men to have some limited intellectual choice and a role in policy formation. The Han preserved the concept of empire, of a supreme autocrat, and of rational units of local administration. In continued the Ch'in [Qin] system of codified law—though with something less than faith in its total efficacy. It drew from many schools and developed a state orthodoxy—which scholars call "Han Confucianism"—and made that orthodoxy the basis of a rudimentary but significant examination system for the recruitment of a meritocracy. Externally the Han extended its hegemony over vast reaches of Central Asia, over the Liao River Valley and northern Korea, over northern Vietnam in the far south. And, for all its foreign adventures, the Han presided—for many decades of its life—over a growing population spreading into previously aboriginal land, over a developing economy that filled the imperial coffers and made possible an opulent life for the fortunate. The second Han Dynasty, which began in A.D. 25 and lasted until A.D. 220, was not as centralized or as successful as the first, but it perpetuated the basic institutions of the first Han, the imperial

Source: Arthur F. Wright, *The Sui Dynasty* (New York: Knopf, 1978), 7–10.

ideology and much else. From a sixth-century vantage point, looking back across three and a half centuries of foreign invasion, political disunion, and cultural fragmentation, the great Han must have appeared a model for the Sui to follow, a model of unity and stable power. So it seemed to the men of Sui, who in considering policies or policy priorities, court ritual, or local administration always had the Han experience in mind. Historical precedent had, for the Chinese, a power not found in other societies; this led Sui statesmen to turn to history for guidance and, within the long history of China, to turn to the Han Empire for a model.

We now turn to the comparative dimension, seeking in world history an example of an attempt at unification roughly comparable to the Sui's in order to elucidate the character of challenges met and to measure the degree of success achieved. To identify such a comparable effort we should look for a historical situation presenting all or most of the following elements: a subcontinental area, an area once under an ecumenical empire but for centuries split into separately evolving cultures and polities; a major effort at reunification, an effort that evokes or revives institutions and symbols of the previous but long dead empire. The example that, despite many differences—notably in population and resources— seems to fit most closely in the Carolingian Empire. Charlemagne, like the Sui founder, was a product of the culturally mixed societies that had developed, as a result of barbarian invasion, on the marches of the previous empire. In the Chinese as in the European case, those invaders had dealt a death blow to the ancient empires; the sack of Rome by the Goths in 410 is comparable in its devastating psychological shock to the sack of Loyang by the Huns in 311. And, in the wake of both these catastrophes the institutions of the ancient empires were preserved by weak legitimist regimes located far from the original centers of empire: the European at Constantinople, the Chinese at the Yangtze [Yangzi] Valley city that, in modern times, we know as Nanking [Nanjing]. Both Charlemagne

and the Sui founder resorted to the old empire's tradition of codified law, Charlemagne first in the cumulative capitularies of old German law and later in an attempted revival of Roman codification. The Sui were able to draw on the codes of many of the successor states of the long-vanished Han and to weave from many strands a new synthetic code applicable to all its subjects. Both Charlemagne and Sui Wen-ti [Wendi] faced, when they came to power, a great diffusion of central authority: Charlemagne the crazy quilt of claimants to local power—hereditary mayors of the palace, dukes, counts, and bishops—Wen-ti the long-entrenched great families of the northeast, the northwest, and the south, people who regarded hereditary access to office as a right and the official appointment function as an inheritable privilege. Both took strong measures to reverse the centrifugal flow of power, but Sui Wen-ti [Wendi] strove to restore the administrative rationality of the ancient Han Empire while Charlemagne resorted mainly to the ties of sworn fealty and the gifts of land and serfs as means of insuring loyalty. Charlemagne did appoint his own official inspectors and his own dukes along the borders, but he consistently followed no one pattern for the civil administration of his empire; indeed the legacy of trained officials which the Sui inherited was lacking in eighth-century Europe.

When we consider what might be called "cultural policy," we again find many similarities in the measures taken by the two reunifiers. Charlemagne made his court the focus of science, art, and literature. He made efforts to revive Latin studies and to restock the libraries of Europe. Sui Wen-ti [Wendi] issued decrees on the purification of Chinese literary style, and both he and his son carried out large projects of recovering and recopying books, both secular and Buddhist, that had been scattered in the chaotic years since the fall of the Han. Toward their weak legitimist rivals the two reunifiers had different policies. Charlemagne at one time contemplated marriage with the Empress Irene who reigned in Constantinople, and he would by this act have united Christendom. But this plan was soon abandoned, and the East Roman Empire was proclaimed illegitimate because it was ruled by a woman! By contrast, once Sui Wen-ti [Wendi] had proclaimed himself Son of Heaven he laid claim to "all under Heaven," and that included the last of the legitimist dynasties at Nanking [Nanjing] which, a few years later, he forcibly extinguished. "All under Heaven" was less ambiguous than the term "Europe," which in Charlemagne's time was just beginning to be used to designate a political entity, or than "Christendom," in which there were both western and eastern spiritual and political centers, not to mention uncertain and ever-shifting boundaries. Though Charlemagne's advisors spoke of "Europe" as a political unit, this usage seems not to have had wide currency nor much effect on his decisions. Toward the end of his life he divided the "Empire of the Franks" among his sons as their patrimonies. All the sons but one died, and in his hands the empire gradually disintegrated.

Advice to a Future Emperor

The reforms of the Sui were not enough to ensure the survival of the dynasty. By 618 their power had been broken and the Tang Dynasty had taken over. In spite of their short-lived rule, the Sui's reforms were critical to the success of the Tang period, one of the most magnificent eras in Chinese history. The Tang, like the Sui before them, were descendants of Turkic tribesmen who had settled in northwest China after the fall of the Han. And like the Germanic dynasties that ruled much of Europe after Rome, the Tang fabricated false lineages that closely tied them to the Han, reinforcing their claims to be legitimate rulers. The Tang also adopted and adapted Sui institutions and practices on a wide scale. In law, government, and even military organization the Tang benefited from the work the Sui had done before them. The Tang were not without their own contributions: They brought about a period of artistic excellence, military dominance, and cultural growth while opening up China to outside influences which enriched Chinese culture. They also sought to invigorate the power of the monarch. In this selection, the second Tang emperor, Taizong (r. 626–649), offers some advice to his son and heir on how to rule effectively and from a position of strength.

>> 93. Emperor Taizong on Effective Government

[648 c.e.]

How a Ruler Should Act

A country cannot be a country without people and a ruler cannot be a ruler without a country. When the ruler looks as lofty and firm as a mountain peak and as pure, bright, and illuminating as the sun and the moon, the people will admire and respect him. He must broaden his will so as to be able to embrace both Heaven and earth and must regulate his heart so as to be able to make just decisions. He cannot expand his territory without majesty and virtue; he cannot soothe and protect his people without compassion and kindness. He conforts his relations with benevolence, treats his officials with courtesy, honors his ancestors with filial respect, and receives his subordinates with thoughtfulness. Having disciplined himself, he practices virtue and righteousness diligently. This is how a ruler should act.

Source: "Emperor Taizong on Effective Government," in *Chinese Civilization: A Sourcebook*, 2nd ed., edited by P. B. Ebrey (New York: The Free Press, 1993), 112–115.

Establishing Relatives

The country is huge and the responsibility for it is heavy. A huge country cannot be evenly governed by the emperor alone; the responsibility is too great for one man. Thus, the emperor should enfeoff relatives to guard the outlying prefectures. Whether the country is at peace or in danger, they cooperate; whether the country is thriving or declining, they work together with one heart. Both distant and close relations are supported and employed; encroachment and rebellion are prevented.

Formerly when the Zhou dynasty was at its height, the empire was divided among the royal clan. Nearby there was Jin and Zheng to help; far off there was Lu and Wei. In this way, the dynasty was able to survive several centuries. Toward the end of the Qin dynasty, however, the emperor rejected Chunyu's scheme [of enfeoffing relatives] and accepted Li Si's plan [to enfeoff nonrelatives]. He thus detached himself from his relatives and valued only the wise. With no relatives to rely on, the dynasty fell after two generations. Isn't this all because of the fact that if a tree has a mass of branches and leaves, it is difficult to root up, but if the limbs are disabled, the trunk has nothing to depend on? Eager to avoid Qin's errors, the Han dynasty, upon stabilizing the land within the passes, enfeoffed the closest relatives generously. Outdoing the ancient system, the largest fiefs were as big as kingdoms, and the smallest had at least several prefectures. But a branch can get so heavy that it breaks the trunk; a tail can get too big to be wagged. Thus, the Six Kings harbored ambitions of overthrowing the throne and the Seven States were destroyed by arms, all because they had gained too much territory, military force, and power. When Emperor Wu established the Wei dynasty, being ignorant of past experience, he did not grant any titles to his descendants nor any fiefs to his kin. He had no one within or without the capital to protect him. Thus, his throne was usurped and his dynasty was overthrown by someone of a different surname. This is a good example of the old saying that a river does not run when its source dries up and branches wither when the root of the tree decays.

Subordinates granted too much power can develop into insurmountable problems for the throne. On the other hand, subordinates granted too little power will not be strong enough to protect the throne. Thus, the best way is to enfeoff many relatives to even up their power and to have them regulate one another and share one another's ups and downs. By so doing, the throne need not suspect its subordinates and the subordinates need not worry about being wronged or injured. These are the precautions one should take in granting fiefs. Neutralizing the power of subordinates so that none of them gets to be too strong or too weak is indeed the key to securing one's throne....

Evaluating Officials

Differentiation of the ranks and duties of officials is a means of improving customs. A wise emperor, therefore, knows how to choose the right person for the right task. He is like a skillful carpenter who knows to use straight timber to make shafts, curved timber to make wheels, long timber to make beams, and short timber to make posts. Wood of all shapes and lengths is thus fully utilized. The emperor should make use of personnel in the same way, using the wise for their resourcefulness, the ignorant for their strength, the brave for their daring, and the timid for their prudence. As a good carpenter does not discard any timber, so a wise emperor does not discard any gentleman. A mistake should not lead the emperor to ignore a gentleman's virtues, nor should a flaw overshadow his merits.

Government affairs should be departmentalized to make the best use of official's abilities. A tripod large enough for an ox should not be used to cook a chicken, nor should a raccoon good only at catching rats be ordered to fight against huge beasts.... Those with low intelligence or capability should not be entrusted with heavy tasks or responsibilities. If the right person is given the right task or responsibility, the empire can be governed with ease. This is the proper way of utilizing people. Whether the emperor gets hold of the right person for the right task determines whether his empire will be well governed....

Welcoming Advice

The emperor, living in the palace, is blocked from direct access to information. For fear that faults might be left untold or defects unattended, he must set up various devices to elicit loyal suggestions and listen attentively to sincere advice. If what is said is right, he must not reject it even though it is offered by a low servant. On the other hand, if what is said is wrong, he must not accept it even though it is given by a high official. He should not find fault with the rhetoric of a comment that makes sense, nor cavil at the wording of a suggestion worth adopting.... If he acts these ways, the loyal will be devoted and the wise will fully employ their resourcefulness. Government officials will not keep any secrets from the emperor and the emperor, through his close ties to them, can thus gain access to the world.

A foolish emperor, in comparison, rebuffs remonstrations and punishes the critics. As a result, high officials do not give any advice lest they lose their salary and low officials do not make any comment lest they lose their lives. Being extremely tyrannical and dissipated, he blocks himself from any access to information. He considers himself more virtuous than the Three Lords and more talented than the Five Emperors. This eventually brings him and his empire to destruction. How sad it is! This is the evil consequence of rejecting remonstrations.

Discouraging Slander

Slanderers and flatterers are as harmful to the country as grubs to seedlings. They devote all their time to getting ahead. At court they compete for power and out of court they compete

for profit. They fawn to prevent the loyal and the worthy from outranking them; they cheat out of fear that others will acquire riches and honor before them. Acting in collusion and copying each other, they succeed all too often. They get close to their superiors by using fine words and pleasant manners; they please the emperor by anticipating and attending to his wishes....

Advice that grates is difficult to take, but words that fall in with one's wishes are easy for one to follow. This is because while the former is like good medicine that tastes bitter, the latter is like poisoned wine that tastes sweet. A wise emperor accepts bitter criticisms that benefit his conduct; a foolish emperor takes sweet flattery that leads him to destruction. Beware!

Avoiding Extravagance

The ruler cultivates his character through frugality and peacefulness. Restraining himself, he will not tire his people or disturb his subordinates. Thus, his people will not complain and his rule will not go off course. If the emperor indulges himself in curiosities, women, music, hunting, or travel, agriculture will be disturbed and labor service will have to be increased, leading to the exhaustion of the people and the neglect of farming. If the emperor indulges himself in magnificent dwelling, precious jewelry, or fine clothes, taxes will have to be increased, leading the people to flee and the country to be impoverished. A chaotic age is marked by a ruler who is arrogant and extravagant, indulging his desires. While his dwelling and garments are richly ornamented, his people are in need of simple clothes; while his dogs and horses are tired of grain, his people do not have enough husks and chaff. As a result, both the gods and the people become resentful and the ruler and the ruled become estranged. The dynast is overthrown before the emperor has satisfied his wishes. Such is the fearsome cost of being arrogant and extravagant.

Maintaining Military Forces

Weapons and armor are a country's tools of violence. A warlike country, however huge and safe it may be, will end up declining and endangering its populace. Military force cannot be entirely eliminated nor used all the time. Teach people military arts when they are free from farming in order to equip them with a sense of military decorum and morale. Remember how Gou Jian, who paid respect to the fighting spirit of frogs, was able to achieve his supremacy, but Xu Yan, who disregarded military forces, lost his state. Why? Because Gou's troops were inspired and Xu was unprepared. Confucius said, "Not teaching people how to fight is the same as discarding them." Hence military might serves to benefit the realm. This is the gist of the art of war.

Esteeming Culture

Music should be played when a victory is gained; ritual should be established when the country is at peace. The ritual and music to be promulgated are rooted in Confucianism. Nothing is better than literature to spread manners and guide customs; nothing is better than schooling to propagate regulations and educate people. The Way is spread through culture; fame is gained through learning. Without visiting a deep ravine, one cannot understand how deep the earth is; without learning the arts, one cannot realize the source of wisdom. Just as the bamboos of the state of Wu cannot be made into arrows without feathers, so a clever man will not achieve any success without accumulating learning. Therefore, study halls and ritual halls should be built, books of various schools of thought should be widely read, and the six arts [propriety, music, archery, charioteering, writing, and mathematics] should be carefully studied....

Literary arts and military arts should be employed by the state alternatively. When the world is in an uproar and a battle will determine the fate of the country, military arts should be highlighted and schools given low priority. Reverse the two when the country is peaceful and prosperous; then slight the military and give weight to the classics. Neither military nor culture can the country do without; which to emphasize depends on circumstances. Neither soldiers nor scholars can be dispensed with.

Japan and the Creation of a State

When the Han and Roman Empires fell, they left behind not only a power vacuum to be filled but also institutions and practices to assist those who followed them to do the filling. Japan did not enjoy those benefits. The history of Japan before the fourth century C.E. is shadowy. Most of what we do know about it comes from Chinese documents. The Chinese sources describe scores of kingdoms dotting the island, of which the most powerful was Yamatai ruled by its witch-queen Himiko. Kenneth Henshall describes the foundation and development of the first Japanese state, Yamato, and its first historically verifiable emperor Suijin. Lacking strong government institutions of their own, Yamato rulers were more than willing to adopt foreign practices from Korea and especially China. The usage of Chinese traditions becomes particularly evident in the Seventeen Article Constitution as well as the strong influence of Confucianism in Japanese thought.

>> 94. A History of Japan: From Stone Age to Superpower

KENNETH G. HENSHALL [1999]

The Early State Emerges: The Kofun/Yamato Period (CA 300–710)

Some believe that Suijin may have been the leader of a group of fourth-century invaders from Korea known as the 'horse-riders', and that it was these horse-riders who established the Yamato state. This is not impossible; but it seems more likely that Suijin was of the Yamato clan, and that his clan increased their power and authority by a gradual process of degree. In this they relied heavily on negotiation and persuasion—and no doubt threat and coercion—rather than simple military confrontation. Their preferred method seems to have been to incorporate local chiefdoms already established in Yayoi times, and give the chieftains themselves places within the Yamato hierarchy. Ranks and titles were used by the Yamato court to give potentially troublesome members of formerly independent local regimes a personal stake in the emerging imperial system.

The tactic of where possible incorporating a powerful threat rather than directly confronting it, and of drawing on a potential opponent's strengths rather than trying simply to destroy them, is still widely seen today as a basic Japanese preference. Its identification at such an early stage of Japanese history is testimony to the depth of such a tradition.

The ranks and titles given to those local kings and chiefs incorporated into the Yamato camp were important in a status-conscious age. The Yamato administrative system was strongly hierarchical. This, too, is a continuing characteristic of Japanese preferences.

Exact dates remain unclear. It is probable that during the fourth and fifth centuries Yamato authority was not absolute but rather 'first among equals' among a coalition of clans. By the early sixth century, however, the Yamato imperial family seems to have emerged as the single prevailing line. It was at this point that the rulers of the Izumo region started to send tribute to the Yamato ruler.

A sense of statehood is also suggested in a poem attributed to the late fifth-century emperor Yūryaku (r. 456–79);

Your basket, with your pretty basket,
Your trowel, with your pretty trowel
Maiden, picking herbs on this hillside,
I would ask you: Where is your home?
Will you not tell me your name?
Over the spacious Land of Yamato
It is I who reign so wide and far,
It is I who rule so wide and far.
I myself, as your lord, will tell you
Of my home, and my name.

The Yamato state soon entrenched its position by the adoption and promotion of Buddhism. This was especially favoured by the Soga, a particularly powerful clan within the Yamato structure. The Soga were of Korean descent, like many of the aristocratic families of the day, and probably felt more of an affinity with Buddhism than did native Japanese. It was from Korea—specifically priest-scholars from the Korean kingdom of Paekche—that Buddhism was introduced in the mid-sixth century. Its adoption was greatly aided by the practice of writing, which had also been introduced by scholars from Paekche a century earlier.

The Soga saw Buddhism as a means of developing a state religion that would further their political control, which by means such as intermarriage they were starting to assert over the imperial family. They

Source: Kenneth G. Henshall, *A History of Japan: From Stone Age to Superpower* (New York: St. Martin's Press, 1999), 11–4.

were undoubtedly a persuasive element in the acceptance of the religion by the imperial family from Emperor Yōmei (r. 585–7) on.

For its part, the imperial line also saw Buddhism as politically very useful. It provided a unifying ideology for the new nation. Its identification with the imperial family also meant that the spread of Buddhism helped spread acceptance of imperial authority. Moreover, and very importantly, it conferred a degree of Chinese-style dignity and civilisation on the newly emerging state.

Japan did very much want to be taken seriously. This was not just as a deterrent against possible further invasion. It was a genuine wish to achieve the best, to become a strong nation. To this end it was soon to adopt a range of Chinese practices, till eventually it could feel it had outdone China and had nothing left to learn. Here again we see an early example of the incorporation of the strengths of others, combined with a willingness to learn and emulate. [...]

Japan's emulation of China was particularly seen in the activities of Yōmei's second son, Prince Shōtoku (Shōtoku Taishi 574–622), who was half Soga by blood. Probably the best-known figure of those times, from 594 till his death in 622 Shōtoku was regent under Empress Suiko (r. 593–628). He greatly contributed not only to the promotion of Buddhism by the building of numerous temples but to the promotion of all things Chinese. Among other things he was responsible for re-establishing missions to a new reunified China, and for introducing Chinese-style 'cap rank' system in which, as the name suggests, the rank of officials was indicated by their hat.

Shōtoku is also credited with drawing up the so-called Seventeen Article Constitution of 604, which was intended to strengthen central government. It had a strong Chinese flavor, particularly in its Confucianism. Though deemed a constitution it was, however, largely a set of guidelines for officials, with a particular emphasis on harmony (*wa*) and loyalty to the divine and therefore legitimate authority of the imperial line. Something of its nature can be seen from the opening words of Article One, which quote Confucius and state that 'Harmony is to be valued', and from the opening words of Article Eight, which are of a less grand and more specific character: 'Let the ministers and functionaries attend the court early in the morning, and retire late.'

>> 95. The Seventeen Article Constitution, 604 A.D.

[C. 604 C.E.]

The Seventeen Article Constitution, 604 A.D. Summer, 4th month, 3rd day [12th year of Empress Suiko, 604 A.D.]. The Crown Prince personally drafted and promulgated a constitution consisting of seventeen articles, which are as follows:

I. Harmony is to be cherished, and opposition for opposition's sake must be avoided as a matter of principle. Men are often influenced by partisan feelings, except a few sagacious ones. Hence there are some who disobey their lords and fathers, or who dispute with their neighboring villages. If those above are harmonious and those below are cordial, their discussion will be guided by a spirit of conciliation, and reason shall naturally prevail. There will be nothing that cannot be accomplished.

II. With all our heart, revere the three treasures. The three treasures, consisting of Buddha, the Doctrine, and the Monastic Order, are the final refuge of the four generated beings, and are the supreme objects of worship in all countries. Can any man in any age ever fail to respect these teachings? Few men are utterly devoid of goodness, and men can be taught to follow the teachings. Unless they take refuge in the three treasures, there is no way of rectifying their misdeeds.

Source: "The Seventeen Article Constitution, 604 A.D.," in *Sources of Japanese History* vol. 1, by David Lu (New York: McGraw Hill, 1974), 21–23.

III. When an imperial command is given, obey it with reverence. The sovereign is likened to heaven, and his subjects (*yatsuko*) are likened to earth. With heaven providing the cover and earth supporting it, the four seasons proceed in orderly fashion, giving sustenance to all that which is in nature. If earth attempts to overtake the functions of heaven, it destroys everything. Therefore when the sovereign speaks, his subjects must listen; when the superior acts, the inferior must follow his examples. When an imperial command is given, carry it out with diligence. If there is no reverence shown to the imperial command, ruin will automatically result.

IV. The ministers (*machikimitachi*) and functionaries (*tsukasa tsukasa*) must act on the basis of decorum, for the basis of governing the people consists in decorum. If the superiors do not behave with decorum, offenses will ensue. If the ministers behave with decorum, there will be no confusion about ranks. If the people behave with decorum, the nation will be governed well of its own.

V. Cast away your ravenous desire for food and abandon your covetousness for material possessions. If a suit is brought before you, render a clear-cut judgment.... Nowadays, those who are in the position of pronouncing judgment are motivated by making private gains, and as a rule, receive bribes. Thus the plaints of the rich are like a stone flung into water, while those of the poor are like water poured over a stone. Under these circumstances, the poor will be denied resources to justice, which constitutes a dereliction of duty of the minister (*yatsuko*).

VI. Punish that which is evil and encourage that which is good. This is an excellent rule from antiquity. Do not conceal the good qualities of others, and always correct that which is evil which comes to your attention. Consider those flatterers and tricksters as constituting a superb weapon for the overthrow of the state, and a sharp sword for the destruction of people. Smooth-tongued adulators love to report to their superiors the errors of their inferiors; and to their inferiors, castigate the errors of their superiors. Men of this type lack loyalty to the sovereign and have no compassion for the people. They are the ones who can cause great civil disorders.

VII. Every man must be given his clearly delineated responsibility. If a wise man is entrusted with office, the sound of praise arises. If a wicked man holds office, disturbances become frequent.... In all things, great or small, find the right man, and the country will be well governed. On all occasions, in an emergency or otherwise, seek out a wise man, which in itself is an enriching experience. In this manner, the state will be lasting and its sacerdotal functions will be free from danger. Therefore did the sage kings of old seek the man to fill the office, not the office for the sake of the man.

VIII. The ministers and functionaries must attend the court early in the morning and retire late. The business of the state must not be taken lightly. A full day is hardly enough to complete work, and if the attendance is late, emergencies cannot be met. If the officials retire early, the work cannot be completed.

IX. Good faith is the foundation of righteousness, and everything must be guided by good faith. The key to the success of the good and the failure of the bad can also be found in good faith. If the officials observe good faith with one another, everything can be accomplished. If they do not observe good faith, everything is bound to fail.

X. Discard wrath and anger from your heart and from your looks. Do not be offended when others differ with you. Everyone has his own mind, and each mind has its own leanings. Thus what is right with him is wrong with us, and what is right with us is wrong with him. We are not necessarily sages, and he is not necessarily a fool. We are all simply ordinary men, and none of us can set up a rule to determine the right from wrong.... Therefore, instead of giving way to anger as others do, let us fear our own mistakes. Even though we may have a point, let us follow the multitude and act like them.

XI. Observe clearly merit and demerit and assign reward and punishment accordingly. Nowadays, rewards are given in the absence of meritorious work, punishments without corresponding crimes. The ministers, who are in charge of public affairs, must therefore take upon themselves the task of administering a clear-cut system of rewards and punishments.

XII. Provincial authorities (*mikotomochi*) or local nobles (*kuni no miyatsuko*) are not permitted to levy exactions on the people. A country cannot have two sovereigns, nor the people two masters. The people of the whole country must have the sovereign as their only master. The officials who are given certain functions are all his subjects. Being the subjects of the sovereign, these officials have no more right than others to levy exactions on the people.

XIII. All persons entrusted with office must attend equally to their functions. If absent from work due to illness or being sent on missions, and work for that period is neglected, on their return, they must perform their duties conscientiously by taking into account that which transpired before and during their absence. Do not permit lack of knowledge of the intervening period as an excuse to hinder effective performance of public affairs.

XIV. Ministers and functionaries are asked not to be envious of others. If we envy others, they in turn will envy us, and there is no limit to the evil that envy can cause us. We resent others when their intelligence is superior to ours, and we envy those who surpass us in talent. This is the reason why it takes five hundred years before we can meet a wise man, and in a thousand years it is still difficult to find one sage. If we cannot find wise men and sages, how can the country be governed?

XV. The way of a minister is to turn away from private motives and to uphold public good. Private motives breed resentment, and resentful feelings cause a man to act discordantly. If he fails to act in accord with others, he sacrifices the public interests for the sake of his private feelings. When resentment arises, it goes counter to the existing order and breaks the law. Therefore it is said in the first article that superiors and inferiors must act in harmony. The purport is the same.

XVI. The people may be employed in forced labor only at seasonable times. This is an excellent rule from antiquity. Employ the people in the winter months when they are at leisure. However, from spring to autumn, when they are engaged in agriculture or sericulture, do not employ them. Without their agricultural endeavor, there is no food, and without their sericulture, there is no clothing.

XVII. Major decisions must not be made by one person alone, but must be deliberated with many. On the other hand, it is not necessary to consult many people in minor questions. If important matters are not discussed fully, there may always be a fear of committing mistakes. A thorough discussion with many can prevent it and bring about a reasonable solution.

>> Mastering the Material

1. How did the heirs of empires use imperial institutions, practices, and ideas to advance their own conquests and efforts of state building?

2. Why was political legitimacy so important to the rulers of the successor states?

3. Why was fragmentation so common after the collapse of an empire? Is fragmentation a positive or a negative development?

4. How did the state-building model for Japan differ from that of other regions discussed in this chapter? Why is this important?

>> Making Connections

1. Considering that many imperial institutions, customs, ideas, and cultural practices survived the political collapse of the empires, can we truly say that these empires collapsed? How do we measure processes like decline and collapse? Is it more accurate to say that the empires we have been discussing so far collapsed or were transformed?

2. How did natives and newcomers work together to fill the political void left behind by the collapse of an empire?

Chapter 13

The Diffusion of Culture

We have seen in previous chapters of Part 3 that the collapse of empires, especially in Eurasia and North Africa, did not cut off regional or even continental exchange. Indeed, successor societies were often intensely interested in interaction. The barbarians who arrived during the migrations melded with settled peoples into a fluid patchwork of states and stateless societies. These immigrants brought with them new ideas and technologies from the regions from which they came. Sometimes they imposed their beliefs and organization on the people they conquered. Other times the native state-builders were interested in adopting and adapting foreign culture as a tool for survival. In both cases, much of what diffused from region to region was culture. The transmission of these **innovations**—new ideas, languages, religious beliefs, and institutions—from one civilization to another is a complex process that often took decades and even centuries to accomplish. A very simplified model of how **diffusion** works follows: First open lines of communication are required so that innovations can move from one area to another. These innovations need carriers who can take from one place to another. Finally, recipient populations must be willing to adopt the innovations, and for this to occur the innovation has to be somehow better or more prestigious than what the locals already use.

The examples given in the readings of this chapter share all these characteristics. Buddhism, the focus of the first three selections, provides a good case study for the diffusion of a religious system. Buddhism originated in India and within a few centuries of its inception had amassed a large number of adherents there. Its spread into China, however, was waylaid by difficulties as described is Reading 97 by Fairbank and Goldman. China already had a strong system of beliefs based on the philosophy of Confucius as well as the religious tradition of Daoism. So most Chinese were not very receptive at first to some of the ideas and practices found in Buddhism. Eric Zürcher explains in Reading 96 that many of these obstacles began to disappear after the collapse of the Han Empire and the discrediting of many Confucian ideals. With the help of receptive ruling elites who founded Buddhist monasteries and financed missions, Buddhism was able to spread to a population that became increasingly interested in the ideas the Buddhist faith had to offer.

Similar processes are also evident in the spread of other major religions such as Christianity and Islam. When Christian missionaries, the carriers of this particular innovation, traveled to regions where Germanic religions dominated, their efforts to convert the locals often centered on the performance of miracles. These miracles not only demonstrated the usefulness of Christianity—typical miracles included healing the sick, fighting off enemies, and helping with agricultural problems—but also showed just how powerful the Christian God was. The point that the missionaries tried to impress upon their Germanic audiences was that this new God was an improvement over the old gods. When they were successful, conversion usually followed. In the early stages of this conversion process, however, Christianity often toiled under very difficult conditions at the mercy of local, non-Christian elites. As was the case with Buddhism, Christianity simply adapted to meet local needs. That is the essential message of the letter from Pope Gregory the Great to the missionaries in England (Reading 99).

Innovations could diffuse more readily when the state used its power to encourage adoption. The transmission of religious beliefs again serves as a useful case study with Charlemagne's "Capitulary to the Saxons." The laws of the "Capitulary" served to "persuade" local populations to adopt Christianity. The backing of the state, which amounted to imposing harsh penalties on non-adopters, made Christianity a better option than the alternatives in this case.

Not all cultural innovations were religious in nature. The last three examples in this chapter involve the transmission of a technology and a language, yet the same diffusion guidelines apply. In Reading 101, Thomas Glick explains how the introduction of new crops into Spain after the Muslim conquest was possible because as part of the wider Muslim world, Spain was opened up to contact with other parts of the world that had up to then been largely inaccessible. The innovation—in this case, the crops— arrived with the new emigrants from the Middle East who sought to recreate some of their native agricultural environment in this foreign Spanish soil. The advantages of these new crops, moreover, would have been obvious to native farmers who quickly adopted them. Jan Vansina describes a similar if much more prolonged process in sub-Saharan Africa. Vansina's piece also offers a good review of how and why people adopt innovations as well as some of the hurdles that prevent adoption. Sometimes religions, technology, and languages spread as a package, which may explain the rapid spread of the Arabic language. In this case, the diffusion of Arabic was closely tied to the spread of Islam. Arabic did not have any tremendous advantages over existing languages such as Greek, Latin, and Persian, but it did enjoy great prestige because of its association with the Islamic religion.

Buddhism in China

Buddhism traces its origins to sixth century B.C.E. India and the teachings of Siddhartha Gautama, the Buddha. After receiving revelations, the Buddha embarked on a career of preaching to teach others what he had learned. From these modest beginnings began one of the world's great religions. Buddhism had spread throughout India and Sri Lanka by the third century B.C.E., with significant support from the emperor Aśoka (r. 273–232 B.C.E.) and reached China no later than 65 C.E. There it faced difficult challenges, mostly because Confucianism dominated Chinese religious and intellectual thought. Buddhism's ability to expand into China was also hampered by cultural differences between Buddhist practices and Chinese society. Under these circumstances, Buddhism had to adapt to its new surroundings, leading to the development of what Eric Zürcher calls a "distinctively Chinese form of Buddhism." The following three selections work as a group to illustrate some of these ideas. In the first selection, Zürcher describes how the collapse of the Han Empire finally allowed Buddhism to flourish in China. He also describes the appeal Buddhism had for many during this troubled period. In the second selection Fairbank and Goldman offer some specific examples of the problems that Buddhism encountered in its penetration of China as well as some of the compromises that it had to make. The last selection, Mozi's Disposition of Errors *(with commentary), is an example of the way in which societies that received culture both molded the ideas that were brought to them and adapted to the new concepts. The* Disposition, *in the form of a dialogue by an unknown author, makes the argument that Buddhism can exist happily in Chinese society in spite of its non-Chinese origins and its differences with accepted Chinese customs.*

>> 96. Buddhism: Its Origin and Spread in Words, Maps and Pictures

ERIC ZÜRCHER [1962]

The political disintegration of the Han empire after the middle of the second century was hastened by an enormous uprising under Taoist [Daoist] guidance which, in 184 A.D., broke out in several parts of the empire and marked the beginning of a period of chaos and 'warlordism'. In the centuries that followed, the medieval period between the breakdown of Han and the reunification of the empire in 589 A.D., the political unity of China was lost. A 'ghost' of a unified empire was evoked in the second half of the third century, but it was lost almost as soon as it had been established, and the court had to flee in disgrace to the region south of the Yangtze [Yangzi] when, in the first years of the fourth century, Huns and other 'northern barbarians' invaded the ancient homeland of Chinese civilisation, sacked the capital, and occupied most of northern China. From 311 onward, China was divided into two parts: the north ruled by non-Chinese rulers, and the region of the Yangtze [Yangzi] basin and further southward governed by a series of feeble Chinese dynasties.

The breakdown of the Han empire was accompanied by changes in the field of thought. Confucianism, the doctrine of the universal state, had lost much of its prestige—it had clearly failed to save the world from chaos and ruin. Instead we find a sudden revival of several non-Confucian schools of thought and a new intellectual atmosphere, less rigid, more speculative and more inclined to seek for other ways and means. Taoism [Daoism] gained many adherents among the cultured class, and there was a heightened interest in metaphysical and philosophical problems ('Dark Learning'). All these factors stimulated the spread of Buddhism among the cultured part of the population as well. Withdrawal from the world became attractive at a time of incessant warfare, chaos and misery, and to the masses of exploited peasants the Buddhist monastery offered a quiet refuge free from the burden of military service, taxes and forced labour. In the north Buddhism was, for various reasons, generally patronized by the foreign rulers. At first they welcomed Buddhist monks as a new type of shaman, able to ensure their prosperity and military victories by means of prayers and spells. Later on they regularly employed monks as counselors, using the foreign doctrine as a means to counter-balance Confucianism.

Source: Eric Zürcher, *Buddhism: Its Origin and Spread in Words, Maps and Pictures* (New York: Saint Martin's Press, 1962), 59–60.

This close connection between church and temporal power remains characteristic of northern Buddhism: government patronage and donations on an enormous scale (of which the Yün-kang [Yungang] cave temples, founded by the Toba Wei rulers in the fifth century, form the most impressive example); on the other hand close supervision of the church by means of monk-officials held responsible for the activities of the clergy, and occasional outbursts of anti-clericalism such as the ruthless persecutions of the years 446–452 and 574–578. Doctrinally the most important event was the arrival in 402 A.D. of Kumârajîva, the great missionary and translator from Kucha, at Ch'ang-an [Chang'an], then the capital of a fervently Buddhist ruling house of Tibetan origin. He introduced Mâdhyamika philosophy into China and produced an enormous amount of Chinese versions with the help of the largest 'translation team' known in history. About the middle of the sixth century northern China is said to have contained more than 30,000 temples.

In the south, Buddhism flourished from the early fourth century. Scholar-monks such as Chih Tun [Zhi Dun] (314–366) and Huiyüan [Huiyuan]

(334–416), explained the doctrine to the cultured public in terms of traditional Chinese thought and thereby laid the foundations of Chinese Buddhist philosophy. Of the many imperial sponsors of Buddhism in the south we must mention the emperor Wu of the Liang dynasty (reigned 502–549). He took the Buddhist vows, personally propagated Buddhism, forbade the slaughter of animals, and officially prohibited Taoism [Daoism]. It is under his reign that Bodhidharma, the reputed founder of Ch'an [Chan] (Zen) Buddhism, is said to have arrived in China.

In 589 China was again united. The following (second) period of political unification, the period of the Sui and T'ang dynasties (589–907), forms the golden age of Chinese Buddhism. There was great activity and growth in every field. Sects arose, partly based on indigenous doctrinal developments, partly transplanted from India. Pilgrims travelled to the ends of the known world; Chinese Buddhism had some influence in Tibet, and several of its sects were transferred to Japan. Buddhism permeated art and literature; Chinese Buddhist art, now fully emancipated from its foreign prototypes, followed its own lines of development.

>> 97. China: A New History

J. K. FAIRBANK AND MERLE GOLDMAN [1998]

The Buddhist teachings were set forth in the great Buddhist canon or tripitaka. Translation of sutras from this canon became the chief work of the first Buddhist monks in China. They and their followers faced enormously complex linguistic as well as intellectual problems—how to translate from Sanskrit, which was polysyllabic, highly inflected, and alphabetic like English and other Indo-European languages, into the monosyllabic, uninflected, ideographic script of China; how to convey, in that rather terse and concrete medium, the highly imaginative and metaphysical abstractions of Indian mysticism.

In attempting to transfer or "translate" their new and alien ideas into terms meaningful for their Chinese audience, the early Buddhist missionaries ran into the problem that has faced all purveyors of foreign ideas in China ever since: how to select certain Chinese terms, written characters already invested with established meanings, and invest them with new significance without letting the foreign ideas be subtly modified, in fact sinified, in the process. For example, the Chinese character *dao* ("the way"), already so much used in Daoism and Confucianism, might be used variously for the Indian dharma or for yoga or for the idea of enlightenment, while *wuwei,* the "nonaction" of Daoism, was used for nirvana. The result was at least ambiguity, if not some watering down of the original idea.

Source: J. K. Fairbank and Merle Goldman, *China: A New History* (Cambridge, MA: Belknap Press, 1998), 75–76.

Abstract ideas from abroad when expressed in Chinese characters could hardly avoid a degree of sinification. In addition, exotic and socially disruptive values were resisted. As Arthur Wright [...] remarks, "The relatively high position which Buddhism gave to women and mothers was changed in these early translations. For example 'Husband supports wife' became 'The husband controls his wife;' and 'The wife comforts the husband' became 'The wife reveres her husband.' "

Non-Chinese invaders of North China, in the fourth century and after, accepted Buddhism partly because, like themselves, it came from outside the old order that they were taking over. Buddhist priests could be allies in fostering docility among the masses. For the Chinese upper class who had fled to the south, Buddhism also offered an explanation and solace, intellectually sophisticated and aesthetically satisfying, for the collapse of their old society. Emperors and commoners alike sought religious salvation in an age of social disruption. Great works of art, statues, and rock-cut temples have come down from this period. Fruitful comparisons and contrasts can be made between the roles of clergy and monasticism, the growth of sects, and relations of church and state, during this age of Buddhist faith in China and its later Christian counterpart in medieval Europe. Buddhist monasteries, for example, served as hostels for travelers, havens of refuge, and sources of charity. They also became great landowners and assumed quasi-official positions in the administration.

The early period of borrowing and domestication was followed by one of acceptance and independent growth. Chinese native Buddhism was influenced by Daoism, and influenced it in return, to an extent still being debated. New sects arose in China, catering to Chinese needs. Best known to us today through its influence on Oriental art was the school which sought enlightenment through practices of meditation (called in Chinese Chan, or in the Japanese pronunciation, Zen). Perhaps enough has been said to indicate the very complex interaction among such elements as Indian Buddhism, the barbarian invaders, native Daoism, and the eventual growth, flowering, and decay of Chinese Buddhism.

>> 98. The Disposition of Error

Mozi [5th century c.e.]

The author takes the stand that it is possible to be a good Chinese and a good Buddhist at the same time, that there is no fundamental conflict between the two ways of life, and that the great truths preached by Buddhism are preached, if in somewhat different language, by Confucianism and Taoism as well.

Why is Buddhism Not Mentioned in the Chinese Classics?

The questioner said: If the way of the Buddha is the greatest and most venerable of ways, why did Yao, Shun, the Duke of Chou [Zhou], and Confucius not practice it? In the seven Classics one sees no mention of it. You, sir, are fond of the *Book of Odes* and the *Book of History,* and you take pleasure in rites and music. Why, then, do you love the way of the Buddha and rejoice in outlandish arts? Can they exceed the Classics and commentaries and beautify the accomplishments of the sages? Permit me the liberty, sir, of advising you to reject them.

Mozi said: All written works need not necessarily be the words of Confucius, and all medicine does not necessarily consist of the formulae of [the famous physician] P'ien-ch'üeh [Pianque]. What accords with principle is to be followed, what heals the sick is good. The gentleman-scholar draws widely on all forms of good, and thereby benefits his character. Tzu-kung [Zigong] [a disciple of

Source: Mou Tzu, "The Disposition of Error," in *Sources of Chinese Tradition,* edited by W. T. Barry et al. (New York: Columbia University Press, 1960), 314–318.

Confucius] said, "Did the Master have a permanent teacher?" Yao served Yin Shou, Shun served Wu-ch'eng [Wucheng], the Duke of Chou [Zhou] learned from Lü Wang, and Confucius learned from Lao Tzu [Laozi]. And none of these teachers is mentioned in the seven Classics. Although these four teachers were sages, to compare them to the Buddha would be like comparing a white deer to a unicorn, or a swallow to a phoenix. Yao, Shun, the Duke of Chou [Zhou], and Confucius learned even from such teachers as these. How much less, then, may one reject the Buddha, whose distinguishing marks are extraordinary and whose superhuman powers know no bounds! How may one reject him and refuse to learn from him? The records and teachings of the Five Classics do not contain everything. Even if the Buddha is not mentioned in them, what occasion is there for suspicion?

Why Do Buddhist Monks Do Injury to Their Bodies?

One of the greatest obstacles confronting the early Chinese Buddhist church was the aversion of Chinese society to the shaving of the head, which was required of all members of the Buddhist clergy. The Confucianists held that the body is the gift of one's parents, and that to harm it is to be disrespectful toward them.

The questioner said: The *Classic of Filial Piety* says, "Our torso, limbs, hair, and skin we receive from our fathers and mothers. We dare not do them injury." When Tseng Tzu [Zeng Zi] was about to die, he bared his hands and feet. But now the monks shave their heads. How this violates the sayings of the sages and is out of keeping with the way of the filially pious!...

Mozi said:...Confucius has said, "He with whom one may follow a course is not necessarily he with whom one may weigh its merits." This is what is meant by doing what is best at the time. Furthermore, the *Classic of Filial Piety* says, "The kings of yore possessed the ultimate virtue and the essential Way." T'ai-po [Taibo] cut his hair short and tattooed his body, thus following of his

own accord the customs of Wu and Yüeh and going against the spirit of the "torso, limbs, hair, and skin" passage. And yet Confucius praised him, saying that his might well be called the ultimate virtue.

Why Do Monks Not Marry?

Another of the great obstacles confronting the early Chinese Buddhist church was clerical celibacy. One of the most important features of indigenous Chinese religion is ancestor worship. If there are no descendants to make the offerings, then there will be no sacrifices. To this is added the natural desire for progeny. For a Chinese traditionally there could be no greater calamity than childlessness.

The questioner said: Now of felicities there is none greater than the continuation of one's line, of unfilial conduct there is none worse than childlessness. The monks forsake wife and children, reject property and wealth. Some do not marry all their lives. How opposed this conduct is to felicity and filial piety!...

Mozi said:...Wives, children, and property are the luxuries of the world, but simple living and inaction are the wonders of the Way. Lao Tzu [Laozi] has said, "Of reputation and life, which is dearer? Of life and property, which is worth more?"...Hsü Yu [Xu Yu] and Ch'ao-fu dwelt in a tree. Po-i [Boyi] and Shu-ch'i [Shuqui] starved in Shou-yang [Shouyang], but Confucius praised their worth, saying, "They sought to act in accordance with humanity and they succeeded in acting so." One does not hear of their being ill spoken of because they were childless and propertyless. The monk practices the way and substitutes that for the pleasures of disporting himself in the world. He accumulates goodness and wisdom in exchange for the joys of wife and children.

Death and Rebirth

Chinese ancestor worship was premised on the belief that the souls of the deceased, if not fed, would suffer. Rationalistic Confucianism, while taking over and canonizing much of Chinese tradition, including the ancestral sacrifices, denied the existence of spirits and hence the immortality of the soul.

The Buddhists, though likewise denying the existence of a soul, accepted transmigration, and the early Chinese understood this to imply a belief in an individual soul which passed from one body to another until the attainment of enlightenment. The following passage must be understood in the light of these conflicting and confusing interpretations.

The questioner said: The Buddhists say that after a man dies he will be reborn. I do not believe in the truth of these words ....

Mozi said:...The spirit never perishes. Only the body decays. The body is like the roots and leaves of the five grains, the spirit is like the seeds and kernels of the five grains. When the roots and leaves come forth they inevitably die. But do the seeds and kernels perish? Only the body of one who has achieved the Way perishes....

Someone said: If one follows the Way one dies. If one does not follow the Way one dies. What difference is there?

Mozi said: You are the sort of person who, having not a single day of goodness, yet seeks a lifetime of fame. If one has the Way, even if one dies one's soul goes to an abode of happiness. If one does not have the Way, when one is dead one's soul suffers misfortune.

Why Should a Chinese Allow Himself to be Influenced by Indian Ways?

This was one of the objections most frequently raised by Confucianists and Taoists [Daoists] once Buddhism had acquired a firm foothold on Chinese soil. The Chinese apologists for Buddhism answered this objection in a variety of ways. Below we see one of the arguments used by them.

The questioner said: Confucius said, "The barbarians with a ruler are not so good as the Chinese without one." Mencius criticized Ch'en Hsiang for rejecting his own education to adopt the ways of [the foreign teacher] Hsü Hsing, saying, "I have heard of using what is Chinese to change what is barbarian, but I have never heard of using what is barbarian to change what is Chinese." You, sir, at the age of twenty learned the way of Yao, Shun, Confucius, and the Duke of Chou [Zhou]. But now you have rejected them, and instead have taken up the arts of the barbarians. Is this not a great error?

Mozi said:... What Confucius said was meant to rectify the way of the world, and what Mencius said was meant to deplore one-sidedness. Of old, when Confucius was thinking of taking residence among the nine barbarian nations, he said, "If a gentleman-scholar dwells in their midst, what baseness can there be among them?"... The Commentary says, "The north polar star is in the center of heaven and to the north of man." From this one can see that the land of China is not necessarily situated under the center of heaven. According to the Buddhist scriptures, above, below, and all around, all beings containing blood belong to the Buddha-clan. Therefore I revere and study these scriptures. Why should I reject the Way of Yao, Shun, Confucius, and the Duke of Chou [Zhou]? Gold and jade do not harm each other, crystal and amber do not cheapen each other. You say that another is in error when it is you yourself who err.

Two Faces of Christianity

After the fall of the Roman Empire, Christian missionaries—aided by newly converted Germanic kings such as Clovis—began the process of converting the people of western Europe to the Christian faith. This proselytizing took on different forms, with the missionaries often having to depend on the goodwill of the people to whom they were preaching. When this goodwill was missing, the missions typically failed and could even end in martyrdom for the missionary. Moreover, some Church leaders understood that

Christianity was a difficult religion whose complexities were often beyond the grasp of the illiterate people who were the target of these conversion efforts. Consequently, as was the case with Buddhism in China, Christianity tried to adapt to local conditions. A good example of this **cultural accommodation** *is the selection from Bede's* Ecclesiastical History. *The source is a letter sent by Pope Gregory the Great in 601 to the missionaries he had dispatched to England four years earlier. In this case, the missionaries were heavily dependant on the support of the Anglo-Saxon kings and their subjects and had to tread with care. Over the next two hundred years, the situation improved considerably for Christianity. By the time Charlemagne became king of the Carolingian Franks and master over most of Europe, Christianity was operating from a position of strength with the power of the Carolingians backing its efforts. The second source is a capitulary that Charlemagne promulgated for his newly captured territories in Saxony. The Saxons (not to be confused with the Anglo-Saxons) had consistently refused to accept Carolingian authority or that of the Church. The capitulary, with its draconian punishments, is an effort to enforce Carolingian power in this region and to ensure that the Saxons behaved like good Christians.*

>> 99. Ecclesiastical History of the English People

BEDE [C. 731 C.E.]

When these messengers had left, the holy father Gregory sent after them letters worthy of our notice, which show most clearly his unwearying interest in the salvation of our nation. The letter runs as follows:

'To our well loved son Abbot Mellitus: Gregory, servant of the servants of God.

'Since the departure of those of our fellowship who are bearing you company, we have been seriously anxious, because we have received no news of the success of your journey. Therefore, when by God's help you reach our most reverend brother, Bishop Augustine, we wish you to inform him that we have been giving careful thought to the affairs of the English, and have come to the conclusion that the temples of the idols among that people should on no account be destroyed. The idols are to be destroyed, but the temples themselves are to be aspersed with holy water, altars set up in them, and relics deposited there. For if these temples are well-built, they must be purified from the worship of demons and dedicated to the service of the true God. In this way, we hope that the people, seeing that their temples are not destroyed, may abandon their error and, flocking more readily to their accustomed resorts, may come to know and adore the true God. And since they have a custom of sacrificing many oxen to demons, let some other solemnity be substituted in its place, such as a day of Dedication or the Festivals of the holy martyrs whose relics are enshrined there. On such occasions they might well construct shelters of boughs for themselves around the churches that were once temples, and celebrate the solemnity with devout feasting. They are no longer to sacrifice beasts to the Devil, but they may kill them for food to the praise of God, and give thanks to the Giver of all gifts for the plenty they enjoy. If the people are allowed some worldly pleasures in this way, they will more readily come to desire the joys of the spirit. For it is certainly impossible to eradicate all errors from obstinate minds at one stroke, and whoever wishes to climb to a mountain top climbs gradually step by step, and not in one leap. It was in this way that the Lord revealed Himself

Source: Bede, *Ecclesiastical History of the English People with Bede's Letter to Egbert and Cuthbert's Letter on the Death of Bede* (London: Penguin Books, 1990), 91–93.

to the Israelite people in Egypt, permitting the sacrifices formerly offered to the Devil to be offered thenceforward to Himself instead. So He bade them sacrifice beasts to Him, so that, once they became enlightened, they might abandon one element of sacrifice and retain another. For, while they were to offer the same beasts as before, they were to offer them to God instead of to idols, so that they would no longer be offering the same sacrifices. Of your kindness, you are to inform our brother Augustine of this policy, so that he may consider how he may best implement it on the spot. God keep you safe, my very dear son.

'Dated the seventeenth of June, in the nineteenth year of the reign of our most pious Lord and Emperor Maurice Tiberius Augustus, and the eighteenth after his Consulship: the fourth indiction.'

>> 100. Capitulary Concerning the Regions of Saxony

CHARLEMAGNE [782 C.E.]

1. Decisions were made first on the more important provisions. It was the will of all that the churches of Christ which are now being built in Saxony and are consecrated to God should enjoy not less but greater and higher *honor* than the shrines of idols have had.

2. If anyone takes refuge in a church, no one is to presume to drive him out by force but he is to have asylum until he is brought to court; moreover, he is to be granted his life and freedom from mutilation in honour of God and out of reverence for the saints of that church. But he is to pay for his offence, to the extent that he can and is required by the judgement; and then he is to be brought to the presence of the lord king, that the latter may send him wherever his clemency shall please.

3. If anyone enters a church by force and takes something from it, by violence or stealth, or sets fire to the church, he is to be put to death.

4. If anyone scorns the holy Lenten fast out of contempt for Christianity and eats meat, he is to be put to death; but let the matter yet be investigated by a *sacerdos* lest it should perchance happen that someone eats meat by reason of necessity.

5. If anyone kills a bishop, priest or deacon, he is likewise to suffer capital punishment.

6. If anyone, deceived by the devil, believes, in the way pagans do, that some man or woman is a witch and eats people and if for this reason he burns her and gives her flesh to be eaten, or eats it himself, he is to suffer the capital sentence.

7. If anyone has the body of a dead man consumed by fire, according to the· usage of the pagans, and reduces his bones to ashes, he is to suffer capital punishment.

8. If henceforth anyone from the people of the Saxons, lurking unbaptised among them, wishes to conceal himself, and scorns to come to baptism, and wishes to remain a pagan, he is to be put to death.

9. If anyone sacrifices a man to the devil and offers him as a sacrifical victim to demons after the fashion of the pagans, he is to be put to death.

10. If anyone forms a plot with pagans against Christians or wishes to remain with them, in hostility to Christians, he is to be put to death; and whoever consents to this same action, in treachery against the king or the people of the Christians, is to be put to death.

11. If anyone shows himself unfaithful to the lord king, he is to suffer the capital sentence.

12. If anyone rapes the daughter of his lord, he is to be put to death.

13. If anyone kills his lord or lady, he is to be punished in like fashion.

Source: Charlemagne, "Capitulary Concerning the Regions of Saxony," in *Charlemagne: Translated Sources,* edited and translated by P. D. King (Cumbria, UK: P. D. King, 1987), 205–207.

14. But if, on account of these capital crimes anyone who is not known to have committed them takes refuge of his own accord with a *sacerdos,* makes confession and wishes to do penance he is to be excused death on the testimony of the *sacerdos.*

15. All were agreed concerning the less important provisions. To each church the people of the area of its jurisdiction are to make over a homestead and two *mansi* of land; and for every 120 men among them, nobles and likewise freemen and *liti,* they are to hand over one *servus* and one *ancilla* to the said church.

16. This too was decided with Christ's favour, that when any revenue, from whatever source, comes to the fisc, whether in the form of a fine *[fredus]* or in that of a *bannus* of some sort or in that of any due belonging to the king, a tenth part is to be given to the churches and *sacerdotes.*

17. We likewise order in accordance with God's command, that all are to give a tenth part of their [acquired] wealth and produce to the churches and *sacerdotes*; in proportion to what God has given each Christian, let nobles no less than freemen, and likewise *liti,* make partial return to God.

18. That no public meetings or court-sessions are to take place on Sundays, except perhaps in a case of great necessity or under the compulsion of war, but that all are to resort to the church to hear the word of God and are to give themselves over to prayer and righteous works. On special feast-days also they are likewise to devote themselves to God and to congregating at church and are to forgo secular assemblies.

19. It was also decided to include among these decrees a ruling that every infant be baptised within a year; and we ordain that if, without the counsel and authorisation of a *sacerdos,* anyone scorns to offer an infant for baptism within the span of a year he is to pay 120 *solidi* to the fisc if of noble stock, sixty if a freeman, thirty if a *litus.*

20. If anyone contracts a prohibited or illicit marriage, sixty *solidi* if a noble, thirty if a freeman, fifteen if a *litus.*

21. If anyone offers a prayer to springs or trees or groves or makes any offering after the fashion of the pagans and eats it in honour of demons, sixty *solidi* if he is a noble, thirty if a freeman, fifteen if a *litus.* And if they do not have the wherewithal to pay immediately they are to be given to the service of the church until those *solidi* are paid.

22. We command that the bodies of Christian Saxons be brought to the church's cemeteries and not to the burial-mounds of the pagans.

23. We decree that diviners and soothsayers be given to the churches and *sacerdotes.*

New Crops in Spain

The Islamic conquests of the seventh and eighth century served to bridge the farther reaches of the Eurasian landmass as Muslim rulers held dominion from the Atlantic to the Indian Ocean. The unification of much of this vast area under a single faith with similar cultures and institutions allowed for widespread diffusion of customs and ideas. One of the most significant was the introduction of agricultural and irrigation practices to al-Andalus, the Muslim name for Spain, from the Middle East and Asia. The Muslims had conquered most of Spain from the Visigoths in a whirlwind campaign that began in 711. Their conquest brought a massive influx of people from North African, Egypt, and Syria, and these people brought with them the agricultural knowledge they used in their home countries. In this selection, Thomas Glick describes how the introduction of new irrigation techniques to Spain allowed Muslim cultivators to bring in a host of new crops to Spain and the Western Mediterranean.

>> 101. Islamic and Christian Spain in the Early Middle Ages

THOMAS F. GLICK [1979]

The introduction and acclimatization of new crops, a powerful component of the economic growth of al-Andalus, followed the same pattern of diffusion as the irrigation systems and techniques used to grow them. Of the plants brought by the Arabs to the peninsula (those whose Arabic names passed into the Spanish languages are noted in Table I), the seeds of many must have been brought by anonymous cultivators. Yet more formal methods of introduction are recorded. 'Abd al-Rahmān I, whose nostalgia for the Syrian landscape has been mentioned before, was personally responsible for the introduction of several species, including the date palm. A variety of pomegranate was introduced from Damascus by the chief judge of Córdoba, Mu'āwiya b. Sālih, who personally presented the plant to the Emir. From the palace at Córdoba a Jordanian soldier

named Safar took a cutting and planted it on his estate in the Málaga region. This species, called *safrī* after the soldier, subsequently became widely diffused. Early in the ninth century the poet al-Ghazāl of Jaén returned from a mission to the east with the doñegal fig, which became one of the four or five staple fig varieties in the country. The full description of the poet's modus operandi is symptomatic of the way cultural elements were diffused in that cosmopolitan world:

"The doñegal (*dunaqāl*) fig was introduced by al-Ghazāl when he went from Córdoba to Constantinople as an envoy. He saw that fig there and admired it. It was forbidden to take anything from Constantinople.

He took the green figs and put them with his books that he had wrapped up, after he had unfolded the strings and wrapped them again. When he made his departure, he was searched and no sign was found of it. When he arrived in Córdoba he removed the plant from the middle of the twine, planted it, and cared for it. When it bore fruit, he went with the fig to the lord of Córdoba and it amazed him. He told him about his ruse in procuring it. The lord thanked him for his deed and asked him about its name. Al-Ghazāl replied: 'I do not know what its name is except that when the one who picks it gives some of it to someone he says "Dūnahu qawli" which means "Oh my lord, look!" and so the Commander of the Faithful named it Dunaqāl.' "

Such details are all too infrequent in the literature, but represent what must have been a common pattern.

Newly introduced plants were frequently acclimatized in royal gardens, first in that of the Umayyads in Córdoba and, in the eleventh century, in the royal gardens of Toledo (where the agronomists ibn Bassāl and ibn Wāfid were both employed) and Almería. Many of the new plants were either tropical or semi-tropical

Edible Crops Introduced by the Arabs

Spanish Derivation	Meaning	Arabic Form
aceituna	olive	al-zaitūna
albaricoque	apricot	al-barqūq
alcachofa	artichoke	al-kharshuf
algarrobo	carob	al-kharrūba
arroz	rice	al-ruz
azafrán	saffron	al-za'farān
azúcar	sugar	al-sukkar
azufaifa	jujube	al-zufayzaf
berenjena	egg plant	bādhinjāna
chirivia	parsnip	jiriwiyya
limón	lemon	laimūn
naranja	orange	nāranjā
toronja	grapefruit	turunja
zanahoria	carrot	isfannāriya

Source: Thomas F. Glick, *Islamic and Christian Spain in the Early Middle Ages* (Princeton: Princeton University Press, 1979), 76–8.

varieties that required irrigation, or were temperate species that could only be stabilized in a semi-arid environment by irrigation. Therefore the Andalusi agronomists paid particular attention to the water requirements of each species. Ibn al-'Awwām was precise in stipulating the water needs of mountainous plants transplanted in the lowlands.

Chief among the newly introduced irrigated crops were sugar cane, which in al-Andalus was watered every four to eight days, and rice, which had to be continually submerged. Cotton was cultivated at least from the end of the eleventh century and was irrigated, according to ibn Baṣṣāl, every two weeks from the time it sprouted until August I. The Andalusis were self-sufficient in cotton and exported it, according to al-Ḥimyarī, to Ifriqiya and as far south as Sijlmāsa. Oranges and other citrus plants were also irrigated, as were many fruit trees and dry-farming crops which do not need to be watered but which produce greater yields if they are.

The introduction of new crops, combined with extension and intensification of irrigation, gave rise to a complex and varied agricultural system, whereby a greater variety of soil types were put to efficient use; where fields that had been yielding one crop yearly at most prior to the Islamic invasion were now capable of yielding three or more crops, in rotation and where agricultural production responded to the demands of an increasingly sophisticated and cosmopolitan urban population by providing the towns with a variety of products unknown in northern Europe.

The Spread of Arabic

The names of new crops were not the only Arabic words to spread across the vast new Muslim empire. As Muslim dominion spread, so did the influence of Islam with new converts coming slowly at first and then accelerating thereafter. Closely tied to the diffusion of the Muslim faith was the Arabic language. Much like Latin in western Europe, Arabic became a language of religious dialogue and administration spoken throughout the Muslim world. Unlike Latin, Arabic was considered the divine language in which the Angel of God had dictated the divine revelations (the Koran) to Muhammad from an original in Heaven. In the following selection, Anwar Chejne describes the deep reverence Muslims held for Arabic.

>> 102. The Arabic Language: Its Role in History

ANWAR G. CHEJNE [1969]

In its birthplace in the northwestern region of the Arabian Peninsula, Arabic was one of several dialects spoken by the Quraysh aristocracy to which the Prophet Muhammad belonged. Before the rise of Islām, Arabic lacked any literary tradition to speak of, yet it seems to have been important in Arabic society as a medium of oral poetry. This poetry, abundant and rich, not only occupied a special place in the life of the several tribes, but also served as a koine and unifying force among them. It is to the poetry that the Arabs owed their awareness of being one people, for it gave focus to their artistic, intellectual, and spiritual expression. [...]

Source: Anwar G. Chejne, *The Arabic Language: Its Role in History* (Minneapolis: University of Minnesota Press, 1969), 6–9.

Besides appreciation of the artistic value of poetry, eloquence (*faṣāḥah*) or the ability to express oneself correctly was also considered in preIslamic and Islamic times one of the basic attributes of the "perfect man," and a mark of wisdom. Correct speech and eloquence became all the more significant following the Arab expansion when the spoken language and that of the Qur'ān were undergoing what Muslim scholars refer to as corrupting influences. [...]

Although correct speech and oral eloquence remained goals never reached in practice, they were admired and appreciated much more than the advantages of the natural, easy, yet faulty everyday speech (*laḥn*) common to both the literati and the masses. This situation, no doubt influenced by religious considerations, contributed greatly to the preservation of Arabic as the sole literary medium and prevented it from branching out into several languages as had been the case with Latin.

Closely related to the aesthetic appreciation of correct speech was the great reverence for the Qur'ān, which exerted from the outset an enormous influence on the religious, political, social, and intellectual life of the Arab-Muslim people. It was the Qur'ān—the Revealed Book—that was believed to represent the highest linguistic achievement of the Arabic language. This conviction facilitated the rapid development and dissemination of Arabic and contributed to its transformation from an obscure dialect into one of the great languages of medieval and modern times.

The intimate relationship between Arabic and Islām is reflected in the attitudes and beliefs of the Arab-Muslims over the centuries. The interaction between language and religion led to the development of a number of traditions and the establishment of a linguistic dogma. To begin with, was it not true that God revealed His message to Muhammad in an "Arabic Qur'ān" meant to be understood by the Arabs and by all those who may aspire to eternal salvation? The belief in the divine nature of the Qur'ān was further strengthened by strong religious traditions whereby the Revealed Book was regarded as a transcript of the Word of God from a preserved tablet (*lawḥ maḥfūẓ*) containing the Mother of the Book (*umm al-kitāb*) found in the seventh heaven from eternity.

As such, the Qur'ān constitutes a miracle, and cannot be imitated in any shape or form by any mortal. It is unique in style, pure in origin, and unexcelled in beauty. Such beliefs became current not only among commentators, theologians, and traditionalists but among philologists, grammarians, and literary critics as well. These beliefs remained unchanged even after the development of literary criticism and philological and grammatical studies, which appraised the style and discussed the origin of the language, the detection of foreign words, and other linguistic peculiarities. Muslim scholars were not inclined to admit the presence of foreign words in the Qur'ān, or to sanction its translation into any foreign language, in the strong belief that it would lose the superior qualities which Arabic alone is able to convey. According to them, it is by virtue of its divine nature that the language of the Qur'ān stands unique. For instance, Abū 'Ubaydah (died c. 825), an able philologist and author of numerous works, categorically denied the presence of foreign words in the Qur'ān in a famous statement: "Whoever pretends that there is in the Qur'ān anything other than the Arabic language has made a serious charge against God." Others said that the so-called foreign words were coincidental—that Arabic and foreign tongues happen to use the same expression for the same thing. Although foreignism in the Qur'ān could not be dismissed lightly by later authors, this did not in any way shake their belief in its essential Arabism.

The doctrine of the divine nature of the Qur'ān with respect to its meaning, wording, and even its most minute details, came to encompass the Arabic language as a whole. The issue of whether Arabic was God's gift, and hence superior to all languages in beauty, wealth, and nobility, has deeply concerned philologists, theologians, philosophers, religious scholars, and others.

To Make or Not to Make Ceramics

Adoption of an innovation was not always a given. Social, cultural, environmental, and political factors could discourage adoption even when it was clear that the innovation was beneficial. In this final selection, Jan Vansina, a renowned Africanist, challenges the notion that some African societies accepted new technologies, or packages of related technologies, quickly and with little opposition. Instead, Vansina describes an adoption process that may have taken over a millennia to complete as new technologies created social changes that slowed down the acceptance of future innovations. The transmission of cultural and technological innovations into Angola represents the very southern edge of the diffusion of Bantu language and culture and movement of Bantu peoples (discussed by Christopher Ehret in Reading 88 [Chapter 11]).

>> 103. How Societies Are Born: Governance in West Central Africa before 1600

JAN VANSINA [2004]

A Coming Together

We have completed our journey across the historical landscape of West Central Africa. We have seen that during a first period before societies with their overarching institutions of governance could arise, individual communities in the area had to better secure and control their food supplies. They adopted the use of ceramics, which allowed them to use more plants as food by cooking them and they then began to produce food themselves rather than simply relying on the less secure bounty provided by foraging. Once this was achieved, communities became sedentary wherever possible. Where that was not possible, they formed nomadic groups around the management of sufficiently large herds of bovines. [...]

Not so long ago, scholars still understood the underlying dynamic of the first period as one in which Bantu-speaking immigrants introduced the whole package of technologies as they colonized the area. Gradually it became evident that there was neither a single package nor any large-scale immigration. As demonstrated in Part 1 of this book, the dynamics were different. First of all, the adoption of new technologies proceeded slowly, and the technologies were adopted in a piecemeal fashion rather than as a package. Starting with the acquisition of ceramics and pursuing this with all the acquisitions which followed, autochthons first experimented with a novelty because they foresaw, that is, they imagined ahead of time, that it would help either to increase their food supply or to render it more secure. Over time, they became familiar with less desirable side effects and learned to cope with them while they also learned how to insert the new technology into the overall economic management of their lives and to better fit it to the needs of the moment. After all this trial and error, the innovation was then internalized and community after community made the final choice to adopt or to reject it. Rejection transpired when an innovation could not be adopted or be sustained: for example, there was no suitable clay to make pots, the environment did not allow the introduction of the main crops around which horticulture was practiced so that only cowpeas and cucurbits continued to be planted, game and vegetal food was so abundant that

Source: Jan Vansina, *How Societies Are Born: Governance in West Central Africa before 1600* (Charlottesville: University of Virginia Press, 2004), 261–2.

there was not much incentive to adopt food production, and so on.

Moreover, each new technology brought about social changes as well. To make ceramics enhanced the status of women potters, horticulture required a new sort of coordination of male and female labor to prepare fields and it could lead to a seasonal separation of women and men as the women stayed put to plant while the men roamed about for game. The smelting and the forging of metals widened gender distinction and created new prestigious careers, and some of its products became highly prized valuables that gave a new sort of power to those who detained them. Indeed once metal hoes became the preferred tool for cereal cultivation, women farmers became dependent on men in a way they never had been before and a gender hierarchy developed. As argued earlier, keeping large herds had to be preceded by the acceptance of delayed returns on labor, yet that provoked new divisions of labor (by gender, and age), fostered social inequality, created new notions of wealth and inheritance, and thus seems to have led to the invention of unilinear matrilineal descent and its consequences.

No wonder then that the adoption of new technologies had to be piecemeal and stretched out over half a millennium or more, even if one excludes earlier, more modest innovations such as the introduction of ground stone tools. The entire process was complete everywhere only by the ninth or even tenth centuries with the full spread of cereal farming and with an intensified production of metals. Compared to other parts of Africa, this is remarkably late, centuries later than anywhere else except for arid southwestern Africa.

>> Mastering the Materials and Making Connections

For the questions below, concentrate on the material in Part 3, but consider also sources from previous chapters where appropriate.

1. Why is cultural diffusion an important element in the development of human societies?

2. How do local conditions affect whether an innovation is going to be adopted or not?

3. Based on what you have read in this chapter, what are some ways that innovations diffuse from one part of the world to another?

4. Can the interference of the state help or hinder the adoption of innovations? Can you think of some cases not mentioned in these readings in which state support may have helped or hindered the adoption of a particular innovation?

5. Do religions, languages, ideas, technologies, and other cultural elements diffuse in the same way or are there differences in the way they spread from one region to another?

6. Does political disruption and fragmentation limit or accelerate the diffusion of ideas, culture, and technology?

Part 3 Conclusion

In the year 962, in early February, the city of Rome witnessed the coronation of a new emperor as it had many times before. The difference here is that it occurred almost 500 years after the Western Roman Empire had ceased to exist as a political entity. The new emperor, moreover, was not a Roman or even a citizen of Rome's old empire. Instead, he was a Germanic Saxon king, born far from the heart of the empire and burdened with the clearly "barbaric" name of Otto. It was a situation that the emperor Hadrian, whose travels began Part 3, would have found unsettling had he been able to see it. But Otto's coronation—despite the repugnance it may have caused Hadrian and his contemporaries—is a useful event to help us summarize the concepts covered in this part.

Otto was a descendant of those very same people that the Romans would have considered barbarians and whose raids and attacks had hastened the decline of the Western Roman Empire. Yet, almost immediately after the empire had disintegrated under the weight of internal and external problems, these Germanic people, who had migrated for generations over large regions of Eurasia, began the process of carving out new polities with themselves in charge. It was through their efforts that the modern nation-states of Europe began. Lacking much experience in governing static peoples and kingdoms, they borrowed much from the Romans: laws, institutions, and bureaucratic expertise for example. In this they were like other people on the peripheries of the great empires (and in this part we have seen similar cases in Japan and with the Muslim Caliphate). Yet, they also had much to contribute including a remarkable skill in war craft.

As they mixed and integrated with the Romans, they learned and adopted much of their culture and traditions. They wanted to be Romans. As one late fifth century Gothic king put it, "an effective Goth wants to be like a Roman; only a poor Roman would want to be a Goth." In an effort to seem more Roman, they even created stories about shared ancestors, linking themselves to the Trojans and other ancient peoples. One of the many things they adopted from the Romans was Christianity, the state religion of the Roman Empire by the fifth century. Within a few generations, many of these one-time Germanic tribesmen were also serving as Christian missionaries and helping to diffuse the innovation of Christianity to those who had not been exposed to it.

The title of Roman Emperor that Otto took was a perfect symbol for the disruptions, migrations, diffusions, and changes that Europe had experienced in the preceding half millennium. His Saxon heritage was a clear indicator of the importance the Germanic invaders and migrants had attained in the new European order. The one-time barbarians were now ruling their own empire. Otto, moreover, was crowned by the Pope, who was not only the spiritual leader of Latin Christendom, but who, based on a forged document, claimed the right to name the Western

Emperor. And for this they chose the Germanic king. Otto's claim to be a Roman sought to give him additional legitimacy and tried to link him to the Roman authority and prestige that still reverberated centuries after the Western Empire had collapsed. Considering that Roman Law still had a place in Europe, that bishops (who had been quasi-official Roman functionaries) helped with the administration of his realm, and that Latin was still the language of authority in Otto's realm, the claim to be Roman was not as far fetched as it might seem.

The coronation by the Pope was also a clear sign that Otto had the backing of the Christian Church and its powerful God. Moreover, his imperial title not only empowered him to rule but it raised his status to that of an equal with the Byzantine (or Eastern Roman) Emperor—or so at least he and his supporters claimed. It placed him in a long line of imperial rulers dating back to the great Augustus and including such stalwart figures as Hadrian, Constantine, and Justinian. In short, Otto had appropriated and adapted these diverse cultural elements and used them to forge a new empire. To our modern eyes, this may seem like rule by smoke and mirrors, and that is partially true, but we must never fail to recognize that this was a society in which symbols mattered. Otto was a symbol of the Roman Empire reborn: the ultimate result of the exchanges and diffusion of peoples and ideas that had characterized the history of Europe for much of the preceding few centuries. His legitimacy and authority depended on his adoption, adaptation, and fusion of diverse cultural and political innovations into a new unified whole.

Further Reading

There are many sources available on the empires covered in Part 3 and their heirs. Peter Brown's *The World of Late Antiquity* (London: Thames and Hudson, 1971) remains a magisterial introduction to the Western world after the collapse of Rome. Peter Heather's *The Fall of the Roman Empire* (Oxford: Oxford University Press, 2006) offers a recent and very readable interpretation of that fall. Roger Collin's *Early Medieval Europe, 2nd ed.* (New York: St. Martin's Press, 1999) and Marshall Hodgson's first volume of *The Venture of Islam* (Chicago: University of Chicago Press, 1974) are useful introductions to the world after Rome in Europe and the Islamic world, respectively. Christopher Ehret's *An African Classical Age* (Charlottesville, VA: University of Virginia Press, 1998) offers an overview of African history from 1000 B.C.E. to 400 C.E. as well as engaging in useful discussions on archaeology and linguistics. For India, the works of Romila Thapar, notably *Early India* (Berkeley: University of California Press, 2004) remain among the most accessible introductions. The same can be said for John King Fairbanks and Merle Goldman's *China: A New History* (Cambridge, MA: Belknap Press, 1998). For more in-depth coverage one can always turn to the relevant volumes of *The Cambridge History of China.* Finally, recent historical scholarship has served the Americas well, including Geoffrey Baswell's edited collection, *The Maya and Teotihuacan* (Austin: University of Texas Press, 2004).

Terms to Know

political fragmentation
  (p. 244)

successor states
  (p. 244)

cultural accommodation
  (p. 268)

innovations
  (p. 261)

master narrative   *(p. 240)*

diffusion   *(p. 261)*

Part 4

The Medieval World System, 1000–1500

In his 1963 seminal world history text *The Rise of the West,* William McNeill argued that the two most significant events to occur between the years 1000 and 1500 were the emergence of the Turks and Mongols as major world powers and the rebirth of Europe as a significant participant in world events. This is not to downplay the importance of events in Africa and the Americas, as McNeill later acknowledged and as we discuss in Part 4. However, these two Eurasian themes were of vital importance in the construction of a global system of interaction in the first half of the second millennium, and they serve as useful themes for some of the broader issues discussed in this part.

A quick glance at Eurasia in the year 1000 would reveal societies with a wide array of social organizations and levels of technological sophistication. China, in the far eastern end of the continent, was thriving under the energetic Song Dynasty and its reformed educational system and bureaucracy. Under the Song, Chinese inventors and scholars quickly outpaced their counterparts in other regions of Eurasia, and China became a major trading power as great mercantile cities, such as Hangzhou, emerged in southern China. Not all was good for the Song, however, as they also suffered momentous setbacks, including the capture and loss of their capital city (Kaifeng) and much of the North with it to Ruzhen invaders in 1127. This invasion was but a sign of things to come; by the late thirteenth century the Mongols under Kublai Khan had toppled the Song completely and placed China under their control. Kublai Khan established the Yuan Dynasty and in so doing began a process by which the Mongols embraced Chinese tradition and customs while maintaining much of their central Asian heritage. China's influence also continued to extend beyond its borders during this period, especially in relation to neighbors like Korea and Japan. Yet this influence did not suffocate native culture and traditions. Japan, in particular, adapted many of the ideas and traits borrowed from the Chinese to a more militaristic lifestyle led by its samurai warriors. Finally, the Mongols opened China to influences from the outside world, especially other regions of their vast Empire. Muslims became influential in the Mongol court as merchants and functionaries, and Islam began to make headway in China and to gain converts. Concurrently, in 1295, a Franciscan friar set up the first Christian mission in China.

The Muslim world was also experiencing a period of expansion as well as cultural and scientific innovation in the eleventh century. Led by scholars working in cities like Baghdad, Damascus, and Córdova, Islam was at the height of its intellectual achievement as Muslim scholars made significant breakthroughs in medicine, mathematics, and philosophy. The highly favorable position of Muslim states astride some of the most important trade routes in Eurasia ensured Islam's continued pivotal, and at times dominant, role in trade. The expansion of Islam also continued apace, especially in India and Africa where new and numerous Muslim polities developed over the 500 years covered in Part 4. The Muslim founders of these new states brought with them all the apparatus of Islamic civilization including religion, the Arabic language, customs and traditions, and trade practices to regions that had little previous exposure to them. In so doing, Islam integrated (or in some cases, reintegrated) the geographic core of Eurasia with much of its periphery including western Europe, parts of Africa, and the Indian Ocean, which tremendously facilitated exchanges between these diverse cultures. Yet the favorable geographic location of Islamic states also made them logical targets for invasions. Over the first half of the second millennium, numerous foreign invaders including Turks from central Asia, Crusaders from western Europe, and Mongols from eastern Asia, invaded and conquered significant regions of the Muslim heartland. Some—like the Crusaders—created temporary states that Muslim military might eventually dislodged, while others—like the Turks—were assimilated, converted to Islam, and remain an integral part of the Muslim world to this day. One of the most remarkable of the latter cases were the Ottoman Turks, outsiders who not only embraced Islam and its traditions but also came to dominate the Muslim world; the Ottomans carved out an impressive empire for themselves in western Asia, the Mediterranean, North Africa, and Europe between the fourteenth and sixteenth centuries.

The Mongols were even more impressive than the Ottoman Turks in their ability to join far-flung regions into a substantial and viable empire. Beginning as a loose alliance of central Asian tribes, the Mongols were united under the leadership of the great Genghis Khan in the early thirteenth century. Genghis Khan's political and military skill as well as that of his successors guided the Mongols in their quest for Eurasian domination. Their vast empire included parts of eastern Europe, much of Russia and Ukraine, central Asia, large sections of the Muslim world and East Asia, and the bulk of China. It was truly a world empire. Under Mongol protection—sometimes dubbed the *Pax Mongolica* (Mongol Peace) by modern scholars—mercantile routes that had fallen into disuse returned to their former grandeur becoming pathways for people, trade, ideas, and disease. Journeys that began in western Europe and ended in central and East Asia—like those of William of Rubruck, Marco Polo, and later Ruy Gonzalez de Clavijo—became increasingly frequent thanks to Mongol caravan routes and mail posts. Travel from East Asia to western Europe, although less common, was not unheard of as evidenced by the journey of Rabban Mar Sauma, a Nestorian Christian born in Peking who visited Constantinople, Rome, and Paris in the late 1280s. Although the Mongols were critical in helping to connect many of the far-flung regions of Eurasia thereby increasing communication and exchanges, their destructive campaigns were also responsible for much ruin and disruption. Their sack of Baghdad in 1258, for example, wiped out the great libraries and schools housed in the city with their centuries of accumulated knowledge. Their expansion into southeast Asia into what is now Vietnam and Burma left cities devastated and ended the spread of Indian culture in the region. Consequently, the Mongols must be viewed in terms of their seemingly contradictory accomplishments: They had created the conditions that encouraged and facilitated extended contact and exchange between East and West, but they were also responsible for incredibly destructive campaigns in which millions are likely to have perished and centuries of human accomplishment wiped out.

The trade routes that the Mongols connected reached not only across Eurasia but also deep into Africa. Stretching across the Sahara desert (a sea of sand) and the Indian Ocean (a sea of water), Arab and Indian traders forged relationships with coastal African merchants and connected themselves to a burgeoning commercial network within the continent of Africa. In West Africa, the trans-Saharan trade helped stimulate empires like Mali and Songhay, which adopted Islam as a state religion. Most of Africa, however, was covered in very small states, sometimes linked to each other as confederation. Among these were the Swahili trading cities of the eastern coast, which flourished as middlemen for the Africa-to-Indian-Ocean trade.

Perhaps the chief beneficiaries of the increased communication and trade that was occurring in Eurasia after the eleventh century were the relatively small and weak kingdoms of western Europe. Compared to societies in other parts of Eurasia, western Europe—or Latin Christendom as it is often called—was a backward and poor region on the borders of the known world. In the early eleventh century, it was still recovering from the destruction of the classical world. Yet even in its backwardness, Europe was cultivating the building blocks of a renaissance. The hundreds of feudal principalities that dotted the western European landscape and the almost continuous warfare that existed served to create an elite military class that would spearhead European expansion in the Crusades and other colonial efforts. There was also an emerging merchant class characterized by its willingness to take risks and its reluctance to be tethered by restrictive regulations. Members of this merchant class in cities like Venice, Genoa, and Pisa in Italy and Ghent and Bruges in Flanders would be responsible for helping to reestablish the long-distance trade routes lost after the fall of Rome. Europeans also showed a tremendous willingness to embrace ideas, innovations, and technologies from their neighbors. The long military struggle with Islam, of which the Crusades were the most famous manifestation, did not deter European scholars from adopting and adapting Muslim knowledge in philosophy, agriculture, algebra, the sciences, and even chess. Europeans likewise took over inventions originating in China—like paper, gunpowder, and printing—and often improved upon them. In short, western Europe, even with its weaknesses, was ideally situated to benefit from its more advanced neighbors and rapidly catch up to them in terms of development. The Middle Ages witnessed the emergence of European nations as major, indeed leading, participants on the world stage.

Many of the advances made in the European Middle Ages were directly related to shipping, navigation, and cartography. And it was using these tools that in 1492 Christopher Columbus, a Genoese explorer in the service of the kings of Spain, crossed the Atlantic Ocean and established permanent contact between Eurasia and Africa and the Americas, joining the **Old World** and the **New World.** The world that awaited Columbus and those who followed him was distinctly different from the one he had left behind. Among the major political entities they encountered were the large, urban empires of the Aztecs and the Incas (Tawantinsuyu). These two empires were relatively recent creations as both the Incas and Aztecs had significantly expanded their territorial reach in the fifteenth century. They had also followed different paths to empire. The Incas were one of numerous Andean cultures fighting for domination; they would eventually emerge victorious over their neighbors and come to rule over much of what is now western South America including Peru, Ecuador, and southern Colombia. The Aztecs, for their part, were barbarian nomads from northern Mexico who made their way toward the much more culturally advanced valley of Mexico in the south. Beginning as allies and tributaries of stronger regional powers, the Aztecs in conjunction with their allies from Texcoco and Tlacopan—the Triple Alliance—eventually became the dominant power in central Mexico. They united many of the local warring city states under their control, forcing them to pay regular tribute in both goods and human sacrificial victims, which the Aztecs then offered up to their gods. Beyond these two large empires, much of the remaining population lived in independent villages or in confederations of allied communities led by elders.

In addition to the unfamiliar political realities they encountered in the New World, the Spaniards had to come to grips with cultures, religions, and traditions that were very different from their own. Christianity and Islam, the two religions with which a sixteenth-century European would have been most familiar, were unknown by the local populations. The same held true for technologies, crops, and animals that were common in Eurasia and North Africa like guns, sugar, and horses. In their place were indigenous knowledge systems that ranged from animistic worship of natural phenomena to complex, ritualistic polytheistic faiths, crops like maize and work animals like the llama, and stunningly beautiful cities decorated with lagoons and ceremonial pyramids that affirmed the vibrancy and development of these American societies. Perhaps most relevant to the newcomers was the wealth in gold and silver displayed everywhere they went. The unending search for precious metals that drove many greedy Europeans to American shores as well as the quest for new converts to Christianity that animated many of the pious ones ensured that the meetings between Europeans and the natives of the Americas would be anything but peaceful.

Part 4 Timeline

960–1279 C.E.	Song Dynasty rules China.
987	Prince Vladimir of Kiev begins his search for a monotheistic faith.
c. 950–1050	Viking voyages to North America.
1096–1291	Christian crusades in the Holy Land.
1127	The partition of China follows the Ruzhen invasions.
c. 1162–1227	Life of the great conqueror and ruler Genghis Khan.
c. 1230–1240	Sunjata Keita constructs the Mali Empire in the West African sahel.
1258	The sack of Baghdad by the Mongols.
1271–1296	Marco Polo (probably) travels in Asia.
1279–1368	Yuan (Mongol) Dynasty rules China.
1331–1353	The Black Death makes its way from China to the Middle East, North Africa, and western Europe.
1336–1405	Life of Tamerlane, who resurrects much of the Mongol Ilkhanate in central Asia.
1353	Ibn Battuta visits Mali.
c. 1380–1430	Construction of many of the most prominent independent Swahili-speaking city-states in western Africa.
1394–1460	Life of Henry the Navigator, who sponsors Portuguese exploration of the Atlantic Ocean and the coast of Africa.
1442–1444	Abd-er-Razzák travels in India.
1492	Columbus's first voyage to the Americas; last Muslim kingdom in Spain conquered by Christians.
1521	Overthrow of the Aztec Empire by Spanish Conquistadors.
1531	Overthrow of the Inca Empire by Spanish Conquistadors.

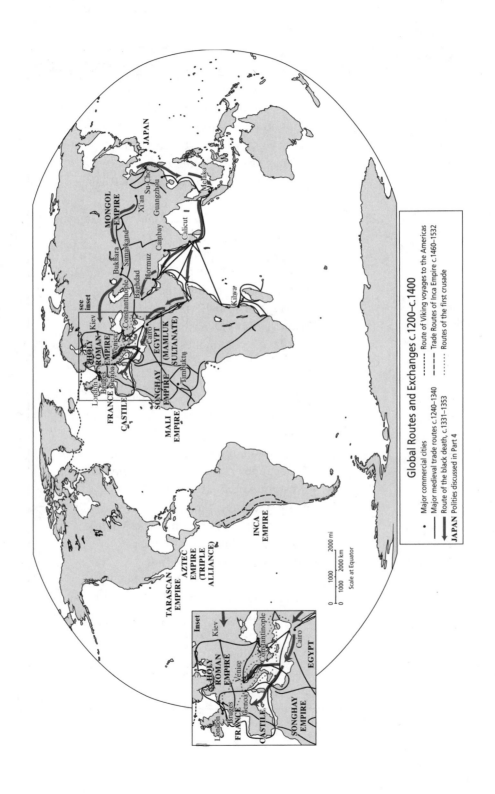

Global Routes and Exchanges c.1200–c.1400

JAPAN

MONGOL EMPIRE

Su-Cho
Xi'an
Guangzhou
Cambay
Calicut
Bukhara
Samarkand
Hormuz
Baghdad
Constantinople
Melaka

see inset

Kiev
Venice
HOLY ROMAN EMPIRE
Genoa
Cairo
London
Bruges
FRANCE
CASTILE
EGYPT (MAMLUK SULTANATE)
SONGHAY EMPIRE
Timbuktu
Kilwa
MALI EMPIRE

TARASCAN EMPIRE
AZTEC EMPIRE (TRIPLE ALLIANCE)
INCA EMPIRE

0   1000   2000 mi
0 1000 2000 km
Scale at Equator

- Major commercial cities
- - - - - Major medieval trade routes c.1240–1340
→ Route of the black death, c.1331–1353
JAPAN Polities discussed in Part 4

- - - - - Route of Viking voyages to the Americas
- - - - - Trade Routes of Inca Empire c.1460–1532
········· Routes of the first crusade

Inset

Kiev
HOLY ROMAN EMPIRE
Venice
Constantinople
London
Bruges
Genoa
FRANCE
CASTILE
SONGHAY EMPIRE
EGYPT
Cairo

Chapter 14

Global Trade Networks

Between the eleventh and the thirteenth centuries, the lands ruled over by Islamic Caliphs were the center of the world, at least of the economic world. The Middle East was the hub through which numerous trade routes crossed connecting China, eastern Asia, and the lands that bordered the Indian Ocean to Africa and Europe. Cities like Cairo, Alexandria, Baghdad, and the Byzantine city of Constantinople were **entrepôts** where merchants brought goods from all over the world to buy and to sell, to export local items to foreign lands, and to bring exotic goods back to their home regions. This central location and extensive trade produced great revenue for Muslim rulers. Thus it is not surprising that these rulers encouraged merchants to come to their lands with offers of wealth and protection, often in official edicts such as the one by the Egyptian sultan Qalawun, as recorded by al-Qalqashandi in the chapter's first selection.

The Middle East was more than just the economic center of Eurasia. It was also of primary importance as a religious center to Muslims, Christians, and Jews, all of whom hold the city of Jerusalem to be holy. In the eleventh century, the Muslims held Jerusalem, but European Christians coveted it. Europe had begun its dramatic transformation over the course of the eleventh century. Popes—the religious leaders of Latin Christianity—grew more powerful and influential; secular kingdoms became bigger, more centralized, and better organized; and the economy created more wealth and slowly began to diversify on the success of richer agricultural harvests and a highly profitable trade in cloth. Europe was on the verge of a remarkable period of expansion and development. The first outward manifestation of this European upsurge were the **Crusades,** a series of holy wars waged by European knights at the behest of the Church against Muslims in an effort to control Jerusalem. Although the Crusades were wars of conquests, they had several other consequences for Europeans and Muslims alike. For one, as Janet Abu-Lughod explains, the Crusades were critical in connecting—or more accurately, reconnecting—Europe to the wider Eurasian trade routes that passed through the Middle East. Likewise, under the banner of the Crusades, Europe also began to expand not only with its enclaves in the Middle East, but also with far more successful conquests and settlements in Spain, eastern Europe, the Baltic Region, and the Balkans. Finally, as discussed in Chapter 16, the Crusades not only encouraged trade in goods, but also trade in ideas and served as a conduit for knowledge from the Middle East, Africa, and Asia to flow freely into Europe.

The **trade networks** that crisscrossed the Middle East radiated both locally and intercontinentally. On a local level were the markets of East Africa. These markets illustrate some of the processes that we have presented in this text. Many of the local merchants were converts to Islam and writers of Arabic, inheriting and adapting these innovations to their own needs as they diffused from their place of origin in the Arabian Peninsula in the waning centuries of the first millennium. But they were also closely tied to older mercantile traditions and trade zones in eastern Africa and its interior. As such, these merchants and their markets served to connect their home regions with the wider Islamic world and beyond. As the reading by Chapurukha Kusimba makes clear, East African merchants of the thirteenth and fourteenth centuries were dealing in goods from as close as Mogadishu and as far away as China, undoubtedly benefiting from the wide reach of Middle East–centered trade networks.

European cities like Genoa and Venice also benefited from and contributed to these Eurasian and African trade routes. Italian merchants, and those from other Mediterranean cities, established numerous merchant colonies throughout cities in the Middle East, Anatolia, and even the Black Sea. It was from these advance positions that merchant travelers like Marco Polo launched themselves into the interior of Asia along roads and cities that were now part of the Mongol Empire. When Marco Polo reached Khan-Balik, the capital of the Mongol Emperor Kublai Khan, he was astounded by its splendor, grandeur, and curiosities including paper money. He also described the numerous hostels reserved for merchants from diverse parts who gathered in the city, illuminating for his European readers the cosmopolitan nature of Asian cities. His description is not unique, as those given by the Korean traveler Ch'oe Pu and the Muslim ambassador Abd-Er-Razzák confirm the international flavor of medieval Asian cities. They were places where people came to trade goods, to make fortunes, and to exchange ideas.

A similar network of trade routes existed in the Americas. Although their scope was smaller, the types of goods traded was different, and the nature of mercantile relations diverged from those found in Eurasia and Africa, these trade routes similarly served to connect the different societies of the Americas and served as conduits for goods, peoples, and ideas. However, trade in the Americas encountered different problems than those found in Eurasia. The absence of wheeled vehicles and large pack animals like horses, camels, and donkeys limited the movement of goods in both quantity and distance. A professional merchant class similar to that found in China, the Muslim world, and Europe seems not to have developed in the Americas. Finally, there was significant, perhaps even stifling, state control over the trade of goods, especially by the massive empires of the Aztecs and the Incas. In these and other states luxury, or prestige, goods were controlled and distributed by local rulers for political purposes, as described by historian David Drew or demanded as tribute as shown by the Aztec tribute roll in Reading 111. This was a pattern that seems to have extended all over the Americas from the Mississippian chiefdoms of North America all the way south to the territories of the Incas in Peru.

The Islamic World as the Hub of Eurasian Trade

Due to its central geographic location, the Islamic world sat astride the major trade routes that linked East to West and Eurasia to Africa. Benefiting from their central locations, Muslim cities such as Baghdad and Damascus had long played an important role in Eurasian trade. By the late thirteenth century, after the destruction of Baghdad by the Mongols in 1258, the Egyptian city of Cairo assumed the mantle of leading Muslim commercial center. Cairo, which was connected to the European trade market through Venetian traders, also had easy access to the Indian Ocean via the Red Sea and beyond it to the great markets of India and China. In this selection from the Subh al-a 'shā, *an encyclopedia compiled in the early fifteenth century by the Egyptian writer al-Qalqashandī, the Egyptian Sultan al-Manṣūr Qalawun (r. 1280–1290) invites merchants from Iraq, Persia, Asia Minor, the Arabian Peninsula, India, and China to come to trade in Egypt. He promised them that they would find everything they could want as well as justice and protection.*

>> 104. Subh al-a 'shā

AL-QALQASHANDĪ [EARLY FIFTEENTH CENTURY C.E.]

A decree has been issued, may God exalt the Sultan's exalted command, and may his [the Sultan's] justice keep the subjects in assured protection. He requests the prayers of the people of both east and west for his thriving reign, and let all of them be sincere. He offers a genuine welcome to those who come to his realm, as to the garden of Eden, by whatever gate they may choose to enter, from Iraq, from Persia, from Asia Minor, from the Hijāz, from India, and from China. Whoever wishes to set forth—the distinguished merchants, the men of great affairs, and the small traders, from the countries enumerated and also those which have not been enumerated—and whoever wishes to enter our realms may sojourn or travel at will and to come to our country of broad lands and leafy shades, then let him, like those whom God has destined for this,

make firm resolve on this worthy and beneficial act, and let him come to a country whose inhabitants have no need either of supplies or reserves of food, for it is an earthly paradise for those who dwell in it, and a consolation for those who are far from their own homes, a delight of which the eye does not weary, a place from which one is never driven by excessive cold, for one lives there in perpetual spring and permanent well-being. It is enough to say that one of its descriptions is that it is God's beauty spot on His earth. God's blessing accrues in the baggage of whoever does a good deed by lending or receives a good deed by borrowing. Another of its features is that anyone who comes there hoping for anything, gets what he wants, for it is a land of Islam, with armies whose swords are beyond reproach. For justice has made its lands prosper and has multiplied its inhabitants. The buildings have increased so that it is a land of great cities. The needy is at ease there, and does not fear the violence of the creditors, for demands there are not exacting and

Source: al-Qalqashandī, *Subh al-a 'shā*, in "An Invitation to Merchants (ca. 1280–1290)," in *Islam: From the Prophet Muhammad to the Capture of Constantinople*, vol. 2, edited and translated by Bernard Lewis (New York: Harper Torchbooks, 1974), 166–168.

deferments easily obtained. The rest of the people and all the merchants have no fear there of any oppression, for justice protects.

Whoever becomes aware of this our decree, among the merchants who live in Yemen and India and China and Sind and elsewhere, let them prepare to travel and come to our country, where they will find the reality better than the word and will see a beneficence beyond the mere fulfillment of their promises and will sojourn in "a fair land under a forgiving Lord" [Qur'ān, xxxv, 15] and in comfort deserving of gratitude (for only the grateful is rewarded) and in security of person and property, and felicity which illuminates their circumstances and fulfills their hopes. They will receive from us all the justice that they expect. Our justice responds to those who call on it, has procedures which will be praised by their way of life, will leave their property to their descendants, and will protect and preserve them so that they will take shelter under its shadow and be protected. Whoever brings merchandise with him, such as spices and other articles imported by the Kārimī[1] merchants, will suffer no unjust impost nor be subjected to any burdensome demand, for [our] justice will leave with them what is desirable and remove what is burdensome. If anyone brings [white] male slaves [mamlūk] or slave-girls, he will find their sale price beyond his expectations and [will be accorded] the tolerance in fixing a profitable price which is customarily accorded to those who import such slaves from near and all the more

from distant lands; for our desire is directed toward the increase of our troops, and those who import mamlūks have gained a title to our generosity. Let whoever can do so increase his import of mamlūks, and let him know that the purpose in demanding them is to increase the armies of Islam. For thanks to them, Islam today is in glory with flag unfurled and the Sultan al-Manṣūr [Qalawun]. The mamlūk who is thus imported is removed from darkness to light. Yesterday he was blamed for unbelief; today he is praised for faith and fights for Islam against his own tribe and people.

This is our decree for all traveling merchants to whose knowledge it comes, 'They seek the bounty of God, while others fight in the cause of God.' [Qur'ān, lxxiii, 20] Let them read in it the orders which will ease their task; let them be guided by its star, nourished by its wisdom. Let them mount the neck of the hope which impels them to leave their homes and stretch out their hands in prayer for him who wishes people to come to his country, so that they may benefit from his generosity in all clarity and in all beneficence; and let them take advantage of the occasions for profit, for they are ripe for picking. These true promises are sent to them to confirm their high hopes and reaffirm to them that the noble rescript is valid, by the command of God, in accordance with what the pens have written, and [God is] the best Guarantor.

Al-Qalqashandī, *Ṣubḥ al-aʿshā*, xiii, pp. 339–342.

Rebuilding Europe: The Origins of Its Hegemony

One of the most significant developments that took place in the early centuries of the second millennium was the recovery of the European economy and the reintegration of Europe into the larger Eurasian and African worlds. The ninth and tenth centuries had been difficult for Europe as it once again became the target of invasions, this time

---

[1] An association of merchants in Egypt and Arabia, engaged in the eastern trade.

by Vikings from the north, Magyars from the east, and Muslims from the south. These invasions shattered the fragile empire left behind by Charlemagne (d. 814) into scores of small feudal polities whose main purpose was to survive. Yet by the eleventh century, a revival was becoming evident as an agricultural recovery swept through Europe, fueling an economic revival and a population explosion. Moreover, having beaten off or absorbed its invaders, Europe entered a phase of expansion and colonization of which the Crusades (1096–1291) to the Holy Land were the most famous, but far from unique, example. In the following selection, historian and sociologist Janet Abu-Lughod highlights the connection between the Crusades, trade, and Europe's reintegration into the world system. It should be noted, however, that Europe was not only on the receiving end of goods coming from other markets in Eurasia and Africa but that, in fact, Europe was also a significant supplier of certain items such as cloth, silver, and armaments that were highly prized by its neighbors.

>> 105. Before European Hegemony: The World System A.D. 1250–1350

JANET ABU-LUGHOD [1989]

Between the beginning of the twelfth century and the end of the thirteenth—signaled by the recapture of Palestine from the Crusader kingdoms, an event referred to by European historians as the "fall" of Acre in 1291—there was intense if mostly violent contact between western Europe and the countries bordering the eastern and southern shores of the Mediterranean. Crusade followed crusade, solidifying the competitive alliance between northern and southern Europe and, most importantly for our purposes, establishing regular trading channels that connected northern Europe, through the Italian intermediaries, to the preexisting circuits of commerce that joined the Middle East with India and China.

Thus, although the Crusades eventually failed, they had a significant consequence. They were the mechanism that reintegrated northwestern Europe into a world system from which she had become detached after the "fall of Rome." It is no wonder that the thirteenth century should have been such a time of efflorescence on the continent. Not only were her horizons expanded; so were her resources.

Much has been made of the new "tastes" that were whetted in Europe by her contacts with the East. Spices, silk cloth and brocades, damascene blades, porcelain, and a variety of luxury goods previously undreamed of made a rich prize for the Crusaders. The Crusades may have been initiated by a desire to capture souls, but they were sustained, in part, by the capture of booty. When conquest failed, however, purchases were necessary. At first, Europe had little to offer in this exchange, except for slaves, precious metals (primarily silver), and wood and furs (the former a scarce resource in a land area with extensive deserts, the latter unobtainable but scarcely "needed" in hot climes). But it appears that the need for items to sell in eastern markets stimulated European production, particularly of the fine woolen cloth made from the fleece of sheep that grazed on its plains and plateaus.

Source: Janet L. Abu-Lughod, *Before European Hegemony: The World System A.D. 1250–1350* (New York: Oxford University Press, 1989), 46–49.

The renaissance of agriculture, mining, and finally manufacturing in northwestern Europe during the twelfth and thirteenth centuries must be attributed at least in part to the expansion of its horizons and to the heightened opportunities for trade generated by the Crusades. This was a time of rapid urbanization throughout the continent, both in Flanders and France—which had access to the western Mediterranean basin through Marseille, Aigues-Morte, Montpellier, and particularly, its chief seaport, Genoa—and in the central section served by the Rhine, which allowed a connection from the North Sea all the way to Venice, its chief outlet to the Mediterranean [...]. Although originally such trade was conducted at "Fairs" held periodically at first and then continuously in towns designed to host merchants from a variety of directions, eventually the heightened industrialization, stimulated by a rapid population increase and the growing demands of the eastern trade, led to the growth of true trading emporia with outlets to the sea, of which Bruges was a chief example.

Connections with the East through Constantinople were maintained throughout the Middle Ages, but this gave access only to the northern overland route to China, which was neither secure (it was traditionally a battleground for seminomadic tribes in a war of all against all) nor cheap, since travel by land was always more expensive than by sea. Not until the area was "unified" in the early days of the Mongols under the "world conqueror," Genghis Khan (d. August 18, 1227), did it become feasible for Europeans to traverse this long and treacherous route.

Eastern Africa, the Indian Ocean, and Beyond

The great trade networks that extended from the Muslim world like so many spokes on a wheel also reached into East African kingdoms such as Great Zimbabwe and many smaller confederations of the African interior. As anthropologist Chapurukha Kusimba explains in the following selection, these African kingdoms exchanged products and wares with Egypt, the Arabian Peninsula, India, Southeast Asia, and China. Cities on the eastern African coast played a critical role as intermediaries, and it was here where African goods brought from the interior by human caravans were bartered for foreign items. As in other parts of the Eurasian trade networks, Islam played a critical role. The conversion of East African merchants to Islam incorporated them into the wider world of Muslim commerce, giving them protections and benefits they would not have had otherwise. However, these merchants did not adopt the Islamic faith wholesale. Instead, they built a distinctive way of living that incorporated local environmental factors, East African culture and worldviews, and Islamic lifestyles. The unique urban society they built was exemplified by the shared KiSwahili language, which is structurally rooted in eastern African languages but uses many Arabic terms and is generally written using Arabic script. The development of the Swahili cities is merely one example of how Islam and trade went hand in hand, each helping with the diffusion of the other and enveloping large areas of Africa and western Asia in complex networks of religious, cultural, and economic exchange.

>> 106. The Rise and Fall of Swahili States

CHAPURUKHA M. KUSIMBA [1999]

East Africa's growing prosperity increased the market for *exotica* both from the African interior and from around the Indian Ocean: Islamic *sgraffiato* pottery, Chinese wares, jars from Annan or Cambodia, and minerals from Madagascar and Zimbabwe were imported for use in the homes of Coastal peoples. Although the proportion of imported wares to local ones remained the same, the volume and distribution of imported ones increased. New luxury items were imported in fairly regular quantities. Appearance and body care gained new significance as reflected in the addition of bronze mirrors, kohl sticks, and glass and rock crystal beads to the women's wardrobe. Both elite and non-elite women wore elaborate ornaments including gold, silver, and bronze bracelets and rings. Large quantities of Indian beads and Egyptian and Siraf glass were imported, as well as sprinkler bottles and bowls in green, white, smoky, and cobalt glass [...].

The many spindle whorls at Kilwa, Pate, and Mogadishu demonstrate growth of weaving and textile industries. The shift to a cash-based economy was signaled by the minting of copper and silver coins at Kilwa, Manda, and Shanga beginning in the twelfth century, unifying the system of exchange, while extending and exerting political control beyond the town's boundaries. Although each city made its own coins, many coins were used everywhere [...].

The Coastal cities reached their zenith in the thirteenth century. Settlements that had begun as modest fishing or farming hamlets gradually developed into towns and cities closely connected to Indian Ocean commerce. The volume of imported pottery testifies to the impressive volume of fifteenth-century trade through East African ports [...]. Major trading partners continued to be Egypt, Yemen, and the Indian sub-continent. Textiles, beads, ceramics, and pottery ranked high among the imports. Timber, ivory, cereals, furniture, and iron were among the principle exports [...].

Chinese Longquan, Tongan, and Ying Ch'ing were the most popular fifteenth-century imports [...]. The volume of goods from China declined in the early fifteenth century. Late in the century, though, the internal disruptions in China ceased sufficiently to allow China to begin exporting the popular Blue-on-White bowls. By the end of the century, the Chinese Blue-on-White porcelain market regained its popularity in the Indian Ocean as well [...]. In the midst of this market unrest, the Persian Gulf trade was rejuvenated filling in the void. There was an attempt to duplicate Chinese motifs as Muslim potters, desiring to participate in lucrative East African markets, made Chinese imitations to appeal to East African tastes. The Islamic pottery varied greatly in quality, but so too did the reintroduced ceramics from China, though it is also possible that some putatively Chinese pottery was actually made in Thai and Vietnamese kilns [...].

Marco Polo and the Post System in the Mongol Empire

The Muslim world, sub-Saharan Africa, and Europe traded extensively with China and other parts of Asia. By the thirteenth century, the sprawling Mongol Empire of Genghis Khan and his successors dominated much of eastern and central Eurasia, linking vast

Source: Chapurukha M. Kusimba, *The Rise and Fall of Swahili States* (Walnut Creek, CA: Altamira Press, 1999), 130–131.

regions with roads and protecting these regions by the Mongol Peace. It was to this Mongol Empire that the Venetian merchant Marco Polo traveled in 1271 with his father and his uncle (some scholars question the veracity of his narrative). While there, Marco Polo became a favorite of Kublai Khan (Genghis's grandson) and traveled widely through the Mongol Empire. In 1295, after over two decades abroad, he returned to Venice. In 1298, he was captured in a Venetian-Genoese war and spent the better part of a year as a Genoese captive. While in prison he befriended Rusticello de Pisa, a writer of Romances, and the two collaborated in writing the memoirs of Marco Polo's travels in the east. Their effort was entitled "The Description of the World" in French, but is better known as The Travels of Marco Polo, *its English title. Among the many innovations that Marco Polo encountered in China was the highly efficient Mongol post system, which allowed the Khans to exert control over their vast domains. The post system allowed the Mongols to send and receive information and goods quickly over vast distances. Moreover, networks such as this one were critical in linking the far-flung regions of the Mongol Empire together and accelerated exchanges between East and West.*

>> 107. The Travels of Marco Polo

MARCO POLO AND RUSTICELLO DE PISA
[1298–1299 C.E.]

You must know that the city of Khan-balik is a centre from which many roads radiate to many provinces, one to each, and every road bears the name of the province to which it runs. The whole system is admirably contrived. When one of the Great Khan's messengers sets out along any of these roads, he has only to go twenty-five miles and there he finds a posting station, which in their language is called *yamb* and in our language may be rendered 'horse post'. At every post the messengers find a spacious and palatial hostelry for their lodging. These hostelries have splendid beds with rich coverlets of silk and all that befits an emissary of high rank. If a king came here, he would be well lodged. Here the messengers find no less than 400 horses, stationed here by the Great Khan's orders and always kept in readiness for his messengers when they are sent on any mission. And you must understand that posts such as these, at distances of twenty-five or thirty miles, are to be found along all the main highways leading to the provinces of which I have spoken [...].

When the messengers are travelling through out-of-the-way country, where there are no homesteads or habitations, they find that the Great Khan has had posts established even in these wilds, with the same palatial accommodation and the same supply of horses and accoutrements. But here the stages are longer; for the posts are thirty-five miles apart and in some cases over forty miles.

By this means the Great Khan's messengers travel throughout his dominions and have lodgings and horses fully accoutred for every stage. And this is surely the highest privilege and the greatest resource ever enjoyed by any man on earth, king or emperor or what you will. For you may be well assured that more than 200,000 horses are stabled at these posts for the special use of these messengers. Moreover, the posts themselves number more than 10,000, all furnished on the same lavish scale. The whole organization is so stupendous and so costly that it baffles speech and writing [...].

Source: Marco Polo and Rusticello de Pisa, *The Travels of Marco Polo*, translated by Ronald Latham (London: Penguin Books, 1958), 150–153.

Now let me tell you another thing which I forgot to mention—one that is very germane to the matter in hand. The fact is that between one post and the next, at distances of three miles apart, there are stations which may contain as many as forty buildings occupied by unmounted couriers, who also play a part in the Great Khan's postal service. I will tell you how. They wear large belts, set all round with bells, so that when they run they are audible at a great distance. They always run at full speed and never for more than three miles. And at the next station three miles away, where the noise they make gives due notice of their approach, another courier is waiting in readiness. As soon as the first man arrives, the new one takes what he is carrying and also a little note given to him by the clerk, and starts to run. After he has run for three miles, the performance is repeated. And I can assure you that by means of this service of unmounted couriers, the Great Khan receives news over a ten days' journey in a day and a night. For it takes these runners no more than a day and a night to cover a ten days' journey, or two days and two nights for a twenty days' journey. So in ten days they can transmit news over a journey of a hundred days. And in the fruit season it often happens that by this means fruit gathered in the morning in the city of Khan-balik is delivered on the evening of the next day to the Great Khan in the city of Shang-tu, ten days' journey away.

Markets in China and India

The Travels of Marco Polo offers some rich descriptions of eastern market cities including the ten bustling markets of Kinsai (modern Hangzhou). But Marco Polo was not the only foreign traveler to be captivated by markets in Asia. In the first selection here, the Korean traveler/prisoner Ch'oe Pu describes the markets of the city of Su-chou [Suzhou] and the gathering of merchants from nearby regions. Ch'oe Pu was a Korean official whose ship drifted off course into China in 1487. He was captured and taken under escort through much of eastern China. On his release in 1488, he wrote down the story of his travels. The second selection was written by Abd-Er-Razzák, a Muslim ambassador traveling through India between 1442–1444. On arriving in the city of Calicut (in southwest India), Abd-Er-Razzák was struck by the security and vigor of its harbor and markets. This positive description is quite telling as he was not very impressed with Calicut as a whole—he calls it a "disagreeable place" in a later passage—and the affirmative portrayal of the harbor and markets only hints at their vitality and importance.

>> 108. Diary: A Record of Drifting Across the Sea

Cʜ'ᴏᴇ Pᴜ [1488 CE]

XXX In olden times, Su-chou [Suzhou] was called Wu-k'uai [Wukuai]. It borders the sea in the east, commands three large rivers and five lakes, and has a thousand *li* of rich fields.

Learned men and gentry abound there; and all the treasures of the land and sea, such as thin silks, gauzes, gold, silver, jewels, crafts, arts, and rich and great merchants, are there. It has been accepted in China from olden times that the land south of the Yangtze [Yangzi] River is the beautiful and good land and that within that land Su-chou [Suzhou] and Hang-chou [Han Zhou]

Source: *Ch'oe Pu's Diary: A Record of Drifting Across the Sea,* edited and translated by John Meskill (Tucson: University of Arizona Press, 1965), 93–4.

are the first departments, especially Su-chou [Suzhou]. Yüeh [Yue] Bridge is inside the wall and separates Wu and Chang-chou [Zhangzhou] counties. Market quarters are scattered like stars. Many rivers and lakes flow through [the region], refreshing and purifying it. The people live luxuriously. There are solid rows of towers and stands, and in such places as the space between Ch'ang-men [Changmen] and Ma-t'ou [Matou] [the wharves?], merchantmen and junks from Honan [Henan], Hopei [Hebei], and Fukien [Fujian] gather like clouds. The lakes and mountains are fresh and stimulating, the scenic splendors innumerable.

>> 109. Narrative of the Voyage

ABD-ER-RAZZÁK [1442–1444 C.E.]

Calicut is a perfectly secure harbour, which, like that of Ormuz, brings together merchants from every city and from every country; in it are to be found abundance of precious articles brought thither from maritime countries, and especially from Abyssinia, Zirbad, and Zanguebar; from time to time ships arrive there from the shores of the House of God and other parts of the Hedjaz, and abide at will, for a greater or longer space, in this harbour; the town is inhabited by Infidels, and situated on a hostile shore. It contains a considerable number of Mussulmauns, who are constant residents, and have built two mosques, in which they meet every Friday to offer up prayer. They have one Kadi, a priest, and for the most part they belong to the sect of Schafei. Security and justice are so firmly established in this city, that the most wealthy merchants bring thither from maritime countries considerable cargoes, which they unload, and unhesitatingly send into the markets and the bazaars, without thinking in the meantime of any necessity of checking the account or of keeping watch over the goods. The officers of the custom-house take upon themselves the charge of looking after the merchandise, over which they keep watch day and night. When a sale is effected, they levy a duty on the goods of one-fortieth part; if they are not sold, they make no charge on them whatsoever.

In other ports a strange practice is adopted. When a vessel sets sail for a certain point, and suddenly is driven by a decree of Divine Providence into another roadstead, the inhabitants, under the pretext that the wind has driven it there, plunder the ship. But at Calicut, every ship, whatever place it may come from, or wherever it may be bound, when it puts into this port is treated like other vessels, and has no trouble of any kind to put up with.

Tribute and Gift Exchange in the Americas

The people of the Americas also exchanged goods, ideas, and cultural elements using trade networks, although these appear to have been less developed than those found in Eurasia and Africa. To supplement the limited trade networks, there were other systems of exchange that played critical roles not only in the transfer of goods from one

Source: Abd-Er-Razzák, "Narrative of the Voyage," in *India in the Fifteenth Century: Being a Collection of Narrative Voyages to India in the Century Preceding the Portuguese Discovery of the Cape of Good Hope*, edited by R. H. Major (New York: Burt Franklin Publisher, 1970 repr.), 13–14.

area to another, but also as forms of political power. The following selection by historian David Drew captures some of the complexities of trade among the Maya in the highlands of Central America and southern Mexico. Drew highlights not only the goods that were being traded, but also the role of certain high-prestige items in the Mayan political system in which gift giving helped to accentuate and strengthen political alliances. The second selection, Records of Tribute Received by the Aztec Capital, shows the Tribute Roll of Emperor Moctezuma, which comes from the Aztec empire in Mexico from the period just before the Spanish conquest of 1520–1521. Here we see **tribute** *paid by defeated peoples to the Aztecs as a system of exchange, and its associated political implications. The Tribute Roll is an impressive tally of goods owed to the Aztec emperor by fourteen conquered cities and towns. When the Aztecs went to war, their primary goal was to compel their enemies to pay them tribute and to secure future victims for their sacrifices, not to conquer them. The tribute system was both a cheaper and more efficient way of controlling and administering their empire than direct rule, and tribute systems are found historically in many parts of the world. In Mesoamerica, however, the tribute system would eventually help to undermine the Aztecs: many of the tributary towns, tired of paying the high levies, formed alliances with the incoming Spanish conquistadors to overthrow this oppressive system. In spite of this, the Tribute Roll is an excellent example of Aztec power and of the complex exchange network that existed in pre-conquest Mexico.*

>> 110. The Lost Chronicles of the Maya Kings

DAVID DREW [1999]

Contrasting environments also meant diverse natural resources or finished products that were exchanged for those from other regions. Trade networks, local and long-distance, in utilitarian and luxury items, ranged across the Maya world from Preclassic times. From highlands to lowlands, for example, went grinding stones of granite or volcanic lava and obsidian, much sought after for spear-points, knives and blades for a multiplicity of craft and ritual uses. In return traveled lowland products such as feathers, beeswax, cotton and animal skins. Salt, a dietary necessity, was a particular speciality of the northern Yucatán, where it was produced in pans along the coast. Cacao, or chocolate, made into the frothy, ancestor of the modern mug of cocoa and the high-status drink of the aristocracy, was an extremely sought-after trade item which only grew in regions of high rainfall such as the lower slopes above the Pacific and around the Gulf of Honduras.

Maya kings themselves controlled the acquisition and use of particularly precious commodities such as jade, only to be found in the Motagua valley of eastern Guatemala, and the tail-feathers of the resplendent quetzal bird, whose habitat was the remote cloud forests of the transitional zone between mountains and jungle. The status and authority of Maya rulers was expressed by the personal use of such rare

Source: David Drew, *The Lost Chronicles of the Maya Kings* (Berkeley, University of California Press, 1999), 8–9.

materials. Each had a particular symbolic value, decorating and accompanying the lord in life and going with him to his grave. The gift-giving of rare jades and finished objects such as finely painted pottery to retainers and subordinates was another token of the ruler's power, and the wider circulation of these objects helped to cement political relationships between kingdoms.

>> 111. Records of Tribute Received by the Aztec Capital, 1502–1520

[c. 1502–1520 C.E.]

Tribute varied from province to province according to the natural resources and artisan traditions of each. But overall it fell into the four main categories mentioned by Castillo [...] and in the Aztec Priests' Speech [...]; they are all represented on this page. Reading from top left, we have first the category mantle (*tilmatli*). This is the woven blanket-cape with knotted ends, worn by the ruling class, which was of various thickness (shown by fingers) and could be quilted, striped, ornate or plain; the third mantle here has a Tlaloc-mask device. The mantle design also served as a glyph for clothing in general: the fourth mantle has a *huipil*-blouse drawn in it (loin-cloths were also itemized in this way). In the second category are the luxurious feather and gold Eagle and Jaguar outfits of the warriors; of the Eagle type, fashioned with small feathers, 20 are required. The shields denote rank. Third comes the Flower of plant life and its derivatives: bushels of white maize and black beans (each with its flour/flower), purslane and sage (*chia* and *guauhtli*), all being staple foods; 400 baskets of refined, and 8,000 buds of unrefined copal; 200 jars of honey. Items in the miscellaneous fourth category are read back up the page to the right: 5 jade necklaces, 1,200 wooden bowls, and 100 axe-heads made from copper (*teputzli*) mined in the region.

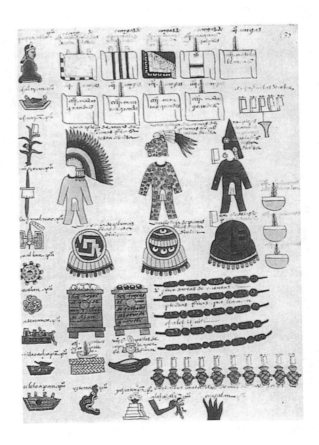

Source: "Records of Tribute Received by the Aztec Capital, 1502–1520" in *Image of the New World: The American Continent Portrayed in Native Texts,* edited by Gordon Brotherston (London: Thames and Hudson, 1979), 234–236.

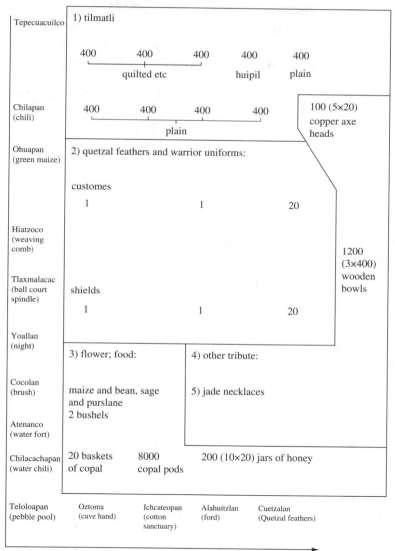

Tepecuacuilco — 1) tilmatli

400	400	400	400	400
	quilted etc		huipil	plain

Chilapan (chili)

400	400	400	400
	plain		

100 (5×20) copper axe heads

Ohuapan (green maize) — 2) quetzal feathers and warrior uniforms:

customes

| 1 | 1 | 20 |

Hiatzoco (weaving comb)

1200 (3×400) wooden bowls

Tlaxmalacac (ball court spindle) — shields

| 1 | 1 | 20 |

Yoallan (night)

Cocolan (brush) — 3) flower; food:

maize and bean, sage and purslane 2 bushels

Atenanco (water fort)

4) other tribute:

5) jade necklaces

Chilacachapan (water chili)

20 baskets of copal   8000 copal pods   200 (10×20) jars of honey

Teloloapan (pebble pool)   Oztoma (cave hand)   Ichcateopan (cotton sanctuary)   Alahuitzlan (ford)   Cuetzalan (Quetzal feathers)

(conventional place – names endings – co – (t)lan – pan are not translated)

>> Mastering the Material

1. Consider the location of Islamic states in Europe, Asia, and Africa in the thirteenth through fifteenth centuries. What do you think were the advantages and disadvantages of their geographic positions in terms of commerce and defense?

2. We often think of the Mongols as "barbarians" and "destroyers," which is how their enemies often depicted them. However, under their rule marketplaces and long-distance trade flourished. Does this suggest we should view them a different way, and if so how?

3. In a tribute system, outlaying regions pay an annual or monthly tribute to central authorities or more powerful states in the form of goods they produce, but are largely left to rule themselves otherwise. What do you think are the advantages of this system from the perspective of the central authorities? What were the disadvantages?

Chapter 15

Exploration and Conquest

Being on the borders of the known world in the eleventh century made Europe peripheral to many of the events occurring in the core of Eurasia, but there were also some distinct advantages to living at the edge. For one, its distance from the Mongol heartland meant that Europe was spared the worst of the Mongol invasions. The brunt of their rule instead was borne by regions like China, which endured almost a century of Mongol occupation, and Mesopotamia, which suffered through atrocities like the sacking of Baghdad. Nor did Europe later have to endure the campaigns of conquest of Temür the Lame, a successor to the Mongols. Likewise, because of its geographic position on the periphery, Europe had extensive coastlines and access to the sea as well as a distinguished naval history dating back to antiquity. Over the last half of the first millennium, Europeans continually improved their maritime capabilities as the Venetians, Genoese, Catalans, Irish, and English (among others) took to the seas in numbers to trade, conquer, and explore. Perhaps no European people mastered the seas with as much skill and ferocity as the Scandinavians. Originating in modern Sweden, Norway, and Denmark, in regions where the only habitable areas were on the coasts—the interior of most of Scandinavia is either too cold or too mountainous to be suitable for agriculture—the Scandinavians relied extensively on the sea for food, communication, trade, and booty taken in raids. It was due to their plundering raids that Scandinavian seamen acquired their less savory moniker: Vikings. The combination of geography, naval skills, and daring made Vikings ideal explorers. Between the eighth and eleventh century, their travels took them all over western Eurasia, into the Atlantic Ocean, and beyond. In Constantinople, a group of Vikings served as bodyguards to the Byzantine emperor. In Russia, they established a Viking kingdom known as the Kievan Rus, actively trading with the Slavs and other inhabitants of the region. And in the North Atlantic they savagely raided the coasts of western Europe, but also explored and discovered many of the major islands of the North Sea and eventually the northeast coast of North America (an expedition described in Reading 112), arriving in the New World some 500 years before Columbus. Like the Mongols, although to a lesser extent, the Vikings helped to connect regions that had hitherto lacked any significant links.

The Vikings were among the last outside invaders to score any major military successes against Christian Europe in the Middle Ages. After the Viking invasions, Europe became stronger, better organized, and expansionistic. This colonizing spirit was evident in the Crusades to the Middle East, but also in concurrent crusading offensives against the non-Christian people of eastern Europe and the Baltic region and the

Muslims in Spain, a crusading venture better known as the **Reconquista.** The Crusades and similar holy wars were driven by greed, pugnacity, and zealous piety and were inspired by preaching such as the sermon given by Pope Urban II at Clermont, which served to launch the First Crusade against the Holy Land. The Crusades were initially successful, but in the end were military failures; by 1291 the Muslims had recaptured Acre, the last Christian stronghold in the Holy Land, effectively ending the Crusades. However, while these defeats ended the Crusades themselves, the spirit that animated them had not abated. This was true especially in Spain where Christian kings continued their slow but successful efforts to once again place the entire Iberian Peninsula under Christian control and conclude the Reconquista.

One of the consequences of the Reconquista was the creation of the kingdom of Portugal. Pressed against the ocean by Castile (its powerful neighbor to the east), by the fourteenth century the Portuguese turned to the sea as they sought to expand and enrich their small and poor kingdom. Lured by the prospects of African gold, the possibility of expanding the Reconquista to western North Africa, and the chance of finding a route to the East that did not pass through the Muslim world, Portuguese sea captains and adventurers gradually ventured farther and farther away from Europe into the Atlantic and to the coast of West Africa. By 1450, they had settled numerous islands in the Atlantic including Madeira and the Azores. In 1497, Vasco de Gama was able to sail past the Cape of Good Hope in the tip of southern Africa and on to India. At each step, the Portuguese also established a series of forts on the African coast. From these forts they traded for the precious gold and for slaves. Their arrival in West Africa coincided with a long period of warfare in the region that produced a stream of captives, which the Portuguese bought as slaves that they then shipped off to Europe, the newly settled Atlantic islands, or the New World. It is still debated to what degree these wars were caused by a struggle for domination, and to what degree they were produced by the burgeoning demand for slaves. In the context of this expansion of warfare, states such as Songhay struggled for supremacy, partly to avoid becoming victims themselves as described by Roland Oliver & Anthony Atmore in Reading 115.

When these slaves arrived in the New World in the sixteenth century, they found a world increasingly dominated by Europeans despite ongoing resistance from the highly skilled warrior classes that maintained and expanded the larger American states like those of the Aztecs, Incas, and their competitors. They also faced resistance from the militias of smaller confederations and independent villages, which could call out their entire male population to fight. However, none of these societies were, in the long term, able to withstand European (initially especially Spanish) forces. There are several theories as to why this is so. Through diffusion and exchange the Spaniards were the heirs of all the technological sophistication of the densely populated societies of Eurasia and Africa. They brought with them an exceedingly large array of knowledge, technologies, and species (such as horses) against which the Americans—with access to smaller populations, fewer specialists, and less-developed arteries of continental communication— simply could not compete. Recent scholarship, however, suggests that the difference may not have been as great as once thought, and that the most important difference was the many diseases that traveled to the Americas with both Europeans and Africans, against which the American populations had little resistance. These diseases—smallpox, cholera, influenza, and others—devastated armies, killed off kings, depopulated entire regions, and may have been the key factor in the demise of many American states.

Vikings in North America

Some of the most remarkable events associated with the early history of medieval Europe were the expeditions of exploration by Scandinavian adventurers to North America in the late tenth century. These expeditions were part of what modern scholars have called the Viking Age, a period of expansion, conquest, and settlement by the people of Norway, Denmark, and Sweden. Over the course of the ninth and tenth centuries Viking ships plied the waters of the North Sea with impunity as they raided all along the coasts of Germany, England, France, and even southern Europe, leaving chaos and destruction in their wake. But the Vikings were more than mere pirates and raiders; they were also out-standing merchants and excellent sailors. Their formidable navigation skills, their expertly engineered vessels—the longships—and a high level of daring and courage meant that Viking captains often sailed into or got lost in uncharted waters. Many of these seemingly doomed voyages instead turned into journeys of exploration as the Vikings discovered or visited places that were barely known or completely unfamiliar to the residents of Eurasia. Among them were the Faeroe Islands, Iceland, and Greenland. Perhaps the most spectacular, if least successful, voyages of all were those to eastern Canada by Leif "the lucky" Eriksson and others. The purpose of Eriksson's expedition was to investigate a sighting of land made to the west of Greenland by the Norwegian merchant Bjarni Herjólfsson. During his journey, Eriksson made landfall in several places including Helluland (most likely Baffin Island), Markland (probably Labrador), and ultimately in Vinland or Wine Land, referring to Newfoundland, Canada. The following selection from the Grælendinga Saga (Saga of the Greenlanders) was written down in the early thirteenth century, based on stories told orally since the eleventh century, and describes Eriksson's voyage. After Eriksson returned to Greenland, several others returned to Vinland but after some early success at trading with the Native Americans they found increasingly hostile receptions and no permanent settlement was ever established.

>> 112. Grœlendinga Saga

[RECORDED THIRTEENTH CENTURY C.E.]

They made their ship ready and put out to sea. The first landfall they made was the country that Bjarni had sighted last. They sailed right up to the shore and cast anchor, then lowered a boat and landed. There was no grass to be seen, and the hinterland was covered with great glaciers, and between glaciers and shore the land was like one great slab of rock. It seemed to them a worthless country.

Then Leif said, 'Now we have done better than Bjarni where this country is concerned—we at least have set foot on it. I shall give this country a name and call it *Helluland*.'

Source: "Grœnlendinga Saga" in *The Vinland Sagas: The Norse Discovery of North America* edited and translated by Magnus Magnusson and Hermann Pálsson, (Baltimore: Penguin Books, 1965), 55–58.

They returned to their ship and put to sea, and sighted a second land. Once again they sailed right up to it and cast anchor, lowered a boat and went ashore. This country was flat and wooded, with white sandy beaches wherever they went; and the land sloped gently down to the sea.

Leif said, 'This country shall be named after its natural resources: it shall be called *Markland.*'

They hurried back to their ship as quickly as possible and sailed away to sea in a north-east wind for two days until they sighted land again. They sailed towards it and came to an island which lay to the north of it.

They went ashore and looked about them. The weather was fine. There was dew on the grass, and the first thing they did was to get some of it on their hands and put it to their lips, and to them it seemed the sweetest thing they had ever tasted. Then they went back to their ship and sailed into the sound that lay between the island and the headland jutting out to the north.

They steered a westerly course round the headland. There were extensive shallows there and at low tide their ship was left high and dry, with the sea almost out of sight. But they were so impatient to land that they could not bear to wait for the rising tide to float the ship; they ran ashore to a place where a river flowed out of a lake. As soon as the tide had refloated the ship they took a boat and rowed out to it and brought it up the river into the lake, where they anchored it. They carried their hammocks ashore and put up booths. Then they decided to winter there, and built some large houses.

There was no lack of salmon in the river or the lake, bigger salmon than they had ever seen. The country seemed to them so kind that no winter fodder would be needed for livestock: there was never any frost all winter and the grass hardly withered at all.

In this country, night and day were of more even length than in either Greenland or Iceland: on the shortest day of the year, the sun was already up by 9 a.m., and did not set until after 3 p.m.

When they had finished building their houses, Leif said to his companions, 'Now I want to divide our company into two parties and have the country explored; half of the company are to remain here at the houses while the other half go exploring—but they must not go so far that they cannot return the same evening, and they are not to become separated.'

They carried out these instructions for a time. Leif himself took turns at going out with the exploring party and staying behind at the base. [...]

One evening news came that someone was missing: it was Tyrkir the Southerner. Leif was very displeased at this, for Tyrkir had been with the family for a long time, and when Leif was a child had been devoted to him. Leif rebuked his men severely, and got ready to make a search with twelve men.

They had gone only a short distance from the houses when Tyrkir came walking towards them, and they gave him a warm welcome. Leif quickly realized that Tyrkir was in excellent humour.

Tyrkir had a prominent forehead and shifty eyes, and not much more of a face besides; he was short and puny-looking but very clever with his hands.

Leif said to him, 'Why are you so late, foster-father? How did you get separated from your companions?'

At first Tyrkir spoke for a long time in German, rolling his eyes in all directions and pulling faces, and no one could understand what he was saying. After a while he spoke in Icelandic.

'I did not go much farther than you,' he said. 'I have some news. I found vines and grapes.'

'Is that true, foster-father?' asked Leif.

'Of course it is true,' he replied. 'Where I was born there were plenty of vines and grapes.'

They slept for the rest of the night, and next morning Leif said to his men, 'Now we have two tasks on our hands. On alternate days we must gather grapes and cut vines, and then fell trees, to make a cargo for my ship.'

This was done. It is said that the tow-boat was filled with grapes. They took on a full cargo of timber; and in the spring they made ready to leave and sailed away. Leif named the country after its natural qualities and called it *Vinland.*

The Crusades

The Vikings were only the vanguard of territorial expansion by Europeans. After centuries of being the target of numerous invasions, western Europeans went on the offensive to begin an age of conquest and colonization that continued until the twentieth century. The first of these efforts were the Crusades. The Crusades began in 1095 when Pope Urban II (r. 1088–1099) addressed the nobles of France in a field in Clermont. Urban's speech is the topic of the following selection from the Chronicle of Fulcher of Chartres. *Fulcher was a witness to the speech, but did not begin writing his chronicle until 1101. At Clermont Urban urged the knights present to go to the aid of the Christian Byzantines who were being attacked by the Seljuk Turks, a tribe originating in central Asia that had recently converted to Islam and had captured large regions of the Byzantine Empire. He framed his appeal in the context of a holy war that had as its ultimate aim the liberation of Jerusalem from its current Muslim masters. In return for their military service, Urban promised the participants a remission of their sins and the possibility of booty and conquest. Tens of thousands answered his call and by 1099 the participants of the First Crusade had accomplished a near miracle when they captured Jerusalem and established a series of principalities in the Holy Land. These crusader states would serve as European outposts and gateways to western Asia, India, and China for Christian merchants, missionaries, and adventurers. Over the course of the next two centuries there would be seven other major and numerous minor crusades. They continued until 1291 when Muslim forces recaptured the last of the Crusader strongholds in the Holy Land, the city of Acre. By the time that Acre fell, the Crusades had transformed Europe, drawing it closer to the other Eurasian civilizations, opening new intellectual, cultural, and mercantile opportunities, and whetting the European appetite for conquest and expansion.*

>> 113. The Chronicle of Fulcher of Chartres, Book I

[1101 C.E.]

1. These and many other things having been suitably disposed of, all those present, both clergy and people, at the words of Lord Urban, the Pope, voluntarily gave thanks to God and confirmed by a faithful promise that his decrees would be well kept. But straightway he added that another thing not less than the tribulation already spoken of, but even greater and more oppressive, was injuring Christianity in another part of the world, saying:

2. "Now that you, O sons of God, have consecrated yourselves to God to maintain peace among yourselves more vigorously and to uphold the laws of the Church faithfully, there is work to do, for you must turn the strength of your sincerity, now that you are aroused by divine correction, to another affair that concerns you and God. Hastening to the way, you must help your brothers living in the Orient, who need your aid for which they have already cried out many times.

Source: "The Chronicle of Fulcher of Chartres, Book I," translated by Martha E. McGinty, in *The First Crusade: The Chronicle of Fulcher of Chartres and Other Source Materials*, edited by Edward Peters (Philadelphia: University of Pennsylvania Press, 1971), 29–31.

3. "For, as most of you have been told, the Turks, a race of Persians, who have penetrated within the boundaries of Romania even to the Mediterranean to that point which they call the Arm of Saint George, in occupying more and more of the lands of the Christians, have overcome them, already victims of seven battles, and have killed and captured them, have overthrown churches, and have laid waste God's kingdom. If you permit this supinely for very long, God's faithful ones will be still further subjected.

4. "Concerning this affair, I, with suppliant prayer—not I, but the Lord—exhort you, heralds of Christ, to persuade all of whatever class, both knights and footmen, both rich and poor, in numerous edicts, to strive to help expel that wicked race from our Christian lands before it is too late.

5. "I speak to those present, I send word to those not here; moreover, Christ commands it. Remission of sins will be granted for those going thither, if they end a shackled life either on land or in crossing the sea, or in struggling against the heathen. I, being vested with that gift from God, grant this to those who go.

6. "O what a shame, if a people, so despised, degenerate, and enslaved by demons would thus overcome a people endowed with the trust of almighty God, and shining in the name of Christ! O how many evils will be imputed to you by the Lord Himself, if you do not help those who, like you, profess Christianity!

7. "Let those," he said, "who are accustomed to wage private wars wastefully even against Believers, go forth against the Infidels in a battle worthy to be undertaken now and to be finished in victory. Now, let those, who until recently existed as plunderers, be soldiers of Christ; now, let those, who formerly contended against brothers and relations, rightly fight barbarians; now, let those, who recently were hired for a few pieces of silver, win their eternal reward. Let those, who wearied themselves to the detriment of body and soul, labor for a twofold honor. Nay, more, the sorrowful here will be glad there, the poor here will be rich there, and the enemies of the Lord here will be His friends there.

8. "Let no delay postpone the journey of those about to go, but when they have collected the money owed to them and the expenses for the journey, and when winter has ended and spring has come, let them enter the crossroads courageously with the Lord going on before."

The Portuguese in the Atlantic

The Holy Land was not the only region where Christian and Muslims fought each other in holy wars. Spain was also an active crusading front. In 711 a Muslim army had conquered much of Spain and over the next 800 years Christian forces battled to regain control over the peninsula. Over the course of these reconquest efforts several Christian kingdoms were formed including Castile, in the center of the Iberian Peninsula (which shouldered the bulk of the offensive against the Muslims), and the kingdom of Portugal, on the western coast of the peninsula. By the mid-thirteenth century, Portugal had completed the conquest of Muslim territories within its sphere of influence. Unable to expand any further in Iberia, the Portuguese increasingly turned their attention to the Atlantic and the prospect of exploration and colonization overseas. By the fifteenth century these endeavors had begun to yield some remarkable results under the patronage of Prince Henry, called the Navigator by his admirers. In this selection, the fifteenth-century Portuguese chronicler Gomes Eannes de Azurara explains why Henry (the Infant) sponsored missions of exploration to the west coast of Africa. It should be noted that Eannes de Azurara's account, written in the 1450s, is highly complimentary of Prince Henry and there is little evidence beyond this chronicle to support the reasons he gives.

Nonetheless, whether the reasons are true or simply a portrayal of Henry through Eannes de Azurara's admiring pen, the chronicle still provides insights into how people of the age viewed exploration. The actual missions were to be of tremendous historical importance as they helped to pave the way for the later voyages of Christopher Columbus and initiated the Atlantic Slave Trade that would ultimately uproot and enslave millions of Africans.

>> 114. The Chronicle of the Discovery and Conquest of Guinea

GOMES EANNES DE AZURARA [C. 1452 C.E.]

We imagine that we know a matter when we are acquainted with the doer of it and the end for which he did it. And since in former chapters we have set forth the Lord Infant as the chief actor in these things, giving as clear an understanding of him as we could, it is meet that in this present chapter we should know his purpose in doing them. And you should note well that the noble spirit of this Prince, by a sort of natural constraint, was ever urging him both to begin and to carry out very great deeds. For which reason, after the taking of Ceuta he always kept ships well armed against the Infidel, both for war, and because he had also a wish to know the land that lay beyond the isles of Canary and that Cape called Bojador, for that up to his time, neither by writings, nor by the memory of man, was known with any certainty the nature of the land beyond that Cape. Some said indeed that Saint Brandan had passed that way; and there was another tale of two galleys rounding the Cape, which never returned. But this doth not appear at all likely to be true, for it is not to be presumed that if the said galleys went there, some other ships would not have endeavoured to learn what voyage they had made. And because the said Lord Infant wished to know the truth of this,—since it seemed to him that if he or some other lord did not endeavour to gain that knowledge, no

mariners or merchants would ever dare to attempt it—(for it is clear that none of them ever trouble themselves to sail to a place where there is not a sure and certain hope of profit)—and seeing also that no other prince took any pains in this matter, he sent out his own ships against those parts, to have manifest certainty of them all. And to this he was stirred up by his zeal for the service of God and of the King Edward his Lord and brother, who then reigned. And this was the first reason of his action.

The second reason was that if there chanced to be in those lands some population of Christians, or some havens, into which it would be possible to sail without peril, many kinds of merchandise might be brought to this realm, which would find a ready market, and reasonably so, because no other people of these parts traded with them, nor yet people of any other that were known; and also the products of this realm might be taken there, which traffic would bring great profit to our countrymen.

The third reason was that, as it was said that the power of the Moors in that land of Africa was very much greater than was commonly supposed, and that there were no Christians among them, nor any other race of men; and because every wise man is obliged by natural prudence to wish for a knowledge of the power of his enemy; therefore the said Lord Infant exerted himself to cause this to be fully discovered, and to make it known determinately how far the power of those infidels extended.

The fourth reason was because during the one and thirty years that he had warred against the

---

Source: Gomes Eannes de Azurara, *The Chronicle of the Discovery and Conquest of Guinea*, vol. 1, edited and translated by Charles Raymond Beazley and Edgar Prestage (New York: B. Franklin, 1963), 27–30.

Moors, he had never found a Christian king, nor a lord outside this land, who for the love of our Lord Jesus Christ would aid him in the said war. Therefore he sought to know if there were in those parts any Christian princes, in whom the charity and the love of Christ was so ingrained that they would aid him against those enemies of the faith.

The fifth reason was his great desire to make increase in the faith of our Lord Jesus Christ and to bring to him all the souls that should be saved,—understanding that all the mystery of the Incarnation, Death, and Passion of our Lord Jesus Christ was for this sole end—namely the salvation of lost souls—whom the said Lord Infant by his travail and spending would fain bring into the true path. For he perceived that no better offering could be made unto the Lord than this; for if God promised to return one hundred goods for one, we may justly believe that for such great benefits, that is to say for so many souls as were saved by the efforts of this Lord, he will have so many hundreds of guerdons in the kingdom of God, by which his spirit may be glorified after this life in the celestial realm. For I that wrote this history saw so many men and women of those parts turned to the holy faith, that even if the Infant had been a heathen, their prayers would have been enough to have obtained his salvation. And not only did I see the first captives, but their children and grandchildren as true Christians as if the Divine grace breathed in them and imparted to them a clear knowledge of itself.

But over and above these five reasons I have a sixth that would seem to be the root from which all the others proceeded: and this is the inclination of the heavenly wheels. For, as I wrote not many days ago in a letter I sent to the Lord King, that although it be written that the wise man shall be Lord of the stars, and that the courses of the planets (according to the true estimate of the holy doctors) cannot cause the good man to stumble; yet it is manifest that they are bodies ordained in the secret counsels of our Lord God and run by a fixed measure, appointed to different ends, which are revealed to men by his grace, through whose influence bodies of the lower order are inclined to certain passions. And if it be a fact, speaking as a Catholic, that the contrary predestinations of the wheels of heaven can be avoided by natural judgment with the aid of a certain divine grace, much more does it stand to reason that those who are predestined to good fortune, by the help of this same grace, will not only follow their course but even add a far greater increase to themselves. But here I wish to tell you how by the constraint of the influence of nature this glorious Prince was inclined to those actions of his. And that was because his ascendent was Aries, which is the house of Mars and exaltation of the sun, and his lord in the XIth house, in company of the sun. And because the said Mars was in Aquarius, which is the house of Saturn, and in the mansion of hope, it signified that this Lord should toil at high and mighty conquests, especially in seeking out things that were hidden from other men and secret, according to the nature of Saturn, in whose house he is. And the fact of his being accompanied by the sun, as I said, and the sun being in the house of Jupiter, signified that all his traffick and his conquests would be loyally carried out, according to the good pleasure of his king and lord.

The Kingdom of Songhay

When the Portuguese arrived on the coast of West Africa, they largely encountered numerous small kingdoms and confederations as well as village-based societies. In the interior of the region, however, existed a heritage of large empires and states. In the fifteenth century the greatest of these kingdoms was Songhay, which was in the process of replacing Mali as the dominant power in West Africa. In the following selection, Roland Oliver and Anthony Atmore, both senior African historians, discuss the process and some of the results of

Songhay's expansion. In many ways Songhay's growth followed a common pattern of state expansion shared by the Mongols, Aztecs, and Incas among others. Their military fortunes improved with the arrival of a first-rate military commander, Sonni Ali, whose conquests aimed not only to expand his territories but also to control key communication routes. Once a region had been conquered, much of its administration was turned over to skilled local officials who did much to incorporate local regions into the larger kingdom. Sonni Ali and his successor, Muhammad Ture, also took over important trade routes in salt and slaves, which tied Songhay to a wider African, Mediterranean, and, increasingly, Atlantic economy.

>> 115. Medieval Africa, 1250–1800

ROLAND OLIVER AND ANTHONY ATMORE
[2001]

The fifteenth century did indeed see a change in the main overarching system of political control in the western Sudan, but this was in no sense a consequence of Portuguese outreach. Already from about 1360 onwards the Keita dynasty of Mali had been subject to severe internal dissensions based on the rivalry between the descendants of Mansa Musa and those of his brother and successor Mansa Sulayman. Trouble at the centre of the system was soon reflected in disintegration at the periphery. Of the tributary states, Songhay in the east and in the west the Wolof kingdom south of the lower Senegal were the first to break away. Next, from the region enclosed by the Niger bend, Mossi horsemen made swift, devastating raids on the rich riverside towns from Jenne to Timbuktu. The Fulbe pastoralists from the upper Senegal moved in upon the areas of cereal production around the inland delta of the Niger. Finally, the Tuareg nomads of the desert advanced southwards upon the cities of the Niger bend, occupying Timbuktu in 1433. Thus, although the great king of the interior whose existence was reported by the Dyula traders to the Portuguese on the Gambia in 1455 was still the Mansa of Mali, the range of his effective rule was already limited to the Mande-speaking heartland of the former imperial system. Within twenty years, it was to be reduced still further, to the southern half of that core region.

The state which expanded to fill the power vacuum left by the break-up of Mali was Songhay. As a kingdom embracing much of the eastern arm of the Niger bend, it already had a long history. It had been the contemporary, and in some respects the counterpart, of ancient Ghana, commanding the caravan routes leading northwards and eastwards from the Niger bend in much the same way as Ghana had controlled those leading to the north and west. With the expansion of Mali in the thirteenth century, Songhay had lost its northern province and its control of the desert routes. For much of the fourteenth century the remainder of the kingdom paid tribute to Mali. Yet the Songhay-speakers were still the predominant population of the river valley far beyond the political boundaries of the state. They were the fishermen, the boat-builders and the river traders right round the great bend of the Niger, forming the main ethnic stratum at Jenne and Timbuktu as well as at Gao and Kukya. Moreover, eastern Songhay, along with the neighbouring country of the Mossi, offered the best conditions for horse-breeding to be found anywhere to the south of the Sahara, and the mounted lancers of the Songhay aristocracy were swift and terrible, whether as slave-raiders on the eastern frontier or as the pillagers of the Sahel cities. Thus the potential existed for a Songhay revival, given only the leadership capable of directing it, and in 1464 this was found with the accession to the throne of Sonni Ali, who in a reign of twenty-eight years placed Songhay in the position formerly occupied by Mali.

Source: Roland Oliver and Anthony Atmore, *Medieval Africa, 1250–1800* (Cambridge: Cambridge University Press, 2001), 66–69.

Sonni Ali is remembered in the oral tradition of Songhay as a magician of unparalleled power, and in the chronicle of al-Sa'di of Timbuktu as an impious and unscrupulous tyrant. In reality, he was first and foremost a great military commander with a well-conceived strategy of conquest, based upon the Niger waterway. Whenever possible, he manoeuvred his land forces within the arc of territory enclosed by the river, ferrying them to the north bank only to attack specific targets. In 1469 he took Timbuktu from the Tuareg, making his own headquarters at the river-port of Kabara, but sacking the rich city and driving out the Tuareg and Sanhaja clerics who had been the civil functionaries and the teachers and preachers at the famous Sankore mosque. A poignant passage of al-Sa'di's chronicle describes their departure northwards to the desert city of Walata.

On the day they left Timbuktu you could see grown men with beards anxious to mount a camel, but trembling in fear before it. When they mounted the camel, they were thrown off when the beast rose, for our righteous forefathers used to keep their children indoors until they grew up. Hence they had no understanding of practical matters, since they did not play in their youth, and play makes a child smart and gives him insight into many things!

Having established this vital junction between the land and water routes, Sonni Ali pursued his conquests upstream, reaching Jenne, which he besieged with the aid of 400 river boats in 1473. This gave him command of the gold and kola trade routes leading southwards to the Volta basin. It remained to secure the important grain-producing region around the inland delta from raids by Mossi from the south and Fulbe from the west. It was only towards the end of his reign that Sonni Ali's forces were in direct contact with those of the already much reduced kingdom of Mali in the region to the west of the upper Niger. Here, broadly speaking, he was successful in the savanna, but not so in the forest, where his cavalry, impeded by the dense vegetation, was at the mercy of the Malian archers.

In methods of government, it seems that the new Songhay leadership mainly took over the old Malian system, and this tendency became clearer when, soon after the death of Sonni Ali, power was seized by one of his generals, the Askiya Muhammad Ture, whose name would strongly suggest that he was not of Songhay but of Soninke (i.e., northern Mande) origin, and that his *coup d'état* represented a return to Mande leadership in what was predominantly a Mande-speaking empire. In another important respect Muhammad Ture's accession signified a return to the traditional Malian ethic. Before all else he was an orthodox and pious Muslim, who was able to re-enlist the support of the literate class of the great cities of Gao, Timbuktu and Jenne. During his reign the scholars returned to Timbuktu, the princes were educated in the Sankore mosque and the princesses were married to the rich merchants who managed the trans-Saharan trade. Relations with the Tuareg and the Sanhaja were restored, and through them Songhay established virtual control over the salt mines of Taghaza and the copper mines of Takedda, which were the keys to the successful working of the long-distance trade. Again, the Muslim clerics, once restored to favour, supplied the ideological support and the legal framework necessary for the efficient government of a large territory within which many people were constantly moving around outside their traditional ethnic areas.

At a more material level, the Songhay empire depended greatly on its colonies of royal slaves and on its privileged castes of craftsmen, which had probably been built up originally from the more skilled groups of war captives, such as smiths, weavers and leather-workers. Here again, Songhay took over a system already initiated in Mali, while adding greatly to the numbers of slaves by means of the regular, annual raids carried out by the Songhay cavalry among the unprotected, stateless peoples living south of the Niger bend. Many of these captives went to the trans-Saharan markets, especially at this time those of southern Morocco, where a sugar industry was being actively developed. Others were sold to the free citizenry of Songhay. Others again became the property of the ruler and were either recruited into the army or settled in colonies on the state farms. These were spread right across the empire, to supply the government and the garrisons, but the largest concentration was still to be found in the well-watered inland delta, whose grain harvests were so vital to the towns of the Sahel, the desert caravans and even the workers in the desert salt mines.

The Mongols

Just as Muslim forces were beginning their efforts to push the Crusaders completely out of the Holy Land, the Muslims had to deal with a second, and perhaps more dangerous, group of foreign invaders: the Mongols. In the mid-1250s a vast Mongol army under the leadership of Hugalu Khan, grandson of Genghis Khan, invaded the Muslim world, aiming for Baghdad. They besieged the city in early 1258, as described in selection by the Syrian scholar Ibn Kathir, who would write about it almost a century later in his History *(or* Al-Bidayah wa al-Nihayah*). Despite the fact that the city surrendered very quickly, according to Ibn Kathir, the Mongols—or the Tatars as this and other sources call them—completely obliterated Baghdad and butchered tens, perhaps hundreds, of thousands of its inhabitants. Among those killed was the caliph, the nominal leader of the Muslim world, and many of his relatives. Their deaths effectively ended the Abbasid Dynasty, which had held the caliphate since 749. Baghdad, which had been the center of the Islamic world and a bastion of learning and science, took centuries to recover. After Baghdad, the Mongols were able to subjugate Damascus and then tried advancing toward Egypt. In 1260, however, the Mamluks, the Muslim rulers of Egypt, defeated a Mongol army at the Battle of Ain Jalut and put a stop to Mongol expansion in the West.*

By the time of Ain Jalut, the Mongols already had an expansive empire that included much of China and large parts of central Asia. The extent of their conquests meant that the Mongols also had to be efficient and able rulers. To govern their sprawling and multiethnic empire, the Mongols left much of the administration of the conquered territories to local officials working under the supervision of Mongol governors. The second selection, written in the late thirteenth century, is a brief biography of the governor Menggu written by a Chinese official and meant to highlight the governor's achievements. While the selection shows the strictness of Mongol rule over their subject people, it also describes the security and stability that Mongol power was capable of achieving.

>> 116. The Fall of Baghdad (1258)

IBN KATHIR [1351–1358 C.E.]

Then came the year 656 [1258], in which the Tatars captured Baghdad and killed most of its people, including the Caliph, and the dominion [*dawla*] of the sons of 'Abbās ended there.

When this year began, the Tatar armies had already attacked Baghdad, under the two amirs who commanded the troops of the Sultan of the Tatars, Hülegü Khan. To them came the auxiliaries

Source: Ibn Kathir, "The Fall of Baghdad (1258)," in *Islam: From the Prophet Muhammad to the Capture of Constantinople* vol. 1, edited and translated by Bernard Lewis (New York: Harper Torchbooks, 1974), 81–84.

of the lord of Mosul, to help them against the Baghdadis, with provisions and gifts and offerings from him. He did all this because he feared for himself from the Tatars and wished to ingratiate himself with them, may God condemn them. Baghdad was defended, and mangonels and onagers were set up, with other instruments of defense, which, however, cannot avert any part of God's decree. As the Prophet said, "Caution does not avail against fate" and as God said, "When God's term comes it cannot be deferred" [Qur'ān, lxxi, 4] and, also: "God does not change what is in a people until they change what is in themselves; when God wishes evil for a people, they cannot avert it, and they have no other protector" [Qur'ān, xiii, 11].

The Tatars surrounded the seat of the Caliphate and rained arrows on it from every side until a slave-girl was hit while she was playing before the Caliph and amusing him. She was one of his concubines, a mulatto called 'Urfa, and an arrow came through one of the windows and killed her while she was dancing before the Caliph. The Caliph was alarmed and very frightened. The arrow which had hit her was brought to him, and on it was written, "When God wishes to accomplish His decree, he deprives men of reason of their reason." After this the Caliph ordered increased precautions, and the defenses of the seat of the Caliphate were multiplied.

The arrival of Hülegü Khan at Baghdad with all his troops, numbering nearly 200,000 fighting men, occurred on Muharram 12 of this year [January 19, 1258]…he came to Baghdad with his numerous infidel, profligate, tyrannical, brutal armies of men, who believed neither in God nor in the Last Day, and invested Baghdad on the western and eastern sides. The armies of Baghdad were very few and utterly wretched, not reaching 10,000 horsemen. They and the rest of the army had all been deprived of their fiefs [iqṭā'] so that many of them were begging in the markets and by the gates of the mosques. Poets were reciting elegies on them and mourning for Islam and its people. All this was due to the opinions of the vizier Ibn al-'Alqamī the Shi'ite, because in the previous year, when heavy fighting took place between the Sunnis and

the Shi'a, Karkh and the Shi'ite quarter were looted, and even the houses of the vizier's kinsmen were looted. He was filled with spite because of this, and this was what spurred him to bring down on Islam and its people the most appalling calamity that has been recorded from the building of Baghdad until this time. That is why he was the first to go out to the Tatars. He went with his family and his companions and his servants and his suite and met Sultan Hülegü Khan, may God curse him, and then returned and advised the Caliph to go out to him and be received by him in audience and to make peace on the basis of half the land tax of Iraq for them and half for the Caliph. The Caliph had to go with 700 riders, including the qāḍis, the jurists, the Sufis, the chief amirs, and the notables. When they came near the camp of Sultan Hülegü Khan, all but seventeen of them were removed from the sight of the Caliph; they were taken off their horses and robbed and killed to the very last man. The Caliph and the others were saved. The Caliph was then brought before Hülegü, who asked him many things. It is said that the Caliph's speech was confused because of his terror at the disdain and arrogance which he experienced. Then he returned to Baghdad in the company of Khoja Naṣir al-Dīn al-Ṭūsī, the vizier Ibn al-'Alqamī, and others, the Caliph being under guard and sequestration, and they brought great quantities of gold and jewels and gold and silver objects and precious stones and other valuables from the seat of the Caliphate. But this clique of Shi'ites and other hypocrites advised Hülegü not to make peace with the Caliph. The vizier said, "If peace is made on equal shares, it will not last more than a year or two, and then things will be as they were before." And they made the killing of the Caliph seem good to him so that when the Caliph returned to Sultan Hülegü he gave orders to kill him….

They [the Tatars] came down upon the city and killed all they could, men, women and children, the old, the middle-aged, and the young. Many of the people went into wells, latrines, and sewers and hid there for many days without emerging. Most of the people gathered in the caravanserais and locked themselves in. The

Tatars opened the gates by either breaking or burning them. When they entered, the people in them fled upstairs and the Tatars killed them on the roofs until blood poured from the gutters into the street; "We belong to God and to God we return" [Qur'ān, ii, 156]. The same happened in the mosques and cathedral mosques and dervish convents. No one escaped them except for the Jewish and Christian *dhimmīs,* those who found shelter with them or in the house of the vizier Ibn al-'Alqamī the Shī'ite, and a group of merchants who had obtained safe-conduct from them, having paid great sums of money to preserve themselves and their property. And Baghdad, which had been the most civilized of all cities, became a ruin with only a few inhabitants, and they were in fear and hunger and wretchedness and insignificance.

>> 117. A Mongol Governor [late thirteenth century C.E.]

Emperor Taizu [Chinggis Khan] received the mandate of Heaven and subjugated all regions. When Emperor Taizong [Ogodei Khan] succeeded, he revitalized the bureaucratic system and made it more efficient and organized. At court, one minister supervised all the officials and helped the emperor rule. In the provinces, commanderies and counties received instructions from above and saw that they got carried out. Prefects and magistrates were as a rule appointed only after submitting [to the Mongols]. Still one Mongol, called the governor, was selected to supervise them. The prefects and magistrates all had to obey his orders. The fortune of the common people and the quality of the government both were entirely dependent on the wisdom of the governor.

Zhangde, one of the ten routes, is crucial to communication between north and south. In the fourth month of 1236, the court deemed Menggu capable of handling Zhangde, so promoted him from the post of legal officer of the troops of Quduqu to be its governor. At the time, the Jin had fallen only three years earlier. The common people were not yet free of the army, the injured had not yet recovered, those who had fled had not yet returned, and the residents were not yet contented. Because regulations were lax, the soldiers took advantage of their victory to plunder. Even in cities and marketplaces, some people kept their doors closed in the daytime. As soon as Menggu arrived, he took charge. Knowing the people's grievances, he issued an order, "Those who oppress the people will be dealt with according to the law. Craftsmen, merchants, and shopkeepers, you must each go about your work with your doors open, peacefully attending to your business without fear. Farmers, you must be content with your lands and exert yourselves diligently according to the seasons. I will instruct or punish those who mistreat you." After this order was issued, the violent became obedient and no one any longer dared violate the laws. Farmers in the fields and travelers on the roads felt safe, and people began to enjoy life.

In the second month of 1238, Wang Rong, prefect of Huaizhou, rebelled. The grand preceptor and prince ordered Menggu to put down this rebellion, telling him to slaughter everyone. Menggu responded, "When the royal army suppresses rebels, those who were coerced into joining them ought to be pardoned, not to mention those who are entirely innocent." The prince approved his advice and followed it. When Wang Rong surrendered, he was executed but the region was spared. The residents, with jugs of wine and burning incense, saw Menggu off tearfully, unable to bear his leaving. Forty years later when he was put in charge of Henei, the common people were delighted with the news, saying, "We will all survive—our parents and relatives through marriage all served him before."

Source: "A Mongol Governor," translated by Patricia Ebrey; in *Chinese Civilization: A Sourcebook,* edited by Patricia B. Ebrey (New York: The Free Press, 1981), 192–194.

In 1239 locusts destroyed all the vegetation in Xiang and Wei, so the people were short of food. Menggu reported this to the great minister Quduqu who Issued five thousand piculs of army rations to save the starving. As a consequence no one had to flee or starve.

During the four years from 1240 to 1243, the great southern campaigns took place. Wherever the armies passed, the local officials complained. Menggu, through loyal and diligent preparations, was able to supply the troops without hurting the people.

In 1247 some previously pacified cities in the Huai and Han areas rose in revolt. Refugees fled north and south. Border generals and local officials joined the fray, fighting and plundering. Menggu, by establishing trust, was able to gather together more than ten thousand households and settle them down as commoners. Even children were included.

At that time the harvest failed for several years in a row, yet taxes and labor services were still exacted. Consequently, three or four of every ten houses was vacant. Menggu ordered the officials to travel around announcing that those who returned to their property would be exempt from taxes and services for three years. That year seventeen thousand households returned in response to his summons. [...]

General Chagan recognized Menggu's honesty and humanity. Whenever the other circuits condemned prisoners to death, he had Menggu conduct the review investigation. Innumerable times, Menggu relied on the law to redress grievances and reduce penalties. Ten years before, a peasant in Anyang had offended a noble and been ordered to turn over six young girls. Menggu ordered the noble official Alachur to marry them all out to commoners. There was a drought in the summer of 1250. After Menggu prayed for rain, moisture became adequate.

In the spring of 1262, Li Tan revolted and sent his henchmen to far away places disguised as mounted couriers. They traveled through many routes, east and west, the officials unable to recognize them. Menggu discovered them and got them to admit their treacherous conspiracy, thus defeating them. When there was a drought in 1263, Menggu prayed for rain and it rained. That year he was given the title Brilliant and August General and made governor of Zhongshan prefecture. In 1270 he was transferred and became governor of Hezhong prefecture. In the spring of 1274 he was allowed to wear the golden tiger tablet in recognition of his long and excellent service, his incorruptibility, and the repute in which he was held where he had served. He was advanced out of order to great general of Huaiyuan, governor of Huaimeng route, and military administrator of several armies. On the 29th of the second month he died of illness in the main room of his private residence at the age of seventy-one.

Ambassadors, Post Systems, and Lame Conquerors

In spite of its vastness and power, the Mongol Empire was not destined to last. By the mid-fourteenth century, the Mongol khans had lost control over many regions of their former empire including China, Iran, and much of central Asia. In central Asia, power often passed to local Turco-Mongolian tribes. Around 1360, a local noble named Temür the Lame (Tamerlane or Tamburlaine in the West) began the process of harnessing the military power of these nomadic warriors into a fearsome war machine whose conquests would echo those of Genghis Khan some 150 years earlier. At the height of his power Temür had control over much of modern western and central Asia, Egypt, Turkey and India, and Russia, only to have his empire collapse soon after his death in 1405. The following selection give some insights into the role played by Temür and his empire in bridging the gap among the far-flung people of Eurasia. The selection is from the account left behind by Ruy Gonzalez de Clavijo, a Spanish ambassador who visited Temür at his court in Samarkand in 1404. He describes meeting some Egyptian ambassadors who were also on their way to Samarkand and describes the Spanish delight upon seeing a giraffe for the first time. Then, as the party stopped in the city of Tabriz, Clavijo describes Temür's post system, an inheritance from the earlier Mongol rulers. Finally, upon reaching Temür's court, Clavijo and his party also meet some ambassadors from China, who, as the reading explains, were not held in very high regard at Temür's court. This selection shows the importance of a powerful central polity in bringing different peoples (and in this case, exotic animals) and ideas together. Not only was Samarkand the point to which all roads in Temür's empire led, it was able to draw ambassadors from the farthest corners of Eurasia and Africa.

>> 118. Clavijo: Embassy to Tamerlane, 1403–1406

[C. 1406 C.E.]

When we had arrived at this city of Khoy we found here already come an ambassador sent to Timur, from [Násir-ad-Dín Faraj the Mamlúk] Sultan of Egypt, who was voyaging with twenty horsemen, and fifteen camels. They carried presents which the Sultan was offering to Timur. Among these presents were counted six ostriches brought hither from Egypt, also a beast called a Jornufa [namely a Giraffe] which was strangely made and after a fashion unknown to us.

This animal has a body as big as a horse but with an extremely long neck. Its forelegs are very much longer than the hind legs, and its hoofs are divided like those of cattle. The length of the foreleg from the shoulder down to the hoof measured, in this present beast, sixteen palms, and from the breast thence up to the top of the head measured likewise sixteen palms: and when the beast raised its head it was a wonder to see the length of the neck, which was very thin and the head somewhat like that of a deer. The hind legs in comparison with the forelegs were short, so that any one seeing the animal casually and for the first time would imagine it to be

seated and not standing, and its haunches slope down like those of a buffalo. The belly is white but the rest of the body is of yellow golden hue cross marked with broad white bands. The face, with the nose, resembles that of a deer, and in the upper part it projects somewhat acutely. The eyes are very large, being round, and the ears like those of a horse, while near its ears are seen two small round horns, the bases of which are covered with hair: these horns being like those of the deer when they first begin to grow. The animal reaches so high when it extends its neck that it can overtop any wall, even one with six or seven coping stones in the height, and when it wishes to eat it can stretch up to the branches of any high tree, and only of green leaves is its food. To one who never saw the Giraffe before this beast is indeed a very wondrous sight to behold. [...]

It is to be noted that from Tabriz all the distance to Samarqand Timur has established relays of horses kept ready at command so that his messengers may ride on his missions night and day without let or hindrance. The post-houses have been built at intervals of a day's journey apart, or sometimes of half a day's journey. In some post-houses a hundred horses will be found, in others only fifty, while in a few there may be as many as two hundred: and thus the

Source: Clavijo: Embassy to Tamerlane, 1403–1406 edited by E. Denison Ross and Eileen Power, and translated by Guy le Strange (New York: Harper and Brothers, 1928), 149–50, 155, 222–223.

high road all the way to Samarqand is served. We were told that from Tabriz to Cairo they count it to be ten days' journey, and the city of Baghdad lies to the right hand of one going thither. [...]

Those lords now conducting us began by placing us in a seat below that of one who it appeared was the ambassador of Chays Khán, the emperor of Cathay. Now this ambassador had lately come to Timur to demand of him the tribute, said to be due to his master, and which Timur year by year had formerly paid. His Highness at this moment noticed that we, the Spanish ambassadors, were being given a seat below that of this envoy from the Chinese Emperor, whereupon he sent word ordering that we should be put above, and that other envoy below. Then no sooner had we been thus seated than one of those lords came forward, as from Timur, and addressing that envoy from Cathay publicly proclaimed that his Highness had sent him to inform this Chinaman that the ambassadors of the King of Spain, the good friend of Timur and his son, must indeed take place above him who was the envoy of a robber and a bad man the enemy of Timur, and that he his envoy must sit below us: and if only God were willing, he Timur would before long see to and dispose matters so that never again would any Chinaman dare come with such an embassy as this man had brought. Thus it came about that later at all times during the feasts and festivities to which his Highness invited us, he always gave command that we should have the upper place. Further on the present occasion, no sooner had his Highness thus disposed as to how we were to be seated, than he ordered our dragoman to interpret and explain to us the injunction given in our behalf. This Emperor of China, as we have said, is called Chays Khán, a title which signifies Emperor of Nine Empires, but the Tartars call him Tanguz, a name given in mockery, for this with them is as who would say the Pig Emperor.

Conquest in the New World

Warfare and conquest in the Americas was as bloody and widespread as it was in Eurasia. Mighty empires like those ruled by the Incas and the Aztecs held sway over vast regions and their populations. These empires, much like the Mongols, kept themselves together through a combination of strong central administration and fearsome military force. The administration and military power were necessary not only to keep subject peoples in line, but also to extract the mercantile and human tribute upon which both the Incas and Aztecs depended (see Chapter 14). The importance of warriors to these American societies is obvious in the first selection by Aztec historian Inga Clendinnen. Clendinnen describes a society in which war was of paramount importance and the warrior was a highly exalted individual. The second selection from the Narrative of the Incas, *written by Juan de Betanzos between 1551 and 1557, is one of our best sources of Inca history, covering both the period immediately preceding the Spanish conquest and much of the conquest itself. De Betanzos, a Spaniard who lived most of his adult life in Peru, was one of the foremost translators of Quechua (the native language of the Incas and the official language of their state of Tawantinsuyu) and was married to an Inca princess. These skills and circumstances gave him access to people and sources that allowed him to reconstruct much of the history of the Inca Empire in the fifteenth and sixteenth century. In this passage from the* Narrative *Betanzos describes how the Inca Yupanque gathered his armies and went to war against the neighboring Soras. The reading also highlights Yupanque's effort to strengthen his lines of communication and improve his ability to conquer as well as rule.*

>> 119. Aztecs: An Interpretation

INGA CLENDINNEN [1991]

To be born a male in Tenochtitlan was to be designated a warrior. The attending midwife met the birth of a boy child with war-cries, and lifted the baby, still slippery with the birth fluid, away from his mother's body to dedicate him to the Sun, and to the 'flowery death' of the warrior in battle or on the killing stone. The umbilical cord would be entrusted to a seasoned warrior, to be buried 'in the midst of the plains where warfare was practiced'. At the child's naming a few days after birth the small boys of the neighbourhood were recruited to shout the name of the tiny warrior through the streets and at the house entrances, so awarding him his first triumph. After the ceremonious dedication at birth came the first marking of warriordom into the flesh. A few days after the naming ceremony the priests drilled the male infant's lower lip in preparation for the warrior lip-plug. With each year to follow there were new markings, when at the close of the warrior festival of Toxcatl all young males down to infants on their cradleboards were cut on stomach, chest, and arms by the priests, to sign their commitment to Huitzilopochtli, god of the Sun and of War. Males also bore a line of scars burned into the skin of the left wrist to indicate their dedication to the Turquoise Prince, the Sun, through his association with the Turquoise Lord of Fire. (Girl children were not exempt from this physical signing, those dedicated at the priest house being cut on hip and chest to affirm their affiliation with the deities of the earth.) For their infant years commoner lads stayed in the care of their mothers, but by the age of three more of their instruction devolved on their fathers, as they began to learn the skills and tasks of men. At six they were allowed the freedom of the streets. From the age of ten they began to be shaped for their warrior future; while most of their hair continued to be close cropped a single tuft was left to grow at the back of the head.

All young Mexica males were exposed to warrior training; all were given the opportunity to excel; those who did excel were lavishly rewarded. At puberty most commoner boys, save for those few specifically dedicated to the calmecac or priest house, came under the full jurisdiction of the *telpochcalli*, the 'House of Youth' of the local warrior house, although they had probably spent as much time as their fathers allowed close by that magnet of male activities in their younger years. Their days were spent in work details for the ward, under the direction of a more senior lad, and in the further practice of a range of masculine skills, few commoners being so successful in battle as to emancipate themselves entirely from ordinary labour. The mass of Mexica warriors was parttime, returning from campaigns to their usual pursuits of horticulture, peddling, fishing or hunting, sandal-making, pulque-brewing, or any one of the other trades the city supported. A trade was a necessary safeguard, should fortune not be with them. 'Fortune' came through battle, in the tangibles of material goods, of sexual pleasures, a desirable Mexica girl for marriage, and—most important—prestige, honour, fame. 'Success' was measured narrowly by the number and status of enemy warriors taken alive in one-to-one combat.

The city folk knew the penalties of war: the fate of the warrior outmatched or momentarily off guard, captured, then bloodily and ceremoniously killed, was constantly enacted in the streets and temples. They knew the desolated households, the young wives suddenly bereft. They knew its lesser costs, too, in the incidence of the casual, semi-licensed violence and depredations of restless young men with small respect for the peaceable trades and those who practised them. In the most solemn ceremonials the probability,

Source: Inga Clendinnen, *Aztecs: An Interpretation* (Cambridge: Cambridge University Press, 1991), 112–113.

indeed the inevitability, the necessity, and the desirability of the warrior's death in battle or on the killing stone was insisted upon. But these darker notes were muted in the public display, where it was the splendour of the warrior which was most lavishly glorified.

>> 120. Narrative of the Incas

JUAN DE BETANZOS [1551–1557 C.E]

Since Inca Yupanque saw that he became lord in the way that this account has related to you and he no longer had to deal with construction in the city, after relaxing with his people, he ordered that all of the lords of the city of Cuzco and the rest of the caciques and important people assemble in the square, which they did all together. With them all there, he told them that he had information that surrounding that city there were a great many towns and provinces. For him, since he was powerful, it was bad to live with so little. Thus he had made up his mind and given the order to go out from that city two months hence in an effort to subjugate those towns and provinces to the city of Cuzco and remove the title of *capac* that was held by every one of those little lords of those towns and provinces. There should be only one *capac* and he was that one. And if it happened that during that campaign he should meet some lord with whom he did battle and lost, he would be happy to serve him. But he did not fear this would happen because, as they could see, the Sun was with him. For the campaign he would need one hundred thousand warriors. Within those two months he wanted to have them assembled in the city of Cuzco with their weapons and the rest of the provisions necessary for the campaign. To this they answered that they would be glad to give him these soldiers and serve with them, for they would go along themselves. They begged him to take them along with him and to see fit to give them three months' time, because they needed that much time to raise the forces.

Pachacuti Inca Yupanque was pleased with this. He ordered that they leave everything in their lands with their leaders and stewards, who were to take great care to sow many large fields, because he knew that the time he planned to spend in the war would make it necessary. Then he ordered them to leave and, when they reached their lands and provinces, to give the order to assemble the forces which would come there in three months. Thus the lords left, and Pachacuti Inca Yupanque remained in the city with his people. During the following three months, he did nothing but enjoy himself with his people and make great sacrifices to the Sun and the rest of the idols and *guacas*. During these sacrifices, he fashioned a small idol that a man could carry easily in his hands. This idol was of gold; made for them to worship when they were at war and the time they spent on it. They worshiped this idol as the god of battles and named him Caccha. He gave this god as a favor to his closest relative so that during the war he could take charge of carrying it on his shoulders or however he could. On the day when they were going into battle, he would carry it in his hands all dressed and adorned with its diadem, and the bearer would wear another diadem on his head, all the while taking a young man along with him who, with a small parasol, called *achigua* by them, would shade the idol whenever they stopped, exactly as they did for the Inca. This parasol would be carried on a long pole so that during the battle it would be known where the Inca was and the people would take care to watch out for him and defend him and the idol. Great sacrifices were made to this idol, from the time it was made until the end of the three months, when the people assembled. After the three months elapsed, the people gathered. The day before they were to leave, Inca Yupanque himself made great sacrifices

Source: Juan de Betanzos, *Narrative of the Incas,* translated and edited by Roland Hamilton and Dana Buchanan (Austin: University of Texas Press, 1996), 81–83, 85–86.

to all the *guacas* and idols, especially to the Sun and to this idol Caccha, and ordered that the people who remained in the city always take care to offer a sacrifice to the Sun, the *guacas,* and idols, whom they were to beg for success as long as the Inca was away at war. [...]

Thus the Inca went on his way and reached the Abancay River, where he ordered his soldiers and captains to have those who could swim jump into the river and swim across. Then they were to get to work on the supports for two more bridges just like the last ones. They acted on this order right away and made them. Right there many other caciques and lords offered peace. The Inca asked them if the people from towns and provinces that were ahead of them had news of his arrival. They said that past their towns there was a province with a very great number of people. These people were called Soras, and also farther ahead of this one there were two provinces with very many people, who were called Lucanas. [...]

There the Inca told his captains and leaders of the city of Cuzco that when they went to ask him to take the *borla* fringe, it was the painting and drawing that they had seen him make of the bridges and roads that they had made up to there. And he ordered them to have roads constructed and bridges made over the rivers, just as he had done up to there, wherever they went on military campaigns. Thus he left there with his army. He gave the order to march to the province of the Soras. Thinking they were powerful and planning their defense and resistance, when they got word that Pachacuti Inca Yupanque was coming against them, they had readied their forces, barriers, and forts through all their land, which had big ravines, mountains, and very rough terrain with high cliffs and bad roads.

When Pachacuti arrived with his powerful forces, he divided his squadrons and made war from all sides, in such a way that very quickly he defeated them, subjugated them, and captured the lords of those towns and provinces. After this was done, the Inca had his men divide into three groups. He put two of the groups under certain captains of his who were lords of Cuzco. He ordered them to leave there and for one group to go in one direction, not going off very far from the city of Cuzco, to conquer and subjugate the people of the province called Condesuyo today. The other squadron of soldiers, along with the other lords of Cuzco and captains to whom he had given command, were to go across the province today called Andesuyo, winning and subjugating the towns and provinces they might find. He also ordered them not ·to go too far from the city of Cuzco. They might run into some provinces with so many soldiers that they could not overcome them and for that reason would need help. If so, they were to send him word of it. And he would come to their rescue. They asked him where the messengers they would send would find him if they found themselves in such straits. He told them he planned to relax there for a few days. From there he would return to the city of Cuzco. Therefore they should send their messenger to the city of Cuzco because there they would be able to inform him of what was happening.

So that he could receive messages better and faster, he ordered each one of the lords from there on to the city of Cuzco to put runners in their territory along the road. There were always to be runners there who would be provided by the communities as necessary. The post stations were to be close together so that news would reach the city of Cuzco quickly and his captains could keep him informed. For this purpose, he immediately ordered an *orejon* lord of the city of Cuzco to start setting up these post stations. Each one should have little huts set up in the places designated. Then that *orejon* lord who had been given that assignment asked the Inca how far one station should be put from the next. The Inca showed him a certain distance, which was one-quarter of a league [less than a mile] and not very far. Then the captains left with their men, going across the provinces that you have heard about. And that *orejon* lord left to set up the post stations. Finally, the Inca remained with that other part of the soldiers whom he had ordered to stay as his personal guard.

>> Mastering the Material

1. Based on the readings in this chapter, what do you think is the role of war in making connections and establishing exchanges between peoples?

2. What are the advantages possessed by land-bound societies in comparison to the advantages possessed by those cultures who depend significantly on the sea?

3. Why do human societies seek to expand themselves even at the expense of their neighbors? Use some of the sources in this chapter to support your argument.

>> Making Connections

1. Many of the selections in this text, including the selections in Part 4 on crusading, highlight the relationship between religion and war. What is the relation between religion and war, and why are the two so closely tied in human societies?

Chapter 16

Exchanges of Inventions, Ideas, and Disease

China may have been the most advanced of all medieval societies. Its centuries of accumulated knowledge, skilled artisans and craftsmen, large population, and stability brought about by dynasties like the Tang and the Song ensured that by the eleventh century China was far ahead of the Muslim world, not to mention Europe and Africa, in the development of many technologies. The Chinese, over the course of the first millennium, had developed paper, gunpowder, and the compass, just to name a few innovations. By the eleventh century they were using movable type and producing high-quality iron and steel in quantities that were truly awe-inspiring. In the late eleventh century, for example, China was capable of producing over 114,000 tons of pig iron—double England's output during the industrial revolution. This massive production capacity and high level of technological proficiency have prompted some scholars of China to argue that the country underwent an industrial revolution in the Middle Ages. Its production and might were also reflected in the manufacture of luxury goods such as silk and porcelain, two industries dominated by the Chinese. Powering this economic and technological giant was an equally large population that was closing in on 100 million people by the end of the eleventh century—for comparison, Europe may have had about 35 million people at this time. Moreover, the Chinese elite were highly skilled and educated, relying on an ever-growing collection of printed texts to enhance their learning. Over 200,000 students were in Chinese schools in 1100 and from these emerged the literati, the innovators, the inventors, and the administrators who staffed the civil service.

All of this technology and industrial might was not enough to keep the Chinese free from invaders. In 1127 Ruzhen invaders not only captured northern China but also adopted Chinese military technology, which they then turned on the Chinese themselves. The Mongols, when they conquered China in the thirteenth century, also co-opted Chinese technological advances, particularly the excellent metal weapons and armor produced by Chinese foundries. The most significant result of the Mongol encounter with Chinese technology was to help bring it to other parts of Eurasia. The vastness of the Mongol Empire and the peace that it imposed did much to increase contact between the eastern and western ends of Eurasia, as Mongol roads became pathways for contact and exchanges between China and Europe and everywhere in between.

As with almost all the other processes discussed in Part 4, Europe again proved to be the biggest beneficiary of knowledge and ideas coming from beyond its borders.

Slowly, inventions, innovations, and ideas from China, India, and the Muslim world filtered into Europe during the medieval period. The readings by Needham, White Jr., and Yolom all address this diffusion. This trickle, which eventually became a flood, was at the center of the **Renaissance of the Twelfth Century,** the great medieval European scientific, intellectual, and cultural reawakening. Yet Europe was more than just a passive receptacle for foreign discoveries and inspiration. As David Landes argues in Reading 122, Europeans were innovators in their own right as they took the inventions of others and changed them to increase efficiency, make them easier to use, or put them to a brand new purpose altogether. Europe's great strength during the Middle Ages was its willingness to embrace the foreign—even over the objection of the Church and other authorities—and to adapt it and improve it for local needs.

Europe certainly benefited a great deal from the global system created by the Mongol Empire, but not all that traveled on Mongol roads was benign or helpful. William McNeil demonstrates how the connection between disparate areas that the *Pax Mongolica* had facilitated also connected distinct disease environments with each other. The ease of travel ensured that pathogens could swoop in on unsuspecting regions before local populations had time to build up immunities or to properly prepare themselves, as far as was possible, for an approaching disease. This was certainly the case when the **Black Death,** a pandemic like none seen before or since, used trade routes to sweep across the Eurasian landmass and Africa. The reading by al-Wardī and de' Mussis are indicative of the untold devastation, suffering, and death left in its wake. Some afflicted parts of the world did not fully recover demographically until the sixteenth or seventeenth century. More than any Chinese porcelain found in East Africa, Persian crop grown in Spain, or European silver used to pay for wages in India, the Black Death demonstrated how intimately connected the medieval world had become.

During this period, ideas, skills, and innovations were diffusing in regions other than Eurasia. Nevertheless, the vast exchange of technologies and diseases across the Mongol Empire, Europe, and the Mediterranean was especially significant because it provided many of the tools for the development of the great maritime trade routes of the next age—the Spanish conquest of the Atlantic Ocean and the Portuguese circumnavigation of Africa. Gunpowder, cannon, and the lateen sail all made their way to Europe from Asia in this period. In this way, Columbus's voyage to the Americas and their subsequent conquest by Europeans is a story with Asian, as well as European, roots.

China: Hotbed of Inventions

In the Middle Ages Chinese inventors conceived machines, artifacts, and technological processes that would later make their way through the Eurasian landmass extending from Japan to England. In the first selection, Joseph Needham, perhaps the foremost Western scholar on Chinese technology, discusses some of the most important Chinese innovations and the problems associated with trying to understand their transmission to the Islamic World and Europe. It often took centuries for a Chinese invention to make its way westward and, as Needham points out, inventions flowing from Europe to Asia also took centuries to diffuse. The key question that Needham asks is whether Western inventors reinvented many of these innovations on their own or whether their creativity was influenced by knowledge of Chinese originals. Whether the West benefited from transmission or reinvention it is clear from Needham's conclusion that Western technicians often adapted and improved the ideas that filtered in from Asia. This point is taken up by Harvard historian David Landes in his book The Wealth and Poverty of Nations, *a section of which is the second source here. Landes considers gunpowder, both in terms of how the Chinese used it and the improvements made to its use by Europeans. Those improvements would prove crucial in giving Europe military superiority as it set out on its colonial ventures in the late fifteenth century and beyond.*

>> 121. Science and Civilisation in China

JOSEPH NEEDHAM [1978]

General remarks

Of all the river-valley civilisations of antiquity, China was unique in its geographical isolation. In spite of this, and notwithstanding the difficulties in making contact, we can see that there was a virtually continuous diffusion of techniques to the West, if not of scientific ideas. This transmission was of vital importance for the development of Europe. With civilisations less complex and less advanced than now, independent invention was less likely and transmission more important. A combination of gears to make a device like a hodometer for measuring distance travelled by a vehicle would have been a work of genius in the third century B.C. while it could be readily devised by any young mechanic today.

Yet although transmission was paramount, it is still frequently difficult to award priorities. To take an extreme example, the German astronomer Joseph von Fraunhofer invented in 1842 a special clock to drive a telescope so that it could follow the stars continuously in spite of the rotation of the Earth, and thus make observing more convenient. He did not know that even though they had no telescopes, the Chinese had done

this eight centuries earlier with their own astronomical instruments. Was this development truly a re-invention? Again, there are other apparently independent discoveries that one feels convinced were really due to transmission even though we have no absolute proof. Suspension-bridges with wrought-iron chains are a case in point: first constructed in China in the sixth century A.D.; they soon had successors in that part of the world, especially Tibet and other Himalayan countries, but they did not appear in Europe until the eighteenth century. Was this a case of independent invention or delayed diffusion? Here, as in so many other cases, dates of transmission are hard if not impossible to find, and we cannot be sure, though we do know that some of the European engineers knew of the Chinese bridges before any were built in Europe itself. Nevertheless it is clear that a host of technical devices—the wheelbarrow, the piston-bellows, the cross-bow; the technique of deep borehole drilling, the art and mystery of cast iron—were all known in China before, and often long before, they were known in the West. On the other hand, the Chinese also had to wait a very long time for some basic inventions to penetrate from the West, e.g. the screw and the crankshaft, to name only two; and there were some Chinese inventions which were known in the West but not adopted: paper money, the use of coal, and the

Source: The Shorter Science and Civilisation in China: An Abridgement of Joseph Needham's Original Text, vol I., edited by Colin A. Ronan (Cambridge: Cambridge University Press, 1978), 74–77.

adoption of water-tight compartments in ship-building for example. The whole situation of transmission of inventions and techniques has many facets, as Tables 6 and 7 show.

Lastly there is the question of what has been called 'stimulus diffusion', where an idea is transmitted without any details of the technique. The windmill is just such a case. An eighth-century Persian invention, it was always mounted horizontally, and it was in this form that it was introduced into China at the beginning of the Mongol period some five centuries later. From the first, however, the European windmill was vertical, as fourteenth-century illustrations show, and it seems that what was transmitted here was the idea of wind-driven vanes but nothing more. The concept alone came through and European millwrights adopted their own techniques, using right-angle gearing, to put it into practice. It was indeed as if someone, perhaps returning from the Crusades, had reported that the Saracens had harnessed the wind to grind their corn, and left it at that. The technicians had to go on from there and, in doing so, followed a different path. Again, the windmill is not an isolated case: there are plenty of others that could be cited.

It was in a variety of ways such as these, directly or indirectly, by travels of merchants and ambassadors, by capture of prisoners, or immigration of deserters, that there was cultural interchange between East and West, an interchange which seems, from more recent research, to have been greater than ever previously supposed.

Table 6 Transmission of mechanical and other techniques from China to the West

		Approximate lag in centuries
(a)	Square-pallet chain-pump	15
(b)	Edge-runner mill	13
	Edge-runner mill with application of water-power	9
(c)	Metallurgical blowing-engines, water-power	11
(d)	Rotary fan and rotary winnowing machine	14
(e)	Piston-bellows	c. 14
(f)	Draw-loom	4
(g)	Silk-handling machinery (a form of flyer for laying thread evenly on reels appears in the eleventh century A.D., and water-power is applied to textile mills in the fourteenth)	3–13
(h)	Wheelbarrow	9–10
(i)	Sailing-carriage	11
(j)	Wagon-mill	12
(k)	Efficient harness for draught-animals:	
	Breast-strap (postilion)	8
	Collar	6
	Variolation	1–7
(l)	Cross-bow (as an individual arm)	13
(m)	Kite	c. 12
(n)	Helicopter top (spun by cord)	14
	Zoetrope (moved by ascending hot-air current)	c. 10
(o)	Deep borehole drilling	11
(p)	Iron casting	10–12
(q)	'Cardan' suspension	8–9
	Clockwork escapement	6

(r)	Segmental arch bridge	7
(s)	Iron-chain suspension-bridge	10–13
(t)	Canal pound-lock.	7–17
(u)	Nautical construction principles	> 10
(v)	Axial rudder	c. 10
(w)	Gunpowder	4
	Firearms	4
(x)	Magnetic compass	11
	Magnetic compass with needle	4
	Magnetic compass used for navigation	2
(y)	Paper	12
	Printing (block)	6
	Printing (moveable type)	4
	Printing (metal moveable type)	1
(z)	Porcelain	11–13

Table 7 Transmission of mechanical techniques from the West to China

		Approximate lag in centuries
(a)	Screw	14
(b)	Force-pump for liquids	18
(c)	Crankshaft	3

>> 122. The Wealth and Poverty of Nations: Why Some Are So Rich and Some So Poor

DAVID S. LANDES [1999]

Gunpowder. Europeans probably got this from the Chinese in the early fourteenth, possibly the late thirteenth century. The Chinese knew gunpowder by the eleventh century and used it at first as an incendiary device, both in fireworks and in war, often in the form of tubed flame lances. Its use as a propellant came later, starting with inefficient bombards and arrow launchers and moving on to cannon (late thirteenth century). The efficiency and rationality of some of these devices may be inferred from their names: "the eight-sided magical awe-inspiring wind-and-fire cannon" or the "nine-arrows, heart-penetrating, magically-poisonous fire-thunderer." They were apparently valued as much for their noise as for their killing power. The pragmatic mind finds this metaphorical, rhetorical vision of technology disconcerting.

The Chinese continued to rely on incendiaries rather than explosives, perhaps because of their superior numbers, perhaps because fighting against nomadic adversaries did not call for siege warfare.[1] Military treatises of the sixteenth century describe hundreds of variations: "sky-flying

Source: David S. Landes, *The Wealth and Poverty of Nations: Why Some Are So Rich and Some So Poor* (New York: W. W. Norton, 1999), 52–53.

[1]The Chinese would seem to have been more afraid of rebellion from within than invasion from without. More modern armaments might fall into the wrong hands, and these included those of the generals. Cf. Hall, *Powers and Liberties*, pp. 46–47.

tubes," apparently descended from the fire lances of five hundred years earlier, used to spray gunpowder and flaming bits of paper on the enemy's sails; "gunpowder buckets" and "fire bricks"—grenades of powder and paper soaked in poison; other devices packed with chemicals and human excrement, intended to frighten, blind, and presumably disgust the enemy; finally, more lethal grenades filled with metal pellets and explosives. Some of these were thrown; others shot from bows. One wonders at this delight in variety, as though war were a display of recipes.

The Chinese used gunpowder in powder form, as the name indicates, and got a weak reaction precisely because the fine-grain mass slowed ignition. The Europeans, on the other hand, learned in the sixteenth century to "corn" their powder, making it in the form of small kernels or pebbles. They got more rapid ignition, and by mixing the ingredients more thoroughly, a more complete and powerful explosion. With that, one could concentrate on range and weight of projectile; no messing around with noise and smell and visual effects.

This focus on delivery, when combined with experience in bell founding (bell metal was convertible into gun metal, and the techniques of casting were interchangeable), gave Europe the world's best cannon and military supremacy.

The Perpetual Motion Machines of India

China was not the only significant technological innovator in Asia. Medieval scholars have traced inventions like vertical axle windmills and hot-air turbines to Tibet where they were used for prayer. The blow gun, important for the later development of the steam engine, was indigenous to Malaya. And stirrups, essential for making horses suitable for cavalry charges, may have origins in India. India was also the birth place of perpetual motion machines as described in this selection by Lynn White, Jr., the foremost scholar on the history of European medieval technology. A common theme to all these inventions is how Europeans adopted and improved them. Perhaps due to their relatively small populations and less reliance on slave labor, inventors in some parts of Europe at this time were always looking for innovations that made labor more efficient and less dependent on manpower. The idea of perpetual motion and its perceived impact on work received an enthusiastic response in Europe and enabled Europeans to think more creatively on work, science, and the nature of the universe.

>> 123. Tibet, India, and Malaya as Sources of Western Medieval Technology

LYNN WHITE, JR. [1960]

But it is India that supplied an even more significant element in Europe's thinking about mechanical power: the concept of perpetual motion. Writing about A.D. 1150, the great Hindu astronomer and mathematician Bhāskarā describes two gravitational *perpetua mobilia*. In India such an idea was consonant with, and was probably rooted in, the Hindu belief in the cyclical and self-renewing nature of all things. Almost immediately it was picked up in Islam, where it amplified the tradition of automata, inherited from the Hellenistic age. An Arabic treatise of uncertain date, but which in the manuscript collections is associated with the works of Ridwān (ca. A.D. 1200), contains six perpetual motion machines, all gravitational. One of them is identical with Bhāskarā's mercury wheel with slanted rods,

Source: Lynn White, Jr., "Tibet, India, and Malaya as Sources of Western Medieval Technology," *The American Historical Review* 65 (1960): 522–526.

whereas two others are the same as the first two perpetual motion projects to appear in Europe: the architect and engineer Villard de. Honnecourt's wheels of pivoted hammers and of pivoted tubes of mercury of about 1235. In an anonymous Latin work of the later fourteenth century we find a *perpetuum mobile* very like Bhāskara's second proposal, that is, a wheel with its rim containing mercury. We may thus be sure that about A.D. 1200 Islam transmitted the Indian concept of perpetual motion to Europe, just as it was transmitting at the same moment Hindu numerals and positional reckoning: Leonard of Pisa's *Liber abaci* appeared in 1202.

The significant things about perpetual motion in thirteenth-century Europe, in contrast to India and Islam, are the indications of intense and widespread interest in it, the attempt to diversify its motors, and the effort to make it do something useful.

The contemporaries of St. Thomas Aquinas were far more power conscious than any previous culture had ever been. Industrial applications of water and wind power were revolutionizing manufacture. But the thirteenth-century Occident saw two forces, gravity and magnetism, which operated with a constancy unrivaled by wind and water. By 1199 the trebuchet, powered by counterweights, had begun to sweep earlier forms of artillery from the field, and by 1271 we are told by Robert the Englishman that technicians were laboring to invent an escapement to make possible a weight-driven clock. As for magnetism, the compass had presumably come from China, not by way of Islam, but overland, probably as an astronomical instrument for determining the meridian, and it had arrived in Europe by the end of the twelfth century. Could gravity and magnetism be harnessed further?

Attached to his sketch of a gravitational *perpetuum mobile,* Villard appends a note: "Many a day have the masters disputed how to make a wheel turn by itself. Here is how it can be done, by unequal hammers or by quicksilver." And in 1269, in his epochal *Epistola de magnete,* which is the cornerstone of all subsequent work in magnetism, the military engineer Peter of Maricourt, presenting a diagram of the first project for a magnetic perpetual motion machine, confirms Villard's testimony of the general interest in such matters by adding: "I have seen many men floundering exhausted in their repeated efforts to invent such a wheel." [...]

In his *De magnete* of 1600, William Gilbert is more indebted to Peter of Maricourt than to any other author. Although Gilbert repudiates the idea of perpetual motion machines and is dubious of the *terrella's* supposed rotation, nevertheless Edgar Zilsel was correct in perceiving that he "would like to accept the statement of Peter of Maricourt that a spherical magnet rotates continuously by itself," because from it he had conceived by analogy the idea that the earth itself is a vast magnet that rotates because it is such. Although Gilbert's hypothesis of the magnetic diurnal revolution of the earth's globe could not yet be conclusively demonstrated, it was by then so plausible an idea that even with inadequate proof it quickly abolished one of the major physical objections to the Copernican system. Thus the Indian idea of perpetual motion, first found in Bhāskara's *Siddhānta śiromaṇi* of about 1150, not only helped European engineers to generalize their concept of mechanical power, but also provoked a process of thinking by analogy that profoundly influenced Western scientific views.

The Chess Queen

Like the perpetual motion machines described in the previous selection, the game of chess also originated in India, probably sometime before the sixth century C.E. As a war game and one dominated by male players and pieces, chess seems like an unlikely source for modern historians to use to trace shifting attitudes toward women, but that is exactly what Marilyn Yalom has done in her book Birth of the Chess Queen. *Yalom has followed the evolution and diffusion of chess from its beginnings in India to its adoption by the Persians and later the Arabs. Much like Islam, Arabic, and certain crops (discussed in Part 3), chess also made its way to western Eurasia by way of Muslim conquerors, scholars, and merchants. As Yalom explains in the following selection, its arrival in Europe led to a definitive change in the game: the introduction of the queen as a piece and its eventual development into the most powerful piece on the board. The ascendancy of the chess queen in medieval Europe owed much to the relative importance of female rulers, Mariolatry (the worship of the Virgin Mary), and courtly love. By the late fifteenth century, the queen had become the most powerful piece on the chess board, a position it still holds today in most of the world, and the culmination of an odyssey of diffusion and adaptation that had begun 1,000 years earlier on the other side of the world.*

>> 124. Birth of the Chess Queen

Marilyn Yalom [2005]

In India, where chess had originated in the fifth century, it would have made no sense to have a queen on the board. Chess was resolutely and exclusively a war game enacted between male fighters mounted on animals or marching on foot. This same pattern made its way into Persia and the Arabic lands, with only slight modifications. To this day, the Arabic game is played with a vizier and an elephant, having resisted the changes that took place in Europe a thousand years ago.

When the Arabs carried the game across the Mediterranean into Spain and Sicily, chess began to reflect Western feudal structures and took on a social dimension. The queen replaced the vizier, the horse was transformed into a knight, the chariot into a tower (today's castle or rook), the elephant into a bishop (though in France, it became a jester, and in Italy, a standard bearer). Only the king and the foot soldier (pawn) at the two ends of the hierarchy remained exactly the same. [...]

During the eleventh and twelfth centuries, when the chess queen was driving the vizier from the European board, there were numerous currents favorable to the idea of female power. The first was the reality of Christian queenship, which had taken its distinctive shape during the early Middle Ages. The queen was, first and foremost, the king's wife, his faithful partner, helpmate, and loyal subject. Like the Eastern vizier, she was also

a giver of advice, especially on issues concerning kinship, but even in matters of diplomacy and warfare. Her official duties included intercession with the king on behalf of various petitioners, be they members of the nobility, clergy, or laity.

On a more intimate level, she was expected to preside over the royal household, with chief administrative responsibility for providing food, clothing, rest, and entertainment. Even more intimately, she was expected to produce children. This was her most important function, since only the King and queen's heirs could ensure dynastic stability.

Most queens, as well as duchesses and countesses, became rulers by virtue of marriage to a reigning sovereign and were then known as queens consort. If they were widowed, some were appointed queens regent until the heir apparent came of age. Precious few women were queens regnant, ruling by right of inheritance, like the Spanish queen Urraca of León and Castile, who received her kingdom directly from her father in 1109. At a somewhat lower level, many noblewomen with inherited titles assumed full responsibility for their fiefs. Even after marriage, they did not automatically turn over authority to their husbands. Such heiresses did homage to their superiors—kings, emperors, and popes—in formal ceremonies that acknowledged their feudal allegiance. Some became de facto rulers of their domains when their husbands went off to the Crusades, beginning with the First Crusade in 1095.

Source: Marilyn Yalom, *Birth of the Chess Queen* (New York: Perenial, 2005), xix, xxi–xxii.

A second cultural current that coincided with the chess queen's birth and reinforced the institution of queenship was the cult of the Virgin Mary. From the eleventh century onward, the miraculous birth of Jesus became the subject of countless poems, hymns, narratives, and theological treatises. Hundreds of churches were dedicated to Our Lady, with mother and child represented in sculpture, wall paintings, and stained glass. In her privileged maternal position, Mary could be appealed to for intercession with the Lord, or she might produce miracles on her own. Mary in her various incarnations as the Mother of God, the Bride of Christ, and the Queen of Heaven became an object of unrivaled worship throughout medieval Christendom.

A third influence was the cult of romantic love. The adoration of a beautiful lady, often the wife of a king or powerful noble, was first celebrated by troubadours in the South of France and then exported to all the courts of Europe. Chess soon became associated with good breeding and "courtesy." The knight who wanted to be considered "courteous" was expected to be able to play chess well, with female as well as male adversaries. The game allowed the two sexes to meet on equal terms, and sometimes served as a cover for romance. Both Mariolatry and its secular opposite—the cult of romantic love—contributed to the rise of the chess queen.

Networks of Disease

Inventions, ideas, and trade goods were not the only travelers on Eurasia's vibrant trade routes. These networks also proved to be ideal pathways for the transmission of disease. The Black Death, a catastrophic pandemic that devastated Eurasia and North Africa in the fourteenth century, originated in China and Mongolia and made its way west on Mongol roads and shipping lanes. This massive outbreak of disease has traditionally been blamed on plague; plague that manifested itself in bubonic, pneumonic, and septicemic varieties. Although this plague hypothesis has recently come under scrutiny from some scholars, it is clear that whatever disease was responsible for the Black Death, it was a ferocious killer. As the outbreak made its way from China to England between 1331–1332 and 1353, it left devastation and demographic calamity in its wake. In Europe, where some of the best estimates for the number of dead are available, between one-third and one-half of the population died; Egypt and Syria seem to have experienced similar loses. In the first selection, from William McNeill's famed book Plagues and Peoples, *McNeill points to the importance of the Mongols in reestablishing old trade routes and creating new ones that made travel across the Eurasian landmass much easier and more common than it had been in the past. This new permeability also made it much easier for isolated diseases to come into contact with new and unsuspecting hosts as traditional "epidemiological frontiers" collapsed in the face of Mongol efforts to unite their empire. The next two sources capture contemporary reactions to the Black Death. The first comes from Ibn al-Wardī, a Muslim scholar living in Aleppo, Syria. Al-Wardī recounts the path of the epidemic as it made its way from eastern Asia to the Middle East. Ultimately he would succumb to the pestilence in 1349. Much luckier was Gabriele de' Mussis, a lawyer from Piacenza in northern Italy who also experienced the pestilence but was able to live through it. De' Mussis's account of the disease is among the most often quoted chronicles of the Black Death because of its details about the spread of the epidemic: de' Mussis blames the Tartars (Mongols) and their biological warfare against the Genoese city of Caffa for helping to propagate the disease. De' Mussis's account is also notable for its haunting passages highlighting the human cost of the pandemic.*

>> 125. Plagues and Peoples

WILLIAM H. McNEILL [1977]

The first such change that affected both macro- and micro-parasitic patterns in far-reaching ways was the intensification of overland caravan movement across Asia that reached its climax under the Mongol empires founded by Genghis Khan (1162–1227). At the height of their power (1279–1350), the Mongol empires embraced all of China and nearly all of Russia (the distant Novgorod alone remained independent), as well as central Asia, Iran, and Iraq. A communications network comprising post messengers capable of traveling one hundred miles a day for weeks on end, and slower commercial caravans and armies, marching to and fro across vast distances, knitted these empires together until the 1350s, when rebellion flared within China, leading by 1368 to the complete expulsion of the Mongols from their richest conquest.

Before that upheaval, however, literally thousands of persons moved to and fro across Eurasia, often leaving scant trace in written records. Marco Polo's famous account of his travels, for instance, came into existence merely by accident. Captured in war and imprisoned in a Genoese jail, a fellow prisoner thought it worthwhile to write down Marco's stories. Otherwise, there would be absolutely no surviving record of the Polos' existence. Other records casually reveal how permeable the Eurasian continent became under the Mongols. When, for instance, the Flemish friar William of Rubruck, arrived as the French king's emissary in the Mongol capital of Karakorum in 1254, he met a woman, native to a village near his own birthplace, who had been captured fourteen years before in the course of a Mongol raid into central Europe.

Mongol communications had another important effect. Not only did large numbers of persons travel very long distances across cultural and epidemiological frontiers; they also traversed a more northerly route than had ever been intensively traveled before. The ancient Silk Road between China and Syria crossed the deserts of central Asia, passing from oasis to oasis. Now, in addition to this old route, caravans, soldiers and postal riders rode across the open grasslands. They created a territorially vast human web that linked the Mongol headquarters at Karakorum with Kazan and Astrakhan on the Volga, with Caffa in the Crimea, with Khanbaliq in China and with innumerable other caravanserais in between.

From an epidemiological point of view, this northward extension of the caravan trade net had one very significant consequence. Wild rodents of the steppelands came into touch with carriers of new diseases, among them, in all probability, bubonic plague. In later centuries, some of these rodents became chronically infected with *Pasteurella pestis*. Their burrows provided a microclimate suited to the survival of the plague bacillus winter and summer, despite the severities of the Siberian and Manchurian winters. As a result, the animals and insects inhabiting such burrows came to constitute a complex community among which the plague infection could and did survive indefinitely. [...]

What seems most likely; therefore, is that *Pasteurella pestis* invaded China in 1331, either spreading from the old natural focus in Yunnan-Burma, or perhaps welling up from a newly established focus of infection among the burrowing rodents of the Manchurian-Mongolian steppe. The infection must then have traveled the caravan routes of Asia during the next fifteen years before reaching the Crimea in 1346; whereupon the bacillus took ship and proceeded to penetrate almost all of Europe and the Near East along routes radiating inland from seaports.

Assuredly, the far-flung network of caravanserais extending throughout central Asia and eastern Europe offered a readymade pathway for the propagation of *Pasteurella pestis* across thinly inhabited regions. Each regular resting

---

Source: William H. McNeill, *Plagues and Peoples* (New York: Anchor Books, 1977), 162–163, 175.

place for caravans must have supported a complement of rats and fleas, attracted there by the relatively massive amount of foodstuff necessary to keep scores or even hundreds of traveling men and beasts going. Such populations of rats and fleas stood ready, like similar concentrations of rats at gristmills in the interior parts of western Europe, to receive and propagate

Pasteurella pestis whenever it might appear, whether introduced initially by rat, flea, or human carrier. Then, when the humanly lethal consequences of the local propagation of the infection became apparent, one can be certain that everyone able to flee would do so, thus transferring the bacillus to some new, similar locus for still further propagation.

>> 126. Risālah al-naba' 'an al-wabá

IBN AL-WARDĪ [C. 1348 C.E.]

The plague frightened and killed. It began in the land of darkness. Oh, what a visitor! It has been current for fifteen years. China was not preserved from it nor could the strongest fortress hinder it. The plague afflicted the Indians in India. It weighed upon the Sind. It seized with its hand and ensnared even the lands of the Uzbeks. How many backs did it break in what is Transoxiana! The plague increased and spread further. It attacked the Persians, extended its steps toward the land of the Khiṭai, and gnawed away at the Crimea. It pelted Rūm with live coals and led the outrage [...] to Cyprus and the islands. The plague destroyed mankind in Cairo. Its eye was cast upon Egypt, and behold, the people were wide-awake. It stilled all movement in Alexandria. The plague did its work like a silkworm. It took from the ṭirāz factory its beauty and did to its workers what fate decreed.

Oh Alexandria, this plague is like a lion which extends its arm to you.
Have patience with the fate of the plague, which leaves of seventy men only seven.

Then, the plague turned to Upper Egypt. It, also, sent forth its storm to Barqah. The plague

attacked Gaza, and it shook 'Asqalān severely. The plague oppressed Acre. The scourge came to Jerusalem and paid the *zakāt* [with the souls of men]. It overtook those people who fled to the al-'Aqsā Mosque, which stands beside the Dome of the Rock. If the door of mercy had not been opened, the end of the world would have occurred in a moment. It, then, hastened its pace and attacked the entire maritime plain. The plague trapped Sidon and descended unexpectedly upon Beirut, cunningly. Next, it directed the shooting of its arrows to Damascus. There the plague sat like a king on a throne and swayed with power, killing daily one thousand or more and decimating the population. It destroyed mankind with its pustules. May God the Most High spare Damascus to pursue its own path and extinguish the plague's fires so that they do not come close to her fragrant orchards.

Oh God, restore Damascus and protect her from insult.
Its morale has been so lowered that people in the city sell themselves for a grain.

The plague struck al-Mazzah and appeared in Barzah. The plague, then, came to Ba'labakk and compounded itself with the town as its name is compounded. It recited in Qārā: "Halt, friends both! Let us weep." The plague cleansed al-Ghasūlah. It eclipsed totally the sun

Source: "Ibn al-Wardī's *Rislat al-naba' 'an al-waba':* A Translation of a Major Source for the History of the Black Death in the Middle East," Translated by Michael Dols, in *Near Eastern Numismatics, Iconography, Epigraphy and History: Studies in Honor of George C. Miles,* edited by Dickran K. Kouymjian (Beirut: American University of Beirut, 1974), 448–452.

of Shemsin and sprinkled its rain upon al-Jubbah. In al-Zababāni the city foamed with coffins, and the plague brought misfortune on Ḥims and left it with three. The plague domesticated itself in Ḥamāh, and the banks of the river 'Aṣī became cold because of the plague's fever.

Oh Plague, Ḥamāh is one of the best lands, one of the mightiest fortresses.
Would that you had not breathed her air and poisoned her, kissing her and holding her in your embrace.

The plague entered Ma'arrah al-Nu'mān and said to the city: "You are safe from me. Ḥamāh is sufficient for your torture. I am satisfied with that."

It saw the town of Ma'arrah, like an eye adorned with blackness, but its eyebrow decorated with oppression.
What could the plague do in a country where every day its tyranny is a plague?

The plague and its poison spread to Sarmīn. It reviled the Sunnī and the Shī'ī. It sharpened its spearheads for the Sunnī and advanced like an army. The plague was spread in the land of the Shī'ī with a ruinous effect. To Antioch the plague gave its share. Then, it left there quickly with a shyness like a man who has forgotten the memory of his beloved. Next, it said to Shayzar and to al-Ḥārim: "Do not fear me. Before I come and after I go, you can easily disregard me because of your wretchedness. And the ruined places will recover from the time of the plague." Afterward, the plague humbled 'Azāz, and took from the people of al-Bāb its men of learning. It ravished Tel Bāshar. The plague subjected Dhulūl and went straight through the lowlands and the mountains. It uprooted many people from their homes.

Then, [...] the plague sought Aleppo, but it did not succeed. By God's mercy the plague was the lightest oppression. I would not say that plants must grow from their seeds.

The pestilence had triumphed and appeared in Aleppo.
They said: it has made on mankind an attack.
I called it a pestilence.

How amazingly does it pursue the people of each house! One of them spits blood, and everyone in the household is certain of death. It brings the entire family to their graves after two or three nights.

I asked the Creator of mankind to dispel the plague when it struck.
Whoever tasted his own blood was sure to die.

Oh God, it is acting by Your command. Lift this from us. It happens where You wish; keep the plague from us. Who will defend us against this horror other than You the Almighty?

>> 127. Historia de Morbo

GABRIELE DE' MUSSIS [C. 1348–1349 C.E.]

In 1346, in the countries of the East, countless numbers of Tartars and Saracens were struck down by a mysterious illness which brought sudden death. Within these countries broad regions, far-spreading provinces, magnificent kingdoms, cities, towns and settlements, ground down by illness and devoured by dreadful death, were soon stripped of their inhabitants. An eastern settlement under the rule of the Tartars called Tana, which lay to the north of Constantinople and was much frequented by Italian merchants, was totally abandoned after an incident there which led to its being besieged

Source: Gabriele de' Mussis, "Historia de Morbo," in *The Black Death* edited and translated by Rosemary Horrox (Manchester: Manchester University Press, 1994), 16–18, 22–23.

and attacked by hordes of Tartars who gathered in a short space of time. The Christian merchants, who had been driven out by force, were so terrified of the power of the Tartars that, to save themselves and their belongings, they fled in an armed ship to Caffa, a settlement in the same part of the world which had been founded long ago by the Genoese.

Oh God! See how the heathen Tartar races, pouring together from all sides, suddenly invested the city of Caffa and besieged the trapped Christians there for almost three years. There, hemmed in by an immense army, they could hardly draw breath, although food could be shipped in, which offered them some hope. But behold, the whole army was affected by a disease which overran the Tartars and killed thousands upon thousands every day. It was as though arrows were raining down from heaven to strike and crush the Tartars' arrogance. All medical advice and attention was useless; the Tartars died as soon as the signs of disease appeared on their bodies: swellings in the armpit or groin caused by coagulating humours, followed by a putrid fever.

The dying Tartars, stunned and stupefied by the immensity of the disaster brought about by the disease, and realising that they had no hope of escape, lost interest in the siege. But they ordered corpses to be placed in catapults and lobbed into the city in the hope that the intolerable stench would kill everyone inside. What seemed like mountains of dead were thrown into the city, and the Christians could not hide or flee or escape from them, although they dumped as many of the bodies as they could in the sea. And soon the rotting corpses tainted the air and poisoned the water supply, and the stench was so overwhelming that hardly one in several thousand was in a position to flee the remains of the Tartar army. Moreover one infected man could carry the poison to others, and infect people and places with the disease by look alone. No one knew, or could discover, a means of defence.

Thus almost everyone who had been in the East, or in the regions to the south and north, fell victim to sudden death after contracting this pestilential disease, as if struck by a lethal arrow which raised a tumour on their bodies. The scale of the mortality and the form which it took persuaded those who lived, weeping and lamenting, through the bitter events of 1346 to 1348— the Chinese, Indians, Persians, Medes, Kurds, Armenians, Cilicians, Georgians, Mesopotamians, Nubians, Ethiopians, Turks, Egyptians, Arabs, Saracens and Greeks (for almost all the East has been affected)—that the last judgement had come. [...]

Listen to the tearful voices of the sick: 'Have pity, have pity, my friends. At least say something, now that the hand of God has touched me.'

'Oh father, why have you abandoned me? Do you forget that I am your child?'

'Mother, where have you gone? Why are you now so cruel to me when only yesterday you were so kind? You fed me at your breast and carried me within your womb for nine months.'

'My children, whom I brought up with toil and sweat, why have you run away?'

Man and wife reached out to each other, 'Alas, once we slept happily together but now are separated and wretched.'

And when the sick were in the throes of death, they still called out piteously to their family and neighbours, 'Come here. I'm thirsty, bring me a drink of water. I'm still alive. Don't be frightened. Perhaps I won't die. Please hold me tight, hug my wasted body. You ought to be holding me in your arms.'

At this, as everyone else kept their distance, somebody might take pity and leave a candle burning by the bed head as he fled. And when the victim had breathed his last, it was often the mother who shrouded her son and placed him in the coffin, or the husband who did the same for his wife, for everybody else refused to touch the dead body. No prayer, trumpet or bell summoned friends and neighbours to the funeral, nor was mass performed. Degraded and poverty-striken wretches were paid to carry the great and noble to burial, for the social equals of the dead person dared not attend the funeral for fear of being struck down themselves. Men were borne to burial by day and night, since needs must, and with only a short service. In many cases the houses of the dead had to be shut up, for no one dared enter them or touch the belongings of the dead. No one knew what to do. Everyone, one by one, fell in turn to death's dart.

>> Mastering the Material

1. From your reading of the sources, what were the advantages and disadvantages for Europe of the rapid communications allowed by the sophisticated trade routes that connected it to China and India in the fourteenth century?

2. This chapter argues that diseases and ideas tend to move from one society to another in similar patterns. Do you agree with this view, or is the diffusion of ideas in some way fundamentally different from the diffusion of diseases? Explain.

>> Making Connections

1. As White, Needham, and Landes suggest, there is some debate over whether Europeans "adopted" Chinese technology, improved and "adapted" it to their own needs, or simply developed a lot of inventions similar to Chinese inventions on their own. This debate brings to light questions historians ask about diffusion and innovation. In many cases in this text, both in this part and others, we have seen innovations and ideas that seem to occur simultaneously or clearly to diffuse from one area to another, but nevertheless are expressed differently in different areas.

   a. In terms of the development of societies, how important is diffusion as a source of change? How important is internal innovation? Which do you think, historically, has proven to be more important?

   b. What factors might influence societies in deciding whether or not they want to adopt an innovation from another society?

   c. What factors might influence the speed by which ideas or technologies diffuse between societies?

   d. Some world historians have begun to suggest that it is a mistake to see innovation and diffusion as different processes. Instead, they argue, societies do not "adopt" innovations from their neighbors, but rather "adapt" them, or innovate them further. Do you agree? Is there evidence for or against this view in this or other chapters of this text?

2. Jared Diamond (Reading 10, Chapter 2) suggests reasons for the spread of disease among and within early urban societies. How can his arguments explain the development and rapid spread of the Black Death in the fourteenth century?

Chapter 17

Exchanges and Perceptions of the Other

When Christopher Columbus headed west into the Atlantic, he believed that his voyage would take him to China and India; that is, he did not conceive that part of the world had escaped the curious eyes of Eurasian travelers and explorers and was still unknown to him. Columbus would die claiming that he had indeed reached the Indies and made landfall on the coast of Cathay (China). It is not surprising that he called the people that he met in the New World by the name Indians.

Columbus was not the only one who misunderstood exactly what he had found. Centuries after his voyages, Europeans were still trying to figure out exactly who the inhabitants of the Americas were, with some subscribing to the theory that they were the descendants of the Ten Lost Tribes of Israel, scattered to the winds by the Assyrians in the eighth century B.C.E. and somehow reconstituted in the valleys of Mexico and the mountains of Peru. For early modern Europeans the shocking discovery of a previously unknown landmass and the people who lived there shattered much of the accumulated knowledge that passed as truth in the Old World. For many, the simplest way to deal with the new information that did not fit into their worldview was somehow to make it fit. Both Columbus's repeated claim that he had indeed made it to Asia by traveling west and the connection made between Native Americans and the Lost Tribes of Israel illustrate the point: Human beings form their opinions and impressions of others based on their own past experiences, their cultural and social outlook, and on any past information, accurate or not. Consequently, descriptions like those found in this chapter must always be considered not only for what they say about the observed, but also for what they say about the observer. This makes these sources doubly rich to the historian.

Beyond the worldview—or mental baggage, if you will—that all the various observers carried with them, there were also the vastly different circumstances under which contacts and exchanges occurred. Some, like Marco Polo, Li Chih-ch'ang [Li Zhichang], and Ibn Khaldun, were often welcomed and treated well by the people they encountered in their travels. The ambassadors sent by Vladimir of Kiev were sent as observers to report back to their prince on the religious practices of the regions they visited. Others like Ch'oe Pu were prisoners as they journeyed in far off places. And still others like the Vikings, Mongols, Crusaders, and Conquistadors came across foreign cultures in the midst of conquering them. The conditions under which contact took place undoubtedly influenced the perception that one group had for the other.

The sources in this chapter reflect these points well. Usāmah Ibn-Munqidh and Ibn Battūta were educated and worldly Muslims confronting alien societies, Crusaders in the case of Ibn-Munqidh and sub-Saharan Africans for Ibn Battuta. Both seem to have been on friendly terms with the people they were describing and found things to praise in them. Yet the cultural differences between the two Muslim writers and their subjects are obvious. Both, for example, are quick to note the laxity which the Crusaders and Sudanese had toward sexuality and the relative ease with which men and women interacted. In describing this laxity, however, Ibn-Muqidh and Ibn Battūta also reveal the conservative nature of their own societies. In his writing, William of Rubruck exhibited a similar disdain for foreign practices and customs, in this case Mongol marriage practices among a son and the wives of his father. William called them "abominable and filthy." Yet, what William found so distasteful obviously presented no problems to the Mongols. What made the practice "abominable and filthy" were William's own European preconceptions and prejudices that he used to interpret, understand and, in this case, judge the world he was discovering.

In spite of episodes like these, the sources in this chapter—indeed in this entire text—also reveal members of different societies trying as best they could to understand, commend, and learn from each other. Ibn Battūta praised the Sudanese for their security and lack of oppression. Diego de Landa, when he was not expressing disapproval over the drinking practices of the natives of the Yucatan, could laud them for their hospitality and friendliness. Li Chih-ch'ang [Li Zhichang] commented soberly on different Mongol technologies, noting that they were different from their Chinese equivalent, yet apparently equally effective. And we must not forget that Li Chih-ch'ang [Li Zhichang] and his master took their journey because the Mongol emperor Genghis Khan was interested in learning more about Taoism [Daoism]. A similar motive holds true for Vladimir's ambassadors. It was in moments like these, when the value of foreign practices and innovations could be understood and appreciated that exchanges took place: Ibn-Munqidh realizing that even Muslims with their glorious medical traditions could learn something from the Franks and their medicine; Marco Polo appreciating the usefulness of the Mongol post system; or Kublai Kahn learning to accept some of the tranquility of Buddhist teachings and exchanging the tents of his ancestors for the pleasure palace he had constructed at the fabled Xanadu. The continued progress of humanity has depended on exchanges such as these.

Russia Searches for a Monotheistic Religion

Over the course of their expansionary phase, the Vikings also migrated east. In the ninth and tenth centuries, they used the extensive Russian river system to explore, settle, and trade with various parts of eastern Europe and western Asia. Their journeys led them as far as the Byzantine Empire. In Russia, a Viking leader by the name of Rurik became the legendary founder of the royal dynasty that ruled Russia until 1562.

Our knowledge of Rurik comes from The Russian Primary Chronicle, *a source compiled by Christian monks between 1037 and 1118 and the most important source for early Russian history. According to the* Primary Chronicle, *Rurik and his Scandinavian followers—the Rus'—were invited to settle and rule in Novgorod in 862. From there they extended their power to Kiev and founded the Russian state. Rurik and his place in founding Russia remain a matter of debate among scholars. Equally disputed is the adoption of Christianity by Vladimir, Prince of Kiev, one of Rurik's descendants. The story presented in the following selection details Vladimir's efforts to adopt a monotheistic faith that he could use to help him enhance his political power. In 987, Vladimir sent his ambassadors to explore the religions of the different confessional groups in his geographical proximity: Islam (represented here by Turkic Bulgars), Catholic Christianity (the Germans), and Byzantine or Greek Christianity. As the story suggests, Vladimir ultimately chose Greek Christianity and sealed his decision by marrying the sister of the Byzantine emperor and having a mass baptism ceremony for the people of Kiev. Although the story is probably only partially accurate, it does highlight the willingness of Vladimir and his nobles (the boyars) to be receptive to foreign cultural influences and to evaluate and then reject or adopt foreign practices.*

>> 128. The Russian Primary Chronicle: Laurentian Text

[1037–1118 C.E.]

Vladimir summoned together his boyars and the city-elders, and said to them, "Behold, the Bulgars came before me urging me to accept their religion. Then came the Germans and praised their own faith; and after them came the Jews. Finally the Greeks appeared, criticizing all other faiths but commending their own, and they spoke at length, telling the history of the whole world from its beginning. Their words were artful, and it was wondrous to listen and pleasant to hear them. They preach the existence of another world. 'Whoever adopts our religion and then dies shall arise and live forever. But whosoever embraces another faith, shall be consumed with fire in the next world.' What is your opinion on this subject, and what do you answer?" The boyars and the elders replied, "You know, oh Prince, that no man condemns his own possessions, but praises them instead. If you desire to make certain, you have servants at your disposal. Send them to inquire about the ritual of each and how he worships God."

Their counsel pleased the prince and all the people, so that they chose good and wise men to the number of ten, and directed them to go first among the Bulgars and inspect their faith. The emissaries went their way, and when they arrived at their destination they beheld the disgraceful actions of the Bulgars and their worship in the mosque; then they returned to their country. Vladimir then instructed them to go likewise among the Germans, and examine their faith, and finally to visit the Greeks. They thus went into Germany, and after viewing the German ceremonial, they proceeded to Tsar'grad, where they appeared before the Emperor. He inquired on what mission they had come, and they reported to him all that had occurred. When the

Source: The Russian Primary Chronicle: Laurentian Text, translated and edited by Samuel H. Cross and Olgerd P. Sherbowitz-Wetzor (Cambridge, MA: The Medieval Academy of America, 1953), 110–111.

Emperor heard their words, he rejoiced, and did them great honor on that very day.

On the morrow, the Emperor sent a message to the Patriarch to inform him that a Russian delegation had arrived to examine the Greek faith, and directed him to prepare the church and the clergy, and to array himself in his sacerdotal robes, so that the Russes might behold the glory of the God of the Greeks. When the Patriarch received these commands, he bade the clergy assemble, and they performed the customary rites. They burned incense, and the choirs sang hymns. The Emperor accompanied the Russes to the church, and placed them in a wide space, calling their attention to the beauty of the edifice, the chanting, and the pontifical services and the ministry of the deacons, while he explained to them the worship of his God. The Russes were astonished, [...] and in their wonder praised the Greek ceremonial. Then the Emperors Basil and Constantine invited the envoys to their presence, and said, "Go hence to your native country," and dismissed them with valuable presents and great honor.

Thus they returned to their own country, and the Prince called together his boyars and the elders. Vladimir then announced the return of the envoys who had been sent out, and suggested that their report be heard. He thus commanded them to speak out before his retinue. The envoys reported, "When we journeyed among the Bulgars, we beheld how they worship in their temple, called a mosque, while they stand ungirt. The Bulgar bows, sits down, looks hither and thither like one possessed, and there is no happiness among them, but instead only sorrow and a dreadful stench. Their religion is not good. Then we went among the Germans, and saw them performing many ceremonies in their temples; but we beheld no glory there. Then we went to Greece, and the Greeks led us to the edifices where they worship their God, and we knew not whether we were in heaven or on earth. For on earth there is no such splendor or such beauty, and we are at a loss how to describe it. We only know that God dwells there among men, and their service is fairer than the ceremonies of other nations. For we cannot forget that beauty. Every man, after tasting something sweet, is afterward unwilling to accept that which is bitter, and therefore we cannot dwell longer here." Then the boyars spoke and said, "If the Greek faith were evil, it would not have been adopted by your grandmother Olga who was wiser than all other men." Vladimir then inquired where they should all accept baptism, and they replied that the decision rested with him.

Muslims and Crusaders

The Crusades are often represented as violent confrontations between Christians and Muslims caught in the zeal of holy war. While this is true, it does not tell the whole story of the encounters and relationships between Muslims and Christians during this period. After the success of the First Crusade and the establishment of the Christian Kingdom of Jerusalem, those Europeans who settled in the Holy Land slowly became integrated into local networks of political alliances, trade, and friendship with the neighboring Muslims. The Muslim views of these Europeans were a mixture of admiration for their martial abilities and courage combined with a disdain for their cultural backwardness, hostility, and religious views. One of our best sources for Muslim attitudes toward Crusaders comes from Usāmah Ibn-Munqidh (1095–1188), a Syrian noble, warrior, and writer. Ibn-Munqidh seems to have known the Franks, as Crusaders were called by non-Europeans, well. He had close Frankish friends and seems to have been at ease in their company. This did not preclude him from criticizing and mocking some of their practices. In this selection Ibn-Munqidh describes some of the more savage aspects of Frankish surgery; but he is also quick to acknowledge that numerous Frankish remedies were quite efficacious and quickly appropriated by Muslim medical practitioners. He also depicts gender relations between Frankish men and women that were shocking to a chivalrous and aristocratic Muslim.

>> 129. Kitāb al-I'tibār

USĀMAH IBN-MUNQIDH [C. 1175 C.E.]

A case illustrating their curious medicine is the following:

The lord of al-Munaytirah wrote to my uncle asking him to dispatch a physician to treat certain sick persons among his people. My uncle sent him a Christian physician named Thābit. Thābit was absent but ten days when he returned. So we said to him, "How quickly hast thou healed thy patients!" He said:

They brought before me a knight in whose leg an abscess had grown; and a woman afflicted with imbecility. To the knight I applied a small poultice until the abscess opened and became well; and the woman I put on diet and made her humor wet. Then a Frankish physician came to them and said, "This man knows nothing about treating them." He then said to the knight, "Which wouldst thou prefer, living with one leg or dying with two?" The latter replied, "Living with one leg." The physician said, "Bring me a strong knight and a sharp ax." A knight came with the ax. And I was standing by. Then the physician laid the leg of the patient on a block of wood and bade the knight strike his leg with the ax and chop it off at one blow. Accordingly he struck it—while I was looking on—one blow, but the leg was not severed. He dealt another blow, upon

which the marrow of the leg flowed out and the patient died on the spot. He then examined the woman and said, "This is a woman in whose head there is a devil which has possessed her. Shave off her hair." Accordingly they shaved it off and the woman began once more to eat their ordinary diet—garlic and mustard. Her imbecility took a turn for the worse. The physician then said, "The devil has penetrated through her head." He therefore took a razor, made a deep cruciform incision on it, peeled off the skin at the middle of the incision until the bone of the skull was exposed and rubbed it with salt. The woman also expired instantly. Thereupon I asked them whether my services were needed any longer, and when they replied in the negative I returned home, having learned of their medicine what I knew not before.

I have, however, witnessed a case of their medicine which was quite different from that.

The king of the Franks had for treasurer a knight named Bernard [*barnād*], who (may Allah's curse be upon him!) was one of the most accursed and wicked among the Franks. A horse kicked him in the leg, which was subsequently infected and which opened in fourteen different places. Every time one of these cuts would close in one place, another would open in another place. All this happened while I was praying for his perdition. Then came to him a Frankish physician and

---

Source: An Arab–Syrian Gentleman and Warrior in the Period of the Crusades: Memoirs of Usāmah Ibn-Munqidh, translated by Philip K. Hitti (New York: Columbia University Press, 2000), 162–165.

removed from the leg all the ointments which were on it and began to wash it with very strong vinegar. By this treatment all the cuts were healed and the man became well again. He was up again like a devil.

Another case illustrating their curious medicine is the following:

In Shayzar we had an artisan named abu-al-Fath, who had a boy whose neck was afflicted with scrofula. Every time a part of it would close, another part would open. This man happened to go to Antioch on business of his, accompanied by his son. A Frank noticed the boy and asked his father about him. Abu-al-Falh replied, "This is my son." The Frank said to him, "Wilt thou swear by thy religion that if I prescribe to thee a medicine which will cure thy boy, thou wilt charge nobody fees for prescribing it thyself? In that case, I shall prescribe to thee a medicine which will cure the boy." The man took the oath and the Frank said:

Take uncrushed leaves of glasswort, burn them, then soak the ashes in olive oil and sharp vinegar. Treat the scrofula with them until the spot on which it is growing is eaten up. Then take burnt lead, soak it in ghee butter [samn] and treat him with it. That will cure him.

The father treated the boy accordingly, and the boy was cured. The sores closed and the boy returned to his normal condition of health.

I have myself treated with this medicine many who were afflicted with such disease, and the treatment was successful in removing the cause of the complaint. [...]

The Franks are void of all zeal and jealousy. One of them may be walking along with his wife. He meets another man who takes the wife by the hand and steps aside to converse with her while the husband is standing on one side waiting for his wife to conclude the conversation. If she lingers too long for him, he leaves her alone with the conversant and goes away.

Here is an illustration which I myself witnessed:

When I used to visit Nāblus, I always took lodging with a man named Mu'izz, whose home was a lodging house for the Moslems. The house had windows which opened to the road, and there stood opposite to it on the other side of the road a house belonging to a Frank who sold wine for the merchants. He would take some wine in a bottle and go around announcing it by shouting, "So and so, the merchant, has just opened a cask full of this wine. He who wants to buy some of it will find it in such and such a place." The Frank's pay for the announcement made would be the wine in that bottle. One day this Frank went home and found a man with his wife in the same bed. He asked him, "What could have made thee enter into my wife's room?" The man replied, "I was tired, so I went in to rest." "But how," asked he, "didst thou get into my bed?" The other replied, "I found a bed that was spread, so I slept in it." "But," said he, "my wife was sleeping together with thee!" The other replied, "Well, the bed is hers. How could I therefore have prevented her from using her own bed?" [...] "By the truth of my religion," said the husband, "if thou shouldst do it again, thou and I would have a quarrel." Such was for the Frank the entire expression of his disapproval and the limit of his jealousy.

Mali in the Fourteenth Century

The bridging of the Eurasian landmass and Africa and the strengthening of the world system led to a substantial increase in travel and communication between diverse regions. Medieval literature is full of narratives produced by contemporary travelers. These narratives often highlighted the exotic and the strange, the outlandish and the fanciful; in short, travelers typically noted those aspects of the civilization they were visiting that differed from their own. One of the most famous of all medieval travelers was the Islamic scholar Ibn Battūta (1304–1368), whose peripatetic life took him across the breadth of the Muslim world from Morocco into China, India, and the Indian Ocean. His last trip between February 1352 and December 1353 took him to the Muslim kingdom of Mali in sub-Saharan Africa. When Ibn Battūta visited, Mali was a vibrant, rich, and powerful kingdom that controlled much of the world's gold supply and whose rulers spent lavishly on mosques, schools, and the furthering of education. In the following passages, Ibn Battūta reflects on what he has seen in Mali and offers praise or condemnation based on his own cultural and religious outlook. Notice, moreover, that like Ibn-Munqidh, he is scandalized upon seeing men and women who were not married interacting socially. The difference here is that he is observing other Muslims, not Frankish Christians.

>> 130. Rihla

IBN BATTŪTA [1355–1356 C.E.]

The Qadi and His Lady Friend

One day I went into the presence of the qadi of Iwālātan, after asking his permission to enter, and found with him a young and remarkably beautiful woman. When I saw her I hesitated and wished to withdraw, but she laughed at me and experienced no shyness. The qadi said to me: "Why are you turning back? She is my friend." I was amazed at their behaviour, for he was a faqih and a pilgrim. I was informed that he had asked the sultan's permission to make the Pilgrimage that year with his lady friend (I do not know whether it was this one or not) but he had not allowed him.

A Similar Anecdote

One day I went into the presence of Abū Muḥammad Yandakān al-Masūfi in whose company we had come and found him sitting on a carpet. In the courtyard of his house there was a canopied couch with a woman on it conversing with a man seated. I said to him: "Who is this woman?" He said: "She is my wife." I said: "What connection has the man with her?" He replied: "He is her friend." I said to him: "Do you acquiese in this when you have lived in our country and become acquainted with the precepts of the Shar'?" He replied: "The association of women with men is agreeable to us and a part of good conduct, to which no suspicion attaches. They are not like the women of your country." I was astonished at his laxity. I left him, and did not return thereafter. He invited me several times but I did not accept. [...]

What I Approved of and What I Disapproved of among the Acts of the Sūdān

One of their good features is their lack of oppression. They are the farthest removed of people from it and their sultan does not permit anyone to practise it. Another is the security embracing the whole country, so that neither traveller there nor dweller has anything to fear from thief or usurper. Another is that they do not interfere with the wealth of any white man who dies among them, even though it be *qinṭār* upon *qinṭār*. They simply leave it in the hands of a trustworthy white man until the one to whom

---

Source: Ibn Battūta, "Rihla," in *Corpus of Early Arabic Sources for West African History*, translated and edited by J. F. P. Hopkins and N. Levtzion (Cambridge: Cambridge University Press, 1981), 285–286, 296–297.

it is due takes it. Another is their assiduity in prayer and their persistence in performing it in congregation and beating their children to make them perform it. If it is a Friday and a man does not go early to the mosque he will not find anywhere to pray because of the press of the people. It is their habit that every man sends his servant with his prayer-mat to spread it for him in a place which he thereby has a right to until he goes to the mosque. Their prayer-carpets are made from the fronds (*sa'af*) of the tree resembling the palm which has no fruit. Another of their good features is their dressing in fine white clothes on Friday. If any one of them possesses nothing but a ragged shirt he washes it and cleanses it and attends the Friday prayer in it. Another is their eagerness to memorize the great Koran. They place fetters on their children if there appears on their part a failure to memorize it and they are not undone until they memorize it.

I went into the house of the qadi on the day of the festival and his children were fettered so I said to him: "Aren't you going to let them go?" He replied: "I shan't do so until they've got the Koran by heart!" One day I passed by a youth of theirs, of good appearance and dressed in fine clothes, with a heavy fetter on his leg. I said to those who were with me: "What has this boy done? Has he killed somebody?" The lad understood what I had said and laughed, and they said to me: "He's only been fettered so that he'll learn the Koran!"

One of their disapproved acts is that their female servants and slave girls (*al-khadam wa-'l-jawārī*) and little girls appear before men naked, with their privy parts uncovered. During Ramaḍān I saw many of them in this state, for it is the custom of *farāriyya* to break their fast in the house of the sultan, and each one brings his food carried by twenty or more of his slave girls, they all being naked. Another is that their women go into the sultan's presence naked and uncovered, and that his daughters go naked. On the night of 25 Ramaḍān I saw about 200 slave girls bringing out food from his palace naked, having with them two of his daughters with rounded breasts having no covering upon them. Another is their sprinkling dust and ashes on their heads out of good manners. Another is what I mentioned in connection with the comic anecdote about the poets' recitation. Another is that many of them eat carrion, and dogs, and donkeys.

The Mongols through the Eyes of Their Neighbors

Over the course of the thirteenth century as the Mongols expanded their vast empire, they subjugated and encountered numerous peoples, some of who recorded their experiences and observations. Many of these outside observers were, like Ibn Battūta, travelers who, thanks to the Mongol efforts at empire building, were able to move from one geographic region to another with relative ease. These foreign travelers wrote some of the best surviving sources on Mongol society and history. One of them was the Franciscan friar William of Rubruck (c. 1220–c. 1293), one of the first medieval Europeans to record his travels to East Asia and China—his trip preceded Marco Polo's by almost two decades. William's trip was a direct result of the Crusades. In 1253, during the course of the Seventh Crusade, Louis IX (r. 1226–1270), king of France and leader of the Crusade, sent William on a mission to the Mongols. Louis's goal was to try to engage the Mongols in a Christian–Mongol alliance against the

Muslims. He was to be sorely disappointed. William shuttled from one Mongol court to another across the breadth of Asia until he arrived at the court of Möngke, the Mongol ruler. After a few months, Möngke sent William back with a letter demanding Louis's submission to Mongol rule. Upon his return to the West in 1255, William wrote a thorough and fascinating report of his journey for Louis. His extensive curiosity and reflective comments made him an excellent observer of the Mongols and their customs. In this selection, William describes the gender-based division of labor that he witnessed in Mongol society. He also provides insights into the lives of Mongol women and marriage practices. These marriage practices were obviously a source of curiosity for outsiders; the Chinese Taoist [Daoist] monk Li Chih-ch'ang [Li Zhichang] (1193–1278) also comments on them in his narrative. Li Chih-ch'ang [Li Zhichang] wrote his account after accompanying his master, Ch'ang Ch'un [Chang Chon], to Genghis Khan's battle camp in the Hindu Kush in the early 1220s. Genghis Khan had summoned the master to learn more about Taoism [Daoism]. In traditional Chinese literary style, Li Chih-ch'ang's [Li Zhichang] account is impersonal, but full of useful and observant details.

>> 131. The Journal of Friar William of Rubruck

WILLIAM OF RUBRUCK [1255 C.E.]

The duties of women are: to drive carts, to lay their houses upon the carts and to take them down again, to milk cows, to make butter and *gryut*, to dress skins and to sew them, which they usually do with thread made of tendons. They divide the tendons into slender threads, and then twine them into one long thread.

They make sandals and socks and other garments. However, they never wash any apparel, for they say that God is thus angered, and that dreadful thunder will come if washed garments be hanged out to dry. Yes, they beat such as wash, and take their garments from them. They are terribly afraid of thunder, and when it thunders they put all strangers out of their houses, and then wrap themselves in black felt and lie hidden till the thunder is over.

They never wash their dishes or bowls, but when their meat is cooked they wash the bowl with scalding hot broth out of the pot; and then pour the broth into the pot again. They also make felt and cover their houses with it.

The duties of the men are: to make bows and arrows, stirrups, bridles, and saddles; to build houses and carts; to keep horses; to milk mares; to churn *cosmos*, and to make bags into which to put it; they keep camels also and lay burdens upon them. As for sheep and goats, both men and women tend and milk them.

With sheep's milk thickened and salted they dress and tan their hides. When they desire to wash their hands or their heads, they fill their mouths full of water and spout it into their hands a little at a time; and in this way they wet their hair and wash their heads.

As to their marriages, you must understand that no man can have a wife till he has bought her. Sometimes it happens their girls are very stale before they are married, for their parents keep them till they can sell them. They keep the first and second degrees of blood kin inviolable, as we do; but they have no regard of the degrees of affinity: for they will marry at one time, or by succession, two sisters. Their widows marry not at

Source: William of Rubruck, "The Journal of Friar William of Rubruck," in *Contemporaries of Marco Polo*, edited by Manuel Komroff (New York: Liveright Publishing, 1928), 70–72.

all, for this reason; because they believe that all who have served them in this life, shall do them service in the life to come. Therefore, they are persuaded that every widow after death shall return to her own husband. And hence comes an abominable and filthy custom among them, namely, that the son marries sometimes all his father's wives except his own mother. The court or house of the father or mother falls by inheritance always to the younger son. He is to provide for all his father's wives, because they are part of his inheritance as well as his father's possessions.

And then if he will he uses them as his own wives; for he thinks it no injury if they return to his father after death. Therefore, when any man has bargained with another for a maid, the father of the said damosel makes him a feast; in the meanwhile she flies to some of her kinsfolk to hide herself. Then her father says to the bridegroom: "Lo, my daughter is yours, take her wheresoever you can find her." He and his friends then seek her till they find her, and having found her he must take her by force and carry her off with a semblance of violence to his own house.

>> 132. The Travels of an Alchemist

LI CHIH-CH'ANG [LI ZHICHANG] [1224 C.E.]

Both men and women plait their hair. The men's hats are often like *yüan-shan-mao* [Yuanshanmao], trimmed with all kinds of coloured stuffs, which are embroidered with cloud-patterns, and from the hats hang tasseled pendants. They are worn by all holders of official rank, from the notables downwards. The common people merely wear round their heads a piece of white muslin about six feet long. The wives of rich or important people wind round their heads a piece of black or purple gauze some six or seven feet long. This sometimes has flowers embroidered on it or woven patterns. The hair is always worn hanging down. Some cover it in a bag of floss-silk which may be either plain or coloured; others wear a bag of cloth or plain silk. Those who cover their heads with cotton or silk look just like Buddhist nuns. It is the women of the common people who do so. Their clothes are generally made of cotton, sewn like a straining-bag, narrow at the top and wide at the bottom, with sleeves sewn on. This is called the under robe and is worn by men and women alike. Their carriages, boats and agricultural implements are made very differently from ours. Their vessels are usually of brass or copper; sometimes of porcelain. They have a kind of porcelain that is very like our Ting [Ding] ware. For holding wire they use only glass. Their weapons are made of steel. In their markets they use gold coins without a hole in the middle. There are native written characters on both sides. The people are often very tall and strong; so much so that they can carry the heaviest load without a carrying-beam. If a woman marries and the husband becomes poor, she may go to another husband. If he goes on a journey and does not come back for three months, his wife is allowed to marry again. Oddly enough some of the women have beards and moustaches. There are certain persons called *dashman* who understand the writing of the country and are in charge of records and documents.

At the end of the winter they have a great fast that goes on for a month. Every evening the head of the family himself slays a sheep and divides it among those present, the meal going on continuously until next morning. In the remaining months there are six other fasts. Again, from the top of a high building they

---

Source: Li Chih-Ch'ang, *The Travels of an Alchemist*, translated by Arthur Waley (New York: AMS Press, 1979), 106–108.

project great logs of wood like flying eave-beams (that make a platform) some ten foot square, and on it they construct a small bare chamber hung round with tasseled pendants. Every morning and evening the leading man goes up there and bows to the west. This is called "addressing Heaven". They do not pray either to Buddha or to the Taoist [Daoist] divinities. He sings up there in a long drawn-out chant and when they hear his voice all able-bodied men and women must at once run thither and bow down. This happens all over the country. Any one who disobeys is slain and his body cast into the market-place. The leader's clothes do not differ from those of his country-men, save that his head is bound with a scarf of fine muslin thirty-two feet long, supported on a frame-work of bamboo.

The Old and the New World Confront Each Other

The joining of the Old World and the New after the voyages of Christopher Columbus and those who followed him created many opportunities for cross-cultural observations. When Europeans began to arrive in the Americas, many of them recorded what they saw and commented, often in a negative manner, about the religion, lifestyle, and customs of the indigenous population. One of the most notorious narratives was written by Diego de Landa, the Francisco bishop of Yucatan and a zealous proponent of converting the native Maya to Christianity. In his efforts to understand the Maya and their religion, de Landa wrote the Relación de las Cosas de Yucatan, *perhaps our best surviving source on Maya spirituality, language, and customs. But in his efforts to convert the Maya to Christianity de Landa had few qualms against imprisoning, interrogating, and torturing those whose Christianity he felt to be less than sincere. In 1562, as part of his efforts to wipe out idolatry in Yucatan, he ordered the burning of 27 Maya codices and thousands of religious images during the course of a ceremony of religious affirmation known as an auto de fé. He believed the codices and the images to be the work of the devil and a hindrance to the spread of the Christian faith. The destruction of so many sources helps to explain why modern historians are so dependent on de Landa's work to understand the Maya; de Landa burned much of the other source material. In the following selection de Landa describes various cultural practices of the Maya. The passage bears evidence of de Landa's keen observation, but also his paternalism and criticism of the Maya way of life.*

Diego de Landa's heavy handed approach to the Maya was common in the New World; the charges of Spanish—and other European—excesses against the Native Americans are many and well documented. Not surprisingly, these episodes of brutality tainted the attitude of the native peoples toward the Spanish. The brutality, moreover, began soon after contact was made for the first time. The selection from the Codex Ríos, *found in the work of Gordon Brotherston, comes from the heartland of the Aztec empire and it is written in the Toltec pictographic language that was widely used in the region. The images depict the conquest of Tenochtitlan by Cortes and his conquistadors while the accompanying text by Aztec scholar Gordon Brotherston explains some of the more subtle details about the calendar and the language.*

>> 133. Yucatan Before and After the Conquest

DIEGO DE LANDA [1566 C.E.]

They tattoo their bodies and are accounted valiant and brave in proportion to its amount, for the process is very painful. In doing it the craftsman first covers the part he wishes with color, and then delicately pierces the pictures in the skin, so that the blood and color leaves the outlines on the body. This they do a little at a time, on account of the pain and because of the disorders that ensue; for the places fester and form matter. But for all this they ridicule those who are not tattooed. They set much store on amiability and the showing of graces and natural accomplishments; today they eat and drink as we do.

The Indians are very dissolute in drinking and becoming intoxicated, and many ills follow their excesses in this way. They kill each other; violate their beds, the poor women thinking they are receiving their own husbands; they treat their own fathers and mothers as if they were in the houses of enemies; they set fire to their houses, and so destroy themselves in their drunkenness. When the carouse is general, and for the sacrifices, all contribute to it; when private, the cost is borne by the entertainer, with the aid of his parents. Their wine they make of honey and water and the root of a certain tree they grow for the purpose, and which gives the wine strength and a very disagreeable odor. At their dances and merry-makings they eat seated two by two, or in fours. After the eating the cup-bearers, who have had to remain sober, help themselves from great jars until they are overcome, and their wives have great trouble in getting their drunken husbands home.

They often spend on one banquet all they have made by many days of trading or scheming. They have two methods of making these feasts; the first of these (that of the chiefs and leading men) obliges each guest to return an invitation to his host; to each guest the host must give a roast fowl and cacao and drinks in abundance, and after the banquet it is the custom to present each with a mantle to wear, with a small stand and a cup, as fine as the host can afford. If one of the guests has died, the obligation to give the return invitation lies on his house or parents.

The other kind is between kinsfolk, when they marry their children or celebrate the deeds of their ancestors. This does not have to be returned, except that if a hundred Indians have invited one to a feast, all are invited by him when he makes a feast or marries his children. They think much of friendship and remember these invitations even when separated far from each other. At the banquets the drink is passed by beautiful women, who, after handing the goblet, turn the back until it is emptied.

The Indians have delightful ways of entertainment; particularly they have actors who perform with great skill, to such an extent as that they hire themselves to the Spaniards for nothing other than to observe the jests the Spaniards pass with their servants, their wives, and on themselves over their good or bad serving; all of this they act later with as much art as attentive Spaniards could.

They have small drums which they strike with the hand, and another drum of hollow wood that gives a deep, mournful sound. This they hit with a longish stick at the end of which is a ball of a certain gum that exudes from a tree. They have long, thin trumpets of hollow wood, the end of which is formed of a large twisted gourd. They have another instrument made of a whole tortoise with its shells, from which the flesh has been removed; this they strike with the palm of the hand, giving a mournful, sad sound.

They have whistles of cane and of deer bones, also large conchs and reed flutes; with these instruments they accompany the dancers. Two of their dances are especially virile and worth seeing; one is a game of reeds, whence they call it colomché,

---

Source: Diego de Landa, *Yucatan Before and After the Conquest,* translated by William Gates (New York: Dover, 1978), 35–37.

the word having that meaning [a 'palisade of sticks']. To perform it they make a large circle of dancers, whom the music accompanies, and in time with which two come into the circle; one of these dances erect, holding a handful of reeds, while the other dances squatting, both keeping time around the circle. The one with the reeds throws them with all his force at the other, who with great skill catches them with a small rod. When all are thrown they return, keeping time, into the circle, and others come out to do the same.

There is another dance in which 800 Indians, or more or less, dance with small flags in a great war measure, among all of them not one being out of time. They are heavy in their dances, since they do not cease dancing for the entire day, food and drink being brought to them. The men do not dance with the women.

>> 134. Image of the New World: The American Continent Portrayed in Native Texts

GORDON BROTHERSTON [1979/c. 1562–1566 C.E.]

Cortés's appropriation of the Aztec empire, centred on Tenochtitlan, in the highland Valley of Mexico, was recorded by many of its citizens, in native and in European script. This account is copied from a screenfold which recorded the history of the metropolitan area from the twelfth to the sixteenth centuries. It is in Toltec writing, used by the Aztecs and many other Mesoamerican peoples as an official script. Like all historical narratives in Toltec writing, it is calendrical. Events are narrated year by year, with the annual dates appearing here in Aztec style, in a row of boxes. The period covered in this extract goes from the year II Flint (=1516) to 7 House (=1525); the Toltec system of dating, [...] involves the use of four 'Year-Bearer' signs, House, Rabbit, Reed and Flint, with co-efficients from one to thirteen; thus, 1978 is 5 Rabbit, and 1979 is 6 Reed.

In part, Toltec 'writing' is obviously pictographic. We see that there was conflict in the year 12 House because a warrior, holding spears and shield, brandishes a sword (of wood inset with obsidian blades). Two years later, in I Reed, the appearance of a horseman with metal shield and sword and a trefoil cross announces that the Spaniards have landed; they are greeted by an envoy of Moctezuma's, whose gift to them shows that the Aztecs were fully apprised of their journey from Cuba. Similarly graphic are: the fight at Tenochtitlan, in which Aztec priests are dismembered by the foreigners' steel swords on the very steps of the main pyramid of the city, topped by twin sanctuaries (2 Flint); Cortés's second and successful attack on the capital (3 House); the surrender of Moctezuma's successor, Cuauhtemoc, in his canoe (4 Rabbit); and the hanging of Cuauhtemoc near the Usumacinta river (6 Flint).

Toltec writing is also ideographic: clothing, weaponry, furniture, buildings, plants, and animals, hand-gestures and many other phenomena all have their precise shapes and meanings. A mummy on a wickerwork throne or seat means a royal funeral (II Flint); spears and shield mean war (13 Rabbit, I Flint, etc.). By occupying a native house or sanctuary, Christian friars usurp the priests of the Toltec religion (4 Rabbit, 6 Flint), just as native royalty, with their seats of authority, are displaced by the introduction of folding chairs of Frankish design (6 Flint to 8 House).

Conventional objects and shapes are also used as numbers, and to identify people and places. Eastern neighbours of the Aztecs, the Tlaxcalans, bear a crescent under the chin as their characteristic: they appear as opponents of the Aztecs both before the Spanish conquest (12 House, 13 Rabbit) and during it, as allies of the Spaniards. Under the year 3 House, we see that Cortés's second attack cost him a hundred of his own men (bearded

Source: Gordon Brotherston, *Image of the New World: The American Continent Portrayed in Native Texts* (London: Thames and Hudson, 1979), 28–32.

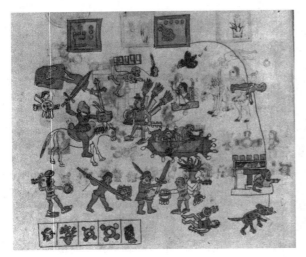

corpse with 5 banners each having the value of twenty) and four hundred Tlaxcalans (head, with a feather denoting that quantity). In Nahua, the language of the Toltecs and the Aztecs, Cuauhtemoc means 'Eagle Falling': the emperor's name glyph has this bird on a downward trail of footprints (4 Rabbit and 6 Flint). The glyph of the Aztec capital Tenochtitlan (seen in 13 Rabbit, I Reed, etc.) comprises a stone (*te-tl*) and a cactus (*nochtli*). Other place names are indicated by a House or by a hill sign, and, like the names of the Aztecs' allies (listed from I Reed to 3 House), they can often be read by equivalent elements in languages other than Nahua. That these readings of Toltec writing were phonetic as well as ideographic, however, is shown by the approximate rendering of Spanish sounds by Nahua word-signs. Cortés corresponds to *coatl* (snake) while the Franciscan Juan Tecto (see 5 Reed) is transcribed as *oua-tl* (cane) and *totec* (grown maize).

>> Mastering the Material

1. William of Rubruck and Li Chih-Ch'ang both describe Mongol marriage practices, but their descriptions are not exactly identical. What do you think accounts for this discrepancy?

2. What do the sources in this chapter tell us about the home society of each author? Do the sources tell us more about the observer or the observed?

3. Some scholars have argued that Europeans came to dominate in the New World both because of their advantages in technology and because the many diseases they brought with them wiped out the indigenous population who had no immunity. Do you agree with this view? What gave Europeans the advantages they had when they arrived in the New World?

>> Making Connections

1. The Muslim and Christian "worlds" are often depicted today as being locked in a centuries-old "clash of civilizations." From the sources in Part 4, including Usāmah Ibn-Munqidh's writings, consider whether this model is correct for the eleventh through fifteenth centuries. To what extent was the relationship between practitioners of the two religions exemplified by warfare and the Crusades? To what degree was it expressed through trade, intellectual exchange, and mutually beneficial relationships?

2. How do sources in other parts of this book reflect each author's perceptions of "others"? Pick several and evaluate them separately and together.

Part 4 Conclusion

The year 1492 was critical in the history of the world as Columbus's voyage definitively linked Africa and Eurasia to the Americas. After 1492, we can truly speak of a global system, deeply interconnected. But this was not the first Eurasian voyage to the New World. The sources in this part show that 500 years before Columbus's fateful trip, the Vikings had already made landfall and established settlements on the coast of eastern Canada, albeit settlements that ultimately failed. And there may have been other transoceanic expeditions undertaken by explorers who left few if any records of their deeds. The question to ask is what made Columbus successful while others failed. Why had the Vikings been forced to abandon their settlements after only a short time, while Columbus and those who followed him succeeded in establishing a vast transoceanic empire that included Spain, Peru, and Mexico? Comparing Columbus's effort to Leif Eriksson's, it quickly becomes obvious that they came from very different societies in terms of technological development. Eriksson's Europe at the turn of the millennium was a backward, insignificant, and peripheral region on the Eurasian continent. The settlements he and other Scandinavians founded were easily overrun by small bands of native warriors, ending any hope of long-term colonization. On the other hand, Columbus's Europe, 500 years later, was a much more advanced society with a host of technologies, innovations, and diseases at its disposal. The Middle Ages had transformed Europe, and Columbus, unlike his Viking predecessors, came armed with a wide range of weapons, technologies, and germs against which the natives of the Americas had no defense. Within a few decades Spanish conquistadors had toppled the once-mighty empires of the Aztecs and the Incas.

It is also worth remembering, especially in the context of this text, that European successes in the Americas were the direct result of centuries of exchanges in the Old World. The medieval transformation of Europe was deeply indebted to changes taking place outside European borders, which enabled the Latin West to learn and benefit from the skills and knowledge of its Eurasian neighbors. Columbus's success becomes unthinkable without the many events and innovations that helped him on his way and which originated outside of Europe: the Turkish invasion of the Byzantine Empire, which helped launch the Crusades and what they meant to Europe's development and its reintegration into the Eurasian and African world systems; the collection and preservation of knowledge in Muslim libraries and the innovative work done by Muslim scholars, which would help to fuel the revival of learning in Europe during the Renaissance of the Twelfth Century; the expansion of the Mongols and the vast areas of Eurasia that they brought under their control, which made the transfer of people, goods, ideas, and diseases much easier; Muslim control over major trade routes between East and West, which motivated numerous European countries, including the Portuguese, to seek alternate routes to East Asia, extensively developing their seagoing capabilities in the process; the numerous inventions that were critical to a transoceanic trip such as the lateen or triangular sail, which came from the Muslims, and the compass, gunpowder, and many others that originated in China and India. Thus, by the time he set sail,

Columbus was the heir of thousands of years of technological, philosophical, religious, and scientific development and exchanges that had taken place all over Eurasia and Africa. His successful expeditions owed as much to Chinese inventors, Mongol conquerors, and Muslim merchants as they did to his own efforts and determination.

Further Reading

The literature that covers the themes developed in this unit is vast. For China, *The Cambridge History of China: Vols. 6–8* (Cambridge: Cambridge University Press, 1988–1994) are a good introduction on many of the topics covered here. For the Mongols, Peter Jackson's *The Mongols and the West* (Harlow, UK: Pearson Longman, 2005) engages many of the topics discussed here and has the added virtue of being recent. Medieval Islam is well covered by the second volume of Marshall G. S. Hodgson's *The Venture of Islam* (Chicago: University of Chicago Press, 1974). For Islam in western Africa as well as the rise and decline of the western African Empires, Nehemiah Levtzion's *Ancient Ghana and Mali* (London: Methuen, 1973) is useful. For European expansion, Robert Bartlett's *The Making of Europe* (Princeton: Princeton University Press, 1993) is a very good place to start, and Jonathan Riley's Smith's *The Crusades: A History* (New Haven: Yale University Press, 2005) is a fine overview of crusading. The origins of exploration in the Atlantic are nicely described by Felipe Fernández-Armesto in *Before Columbus* (Philadelphia: University of Pennsylvania Press, 1987), and for Vikings one can turn to Eric Christiansen's *The Norsemen in the Viking Age* (Oxford: Blackwell, 2002). For the Americas, Nicholas Saunders' *Ancient Americas: The Great Civilizations* (Stroud: Sutton, 2004) offers a very readable introduction to complement the more in-depth *The Cambridge Histories of the Native Peoples of the Americas: Vols. 1–3* (Cambridge: Cambridge University Press, 1996–2000). Alfred Crosby's *The Columbian Exchange* (Westport, CT: Greenwood, 1972) is still a must read for the biological and cultural consequences of the meetings of the Old World and the New. Finally Michael Dols' *The Black Death in the Middle East* (Princeton: Princeton University Press, 1977) and Samuel Cohn's *The Black Death Transformed* (New York: Oxford University Press, 2003) are critical to understanding the spread of the disease, even though the latter has a highly controversial argument.

Terms to Know

Black Death *(p. 320)*

Crusades *(p. 285)*

Reconquista *(p. 300)*

entrepôts *(p. 285)*

New World *(p. 281)*

Old World *(p. 281)*

Renaissance of the Twelfth Century *(p. 320)*

trade networks *(p. 286)*

tribute *(p. 295)*

Chapter 18

Transition

Bridging the Divide in World History
Continuity and History

We all sit on top of thousands of years of human history. In many ways, it is a shared history. Because of the interrelated nature of human societies and individuals, history is global in nature. Archaeological and scientific evidence suggests that we all share ancestors, no matter where we live, and moreover history is full of events and trends that had global impact. Thus, even though we live in different localities, we share aspects of our personal histories with people on different continents.

History is not only global, but also continuous. Although the great historical transformations are most dramatic—the rise and collapse of empires, wars, technological revolutions—underneath them much stays the same. Thus we share certain experiences with people not only in different places, but in different times as well. This does not mean that "history repeats itself"—it cannot, because conditions are never identical. Rather, it means that humans often react to similar challenges and opportunities in similar ways. This is true only partly because humans are genetically closely related to each other and thus "programmed" in similar ways. Of equal importance is the fact that the decisions humans make and the identities they feel are informed by their understandings of history and their knowledge of what has happened before. Thus, history is alive in each of us.

Nevertheless, our understanding of the world around us is grounded firmly in our location in place and time. We all perceive our world, and our histories, from a certain vantage point. This leads to some interesting interpretations. In the mid-twentieth century, for example, most historians understood history in terms of the progress of certain groups—and especially "Westerners"—to global dominance. This made sense to them because they had witnessed several centuries of expansion and domination by western Europeans and, more latterly, the United States. This trend seemingly began in the 1500s, as Spain and Portugal built vast military and colonial empires in the Americas as well as economic empires in the Indian Ocean. They were rather quickly followed by other European states. The industrial revolution, which began in Great Britain and spread first through Europe and later the United States and Japan, fueled further expansionism that resulted in the occupation of Africa and much of Asia by these states. Thus western historians in the late 1940s could be forgiven for thinking this trend would go on forever. It did not, of course. The formal European-led empires collapsed between 1948–1994, and soon China and India rose as economic powerhouses for the twenty-first century.

This example illustrates the dangers of looking at history *solely* from the perspective of a certain place and time. It is more useful to try to understand history from a variety of perspectives. In 1400, for example, nobody could have predicted the impact of Columbus's voyages to the Americas, or the subsequent rise to prominence of Spain and Portugal. Indeed, the world in 1400 looked very different from the world in 2000, and only at times did it function in similar ways.

The Fifteenth Century World

What was the world like in the fifteenth century? As we have seen, that question has many answers, depending in part on the location, status, occupation, and worldview of the respondent.

In many parts of Europe, Asia, and North Africa, the fifteenth century was a time of recovery following the Black Death that had swept across much of the region in the previous century. This recovery entailed not only population increase, but the appearance of new technologies and skill sets. The evidence suggests that much of this new innovation was a result of increasing diffusion and exchange among societies rather than solely by a great shift in any one area. By the 1430s, commerce had recovered across much of the world's largest landmass. Great fleets, many of them Chinese, traversed the Indian Ocean from Japan around southeast Asia and India to Arabia and East Africa. These vast flotillas were impressive, but their importance was exceeded by the many independent Indian, Arabian, and Indonesian ships that traveled the same routes. In the Mediterranean as well, maritime commerce was on the increase, and new ship types such as the square-and-lateen-sailed caravel would soon prove able to cross the Atlantic Ocean as well. Only in central Asia was trade decreasing, as the Mongol Empire that had once ensured the safety of convoys began to spin out of control.

Meanwhile, Africans were linked to this and other trading networks through a complex series of overland routes. Convoys of heavily laden camels carried salt, gold, and the Muslim religion across the Sahara in both directions. Dhows and other sailing vessels left East African shores carrying valuable goods and returned with manufactured products from Asia. On the Atlantic coast of Africa, Portuguese merchants and royal agents were increasingly important trading partners. Within the waterways of the continent, canoes plied Africa's vast rivers, and humans and animals carried valuable goods between the continent's many different ecological zones.

A separate, but similarly intricate, trade network meanwhile connected the states of the Americas, from the confederations of the North-East through the great kingdoms of Mesoamerica, such as the Aztec triple alliance, and arguably down to the well-established states of the Peruvian highlands. There is even evidence of important regional trade networks in the Amazon basin. Although less-well proven, these networks are evidenced by shared crops and gods, and in some cases natural resources found thousands of miles from their place of origin.

At the very edges of each of these trade routes the explorers could be found, whether the Islamic traveler par excellence Ibn Battūta, the Vikings settled in Greenland, or the great Chinese admiral Zheng Ho. Behind them stretched long strings of cities engaged in commerce with each other: London, Bruges, Genoa, Venice, Constantinople, Cairo, Timbuktu, Bukhara, Samarkand, Hormuz, Kilwa, Cambay, Calicut, Mallaca, Guangzho, Hangzhou, Qosqo, Tenotchtitlán. These cities served as manufacturing centers, markets, and political capitals. Nevertheless, aside from a few highly urbanized regions like northern Italy, parts of China, and the Netherlands, most humans lived in rural areas. For these people, the state was a distant, sometimes hazy entity. Whether they lived in a vast empire or a relatively small kingdom, the centralized government was generally only moderately intrusive most of the time, although this could easily change during periods of conflict or upheaval. Instead, local leadership was more important and more invasive—whether village elders, feudal lords in their manors, or religious authorities.

Because fifteenth century states were generally relatively weak (by today's standards), borders and frontiers were often fluid and porous. We have seen this in this text, in the commercial activity of long-range traders, the ebb and flow of language, and the ability of people to alter their identities if they chose to. Nevertheless, in the fifteenth century the state was growing in importance in some regions, especially Eurasia and parts of Africa. Across this vast region, a host of strong, centralized states was coming into existence. Among the most important were those that would become the great empires of the sixteenth century: the Ottoman, Austrian Habsburg, Mughal, Safavî, Russian, Chinese (Ming), French, and Iberian (Portuguese and Spanish) Empires.

Even more impressive than the march of political entities was the ongoing expansion of organized religions. Four deserve special attention in this period: Christianity, Islam, Buddhism, and the Aztec worship of Huitzilopochtli, the god engaged in a struggle against his brothers to save the universe. In each case, the religion, often hitched to the fortune of an expanding state or states, was increasing its influence across wide stretches of the world in the fifteenth century.

From Many Worlds to One?

At the very end of the fifteenth century, Christopher Columbus stumbled upon the Americas while searching for a westerly route to Asia. He was not the first Eurasian or African to reach the Americas—there is much evidence of Vikings in Vinland and somewhat less evidence for Chinese, West African, and Basque expeditions. Nevertheless, it was only following Columbus's returns that the two great landmasses of the Old World (Europe, Asia, and Africa) and the New World (the Americas) were brought into sustained, permanent contact with each other. Coupled with the opening of new, permanent maritime routes around Africa and—after 1517—across the Pacific, this reunification marked a major development in world history with long-term repercussions for humans everywhere. Millions of humans flowed across these new ocean routes as settlers, both willing and unwilling, free and enslaved. They brought with them technologies and culture to be shared and merged. Similarly, after Columbus the world experienced an unprecedented exchange of organisms. Europeans brought cattle, horses, and pigs to the Americas along with wheat and sugarcane and diseases like cholera and smallpox. In return, they brought to the Old World American crops like maize (corn), cocoa, and potatoes and possibly, but less profitably, syphilis. Historian Alfred W. Crosby, Jr., has labeled this process the "Columbian Exchange."

Many European scholars, and now many world scholars, feel that these reconnections at the end of the fifteenth century were of such immense significance that they are the logical place at which to divide the history of the world. Before 1492, the globe was fractured into many worlds. After 1492, it became one world, a truly "global" world. Admittedly, there are many reasons to support this argument. The Columbian Exchange had an impact on societies in every region of the world. Thus if the word *global* is read literally, 1492 seems to indicate the beginning of a new era—the first truly global era—which could conveniently be labeled the *modern* age. Modernity, in this sense of the word, refers not to the technological sophistication or cultural attitudes of certain peoples, but rather to the joint experience of a truly global world—an experience that could only occur after 1492.

However, there are problems with this construction of history. As we have seen, Europe, Asia, and Africa were tied together by many links in a large and diverse world long before the Columbian age. Among the most important of these links were commercial ties between the different regions. For example, European consumers demanded spices and manufactured goods like porcelain from Asia, which were difficult and expensive to obtain. Similarly, Europeans imported African gold and other precious metals, largely through North African and Arab Muslim intermediaries. Asian societies too—especially India and China—demanded African gold as well as other precious metals to feed their expanding economies. Meanwhile the Americas, while they might have been for all practical purposes separated from Eurasian and African societies, were independently engaged in a world of great richness and interactivity.

This set of trading relationships points to the many continuities of the pre-1500 and post-1500 age. Among the principal motives of Columbus and those who followed him was the search for a new, more accessible route to Asian spices and manufactured products. An additional impetus was political and religious. For the explorer-kings of Portugal and Spain, sponsoring voyages around Africa or west to the Americas was one potential way to outflank Muslim rulers and to reach African goldfields and Asian producers. When the silver mines of the Americas were discovered by chance, this precious metal was quickly appropriated by Europeans to exchange for the luxury goods of Asia. Meanwhile, Chinese and Indian producers eagerly embraced the new European trade because of their demand for silver and gold currency.

By expanding abroad—initially for Asian goods but later for the silver and crops of the Americas—western Europeans transformed the world. They unwittingly brought diseases that ravaged the populations of the Americas and left the countries open to colonization. They imported Africans as slaves to work mines and plantations, in the process substantially altering the demographics of large portions of both Africa and the Americas. The profits from this intercontinental commerce eventually helped to fund western Europe's industrial revolution, although in Britain rather than Spain or Portugal. In fact, it was a major factor in setting the groundwork for the European preeminence of the nineteenth and twentieth centuries: the "modern" age in which western Europeans possessed superior armies and navies, the most vibrant economies, and the most innovative and powerful research institutions. An age, also, in which Europe ruled much of the world.

What Happens Next? The Twenty-First Century World

This is not, however, the age in which we live. Starting directly after the Second World War (1939–1945), the great European empires began to crumble under an onslaught of independence movements in their colonies. For a while, they were replaced by two great powers—the Soviet Union and the United States—who faced each other like ponderous giants across Europe and the Pacific. The collapse of the Soviet Union ended this face-off, however, and soon a multitude of new economic and military powers arose.

The world today seems in some ways a repeat of earlier worlds. The great rising economies are those of the ancient powerhouses, China and India. The economies of Islamic states are increasingly important once again, although they remain disunited. Yet there are differences, as well. Europe is largely unified in a single economy as never before—not even under the Romans. Moreover, the vast economies of the Americas—especially Brazil and the United States—are integrated into global marketplaces. Finally, some regions, such as Africa, remain economically hobbled by the effects of the slave trade and colonialism. Still, while the details vary, the twenty-first century economy arguably bears much more resemblance to the fifteenth than the nineteenth century economy in at least one way: it is multilateral. No single region dominates. Instead, trade between many manufacturing centers, largely located in cities, resembles the commerce of the fifteenth century once again.

What will the future bring? This is not a question for historians, whose job is to study the past. We can say, however, that although history does not repeat itself, it does shape the present, and as such it has an enormous influence on the future.

Credits

Page 11: From *A History of Civilizations* by Fernand Braudel translated by Richard Mayne (Allen Lane The Penguin Press, 1994). Translation copyright © Richard Mayne, 1993. Used by permission of Penguin Group (UK).

Page 13: Reprinted by permission of *Foreign Affairs*, Summer 1993 (72). Copyright © 1993 by the Council on Foreign Relations, Inc.

Page 13: Diop, Cheikh Anta, *The African Origins of Civilization: Myth or Reality*, Chicago: Lawrence Hill, 1974. Originally published in French, 1955.

Page 17: From "Dialogues-YES, Civilizations-NO" by Andre Gunder Frank, a paper originally presented at United Nations Conference on Dialogue of Civilizations Tokyo and Kyoto, 31 July-3 August, 2001.

Page 26: From *A History of Civilizations* by Fernand Braudel translated by Richard Mayne (Allen Lane The Penguin Press, 1994). Translation copyright © Richard Mayne, 1993. Used by permission of Penguin Group (UK).

Page 28: Excerpt as submitted J.N. Postgate, *Early Mesopotamia* (New York: Routledge, 1992), 3.

Page 30: From *The Epic of Gilgamesh* translated with an introduction by N.K. Sandars (Penguin Classics 1960, Third edition 1972). Copyright © N.K. Sandars, 1960, 1964, 1972. Used by permission of Penguin Group (UK).

Page 32: From *Ancient Egyptian Literature: Volume I, The Old and Middle Kingdoms*, edited by Miriam Lichtheim. Reprinted by permission of University of California Press and the Estate of Miriam Lichtheim.

Page 35: Reprinted with the permission of Simon & Schuster Adult Publishing Group from *Popol Vuh* by Dennis Tedlock. Copyright © 1985, 1996 by Dennis Tedlock.

Page 41: "The First Farmers" by Jared Diamon from *Science* 278 (Novermber 14, 1997). Reprinted with permission from American Association for the Advancement of Science.

Page 44: From *Ancient Egyptian Literature: Volume I, The Old and Middle Kingdoms*, edited by Miriam Lichtheim. Reprinted by permission of University of California Press and the Estate of Miriam Lichtheim.

Page 45: Francesca Bray, "Agriculture," from *Science and Civilization of China*, Volume 6 edited by Joseph Needham. Reprinted with the permission of Cambridge University Press.

Page 77: "Shang Oracle Bone Inscriptions" by David N. Keightley in *New Sources of Early Chinese History,* edited by Edward Shaughnessy, The Society for the Study of Early China. Used by permission.

Page 79: Pritchard, James, *The Ancient Near East,* Volume II. © 1975 Princeton University Press, 2003 renewed Princeton University Press. Reprinted by permission of Princeton University Press.

Page 81: Reprinted with the permission of Simon & Schuster Adult Publishing Group from *Popol Vuh* by Dennis Tedlock. Copyright © 1985, 1996 by Dennis Tedlock.

Page 82: From *Archaic Greece: The Age of Experiment* by Anthony Snodgrass. Reprinted by permission of University of California Press and Anthony Snodgrass.

Page 83: Reprinted with permission of The Free Press, a Division of Simon & Schuster, Inc. from Aristotle's Constitution of Athens & Related Texts. Translated with an Introduction and Notes by Kurt von Fritz and Ernst Kapp. Copyright © 1950 and 1974 Hafner Press.

Page 85: Goldman, Robert, *The Ramayana of Valmiki,* Volume 1, © 1984 Princeton University Press. Reprinted by permission of Princeton University Press.

Page 89: Chester G. Starr, *Rise and Fall of the Ancient World* (Chicago: Rand McNally, 1960), 28–30.

Page 91: Pritchard, James, *The Ancient Near East,* Volume II. © 1975 Princeton University Press, 2003 renewed Princeton University Press. Reprinted by permission of Princeton University Press.

Page 93: From *Protagoras and Meno* by Plato, translated by W.K.C. Guthrie (Penguin Classics, 1956). Copyright © W.K.C. Guthrie, 1956. Used by permission of Penguin Group (UK).

Page 95: From *Ancient Egyptian Literature: Volume II, The New Kingdoms,* edited by Miriam Lichtheim. Reprinted by permission of University of California Press and the Estate of Miriam Lichtheim.

Page 97: Reprinted with the permission of Simon & Schuster Adult Publishing Group from *Popol Vuh* by Dennis Tedlock. Copyright © 1985, 1996 by Dennis Tedlock.

Page 98: Pritchard, James, *The Ancient Near East,* Volume II. © 1975 Princeton University Press, 2003 renewed Princeton University Press. Reprinted by permission of Princeton University Press.

Page 100: Shi Jing 178, from the University of Virginia Chinese Text Initiative: http://etext.lib.virginiaedu/chinese/shijing/AnoShih.html.

Page 102: Genesis 34 from the New Revised Standard Version of the Bible, copyright © 1989 by the National Council of the Churches of Christ in the USA. Used by permission. All rights reserved.

Page 114: Kaufmann, Yehezkel, *The Religion of Israel*, translated by Moshe Greenberg. Copyright © 1960 University of Chicago Press. Used by permission of the University of Chicago Press.

Page 117: From *The Works and Day: Theogony: The Shield of Herakles* by Hesiod, translated by Richard Lattimore. Copyright © University of Michigan, 1959 renewed 1987 by Alice Lattimore. Reprinted by permission of University of Michigan Press.

Page 120: Reprinted with the permission of Simon & Schuster Adult Publishing Group from *Popol Vuh* by Dennis Tedlock. Copyright © 1985, 1996 by Dennis Tedlock.

Page 123: From *The Laws of Manu* translated with permission of Penguin Group (UK).

Page 124: From *The Ramayana* by R. K. Narayan, copyright © 1972 by R. K. Narayan. Used by permission of Viking Penguin, a division of Penguin Group (USA) Inc.

Page 125: From *The Laws of Manu* translated with permission of Penguin Group (UK).

Page 126: Reprinted with the permission of Simon & Schuster Adult Publishing Group from *Popol Vuh* by Dennis Tedlock. Copyright © 1985, 1996 by Dennis Tedlock.

Page 129: From *Ancient Egyptian Literature: Volume I, The Old and Middle Kingdoms*, edited by Miriam Lichtheim. Reprinted by permission of University of California Press and the Estate of Miriam Lichtheim.

Page 132: Psalm 104 from the New Revised Standard Version of the Bible, copyright © 1989 by the National Council of the Churches of Christ in the USA. Used by permission. All rights reserved.

Page 136: From *The Origin and Goal of History*, by Karl Jaspers, translated by Michael Bullock, © 1953 by Yale University Press. Used by permission.

Page 139: From *Alien Wisdom: The Limits of Hellenization* by Arnaldo D. Momigliano, 1975. Reprinted with the permission of Cambridge University Press.

Page 140: From *History of the Peloponnesian War* by Thucydides, translated by Rex Warner, with an introduction and notes by M.I. Finley (Penguin Classics 1954, Revised edition 1972). Translation copyright © Rex Warner, 1954. Introduction and Appendices copyright © M.I. Finley, 1972. Used by permission of Penguin Group (UK).

Page 142: From *Analects of Confucius,* translated by Simon Leys. Copyright © 1997 by Pierre Ryckmans. Used by permission of W. W. Norton & Company, Inc.

Page 145: "Buddha's First Sermon," version produced by Maitreya Sangha, permanent URL http://sangha.net/messengers/buddha.htm.

Page 289: From *Before European Hegemony: The World System A..D. 1250–1350* by Janet Abu-Lughod, 1989, Oxford University Press.

Page 291: From *The Rise and Fall of Swahili States* by Chapurukha M. Kusimba, 1999, Altamira Press. Used by permission of University Press of America.

Page 292: From *The Travels of Marco Polo,* translated with an introduction by Ronald Latham (Penguin Classics, 1958). Copyright © Ronald Latham, 1958. Used by permission of Penguin Group (UK).

Page 293: From *Ch'oe Pu's Diary: A Record of Drifting Across the Sea*, edited and translated by John Meskill, 1965, University of Arizona Press. Reprinted with permission of the Association for Asian Studies, Inc.

Page 294: Abd-Er-Razzák, "Narrative of the Voyage," in *India in the Fifteenth Century: Being a Collection of Narrative Voyages to India in the Century Preceding the Portuguese Discovery of the Cape of Good Hope,* edited by R. H. Major (New York: Burt Franklin Publisher, 1970 repr.), 13–14.

Page 295: From *The Lost Chronicles of the Maya Kings* by David Drew. Reprinted by permission of Weidenfeld & Nicolson, a division of The Orion Publishing Group.

Page 296: From *Image of the New World* by Gordon Brotherston. © Thames & Hudson Ltd., 1979. Reprinted by kind permission of Thames L& Hudson Ltd., London.

Page 301: From *The Vinland Sagas* translated with an introduction by Magnus Magnusson and Hermann Pálsson (Penguin Classics, 1965). Copyright © Magnus Magnusson and Hermann Pálsson, 1965. Used by permission of Penguin Group (UK).

Page 303: "Fulcher of Chartres' 'Chronicle of the First Crusade'" from *The Chronicle of Fulcher of Chartres and Other Source Materials* edited by Edward Peters, 1971, University of Pennsylvania Press, pp. 29–31. Reprinted by permission of the University of Pennsylvania Press.

Page 305: Gomes Eannes de Azurara, *The Chronicle of the Discovery and Conquest of Guinea,* vol. 1, edited and translated by Charles Raymond Beazley and Edgar Prestage (New York: B. Franklin, 1963), 27–30.

Page 307: Roland Oliver and Anthony Atmore, *Medieval Africa, 1250–1800,* Cambridge University Press, 2001. Reprinted with the permissions of Cambridge University Press.

Page 309: From *Islam: from the Prophet Muhammad to the Capture of Constantinople, Vol I; Politics and War,* edited and translated by Bernard Lewis. Reprinted by permission of Oxford University Press, Inc.